Jalan Singapura

Jalan Singapura

700 Years of Movement in Singapore

Eisen Teo

© Eisen Teo

Independently published through Kindle Direct Publishing

First Edition 2019
(Then published by Marshall Cavendish Editions, an imprint of Marshall Cavendish International)
Second Edition 2024

All rights reserved

No part of this publication may be reproduced, stored in a retrieval system or transmitted, in any form or by any means, electronic, mechanical, photocopying, recording or otherwise, without the prior permission of the copyright owner. Requests for permission should be addressed to the Author, Eisen Teo.
E-mail: eisenteo@gmail.com
Website: www.historybyeisen.com

National Library Board, Singapore Cataloguing-in-Publication Data

Name: Teo, Eisen.
Title: Jalan Singapura : 700 Years of Movement in Singapore / Eisen Teo.
Description: Singapore : Independently Published [2024]
Identifier(s): ISBN 979-834-5613-60-3 (paperback)
Subject(s): LCSH: Transportation—Singapore—History. | Urban transportation—Singapore—History. | Urban transportation policy—Singapore—History.
Classification: DDC 388.095957—dc23

Printed in Singapore

Cover photo by Eisen Teo, 2018: The new above the old—the Punggol Light Rapid Transit Line's West Loop (opened 2014) appears above a section of historic Ponggol Seventeenth Avenue that was closed due to road realignment.

To Tiak, my wife

CONTENTS

INTRODUCTION: A History of Movement 9

CHAPTER 1 — Prehistory to 1819: Lost Tracks 18
    The Creation of an Island 20

CHAPTER 2 — 1819 to 1880: Feet and Hooves 30
    The Early Days of a New Settlement 32
    A Town Plan for 150 Years 37
    From One Empire to Another 44
    The Age of Agriculture 47
    A Little Piece of Britain in Singapore 54
    Moving People, Moving Animals 60
    Forging Channels of Movement 66
    From Old to New Harbour 72
    "Signposts of Daily Activities" 73

CHAPTER 3 — 1880 to 1918: Muscles and Motors 80
    Claiming Land from the Sea 82
    The Age of Public Transport 87
    Rise and Demise of the Steam Tram 94
    Off with the Pedestrians 97
    An "Iron Horse" into the Hinterland 102
    The Tram Returns Electrified 105
    Enter the "Coffee Grinder" 109
    Blood on the Streets 113
    Singapore, Imagined 116
    A Rural Board, a "Miniature City" 125
    The Toponymics of Malaya 126

CHAPTER 4 — 1918 to 1941: Jams and Crashes   128

    A Land Link After 8,000 Years   130

    The Necessary "Mosquitos"   132

    Rise of the Chinese Bus Companies   137

    The New King of the Roads   143

    Reining in a Beast   146

    Of English Towns and Malay Names   150

    Shifting Tracks, Completing Rings   153

    Tending to the "No-Man's Land"   157

    Assembling a Military Jigsaw   159

CHAPTER 5 — 1941 to 1950: Gear Reversal   164

    War on Wheels   166

    Turning Back the Clock   171

    A City of Walkers   174

    Visions of a "New City"   176

    Return of the Old Order   179

CHAPTER 6 — 1950 to 2011: Urban Revolution   184

    New Town, Old Concept   186

    The First Urban Plan in 130 Years   190

    Big Government, Big Bureaucracy   195

    The Death of a City   201

    New Towns Around the Island   217

    A Toponymic Revolution   228

    Claiming Land from the Sea—Again   237

CHAPTER 7 — 1950 to 2011: Mergers and Laws 246
    From Trunk Roads to Expressways 249
    The Roads are for Motorists—to Pay 258
    From 12 to One… Then Two 269
    Turning Around the Bus Industry 273
    Comfort for the Taxi Industry 278
    Moving Mountains for the Mass Rapid Transit 281
    Transport Giants, Mass Movement 286
    Forsaken by the "Book of Fate" 295

CONCLUSION: Speed and Slowness 302
    The Car-Lite Drive 304
    The Road Ahead 311

BIBLIOGRAPHY 320

INDEX 330

ACKNOWLEDGEMENTS 335

ABOUT THE AUTHOR 336

INTRODUCTION
A History of Movement

HIGH STREET is a short, nondescript, one-way road nestled in the heart of the Republic of Singapore's Central Business District (CBD), the city-state's commercial and business nexus. It is just three lanes wide and no longer than 145 metres. However, of the thousands of roads crisscrossing Singapore, a modern metropolis of more than 5.6 million people, High Street can be seen as a microcosm of a history of urbanisation, transport, and traffic in Singapore.

High Street was one of the first roads laid down by the British in 1819 when they colonised the land surrounding the banks of the Singapore River. As the ink was drying on the treaties of trade and friendship between the British Empire and Johor Sultanate, Lieutenant Henry Ralfe, an engineer and gunnery officer of the Bengal Artillery of the British East India Company (EIC), oversaw the clearing of jungle north of the Singapore River for the laying down of High Street.

In those early days, the army cometh and the army maketh, and that applied to roads too. Singapore had almost no cheap labour or convicts—yet. They would come later, in the thousands. It was the sepoys, or Indian soldiers serving the EIC, who did the grunt work of clearing the land of jungle and undergrowth, breaking and laying down the stone chips, and covering the chips with laterite to form macadam roads, a new type of road at the time.

High Street was significant for a few reasons. It ran parallel to the Singapore River just 120 metres away, so the real estate there was coveted by merchants and traders, possibly giving rise to its name—in Britain, "High Street" was a common name given to the primary business streets of towns and cities. It was also literally on higher ground than the land on the other side of the Singapore River, which meant it flooded a lot less frequently, making the land around it more attractive to settlers.

High Street also ran from the sea to an ancient hill with a history going back at least 500 years, a hill once occupied by the Malay kings who ruled the island. The hill was called Bukit Larangan, Malay for "Forbidden Hill". Symbolically, High Street gave the British access to the former seat of Singapore's ancient kings, a direct path to legitimisation as Singapore's next rulers. In 1823, four years after the port of Singapore's founding, when Sir Stamford Raffles (1781–1826) travelled from his residence atop the hill down to the sea to board a ship bound for England for the last time, he did so using High Street.

The year Raffles left for home, there were no more than 10,000 people living in and around the port of Singapore, a settlement of no more than three dozen roads. Most of the population went about their daily lives on foot, with the exception of a few who rode on carriages pulled by horses and donkeys, beasts of burden hauled in by ship from around the Malay Archipelago, Australia, and even far-off Europe.

Over the next 200 years, the Town of Singapore spread outwards from High Street like spokes of a wheel. Plantations and villages mushroomed

Top: High Street in 1905, with the Hotel de l'Europe on the right, and Fort Canning Hill in the background. Above: High Street today, at roughly the same spot. Parliament House is to the left, while the National Gallery is to the right. (Sources: Library of Congress, Eisen Teo)

further and further away from the Singapore River. Hundreds of roads were built. Myriad forms of transport came and went. People could travel longer distances within the same amount of travelling time—or less. As Singapore's population exploded from the thousands to the hundreds of thousands, as the streets became busier, as more people made more trips every day on faster vehicles, Singapore became a town—later a city—of movement.

The face of High Street morphed in tandem with the development of Singapore. In the 1820s, residences were constructed for merchants such as Edward Boustead (1800–1888) and John Argyle Maxwell. An open field was set aside at the seaward end of High Street. It would become the Esplanade, a recreational and social landmark for the European community, where the cream of society headed in the evenings in their horse carriages to meet and gossip. In 1827, Maxwell's home was rented to the authorities to serve as a courthouse, which eventually became the Supreme Court. By the 1870s, it was joined by a multitude of shophouses, a Town Hall, a Printing Office, and over the site of Boustead's residence, the Hotel de L'Europe, which would become one of colonial Singapore's finest hotels. Into the 1880s, rickshaws—a new form of public transport—transformed movement in Singapore. High Street saw the coming up of rickshaw stations—depots for the two-wheeled steel-and-wooden contraptions and their pullers—alongside European textile shops and department stores. The sea gradually receded from the road as reclamation moved the shoreline eastward, growing the size of the Esplanade, known today as the Padang, the Malay word for "Field".

Around the turn of the century, the Town Hall was demolished to make way for the Queen Victoria Memorial Hall and Theatre—known today as the Victoria Theatre and Memorial Hall. The Hotel de L'Europe survived longer, into the 1930s, before it too was demolished for a new Supreme Court, presently part of the National Gallery. After World War II ended in 1945, the Printing Office building was turned over to the Public Works Department—a bureaucratic establishment involved in the building and maintenance of roads, bridges, drains and other public infrastructure. As Singapore took slow but sure steps towards self-government, the original Supreme Court building was refurbished into an Assembly House; with full independence in 1965, it became a Parliament House.

High Street of the 1960s was still the premier shopping belt of the City, the predecessor of today's swanky Orchard Road. "Urban renewal" in the 1970s and 1980s completely changed its appearance, replacing its crumbling shophouses with larger buildings such as High Street Centre and High Street Plaza. Just two city blocks away, the ground opened up like a gaping surgical wound for the construction of the underground Mass Rapid Transit (MRT) system. But at least High Street survived the overhaul of the historic city centre—many roads and urban spaces around it did not.

As the 20th century came to an end, three blocks were added to the historic Printing Office building to form a new Parliament House; the former Parliament House is now the Arts House. To consecrate the move, almost 60 per cent of the length of High Street was renamed Parliament Place. In one fell swoop, High Street retreated further from the sea than at any other time in its history. Today, what remains of High Street is buried in the dense undergrowth of an urban jungle. Like most roads in Singapore, High Street is clean and well-maintained, with smart white lines painted on it for the smooth passage of motor vehicles, flanked by broad pavements fronting glass-and-concrete facades.

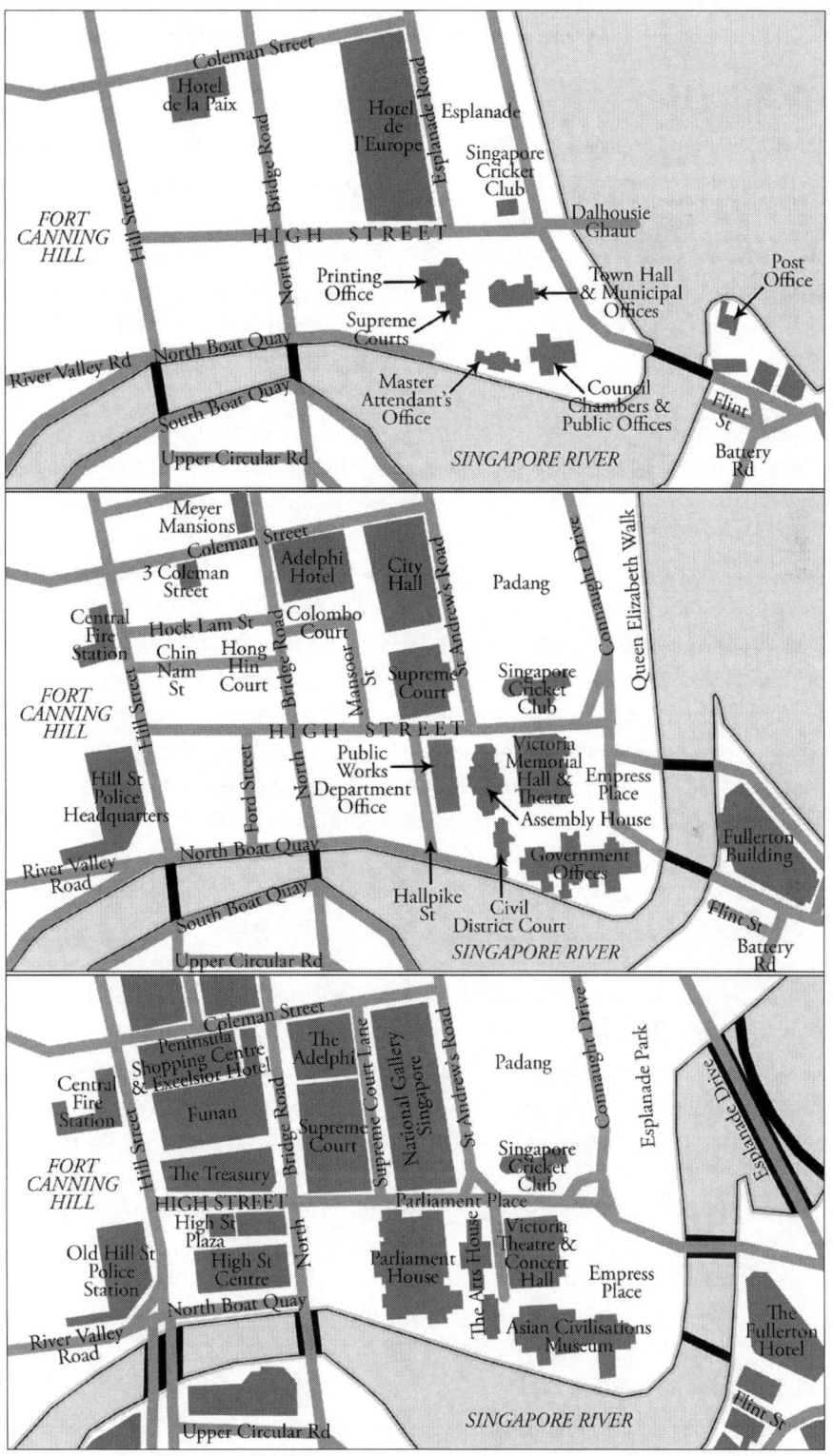

High Street and surrounding areas in (from top to bottom) 1878, 1954, and 2019. The road is a microcosm of a history of urbanisation, transport, and traffic in Singapore. (Source: Eisen Teo)

SINGAPORE IS a city of movement lacking a History of Movement. A history of movement traces the evolution over time of physical and human phenomena that must be studied together, as they interact with and influence each other.

The phenomena include:

- Firstly, the Methods of Movement—modes of land transport, from the horse carriage and rickshaw to the motor car and MRT.
- Secondly, Channels of Movement—which refer to roads and rail systems, and even rivers and streams. For the purposes of this book, I will cover only land-based channels of movement. Also, in the context of a city, a history of channels of movement is inseparable from a history of the urban space in which the channels exist. German urban transportation planner Kurt Leibbrand wrote: "Town building and traffic cannot be separated. One without the other is unthinkable."
- Thirdly, Patterns of Movement—the traffic of a city, and how inhabitants of a city interact with each other through different methods of movement over the same channel of movement.
- Lastly, Experiences of Movement—the social memories of travel. Singapore exists not just as a place, but also a state of mind; likewise, movement exists not just by traversing the space between point A and point B. Travelling exposes people to the scenery from A to B, bequeaths them varying sensations of time, and forces them to interact with other road users, albeit fleetingly. Movement becomes part and parcel of urban existence, and every experience of movement, which is very personal, consciously or subconsciously influences an individual's future travel behaviour. Movement takes place in a continuously changing environment, and people continuously react and adapt to such an environment.

A history of movement for Singapore also unearths the underlying forces or processes governing the evolution of the aforementioned aspects of movement. Why did steam and electric trams die out so quickly in Singapore, as compared to other Asian cities? What explains the presence of grid systems of roads in and around the CBD? What are the stories behind clusters of road names more reminiscent of an English countryside than a tropical island? Did Singapore always possess a "rush hour" and were congested roads, parking problems, and high accident rates always endemic? Answering these questions exposes both the threads of continuity and the interstices that make up a history of movement.

A history of movement for Singapore needs to be written for several compelling reasons. One is historiography. Books on Singapore's political and military history, and "big" personalities in Singapore history, outnumber books on social, cultural, and other aspects of Singapore. Fortunately, the proportions are gradually shifting, but the roads of urban and land transport history are still relatively less trodden.

Which leads to the second reason: perspective. This book will map not just 200 years of modern Singapore, but the 8,000 or so years before it, back to the geological formation of the island presently known as Singapore. This attempt at the *longue durée* departs from short-term approaches to Singapore history, the frequency of which was intensified by SG50, a year-long series of activities held in Singapore in 2015 to commemorate 50 years of independence from Malaysia. Delving so deep into the past serves a pragmatic purpose. We can use the past as a beacon to illuminate the present, and as a compass to steer us into the future.

A history of movement is also crucial for understanding the creation and destruction of history in Singapore. A history of movement charts the creation of the man-made environment in which both epochal events and everyday social memories have unfolded. This book will cover decades-long processes, such as the 19th-century spread of plantation agriculture, and brief episodes such as the British putting down the worst riots in modern Singapore's history in 1854, and the Japanese invasion of Singapore Island in 1942.

As for the destruction of history, look no further than how a new city was built over the ashes of an old city from the 1960s to the 1990s; historic landmarks making way for arterial roads, expressways, and MRT lines; even certain place names being chosen over others for the christening of towns and roads. These and more will be covered in this book.

Finally, a history of movement is an intimate, personal history. I was born in Singapore in 1984, when thousands were working around the clock on dozens of MRT construction sites around the island. Over my lifetime, the MRT—which I use almost every day—has grown from tabletop blueprints to five lines, 200 km of track and 119 stations. My experience of taking the MRT has changed over time. When I was a kid, I could still get a seat on the train even during the rush hour; now, trains are packed even past 10pm on weekdays. Be it in Singapore or another city, we have to move around every day to live our lives. Transport is something we take all the time; traversing urban spaces is part and parcel of existence. A history of movement matters to us because it is part of our DNA as city dwellers.

Other than the Introduction and the Conclusion, there are seven parts to this book. Chapter 1 explores the geological factors that have influenced Singapore's urbanisation and land transport patterns throughout its history. That means starting my story from the birth of what is now known as Singapore Island about 8,000 years ago. I will also touch on the paucity of historical and archaeological records about roads and land transport for ancient Singapore up to the arrival of the British in 1819, and explore the reasons behind this paucity.

Chapter 2 spans 1819 to the arrival of the rickshaw in 1880. During this period, the town of Singapore's grid road network and Singapore Island's trunk roads—channels of movement that would last for at least 150 years—were laid down. Set in stone, too, were a British road and place-naming system, and a bureaucratic framework for road building and maintenance.

Chapter 3 covers 1880 to the end of World War I in 1918. Over these four decades, Singapore's streets were transformed by a flood of new methods of movement—rickshaws, trams, motor cars, motor buses, and more.

Chapter 4 covers only 23 years, from 1918 to 1941; but during this time, Singapore entered the modern age, as motor cars overtook rickshaws as kings of the road. The rapid growth in the car population transformed Singapore traffic and forced the usually laissez-faire authorities to grapple with unprecedented forms of traffic management.

Chapter 5 spans the tumultuous 1940s, from World War II and the Japanese Occupation to the years after the British resumed control of Singapore. While a brutal occupation meant a general regression in transport "progress", there are intriguing "what-ifs" to be explored—from Japanese road names to Japanese plans for a high-speed bullet train from Korea to Singapore. All these never came to be because Nipponese rule over Singapore only lasted three-and-a-half years.

The decades from 1950 to the dawn of the 21st century are covered in chapters 6 and 7. Chapter 6 focuses on Singapore's "Urban Revolution", a state-engineered process that saw a new city—and channels of movement—rise above the ashes of the old; what has remained is as intriguing as what has changed.

Chapter 7 covers land transport and traffic, including the creation of mighty transport oligopolies operating multiple methods of movement, and the introduction of new layers of transportation—the MRT and expressways—freeing millions from the centuries-old vagaries of congested trunk and arterial roads.

Finally, the Conclusion will identify present-day urbanisation, land transport, and traffic issues facing the city-state of Singapore, and draw on lessons learned from a history of movement to suggest panaceas to these real-world problems. Some of the solutions may sound radical, impossible even. They include expanding the MRT network, slashing the number of motor cars by two-thirds, and closing parts of the city to private cars. But these will be solutions borne from a history of movement that is at least 200 years old. Seen from such a broad perspective, these ideas represent not a break from history, but to the contrary, a continuation of history.

In 1956, American urban and transport consultant Wilfred Owen quipped: "Despite all the methods of movement, the problem in cities is how to move." One way of answering the enduring question of "How to move" can be through the study of a history of movement.

AS A Singaporean, this book is my sincere contribution to a national narrative, a narrative that is hopefully fresh, illuminating, and practical at the same time. But while this narrative is a story unique to Singapore, I also hope the historical framework I have crafted—a history of movement—can be employed as a template to construct a history of any urban centre in the world, a history that traces continuities and patterns in urbanisation, land transport, and traffic over time; tackles urbanisation, land transport, and traffic issues as a whole; and proffers radical yet practical solutions to them.

Now is an opportune time to study urban and land transport histories in cities. In 1950, just 30 per cent of the world's population was urban, numbering close to 750 million people. In 2009, the number of people living in urban areas surpassed those living in rural areas for the first time. By 2050, two-thirds of the world's population will be urban—about 6.4 billion people, close to nine times that of 1950's urban population. As the globe's urban population grows, a history of movement will be needed more than ever to shed light on urban and land transport issues, not just in Singapore, but all over the world, from Manila to Mexico City, Tokyo to Toronto, Lagos to London.

BACK TO High Street in Singapore. When Lieutenant Ralfe was overseeing its construction in 1819, it was sited inside the confines of an ancient town that existed 500 years before, in the

14th century. However, the British never found any traces of roads that once crisscrossed this town, giving us little understanding of a history of movement in Singapore before the British arrived in 1819. Why was this the case?

Was it also a coincidence that the ancient town of the 14th century and the British settlement of the 19th century both began in the same part of Singapore Island, an area in the south of the island bounded by the Singapore River and Bukit Larangan? Was it down to human choice or the exigencies of physical geography? The next chapter will explore these questions and set the stage for the dawn of a history of movement in Singapore.

CHAPTER 1
Prehistory to 1819: Lost Tracks

THE STORY of Sang Nila Utama is common folklore in Singapore. It first appeared in the *Sejarah Melayu*, or *Malay Annals*, a piece of classical Malay literature composed sometime in the 1500s.[1] In it, Sang Nila Utama was a prince from Palembang, Sumatra, then the raja of the island of Bintan. One day, seized by wanderlust, he and his entourage travelled to the neighbouring island of Batam. There, "looking across the water he saw that the land on the other side had sand so white that it looked like a sheet of cloth". He was told the sand was "the land called Temasek". Of course, he set sail for it. The year was 1299.

Sang Nila Utama nearly did not reach his destination, because a storm disrupted his ship. Throwing overboard most of the luggage did not appease the raging seas, until the raja did the symbolic thing by throwing out his crown. That calmed the seas and ensured he completed the journey, which takes merely an hour by ferry today.

Thereafter, Sang Nila Utama and his attendants "went inland for sport on the open ground at Kuala (Mouth of the River) Temasek". Then:

> … they all beheld a strange animal. It seemed to move with great speed; it had a red body and a black head; its breast was white; it was strong and active in build, and in size was rather bigger than a he-goat. When it saw the party, it moved away and then disappeared.

The curious raja was told that the strange animal was a lion; since it symbolised strength, courage, and leadership, Temasek was worthy of establishing a new kingdom. Sang Nila Utama decided to act upon this advice, naming his kingdom Singapura—Sanskrit for "Lion City". He became the first of five rajas to rule Singapura for the next century or so. Today, the Malay name for Singapore is still Singapura.

Sang Nila Utama spotted his creature near the mouth of the River Temasek, a river that shared its name with the island. As the island was subsequently known as Singapura, the river was probably the Sungei Singapura, or Malay for "Singapore River". Since the north bank of the Singapore River was on higher ground than the marshy south bank, the open ground where Sang Nila Utama went for sport was probably Empress Place today. That means his ship docked at the original coastline just north of the Singapore River, which presently runs lengthwise down the middle of the Padang. Whether the *Sejarah Melayu* is history, myth, or somewhere in between, the story of the raja from Palembang and the lion-creature is the earliest detailed account of what is now Singapore Island.

It is usually taken for granted that Sang Nila Utama made landfall in the southeastern part of Singapore Island, by the Singapore River. Why not the north or west of Singapore Island, or by the banks of another river? His journey and eventual arrival in Singapore were determined by the waxing and waning of an ice age, the rise and fall of seas, and the power of rivers in creating new land.

THE CREATION OF AN ISLAND

FOR MOST, if not all of human history, Singapore's fate has been intertwined with that of the sea. "Temasek" is probably old Javanese for "Sea Town". The island lies at the southern tip of the Malay Peninsula, conveniently at the point where the monsoons meet, at the confluence of maritime trade routes connecting the great empires of the Middle East, India, and China, commanding the southern entrances to the Straits of Malacca and the South China Sea. But this wasn't always the case. Fourteen thousand years ago, Singapore was a thousand kilometres from the sea.

At the time, large swathes of the northern hemisphere were covered by ice sheets and glaciers. The world was—and is—in the midst of an ice age that had started two million years before and has never truly ended. The past two million years have been made up of periods of "glacials" and "interglacials"—alternating cold and warm climate, and expanding and retreating ice sheets and glaciers. Fourteen thousand years ago, the Earth was at the tail-end of possibly its 20th glacial period, one which had begun about 100,000 years before.

With a significant proportion of the Earth's waters locked in ice, sea levels then were 140 metres—or roughly 45 storeys—lower than present-day sea levels. Much of the continental shelves of Southeast Asia and Australia that are now under water was dry land instead. Present-day mainland Southeast Asia, Sumatra, Java, Borneo, and part of the South China Sea was one land mass called Sundaland, named after the Sunda Shelf. Sundaland was roughly twice the size of present-day India. To the east of Sundaland lay Sahuland, comprising present-day New Guinea, Australia, and the sea that now separates them. Fourteen thousand years ago, there would have been no Singapore Island—just low-lying hills covered by jungle in the middle of Sundaland.

The world's 20th glacial period in two million years came to an end, to be replaced by an interglacial period marked by a warmer climate and retreating ice sheets. Over the next 6,000 years, the Earth thawed. From between 14,000 and 8,000 years ago, three rapid ice melts resulted in three episodes of sudden, cataclysmic flooding.

As thousands of square kilometres of ice sheets melted, sea levels kept rising. In what is now Southeast Asia, an area the size of present-day India was flooded. Mighty rivers, jungle-covered valleys, and ancient human settlements disappeared forever under rising waters. By around 6,000 BCE, new intercontinental seas had appeared. The Straits of Malacca, the Karimata Strait, the Java Sea, and the South China Sea took shape. These water bodies forged the new islands of Sumatra, Java, and Borneo from the Malay Peninsula.

The rising seas also created a narrow waterway just a kilometre wide separating a tiny island from the rest of the Malay Peninsula. The waterway is now known as the Straits of Johor, and the island is now Singapore. The sea level then stabilised. If it had risen another 30 per cent, much of Singapore would have been inundated. If it had stabilised at a level 30 per cent lower, Singapore, Batam, and Bintan would have remained part of the Malay Peninsula. The extent of post-glacial flooding created the right geographical conditions for Singapore's destiny as a maritime port of call, but also stopped short of erasing its existence altogether. Singapore, for all its hills, remains very low-lying. Its tallest natural point is 164 metre-tall

Bukit Timah Hill in the centre of the island.

The transformation of the geography of what was formerly a solid landmass opened it to maritime trade, travel, and that age-old cultural activity so misunderstood by the Europeans—piracy. It also led to the evolution of maritime communities such as the Orang Laut, Malay for "Sea People", comprising the Orang Seletar, Orang Biduanda Kallang, and Orang Gelam, among others. However, because the Straits of Johor was so narrow, Singapore's southern coast—which faced the open sea—was more welcoming to passing ships. Most international voyagers came to Singapore from the south—much like how Sang Nila Utama did in 1299.

At the formation of Singapore Island at 6,000 BCE, most of its geology had already taken shape. The island's oldest rocks lie in the central and northern parts—most of them a solid core of Bukit Timah Granite, formed by the cooling and solidification of magma or lava between 250 and 235 million years ago. Structurally, the Bukit Timah Granite is part of a seam of granite running 200 km north from Singapore to northern Johor. Within Singapore itself, the granite runs from present-day Woodlands in the north to Bukit Timah Hill and the gentle hills surrounding present-day Orchard Road to the south. A small area west of the Bukit Timah Granite, including the cluster of hills that gave rise to the place name Bukit Panjang, or Malay for "Long Hill", has older rocks called Gombak Gabbro.

Then, between 235 and 175 million years ago, when dinosaurs of the Late Triassic and Early Jurassic periods roamed the Earth, sediments from weathered rocks were deposited into a shallow marine basin west of the granite core, and lithified into rocks. They became the present-day Jurong Formation, consisting mostly sedimentary rock. The Jurong Formation runs from the northwest of the island to the southeast, from Sarimbun through Tengah, Clementi, and Queenstown, ending near Telok Blangah.

Fast forward to between 5 million and 500,000 years ago, when rivers draining southern Johor into the Straits of Johor—possibly ancestors of the present-day Sungei Skudai and Sungei Johor—did their work. Alluvium—deposits of clay, silt, and sand—dumped by a river to the west formed solid land which is now part of Lim Chu Kang. More deposits left by another river to the east now make up much of northeastern and eastern Singapore, such as Punggol, Sengkang, Tampines, Bedok, and Changi.

Finally, some of the youngest and most low-lying areas of Singapore Island, called the Kallang Formation, were formed between 140,000 years ago and the present, a period within which the world's last glacial period came and went. These were flood plains surrounding present-day river systems, many of which have been canalised or dammed into reservoirs. The river systems include the Kranji, Jurong, Pandan, Sembawang, Seletar, Punggol, Serangoon, Bedok, Kallang, Rochor, Geylang, and Singapore. Throughout human history, settlements and civilisations are usually born on low-lying flood plains as the river is a source of water and transport, and the land is fertile for farming. Since the southern coast of Singapore Island was more welcoming to passing ships, then the rivers there were natural candidates for maritime settlers.

However, the southeastern coast was less dangerous for ships than the southwestern coast. The seas to the southwest of Singapore Island were replete with smaller islands and coral reefs—not so for the seas to the southeast. That is probably why the first recorded human settlements on Singapore

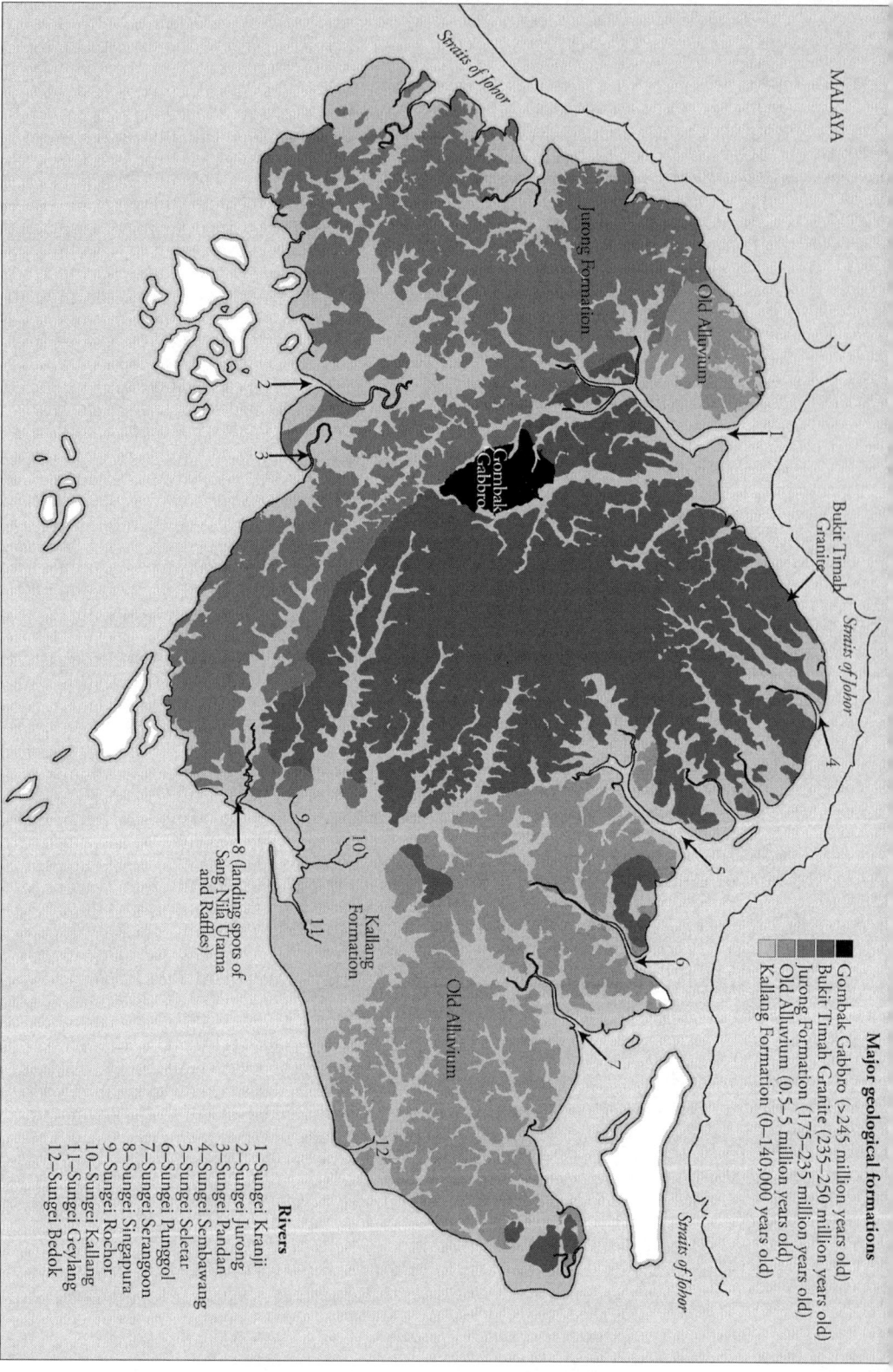

An 1850s map of Singapore Island, showing major geological formations. Many areas covered by the Kallang Formation are low-lying flood plains surrounding rivers, conducive for human settlement. Meanwhile, the southern coast of Singapore Island was more welcoming to passing ships than the narrow Straits of Johor to the north. However, the seas to the southeast were less dangerous for ships than the seas to the southwest, which were replete with smaller islands and coral reefs. Hence, that was probably why Sang Nila Utama (and later Raffles) made landfall by what is now the Singapore River. (Source: Eisen Teo)

began in the southeast of the island, and that was probably why Sang Nila Utama made landfall by what is now the Singapore River.

Hundreds of years later, Stamford Raffles would read about the story of Sang Nila Utama in the *Sejarah Melayu*, and attempt to retrace his journey, sailing towards Singapore Island from the south. He would dock in the same area as did Sang Nila Utama, and the settlement he founded would spread outward and cover whatever remained of Sang Nila Utama's settlement. Singapore's history of movement may have begun with human agency, but it was human agency within geographical and geological parameters.

Ever since, geography and geology would also influence much of modern Singapore's urban and land transport evolution. For example, the relative hilliness of the central and western parts of Singapore Island, which comprise older rocks, as compared to the flatter terrain of the southeastern and eastern parts, would subtly skew urbanisation and road development patterns to the southeast and east of the island. Hence, some of the oldest parts of built-up Singapore are presently in the southeast of the island.

Sang Nila Utama and his four successors chose a hill that commanded a good view of the sea to build their palaces; a hill probably known as Bukit Larangan then, and now known as Fort Canning Hill. A settlement thrived at the foot of the hill, stretching to the sea and to the banks of the Sungei Singapura. It lasted until the end of the 14th century, when it was sacked by either one of two regional powers—the Majapahit Empire to the south, or the Siamese to the north. Today, almost no traces of buildings or roads in this settlement—or any other settlement predating the arrival of the British in 1819—remain. To better elucidate the reasons behind this almost total absence, let us briefly visit a place 4,000 km away that has retained some of its ancient roads.

THE NORTHERN Indian city of Fatehpur Sikri was founded in 1569, 270 years after Singapura. After a string of military victories, Mughal emperor Akbar ordered its construction as his new capital, about 35 km from the existing capital of Agra. Fatehpur Sikri served as such from 1571 to 1585, until the exhaustion of the spring-fed lake that was the city's water supply. It was planned as a walled city, a showcase of Mughal architecture, replete with royal palaces, courts, and mosques.

Over two years from 1980 to 1981, archaeologists excavated roads that originally ran within Fatehpur Sikri. These included the city's main road, complete with crossings with four secondary roads. The main road was paved, about a kilometre in length, and as wide as a present-day four-lane road; each secondary road was as wide as a present-day one-lane road. About three centuries old, they were feats of Mughal engineering, built to outlast the empire itself.

The main road varied in thickness from 35–50 cm, comprising stone blocks set in mortar such that each block had its thinner or sharper part facing down, maximising the surface area of stone bearing the load of pedestrians or vehicles above. This increased the strength and stability of the roads. The road builders had also chosen stronger and harder stones that were not easily eroded, and they had added lime to the mortar to make the entire layer waterproof. As a whole, the roads were designed to withstand constant weathering and traffic stress for hundreds of years. Consequently, archaeologists could unearth the original roads today for historians to construct a plan of 16th-century Fatehpur Sikri.

Such a scrutiny of Fatehpur Sikri's long-lasting roads helps us understand why ancient Singapura's roads have not survived to the present day. The Mughal Empire—which at its height in the 17th century controlled most of modern-day India and ruled 150 million subjects, and fostered advances in the arts, literature, architecture, science—and engineering. Emperor Akbar himself excelled as an engineer and technician. It is no wonder Fatehpur Sikri's roads were built with excellent engineering.

In contrast, ancient Singapura was a largely autonomous entity with a population of possibly no more than 10,000. It arose during a transitional period in regional geopolitics, when the declining Sumatra-based Srivijaya Empire was being supplanted by a rising Java-based Majapahit Empire. As a result, ancient Singapura was never directly ruled by either; it also never fell under direct Siamese influence. In the 1500s, it came under the domain of the Johor Sultanate, which at its height included Pahang, Johor, and the Riau and Lingga Islands. However, even during the sultanate's golden age, Johor's achievements were in the areas of trade and Islamic studies, not engineering. Hence, Singapura had no longstanding tradition of scientific or technical achievement to draw upon. Its roads were most probably no more than dirt tracks laid down with little technology. Moreover, kampungs—a traditional form of settlement throughout the Malay Archipelago—usually possessed only foot paths between houses, with no proper access roads, unlike ancient European or Chinese towns; foot paths were easily washed away by floods or overrun by undergrowth. Hence, compared to Fatehpur Sikri's impressive transport-related archaeological record, ancient Singapura's pales in comparison.

There is another critical factor severely limiting the longevity of Singapura's roads—or for that matter, any man-made structure on the island. Singapore lies just a degree north of the Equator, and receives some of the heaviest rainfall in the world—three times the annual rainfall of Fatehpur Sikri. The ravages of an equatorial climate, coupled with an abundant growth of flora, mould, and insect populations, have obliterated many an archaeological record in the Malay Peninsula.

As for the Orang Laut who inhabited the river banks and coasts of Singapore Island for hundreds, maybe thousands, of years, there was no need for roads in the first place. Rivers and the sea were their channels of movement, using wooden boats—both of which have left almost no archaeological record.

When the archaeological record is found wanting, we have to fall back on scrutinising the literary record. However, literary descriptions of Singapore before the arrival of the British in 1819 do not contribute much towards a history of movement—there is almost no mention of urban development, roads, land transport, or traffic. As for the Orang Laut, they left few, if any, conventional written records.

As early as the 1300s, settlements on Singapore Island were already mentioned in Chinese and Javanese records. One such extensive description lies in *Daoyi Zhilue*, or Mandarin for "A Brief Account of Island Barbarians", penned in 1349 by Wang Dayuan, a merchant from Yuan China. The book is a compilation of his travels throughout Southeast Asia and a treatise on commerce in the region. Wang describes Banzu, probably the kingdom of Singapura centred on present-day Fort Canning Hill; he also describes a settlement on the southern coast of the island—presently the western entrance to Keppel Harbour—inhabited by "Danmaxi (Temasek) barbarians". However, as Wang was possibly preoccupied by trade and economic issues, he focuses on agriculture, soil, and climate; the types of goods traded; and how the "Danmaxi barbarians" were "addicted to piracy". There is no mention of patterns of settlement, roads, or land transport.

The *Sejarah Melayu* of the 1500s does not devote much space to describing the kingdom of Singapura. It simply says: "... Singapura became a great city, to which foreigners resorted in great numbers so that the fame of the city and its greatness spread throughout the world." Again, there is no description of urban development or roads up to the demise of the kingdom.[2] The same pattern follows for its physical descriptions of the kingdom of Malacca, which are limited to the names of its neighbouring kingdoms, population size, and the distance the city extended along the sea (which was one league, or about 5.5 km/3.4 miles).

Portuguese explorers and mariners who wrote about Singapura and Malacca in the 1500s and 1600s were preoccupied with the political intrigue of the region, royal lineages, and the riches of Malacca, which fell under Portuguese control in 1511. For example, the *Suma Oriental*, a book written by apothecary Tome Pires on Asian trade, describes Malacca in terms of physical landmarks at its boundaries, the rivers and farms within its domains, the number of men in its army, the territories which paid tribute to it, and of course the trade it carried out.

Further destruction befell Singapura in 1526 and 1613. First, the Portuguese wiped out a town at the mouth of the Sungei Singapura, possibly because of its association with the defeated Malacca Sultanate. Then, nearly a hundred years later, the Acehnese repeated the feat to strike against their rival, the Johor Sultanate. But this did not spell the end of strife for the island. The *Hikayat Siak*, a book tracing the rise of the Siak Sultanate in central-eastern Sumatra in the 1700s, briefly mentions a battle on the Sungei Singapura in 1767 between forces from Siak and Johor, but it is merely a footnote in history.

Another factor contributing to the sparse knowledge of movement in precolonial Singapura was the absence of a conventional cartographic tradition among the Malays and Orang Laut. Instead, such pictorial depictions were only executed by Chinese and European visitors to the Malay Peninsula and Singapore—and these were few and far between. Detailed maps of Singapore showing off its roads and physical landmarks only appeared after 1819, as the British became interested in mapping its new territory for the purposes of economic exploitation.

What do we know then, that can contribute to a history of movement in Singapore before the British arrived? Not much at all. After Sang Nila Utama decided to set up a new kingdom in 1299 and not return to Bintan as its raja, he composed a message for his adoptive mother in Bintan: "I am not coming back, but if you love me, please send me men, elephants, and horses to establish a city." She duly obliged. From this exchange, it is possible that in ancient Singapura, people walked on foot, or travelled on horses and elephants.

In 1604, Manuel Godinho de Eredia, a cartographer of mixed Bugis (an ethnic group from Sulawesi, part of present-day Indonesia) and Portuguese descent, drew a map of Singapura, one of the earliest maps to depict it in detail. Alas, there were no settlements or roads marked on the map. However, it had five place names: Tanlon Ru (Tanjong Rhu), Sunebodo (Sungei Bedok), Tanamera (Tanah Merah), Tanjon Rusa (Tanjong Rusa), and an island named Blacanmati (Pulau Blakang Mati). Tanjong Rhu is Malay for "Cape of Casuarinas", a reference to the casuarina trees that grew along its beach. "Bedok" could refer to a large Malay drum called *bedoh*, used to sound the alarm or call Muslims to prayer. Tanah Merah is Malay for "Red Earth", a reference to red lateritic cliffs lining the east coast of Singapore Island, visible from the sea. Tanjong Rusa is Malay for "Cape of Deer". And Blakang Mati means "Behind Death", a possible reference to pirates, burial grounds, or spirits haunting the area. Other than the Sungei Singapura, these are possibly the five oldest place names in Singapore; the first three listed are still in use today.

Meanwhile, events in another part of the Johor Sultanate would have a future impact on Singapore. In the mid-1600s, gambier planting started in Sumatra and the west coast of the Malay Peninsula; the Malays planted gambier as a medicine and an ingredient for betel nut chewing. This was converted into a full-fledged industry in the 1730s, when a Bugis minister of Riau, Daeng Chelak, opened Bintan to immigrants from China. This was the first time Chinese farmers arrived en masse in the Malay Archipelago; it was also the first time pepper was cultivated alongside gambier. By the late 1700s, 10,000 Chinese had settled in Bintan, growing gambier for export to Java and China as a tanning agent. Gambier became a cornerstone of the economy of the Johor Sultanate and buttressed the power of the Bugis within the sultanate. However, as the 1700s drew to a close, the Johor Sultanate was in steady decline and the Dutch were encroaching to the south, from Sumatra and Java. By 1818, the Dutch occupied the Riau Islands, forcing the Temenggong, a Johor court official and maritime chief named Abdul Rahman (died 1825), to relocate himself and his followers to the north—to a village in Singapura, near the mouth of the Sungei Singapura. A fitting location, because that is near the site of Parliament House today.

Sources differ on when the Temenggong first set up this village—dates range from 1811 and 1812 to 1818. But the village—named Kampong Temenggong in his honour—was there when Raffles arrived in Singapura in 1819, with the Temenggong himself in residence. No map of the village was ever made, hence we do not know if Kampong Temenggong had any paved or named roads. The village was also founded on part of the original location of ancient Singapura, so we do not know if the village had destroyed any ancient structures, foundations, or roads.

On the eve of Raffles' arrival, other than Kampong Temenggong, there were several settlements on Singapura. To the north of the Sungei Singapura, by the sea, around where Kampong Glam is today, there was a village occupied by Bugis and Chinese settlers, and the Orang Gelam. The Orang Gelam were named after the gelam tree, or *kayu putih*, a tree native to Singapore and used for making medicine, furniture, and boats; the same tree later gave its name to Kampong Glam. Also, because of Singapura's proximity to Bintan, some Chinese planters had migrated from Bintan to Singapura, settling in the forested hills west of Kampong Temenggong with about 20 gambier and pepper plantations. Around the mouths of the Sungei Rochor, Kallang, and Geylang, there lived small communities of Orang Biduanda Kallang. Some Orang Laut still lived around the southern coast of Singapura, as Wang had described in 1349. In the north of the island, Orang Seletar lived along the banks and mouth of the Sungei Seletar, and in the northeast, there was a coastal village named Ponggol. It was said that Ponggol, or Punggol, means "hurling sticks at the branches of fruit trees to bring them down to the ground" in Malay.

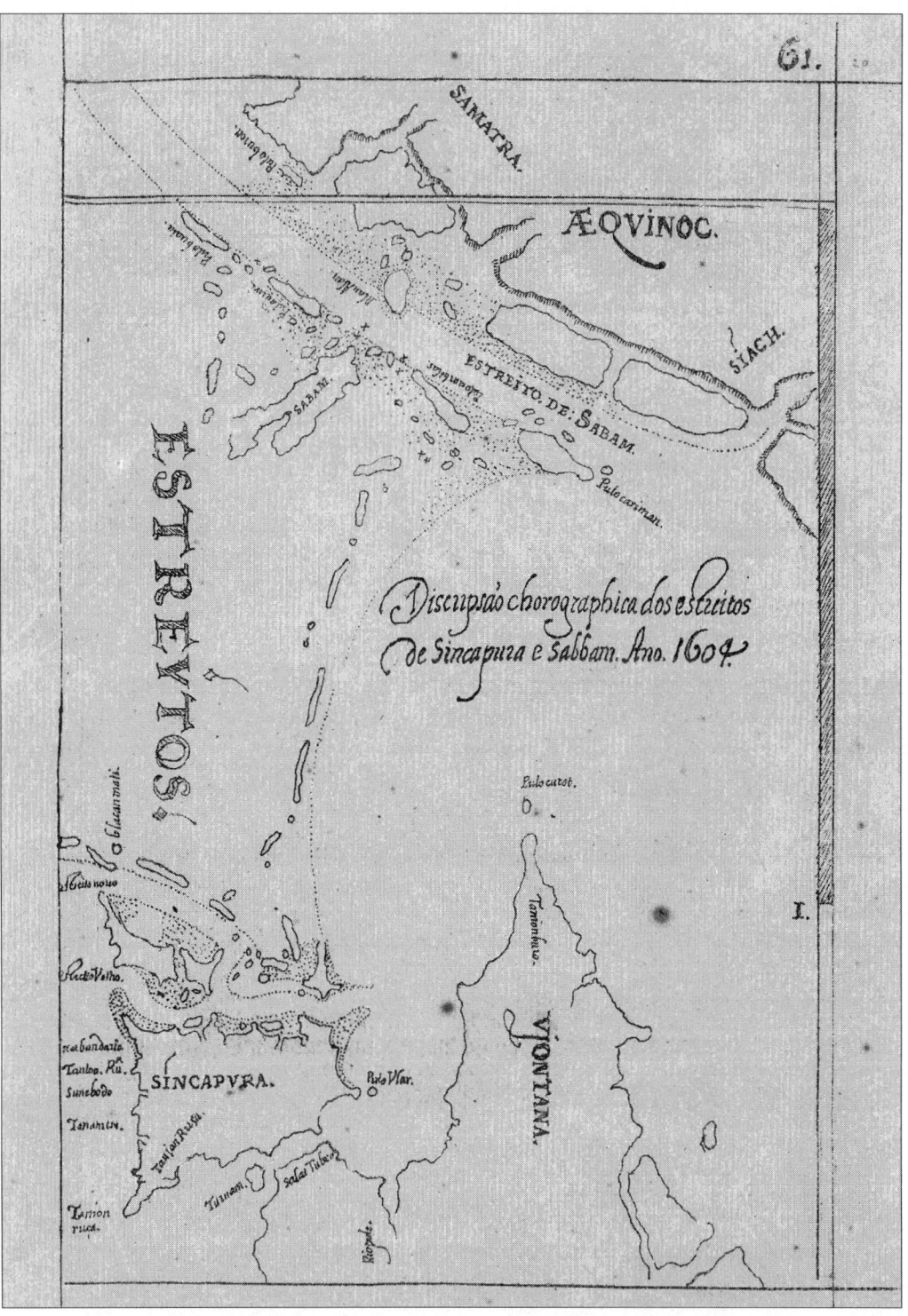

In this 1604 map by cartographer Manuel Godinho de Eredia, Singapura is the island on the bottom left corner. Starting from the bottom of the map, the first four place names on the extreme left are Tanjon Rusa (Tanjong Rusa), Tanamera (Tanah Merah), Sunebodo (Sungei Bedok), and Tanlon Ru (Tanjong Rhu). The eighth name is Blacanmati (Pulau Blakang Mati). (Courtesy of National Library, Singapore [Accession no.: B03013605G])

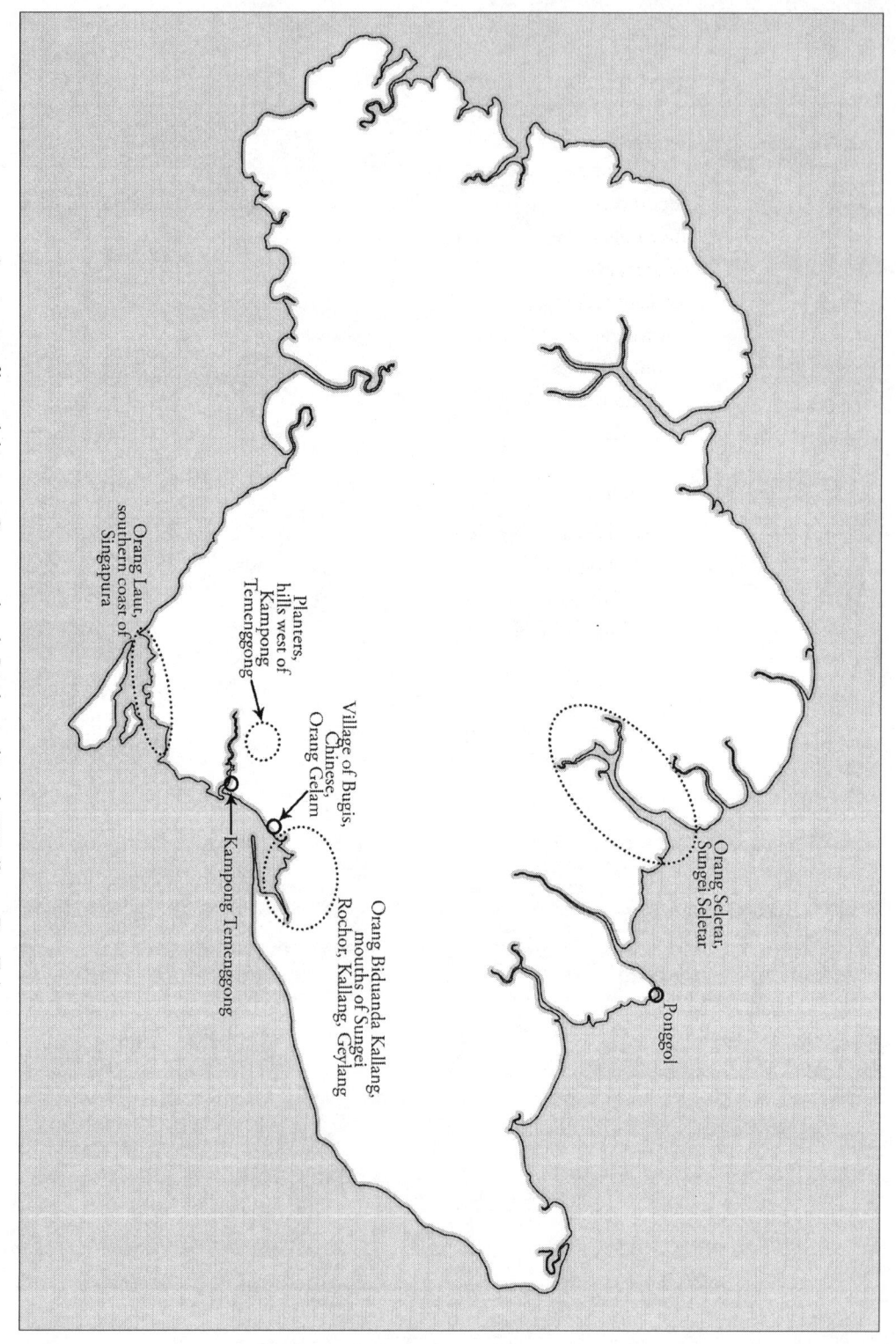

An estimation of human habitation in Singapura when the British arrived in early 1819. (Source: Eisen Teo)

These were more or less the extent of human habitation in Singapura in 1819—in all, the total population numbered no more than 1,200.

In 1822, Singapore's second Resident, John Crawfurd (1783–1868), studied the terrain on which the ancient emporiums of Temasek and Singapura once stood. By then, most traces of these settlements and whatever roads they possessed had disappeared under the onslaught of hundreds of years of rain and vegetation. All Crawfurd found were the remains of foundations of buildings on the northern and western sides of what is now Fort Canning Hill, an earthen wall 2.5–3 metres in height running from the hill to the coast, and at the mouth of the Singapore River, a large piece of sandstone with ancient script on it. The British called the wall the "Old Lines of Singapore", which they believed was part of the limits of the ancient town of Singapura; meanwhile, the large piece of sandstone was blown up in 1843, leaving behind a surviving fragment called the Singapore Stone. Crawfurd did not find any trace of roads.

Limited modes of land transport, a mere handful of place names and villages, part of the boundary of an ancient settlement—these are all that contribute to a history of movement before the British arrived in 1819. Primitive engineering technology, a harsh climate, an absence of a cartographic tradition, and the preoccupation of foreign visitors with economics and politics, are factors that impede efforts to piece together a precolonial history of movement. It is because of these that High Street is one of Singapore's oldest roads, if not the oldest, even though it is only about 200 years old; it is also because of these factors that a detailed history of movement only becomes possible in the last 200 years.

Yet the British could have settled in Singapore a hundred years before 1819—and it could have been a Scot, not an Englishman, to claim credit for the founding of modern Singapore. Scottish sea captain Alexander Hamilton was a good friend of Johor's Sultan Abdul Jalil; in 1703, Hamilton called on the sultan on his way to China. The latter then:

> … treated me very kindly, and made me a present of the island of Singapore, but I told him it could be of no use to a private person, though a proper place for a company to settle a colony on, lying in the centre of trade, and being accommodated with good rivers and safe harbours…

This remains one of the big what-ifs of Singapore history—what if Hamilton had taken up the Sultan's offer? With a hundred-year head-start, predating the arrival of a Temenggong or Chinese planters, could Singapore's history of movement have taken a different turn?

CHAPTER NOTES

1. There are 32 variant editions of the *Sejarah Melayu*, and studies by Dutch and Malay scholars have confirmed that Raffles MS 18 is the oldest version. According to Malaysian historian Cheah Boon Kheng, the first author of the *Sejarah Melayu* "outlived the capture of Malacca by the Portuguese in 1511, wrote his text up to the year 1535 and died sometime after 1535". The text was subsequently passed down to other writers and copyists, which then became Raffles MS 18. I quoted from the English translation of Raffles MS 18 by C. C. Brown, first published in 1952.

2. C. C. Brown's translation of Raffles MS 18 mentions "a man of Pasai called Tun Jana Khatib… (walking) through the streets (of Singapura)". Unfortunately, there is no further description of these streets. John Leyden's translation of the *Sejarah Melayu* mentions Tun Jana Khatib "walking in the market-place of (Singapura)". Again, there is no further description of the area.

CHAPTER 2
1819 to 1880: Feet and Hooves

IN 1819, the British obtained permission from the Sultan of Johor to set up a trading post in the southeastern part of Singapore Island. Over the next six decades, the settlement, also named Singapore, grew from a village of about 150 souls into a bustling town of 95,000.[1] A colonial port-town of largely Asian immigrants ruled by a tiny group of Europeans, built along British lines and with British channels and methods of movement, was transplanted onto an island deep in the heart of the Malay world, effacing centuries of Malay and Orang Laut place names and channels of movement. Before the arrival of the British, transport within Singapore Island was mainly river and sea-based. British authority and large-scale Chinese immigration made possible a permanent transition to a land-based transport network.

The Town of Singapore was concentrated along a four-kilometre stretch of coastline in the southeast, extending no more than a kilometre inland. In 1878, American zoologist William Hornaday visited it, observing:

> Singapore is certainly the handiest city I ever saw, as well planned and carefully executed as though built entirely by one man. It is like a big desk, full of drawers and pigeonholes, where everything has its place, and can always be found in it. For instance, around the (Esplanade) you find the European hotels—and bad enough they are, too; around Commercial Square, packed closely together, are all the shipping offices, warehouses, and shops of the European merchants; and along Boat Quay are all the ship chandlers. Nearby, you will find a dozen large Chinese medicine shops, a dozen cloth shops, a dozen tin shops, and similar clusters of shops kept by blacksmiths, tailors and carpenters, others for the sale of fruit, vegetables, grain... All the washerwomen congregate on a five-acre lawn called Dhobi Green, at one side of which runs a stream of water, and there you will see the white shirts, trousers, and pajamas of His Excellency, perhaps, hanging in ignominious proximity to and on a level with yours. By some means or other, even the Joss houses (Chinese temples), like birds of a feather, have flocked together at one side of the town. Owing to this peculiar grouping of the different trades, one can do more business in less time in Singapore than in any other town in the world.

Hornaday's observation of the Town as "well-planned" and "carefully executed" was astute, because its core had been immaculately designed as a grid plan, the handiwork of a committee guided by the vision of one man. However, as decades passed, the strain of breakneck economic and population growth saw the Town outgrow its original plan, even though the original principle of "roads at right angles to one another" was not completely forgotten.

Outside the Town, a trunk road system stretched to most corners of Singapore Island, connecting the Town to plantations of pepper, gambier, nutmeg, and tropical fruits, and 36,000 rural settlers. It was mostly the Chinese who set up villages and market towns along these trunk roads, becoming almost an authority unto themselves, an authority expressed in the names of some of these villages. Closer to the Town, numerous Europeans set up their own little agricultural fiefdoms, leaving behind legacies in the form of plantation houses and driveways. It was the British who first mapped the interior of the island, all the better to parcel out and trade land, that bountiful commodity in the colonial period. As a result, many places in Singapore Island were given "official" names, some very English, others not so; other Malay or Orang Laut place names which were never made known to the surveyors were lost forever. However, far from everyone in Singapore Island subscribed to the British road and place naming system; Chinese and Indian communities had their own unique methods of "mapping" and negotiating the same urban space they shared with the Europeans.

Most of the time, the roads were far from world-class, and when it rained heavily many turned to mud, but for the most part they were built and maintained by an unlikely source of labour—a proud and independent posse of Indian convicts. Over time, an official bureaucracy was established to handle the constant demand for road maintenance. Meanwhile, for the average inhabitant of Singapore, travelling remained a sweaty, laborious affair. Transportation choices other than walking were sparse. These included carriages and carts pulled by horses, donkeys or buffaloes; and the bicycle and horse-drawn omnibuses in later years. Only the rich had their own "private transport" (the term did not exist at the time) in the form of horse carriages. This state of affairs kept the Town of Singapore compact and walkable.

THE EARLY DAYS OF A NEW SETTLEMENT

TO UNDERSTAND how the British settlement of Singapore developed the way it did in the years after 1819, we need to recognise several factors: firstly, the British were around largely because of a thirst for trade and a quest for maritime dominance; secondly, the British initially gained only permission to set up a port—not full sovereignty—over just one per cent of Singapore Island's land area; thirdly, the handful of individuals who oversaw the settlement's development in its early years had grand ideas, lofty ideas worthy of kingdoms and empires, but did not see eye to eye, and never stayed long enough to see their visions realised.

By 1818, the British had been maritime trade rivals with the Dutch for more than two centuries. The Dutch, acting through the Dutch East India Company, a chartered company established in 1602, controlled much of the spice trade in the Malay Archipelago. Ports such as Batavia (present-day Jakarta) and Malacca ensured they maintained a strong grip on shipping along trade routes between India and China. The British, acting through the British East India Company (EIC), had ports at Penang and Bencoolen (present-day Bengkulu in Sumatra), but they were not as well-placed to attract shipping.

Enter Sir Stamford Raffles. Born in 1781 at sea, the 37-year-old already had a prolific career with the EIC. Starting at the lowly position of clerk at age 14, the precocious teenager who studied at night by candlelight soon distinguished himself through his industriousness, energy, and later, mastery of the Malay language and local conditions. Over the next two decades, he excelled in assignments to Penang and Malacca, led a successful military invasion of Java, was knighted for completing a monumental 500-page tome called *The History of Java* in just 17 months, and dispatched to the malaria-ridden backwater of Bencoolen as lieutenant-governor.

But Raffles was not content with lying low. He realised the importance of establishing a new port for the EIC that would succeed in challenging the Dutch monopoly of the seas. His solution was to look somewhere around the tip of the Malay Peninsula. At the end of 1818, he managed to convince his superior, the governor-general of British India, Francis Rawdon-Hastings, to approve an expedition to the southern end of the Straits of Malacca. The instructions were vague, and that suited Raffles.

In January 1819, Raffles set sail from Penang down the Straits of Malacca. First, he surveyed the Karimun Islands off the island of Sumatra. Then he set his eyes on the island of Singapura, the mythical place he had read about in the *Sejarah Melayu*. He realised its suitability as a port—it lay smack along the key India–China trade routes, yet the Dutch were nowhere to be found—yet. The southern part of the island possessed a river deep enough to accommodate a harbour, with plenty of wood and fresh water. Even better, the island was part of the decaying Johor Sultanate, which was weak and open to exploitation, thanks to an ongoing succession dispute.

In 1812, when Johor's Sultan Mahmud Shah breathed his last, his younger son Abdul Rahman (1780–1830) was appointed successor, bypassing the older son Hussein Shah (1776–1835) as he was away in Pahang getting married at the time. Abdul Rahman had the powerful Dutch as backers, so Hussein Shah quietly opted for exile in the Riau Islands. Seven years on, Raffles decided to draw him out, take him to Singapura, and declare him the rightful Sultan of Johor in exchange for permission to set up a trading post on the island. It was controversial and daring, and bound to infuriate the Dutch, but a brilliant political manoeuvre only Raffles would have dared pull off.

So it came to be that a humble British squadron of six ships, led by Raffles and former Resident of Malacca William Farquhar (1774–1839), docked at the southeastern coast of Singapura on 28 January 1819. Raffles and his men landed on the north bank of the Sungei Singapura, the river he identified as the location for a port. The north bank was relatively drier and on higher ground than the south bank, which was marshy and flooded frequently. The north bank was also where the wooden houses of Kampong Temenggong stood.

Nine days later, on 6 February 1819, Raffles signed a Treaty of Friendship and Alliance with Hussein Shah and Temenggong Abdul Rahman. The treaty spelled the name of the island as "Singapoora", but in a proclamation Raffles issued the same day, presumably to the outside world, he named the island "Singapore". The Johor Sultanate's Singapura had become the EIC trading post of Singapore; the new port was no longer by the Sungei Singapura, but the Singapore River.

Hence, from the beginning, the settlement of Singapore hugged the Singapore River and the coastline north and south of the river. The thickly forested interior was largely left untouched, either too daunting or not of interest to early settlers and traders.

Raffles is often credited as the founder of modern Singapore. But it was Farquhar, appointed the first Resident of Singapore, who saw the island through the chaos of its early years. Just one day after the treaty was concluded, Raffles left matters in Singapore to Farquhar, and set sail for Penang. For the next three years he spent fewer than 30 days in Singapore, while Farquhar ran the show. That was fateful for the settlement's subsequent urban and road development. For while Raffles was an avid planner with grandiose ideas, a micro-manager who worked tirelessly and a man determined to get his way, Farquhar was more laissez-faire and easygoing in running the settlement; he was more approachable and willing to compromise, seek a middle way and go with whatever worked for the moment. In the words of Munshi Abdullah (1796–1854), Raffles' tutor in Malay and a good friend of both Raffles and Farquhar, it was in Farquhar's nature to listen to a man's complaint, no matter how poor or lowly the man, and give "advice and direction until the man's mind was set at rest". Such a measured, flexible approach probably secured Singapore's survival in its first three years, and ensured it developed in a more organic manner than Raffles would have allowed if he had been present.

In the years following its founding, thousands flocked to the port to engage in business. Its growth was nothing short of phenomenal. In 1819, just 120 Malays and 30 Chinese lived in the area around the Singapore River. By 1821, the port's population had grown 31 times to 4,727, and by 1824, more than doubled again to 10,683. Some initially hailed from Malacca as they had prospered under Farquhar's rule as Resident from 1803 to 1818. Many more came from the Middle East, southern India, southern China, and all over the Malay world—"a conglomeration of all eastern and western nations".

The port of Singapore turned into a cash cow. By 1823, the value of Singapore's imports and exports exceeded $13 million, more than that of Penang and Bencoolen combined. Yet running the port cost only 12–14,000 pounds a year (in contrast, Bencoolen bled 100,000 pounds a year). From 1819 to 1826, Singapore was run by a skeleton team of a Resident—directly answerable to the EIC in British India—two assistants, and two or three clerks. Just half a dozen men oversaw almost all civil and political duties for the settlement, including the administration of justice, police, and finance.

The settlement grew from the Singapore River and High Street to the foothills of nearby Bukit Larangan—very much the same area covered by 14th-century Singapura. This time, however, the British mapped the settlement in great detail, recording individual buildings, villages, roads, and natural features, with place and road names they either bequeathed or thought the native population used. For the first time in Singapore's history, there was a cartographical record of its human settlements. However, the maps were made from a British point of view and reflected British interests and biases; place and road names were in English, English transliterations, or English misspellings.

The earliest surviving landward map of the port of Singapore was the Bute Map, drawn sometime between 1819 and 1820. On the map, most of "Singapore Town" occupies a narrow strip on the north bank of the Singapore River between Bukit Larangan and the sea. This was presumably prime riverfront property. Singapore Town had grown up around the old Kampong Temenggong, absorbing it, so in the midst of Singapore Town lay the Temenggong's Palace.

To the north, a large patch of land had been cleared for military cantonments for about 150 EIC sepoys and artillerymen; it lay between High Street and the Old Lines of Singapore 500 metres north.

The cantonments were accompanied by officers' tents, a parade ground, magazines, and stores. On a small knoll by the sea, Lieutenant Henry Ralfe had erected a battery of 12-pounder guns to protect the settlement from a Dutch attack from the sea; this is near the middle of the Padang today.

Beyond the Old Lines to the north, there were nine allotments that made up the "Proposed Site of a European Town". In June 1819, when Raffles was away, he wrote orders to Farquhar to reserve the north bank of the Singapore River for purposes of governance, while allocating this European Town and the seafront from the Old Lines to the Rochor River—dubbed the North Beach—for European merchants. Alas, the seas off North Beach were rough and too shallow for large ships. Merchants such as Alexander Guthrie threatened to leave Singapore if they were not allowed to build their offices and godowns elsewhere. Farquhar gave in, and consequently the merchants mostly lived and worked on the north bank of the Singapore River, in Singapore Town, while the European Town remained a "proposed site". North of the European Town, about 1.5 km from the Singapore River, there was a "Bugis Town", a precolonial village with Bugis, Chinese, and Orang Gelam dwellers. Nearby stood the Palace of Sultan Hussein, possibly made of timber and thatch.

On the south bank of the Singapore River sat a "Chinese Town". It was low-lying, muddy land undesirable to the Europeans, where the rest of the Chinese settled. A bridge was proposed to span the Singapore River and connect Singapore Town to this Chinese Town; it was built after the Bute Map was drawn. South of the mouth of the Singapore River, there was a small cape with a promontory on it, called Tanjong Singapura. A small path ran by the promontory; it was known as Lorong Tambangan. "Lorong" is Malay for "Lane"; "Tambangan" could have been a corruption of *tambatan*, Malay for "mooring", a reference to boats moored by the river mouth.

The Bute Map also marks out several unnamed roads that bear the location and shape of present-day roads. Other than High Street, these roads lie north of Singapore Town, in the space reserved for military cantonments. They include what would later become Coleman Street and Hill Street— some of the oldest roads in Singapore today. There was also another narrow path running north from the Old Lines to Bugis Town; it is part of Beach Road today. Finally, there were more roads on the slopes of Bukit Larangan, but they do not align with present-day roads and have disappeared.

By May 1821, about 24 km of roads had been made, according to the *Anecdotal History of Old Times in Singapore*, a book compiled by newspaper owner Charles Buckley (1844–1912) in 1902. Half of these roads were "carriage roads" 12–15 metres wide. The roads "extended from the (Singapore River) to Rochor; round the hill, afterwards levelled (possibly Tanjong Singapura), where Circular Road is now; and out to Selegie, which is no doubt what is now called Selegie Road". Buckley also listed the lengths of specific roads and their corresponding widths, and even the total cost of construction—$6,447. Unfortunately, these roads were never named, although each was categorised as one of four types: carriage road, horse road, horse path, and footpath. Carriage roads were probably roads wide and strong enough to accommodate the movement of horse carriages, while horse roads could only accommodate horses; paths were probably narrower than roads and were separated into those that were strong enough to handle horses and those that could only handle human feet.

From 1819 to 1821, Lieutenant Ralfe was the Assistant Engineer of Singapore, overseeing the

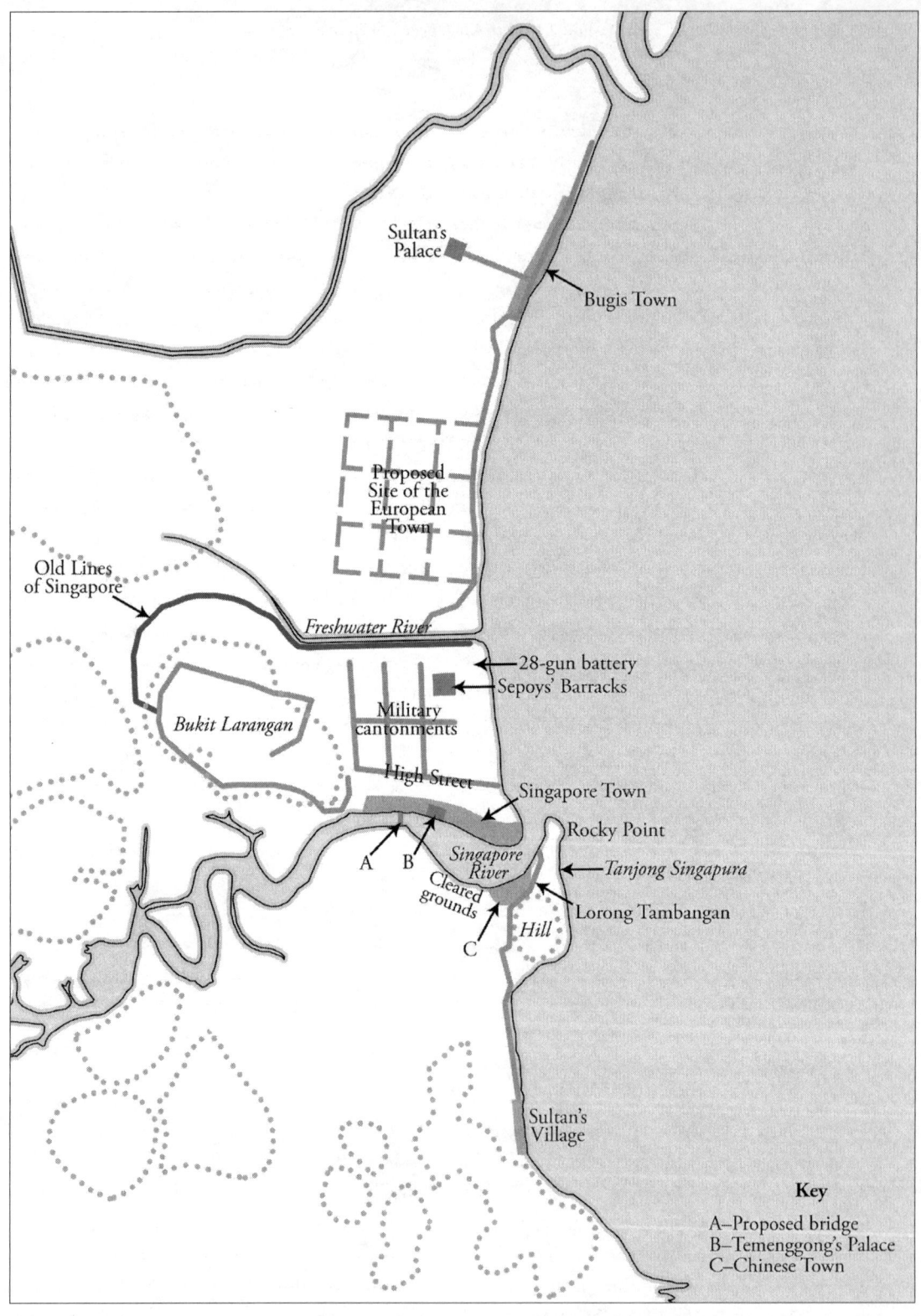

A drawing of the Bute Map, the earliest surviving landward map of the port of Singapore, produced sometime between 1819 and 1820. Hills are marked out with dotted lines. (Source: Eisen Teo)

construction of all roads and buildings. After he left for Calcutta on grounds of ill health, another officer from the Bengal Artillery took his place. He was Lieutenant Philip Jackson (1802–1879).

A TOWN PLAN FOR 150 YEARS

WHEN RAFFLES returned to Singapore for the third and last time on 10 October 1822, he became unhappy at what he perceived as the haphazard growth of the settlement. In a move uncharacteristic of colonial officials at the time, he decided to micro-manage the future development of the port. Farquhar had largely allowed the settlement to grow according to the whims of its residents. Raffles wanted a detailed plan to the growth, separate zones for different races and ethnic groups, and designated spaces allocated for public buildings, European merchants, and a mercantile quarter. As the settlement was now three years old, many things would have to be reworked literally from the ground up. He wanted a master plan for a "new" settlement of Singapore.

Hence, just a week after his return, on 17 October 1822, Raffles appointed a Land Allotment Committee to oversee the reallocation of land. It comprised three men, all friends of Raffles: surgeon and naturalist Dr Nathaniel Wallich (1786–1854), superintendent of Bencoolen's spice plantation Dr James Lumsdaine, and Bencoolen's harbour master Captain Francis Salmond. On 4 November, he established a Town Committee to draw up the master plan. It comprised Captain Charles Edward Davis of the Bengal Native Infantry, Assistant Resident Samuel George Bonham (1803–1863), and Alexander Laurie Johnston (died 1850), one of Singapore's most prominent merchants at the time. He also appointed Assistant Engineer Lieutenant Jackson to make maps of the master plan. Other reputable members of the European community at the time, such as surgeon Dr William Montgomerie (1797–1856) and architect and surveyor George Drumgoole Coleman (1795–1844), were consulted on various issues such as the laying out of roads, building construction, and land reclamation. The resultant Raffles Town Plan, or Jackson Plan, would be Singapore's first and only urban town plan for the next 130 years.

Today, we know what the Town Plan looks like thanks to Jackson's map—although the map reflects what was intended rather than what eventually materialised. Many roads on Jackson's map were not laid out in reality, even though key roads were indeed executed, and the principle of a grid system in road planning, with rectangular plots carved out for buildings, was followed through.

The Raffles Town Plan set down Singapore's first town limits. Raffles wrote that "if a space is reserved from (the sea) inland in every direction of from half a mile to a mile, as the ground may admit", spanning a three-mile seafront from Telok Ayer in the southwest to Sandy Point in the northeast, "it will be sufficient for all the purposes required in a principal town". It was easy to mark out the limits because of natural barriers on all sides. From Telok Ayer to the Singapore River, the town limits were rolling hills; there were marshes on either bank of the Singapore River; north of the Singapore River, the limits were defined by Bukit Larangan, Seligi (Selegie) Hill, and the Rochor River.

The land within occupies only part of the Central Area today, just five MRT stops along the East West Line, or four MRT stops along the North East Line, but it was more than sufficient in 1823 to house a population of over 10,000. This was to be the "new" Town of Singapore.

Inside this town, land was set aside for buildings for administration and to serve the public, such as court houses and government offices. Raffles was adamant that his original vision of 1819 be fulfilled this time. The Town Plan stated that this "Government Ground" was to cover the land from the Singapore River to the Old Lines—covering all of Singapore Town in the Bute Map. Hence, Raffles instructed the Town Planning Committee to oversee the "removal of the native population and buildings" from the north bank of the Singapore River to the opposite side. This was the earliest form of "urban renewal" for modern Singapore—just four years into its existence. Officials had to calculate the value of each building to be demolished and work out compensation for their owners.

The military cantonments north of Singapore Town had to move too. They were first shifted to near the Rochor River, but the area was too low-lying. By the late 1820s, they were moved again to the southern part of Singapore Island, west of Telok Ayer, beyond the town limits. The area became known as the Sepoy Lines, where the EIC's Bengal Artillery and Madras Infantry were stationed.[2]

One of Farquhar's ideas survived though—the Esplanade, an open field next to High Street by the sea, occupying some of the land freed up after the military cantonments moved away. The Esplanade was distinctively colonial. It was similar to other open seaside fields and promenades found in colonial cities all over Southeast Asia, such as Penang's Esplanade and Manila's Malecon Drive (now Bonifacio Drive). Singapore's Esplanade had a road running by the sea; it was called Esplanade Road. When Lieutenant Ralfe's battery moved, the knoll on which it stood—which became part of the Esplanade—took on the name Scandal Point, for Europeans gathered there in the evenings to gossip and share scandals! Scandal Point was another colonial trademark—19th-century British ports in the region each had their own Scandal Points: Penang, Malacca, Rangoon, Hong Kong.

North of the Old Lines, Raffles also realised his initial order of 1819 that the land be turned into a "European Town". The European Town of 1822 was far larger than the European Town of 1819—this time, it stretched lengthwise from the Old Lines to the vicinity of the Sultan's palace compound, and widthwise from the sea to the foot of what are now Mount Sophia and Mount Emily. It was huge for the European community of just 90 in 1824!

However, Raffles did give in to the European merchants' insistence that the North Beach was unsuitable for siting godowns and landing goods by sea. With the north bank of the Singapore River off limits to them now, he decided to site them south of the Singapore River, at its mouth—on the promontory called Tanjong Singapura. Again, this was where Raffles pushed through his bold ideas, and where 19th-century urban renewal took place: he ordered all buildings already erected at Tanjong Singapura to be levelled, the entire hill broken up, and its contents pushed into the marsh on the south bank of the Singapore River. The Chinese Town marked out on the Bute Map had to be demolished for the marshes to be fully reclaimed. This way, flat, dry land was created where there once had been a hill and marshes. This was the first land reclamation project in Singapore's history. Somewhere between 200 and 300 Chinese, Malay, and south Indian labourers were employed for this purpose, with little more than cangkuls, shovels, and baskets to carry earth. Raffles himself came twice a day to give directions, and every evening bags of money were brought to pay the men. In four months Tanjong Singapura was cut down and all hollows, streams, and drains filled up. Lorong Tambangan was also expunged—the first named road in Singapore's history to fall victim to urban renewal, but definitely not the last. In their place a new mercantile quarter arose. It was later named Commercial Square—today's Raffles Place. Many merchants moved into shophouses there, living on the second floor above their ground-floor godowns.

To connect the Government Ground and European Town to Commercial Square, the unnamed bridge spanning the Singapore River was replaced by a wooden drawbridge; the drawbridge was named Presentment Bridge (Elgin Bridge today). Completed in 1822, it was to be the river's only bridge for the next 18 years.

For the non-European races, Raffles instituted a strict policy of physical segregation, parcelling out different parts of the Town to different races, and assigning a headman to each race. This was a framework for keeping them separated, docile and subservient.

North of the European Town, bordered by the banks of the Rochor River and the sea, was land allocated for the Malays, Bugis, Arabs, and other ethnic groups from the region. Altogether, they totalled 6,431 in 1824—about 60 per cent of the population. This was fitting, as the area was already occupied by the Sultan's compound and Bugis Town. However, of Bugis Town, Raffles did not like what he saw. He observed that "at present the houses (were) scattered without any attention to order or convenience", and that it would be "necessary to… (lay) out regular streets inland towards the (Rochor River) and (oblige) the inhabitants to conform thereto". Hence, he ordered more urban renewal—most of the Bugis Town was to be moved to the north, between the Sultan's compound and the mouth of the Rochor River. The area was near to the sand and mudflats of the mouths of the Rochor and Kallang rivers, where the maritime Bugis would be most at home with their high-masted prahus. The Bugis made up a significant 17 per cent of the population of Singapore in 1824. Being trade rivals with the Dutch, the Bugis could be useful in a possible conflict with them. As for the original Bugis Town, Raffles underlined the strictness of the policy of racial segregation, and called for the removal of all Chinese settlers and their seafront houses. A precolonial village was no more.

Other than a Bugis Campong, Raffles also demarcated an Arab Campong; in between lay the Sultan's compound, which at the time stretched inland from the sea to the banks of the Rochor River. Collectively, the Arab Campong, Sultan's compound, and Bugis Campong were known as Kampong Glam. No longer did "kampong" only refer to a traditional village; now, it also referred to an Asian urban neighbourhood.

The Chinese in Singapore—numbering 3,317 in 1824—were allocated land south of the Singapore River, including much of the new land reclaimed with soil from what was once Tanjong Singapura. The new riverfront at the south bank was named Boat Quay—the "belly of the carp" that was the Singapore River. South of it lay the new "Chinese Campong". Inside, Raffles advocated separating the Chinese along topolect lines, such as the Hokkiens, Teochews, and Cantonese, because "it is well known that the people of one province are more quarrelsome than another, and that continued disputes and disturbances take place between people of different provinces".[3]

South of the Chinese Campong and the town limits, to connect it to the southern coast, two roads were laid down from 1823, running past hills and swamps. One was Salat (now Silat) Road; "Salat" was a British spelling of "Selat", the Malay for "Straits". The other was Tanjong Pagar Road;

"Tanjong Pagar" is Malay for "Cape of Stake Fences", referring to the *kelongs* off Tanjong Pagar Village, a coastal village where the road ended.

The Town Plan also set aside land for the Chuliahs—a name for the community of Indians from Tamil Nadu —in an area called the Chuliah Campong, up the Singapore River from the Chinese Campong. However, after Raffles left the settlement in 1823, this plan was never realised and the allocated land remained marshy into the 1830s. Instead of Indians, migrants from Malacca built a village on stilts; the Chuliah Campong on paper became Kampong Malacca in reality.

For the laying down of roads, Raffles left detailed orders for the Town Planning Committee. He wanted the streets lined out at right angles and at fixed breadth—in other words, a grid road network. It is a testament to the simplicity and elegance of the grid pattern that some of Singapore's oldest roads have survived to this day.

Raffles also ordered the Committee to ensure every street was "appropriately named"—an order we take for granted today, but important then as it was not common practice before the arrival of the British. From the 1820s, the duty of naming roads went to officials appointed by the Resident or governor. This persisted until 1849, when a Municipal Committee was formed to run municipal affairs; this committee took over the naming of streets.

Because the men involved in the naming of roads were usually officials from Britain, distinctive British influences emerged in these road names. Inside Government Ground and the European Town, many roads were named after prominent members of the European community, or after physical landmarks. By 1837, Government Ground had roads such as Coleman Street, named after George Coleman; Hospital Street, after a pauper's hospital which closed soon after due to a lack of funds, and by 1850, was renamed Stamford Road after Raffles; Hill Street after Bukit Larangan, the hill which overlooked it; and North Bridge Road after Presentment Bridge. North Bridge Road was the backbone of the grid road system north of the Singapore River. The European Town had roads such as Church Street, named after Thomas Church (1798–1860), who became Resident Councillor in 1837; Flint Street after Captain William Flint (1781–1828), Raffles' brother-in-law and Singapore's first Master Attendant;[4] Queen Street, after Britain's Queen Victoria (1819–1901); Middle Road, because breadthwise, it ran down the middle of the European Town; and Beach Road, because it ran along the beach.

However, over time, there arose exceptions to the rule of naming roads in the European Town after Europeans or prominent landmarks. These exceptions came about because Raffles—the harshest enforcer of his own rules—left Singapore for good in 1823, just months after the Town Plan was finalised. He never lived in Singapore long enough to ensure the long-term physical segregation of races, or the following of specifications of the Town Plan to the letter. Consequently, some merchants never gave up their land and godowns along High Street and the north bank of the Singapore River, even though they were supposed to make way for Government Ground. Merchant Tan Che Sang (1763–1836) was one of them. Eventually, the road running along the north bank was named North Boat Quay, a nod to the loading and unloading of goods between godowns and the river; accordingly, the road running along the south bank was named South Boat Quay. Also, as early as 1828, land parcels along Beach Road and North Bridge Road were leased to Chinese. Bencoolen Malays, attracted to

Singapore because of Raffles' exemplary reputation as governor-general of Bencoolen, settled down in the European Town, influencing the naming of Bencoolen Street and Marbro Street (after Bencoolen's Fort Marlborough). (Marbro Street was renamed Victoria Street in the 1840s after Queen Victoria.) As years passed, people of all races settled all over the Town.

Other exceptions in the European Town included Brass Bassa (now Bras Basah, Malay for "Wet Rice") Road, "originally a pathway beside which a cargo of damaged rice was once spread out to dry". By the 1850s, Bugis Street, Malay Street, Malabar Street, and China Street were also laid down between North Bridge Road and Victoria Street, reflecting the different communities residing there: "Malabar" referred to the western coast of southern India, while there had been an influx of immigrants from Hainan Island, China. Eurasian families had also moved in. What began as a space solely for well-to-do Europeans was gradually shared with Chinese, Bugis, Malays, Indians, and Eurasians.

Down at Commercial Square, the earliest roads built there were mostly named after prominent landmarks or trading communities. They included Market Street, named after the Telok Ayer Market (known today as Lau Pa Sat, or "Old Market"); Battery Road, after Fort Fullerton, a fort built next to Commercial Square in the late 1820s as a replacement for the battery at Scandal Point; Kling Street, after immigrants from southern India (the word "Kling" probably came from the ancient kingdom of Kalinga in southern India); Malacca Street, after the immigrants from Malacca who had flocked to Singapore because of Farquhar.

North of the Singapore River, in the Bugis Campong, later known as Kampong Rochor after the Rochor River, there appeared the first cluster of roads with Malay names and with the word "Jalan" (Malay for "Road" or "Street") or "Lorong" in them. By 1837, a dozen roads had been built. They were named Jalan Chondong ("Leaning Road"), Jalan Trang ("Bright Road"), Jalan Susat, Jalan Sampit ("Narrow Road"), Jalan Sunee, Jalan Passar ("Market Road"), Jalan Ramee, Jalan Bugis, Jalan Malintang, Jalan Henda, Jalan Rochor, and Lorong Jambatan ("Bridge Lane"). By the late 1840s, most of these roads had been renamed. Jalan Malintang was renamed Jalan Sultan after the Sultan of Johor, while seven roads were renamed after islands and cities in the Dutch East Indies, possibly because of settlers from these places: Jalan Henda to Sumbawa Road; Jalan Sunee and Jalan Passar to Palembang Road; Jalan Ramee and Jalan Bugis to Java Road.

The Malay World and Middle East themes for road-naming in Kampong Glam persisted. By the 1850s, Sultan Gate and Sultan Road were built and named after the Sultan of Johor. Arab Street was named after the Arab community. Bally Lane (now Bali Lane) was named after the island of Bali. Sheik Madersaw Lane (later spelled Shaik Madersah) was possibly named after a man called Madersaw Hooseusah,[5] while Jalan Kramat, Malay for "Sacred Shrine Road", was named as such because it passed through a Malay and Muslim cemetery, marked out in early maps as "Tombs of the Malayan Princes"—one part of the cemetery was reserved for Sultan Hussein's household. In the 1870s, Jeddah Street was named after the main city in the Hejaz region of the Ottoman Empire, while Haji Lane was named after the hajj, the pilgrimage to Mecca, also in the Hejaz region. There were exceptions—Jalan Susat and Jalan Sampit were renamed Minto Road, possibly after the 1st Earl of Minto, Gilbert Elliot-Murray-Kynynmound (1751–1814), governor-general of India from 1807 to 1813.

South of the Singapore River, in the Chinese Campong, there appeared roads named after Chinese topolect groups and locations in China—with British transliterations of course. There was China Street (causing confusion because there was another China Street in the European Town); Pekin Street, named after Beijing, the capital of China; Nankin Street after Nanjing; Canton Street after Guangdong Province; Macao Street after Macau; Amoy Street and Chin Chew Street after Xiamen and Quanzhou, Fujian Province; Hokien Street after the Hokkiens, the largest Chinese topolect group in Singapore today.

Other roads were also named after prominent physical landmarks, as was the case in Government Ground and the European Town: North and South Canal Road, after the Singapore Canal, which cut across the width of the Chinese Campong; Circular Road, because it followed the curve of the Singapore River; Cross Street, because it cut across the width of the Chinese Campong; and Telok Ayer (Malay for "Water Bay") Street, a coastal road next to a bay. Finally, there was South Bridge Road, the backbone of the grid road system in the Chinese Campong, linked to North Bridge Road via Presentment Bridge. South Bridge Road was the southern channel out of the Town to the island's southern coast, joined to Tanjong Pagar Road and Salat Road.

As the Chinese Campong became more ethnically diverse, there arose exceptions to the aforementioned toponymic rules. As early as 1827, Singapore's oldest Hindu temple, the Sri Mariamman Temple, and one of its oldest mosques, the Masjid Jamae, built for Tamil Muslims from southern India, were already standing by South Bridge Road. By 1838, Japan Street was named after a Japanese community in the area. Into the 1840s, George Street was named after William Renshaw George (1797–1873), a merchant and son-in-law of Farquhar; Synagogue Street was named after Singapore's first synagogue, set up in 1841 in a shophouse.

After the Town of Singapore's streets were named, the houses along each street had to be built in an orderly fashion. The Town Planning Committee was tasked with fixing the minimum space along a street a house could occupy, hence determining the number of houses a street could accommodate. Each house was to be numbered, and rent charged accordingly. Each house should also have "a verandah of a certain depth, open at all times as a continued and covered passage on each side of the street". The depth was later set at five feet—hence the term "five-foot-way" to describe the covered walkways in front of rows of shophouses. The five-foot-way served as Singapore's first pedestrian walkways, sheltering them from sunlight and rain.

In March 1823, Raffles found time to implement another urban renewal project. The Town Plan had designated the land occupied by Kampong Temenggong and the Temenggong's Palace as Government Ground, but the Temenggong and his followers remained after the Plan was finalised in 1822. Fights and disputes broke out on a regular basis between the Temenggong's men and migrants from Malacca. Raffles used that to persuade the Temenggong and his followers to move to a new plot of land along the southern coast of Singapore Island, in Tulloh (Telok) Blangah—at the time, way beyond the town limits. "Telok Blangah" is Malay for "Cooking Pot Bay", named as such because it faced a bay in the shape of a traditional cooking pot. Raffles claimed that the Temenggong and his followers would have plenty of comfort and living space there.

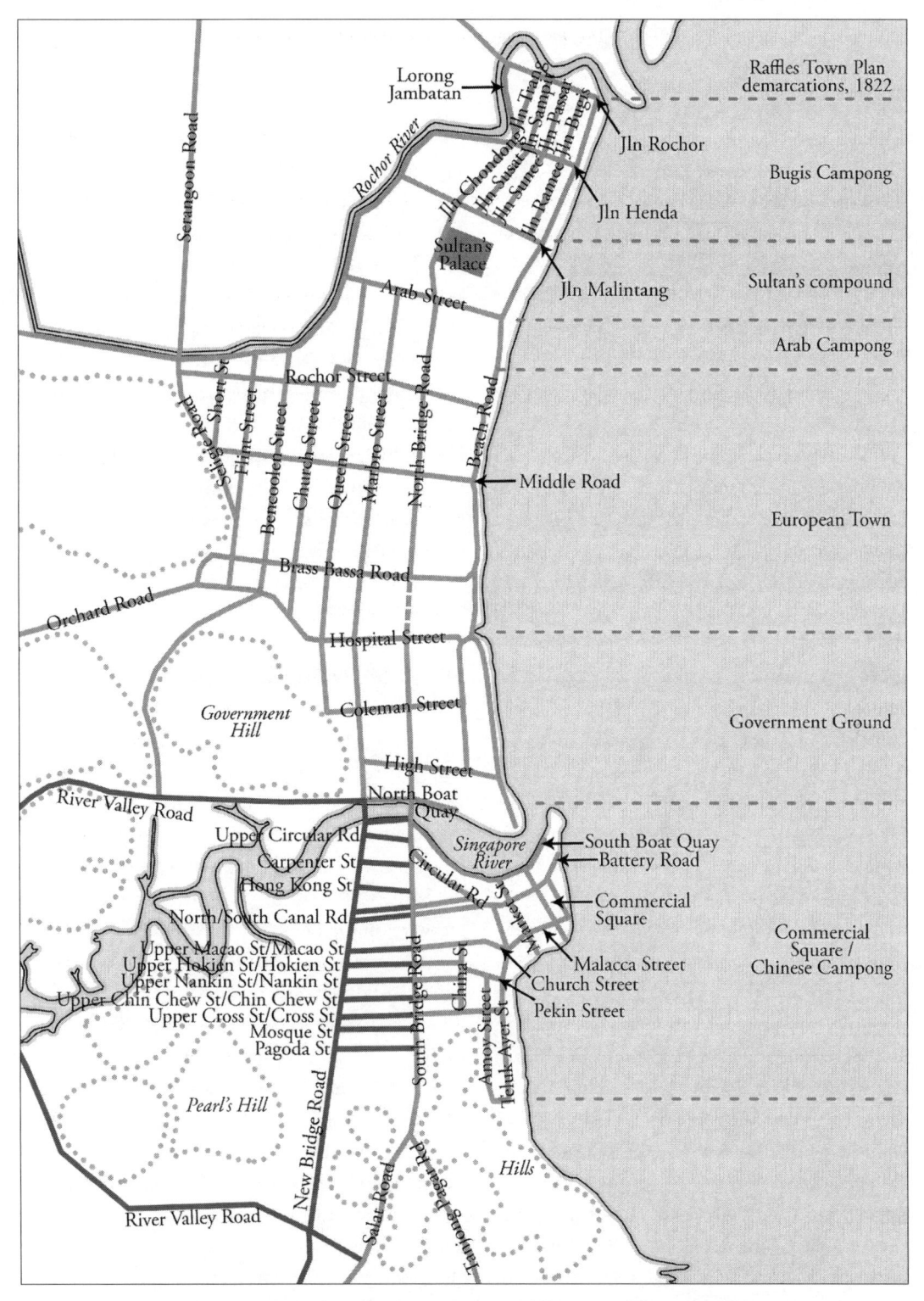

The Town of Singapore. Dashed lines show the parcelling out of different parts of the Town to different races under the 1822 Raffles Town Plan. Light grey solid lines are roads of the Town in 1837, while dark grey solid lines indicate the Chinese Campong Extension and other roads built in the early 1840s. Hills around the Town are marked out with dotted lines to show how the Town was hemmed in by geography. Key channels of movement, such as River Valley Road, Salat Road, and Tanjong Pagar Road, were laid down on valleys among hills. (Source: Eisen Teo)

Eventually, the Temenggong and "60 or 70 households" moved to a 200-acre plot in Telok Blangah. The new Telok Blangah Village lay at the foot of a large hill named Telok Blangah Hill (Mount Faber today). The Temenggong built for himself a new palace ironically called Istana Lama, Malay for "Old Palace". His older palace on the north bank of the Singapore River was pulled down, creating more land for public buildings—exactly what Raffles wanted.

Two months later, in May 1823, Raffles and Farquhar finally fell out; Raffles had had enough of Farquhar's resistance to how the settlement should be run, while Farquhar had had enough of Raffles' insistence of having things done his way. Raffles had Farquhar unceremoniously removed from the post of Resident; this paved the way for John Crawfurd to become Singapore's second Resident, which would have repercussions for the Town's future history of movement.

Just before leaving the island in June 1823, Raffles concluded a fresh agreement with Sultan Hussein and the Temenggong: in return for monthly pensions of $1,500 and $800 respectively, "the whole island of Singapore (with the exception of the land appropriated to the chiefs) and the islands immediately adjacent (were) to be at the entire disposal of the British". This was an important arrangement, for now the British, and the immigrants streaming into the island, could formally settle and develop land outside the town limits, not just within. This, coupled with Crawfurd's encouragement of agriculture, subsequently resulted in large parts of Singapore Island being opened up for plantations and farms.

The same month, Raffles set sail from Singapore for the third and last time; his already feeble health was deteriorating in the tropical climate. Within three years he was dead, his desire to be buried among the ancient Malay kings of Singapura on Bukit Larangan never fulfilled. At the end of the year, with his business in Singapore done, Farquhar also left the island for good. A testimony of his universal popularity and goodwill was the rambunctious sending-off he received. Saying goodbyes, it took two hours for him to board his boat, and hundreds of boats followed him out to sea. Munshi Abdullah later wrote that after the departure of both men, "Singapore at that time was like a woman whose husband has died, her hair unkempt, her face sad, like one who dwells in sorrow because her glory has gone from her." Singapore had seen the exit of two men—Farquhar and Raffles—who had so far influenced the urban development of modern Singapore more than anyone else.

FROM ONE EMPIRE TO ANOTHER

IN MARCH 1824, after five years of tension and negotiation, Singapore's status was settled once and for all. The Netherlands handed Malacca and all factories in India to Britain, and gave up all objections to the British presence in Singapore; in return, Britain ceded Bencoolen to the Netherlands. The Anglo-Dutch Treaty divided the 300-year-old Johor Sultanate down the middle, with no consideration for its two rival kings, Sultans Abdul Rahman and Hussein: Pahang, Johor, and Singapore now lay within a British sphere of influence, while the Riau and Lingga Islands lay within a Dutch sphere of influence.

The path was now clear for Crawfurd to permanently entrench British rule on Singapore Island itself. Unlike Raffles and Farquhar, Crawfurd was "inclined to impatience and outbursts of temper" and had a temperament "intolerant of listening to long-winded complaints". He never respected Sultan Hussein and saw him as a hindrance to British progress. On the other hand, Sultan Hussein led an indolent, extravagant lifestyle, literally growing fat on his monthly EIC allowances, and did not possess the character to challenge or influence British political manoeuvring.

Crawfurd started by withholding the monthly allowances due to the Sultan and Temenggong. The free-spending Sultan was driven to desperation by mounting debts, and in an ensuing meeting Crawfurd slyly suggested the transfer of full sovereignty over Singapore Island to the EIC in return for a large cash handout and a lifetime pension. The Sultan and Temenggong took his bait and agreed. The subsequent Treaty of Friendship and Alliance of August 1824 gave the EIC all rights to Singapore Island and all islands within 10 miles (16 km) of her shores in perpetuity, in return for $30,000 to the Sultan and $1,300 a month for the rest of his life, and $15,000 to the Temenggong and $700 a month for the rest of his life—an amazingly good deal for the British! Munshi Abdullah wrote:

> About five days after the agreement had been concluded Mr. Crawfurd ordered gongs to be sounded all round Singapore and in Kampong (Glam) and a proclamation read: "Be it known to all men in this Settlement that full judicial and legislative control throughout Singapore has passed to the East India Company, and that neither Sultan Shah nor the Temenggong retains any power." When the Sultan heard what the town criers were saying he realised at last that he was in the position of a man bound hand and foot.[6]

Sultan Hussein had a taste of this changed reality two months later, when orders came from India to improve the quality of roads in Singapore. At the time, North Bridge Road ran from the Singapore River to the vicinity of where the European Town ended and Kampong Glam began. Crawfurd ordered it to be extended through Kampong Glam to Jalan Chondong, presumably to link the Singapore River to the Rochor River—never mind that it meant cutting the Sultan's compound right in half. When the Sultan tried to resist, Crawfurd ordered his workmen to smash through the walls of the Sultan's compound. According to Munshi Abdullah, the Sultan "held his peace and said never a word, for he knew that he was no longer possessed of any authority in the Settlement of Singapore". Crawfurd got his road—albeit slightly kinked, because it still had to go around the Sultan's Palace and the mosque he had built, the Masjid Sultan. This kink in North Bridge Road has remained to the present day. But Crawfurd's victory symbolised the triumph of a new empire over an old one. Sultan Hussein was no longer the ruler of a maritime empire stretching from Pahang to the Riau Islands. His domain had shrunk to just a fraction of Kampong Glam.

More geopolitical change was to come. Two years later, in 1826, Singapore, with Penang and Malacca, were organised into the Straits Settlements. The Straits Settlements had a governor, who led a council comprising himself and the resident councillors of Penang, Malacca, and Singapore (replacing the positions of Resident), all responsible to the governor-general in Calcutta, India. Crawfurd, Singapore's Resident, made way for John Prince, Singapore's first Resident Councillor. Sir Robert Fullerton (1773–1831, who later gave his name to Fort Fullerton) became the first governor of the Straits Settlements, and he was based in its capital Penang; the capital shifted to Singapore in 1832.

By the late 1820s, Singapore could be divided into three neat portions—to the north, the Malay part, which covered Kampong Glam; the central part, which contained dwellings of European merchants and public offices; and to the south, the Chinese and commercial quarter, comprising the Chinese Campong and Commercial Square. This neatness and order also extended to the architectural landscape, which had a uniformity of appearance and make—be it the bungalows on spacious grounds in the European Town, or tight rows of shophouses in the Chinese Campong and Kampong Glam. The European Town was dubbed "the Mayfair of Singapore", and in 1832, sailor George Windsor Earl wrote: "On (Beach Road) fronting the sea, are (20) villas of the principal Europeans… large and handsome buildings, fronted by green verandahs and venetian blinds." As for Kampong Glam and the Chinese Campong, Crawfurd wrote in the 1820s: "The whole of the warehouses, and all the dwelling houses in the principal streets… are built of brick and lime, and roofed with red tile."

Commercial Square was the place to do business and make money. According to botanist Frederick William Burbidge, "a morning in the Square gives one a tolerably clear insight into the enterprise and trade of Singapore. You hear a good deal about the price of sago or (gutta-percha) and rice, or about the chartering of steamers or sailing craft, or the freight on home or export goods." The open Square was also a forum to exchange news and debate matters of importance, as described by an editor of Singapore broadsheet *The Straits Times*, John Cameron, in 1865:

(Once you arrive) in town, (10 or 15 minutes) are usually spent in going the rounds of the square to learn the news of the morning. These… gatherings are quite a characteristic of the place and of the community… they serve the purpose of an open air and non-commercial exchange… As scarcely a day passes without the arrival of a steamer with news from England, China, India… there is always ample material for an animated exchange of ideas and information on leading topics, whether they be European politics, the war in America, the position of affairs in China, the combined action at Japan, the affairs of India, Java, Borneo, the administration of the local Government, or the condition and prospects of the adjacent markets.

But to the Europeans, the liveliest and most exotic part of the Town was the Chinese Campong, a window into an alien yet fascinating world. "In the Chinese bazaar are hundreds of small shops in which a miscellaneous collection of hardware and dry goods are to be found, and where many things are sold wonderfully cheap"; "…and here may be procured any article desired, either from Europe, India or China. Any article of which a pattern can be produced, will be imitated by the Chinese."

As years passed and the population of the Town grew, more marshes further up the Singapore River were drained, enabling the construction of more roads and the extension of the town limits. One area of growth was the marshes west of South Bridge Road. It was drained in the late 1830s, allowing for the westward growth of the Chinese Campong from South Bridge Road to the foot of Pearl's Hill. The Chinese Campong Extension (my name) was needed as the Chinese population of Singapore had grown the fastest, from 3,317 in 1824 to 27,988 out of 52,891 souls in 1849—an expansion of nine times in just 25 years!

Because of rapid growth in the population of the Town and in pedestrian and horse carriage traffic, a second, sturdier bridge over the Singapore River was needed to complement Presentment Bridge; hence, Coleman Bridge, a brick bridge named after George Coleman, was built in 1840. It was the first bridge over the Singapore River able to handle horse carriages. This bridge connected Hill Street to a new road, New Bridge Road, which was completed in 1842, forming the backbone of a grid road system in the Chinese Campong Extension. New Bridge Road ran from Coleman Bridge to the Sepoy Lines, joining up with Salat Road. Many smaller roads were also laid down at right angles to New Bridge Road and South Bridge Road.

Two existing roads, North Canal Road and South Canal Road, were extended west of South Bridge Road, names unchanged. Six roads were named after existing roads: Upper Circular Road, Upper Macao Street, Upper Hokien Street, Upper Nankin Street, Upper Chin Chew Street and Upper Cross Street. Hong Kong Street was named after a new British territory ceded by China in 1842. Carpenter Street was named after Chinese carpenters who settled there. The exceptions: Mosque Street, named after the Masjid Jamae, and Pagoda Street, named after the Sri Mariamman Temple. By the 1850s, Smith Street appeared, named after John Colson Smith, a headmaster of the Singapore Institution (now Raffles Institution). As for Sago Street, it referred to sago flour factories which came up along the road.

In 1845, three years after New Bridge Road was completed, the marshes west of the road on which Kampong Malacca stood was reclaimed. Ellenborough Market was constructed on the raised ground, named after a governor-general of India, Edward Law, 1st Earl of Ellenborough (1790–1871). An existing road, Tocksing Street, named after Malacca-born businessman and philanthropist Tan Tock Seng (1798–1850), was renamed Ellenborough Street. By 1847, Tan built a large triangular block of two-storey shophouses between Ellenborough Street and the Singapore River, collectively named Ellenborough Building.

Development moved up both banks of the Singapore River. In the early 1840s, two roads about 2.5 km in length were laid down either side of the river. One ran west from Hill Street; the other, west from New Bridge Road. They eventually met upriver. Since they lay in the valley of the Singapore River, they were both named River Valley Road!

The Town of Singapore began largely as one man's bold vision, but the orderliness and consistency of this vision unravelled as soon as the man departed Singapore. The riverine settlement that was birthed in 1819 also began as a physical manifestation of coexistence between British mercantile interests and a resurrected Malay court. Eventually, however, one subsumed the other. Finally, the growth of the settlement's population beyond all expectations forced the expansion of the Town—the interior was the new frontier.

THE AGE OF AGRICULTURE

IN THE 1820s, the Town of Singapore developed rapidly, but it occupied fewer than half a per cent of the land area of Singapore Island. Once the EIC attained sovereignty over the whole of the island in 1824, both the officials running the Town, and individuals, encouraged the spread of cash crop farming throughout the interior. This began in the 1820s and lasted for a hundred years or so. It changed Singapore Island's jungle landscape forever, facilitated the movement of rich Europeans and Asians from the Town to the "country", planted numerous villages far from

British control and influence, and allowed hitherto unexplored regions to be surveyed and mapped like never before. Eventually, the importation of both Chinese and European agricultural systems created a network of island-wide trunk roads named after Singapore's natural heritage and indigenous ethnic groups, and also clusters of roads nearer to the Town, named after European plantation owners and their mansions. Parts of this agricultural legacy have survived to the present.

The development of agriculture did not come about in Singapore out of the blue. In 1822, Raffles, an avid naturalist, established Singapore's first Botanical and Experimental Garden—the predecessor of today's Botanic Gardens—on the slopes of Bukit Larangan, to explore the cultivation of cash crops such as pepper and nutmeg in Singapore, to challenge the Dutch spice monopoly in the Malay Archipelago. Even though it closed in 1829, the idea of using Singapore Island's vast interior to cultivate cash crops had taken root. While the port of Singapore generated the bulk of revenue for the EIC, the rest of the island was seen as *terra nullius* for attaining regional self-sufficiency in cash crops.

Although the British initiated the process, it was the Chinese that did the grunt work, partly because there were only a handful of Europeans, with the Chinese far outnumbering them. With few restrictions on immigration, thousands of Chinese poured into Singapore from both neighbouring Bintan and China, clearing the interior of jungle for plantations. The authorities doled out allowances of rice to them as an incentive. Non-existent land laws helped the process. Planters could occupy land in the interior without payment or leases. All they had to do was approach the authorities for a free grant. Their plantations largely lay outside the reach of surveyors and taxation.

The Chinese entered the interior by travelling up river systems—at the time, there were no roads into the interior. Since the Town lay in the southeast of Singapore Island, the first river systems to be explored were those in the southeast—the Singapore, Rochor, and Kallang rivers. The Kallang River reached the furthest inland and was lined by thick mangrove, but did not daunt the Chinese. The ensuing pattern of human settlement was very similar to that in nearby Bintan: the first villages and plantations were built on unoccupied land close to the river bank. Just as in Bintan, these settlements were called *kangkars*; *kangkar* was Teochew for "foot of the river". Each *kangkar* came under the control of a *kangchu*, or headman; *kangchu* was Teochew for "lord of the river". Bintan's *kangchu* system spread to Singapore. But while *kangchus* in Bintan paid allegiance to the Kapitan Cina of Riau, *kangchus* in Singapore were largely in the payroll of Chinese merchants who had migrated from both Bintan and China and resided in the Town. One example was Guangdong native Seah Eu Chin (1805–1883), dubbed "the King of Gambier", the pioneer of the industry in Singapore in 1835. Merchants like him paid for the costs of opening and running the plantations in return for a lion's share of the profits. A Chinese economic system had sprouted on the back of Singapore agriculture.

Since Bintan already had a thriving pepper and gambier plantation community, pepper and gambier became the most prevalent of cash crops. Thus began the passing of the pepper and gambier trade from the Riau Islands to Singapore.

The speed of the clearance of the interior is clear in comparing accounts just two years apart. In August 1825, Crawfurd carried out the first circumnavigation of Singapore Island on his ship, the *Malabar*. Of Bukit Timah Hill, the tallest hill on the island, he had this to say: "Although (it was) not above seven or eight miles from the Town… such is the character of the intervening country that it would be almost as easy a task to make a voyage to Calcutta as to travel to it." At the time, a maritime voyage to Calcutta across the Indian Ocean took weeks. Crawfurd's analogy emphasised the impenetrability of the forest.

However, in June 1827, Resident Councillor Prince and the Contractor of Roads took a walk from the Town in the direction of Bukit Timah Hill with the intention of surveying the land so that a road could be built between the Town and the hill. They trekked 22.5 km for five hours; three-quarters of that trek through "undulating hills, marshes and rills" was "gambier and pepper cultivation".

The land area cleared for plantations and farms soon dwarfed the area covered by the Town. In 1823, more than 98 per cent of Singapore Island was swathed in primary forest; by 1840 this had reduced to 82 per cent; by 1860 only 35 per cent was virgin forest. (Today, Bukit Timah Nature Reserve occupies just 0.29 per cent of Singapore Island's land area in 1860.)

To transport agricultural produce from settlements in the interior to the Town, trunk roads were needed. The onus was on the British administration to construct them, but it took years, because of the sheer distances involved. Meanwhile, the Chinese preferred major river systems such as the Kranji, Jurong, Kallang, and Seletar. If a river settlement was near the coast, boats sailed from the coast around the island to the Town. On land, the Chinese cut large trees and laid them across swampy terrain to create rudimentary paths. These paths were called *pyoh* in Hokkien, meaning "duckweed", because the logs were like duckweed floating on a pond.

Without trunk roads, the police and sepoys could not easily move around in the interior to enforce security. Hence, in the 1820s and 1830s, the interior was almost a law unto itself, as the Chinese organised their own *kangkars* and plantations, and Chinese secret societies and robbers thrived, frequently emerging to rob households near the edge of the Town. The Europeans knew very little of what went on beyond the hills surrounding the Town. Rumours swirled of a Chinese secret society a thousand men strong hiding in an armed fort buried in the jungle. Tigers were also prevalent, and as plantations spread, the incidence of tiger attacks skyrocketed. Up to one Chinese a day was killed by tigers, and at dusk their roars could be heard in the distance, sending chills down many a spine. Travel writer Ida Pfeiffer predicted in 1846: "It will be impossible to eradicate (the tiger in Singapore) entirely."

The first trunk road laid down from the Town into the interior was completed between 1836 and 1840. It was about five-and-a-half metres wide (slightly narrower than two lanes today), with the forest cut back a further two metres on each side. The trunk road ran 10.5 km northeast from Selegie Road to the mouth of a river named Saranggong, a portmanteau of the Malay words "satu" ("one") and "ranggong", a local name for the lesser adjutant stork, then common along the river banks. The trunk road took its name from the river. Because of British transliteration, the road had names such as Sirangoon, Saranggong, and Serangoon over the years; Serangoon is the version that has survived to the present.

Serangoon Road offered inroads—literally—into the interior. The land north of Kampong Glam, beyond the Rochor River, was marshy; but after the road was built, Chinese settlers opened paddy fields, and *sireh* (betel nut) and vegetable gardens, watered by the Rochor River. Indian settlers rearing cattle clustered in a new village called Buffalo Village; the area soon became known as Kandang Kerbau, Malay for "Buffalo Cage". Another road was laid down to link Serangoon Road to Jalan Rochor in Kampong Rochor; it was named Rochor Road, which could be confusing as Jalan Rochor was Malay for "Rochor Road" too! Next to Rochor Road, brick kilns opened. In 1842, amateur European racing enthusiasts requested the administration for land for horse racing; a racecourse was built next to Serangoon Road. At the time, it made sense because it was not too far from the European Town, yet it was outside the town limits. Thereafter, the Race Course became a centre of European social life and recreation.

In the 1830s, the pepper and gambier industry in Singapore received a further boost when demand from Europe surged. Gambier was found to be useful for tanning leather and dyeing cotton, wool, and silk. Merchants poured money into more plantations. By 1839, there were 350 pepper and gambier plantations in Singapore; each plantation required a piece of jungle equal in area to that of the plantation for firewood for gambier processing. Annual production of gambier totalled 48,000 piculs, or 2,800 tons. About 3,000 men out of a population of about 35,000 worked in these plantations—roughly one in 12 persons in Singapore.

The swift spread of plantations prompted the EIC to appoint John Turnbull Thomson (1821–1884) as government surveyor for the Straits Settlements. He took up his post in 1841 at the tender age of 20, and his brief was to chart the boundaries of every plantation. By then, the number of pepper and gambier plantations had grown to 500. Planters still cleared land and grew crops without leases, causing many land disputes.

Thomson arrived to clear up the disputes—and map the interior of Singapore, producing multiple maps between 1843 and 1849.

As the interior was mapped in the 1840s, several more trunk roads were laid down from the Town in different directions. Most of them began from the northeast part of the Town, near or within Kampong Glam, because the area was mostly low-lying floodplain alluvium, hence road-building—done with simple tools and no heavy machinery—was easier. In contrast, the land west and southwest of the Town was hillier, largely made up of Bukit Timah Granite and Jurong Formation rocks. Here we see how the island's uneven geology again had a subtle impact on Singapore's history of movement.

Thomson, with the Superintendent of Public Works and Convicts (Coleman from 1833 to 1841, and Colonel Henry Man from 1845), oversaw the building of these trunk roads. Like Serangoon Road, these new trunk roads were named after indigenous ethnic groups, natural features, or flora—probably because the British saw these roads traversing an interior that was wild and mysterious, largely avoided by Europeans who lived and worked in the safety of the Town. The dearth of Europeans in the interior led to a dearth of European place and road names there.

To the northwest of the Town, Bukit Timah Road was laid down from Seligie (Selegie) Road to Bukit Timah Hill, opening in 1843. (Bukit Timah is Malay for "Tin Hill", although there was no record of tin in the area.) Two years later, Bukit Timah Road was extended north from the hill past Bukit Panjang to the Straits of Johor. The road extension was named Kranji Road, after the river and tree of the same name. In all, the Bukit Timah–Kranji trunk road was 22 km long—Singapore's longest trunk road.

Between Bukit Timah Road and the Race Course, vegetable gardens flourished, watered by the upper reaches of the Rochor River. Three small roads emerged—Campong Jawa (now Kampong Java) Road, after a community of Javanese farmers; Garden Road, after the vegetable gardens; and Cross Garden Road, because it was perpendicular to Garden Road. Beyond Garden Road, a dirt track ran north into the interior, meeting the tributaries of the Sungei Seletar. Hence, the track was called Seletar Road. Thomson worked on extending the road to the Straits of Johor, covering a region named Sembawang after another native tree. He completed the job by 1848, and the extended road (and Garden Road) became known as Thomson's New Road, then Thomson Road, the only trunk road thus far named after a European.

To the east of the Town, Victoria Street was extended across the Sultan's compound—the second road after North Bridge Road to run roughshod over the comatose Johor Sultanate, separating the Tombs of the Malayan Princes from Masjid Sultan and the Sultan's Palace. Victoria Street was the start of a trunk road that was given different names at different stretches. Between the Rochor and Kallang rivers, it was named Kallang Road; east of the Kallang River, it was named Gaylang (now Geylang) Road, then Tannah (Tanah) Merah Road; and finally Changi Road, running past Sungei Bedok and ending in the east of the island near Tanjong Changi, formerly known as "Tanjong Rusa" in 1604. The 17.5-km trunk road was completed by 1845. Kallang and Geylang roads were named after the rivers, themselves possibly named respectively after the Orang Biduanda Kallang and *gelang laut*, a creeping plant found on beaches and mangroves; Tanah Merah Road, after the red cliffs named by de Eredia in 1604; Changi Road, after *chengal*, a hardwood used for furniture and houses. By the 1850s, two tracks branched off Changi Road to coastal cliffs—Tanah Merah Kechil, or "Little Red Land", and Tanah Merah Besar, or "Big Red Land".

Present-day Old Upper Thomson Road—formerly part of Thomson Road—is a close approximation of what trunk roads looked in the 19th century. It is a two-lane single carriageway, barely able to fit two cars passing by each other. It has no pedestrian walkways, just the asphalt surrounded by grass and forest on either side. Imagine the same road but with dusty, compacted earth laid over it instead of hardier asphalt, and devoid of lane markings and lampposts—that would have been the trunk and rural roads of the past. The scenery consisted mostly of jungle, fields and plantations—occasionally broken by the welcome sight of a village.

Since trunk roads ran for great distances, both the authorities and the population needed location markers. Enter the milestone, a geographical reference system dating to the ancient Roman Empire. In 1842, a year after Thomson began mapping the interior, 25 milestones were purchased for 62½ Spanish dollars to be laid down by the sides of trunk roads. Milestones marked distances in one-mile graduations from a fixed point in the Town; its exact location in the beginning is unknown, but by the 1860s, it was at the Surveyor-General's Office along North Bridge Road, opposite St Andrew's Cathedral, where Capitol Piazza is today. The milestones were literally made of stone; first sandstone, and then after 1853, sturdier granite. Each was about one metre in height with a pointed top, painted white, with mile numbers written in black paint. The milestones soon became indispensable as geographical points of reference for experiences of movement. They were used

Old Upper Thomson Road in 2012—a portal into the trunk and rural roads of the 19th century. (Source: Eisen Teo)

to record the locations of construction projects, bridges, or stretches of road to be repaired, land purchases, crimes, and tiger attacks and sightings. People began referring to landmarks or villages in terms of milestones; for example, "5th Milestone Bukit Timah Road", or "4th Mile, Serangoon Road"; Geylang Road changed to Tanah Merah Road at the 4th Milestone, which changed to Changi Road after the 6th Milestone. Such terms became formal addresses recognised by the postal service. Even the town limits began to be defined according to milestones—by 1873, the town limits had been extended outwards to the 3rd milestone of most roads from the Town.

Pepper and gambier cultivators began using trunk roads to travel to the Town, trading their produce for food and other essential items, an alternative to making circuitous trips on boats. Many *kangkars* were now connected by trunk roads. The Chinese mostly named these *kangkars* after this format: first, the surname of the headman or family who founded the *kangkar*, followed by "Chu Kang", which means "Residence of the River". For instance, Chan Chu Kang was named after Chan Ah Lak, who purchased 44 acres of land along the Sungei Seletar in 1844 for pepper and gambier plantations. By the 1850s, Thomson Road was a means to access Chan Chu Kang, Yio Chu Kang (also by the Sungei Seletar), and Nam To Kang by the Sungei Sembawang. The Bukit Timah–Kranji trunk road led to Lau Chu Kang, Tan Chu Kang, Bo Ko Kang, and three *kangkars* by the Sungei Kranji—Chu Chu Kang, Whu Hen Kang, and Lim Chu Kang. Some *kangkars* remained far from a trunk road, though: Choa Chu Kang at the Sungei Berih, and Peng Kang (Teochew for "boiling gambier", part of the manufacturing process). These were agricultural settlements with Chinese identities and Chinese populations, a far cry in form and character from the Town of Singapore.

The peak of the pepper and gambier industry in Singapore Island was reached in 1848. That year, there were 7,200 people working in 800 plantations—one in every seven persons on the island! In 1849, Thomson published a detailed report on Singapore agriculture, the first of its kind. A third of the island—close to 35,000 acres—was cultivated; 70 per cent of the cultivation was pepper and gambier, contributing to 60 per cent of gross revenue earned from agriculture.

Thomson's land surveys were the first to divide the lands around the Town into districts. To the northeast, covering the floodplains of the Geylang, Kallang, and Rochor rivers, were the districts of Rochore (Rochor), Kallang, Gaylang (Geylang), Siglap, and Pyah Laebar (Paya Lebar). Paya Lebar is Malay for "Wide Swamp", then covered with sprawling marshes; a rural road, Paya Lebar Road, was laid down to connect Serangoon Road and the Kallang–Changi trunk road. To the north, the districts of Toah Pyoh (Toa Payoh) Chui Kow and Toah Pyoh Lye were named after the logs laid across swampy terrain; "Toah" means "Big" in Hokkien, "Chui Kow" means "Water Canal", referring to tributaries of the Kallang River, and "Lye" could have meant "Fallow Land". There was also the District of Amokiah (Ang Mo Kio); it could have meant "Red Hair Bridge" in Hokkien, "Red Hair" being a somewhat derogatory Chinese epithet for white people. Thomson was said to have constructed a bridge for the Chinese who lived there—although the bridge has been lost to time. To the northwest lay the districts of Tanglin and Claymore; to the southwest, the districts of Tanjong Pagar and Telok Blangah.

Thomson's cartographical work gives us an important insight into the interior of Singapore

Island in the 1840s—through British eyes. Mapping is a process of selection, and what is omitted matters just as much as what is recorded. Thomson worked on what he perceived as a *tabula rasa*. In an 1852 map, large parts of the island outside the Town were left blank; he breezily wrote: "The whole of the Interior is occupied by Pepper and Gambier plantations intermixed with primeval Forest." We may never know what he failed to map. Orang Laut settlements, Chinese villages and plantation estates, Malay place names, and foot paths known only to these non-European communities—landmarks eventually lost in history. Thomson's maps and charts, neatly dividing the land into districts, primarily served the British authorities—the government could use them for greater control over land and resources—and of course, greater security over what they saw as dangerous lawlessness in the countryside.

From 1848, the pepper and gambier industry started to decline. Farmers were running out of virgin forest for new plantations and the firewood needed to process the gambier; persistent secret society violence and tiger attacks in the lawless, untamed interior scared many farmers into quitting the industry; too many plantations also depressed prices, bankrupting many planters. As a result, many planters abandoned Singapore Island for neighbouring Johor at the invitation of the new Temenggong.

Temenggong Abdul Rahman had passed away in 1825; his son, Temenggong Daeng Ibrahim (1811–1862), became the new head of Telok Blangah Village. In a new era where regional sea lanes were in the grip of colonial powers who frowned upon piracy, the Temenggong decided to reinvent himself from a sea lord into a lord of land-based agriculture. He transplanted much of the pepper and gambier industry from Singapore Island to his father's old fiefdom in Johor, adopting the *kangchu* system for Johor's new *kangkars*. The Chinese-dominated pepper and gambier industry, with the riches it earned, buttressed a fledgling Malay state in Johor that soon supplanted the authority of Sultan Hussein, who died in 1835, and his son and successor, Sultan Ali Iskandar Shah (1824–1877). In March 1855, in a treaty brokered by the British, Sultan Ali signed away his sovereignty over Johor to Daeng Ibrahim in return for a pension, formally ending the 300-year-old Johor Sultanate. From 1855 to 1858, Daeng Ibrahim ruled Johor from Telok Blangah Village until he relocated to Iskandar Putri, later Johor Bahru. Finally, the British declared Daeng Ibrahim's son, Abu Bakar (1833–1895), the new Sultan of Johor in 1886. By then, Johor had become the world's greatest producer of pepper and gambier. Singapore's industry declined, and hundreds of plantations were abandoned, to be replaced by other forms of cultivation or secondary forest. But the industry had left an indelible mark on the evolution of Singapore's channels of movement.

A LITTLE PIECE OF BRITAIN IN SINGAPORE

THE EUROPEANS, like the Chinese, also participated in agriculture in Singapore, but they generally stayed away from pepper and gambier, investing instead in nutmeg, sugar cane, coconut, cotton, cloves, coffee, and cinnamon. A group of tropical cash crop enthusiasts and aspiring botanists, such as Montgomerie, the Town's Senior Surgeon Dr Thomas Oxley (1805–1886), and Portuguese naval surgeon and merchant Dr Jose D'Almeida (1784–1850), formed the Agricultural and Horticultural Society in 1836. Their aim: Promote "the improvement of every branch of agriculture in the settlement". However, they were not as adventurous as the Chinese, setting up plantations far closer to the Town, most not more than three kilometres from the town limits. These areas formed a ring around the Town, collectively known to the Europeans as "the country" or "the countryside". Running anticlockwise from the east, there were the District of Geylang, the Balestier-Kallangdale area, the districts of Tanglin and Claymore, and the District of Tanjong Pagar. The first two areas were flat with patches of marshland, while the last two were hilly.

Raffles had allocated the European Town to the Europeans, but many preferred moving out to "the country", where there was more open space. They built large country houses nestled inside private grounds, with winding driveways to main roads. Many were merchants with families in tow; they headed to the Town every morning for business. Marryat wrote in 1846: "The country immediately outside the town of Singapore is spotted with little bungalows, the retreat of the merchants from the monotonous business life which they are compelled to lead."

The District of Geylang was drained by the Sungei Geylang. D'Almeida first opened cotton plantations in the 1820s, but the crop was not suited to the island's soil or climate, and soon failed. From the 1830s, coconut trees were planted instead. One of the plantations was owned by Thomas Owen Crane (1799–1869) and his family; another belonged to Thomas Dunman (1814–1887), Singapore's first Commissioner of Police from 1856. Tanjong Katong (Malay for "Cape of Turtles") Road was laid down from the Kallang–Changi trunk road to near the coast. In 1849, the district was home to 342,608 coconut trees spread over 2,658 acres.

Balestier–Kallangdale lay to the north of the Town, also a marshy area drained by the Kallang River. In the early 1830s, two men bought up large tracts of land for plantations. One was an American, Joseph Balestier (1788–1858), who would later become the first United States Consul for Singapore. The other was Montgomerie. By the 1840s, Balestier's estate covered 1,000 acres; a fifth of this was sugarcane. Three roads cut through it—one was Balestier Road, named after the estate owner; the other two were Garden Road and Cross Garden Road (renamed Moulmein Road in 1900). As for Montgomerie, his estate was called Kallangdale, "dale" being a British term to describe an open valley (creating a name that sounds like a present-day condominium project); he planted nutmeg and sugarcane. After he left Singapore in 1843, his estate was sold to Robert Carr Woods (1816–1875), who was *The Straits Times*' first editor in 1845. Woods renamed the estate after himself—Woodsville, and the cottage in the estate became Woodsville Cottage. Later, Woodsville Road was built through the estate.

In the 1840s, a Chinese merchant purchased land off Serangoon Road for a bungalow and garden. His name was Hoo Ah Kay (1816–1880), although the Europeans called him "Whampoa", a British transliteration of his hometown, Huangpu (in present-day Guangzhou, China). He hired gardeners from China to create the first Chinese garden in Singapore, complete with bridges over ponds, bamboo groves, plant sculptures, even an aviary and a zoo, open to all. His presence in the area for decades contributed Whampoa as a place and road name.

The districts of Tanglin and Claymore experienced a nutmeg craze. A cluster of hills lay to the northwest of Bukit Larangan, renamed Government Hill by the 1830s as Raffles' house became a residence for Straits Settlements governors. By 1849, most of Singapore Island's

71,400 nutmeg trees covering 1,190 acres were found on these hills. Nutmeg was a costly spice used by the Europeans as a flavouring, medicinal, and preservative agent; the British had high hopes for the success of the crop in Singapore.

The first European who settled in the two districts was Captain William Flint, who occupied Bukit Seligie in 1823, renaming it Flint's Hill; after his death in 1828, the hill was renamed Mount Sophia, possibly after his brother-in-law Raffles' second wife. The driveway that ran from the hill to Seligie Road was later named Sophia Road. In the 1840s, the hill and its nutmeg plantation were purchased by lawyer Charles Robert Prinsep (1789–1864). Prinsep left his mark; the Flint Street north of the Singapore River, which was named after Flint, was renamed Prinsep Street.

In 1846, Oxley purchased 173 acres of land to the northwest of Government Hill for a nutmeg plantation of 4,050 trees, described as "the finest nutmeg garden on the island". Being Irish, he named his estate and townhouse Killiney, after a suburb in Dublin, Ireland. Oxley Road and Oxley Rise were named after him, and Killiney Road, after his house. Another house in the estate was named Grange House, so the driveway that led from the house was extended and upgraded to Grange Road in 1863.

North of Killiney Estate, postal officer William Cuppage (1807–1872) secured a grant for a hill in 1845 and after naming it Emerald Hill, grew 1,250 nutmeg trees there. Cuppage Road was named after him.

North of Emerald Hill, another prospective nutmeg planter, Charles Carnie, bought an adjoining hill in 1840. It became known as Carnie's Hill, with 4,370 nutmeg trees, while his hilltop house was named Cairnhill, a portmanteau of "cairn", a human-made stack of stones common in his native Scotland, and "hill". Hence, the driveway that ran from the house was later named Cairnhill Road.

To the northwest of Carnie's Hill, Captain William Scott (1780–1861), a Master Attendant and a good friend of Thomson, set up his own plantation in 1846 named Claymore (hence the district's name). Other than 5,200 nutmeg trees, his plantation grew native fruits such as durians, dukus, rambutans, mangosteens, cocoa, betelnut, and arrowroot. The private carriageway that ran from Scott's house to Bukit Timah Road was named Scotts Road; another road was built between Scotts Road and Bukit Timah Road, named Stevens Road, although the origin of the name is unknown. Claymore Road and Claymore Drive were named in 1926.

To the north of Scott's hill, near Bukit Timah Road, there was another hill named Mount Victoria, possibly after Queen Victoria. In the 1840s, D'Almeida planted more than 1,000 nutmeg trees on it. Consequently, the road running from Stevens Road to Bukit Timah Road, past Mount Victoria, was named Almeida Road.

To the west of the District of Claymore, the Chinese who came before the Europeans had named the hilly area Toa Tang Leng, or "Great East Hills" in Hokkien. The British transliteration of "Tang Leng" was "Tanglin", so "Tanglin" appeared on English-language maps, giving the District of Tanglin and Tanglin Road their names. In the 1850s, lawyer and news editor William Napier (1804–1879) bought 67 acres of land in Tanglin, and his house, completed in 1854, was named Tyersall. Hence the names Napier Road and Tyersall Road.

The main road that connected most of the aforementioned private driveways and estates to the Town was Orchard Road, cut as early as the 1830s from Hospital Street (later Stamford Road).

Orchard Road was originally named for the fruit orchards that lined the road, but by the 1860s, country houses had replaced them, presenting "the appearance of a well-shaded avenue to English mansions", according to a writer, comparable in its "quiet but effective beauty to Devonshire lanes". Another traveller saw Orchard Road as a portal into the wild interior:

> After leaving town (Orchard Road) passes through a narrow valley, with a series of little hillocks on either hand, and upon which many houses have been built. The road is very pretty, being lined by tall bamboo hedges and trees which, uniting above, form a complete shade... Beyond the residences are the remains of many nutmeg plantations... then succeeds a strip of thin jungle, then the Chinese pepper and gambier plantations, and then comes the jungle in earnest, with its gigantic trees, creepers, orchids, parasites, and fallen or decayed trees, plants and vegetables...

Finally, the District of Tanjong Pagar stretched from the Chinese Campong to the southern coast of Singapore Island. The numerous coastal hills formed part of the town limits, offering scenic views of the Town and the sea. First to own a hill was John Palmer (1766–1836), a Calcutta merchant, who purchased what was later named Mount Palmer shortly after the port of Singapore was founded. When his company went bankrupt in 1827, he sold part of the hill to a Parsi who opened a Parsi burial ground, so the hill was also known as Mount Parsee. Then there were Mount Erskine, named after landowner J. J. Erskine, and Mount Wallich, named after Nathaniel Wallich, after his pal Raffles had gifted the hill to him.[7]

During the nutmeg craze of the 1840s, at least four Britons opened plantations in the district—lawyer Charles Scott (1802–1858), merchants Charles Spottiswoode (1812–1858) and Alexander Guthrie, and again, Montgomerie. Scott gave his name to Scott's Hill, while his estate, Raeburn, gave its name to Raeburn Park. Spottiswoode's estate later lived on in the place and road name of Spottiswoode Park. Guthrie gave his name to Bukit Guthrie, a hill with 2,250 nutmeg trees. As for Montgomerie's 79-acre, 1,800-tree plantation, it had two hills named Craig Hill and Duxton Hill. These contributed the place and road names of Craig Road, Duxton Road, and Duxton Hill.

Eventually, Singapore's excessively wet climate, poor soil, and pests took their toll. The cotton struggled; the cloves and indigo died. Heavy duties in Britain on sugar imports contributed to the demise of Balestier's estate. Blight overwhelmed nutmeg in the mid-1850s, decimating most plantations by the next decade.

THE NEXT stage of rural road development unfolded from the 1850s into the 1870s. More rural roads were laid down in the interior of Singapore Island, most from existing trunk roads, not from the Town as before. These new roads connected existing trunk roads or brought land transport to more distant parts of the island; again, because they were far from European centres of population and influence, most of them were named after non-European landmarks or local flora and fauna.

In the west of the island, Jurong Road—about six kilometres in length—was laid down from the Bukit Timah–Kranji trunk road to the Sungei Jurong. Jurong Road and Sungei Jurong were probably named after "Jerung", the Malay word for "shark" (there were no records of sharks in the river though).

In the north, Mandi (now Mandai) Road was constructed to cover the eight kilometres between the Bukit Timah–Kranji trunk road and Thomson Road, and link the villages of Bo Ko Kang and Chan Chu Kang. Mandai Road could have acquired its name from the mandai tree. After Mandai Road was completed, the eight-kilometre stretch of Thomson Road north of Chan Chu Kang to the Straits of Johor was renamed Seletar Road, perhaps because of Thomson Road's sheer length.

In the east, Tampines Road branched off Serangoon Road to Changi Road over 11 km, crossing the Sungei Tampines; both road and river were named after the tempinis tree, valued by the Malays for its strength and durability. In maps, newspaper articles, and official documents, Tampines has been spelled as Tempinis, Tempenis, and Tampenis. And from near where Serangoon Road meets the Sungei Serangoon, a third road, five kilometres long, was laid down to Punggol Village, the coastal settlement predating Raffles' arrival in 1819. The road was named Pongol (later Punggol or Ponggol) Road in 1876.

Of four rural roads built in the south of the island, three took on European names—perhaps because they were closer to the Town. The exception ran west along the coast from Telok Blangah Road to a seaside village called Pasir Panjang Village; the five-kilometre road was called Pasir Panjang Road. "Pasir Panjang" is Malay for "Long Sand", referring to its long, sandy beach. Another road connected Bukit Timah Road to Pasir Panjang Village. It was named Reformatory Road around the turn of the century after the Reformatory, a boys' home located along the road. A third ran west from Napier Road, then curved south to join Pasir Panjang Road. It was named Holland Road before 1891, possibly after Sir Henry Holland, Secretary of State for the Colonies. The fourth road ran from the Town up the Singapore River, then curved south like Holland Road to meet Pasir Panjang Road. It was named in 1865 after a 20-year-old European—Princess Alexandra of Denmark (1844–1925). Two years before, she had married Albert Edward, Prince of Wales, the heir apparent of Queen Victoria—he would later be crowned King Edward VII.

Finally, the central part of the island also had two rural roads in a T-shape, connecting Thomson Road to the Bukit Timah–Kranji trunk road in two places. However, the names of both roads never appeared on maps; the roads and their names have been lost to history, swallowed up by the Central Catchment Area today.

Through the decades, villages grew up at rural road junctions, at the crossroads of the movement of humans and goods. A village was little more than half a dozen shophouses clustered around a junction or along a road, reached by small wooden bridges across open roadside drains; individual houses served by these shops were scattered in the surrounding farms and plantations. There could also be a police station in the vicinity for security.

Early villages included Bedok Village, Serangoon Village (also known as Kangkar Village), Chan Chu Kang, Bukit Panjang Village, and Bukit Timah Village. These villages were gathering and distribution points for farm and animal produce. Fish, livestock, vegetables, and cash crops made their way to these villages from nearby farms, to be transported to the Town. For example, produce from Punggol and Tampines concentrated at Serangoon Village via Tampines Road and the Sungei Serangoon; produce from Bukit Panjang and Jurong gathered at Bukit Timah

CHAPTER 2 1819 to 1880: Feet and Hooves 59

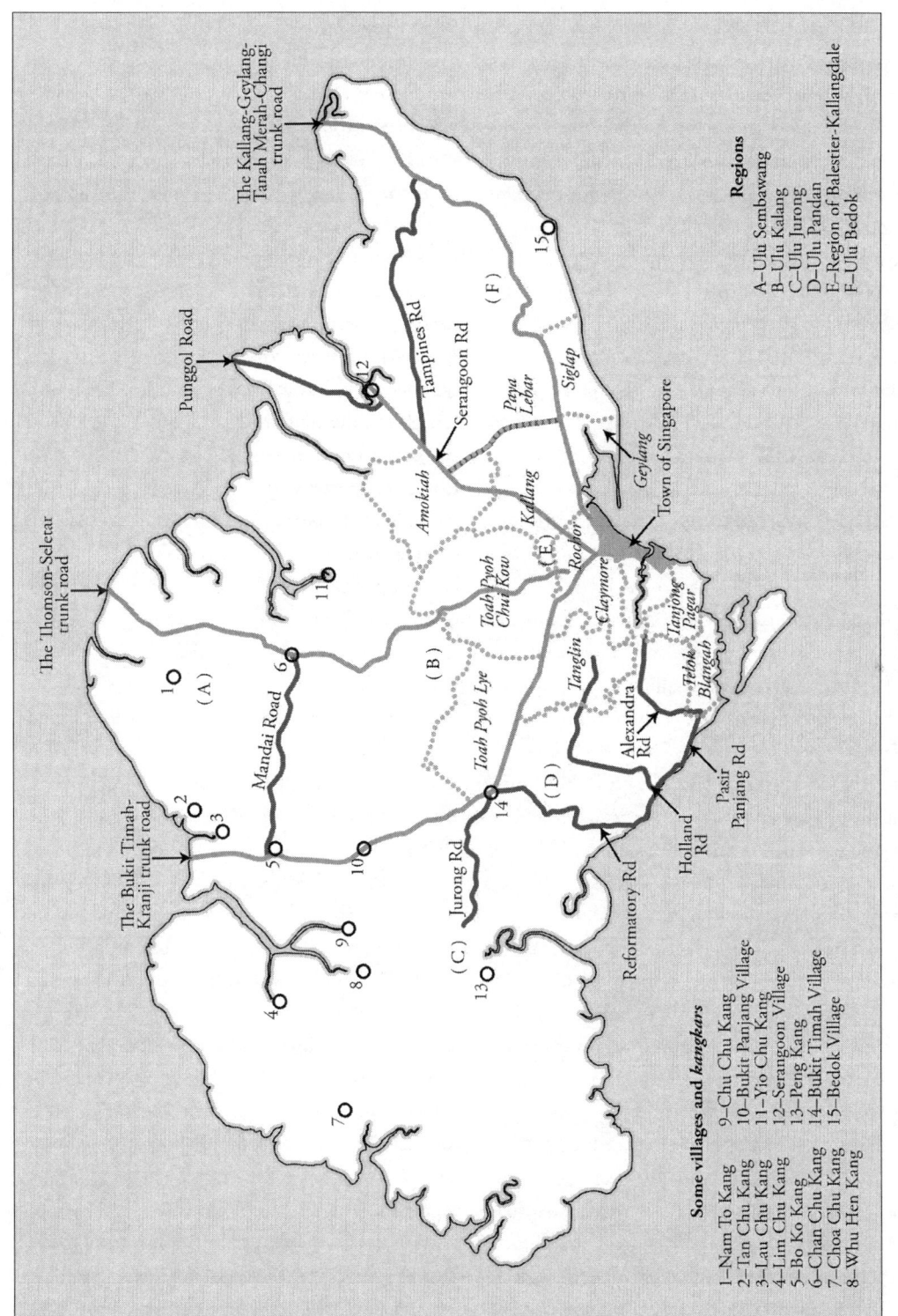

Singapore Island by the 1870s. Light grey solid lines are trunk roads laid down by the 1850s, while dark grey solid lines are trunk roads built by the 1870s. Dotted lines mark out some districts mapped by government surveyor John Turnbull Thomson in the 1840s. Villages mentioned in the text, and place names beginning with "Ulu", are also marked out. (Source: Eisen Teo)

Some villages and *kangkars*

1—Nam To Kang
2—Tan Chu Kang
3—Lau Chu Kang
4—Lim Chu Kang
5—Bo Ko Kang
6—Chan Chu Kang
7—Choa Chu Kang
8—Whu Hen Kang
9—Chu Chu Kang
10—Bukit Panjang Village
11—Yio Chu Kang
12—Serangoon Village
13—Peng Kang
14—Bukit Timah Village
15—Bedok Village

Regions

A—Ulu Sembawang
B—Ulu Kalang
C—Ulu Jurong
D—Ulu Pandan
E—Region of Balestier-Kallangdale
F—Ulu Bedok

Village; produce from Sembawang and Mandai were distributed from Chan Chu Kang.

The spread of trunk and rural roads from the Town throughout the island resembled the veins of a leaf. Many have survived to the present, and their courses have left a permanent impression on the urban development of Singapore. Out of 20 new towns—or satellite towns—built from the 1950s to the 2000s, 10 of them were constructed next to these trunk and rural roads; five more were built atop trunk and rural roads, altering their courses. A hundred years after these roads were laid down, their channels still mattered when it came to a location for a satellite town.

Rivers remained an important channel of transport, though, especially for parts of the island not served by trunk and rural roads. As more of the interior was mapped, a differentiation in place names arose between the upper and lower courses of some rivers. In Malay, "hulu" means "upriver"; "hilir" means "downriver". A variation of "hulu" is "ulu" (which also means "remote, backward, primitive" in Singlish today). Hence, for the upper courses of some rivers, "Ulu" was appended to place names. There were the districts of Ulu Bedok (covering the upper reaches of the Sungei Bedok, where Bedok Reservoir is today), Ulu Kalang (between present-day MacRitchie and Upper Peirce reservoirs), and Ulu Pandan (the place name has survived as Ulu Pandan Road); there were also Ulu Sembawang (where Woodlands town is today) and Ulu Jurong (north of present-day Jurong Lake).

We have seen how the pattern of agricultural development over 40 years influenced the pattern of road development and subsequent road and place names. Collectively, these roads and their names remained long after planters abandoned farms and estates. They would become the skeletal framework upon which future development of the Town's hinterland unfolded.

MOVING PEOPLE, MOVING ANIMALS

IN THE first 60 years of modern Singapore, there were only so many ways one could move around on land. Before the age of motor vehicles, one had to rely on human or animal power.

Singapore was British territory, so some methods of movement were imported from Britain. However, since Singapore was on the other side of the world, it took time for inventions, especially those requiring substantial investment, to arrive from the metropole. Influences also came from British India, the Malay Archipelago, and Australia. Singapore enjoyed free port status, with minimal control over the entry of goods, but it was largely up to private enterprise to import methods of movement. The authorities did not invest in or set up transport companies; they only paid for a portion of the roads.

As a result, most people in Singapore Island went about their daily business on foot, or *jalan kaki* in Malay. The places where one lived, worked, and played were largely within walking distance. This kept almost seven in 10 people in Singapore Island clustered in the Town. Most non-goods vehicles for public hire or private ownership were available only to a small group who could afford it.

For this minority, mostly Europeans and rich Asians, the most common mode of transport was horse- or donkey-drawn carriages. They were known as gharries, hackneys ("hacks"), palanquins, or palankeens; a "horse and gig" had two wheels as opposed to a "horse and victoria" with four. They were the first form of transport for public hire, or "taxis", to serve the Town of Singapore. They could be hired from stables or off the streets, or they could be privately-owned. These vehicles allowed Europeans and rich Asians to travel into the country, yet remain connected to places of work and recreation within the Town. In 1840, there were 170 victorias, 44 gigs, and 266 ponies for a population of 35,389—one carriage for every 166 persons. By 1881, there were 159 cart and hackney carriage owners, 908 carriages, and 2,224 drivers for a population of 139,208—one carriage for every 154 persons.

Carriages for hire usually had just one conductor in charge of maintaining both vehicle and animal. He was called a syce, a term that originated in India, and many were Indians, with sizable minorities of Malays, Javanese, Boyanese, and Chinese. Operating the vehicles, syces practised a custom also from India: they would run on foot by the side of the horse or carriage, rather than sit upon it. The vehicles could be covered or uncovered, and sit one to four people. They were first imported by ship from Britain or India, although as time passed, workshops opened in Singapore manufacturing them. The animals pulling them also had to come from outside of Singapore at first, since Singapore had no endemic pack animals. Horses came from Java, Sumatra, Australia, and England. As soon as Commercial Square was established, horses brought in by ship were sold by auction there, this practice only ceasing in 1890 because of an increase in traffic. Over time, horses began to be bred locally; many stables opened along Cross Street and Upper Cross Street.

Nevertheless, there was no concept of "public transport" then, simply because most of the "public" did not frequent or afford hiring carriages. In fact, the phrase "public transport" only appeared in Singapore-related news in 1918—and carriages were not the main focus.

Europeans and rich Asians who lived in Singapore for the long term, especially households in the country, usually had their own private horse-drawn carriages, or "turn-out". According to Oxley in 1844, hiring a carriage cost a hefty $25 a month, yet they were "dirty, unsightly vehicles and for the most part quite unfit for a Lady's use"; if one was staying in Singapore for some time, it was cheaper to buy a good pony for $50–$100 instead. When Colonel William Butterworth (1801–1856) was the governor of the Straits Settlements from 1843 to 1855, he "imported a large carriage and four horses, and when attending the evening service at St Andrew's (Cathedral) on dark nights, the syces ran at the sides of the horses with lanterns". Some carriages came with a two-man team, comprising a coachman and a footman. This practice originated from Britain, where private chariots or carriages were a mark of status, similar to owning a motor car in Singapore today.

Possessing their own "private transport" shaped the daily schedules of the cream of society. In the 1860s, the work day began at around 10am. In the half hour before, traffic from the country into the Town, and across the Singapore River into Commercial Square, was heavier than usual. The two bridges over the river at the time "(presented) an endless string of (carriages)—by no means an uninteresting spectacle". This was the earliest account of a "rush hour"—even though the term "rush hour" would not appear in a Singapore newspaper until 1906, and traffic would only thicken for a while, not slow down to a jam.

The work day usually ended around 4.30pm, with dinner after that. For the owners of carriages, post-dinner exercise was a carriage ride between 5pm and 7pm along the roads of the Town, especially Beach Road, which skirted the seashore and was blessed by a cool sea breeze. The rides looped around and ended at the grassy Esplanade and Scandal Point, where the rich and powerful gathered to see and be seen, share news, discuss the issues of the day, and gossip the evening away. On Tuesdays and Fridays, a large part of the European community descended upon the Esplanade for military band evenings. Pfeiffer recalled: "The carriages were ranged several rows deep, and surrounded by young beaux on foot and horseback; any one might have been excused for imagining himself in a European city."

Since carriage numbers remained small, it was not until 1867—nearly 50 years into the port of Singapore's existence—that the government drew up a Hackney Carriage Act to register carriage owners, inspect carriages, regulate behaviour on the roads, and set up stands for syces to pick up passengers. A Hackney Carriage Department led by a Registrar of Hackney Carriages was formed under the Municipality; the first Registrar was probably G. C. Evans. He was kept busy pursuing violations of the Act—filthy carriages and drivers, overcrowding of carriages, animals not fit for service, carriages plying without licences, and so on. At the time, the municipal police force, already modest in size to begin with, did not have a dedicated traffic department for maintaining law and order on the roads and cracking down on traffic violations. Nevertheless, the Hackney Carriage Department was the first municipal department to oversee a method of movement, the humble ancestor of the present-day Ministry of Transport.

One man who was not of the wealthy class did ride the "hack-gharries" for free throughout his life—he was Sayyid Habib Noh (1788–1866), a Muslim mystic. Many thought he was a prophet, and syces were in too much awe of him to ask for fares. He would also go into shops and to moneychangers and take what he wished—which he then distributed to the poor. On the day of his death and burial, a syce was allegedly murdered because he had the audacity to ask for money to serve as his hearse! Habib Noh was buried near Tanjong Pagar Village, at the foot of Mount Palmer. His burial site became a *keramat* (sacred burial site), the Keramat Habib Noh.

For the transport of goods, farm produce, and refuse, and water in a time before universal piping, bullock carts were used. Again, the buffaloes— with their jingling bells and horns painted in brilliant colours—had to be imported first from around the region, such as Malacca, Penang, and for black cattle, Bali; then they were bred locally by Indians, many residing along Serangoon Road and in Buffalo Village with their cattle pens. Merchants had to make do with these slow, cumbersome beasts, susceptible to sickness and disease. Other road users also had to endure the animals freely grazing by the roadside, blocking traffic, and fouling the streets with dung!

The government also employed animals and horse-drawn vehicles for essential services such as the police and firefighting. From the 1820s, fire engines were horse-drawn carts carrying hand pumps. The water tanks had to be refilled with buckets. Meanwhile, the police used ponies and bullock carts for patrols.

INTO THE 1860s, new methods of movement had travelled thousands of miles from Europe to Singapore. Two rantoons, a form of tricycle, the first vehicle propelled by human power in Singapore, were imported by auditor T. S. Thomson and chemist Robert Jamie around 1866 or 1867. Soon after, bank manager Andrew Thomas Carmichael got his hands on a bicycle, which Thomson tried out along Chancery Lane, "but he had just started when his foot caught in the treadle and the frame… he landed flat on the road on his face". Comedy turned to

A bullock cart, sometime between 1920 and 1929. Long before motor trucks, these beasts of burden transported goods, farm produce, refuse, and water. (Source: The New York Public Library Digital Collections)

tragedy in 1875 when Lionel Gomes, the son of a clergyman, died of a fractured skull after a vehicle knocked him off his bicycle along Waterloo Street. The following year, a letter was submitted to *The Straits Times* about cyclists not "taking necessary precautions in crowded places": "… almost no horse will stand a bicycle bearing down upon him, and then suddenly swerving when within a few feet of his face. This was what happened to me yesterday afternoon on the Esplanade, and a serious accident was very nearly the result"—something that resonates with road users and pedestrians even today! However, these forms of "private transport" did not become a widespread traffic problem as they were expensive and an "exertion" in the tropical heat.

As for "public transport", the first form accessible to the lower classes in Singapore was the horse-drawn omnibus, the earliest form of public bus, with a capacity of 12–25. It was a far larger version of the horse carriage built specifically for the masses. Introduced in Britain in 1829, it took more than 40 years to reach Singapore, probably because there was little financial incentive for Europeans to start such a venture serving the non-European population.

Omnibuses in Singapore were first mentioned in the *Straits Times Overland Journal* in 1871—an article reported that "some enterprising livery stable owners" had established "a line of omnibuses" to run from the Town to the Sungei Kranji, perhaps to serve people who wanted to travel to Johor. This was Singapore's first public bus service, operating vehicles in which strangers shared a common space on a temporary basis.

Four years later in 1875, *The Straits Times* reported that while hack-gharries remained an "expensive luxury", unidentified omnibus proprietors were "supplying that great want of the native population—cheap conveyance—by running their buses at night". Only one route was mentioned: from Circular Road across the Singapore River, to Kampong Glam via North Bridge Road, and back. Each passenger was charged a uniform fare of three cents. This was Singapore's first night bus service, even though it covered only half the Town. The Town–Kranji omnibus service and the intra-town night service were the earliest forms of "public transport", but they were not prevalent or widespread enough for transport users to coin the term "public transport", or be conscious of it, for years to come.

The enterprising Chinese were never too far away when there was money to be made. By the following year, 1876, they had broken into the business of operating omnibuses, plying the same North Bridge Road route. It was a profitable business as the omnibuses were "generally quite full".

However, due to a desire to earn more profits, omnibus horses began to be overworked. Within a single day on 12 May 1876, three horses in harness collapsed in the streets; two of them died. In fact, most of the cases reported to the recently-formed Singapore Society for the Prevention of Cruelty to Animals were about animals mistreated in the name of transport. Of 84 cases recorded from June to September 1876, three were for cruelty to omnibus horses, 60 for cruelty to ponies pulling hackney carriages, and 17 for the ill treatment of oxen; only four were for the shooting of birds.

In 1879, the Hackney Carriage Act was repealed for a new Hackney Carriage Ordinance. Now, hackney carriages were divided into three classes—first-class was for private use, second-class for public hire, and third-class included omnibuses. Second-class carriage fares were fixed at 15 cents up to half a mile, 20 cents up to a mile, and 10 cents for every additional mile or part thereof. Traffic offences such as dangerous driving, hurting people or damaging property, and speeding, were punished with fines of up to $25, or imprisonment of up to two months.

As the 1870s drew to a close, limited methods of movement kept the size of the Town small—around four square kilometres, walkable within a couple of hours. The Town had a high population density, narrow streets, and little or no wasted space. It was a "foot city"; most people went around on foot. A two- or three-storey shophouse was a migrant coolie's living quarters and workplace; meals were taken from stalls along the streets; entertainment in the form of markets, brothels or storytellers was just around the street corner.

The spartan transport options also contributed to the sense of distance and remoteness for the interior of the island. One took a good part of a day to walk from the Town to, say, Bukit Panjang Village. The dirt tracks that were rural roads were far from even, and when torrential rain fell—which happened often—the roads turned to a watery muck. Throw in roving bandits and tigers, and it is understandable why most Europeans in the early 1800s rarely ventured into the interior. Hence, villages far from the Town had to be mostly self-sufficient. Animals that could pull wagons or carriages, like buffaloes, goats and horses, were valued.

The roads then were far quieter compared to the roads of today. There would be the chatter of pedestrians, the neighing of horses, the clip-clop of hooves, the rumble of carriage wheels, the jingling of bells strapped to the harnesses of buffaloes—that was all. Even in the busiest thoroughfares in the heart of the Town, the flow of traffic was mostly dictated by the movement of people on foot.

Most traffic on the roads occurred during the

THE RIVER AND TOWN OF SINGAPORE, FROM FORT CANNING.
Published by Smith, Elder & Co London 1865.

A view of the Town of Singapore and the Singapore River from Fort Canning Hill in 1865. At the time, limited methods of movement kept the size of the Town small and walkable. Buildings were low and tightly-packed, with narrow streets. Most people went around on foot. (Source: Cornell University Library Digital Collections) day, petering out with the waning of daylight. As early as 1824, major thoroughfares were lit with coconut oil and animal oil lamps, but the lighting was feeble and inconsistent at best, and travelling after dark was difficult and dangerous, even within the Town itself. This state of affairs persisted until 1864, when gasoline lamps were introduced. But only major thoroughfares were lit; the rural roads became pitch-black at night. As darkness spilled over the Town, the exotic dangers of the tiger and the "criminal" Asiatic loomed large in the European consciousness.

FORGING CHANNELS OF MOVEMENT
IN 1847, a witty member of the public posted an advertisement for a fake steeplechase in the *Singapore Free Press*:

> Grand Steeple Chase
> For a purse of 50 dollars
> Added to a sweepstakes of $10 each
> On Tuesday, the 16th Inst., 4pm

> The Course is from Coleman's Bridge along New Bridge Road over the unfinished Faber's Bridge and along South Canal Street into Upper Macao Street, passing over the Buffalo Carts and through or over the Palanquins in Macao or George Street, into South Canal Road, over the sand bank and brick heaps past Messrs Purvis & Guthrie's godowns, into Market Street over the crockery and crates of earthenware, through Malacca Street into Commercial Square, over the logs of timber at Messrs Syme & Co's., thence into Battery Road over the hills of the red earth and granite at Messrs Fraser's and ditches and timber at Messrs Middleton's into Boat Quay, past W S Duncan's and from that to the winning post at Bain's Bridge along Boat Quay.

He or she was creatively expressing a long-standing grievance—the roads south of the Singapore River were in such bad condition, even steeplechase horses would find it a challenge!

In the first 60 years of the Town's existence, building and maintaining the Town's channels of movement, and ensuring they were suitable for methods of movement and patterns of movement at the time, were a constant challenge for the authorities, with simple tools, modest budgets, and only a handful of officials in charge. This was imperative as potholes could snap horse carriage springs and injure horses. Official efforts to better manage roads and execute public works gradually led to the bureaucratisation of movement. A British ruling class had to learn the ropes of running and governing a municipality—and placate the demands of a European mercantile class.

After the Town of Singapore was founded in 1819, Lieutenants Ralfe and Jackson served as its first engineers, overseeing the building of roads and public facilities by EIC sepoys. But as the Town grew beyond all expectations, it became unviable to rely on sepoys from India to do all the building on top of their day job of defending the island. As early as 1823, convicts jailed for committing crimes in Singapore were put to work on roads. After 1824, Bencoolen—Britain's penal colony in Southeast Asia—had to be transferred to Dutch control under the terms of the Anglo-Dutch Treaty. Hence, its convicts were distributed throughout what would become the Straits Settlements. In April 1825, 200 convicts arrived in Singapore to work on roads, and for the next half a century or so, Singapore owed its roads, drainage, and reclaimed land to an army of convicts, armed with nothing more than hand tools and rollers pulled by buffaloes.

At any one time, there were about 1,100–1,200 convicts from India in Singapore, most assigned to roadworks. There was plenty of work for them, not just because the population of the Town grew by leaps and bounds, but also because road-building and maintenance in Singapore was a constant battle against the punishing climate, heavy traffic, and the roads' inherent weaknesses. The principal thoroughfares in the Town were macadam roads, while the rest, including those in the country, were dirt roads. Depending on width and quality, these dirt roads could accommodate carriages, horses, or just human feet. They were built using road construction techniques imported from Britain, with a temperate climate, not a tropical, rainy climate. The British had not studied the 16th-century road construction techniques employed by the Mughals they had subjugated in India—techniques which created roads lasting centuries. Hence, a single bout of heavy rain could reduce Singapore's dirt roads to a muddy morass.

Macadam roads fared no better. These streets were usually bordered by uncovered rainwater ditches on both sides, which the population used as an open trash bin; the drains were never free of rubbish and filth. The choked drainage, coupled with frequent torrential rain, meant that these roads, especially in the low-lying Chinese Campong, were often washed out by floods. Clear days brought other problems. In dry weather, macadam roads became very dusty; pedestrians, horses, and carriages raised clouds of red laterite dust. To keep the dust down, constant watering was needed from bullock carts loaded with water drawn from the sea off the Esplanade.

The convicts were also kept busy reclaiming marshes, mostly around the Singapore, Rochor, and Kallang rivers—the rivers flowing through the Town. In 1831, 200 convicts reclaimed 28 acres of land around Kampong Glam; land was also subsequently reclaimed west of South Bridge Road and in Kampong Malacca. Their reclamation techniques were simple. Swamp was first cleared of trees and undergrowth, and filled in with red earth, usually disintegrated laterite or clay ironstone, to a height of 0.6–1.2 metres; the red earth was taken from the hills surrounding the Town. The earth was then trodden down by foot and graded such that the new land would be as flat as possible. To make it impervious to water, the earth was coated with white sand taken from pits along the Sungei Serangoon.

A dedicated position was needed to oversee these public works and the convicts who did the dirty work. From 1826, the Town had been run directly by the resident councillor, reporting to the governor. Public works were paid for out of the government's general revenues. But in 1833, Governor Bonham appointed Coleman to become Singapore's first Superintendent of Public Works and Convicts. Coleman was the right man as he had been employing convicts to build roads and public buildings since the 1820s. He served as superintendent for the next eight years, overseeing part of the construction of some of Singapore's first trunk roads, such as Bukit Timah Road, with convict labour; he and his team also reclaimed the Chinese Campong Extension west of South Bridge Road.

As road construction involved simple tools, the courses of new roads were influenced by terrain. Where trunk roads ran through low-lying areas, they were usually straight, as was the case for parts of Serangoon Road and Bukit Timah Road; where trunk roads entered hilly terrain, parts of Thomson Road, Kranji Road, Pasir Panjang Road, and Changi Road curved or bent, sometimes at sharp angles, to avoid hills. Generally, trunk roads followed the path of least resistance, because laying down the road itself through thick jungle was already an achievement in the 1830s and 1840s.

On top of terrain, Coleman's men had to deal with tiger attacks. In 1831, as his survey team was laying out a new road in the jungle six kilometres from the Town, a tiger leapt at them. The animal landed on a theodolite and broke it, but no one was injured. After the incident, the men did not work in the jungle without weapons.

Money was also a challenge. Public works were not high on budget priorities. In 1832, to raise extra funds to repair and clean roads, the government levied a five per cent tax on the rent of all houses in the Town for six months. In 1840, taxes on horses and carriages were imposed for the first time to raise more money for improving roads. Nevertheless, Buckley's *Anecdotal History* records persistent complaints about the poor state of roads throughout this period. In 1839, another cheeky individual put up a newspaper advertisement "offering $1,000 reward to any person who could succeed in making a safe and easy conveyance to travel… through the road leading to the Sepoy Lines in particular, and the Singapore roads in general; iron and wood having been found too weak, and springs and wheels impracticable." No one took up his or her challenge to invent a new mode of transport though! In 1847, Dr Charles Curties, a private practitioner, was riding in a horse carriage near the junction of North Bridge Road and Jalan Rochor, when his carriage struck a hole "where the side of the road had fallen in"; "pony and buggy were thrown into the canal, the pony killed, and Dr Curties injured".

More money and better administration were needed for road-building and other public works. This coincided with rising demand from European merchants for greater representation in the running of the Town. In March 1848, the government set up a municipal fund made up of monies to be collected from half-yearly taxes imposed on the rents of all houses, shops, and buildings; agricultural produce derived from all lands; and all carriages, wagons, carts, horses, mules, and elephants in use or kept on the island. In the first 15 days of each year from 1849, the owners of all carriages, carts, and other vehicles would have to register with the police; failure to do so would incur fines which would also go into the fund. The money would go towards paying for the police force, street lighting, drainage, and the "efficient watching, repairing, renewing, cleansing, and keeping in repair the public Roads and Streets and all other public thoroughfares in Town and Country".

To "assist the Government in the management of the Municipal Fund, as well as performing other Municipal Acts", a Municipal Committee was also formed, comprising the resident councillor, the Superintendent of Public Works and Convicts, and three non-officials appointed by the governor. The non-officials had to be resident ratepayers, which of course meant Europeans or very rich and influential non-Europeans. The committee had the power to make rules and regulations, subject to the governor's approval. Committees, funds, taxes, registers, rules—this was the earliest, embryonic form of bureaucratic governance in Singapore that has expanded to thousands of civil servants today.

In November 1848, Temenggong Daeng Ibrahim threw a lavish St Andrew's Day party in his territory in Telok Blangah, inviting many luminaries, including Governor William

Butterworth and his wife. At 10pm the party ended and its participants took to their carriages, and then came "the tug of war":

> (Telok Blangah Road), previously not in a very first-rate condition, had got dreadfully cut up by the passage of the numerous vehicles going to the village, and in returning many carriages fairly stuck fast, including… those of high functionaries, who were thus, for once in their lives, practically convinced of the inconveniences which the public suffer when the roads get out of order. The… material injury… resulting from this state of the roads: broken harness, strained vehicles and jaded horses…

In those days, a traffic jam did not just clog up a road, it could destroy it!

The first Municipal Committee convened on 1 January 1849. From the government, Resident Councillor Thomas Church served as chairman, while Henry Man sat on the Committee as Superintendent of Public Works and Convicts until 1855, when he relinquished his position to Colonel Ronald MacPherson (1817–1869). The first three non-official resident ratepayers chosen by Governor Butterworth were Robert McEwen, Michie Forbes Davidson, and Jose D'Almeida's son Joaquim (died 1870). About 10 per cent of the municipal fund went towards roads and bridges.

The relative peace and calm of the Town was shattered on 5 May 1854 by the worst riots in modern Singapore's short history. The Hokkien-Teochew Riots broke out after an argument over the weight of a *kati* (600g) of rice between a Hokkien shopkeeper and a Teochew buyer; bystanders took sides along linguistic lines; blows were exchanged. Buckley recorded: "The fighting spread into the adjoining streets, in all of which the shops were at once closed, and sticks, stones and knives were used freely on the streets, and bricks thrown from the upper windows…" In no time, hundreds were rioting. Upon hearing about the conflagration, Governor Butterworth foolishly mounted his white horse and rode from Government Hill into the Town; at Hill Street, he was pelted by a mob! He was forced to beat a hasty retreat. The riots soon spread from the Town into the country through the trunk and rural roads, to areas with significant Chinese populations such as Paya Lebar, Bedok, and Bukit Timah. Many villages were swept up in orgies of violence. Dozens were butchered in cold blood.

The modest police force was swiftly overwhelmed; the government had to call in the military, marines from British men-of-war coincidentally berthed in the harbour, and Europeans to volunteer as special constables; even the Temenggong helpfully chipped in 200 Malay soldiers. But the riots were quelled only after the authorities adopted a novel course of action making use of trunk roads. They transported troops and constables on steamers to different corners of Singapore Island, where they landed and marched down the four trunk roads—Kranji Road, Thomson Road, Serangoon Road, and Changi Road—in the direction of the Town, the opposite direction from which the riots spread. Some Chinese put a barrier across Changi Road near the 10½ Milestone, so troops were also landed at Tanah Merah Kechil, which gave them access to the 8½ Milestone—allowing them to cut off the Chinese from behind. This unexpected gambit caught the rioters by surprise and they were taken into custody.

After 10 days, the bloodletting ended. About

500 people were killed, 300 homes destroyed, 500 rioters arrested. The unrest so spooked the European community it contributed to the construction of an artillery fort, Fort Canning, atop Government Hill in 1861, to protect them from internal strife. But the Hokkien-Teochew Riots also showed how trunk roads could serve both as a conduit for the spread of violence between the Town and the interior, and the imposition of government control. Roads were not just a means of colonial control—they could also be the means by which control was lost. 1854 would not be the last time this principle would play out in reality.

MORE MUNICIPAL changes were to come. In 1856, an Act was passed to establish a Municipality of Singapore. The town limits now made up a municipal boundary. The existing Municipal Committee became a Municipal Commission, giving commissioners more power independent of the governor to handle municipal affairs, and control over money raised from the Town. From 1 January 1857, instead of being chosen by the governor, the three non-officials in the Commission were elected by ratepayers paying annual rates of 25 rupees or more. It was a very limited democracy as only a tiny minority in Singapore could vote, but a form of political progress nonetheless. The post of Superintendent of Public Works and Convicts was renamed Municipal Engineer, and he was head of a new Public Works Department (PWD) formed to assist him in solving perennial problems such as poor roads and drainage—the humble ancestor of the present-day Ministry of National Development. The first five municipal commissioners who met at the Town Hall along High Street were its President Captain H. T. Marshall, Municipal Engineer MacPherson, John Harvey, Dunman, and the Commission's first Chinese member, Tan Kim Seng (1805–1864).

The problem of a lack of finances remained, however. More than half of municipal monies were used for the police force, leaving the municipal engineer with a pittance. Some examples of work done included: the raising, remetalling, and repairing of roads; filling up potholes, clearing drains, draining land, repairing bridges. In July 1879, 60-year-old High Street was remetalled.

The Municipality also began differentiating public roads from private roads. The former were maintained at their expense and officially open to the public; the latter ran through or past private land and were paid for by the owners of the land. Many channels of movement in Singapore were private roads. The public could still use private roads if landowners allowed them, but the responsibility and costs of maintaining these roads fell on landowners. From 1856, the Municipality started converting private roads that were frequently used by the public to public roads. For instance, in 1857, the owners of houses along Bali Lane, Haji Lane, and Shaik Madersah Lane in Kampong Glam were served with notices to metal and drain the roads, after which the roads would become public roads maintained by municipal funds.

This greater control also extended to road-naming. The Municipality met on 8 March 1858 to do something unprecedented: a mass road-naming exercise. New roads had to be named; others had been left unnamed; some even shared the same name, causing confusion. Again, since the Municipal Commission was dominated by Britons, most names bequeathed were of fellow Britons or political and military significance to

Britain.

North of the Singapore River in the European Town, Church Street (there was another Church Street near Commercial Square) was renamed Waterloo Street, after the Battle of Waterloo, an epochal British-led military victory over Napoleon's First French Empire in 1815. Flint Street (there was a namesake in Commercial Square) was renamed Prinsep Street. China Street (there was a namesake in the Chinese Campong) was renamed Hylam Street because most of the Chinese living there were Hylam, the British term for the Hainanese. A road between Selegie Road and Waterloo Street was named Albert Street, after Prince Albert (1819–1861), consort to Queen Victoria.

In Kampong Glam, Jalan Rochor had been renamed Market Street; however, since there was another Market Street in Commercial Square, Kampong Glam's Market Street was renamed Crawford Street, after John Crawfurd (although "Crawford" was a misspelling!). Cross Street (there was another Cross Street in the Chinese Campong) was renamed Little Cross Street as it was shorter than its namesake. And to avoid confusion between Rochor Road and Rochor Street, the former was renamed Lavender Street, a tongue-in-cheek reference to the foul-smelling vegetable gardens that lined the road! (However, by 1862, Rochor Street became known as Rochor Road.)

South of the Singapore River, Tavern Street was renamed Bonham Street after the governor of 1836 to 1843. Three roads were named after British generals who had played a part in suppressing the Indian Mutiny, an event that had shaken the foundations of colonial rule in India in 1857. Part of Salat Road was renamed Neil Road, after Brigadier-General James George Smith Neill; a road that ran from River Valley Road to New Bridge Road was named Havelock Road, after Major-General Sir Henry Havelock; part of River Valley Road was renamed Outram Road, after Lieutenant-General Sir James Outram (the River Valley Road north of the Singapore River remained as it was). Finally, Commercial Square, the Town's mercantile heart, was renamed Raffles Place, a tribute to the man who had conceived it.

In 1858, Major John Frederick Adolphus McNair (1828–1910) became Singapore's second municipal engineer. Again, he had his work cut out for him. An unidentified writer to *The Straits Times* in 1861 painted a scene of transport woe:

> With the exception of Orchard Road, Commercial Square, and Circular Road, there is not a yard of really good road inside the (Municipality). The Esplanade is shamefully neglected; China Street is in a fearful condition. Boat Quay from Guthrie's Bridge to North Bridge Road is a continuation of ruts and mud. But (Kallang) Road between Lavender Street and (Kallang) Bridge is the most perfect representation of a Slough of Despond that is to be found in Singapore, if we except (Thomson Road), which is impassable.

In April 1867, after years of agitation, the Straits Settlements was transferred from EIC control in Calcutta to direct Crown rule. The governor now reported to the Secretary of State for the Colonies in London. The PWD of Singapore was expanded to become the PWD of the Straits Settlements, with McNair as its head. McNair's new designation was Colonial Engineer, overseeing a new municipal engineer in Singapore. Henceforth, fresh convicts banished from India were sent to the Andaman Islands in the Indian

Ocean instead of Singapore. In 1873, the last batch of convicts in Singapore were pardoned, paid labour took their place, and the role of Indian convicts in Singapore's history of movement came to a quiet end.

FROM OLD TO NEW HARBOUR

THE SITING of the port of Singapore in 1819 was crucial to its history of movement, for it determined where and how the Town of Singapore evolved. The siting of a second port of Singapore in the 1850s would also be crucial, for it determined where and how the Town—and its channels of movement—subsequently expanded.

The first port of 1819 could have been sited at the location of the second port of the 1850s—in the south of Singapore at Tanjong Pagar and Telok Blangah—if Raffles had been aware that the area was also a shipping route in ancient times. The western entrance to present-day Keppel Harbour is thought to have been described as early as 1349 by Wang Dayuan in the *Daoyi Zhilue*. He wrote about Long Ya Men, Mandarin for "Dragon's Teeth Gate", a craggy granite outcrop which served as a navigational aid to mariners at the time: "The strait runs between the two hills of the (Temasek) barbarians, which look like 'dragon's teeth'. Through the centre runs a waterway."

In September 1819, Farquhar declared in a letter to Raffles that he had found a "new harbour" to the west of the Singapore River; the following year he wrote that it was "capable of affording the most complete protection to ships of the largest size". However, nothing came of his "discovery". In 1821, Crawfurd explored the "new harbour, or Salat Panikam, as it is called by the Malays". He went on to describe: "The entrance is narrow and difficult; but when a ship is once moored within it, she is secure from every danger—from rocks, elements, and even from an enemy, for half a dozen guns would make it impregnable to any attack from sea." At the time, the harbour was a retreat of the native Orang Laut.

To connect the Town with this "New Harbour", Tanjong Pagar Road and Salat Road were built around 1823. For the next three decades, these roads remained dirt paths winding through nutmeg plantations, for the Singapore River sufficed as a harbour.

As years passed, the Singapore River became congested. The growing popularity of steamships running on coal necessitated the building of coal depots; the Singapore River banks soon ran out of space for them and the loading and unloading of coal. The government and Singapore's mercantile community eventually turned their attention towards New Harbour as an alternative. When they did so, they referred to New Harbour as such, and the native name John Crawfurd had recorded—Salat Panikam—disappeared into the abyss of history.

The first victim of the development of New Harbour was a landmark going back at least 500 years—Dragon's Teeth Gate, known to the Malays as Batu Berlayar (Malay for "Sailing Rock") and to the British as Lot's Wife. It was blown up by the British in 1848 to widen the channel for larger vessels. Wang would not have been pleased.

Four years later, in 1852, the Peninsular and Oriental Steam Navigation Company broke new ground by moving to Tebing Tinggi (Malay for "High Bank", where Vivocity is today), just south of Telok Blangah Village. In 1859, New Harbour's first dry dock, No. 1 Dock, was completed off Telok Blangah Road, built by Captain William Cloughton and his Patent Slip & Dock Company. By 1880, New Harbour—from the former Batu

Berlayar in the west to Tanjong Pagar Road in the east—was replete with dry docks and wharves serving shipping and commercial companies. These included the Borneo Company, which had been founded to develop the resources of Borneo, lending its name to Borneo Wharf; and Jardine, Matheson & Company, founded by William Jardine and James Matheson, giving rise to the name for the pier, Jardine's Steps.

Conversely, the swamps that had forced the curvature of Salat Road (part of which was renamed Neil Road in 1858) were reclaimed; so were the sand banks off the coast. The original cape called Tanjong Pagar—the Cape of Stake Fences—disappeared. Tanjong Pagar Village was also levelled to make way for a new mercantile community; only the Temenggong's privileged status prevented Telok Blangah Village from suffering the same fate. But he had to contend with a busier neighbourhood. The agriculture that once was the trademark of Tanjong Pagar was replaced by houses and godowns. The face of the southern coast of Singapore was changing much like how the landscape around the Singapore River changed in the 1820s and 1830s.

But development also brought a sharp rise in traffic. In 1855, the Municipal Committee ordered the widening of "narrow and dangerous" Tanjong Pagar Road, as it was "in a very bad state". By the 1870s, it had grown from a dirt track to a busy macadam road, with houses and godowns on both sides. Neil Road was also lengthened to Telok Blangah Village, the straighter channel of movement allowing traffic to bypass the bends of Salat Road. Other than these improvements, however, the road system connecting New Harbour to the Town remained largely the same from the 1850s to 1880. Nothing like Raffles' Town Plan was ever conceived. This might be for two reasons:

firstly, the hilly terrain of Telok Blangah and Bukit Merah (Malay for "Red Hill") discouraged the PWD from building roads; secondly, the bureaucracy of the Municipal Commission and PWD prevented another strong-minded, Raffles-like personality from bulldozing a town plan from paper to fruition. Only growing traffic congestion and an influential mercantile community could, and would, push the Municipality into serious action.

By the 1870s the writing was on the wall. Bullock carts were still the main method of movement for cargo. Their slowness clogged the roads between New Harbour and the Town. Whenever cattle plague broke out, merchant shipping was delayed.

"SIGNPOSTS OF DAILY ACTIVITIES"

IN AN urban space, road names are a keystone of movement and landmarks crucial for way-finding. In 19th-century Singapore, there were different nomenclatures used by the Europeans and non-Europeans in naming and identifying roads and places. The one primarily used in this book, which has survived to this day, is the English-language road-naming system, the dominant, "official" one imposed and used by government departments. However, there were also unique road-naming systems used among the Chinese and Indian communities in Singapore, but they remained mostly within the respective communities. These systems persisted despite official attempts to override or suppress them, and only disappeared after large-scale resettlement and urban renewal from the 1960s.

We must recognise first that the English-language road-naming nomenclature is a largely British legacy. From 1819, through organised governance, record-keeping, and map-making, the

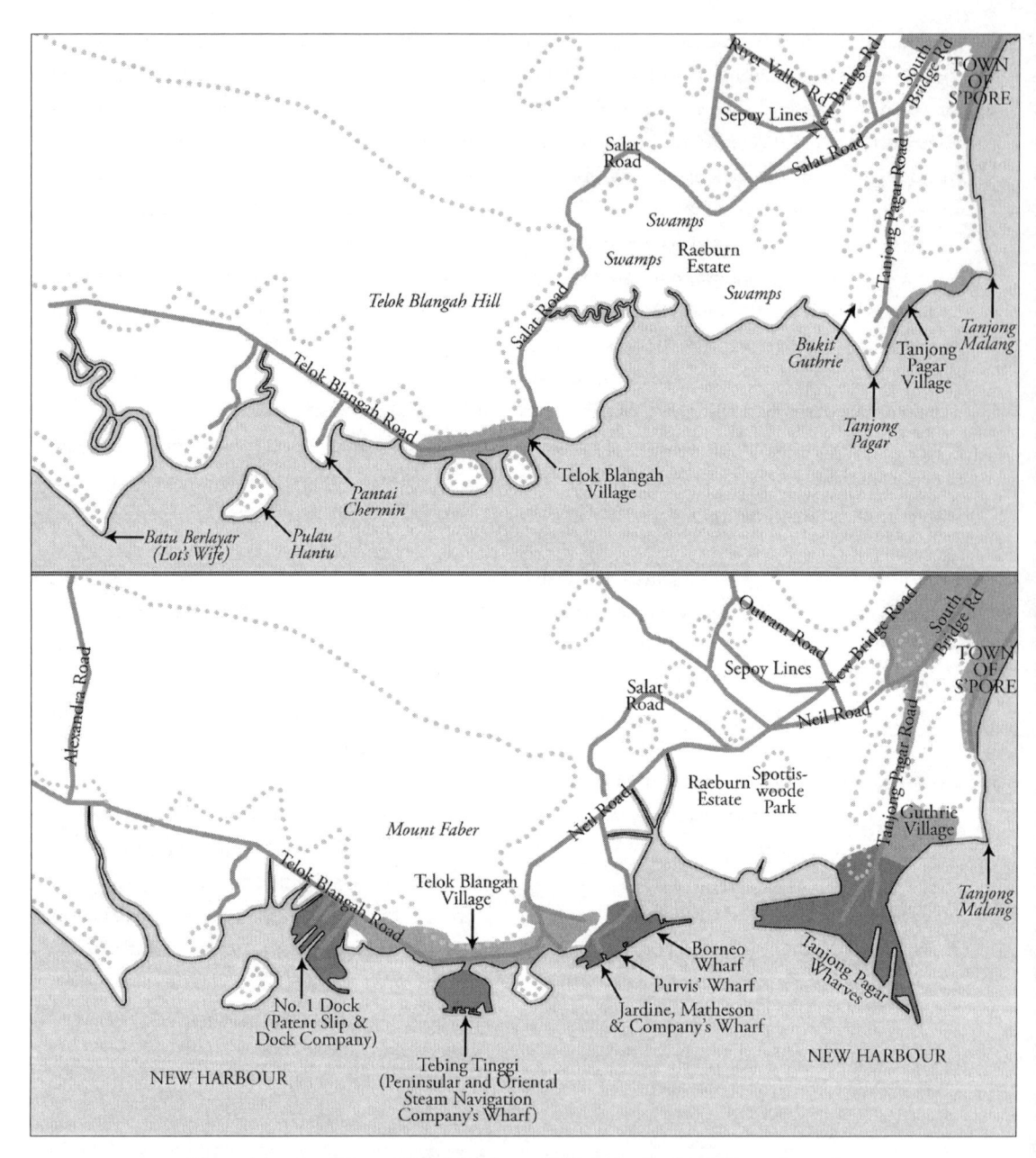

74 **Jalan Singapura**: 700 Years of Movement in Singapore

The southern coast of Singapore Island, based on an 1846 map (top) and an 1881 map (bottom). By 1881, docks and wharves—marked in dark grey—were spreading along the coast of New Harbour, but the road system connecting New Harbour to the Town of Singapore did not experience a sea change. Hills—in dotted lines—may have been a factor. (Source: Eisen Teo) government assigned permanent names to places and roads, a thread of authority that has remained unbroken to the present. The same happened in other successful British port-towns established around the same time, such as Penang (founded 1786) and Hong Kong (1842).

This British road-naming system did not just employ English names. Malay names and geographical terms were incorporated without translation, perhaps because of the special status of the Sultan of Johor and the Temenggong, and the Malays as an indigenous people. Geographical terms included "Bukit", "Jalan", and "Lorong". Numerous Malay names, however, were spelled in various ways by English speakers—for example, "Saranggong" became "Serangoon", "Tempinis" became "Tampines", and "Selat" became "Salat". For one hill, Bukit Guthrie, a Malay geographical term even became attached to an English name.

Chinese names were also adopted, perhaps in acknowledgement of Singapore's large Chinese population, but for names that originated from places in China, the British used common English Romanisations. Hence we have Amoy Street, Canton Street, and Nankin Street, not Xiamen Street, Guangzhou Street, and Nanjing Street. Some Chinese names were even spelled differently, such as Hokien (instead of "Hokkien") Street and Tew Chew (instead of "Teochew") Street.

A Hindi term "Ghat" also entered the British road-naming lexicon, probably originating from British India. "Dhoby Ghaut" appeared in the 1850s as a place name off Orchard Road; there, Indian washermen used the banks and waters of the Sungei Bras Basah as an open-air laundromat. "Dhobi" is "washerman" in Hindi; "Ghat" refers to steps leading down to a body of water; "Dhobi Ghat" evolved into "Dhoby Ghaut". Around the same time, two landing places in the Town were named Dalhousie Ghaut and Butterworth Ghaut. The former was the intersection of Beach Road and High Street, where Raffles departed Singapore for England in 1823; it was named to commemorate the 1850 visit of the governor-general of India, James Broun-Ramsay, 1st Marquess of Dalhousie (1812–1860). Butterworth Ghaut was along the Singapore River at the entrance to Bonham Street. It was named after Governor Butterworth making landfall there when he first arrived in Singapore. Within several decades, however, the place names and landing places of both ghauts fell into disuse. Today, only Dhoby Ghaut has survived as a place name.

Singapore's British road-naming system commemorated individuals who had contributed to the British mercantile and commercial empire in Singapore—and most of these individuals were themselves British. In a 1905 municipal roads study, almost half of all municipal road names were commemorative in nature; two-thirds of these roads were named after Europeans (and probably a couple of Americans), the rest after Asians. This statistic does not cover roads named after places in Britain (for example, Devonshire Road), British colonies (e.g. Bencoolen Street), positive events associated with Britain (e.g. Waterloo Street), and estates belonging to Britons (e.g. Cairnhill Road and Duxton Road). Common road names in Britain have also found their way to Singapore, the most notable being High Street. All these, despite European and American residents making up just half to one per cent of the population of Singapore Island for much of the 19th century.[8]

Under this road-naming system, what would you have to be or do to maximise your chances of getting a road or place in Singapore named after you? First, you should hail from the British Isles—

England, Scotland, Wales or Ireland (Northern Ireland after 1921). Then, you should take up a job with the government developing the port and Town—the earlier the better, when there was more to be done and fewer rivals around. Needless to say, you should also fare relatively well in your job. Singapore's two Residents, Farquhar and Crawfurd, had Farquhar Street and Crawford Street named after them (too bad for the misspelling of "Crawfurd" though). Farquhar's son-in-law Francis James Bernard (1796–1843), Singapore's first Acting Master Attendant and Chief of Police, gave his name to Bernard Street. Superintendents of Public Works and Convicts also had roads named after them—Coleman, MacPherson, and so on.

Even better, you should be a governor of the Straits Settlements, or at least get into the Municipal Committee or Commission. Of the 24 governors and acting governors from 1826 to 1942, 16 had roads named after them, four had bridges named after them, and three had a quay, pier or landing place named after them; only five missed out on these honours. The first five municipal commissioners in 1856—Marshall, Harvey, MacPherson, Dunman, and Tan Kim Seng—all gave their names to roads. Today, we still have Marshall Road (off East Coast Road), Harvey Road off MacPherson Road, Dunman Road, and Kim Seng Road.[9]

Alternatively, you could be a fairly successful merchant or landowner. Usually, if you were one, you were the other. After all, the mercantile and agricultural sectors in Singapore were cornerstones of its economy. Examples of individuals who thrived in these areas included Oxley, Prinsep, and the father-and-son team of Jose and Joaquim D'Almeida, who had not one, but three roads named after them—Almeida Road (off Stevens Road), Almeida Street (off South Bridge Road), and D'Almeida Street (near Raffles Place)!

Tough luck if you fulfilled the above criteria but still had no road or place named after you. Dr Thomas Prendergast was Singapore's first surgeon, brought in by Raffles himself in February 1819, but was soon replaced by Montgomerie, and quickly slipped into obscurity, missing a chance at toponymic immortality. And spare a thought for the five poor Straits Settlements governors who never had a place or road named after them, including the henceforth unfamiliar names of Robert Ibbetson, Kenneth Murchison, and Edmund Augustus Blundell.

If you were non-European, your chances of getting a road or place named after you plunged dramatically. You had to be truly rich, famous, and influential—preferably a landowner, merchant, and government or municipal official rolled into one. One Chinese family gained toponymic favour this way. It started with Municipal Commissioner Tan Kim Seng; then his son, Tan Beng Swee (1828–1884), justice of the peace, gave his name to Beng Swee Place, at the junction of Bras Basah Road and Waterloo Street. Tan Beng Swee's chop, Hong Hin (Hokkien for "Rising Abundance"), also gave its name to Hong Hin Court, off North Bridge Road. Not to be outdone, Tan Beng Swee's son Tan Jiak Kim (1859–1917) was twice municipal commissioner and had Jiak Kim Street named after him!

Syed Omar Ali Aljunied (1792–1852) was one of the few non-Chinese Asians who had a road or place named after him. In 1820, he paid for the construction of Singapore's oldest mosque in Kampong Malacca, presently known as the Masjid Omar Kampong Melaka; Omar Road was also named after him.

These men were in the minority. The majority

of Asian merchants and landowners never received toponymic honours; others had to wait up to a century for immortality. Tan Che Sang once boasted that "he wielded so much influence over the Chinese section that any day he said the word he could empty the place of all the Europeans", yet he never had a road or place named after him. Other rich Chinese men came and went, lost in history: Yeo Kim Swee, Cheong Ann Jan, Ho Chong Lay, Song Hoot Kiam, and so on. Tan Hoon Keat (died 1884) had a hill along Neil Road—Bukit Hoon Keat—named after him, but it was later renamed Dickenson Hill, presently Bukit Pasoh. As for Tamil immigrant Narayana Pillai, he was persuaded by Raffles in 1819 to uproot from Penang and settle in Singapore. He established the island's first brick kiln, ventured into the cotton goods trade, and established the Sri Mariamman Temple at South Bridge Road. But it wasn't until 1957 that Pillai Road off Upper Paya Lebar Road was named after him.

So, this British road-naming nomenclature gave pride and honour largely to the British and Europeans who formed the cream of governance and society in Singapore. But its reach and influence were confined to the English-speaking and reading part of Singapore. In the present day, this covers much of Singapore, since English is the lingua franca and the language of official communication. In the 1800s, however, bazaar Malay was the lingua franca; even by 1921, just 5.6 per cent of the population of the Municipality of Singapore was literate in English. Hence, most Chinese, Malays, and Indians referred to roads and places in Singapore in their own unique ways, in their own languages.

Within the Town of Singapore, Raffles had allocated the best land for the Government Ground and the European Town; the northern and southern peripheries were left to Kampong Glam and the Chinese Campong. To the Chinese, however, the Chinese Campong was their home turf. They knew it as "Greater Town", or Da Po in Mandarin, Toa Po in Hokkien, and so on. To them, Greater Town was the centre of their universe, a little China, a home away from home. Outside Greater Town, north of the Singapore River, was "Lesser Town", or Xiao Po in Mandarin, Sio Po in Hokkien, and so on. Within the Lesser Town, the Chinese used a series of straight, parallel roads as path-finding aids—from North Bridge Road in the east, to Victoria Street, Queen Street, Waterloo Street, Bencoolen Street, and Prinsep Street in the west. These street names—very English in flavour—were for most Chinese alien and hard to pronounce or remember, so they simply assigned numbers to them. North Bridge Road was known as "Main Road", or Da Ma Lu in Mandarin, Toa Beh Lo in Hokkien, and so on. Victoria Street was known as "Second Road" (Er Ma Lu in Mandarin), Queen Street as "Third Road" (San Ma Lu), Waterloo Street as "Fourth Road" (Si Ma Lu), Bencoolen Street as "Fifth Road" (Wu Ma Lu), Prinsep Street as "Sixth Road" (Liu Ma Lu), and Selegie Road as "Seventh Road" (Qi Ma Lu). These names allowed the Chinese to negotiate channels of movement in a part of the Town they were not familiar with.

While the British named many roads after individuals to honour their contributions to the British establishment in Singapore, or after places or events associated with Britain, the Chinese and Indians named most roads after symbols, landmarks, and activities that formed their daily lives; to them, road names served as pragmatic "signposts of daily activities". These names were not arrived at through meetings of committees or officials; they evolved through an informal, ground-up process over time, as specific landmarks and activities grew in importance to a community. Also, while the British made sure a proper, (mostly) unique name was assigned to a fixed length of road which could be clearly demarcated on a map, the Chinese, Indians, and Malays assigned names to a general location which at times covered only part of a road, or conversely, two or more roads at the same time. The aforementioned 1905 municipal roads study unearthed 365 Hokkien and Cantonese names for just 225 roads![10] Clearly, the non-Europeans "mapped" and negotiated the urban landscape of 19th-century Singapore very differently from the Europeans.

North of the Singapore River in Kampong Glam, the Hokkiens knew Sultan Gate as Sio Po Phah Thi Gei, or "Lesser Town's Street of Ironsmiths". The part of Beach Road around Clyde Terrace Market (built in 1873 by the sea) was known as Thi Pa Sat Khau, or "Mouth of the Iron Market". Kandang Kerbau was named Tek Kha, or "The Foot of the Bamboos", describing the bamboo groves that grew along the banks of the Rochor River; this has survived to the present as the place name Tekka.

South of the Singapore River, the Hokkiens did not think of Raffles when they made references to Raffles Place; instead, they called it Tho Kho Huei Hng, or "Flower Garden By The Godowns". Within Greater Town, they named China Street as Kiau Keng Khau, or "Mouth of the Gambling Houses"—no doubt a popular destination for many Chinese. Hokien Street—to the British, the street of the Hokkien people—was known to the Hokkiens themselves as Cho Beh Chia Gei, "The Street Where Horse Carriages Are Made". It helped that the Chinese in one industry congregated in a single street—blacksmiths to one street, carpenters to another, stone masons to a third, and so on. And as an indication of the importance of bullock carts in transporting water around the Town, the Smith Street–Sago Street area was known as Gu Chia Chui ("Bullock Cart Water") to the Hokkiens, Ngau Che Sui ("Bullock Cart Water") to the Cantonese, and Kreta Ayer ("Water Cart") to the Malays.

Bullock carts were also used by the Tamils to convey water from the Balestier Road area to the Town for sale, hence to them, the Balestier Road area was known as Thannir Kampam or "Water Kampung". Albert Street was known as Thimiri Thidal, or "The Place Where People Tread on Fire", a reference to Hindu fire-walking ceremonies. Arab Street was known to the Tamils as Pukadei Sadakku, or "Street of the Flower Shops". And Rochor Street (now Rochor Road) was known as Kammangala Paleia Kuthu Madei Sadakku, "Street of Kampong Glam's Old Hindu Theatre". This was a form of social cartography unlike any physical map the British produced.

As a result of this toponymic heterogeneity, British authority over the Asian communities was not absolute; it complicated and frustrated attempts by the British to survey, monitor, and control them. Addresses could not be recorded accurately for important tasks such as making arrests, issuing court summons, or collecting data to trace house occupancy levels or the spread of infectious diseases. It also meant the experiences and social memories of movement in 19th-century Singapore varied widely among communities. However, the vast majority of recorded experiences and social memories were that of Europeans; with the passage of time, almost total urban renewal of the Town of Singapore from the 1960s, and the prevalence of English as the lingua franca of Singapore today, the non-Europeans' "signposts of daily activities" have all but disappeared in both form and memory. Singapore's history of movement may never be truly complete—a testament to the transience of urban spaces and their communities.

CHAPTER NOTES

1. The "town" refers to the Town of Singapore. The 1871 and 1881 censuses record its population separately from the population of the rest of Singapore Island, labelled "Country".

2. Today, the Singapore General Hospital stands on the site of the Sepoy Lines.

3. Conventionally, at least in Singapore and for historical and political reasons, "Hokkien", "Teochew", "Cantonese", etc. are called "dialects", while Mandarin enjoys an elevated status as a "language". To depart from this, I have decided to use the more neutral term "topolect" in place of "dialect".

4. Singapore's first Acting Master Attendant was Francis James Bernard, who served from February 1819 to April 1820; Flint then took over as Master Attendant from April 1820 to September 1828.

5. Shaik Madersah Lane first appeared as "Sheik Madersaw Lane" in a Singapore newspaper in 1856; in Charles Buckley's *Anecdotal History of Old Times in Singapore*, it is spelled "Shaik Madarsah Lane". A person named "Madersaw Hooseusah" was named in an indenture dated 1854, around the time the road appeared in written records.

6. In Crawfurd's *Journal of an Embassy from the Governor-General of India to the Courts of Siam and Cochin China*, he omitted his deceit.

7. In *One Hundred Years of Singapore*, Mrs. G. P. Owen (Annie Dorothea Caroline Earnshaw) claimed that Mount Wallich used to be called Cursetjee's Hill. However, in an 1878 *Map of the Town and Environs of Singapore* drawn by Major John Frederick Adolphus McNair, Mount Wallich and Cursetjee Hill are marked out as separate hills. I have erred on the side of caution and chosen not to include Mrs. Owen's claim.

8. In 1833, Europeans numbered 119 out of 20,978 people in Singapore (0.57 per cent); in 1901, the European and American resident population was 2,861 out of 228,555 people on Singapore Island (1.25 per cent).

9. That said, Dunman Road in the Tanjong Katong area was not named after Thomas Dunman. Dunman first gave his name to Dunman Street (in present-day Little India) in the 1880s. However, in 1930, Dunman Road was named after Dunman's son William, a former municipal commissioner. To avoid confusion, Dunman Street was renamed Upper Dickson Road.

10. The municipal study is H. W. Firmstone's *Chinese Names of Streets and Places in Singapore and the Malay Peninsula*. Some of the place names identified as Hokkien in the study are actually Teochew. They include names in which "Street" is translated as "Koi"—the Hokkien for "Street" is "Gei", while the "Teochew" for "Street" is "Goi". For such names subsequently mentioned in my book, I have corrected Firmstone's translations.

CHAPTER 3
1880 to 1918: Muscles and Motors

FOR YEARS, Messrs Powell and Co. auctioned horses in front of its godown at Raffles Place, the Town of Singapore's commercial quarter. Sometime in 1878 or 1879, however, its employees dragged out for auction a couple of vehicles never before seen by the crowd in the square, vehicles that would shape the history of movement of Singapore.

For the first time, a pair of rickshaws made their appearance in Singapore. The rickshaw—also known as the jinrickshaw or jinrikisha—was a form of human-powered transport. It was a cart with two wheels made of rims of iron, and either one or two seats for passengers at the back— Messrs Powell and Co.'s rickshaws were double-seated. The rickshaw functioned like a bullock cart or horse carriage, except a human—nicknamed the "chair-coolie"—now took the place of the beast of burden.

The vehicles in Raffles Place were gazed upon "by the astonished populace with the same amazed interest that would have been bestowed upon a pair of unicorns or a two-headed giraffe". Then, a "well-known resident of Singapore", Harry Abrams (1848–1911), a horse dealer, trainer, and veterinarian, intervened.

> ... (With) a long driving whip in hand... (he) rose to the occasion. He burrowed into the crowd and "commandeered" a coolie who had possibly, in the erstwhile, pulled a (rickshaw) in Shanghai... (With)

a great cracking of his long carriage whip, and amid the tumultuous plaudits of the multitude, he rode up and down the side of (Raffles Place) in the first (rickshaw) that ever appeared on the streets of Singapore.

The vehicles were eventually auctioned off for $4 apiece. In February 1880, the first consignment of rickshaws arrived from Shanghai, China, and were put onto the streets for hire. The rickshaw soon became an 19th-century taxi for the masses. It became so popular and numerous, Singapore transformed into a "city of rickshaws" within just 13 years of its introduction.

It is ironic that 32-year-old Abrams had played such a key role in the rickshaw leaving a good first impression on the crowds of Raffles Place. "Daddy Abrams", the founder and proprietor of Abrams' Horse Repository since 1873, represented the age-old horse carriage industry, serving the well-to-do; an industry that would be rivalled and supplanted by the rickshaw.

The rickshaw was not alone in revolutionising movement in Singapore. Before 1880, almost all but the well-to-do walked. By the end of the Great War in 1918, the age of the engine had been ushered in. The electric tram, the railway train, and motor cars and lorries, changed the way people in Singapore moved, worked, and interacted. Rickshaw pulling became an occupation for a large part of the population. The fire brigade and the post office converted their horse-drawn fire engines and mail trucks to motor vehicles, while the port at Tanjong Pagar started using motor trucks in place of bullock carts. These newer, faster, more convenient methods of movement impacted the physical landscape of Singapore, with the laying down of railway lines and tram lines. New roads were cut to connect previously isolated parts of the island. A handful of roads even received the gift of reliable lighting at night. But as moving from point A to point B became easier, the growth in the volume of larger and faster vehicles on major thoroughfares made movement more treacherous too. This despite the expansion of the Town itself, together with the expansion of the Municipality of Singapore to cover a full one-seventh of Singapore Island's land area. Reclamation projects all along the southeast coast of the island created precious new land for houses, commerce, and of course, channels of movement.

Such an evolution was necessary, given the tripling of Singapore's population from 1881 to 1921, from 139,208 to 418,358—almost 40 times the size of the population in 1824. By 1918, Singapore was known as the "Liverpool of the East" and the "Gibraltar of the Far East"—a key port-of-call upholding Pax Britannica. It would have been difficult for Singapore to attain such epithets without a history of movement as vibrant and colourful as the one it experienced from 1880 to 1918.

CLAIMING LAND FROM THE SEA

THE ORIGINAL Town of Singapore laid out in the Raffles Town Plan of 1822 hugged the southeast coast of Singapore Island closely. As its population grew, the volume of traffic also grew, as did the need for more space to accommodate new buildings and traffic. The waters off the southeast coast were shallow, and land reclamation had been accomplished before. It was only a matter of time before more reclamation was carried out—if the political will and funds came together at the right time.

The first part of the Town to grow seawards was Raffles Place. Between 1858 and 1862, Straits Settlements Chief Engineer George Chancellor Collyer (1814–1897) oversaw the building of a seawall a short distance east of the seashore, and reclamation behind it to add to the land area of Raffles Place. Before reclamation, beachcombers collected seashells on the seashore in front of Fort Fullerton. The backs of the shophouses and godowns facing Battery Road and Raffles Place came right up to the water's edge; merchants built private jetties and piers out into the sea for the loading and unloading of goods from vessels. These jetties and piers, standing for almost 40 years, had to make way for the seawall. A new road was laid down atop the seawall; it was named Collyer Quay in 1864 to honour the chief engineer. A row of two-storey terraced buildings arose along Collyer Quay—ground-floor godowns topped by offices—forming the new waterfront of Raffles Place. The upper-floor offices were connected by one long verandah facing the sea, so anyone from one office could walk along the verandah to visit people in another office without having to head downstairs!

By the 1860s, New Harbour was in operation, and the roads between it and the Singapore River and Raffles Place were congested with cargo and horse carriages, constantly wearing them down. The condition of Tanjong Pagar Road was particularly bad. Someone who signed off as "R. L." wrote to *The Straits Times* on 10 March 1869:

> Allow me through the medium of your paper to draw the attention of the

Collyer Quay in 1905. The road was named in 1864 to honour Straits Settlements Chief Engineer George Chancellor Collyer. A row of terraced buildings formed the new waterfront of Raffles Place. (Source: Library of Congress)

Municipal Commissioners to the state of the Tanjong Paggar Road. For months past it has been the worst in the island, when there was rain there were ruts and boulders, sufficient to bring down any horse, or break any set of springs, but now that the Commissioners have taken off the upper crust in their attempt to level the road, it may be described as a vast dust hole with many ruts in it. During this dry weather the dust is at least one foot thick—in many places more so, and a carriage or two raises a cloud of more than Cimmerean darkness.

I could not help thinking on my way to the Dock this day that if the Commissioners were only aware of the condition of the road they would not delay an hour in making the greatest thoroughfare in Singapore, passable without the danger of being choked by dust, and when halfway down, I heard the sound of a conveyance approaching me, and could just catch a glimpse of a pony, which I discerned to be that of the Manager of the Dock. I hailed him, and he stopped—and we conversed but 't'was in a cloud', and I learned what I could scarcely believe, that the attention of the Municipal Commissioners had been called to the subject daily.

Throughout the 1860s and 1870s, Singapore's mercantile community pressed for the filling in of Telok Ayer Bay and the construction of new roads between New Harbour and Raffles Place to relieve the traffic pressure on New Bridge Road, South Bridge Road, Neil Road, and Tanjong Pagar Road. The government dithered, however, and nothing concrete was done until international politics kicked in.

In the 1870s, the British Empire was at loggerheads with the Russian Empire over control of Central Asia. To halt Russian encroachment into British India, Britain even fought a war, the Second Afghan War, against the Afghans in Afghanistan. Britain also feared a Russian attack on its ports, and strategically-placed Singapore was deemed a key target. One coastal fort defending the port at Tanjong Pagar was Fort Palmer, built in 1855 atop Mount Palmer, but its guns were outdated, and the government decided to upgrade them. However, they realised much of the hill was owned by a harbour company, the Tanjong Pagar Dock Company. A deal was then struck by Straits Settlements Governor Sir William Cleaver Francis Robinson (1834–1897)—the company would allow the government to upgrade the fort, while the government would finally fund Singapore's largest land reclamation project yet—the Telok Ayer Reclamation Scheme.

The scheme took place in two stages. The first stage started in 1879 and took 10 long years, ending only in 1889. Previously, the beach along Telok Ayer Bay was used for shipbuilding; it was lined with *tongkangs* (light wooden boats) in various stages of completion. The *tongkangs* and the beach disappeared as the bay was filled up at a cost of $1 million to become the Telok Ayer Reclamation Ground. The shoreline receded from curved Telok Ayer Street, which was never expunged or realigned, surviving as a reminder of the old coastline. Telok Ayer Market, built in 1825 by the sea, had to be demolished, although Market Street lived on as a reminder of the market's original location. The Thian Hock Keng Temple and the Nagore Durgha, respectively a Buddhist/Taoist temple and an

Islamic shrine built along Telok Ayer Street to welcome immigrants fresh off the boat, no longer stood by the sea. Cross Street, Market Street, and Japan Street were extended onto the Telok Ayer Reclamation Ground, almost doubling their lengths. A score of new roads were laid down on the rest of the reclaimed land, and true to the wishes of Stamford Raffles 60 years before, these roads were laid out in a grid pattern at right angles to each other, much like the rest of the Town. Most of their names are a snapshot of British governance and British-led commerce in the 1880s and 1890s, an honour to men who ran the Straits Settlements at the time.

The roads included Finlayson Green, named in 1895 after John Finlayson, a chairman of the Chamber of Commerce and the Tanjong Pagar Dock Company; Cecil Street, after Sir Cecil Clementi Smith (1840–1916), governor from 1887 to 1893; Robinson Road, after William Robinson; McCallum Street, named in 1895 after Major Sir Henry Edward McCallum (1852–1919), colonial engineer for the Straits Settlements from 1885 to 1897; Telegraph Street, named in 1895 after the Eastern Extension Telegraph Company, which occupied an office building there; Palmer Street, named in 1895 after John Palmer; and Cheang Hong Lim Street and Cheang Wan Seng Place, after Cheang Hong Lim (1825–1893), businessman and property, opium, and spirit farm owner; his chop Wan Seng is Hokkien for "Garden of Life". Raffles Quay—named after Raffles—was also laid down along the new shoreline, a full five blocks from Telok Ayer Street. Telok Ayer Market was resurrected along Raffles Quay by 1894, keeping its old name.

Finlayson Green, sometime between 1907 and 1918. It was named in 1895 after John Finlayson, a chairman of the Chamber of Commerce and the Tanjong Pagar Dock Company. (Source: The New York Public Library Digital Collections)

To ease congestion between New Harbour and Raffles Place, Anson Road was built between Mount Wallich and Mount Palmer; it was named after Major-General Sir Archibald Edward Harbord Anson (1826–1925), acting governor in 1877 and from 1879 to 1880. Anson Road, then Robinson Road or Cecil Street, was now a welcome alternative to tired Tanjong Pagar Road.

Further relief for Neil Road arrived between 1881 and 1884, when Keppel Road was laid down between Telok Blangah Road and Tanjong Pagar Road, named after Royal Navy Admiral Sir Henry Keppel (1809–1904). Subsequently, in 1900, New Harbour would also be renamed Keppel Harbour in his honour.

In 1892, Reverend G. M. Reith, a Presbyterian minister, described the refreshing scenery along Keppel Road and Anson Road, a world of difference from Hornaday's account:

> There is more than one road to town from all the wharves, but the best is that skirting the shore, because of the cool breeze from the sea, and also because the road leads straight to the business part of the town. The syce must be instructed, if this route be chosen, to "*jalan tepi laut*" (to drive by the sea shore). It is a well-kept road, laid with tramway lines, and the sea is kept in sight most of the way, a distance of three miles, from the P. & O. Wharf (in Tebing Tinggi). It skirts a number of small laterite hills which are being fast quarried away for road-making purposes. Then Fort Palmer is passed on the right and the Chinese Quarter on the left, and the business part of the town is entered when Robinson Quay is reached. Collyer Quay is then entered— an imposing terrace of offices with the convexity of the curve fronting the sea. At one end is the (Telok) Ayer Fish Market, and at the other Johnston's Pier, whence communication is made by boat with the shipping in the Roadstead. The office of the Hongkong and Shanghai Banking Corporation is almost opposite the Pier...

The business and financial heart of the Town spread from Raffles Place and Market Street to Cecil Street, Robinson Road, Finlayson Green, and Collyer Quay.

THE SECOND stage of the Telok Ayer Reclamation Scheme began in 1907, under the watch of Governor Sir John Anderson (1858–1918). It lasted about six years, drastically altering the shape and coastline of the Town south of the Singapore River.

By 1907, the winds of international politics had shifted. Two decades of Anglo-Russian negotiations and conventions culminated in the 1907 Anglo–Russian Entente, which included a shared understanding of the status of overseas territories of mutual interest, such as Persia, Afghanistan, and Tibet. Conversely, an Anglo–German naval race had commenced since the turn of the century. British warships began to be recalled from imperial policing duties in the Far East to be stationed closer to home. Hence, Fort Palmer was no longer deemed important, and the hill it stood on could now make way for land reclamation.

Two hills that once defined the natural Town limits of 1822, Mount Wallich and Mount Palmer, were flattened. Fortunately, the Keramat Habib Noh was near the foot of Mount Palmer, so it escaped destruction—and has survived to this day.

Wallich Street and Palmer Road, built a few years earlier and also at the respective foothills, survived as memorials to the hills as well.

Thousands of tons of earth were pushed into the sea off the original Reclamation Ground, creating a new Reclamation Ground to the east. Unlike the old Ground, the new Ground was not immediately crisscrossed with roads and opened for development; the exception was Prince Edward Road in the south, named in 1923 after Britain's Prince Edward (1894–1972), who would become King Edward VIII in 1936. A new Telok Ayer Basin was created for the next 60 years. In all, the 30-year Telok Ayer Reclamation Scheme was roughly the size of the Chinese Campong and Raffles Place combined.

The Town north of the Singapore River, from High Street to Rochor Road, also saw reclamation. For more than 70 years, Asian traders had been docking their boats and junks along the coast; residents bathed in the sea, and owners of horses took their steeds for dips. From the early 1890s, reclamation commenced east of Beach Road. Between High Street and Stamford Road, the Esplanade/Padang almost doubled in size, and Scandal Point gradually fell out of favour as a social space. New Esplanade Road was laid down on the reclaimed land on the other side of the Padang. In 1907, to commemorate a visit to Singapore by Queen Victoria's son, Prince Arthur, Duke of Connaught and Strathearn (1850–1942), New Esplanade Road was renamed Connaught Drive. At the same time, the original Esplanade Road, half a century old, was renamed St Andrew's Road, after St Andrew's Cathedral.

Between Stamford Road and Rochor Road, the reclaimed land, known as the Beach Road Reclamation Ground (by 1934, renamed the Raffles Reclamation Ground after the Raffles Hotel), was used for circuses and football matches. Two cinemas, the Alhambra and the Marlborough, opened in 1907 and 1909 near Middle Road. Thereafter, squatter huts sprouted, and firewood and charcoal traders set up shop.

These reclamation schemes set a precedent for far larger projects to come. The timing and form of some projects were also influenced by British relations with Russia and Germany—a reminder that Singapore, as an international port-of-call and a key part of an empire built on maritime dominance, was never isolated from the currents of world events.

THE AGE OF PUBLIC TRANSPORT

AS SINGAPORE was British territory, there was always a chance that innovations in transport in Britain could spread to the island, given enough time, the right conditions, and the interest and capital of investors. One such innovation was steam-powered vehicles. The Industrial Revolution, which started in Britain in the 1760s, saw the rise of steam power. This source of energy was used for both vehicles that plied existing roads, and the railway train, which ran on separate tracks. For the former, steam carriages debuted in Britain in 1801, and steam coaches—effectively steam-powered buses, a form of public transport—in the 1840s. However, their potential for widespread use was somewhat dampened in 1865, with the passing of the Red Flag Act—the maximum speed of steam coaches in the countryside was set at just four miles an hour (6.5 km/h), and two miles an hour (3.2 km/h) in towns and cities. Every steam coach had to be preceded by a man carrying a red flag!

On the other side of the world, the Straits Settlements government began preparing for the advent of the engine. It passed the Light Locomotives Ordinance in 1871, primarily to

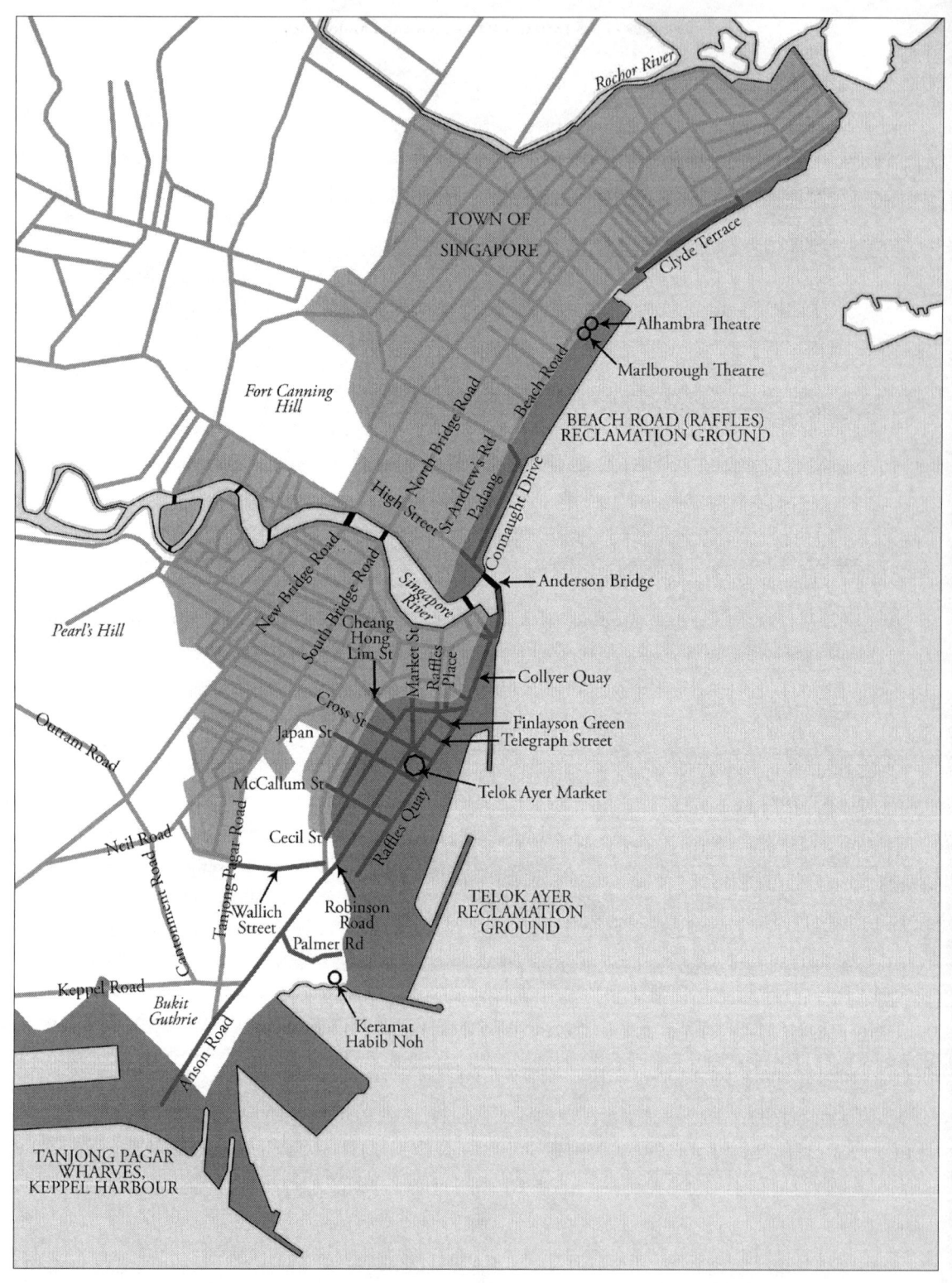

The Town of Singapore in 1913. Reclaimed land (the Beach Road Reclamation Ground, the Telok Ayer Reclamation Ground, and part of the Tanjong Pagar Wharves) and roads made possible by reclamation or the excavation of hills, are shaded in darker grey. The reclamation and new roads changed the form and movement of the Town. (Source: Eisen Teo)

The Telok Ayer Reclamation Ground in 1905, as seen from Mount Erskine. The octagonal-shaped building in the background is Telok Ayer Market, known today as Lau Pa Sat. The road by the sea is Raffles Quay; parallel to it heading inland are Robinson Road and Cecil Street. Perpendicular to them are Japan Street (next to the market) and McCallum Street (south of Japan Street). Today, Lau Pa Sat is surrounded by skyscrapers and is far from the coast. (Source: Library of Congress)

encourage steam coach services between the Town and the north of the island, to promote trade with Johor, then led by the Maharaja Abu Bakar (sampan services crossed the Straits of Johor). The Ordinance took on the terms of the Red Flag Act—four miles an hour for steam coaches in the rural areas, and two miles an hour inside the municipal boundary. However, no steam coach service was ever set up in Singapore.

As for the railway train, while the steam locomotive was pioneered in Britain in 1804, it was not until the 1870s that it became popular as a form of urban transport, and it took even more time to arrive in the Far East. The colonial powers would introduce the railway to the Far East only to open new lands for economic exploitation, and to better control and govern their colonies. After the Straits Settlements was formed in 1826, the British mostly practised a policy of non-intervention with the rest of the Malay Peninsula for the next half-century. This greatly reduced the need for the building of railway lines in Singapore's hinterland, and by extension, in Singapore itself.

Furthermore, a railway line was a significant investment that required deep pockets and a booming economy to pay for rolling stock, stations, and tracks. In Singapore, it was not until 1865 that Europeans applied to Governor Sir William Cavenagh for the right to build a railway between Telok Ayer and New Harbour. Their application was successful, but nothing came of it as New Harbour was still new at the time, so the financial incentive for a railway was weak. Six years later, two harbour companies—the Patent Slip & Dock Company and the Tanjong Pagar Dock Company—competed over the right to build a railway between the Town and New Harbour. Again, nothing came of the discussion.

While steam coaches and the railway took their time to materialise in Singapore, the rickshaw swiftly swept through the Far East, arriving in Singapore by 1880. It was the rickshaw, not steam-powered vehicles, that ushered in the age of public transport in Singapore.

BEFORE THE rickshaw came to Singapore, horse carriages/gharries/hackneys/palanquins were not abundant, and their high charges meant customers were usually Europeans or well-to-do Asians. Bullock carts, also limited in number and more suited to cargo, were not hired by many to get around either. Enter the rickshaw. It was far more abundant and cheaper to hire than any other method of movement, opening it to the masses; its proliferation defined "public transport" in the public consciousness before the term materialised in print. It was only in 1918 that the phrase "public transport" appeared in Singapore-related news—and rickshaws were part of the discussion.

The rickshaw's rise was swift, taking only a couple of years to entrench itself permanently. This was due to several factors. Government policy towards both the importation of contraptions and the passage of labour into Singapore, was largely the same in 1880 as it had been in 1819—laissez-faire. This allowed merchants to bring in large numbers of rickshaws quickly, becoming the first rickshaw capitalists; they also had access to an almost unlimited pool of cheap, willing immigrant labour to become beasts of burden. This combination kept fares low and affordable; after all, the popularity of a type of public transport depends on the ability and willingness of the population to pay for its use.

Furthermore, the rickshaw arrived at just the right time in Singapore's history. It was invented in Japan in 1869, promptly crossing the Sea of Japan to Chinese cities such as Beijing and Shanghai. From China, the first shipment of Japanese-made rickshaws arrived on 16 February 1880, just 11 years after its invention. At the time, Singapore had a population of around 131,000, a critical mass that could both pay for and operate a large rickshaw fleet. Too small a population, and the rickshaw might not have attained a foothold; too large a population, and other rival forms of public transport, such as trams, could have taken root before it.

Only one group of people protested the rickshaw's arrival—gharry drivers. They went on strike, but the strike soon fizzled out, and the rickshaws stayed on—and proliferated. Within just seven years of its introduction, in 1887, there were more than 3,000 rickshaws against an estimated 900 gharries, 1,000 private horse carriages, and several hundred bullock carts. That was when a figure of authority—the Inspector-General of Police Samuel Dunlop—suggested restricting the number of rickshaws at 2,500 vehicles and 3,500 rickshaw pullers; he was possibly concerned at the adverse effect they were having on traffic. However, when the issue was raised with Governor Frederick Weld (1823–1891), he decided there was no basis in the law to limit the number of rickshaws.

In fact, in the first 12 years of the rickshaw's existence in Singapore, there was no dedicated department, official framework, or set of laws to regulate the industry, control who became pullers, train and uphold the service and performance standards of pullers, and impose traffic etiquette. When the rickshaw arrived in Singapore, it was administered under the Hackney Carriage Department, which was soon overwhelmed by their sheer numbers. The department managed to issue and renew rickshaw licences, oversee the opening of rickshaw stands, and even put out notices exhorting pullers to respect the rules of the road, but it was too stretched to do much else. Free to evolve on its own, the rickshaw had an immediate and indelible impact on movement and the social fabric of the Town; it was a boon and a bane to both passengers and pullers.

The rickshaw industry was wholly privatised, but highly fragmented. Only one in 50 pullers owned their vehicles. The rest rented their vehicles from rickshaw owners, who were either pullers themselves, merchants, shopkeepers, or lodging house proprietors, each owning between two and 20 rickshaws. Vehicles were licensed, but not pullers—anyone who could pay the daily rental could take out a rickshaw, making it difficult to regulate them or estimate their numbers. While there were 3,675 rickshaws by 1890, the number of rickshaw coolies was around 5,000—about one rickshaw to 60 persons in Singapore, while one person in 31 was a rickshaw puller.

Most rickshaw pullers were Henghua and Hockchew, two topolect groups from southern China. Years of civil conflict, natural disasters, and famine in southern China left millions with little choice but to migrate to Southeast Asia for a better life, and Singapore was a popular destination. Fresh arrivals were pulled into the trade. They were directed to rickshaw depots or stations, called *Kun*, many of them in the Chinese Campong, or "Chinatown", a term the British began to use by the 1880s. Sago Lane and Banda Street were two examples. The *Kun* provided them everything they needed—lodging, vehicles, wages—but living conditions were extremely crammed and abysmal.

Fresh pullers had to pick up the ropes fast and adapt quickly to a punishing regime. There was no official body to train newcomers; they had to learn from their colleagues. Bazaar Malay was their

An undated photo of an unidentified street where a rickshaw station was located. Rickshaws were parked outside crammed lodgings. (Source: The New York Public Library Digital Collections)

language, and newcomers had to understand basic commands—*kiri* for left, *kanan* for right, *terus* for straight, *berhenti* for stop. Pulling itself was no stroll in the park. It required strong men in the prime of their life, usually 21 to 40 years of age, putting in brutal work for hours on end. *Straits Times* journalist George Peet had advice on how to spot a younger, more energetic puller—they usually ran barefoot, while older pullers wore tattered canvas shoes or wrapped their feet in sacks.

Rickshaws usually plied two shifts. The first stretched from 6am to between 2pm and 3pm. The night shift was either from 2pm to midnight, or from 5pm to 3am. Many sought out the docks along the Singapore River and New Harbour, the commercial areas of Raffles Place and Collyer Quay, and the red-light districts during the graveyard hours.

The cheap fares were a big draw. In 1892, a gharry's charges were 15 cents for up to half a mile (800 metres), 20 cents for between half a mile and one mile (1.6 km), and 10 cents for every additional mile. The rickshaw charged just three cents for every half mile up to five miles (8 km). Like the taxis of today, there was a "night surcharge" of one cent every half mile between 9pm and 5am. Of course, these were "standard" rates. In reality, every fare was negotiable. It depended on the distance, time of day, weather—and haggling. Visitors to Singapore—tourists, soldiers and sailors—were usually generous in tipping and the easiest to rip off. Fares climbed sharply whenever there was rain.

Hardworking pullers with superhuman endurance were considered gems. Around the turn of the century, according to Reverend John Angus Bethune Cook, "it was possible for a rickshaw puller to cover the 14 miles from Kranji to Singapore (Town) in slightly over two hours, with little more than a drink of rice water and a rub down". Shipping company assistant Edwin Brown's experience was even better. Two rickshaw pullers he hired (one to carry him and the other his bicycle) covered Bukit Panjang to Armenian Street—11 miles (17.8 km)—in just 55 minutes!

But these were few and far between. Rogue pullers were more common. They were known to take on passengers, then drop them halfway through a route, leaving them high and dry—some audacious enough to demand the full fare. Others overcharged clueless visitors by up to 10 times the normal fare, or brought them on a long, roundabout journey—"the scenic route"—to earn higher fares. Some refused taking passengers because of the destination—just like some taxi drivers today. And those who did not understand their passengers' instructions simply dumped them at popular landmarks—for example, the Raffles Hotel (opened in 1887) or a brothel in a side street!

Not all customers were angels either. Some suddenly bolted from rickshaws, especially at night under the cover of darkness. Other customers refused to pay the agreed fare at the end of their journeys, responding to their pullers' pleas with verbal and physical abuse. In an industry with no regulations or framework of control, abuses were rife from both pullers and passengers, with few means of redress.

In this harsh, Hobbesian world, the average rickshaw puller did not earn much—in 1893, about 40 cents a day, of which 8–10 cents went to paying the rent for the rickshaw. This meant an immigrant who bought a 33–38-dollar ticket to Singapore from China took three full years just to repay the price of his passage. Only then could he dream about saving up to buy his own rickshaw. Yet many never got past their debts. "The four evils"—opium smoking, prostitution, drinking, gambling—easily wiped out a puller's meagre savings. In the laissez-faire economy created by the British that made rickshaw pulling a major industry in Singapore, pullers were largely left to fend for themselves. As long as pullers did not create trouble, the government did not concern themselves with their welfare.

This was a sobering reality for the pullers—but a reality understood only by their own kind. Europeans usually saw them in another light: an exotic experience, an amusement, a freak show, a pathetic figure preoccupied with squeezing a little more money from his customers. Most surviving first-hand accounts of pullers come from Europeans, and it is through their eyes that we see not just the pullers, but also the Europeans' worldview, prejudices, and biases.

For example, Surgeon-Major John Macgregor looked upon rickshaw pullers with contempt, seeing them as nothing more than pack animals.

> The two-legged ponies are almost invariably Chinamen all over the Far East… they are generally strong sturdy men, but yet perspire a little too freely in such sultry climates. By constant exercise the calves of their legs get so developed, and their hips so plump, that they move between the shafts with all the ease and elegance of sturdy little Highland ponies… The Chinese two-footed ponies in the rickshaws are obtuse enough in their intellect. All ponies are.

His contempt was shared by others frustrated at

the inability of many pullers to speak or understand Malay and English, causing misunderstandings over destinations and fares.

A contributor to the *Singapore Free Press* in 1901 summed up the love-hate relationship between the rickshaw puller and the European in this poem:

> He's not what you'd call handsome, you could hardly say he's neat,
> His clothing is not plentiful – his legs are always bare –
> He has no coat upon his back, no shoes upon his feet,
> For matters such as dress indeed, he really does not care.
>
> He's very odoriferous, you would not call him clean,
> He seldom has a bath and his clothes strong scented are,
> His towel of a neckerchief's the dirtiest ever seen,
> But he's willing, for a trifling sum, to pull you near or far.
>
> His rikisha's most rickety, but he thinks it very neat
> With its cushions (rather hard!) and its oilcloth hood so black,
> It has a bit of carpet bright, on which to put one's feet,
> And the rikisha man believes there is nothing it can lack.
>
> He risks his life, and yours as well, for all rules he does not know,
> And drivers often yell at him for blocking up the way,
> It's no use swearing at him, or telling him to go,
> He speaks an unknown language—he cannot speak Malay.
>
> O Rikisha men! You're dirty, and your faults are manifold,
> You crowd the streets on every side, and vex us evermore,
> But we cannot do without you, and when everything is told,
> We find you very useful in this land of Singapore.

By the 1890s, the rickshaw ride had become a "must-do" for a visitor to Singapore; it was a good way to "see the sights". Like today's experienced taxi drivers, experienced pullers became repositories of local knowledge. They knew the best tourist and entertainment spots to take visitors—including the brothels of Malay Street.

Rickshaw pullers competed fiercely against each other and had to endure being looked down upon or bullied. Within six years of the introduction of rickshaws in Singapore, pullers faced a third challenge, a new, rival form of public transport—the steam tram.

RISE AND DEMISE OF THE STEAM TRAM

THE STEAM tram started plying the heart of the Town in 1886. After rickshaws, horse carriages, and bullock carts, it was the first method of movement in Singapore not powered by humans or animals. The rickshaw and steam tram were as different as light and day. The former was invented in Japan, relied on almost no technology, and was literally powered by Chinese mostly living in penury; the industry in Singapore was highly fragmented. The latter was invented in Britain, symbolised the Industrial Revolution, and was powered by the steam engine; the business in Singapore was monopolised by one company bankrolled by British investors. That the rickshaw and steam tram were imported into Singapore by private enterprise and competed almost freely against each other for passengers was a testament to the openness of Singapore's economy at the time.

Ultimately, the multitudes of barefoot Chinese would run the sleek trams out of business, thanks to the numbers game: there were too many pullers charging too little for their rides.

Unlike rickshaws, it took many decades for the steam tram to move from Britain to Singapore. It took far more money, time, and paperwork to import a steam tram system—tramcars, tracks, permission to build tracks on roads—as compared to rickshaws, which could simply be brought in by ship and carted off the docks. It was not until 1881 when a group approached Governor Weld for permission to build and run a steam tram system in Singapore; perhaps they sensed that the Town had a population large enough to sustain a tram system. They were known as the British East India Syndicate, comprising Joseph Cheney Bolton, William Ker, and John Ross of Glasgow, Scotland; Gilbert McMicking and Robert Jardine of London; and Singapore-based James Graham. The government gave them the green light, and the Tramways Ordinance was drawn up the following year in 1882, demarcating five routes.

The British East India Syndicate formed the Singapore Tramways Company in December 1883. The following year, 14 steam tram locomotives and an unknown number of double-deck passenger cars were ordered from Kitson and Company, a locomotive manufacturer based in Leeds, England.

The first rails of grooved steel were laid down on existing roads in April 1885.

The tramway opened in phases, from May to December 1886. Of the five authorised routes, three materialised with around 12.5 km of single-track rail lines. The routes covered some of the busiest and oldest streets in the Town: from Crawford Street to the Tanjong Pagar wharves via North and South Bridge roads (with a frequency of 15 minutes); Serangoon Road to Middle Road and the wharves (30 minutes); Johnston's Pier (opened in 1856 and named in honour of Alexander Laurie Johnston) to the Telok Ayer Reclamation Ground, the Tanjong Pagar wharves, and Borneo Wharf (20 minutes). For the first time in the Town's history, a mechanical mode of transportation pulled the heart of the Town together.

Each car had a capacity of 60 passengers, and was staffed by a driver and two conductors, one for first-class passengers in the lower deck, the other for second-class passengers in the upper deck. These cars were still smaller than double-decker buses plying Singapore's roads today, but in the 19th century, they were quite a sight. Each weighed 30 tons; spewing sparks and smoke, they were larger, louder, and faster than any other vehicle on the roads. Trams hardly exceeded six miles an hour (9.7 km/h), but they were still faster than rickshaws at five miles an hour (8 km/h), and horse-drawn carriages at four miles an hour (6.5 km/h). The visceral effect of its sheer presence was not lost on the Town's inhabitants, one of whom wrote in to the *Singapore Free Press*:

> (The people of Singapore) were assured that the cars would be noiseless and perfectly safe, and the rails so beautifully laid that no one would know that they were there... Alas! The rattletrap concern... is noisy,

smoky and filthy to the last degree… The tram locomotives have for some months past been of great benefit to the public by liberally distributing free of charge a supply of red hot ashes wherever they run, whereby our horses' hoofs are kept nice and warm, while on a dark night nothing can be more agreeable than the spectacle of three or four of these engines belching forth vast volumes of smoke and steam brilliantly illuminated by myriads of fiery sparks and little gleaming firebrands which subsequently fall about all over the country.

Horse carriage owners and drivers had reason to be concerned: the loud, belching vehicles frightened horses.

To prevent accidents at the junction of Stamford Road and North Bridge Road, one of the busiest junctions in the Town, signalmen were stationed there with a flag by day and a red lamp at night to warn people of the approach of the cars—a first for the Town. Every Sunday between 11am and 1pm and from 5pm to 7pm, tram services near St Andrew's Cathedral were halted for church services!

Ticket pricing took some getting used to. While passengers could haggle with rickshaw pullers, the tram charged fixed prices for different sections. Each section covered the distance between two "stations", which were actually major landmarks such as the junction of Middle Road and North Bridge Road, Central Police Station (along South Bridge Road), and Tanjong Pagar Police Station (at the junction of Tanjong Pagar Road and Keppel Road). Ticket prices ranged from 5–15 cents for first class, and 2–8 cents for second class—in terms of distance, first-class rates were equal to or cheaper than rickshaw rates.

The steam tram was the first method of movement in Singapore with timetables scheduling departures, and fare tables fixed by the location of "stations" on transport lines. Passengers had to get used to planning their activities around timetables and geography. Time and space began creeping into movement. Modernity was coming to Singapore.

On paper, trams could cover the length of the Town from Crawford Street to Tanjong Pagar in half an hour, significantly cutting travel time on foot. In reality though, journey times were usually longer, because passengers could get on or disembark anywhere along routes. This was where the conductor played a key role in upholding or letting down service standards: he was in charge of stopping the tram when passengers wanted to disembark. However, complaints were rife about conductors who delayed in doing so, or ignoring passengers altogether. Similarly, cars did not always stop when passengers flagged them along the roads. Passengers had to engage in new, dangerous activities: running after a car and hopping onto it while it was pulling away ("car-catching"), and stepping off a car while it was still moving. Occasionally, injuries occurred.

In the end, the rickshaw was still more popular than the tram due to cost and convenience. A rickshaw provided door-to-door service, something the tram could never match, since it had to run on fixed tracks. Waiting times for trams at 15–30 minutes were also too long—a rickshaw would usually be available around the corner.

Hence, the tram business suffered from the start. A Singapore Tramways Company ordinary meeting report published in *The Straits Times* on 31 August 1887 admitted revenue "fell far short of what had been anticipated… the company had met with keen competition from (rickshaws)…" Close to 1.39 million passengers took the tram in its first six months, an average of 7,300 a day—a trifle, considering Singapore had a population of about 164,000. Only 4.5 per cent of the population took the tram. The tram had been designed to serve the masses, but most shunned it.

The very nature of the tramway—cars running on fixed, single tracks—made accidents and delays costly. When one tram broke down, the entire route had to be shut down—similar to what the MRT system faces today. To make matters worse, the tram's running costs were high. Cars, machine parts, and coal as fuel had to be imported from England. As a result, the company barely kept its head above water for three years. Its profit from June–December 1887 was $3,214.74; $982.87 for June–December 1888; $3,034.12 from January–June 1889. These paled in comparison to the amount they owed the bank in September 1889: $115,000.

The end came before the decade was out. On 10 December 1889 the company put the tram system up for auction. Bidding ended at $186,000, with businessman Gan Eng Seng (1844–1899) buying the rolling stock for the New Harbour Dock Company. To attract more passengers, the new management slashed both tram intervals and fares—in 1890, the trams ran in intervals of seven minutes between 7am and 10pm, and a ticket cost only three cents. But it was too little, too late. The plug was pulled on the tram on 1 June 1894.

The steam tram was a good idea on paper, but came to Singapore at the wrong time. The cars were built to last 40 years, but were only used for seven. The tracks were quickly cleared, a large quantity of metal purchased by the Hongkong and Shanghai Banking Corporation. The bank, then a three-storey building along Battery Road, used the metal to construct new vaults. After the roadworks were complete, it was as if the smoke-spewing metal monster never existed.

With the tram out of the way, the road was now clear for rickshaws to become the undisputed number one choice of public transport in Singapore. In 1891, there were more than 7,000 rickshaw pullers in Singapore; their numbers ballooned to around 20,000 by 1900, sharing 5,240 vehicles. With a population of about 224,000, that meant one in 11 people in Singapore was a rickshaw puller! Never before in Singapore's history had such a large proportion of the island's population been involved in a method of movement. Photos taken during this time of streets in Chinatown show the roadsides replete with parked rickshaws and pullers catching a breather from a hard day's work. Private rickshaws also began to replace horse carriages as a status symbol among rich Europeans called *tuan besar*, Malay for "big boss". Just as some private carriages had two-man teams, some private rickshaws also had two-man teams, with a runner behind the rickshaw to push it up hills!

OFF WITH THE PEDESTRIANS

THE YEARS from 1886 to 1894 were marked by intense competition between rickshaws and steam trams. In the end, rickshaws won, but the competition forever altered the way people negotiated traffic on the roads.

Before 1880, most people in Singapore went around on foot. Many five-foot-ways were blocked by stalls and goods, forcing pedestrians onto the roads; the roads belonged to pedestrians who walked in all directions. The fastest vehicles, horse carriages, were usually forced to slow down to match the speed of walking pedestrians. That meant traffic moved slowly, haphazardly, as an organised chaos. There were no pavements, no speed limits, no traffic lights or crossings, few traffic laws—because there was no need for them.

After 1880, roads hosted faster-moving vehicles—rickshaws and steam trams—that started to dictate the pace of traffic rather than have their pace dictated by pedestrians. These vehicles were also collectively more numerous. Roads became more bustling, more dangerous. Some of the busiest were Battery Road, North Bridge Road, and South Bridge Road. During the day, such narrow thoroughfares were filled with dozens of rickshaws rushing recklessly in all directions. Pullers were eager to pick up as many fares as possible, and they were notorious for having no regard for traffic order or etiquette, hogging the roads as they wished and not giving way to pedestrians or other vehicles. These on top of trams moving swiftly on tracks fixed in the middle of busy streets. The monstrosity of the tram and the unpredictable chaos of the rickshaw were new coefficients in the traffic equation. Everyone else had to adapt.

For one, pedestrians now had to be careful. Rickshaws could come at them from any direction. A collision would have been very painful—even fatal. As a *Straits Times* reader observed in 1900:

> The... (rickshaw) traffic in North Bridge Road, at its junction with Middle Road, commonly known as Teng Quee's corner, between the hours of 6pm and midnight is so great that it is ofttimes impossible for a foot-passenger to cross the street without running some risks... The erratic movements of some of the (rickshaw) pullers, the headlong rush of others, and the breakneck pace indulged in by a certain class are not only bewildering in the extreme, but

Bustling North Bridge Road. This photo was probably taken after 1905, as the road had the overhead wires and surface tracks of an electric tram system. (Source: The New York Public Library Digital Collections)

positively dangerous... The tendency on the part of the pullers to rush corners and crossings, utterly oblivious to what is before and behind, has often resulted in disaster.

Horse carriage owners also had to be watchful, for their quadrupeds could be frightened by oncoming rickshaws, sometimes even bolting free from their harnesses. One frustrated carriage owner wrote in to *The Straits Times* in 1884:

> Has it ever struck you that the difficulties we experience in crossing the Cavenagh Bridge (not to speak of the others) are very largely increased by the presence of the "jinricksha"? I myself have twice had a collision through one of these humble conveyances suddenly stopping under my horse's nose and causing him to shy; and I have noticed other horses afraid of them too. Only this morning one of these vehicles was occupying the entire width of an already confined passage, while (the puller) was indulging in thought.

Another habit of pullers many found ugly was clustering around a location for business. Today's taxi drivers frequent places such as Changi Airport and popular tourist sites. Similarly, pullers frequented tram terminuses, churches, administrative buildings, and commercial offices. With a lack of rickshaw stands and no tradition of queueing, these entrances, and surrounding roads, were choked with dozens of rickshaws, lying in wait like "sharks". Outside a tram terminus along Bras Basah Road:

> These men rush up, helter skelter to the trams, to the very footboards, to catch passengers almost before they can alight. They are a veritable nuisance, they obstruct the roadway, and they are a source of daily annoyance to tram passengers.

Even the governor became a "shark" victim in May 1892. Weld's successor Cecil Clementi Smith was leaving the Town Hall along High Street in a horse carriage, but the approaches to the building were jammed with rickshaws. One of them caught a wheel of his carriage, another got entangled with his horse. The animal bolted in fright, the carriage broke, and Smith was flung onto the ground. The hapless governor was shaken but uninjured. He might have rued the decision of his predecessor not to restrict rickshaw numbers!

Fortunately, trams were nowhere as reckless as rickshaws, but drivers still had to keep a constant lookout for smaller vehicles and pedestrians who moved without regard to traffic. Statistics on tram accidents in the 1880s and 1890s are not available, but when an accident did occur, it was grisly:

> The fatality, it would appear, happened about 7 o'clock, in the neighbourhood of Police (Bahru) Station (opposite St Andrew's Cathedral), a crowd quickly collecting round the body, or rather the mangled remains, of an unfortunate (15-year-old) Chinese youth, lying scattered at intervals along the tram line, disfigured and mutilated out of all recognition... Inspector Howard was quickly on the spot, and it was found that the entrails of the deceased were strewed all along the up line from near the crossing at Coleman Street and Stamford Road, where the accident apparently occurred, and the Police (Bahru)

Station, at which point an isolated arm was found. The search was then continued, and further up the line at (Bras Basah) Road, nearly half a mile away, the police came upon the headless and eviscerated trunk... eventually, shortly before 8 o'clock, the head was discovered in Sumbawa Road, near the Rochore station, at a distance of nearly a mile from where the trunk had been found. The most revolting feature in the case is the utter callousness and indifference to life shown by the driver of the car, whoever he may be, omitting to turn off steam and pull up the car immediately after the affair took place…

As the streets became busier and more chaotic, the police could barely cope. Most traffic offenders could easily get away, and it was hard for culprits mentioned in complaints to be tracked down and caught. Only the governor's accident in 1892 compelled the police into firmer action against errant rickshaws; the phrase "traffic regulation" first appeared in Singapore's newspapers in 1892.

Also, that September, "shark" victim Governor Smith passed the Jinrikisha Ordinance, to better regulate rickshaw owners and pullers—perhaps his accident had convinced him! The Hackney Carriage Department became the Hackney Carriage and Jinrikisha Department; the Registrar of Hackney Carriages became the Registrar of Hackney Carriages and Jinrikishas. The first registrar was William Edward Hooper (1858–1939), who later gave his name to Hooper Road, off Bukit Timah Road; he would be registrar for the next 31 years. At last, there was a dedicated municipal department for rickshaws; it moved to a new headquarters at the junction of Middle Road and Prinsep Street in 1899.

Some regulations included requiring owners to register with the department for a fee of $12, or be fined $25 and have their rickshaws confiscated; pullers had to keep to the left on roads, and not block the approach to any public building, store or private residence; pullers were not allowed to tout for hire, demand more than the authorised fare, or behave rudely to passengers; pullers had to stop at designated rickshaw stands; offences earned the puller a suspension of one month.

Still, nabbing traffic offenders remained a persistent problem. Also, pullers were still not licensed, which made the regulation of performance standards difficult. And there were no limits on the number of rickshaws or pullers—probably thanks to the lobbying of the only non-European member of the Legislative Council of the Straits Settlements, Tan Jiak Kim. Finally, it was harder to impose controls on a method of movement after it had taken root in a town, as compared to when it was introduced. Belated attempts at introducing and enforcing regulations caused frequent unhappiness between the authorities and rickshaw owners and pullers, exacerbated by language and racial barriers. In 1897, 1901, and 1903, the owners and pullers struck back in the strongest manner possible—by going on strike. When strikes occurred, the Europeans—the apex of society—suffered most.

The 1901 strike started on 21 October after the police, and Hooper, issued fresh demands to rickshaw owners to inculcate road manners in their pullers. The owners went away and told their pullers that the police were going to fine them $5 each! Either something had been horribly lost in translation, or the owners were trying to incite a strike to send the British a message that they were not to be pushed around. Brown vividly described what ensued:

The strike was well arranged, and was complete. With the exception of a few private rickshaws, there were none out on the streets at all... I suppose that 75 per cent of the Europeans used rickshaws then to get back and forth to office, and, for the Eurasians and other portions of the populace they were almost the only means of transport. Private carriages and public gharries—the latter expensive—were the only other methods before the trams and buses came in.

The day the strike occurred was windy, with patches of rain. The mail was in that morning, and the offices had to be reached somehow and there was nothing to be done to "hoof" it. So away went the male portion of the population, carrying Chinese umbrellas and the inevitable tiffin basket, hoping against hope that someone would pass in a horse vehicle and give them a lift.

People trudged along Orchard and Grange roads, their white boots covered with the red mud of a wet laterite road. The clock had been wound back 20 years. The Europeans learned the hard way how dependent they had become on rickshaws. And while most were too young to remember the 1854 Hokkien-Teochew Riots almost half a century before, the Chinese were again showing the British how they were not to be messed around with.

Unfortunately, the matter did not end with the mere strike, and numerous instances of people on bicycles being pelted with missiles, and pedestrians assaulted, were reported, so much so that the police officers were ordered to carry revolvers...

The strike spread to the gharry-wallahs, who were frightened to go on the streets for fear of being attacked... (the following) day there were some ugly scenes, and in Chinatown the police had to make charges, and shots were fired in the air to frighten the crowds. Along Rochor Road and in the district round the rickshaw station, the strikers were active and considerable damage was done.

At last, Governor Sir Frank Athelstane Swettenham (1850–1946) put his foot down and showed the Chinese rickshaw owners who was boss.

It was said that His Excellency kept the *towkays* (businessmen) waiting at Government House for about an hour, sending in biscuits and drinks to them. When he did appear, he talked to them affably about the weather, etc., and said it was very nice of them to call and see him. After a short while he excused himself, saying that he was very busy, and just as he was leaving the room, turned to them and said: "Oh, by the by, gentlemen, there's a rickshaw strike on in town. There's also a boat leaving for China tomorrow. If that strike is not stopped before the ship leaves, you'll be on it! Good morning."

Whether this actually happened or not I cannot say, but certain it is that next day the strike was called off, and in a few hours the vehicles were out on the streets again, and Singapore quickly resumed its normal aspect.

For his role in instigating the strike, a rickshaw owner, Lee Chong Hin, was indeed banished for three years. Governor Swettenham might have won this time, but the towkays had also made a strong point: Singapore could not do without the rickshaw—at least for the next 20 years.

In 1904, single-seated rickshaws were introduced in Singapore for the first time; double-seated rickshaws would be phased out in a decade. Also, in 1904, the Jinrikisha Station was built at the junction of South Bridge Road, Neil Road, and Tanjong Pagar Road. It became a rest-stop for pullers and a venue for the inspection of rickshaws—a fitting location, as it was inside Chinatown, Keppel Harbour was nearby, and South Bridge Road was one of the busiest thoroughfares on the island.

But even as animal and human-powered vehicles controlled patterns of movement in Singapore, their days were numbered. While the steam tram had come and gone, the dawn of the new century would see more machines introduced into the Town, harbingers of a mechanised future: the railway train, a newer version of the tram, and the motor car.

AN "IRON HORSE" INTO THE HINTERLAND

WE HAVE seen the lack of colonial and economic impetus to build a railway in Malaya and Singapore from the 1820s to the 1860s. That changed in the 1870s, with British intervention in Malaya; the tin-rich sultanates of Perak, Selangor, and Negeri Sembilan accepted British "protection" and Residents. The British needed something that could cover hundreds of miles in days, ferrying tons of lucrative tin ore and other natural resources in one trip. The railway train fitted the bill. By the 1880s, separate railway lines had been laid down in Perak, Selangor, and Negeri Sembilan; it was only a matter of time before the railway reached Singapore.

But before that happened, the steam tram debuted in the Town of Singapore in 1886. Then, five years later in 1891, Charles Buckley, known as a "man of many-sided activities", with "ideas that were sometimes not only abreast of the times but ahead of them", boldly proposed a light passenger railway service running the width of the island from the Town to Kranji, and a steamer service between Kranji and Johor Bahru—the first concrete proposal to link the Town to the Malayan hinterland. Called the Kranji Electric Line, the railway would be powered by electricity, not steam. Buckley hoped it would half the time taken to travel between the Town and Kranji, and open up the country—especially the land along Bukit Timah Road—to development.

Like the Singapore Tramways Company, the Kranji Electric Line would be a private venture— Buckley's very own. Acting alone, he first paid for the experiment of an electric railway car on short rails in New Harbour in September, an event attended no less by Johor's Sultan Abu Bakar. The following year in 1892, another test run was conducted on one mile of track in the forests of Kranji, on land granted by the Straits Settlements government. Many guests turned up to witness and experience "the first electric line in Singapore and, possibly, the Far East". The test was a success—and then it was the end of the road. Nothing more was heard of the Kranji Electric Line. The one-mile track disappeared without a trace; termites made short work of the wooden sleepers. Transport historians F. W. York and A. R. Phillips put it aptly: "Late 19th-century transport history is littered with somewhat eccentric schemes which flare into the public domain very briefly and then die away, never to be heard of again." Just two years later, in 1894, the steam tram left the Town of Singapore for good.

Regional events soon pushed the railway train to the fore again. Perak, Selangor, Negeri Sembilan, and Pahang came together as the Federated Malay States (FMS), a British-led federation, in 1895. The following year, Swettenham—then the first Resident-General of the FMS—and Colonial Secretary Joseph Chamberlain plotted the future economic development of British Malaya. Swettenham suggested connecting and extending existing fragmented railway lines across the Peninsula, while Chamberlain wanted a railway link between the state of Johor and Singapore. To them, the railway was a means of strengthening British economic and political control over the vast Malayan hinterland.

Hence, in 1899, Governor Sir Charles Mitchell (1836–1899) approved plans mirroring that of Buckley's in 1891—a railway between the Town and Kranji, then a ferry point for crossing the Straits of Johor. The Straits Settlements government did something unusual—it coughed up the cash and labour for the railway, the first time the authorities invested in and owned a method of movement in Singapore (perhaps because the prosperity of the Straits Settlements was at stake). The railway was accordingly named the Singapore Government Railway, although it was also named the Singapore–Kranji Railway and the Singapore–Johore Railway.

The building of the 15-mile railway line started on 16 April 1900, and took two years and eight months, at a cost of $2 million. The first phase consisted of five stations: the southernmost terminus of Singapore Railway Station at Tank Road, northwest of Fort Canning Hill, on the site of a former police parade ground; Newton Station, named after Howard Vincent Newton (1852–1897), an assistant municipal engineer; Cluny Road Station, near the junction of Cluny Road and Bukit Timah Road; Holland Road Station, at the junction of Holland Road and Bukit Timah Road; and the northernmost terminus of Bukit Timah Station, named after Bukit Timah Village. Singapore Station had two other proposed sites; one at Dhoby Green, a field in Dhoby Ghaut, was dropped because it would have "interfered" with property along Orchard Road; a third site at Kandang Kerbau was too far from the port at the Singapore River.

The first phase opened on the early morning of 1 January 1903:

A few minutes after 6 o'clock one of the few railway officials present waved his hand to the driver as a signal to start, the passengers scrambled in, the engine tootled once or twice, and then slowly steamed out of the station passing a large notice board which proclaimed in English, Malay and Tamil that the station was "Singapore" ... The first bit of excitement occurred on nearing the crossing at the corner of Fort Canning Road and Tank Road. The Sikh in charge of the gates was rather slow in opening them and the engine slowed down as she neared them, her whistle screaming all the time.

Thence the train proceeded up the incline near Oxley Rise, along the backyards of the shophouses in Orchard Road, and across the bridges at Killiney and Orchard roads. There is a slight incline near Cairnhill, but this was safely negotiated and in a few minutes the train puffed into "Newton" where a few more passengers came aboard and those who had come on from "Singapore" jumped out to have a look round. In a few minutes they were off again.

The morning was a lovely one. A little rain had fallen in the Bukit Timah district in the night and this made the morning beautifully cool and fresh. "Cluny Road" was reached without any adventure and the train proceeded to "Bukit Timah", increasing her speed as she swept alongside the Bukit Timah River which runs parallel with the railway line for some distance. Crowds of Chinese had assembled at the different crossings and watched the "iron horse" in silence.

Four trains were in service on the first day, carrying 557 passengers. From third to first class, they paid fares of six to 84 cents.

The second section of the railway opened on 10 April. Two more stations ran north from Bukit Timah Station: Bukit Panjang Station, and the terminus of Woodlands by the Straits of Johor, a short distance from where Kranji Road met the coast and a sampan service transported people from Singapore Island to Abu Bakar Pier at Johor Bahru. At Woodlands, a new ferry service replaced the old sampan service. Buckley had dreamed of the Singapore–Woodlands track 12 years before; the Singapore Government Railway now turned his dream to reality.

Subsequently, the government realised that the Tank Road terminus was too far from Keppel Harbour. Hence, a 7.5-km extension was constructed from Tank Road to Keppel Harbour, with the stations of People's Park (named after an open, recreational field at the foot of Pearl's Hill), Borneo Wharf (at the junction of Keppel Road and Nelson Road), and Pasir Panjang (at the junction of Pasir Panjang Road and Alexandra Road). The three stations opened on 21 January 1907, lengthening the railway to more than 30 km.

At first, there were nine train runs every day—six through trains from the Town to Woodlands, and three stopping at Bukit Timah; the last train of the day left Tank Road for Bukit Timah at 6.40pm. From 1904, the daily schedule was adjusted to eight runs, all to Woodlands. Trains left Tank Road at 6.30am, 7.32am, 10am, 12.30pm, 2.17pm, 3.23pm, 4.43pm, and 5.40pm. At 10–18 miles an hour (16–29 km/h), each train took 54 or 55 minutes to reach Woodlands; it once took up to two hours to travel the same distance on a rickshaw, horse carriage or bullock cart. And now, unlike rickshaw pullers, horses, and buffaloes, trains did not fall sick, and could ferry far larger loads.

The Singapore Government Railway literally broke new ground. For the first time since 1819, it was a new channel of movement on a different plane from that of the existing road system (the steam tramway of 1886 had been constructed on existing roads). Now, trains could travel almost unimpeded, free of traffic jams, pedestrians, the reckless rickshaw, and poor road conditions.

The railway had an immediate impact on trade and commerce. It spelled the death knell for horse-drawn omnibus services that had been plying between Coleman Street and Kranji since 1890. The omnibuses were managed by three proprietors—Messrs Lambert Brothers, Messrs Clarke & Company, and Yeo Chup Hong Guan—and ran twice a day. Their fares matched that of the railway, but did not match its speed. Two months after the railway opened, it also wrestled the contract for delivering mail between the Town and Johor from the horse-drawn omnibus. Within five years of its opening, the railway was moving an average of 1,300 passengers and 156 tons of goods a day. Sunday nights were especially busy—at Tank Road, queues of European planters heading back to their rubber estates in Johor after a lively weekend in the Town; in Johor Bahru, proprietors of gambling farms paid the return fares of all who patronised their tables. Those who gambled away every last cent was assured of a free ride back to Singapore!

Wherever the railway tracks ran, they changed the landscape irrevocably. From the leeward side of Fort Canning Hill, the tracks cut through the backyard of some of the oldest country surrounding the Town: Orchard Road, Emerald Hill, Cairnhill. Formerly covered by plantations, they were now grounds owned by the rich. Between Orchard Road and Newton Station, trains passed by a lake flanked by vegetable gardens. After Newton Station, the tracks ran parallel to Bukit Timah Road, past country houses, open fields, plantations, and forest. Beyond Cluny Road Station lay rural vistas. The three stations between Cluny Road and Woodlands stations were breaks in mostly farms, plantations, and more forest—"some of the prettiest country in the island". Occasionally, people on horseback would race passing trains as an amusement.

But while the railway tracks were their own dedicated channel of movement, the tracks crossed many roads, inconveniencing traffic. Over 30 km of track, there were 55 gate crossings and 23 public level crossings. Timekeepers' sheds had to be constructed at each crossing for gates to be lowered for trains to cross. A railway bridge was erected over Orchard Road, where the malls The Centrepoint and Orchard Central face each other today. The area around the bridge was a vantage point to watch the grand sight of a railway train chugging across a built-up area. People who saw their loved ones off at the Tank Road terminus hurried on their bicycles or carriages to the bridge to wave again as the train passed overhead; meanwhile, all traffic under the bridge temporarily stopped because of superstition!

In 1904, Sultan Abu Bakar's successor, Sultan Ibrahim (1873–1959), signed off on a 194-km line from Gemas, a town near the Negeri Sembilan–Johor border, to Johor Bahru. It was completed by 1910. By then, except for the narrow Straits of Johor, there was a continuous rail link from Singapore to Penang. Three years later, in 1913, in anticipation of a future connection between the railways of the FMS and Singapore, the Straits Settlements government sold its railway to the government of the FMS for $4.136 million—a sale that would have profound urban and transport implications for Singapore in the future. Subsequently, the Singapore Government Railway was renamed the FMS Railway. The FMS government mulled over building a new southern terminus at Fort Canning Hill or what was once Mount Wallich, but nothing came of this.

THE TRAM RETURNS ELECTRIFIED

THE TRAM did not remain dead and buried for long. The Town of Singapore was growing steadily—people believed the venture deserved a second roll of the die. In 1901, seven years after the steam tram's swansong, another group of Europeans with deep pockets proposed an electric tram system. The electric tram was similar in design to the steam tram, but the former was powered by electricity supplied from overhead wires. The time seemed ripe. Every major city in England, including London, had electrified its tramway system; electric tram systems had been established in two major cities in the region, Bangkok (the capital of Siam) and Batavia (the capital of the Dutch East Indies); the railway train was already in Singapore. Eager for an alternative to the chaotic, ill-disciplined rickshaw, the Straits Settlements government approved their proposal.

In September 1901, a company with almost the same name as the one that had folded in 1894—the Singapore Tramways Limited, later the Singapore Electric Tramways Limited—was registered in London, and the Tramways Ordinance resurrected the following year. There were six planned routes covering 24.5 km of roads, about twice the distance covered by the steam tramway.

The electric tramway opened on 25 July 1905, with 50 single-deck tramcars built by Dick, Kerr and Company, a manufacturer based in Preston, England. One model could seat 32 passengers; another seated 40. Each was staffed by a driver and conductor. By 1911, the original six routes had been consolidated into four. Route 1 (with a frequency of six–eight minutes) covered Tank Road (near Singapore Railway Station) to Telok Blangah Road via High Street and Anderson Bridge, a bridge opened in 1910 over the Singapore River and named after Governor Anderson. Route 2 (eight minutes) covered rural Geylang Road through North and South Bridge roads to the Tanjong Pagar wharves. Route 3 (three minutes) served Lavender Street and Route 2 from North Bridge Road to the wharves. Route 4 (eight–15 minutes) was from Bras Basah Road to Serangoon Road, ending in rural Paya Lebar. Outside the Town, the Paya Lebar terminus was surrounded by a dozen attap-roofed shops of the village simply named 5¾ Mile Serangoon Road; the remote Geylang terminus consisted of just a couple of huts in a sea of coconut plantations.

It was clear that just as the layout of Singapore Island's trunk roads showed a bias towards the northeastern and eastern parts of the island, the layout of the tramway followed a similar pattern, because of the same reason—more flat, low-lying terrain to the east, notably the watersheds of the Rochor, Kallang, and Geylang rivers.

Unlike the steam tramway, the electric tramway had compulsory stops for passengers to get on and drop off—the ancestor of the bus stop in Singapore. Each stop had a pole with a circular metal plate bearing the route number. Prominent landmarks and busy road junctions were chosen for stops, such as the Jinrikisha Station, the junction of High Street and North Bridge Road, and Kandang Kerbau Police Station.

Electric trams travelled faster than steam trams, between six and 10 miles an hour (10–16 km/h), although they had to stop at major road junctions, and then cross at no greater than four miles an hour—this was to protect other traffic, since junctions had no traffic lights then. Passengers paid a fixed price for a section in a route—20 cents for a first-class ticket, 15 cents for second class, 10 cents for third class. Charges for freight such as livestock, metal ore, and parcels ranged five to 50 cents per mile.

Unfortunately, *The Straits Times* reported dismal public interest in the tramway on its opening date. "There were not many guests to see the ceremony that celebrated the inauguration," a journalist wrote. "(Governor) Sir John Anderson, who came down to watch the first car load, did not risk himself as a passenger…" Anderson's snub did not augur well for the "kreta (Malay for "car") electric", which faced a litany of problems from the start, some similar to that faced by the steam tram 20 years earlier.

One glaring problem was patchy coverage. Despite it possessing twice as much track as the steam tram, the electric tramway still did not cover significant parts of the Town, such as Orchard

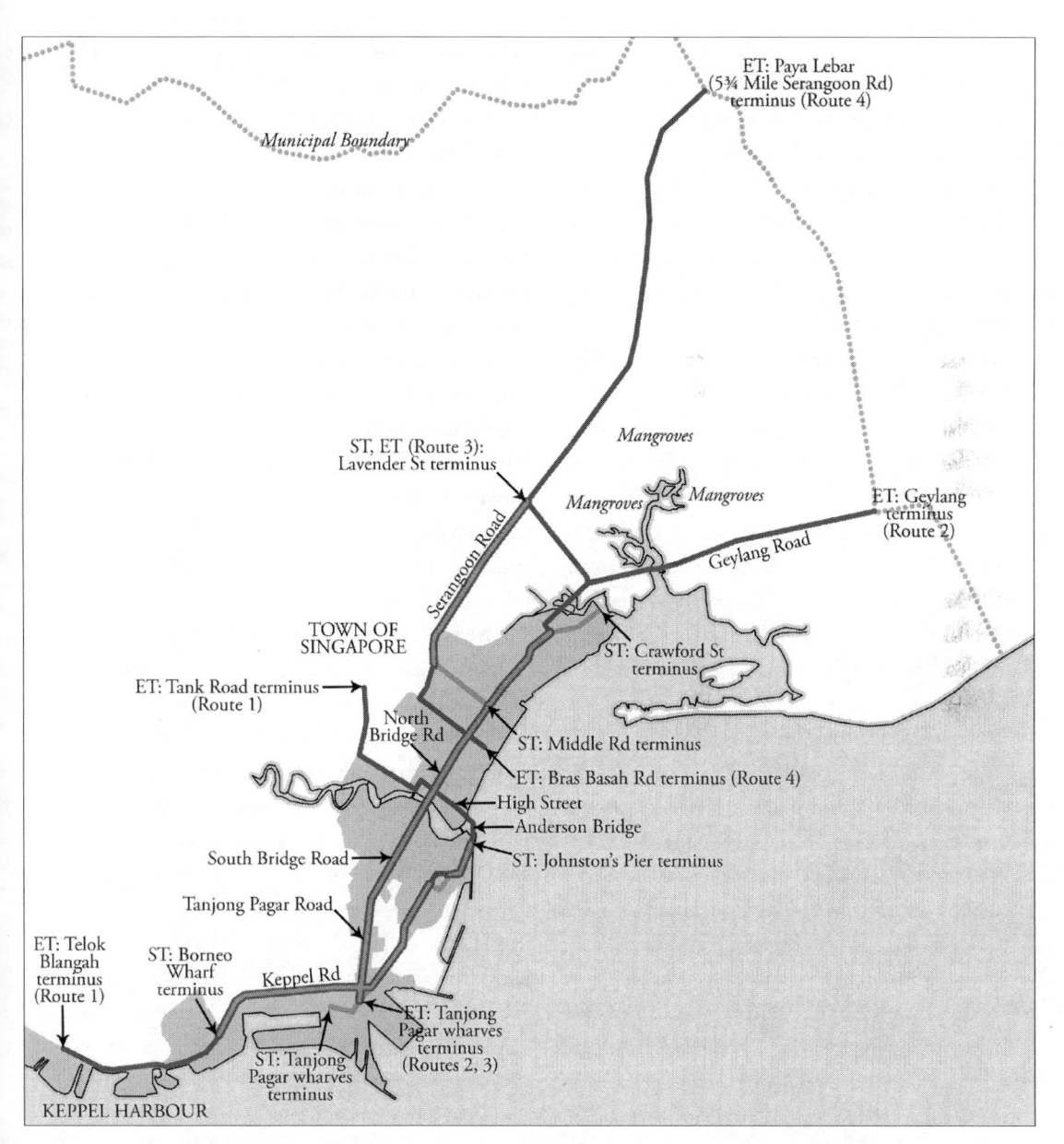

Steam ("ST") and electric tram ("ET") routes in Singapore Island. Steam tram routes are marked in light grey, while electric tram routes are in dark grey. The electric tram network served a significantly larger area than its steam predecessor, and its coverage belied a bias for the northeastern and eastern parts of the island, characterised by more flat, low-lying terrain. Nevertheless, only a small part of the Municipality was served by trams. (Source: Eisen Teo)

Road and New Bridge Road. Some services ceased as early as 11pm, much to the dismay of late-night revellers. No route information was provided on cars, and destination labels were minimal, making the system user-unfriendly. Fares were expensive—a third-class ticket cost 10 cents, while a rickshaw charged six cents a mile. And drivers and conductors were not up to par. Passengers had an old grouse—drivers ignoring people flagging them down. Meanwhile, conductors lacked the change needed for fares. Often, at the junction of High Street and North Bridge Road, a halt had to be made at a moneychanger for spare change!

Another old issue was the tram system having to share the increasingly congested roads with other vehicles. Traffic obstructions on any part of a route—be it slow rickshaws or bumbling bullock carts—affected the entire route. These adversely affected the punctuality and frequency of trams.

There were numerous tram accidents. Understandable, since the tram became the roads' largest and most treacherous vehicle upon its debut, like the steam tram in 1886. In 10 tram accidents reported in the newspapers between 1906 and 1921, there were two deaths and six injuries. The accidents mostly occurred along the busiest streets—North Bridge Road, South Bridge Road, Kallang Road.

Singapore's tropical climate also exposed the shortcomings of importing a method of movement designed for less humid, rainy conditions. Unlike the steam tram, the electric tramway ran on electricity. Within a year of being laid down, the insulating material in miles of underground feeder cables was ruined and had to be replaced at great cost. Tram wheels and tracks wore and tore at a quicker rate. These unexpected costs contributed to the tramway staying in the red in its first three years. Floods also meant bad news. Tracks were made impassable by floodwaters and uprooted trees, and trams were derailed.

But the most serious problem remained that of rickshaws—a formidable bloc, numbering 6,807 vehicles and 20,000 pullers in 1905. The *towkays* and pullers were not above spreading fake news. One was that to ensure the success of the electric tram, the heads of several hundred Chinese coolies were needed to appease a European goddess; another was that the crust of the earth was not strong enough to sustain the weight of tramcars; a third claimed Governor Anderson had disallowed all Chinese from travelling on the trams, threatening a $25 fine. These had the adverse effect of dissuading many Chinese—the majority of Singapore's population—from riding the trams.

Worst of all, anonymous perpetuators frequently attempted to sabotage the tramway by strategically placing stones, wood, or road metal across the tram tracks, occasionally causing accidents or derailments. Even before the tramway opened, in June 1905, broken road metal across the track at the junction of Serangoon Road and MacPherson Road caused a tram to derail, flip on its side and crash into the ditch. Fortunately, the drivers escaped with slight injuries, but the car was wrecked. The following year, saboteurs struck the same stretch of track again. Stones and wood laid across the track derailed a tram; it skidded across the road and into the compound of a house. This time, two bullock cart drivers were arrested—they had argued with a tram driver over who had the right of way, and decided to take revenge. But the main suspects for such incidents were the group of transport operators who stood to lose the most from the electric tram—rickshaw pullers. The Chinese have demonstrated before that they were willing to take matters into their own hands—and they would do so again.

Due to this plethora of problems, the Singapore Electric Tramways struggled from day one. Average daily ridership in its first year was just 11,000, or four per cent of Singapore's population of 263,000, far below its daily capacity of 55,000. The company swiftly revised its fare structure, shortening route sections and reducing charges for most sections to five cents for first class and three cents for second class, making short-distance travel cheaper. This bumped up daily ridership to 32,000 by 1909, about 11 per cent of the population. Even then, its financial year closed with a profit of just 134 pounds ($1,149). That year, the company admitted in its annual report that "the most persistent difficulty remained the popularity of the rickshaw"—the same challenge faced by the steam tram 20 years earlier.

Nevertheless, the kreta electric persisted. To its credit, it did benefit the Town. Its tracks had to be regularly maintained, so the roads over which the tracks ran also had to be maintained. The Municipality gave the Singapore Electric Tramways the liberty to modify or widen roads and bridges, and even divert streams, for their tracks. Roads further away from the Town and in rural areas, such as Geylang Road and Upper Serangoon Road, benefited; for example, Geylang Road had to be widened to accommodate the tram tracks.

The Singapore Electric Tramways also purchased land between MacKenzie Road and Bukit Timah Road by the banks of the Rochor River, for storage and repair facilities—and a power station with eight massive boilers and a 150-feet-tall chimney. The Municipality then bought some current to power street lights within the Town. This brought reliable electric street lighting to busy roads such as Raffles Place and North Bridge Road by 1906—for the first time in modern Singapore's 87-year history.

The electric tram even served an otherworldly purpose as a military hearse. Just south of Singapore Island lay an island called Pulau Blakang Mati, a disease-ridden outpost for Britain's Royal Artillery. (Today, it is the resort island of Sentosa.) Occasionally, a soldier perished from a tropical disease such as malaria. Subsequently:

> The deceased soldier would be brought, in his coffin, by ferry to Jardine's Steps. Close by, at the Nelson Road terminus, one of the freight motors would be waiting, with both side doors open and the floors both clear and clean. The coffin would be placed aboard, the officer in command of the detail take a seat in the rear driving compartment with the rest of the burial party being seated on the floor at each doorway. The car would then be driven at a funereal pace through the town by way of Tanjong Pagar Road and the junction used by depot bound cars from North Bridge Road into Bras Basah Road, thereafter to follow the Paya Lebar route as far as the Christian cemetery (Bidadari Cemetery) located in Upper Serangoon Road.

ENTER THE "COFFEE GRINDER"
THROUGHOUT THE 1880s, engineers in Europe worked on a small, metal "horseless carriage" for one to four passengers. The carriage was known as the motor car in Britain and the automobile in the United States. Karl Benz, a German engineer, would be credited as the father of the modern motor car with his gasoline engine-powered machine in 1885. It took three years for

the motor car to reach Britain, and just 11 years to reach Singapore—the same amount of time it took for the rickshaw to travel from Japan to Singapore—again, thanks to Singapore's open port and laissez-faire governance.

In 1896, the company Katz Brothers imported one of Karl Benz's "motor-velocipeds". The *Singapore Free Press* dubbed the "autocar" "the carriage of the future". It had a hefty price tag of $1,600, weighed 280 kg, had bicycle wheels fitted with rubber tyres, and its 1½-horsepower engine was in the back, powered by benzene at the cost of one cent a mile. The driver controlled the vehicle using just two gears, a steering handle (instead of a steering wheel), and buttons for starting the engine and controlling the volume of explosive vapour admitted into the engine. Other than the driver, the motor car sat just one more passenger—next to the driver. The first trial of the vehicle took place on Bukit Timah Road, one of Singapore's oldest—and straightest—trunk roads. Subsequently, Mr. B. Frost of the Eastern Extension Telegraph Company purchased the vehicle, going on record as the first person in Singapore to own a motor car.

Eventually, Frost sold his car to Buckley. Buckley affectionately called the contraption his "toy", even though operating it was far from smooth. Starting the engine sometimes required pouring a teaspoon of petrol into the carburetor, and lighting it with a match; also, it could not go up hills without being pushed! It was so noisy it was described as "a cross between a perambulator and a concrete-mixer" and a "coffee grinder". Nevertheless, Buckley's "toy" became a familiar sight—and sound—in the Town for many years. At 18 miles an hour (29 km/h), it was the fastest method of movement to grace Singapore's roads, ever—within a decade, this went up to 30 miles an hour (48 km/h). No wonder Buckley was fiercely protective of his "coffee grinder". When an acquaintance remarked how it was a pity the car was unable to reverse, he exclaimed: "Reverse! Rubbish! The man who gets into a situation from which he has got to back out is a damned fool!"

In its early days, the motor car was so rare that whoever owned one garnered plenty of attention. Engineer William Kennedy imported an American Oldsmobile in 1900. When the authorities began registering motor cars and licensing drivers in 1906, Kennedy became the first registered motor car owner and the first licensed driver. His Oldsmobile's licence plate: S-1. Kennedy also became the first official tester of applicants for driving licences. His custom was to make an applicant drive around the pillars of the Central Police Station in South Bridge Road and make a right and left figure eight before heading out into traffic. (The chief of police later took on the task of testing applicant drivers.)

Kennedy later proved to be a gentleman, giving up the licence plate S-1 to a lady, Annie Dorothea Caroline Earnshaw (later Mrs George Mildmay Dare, then Mrs G. P. Owen; 1857–1927), who had requested it for her own motor car, a 12-horsepower Star imported from Britain in 1905 for a cool $3,600. She became the first woman in Singapore to drive a motor car. With her car, she taught a Malay man, Hassan Mohamed, to drive; he became Singapore's first licensed chauffeur, then called a syce in the tradition of gharries and horse carriages. The Asians, astounded at seeing a woman operating a car, dubbed it the "Devil Wind Carriage"; the Europeans called it "Ichiban", Japanese for "Number One". She eventually took S-1 home to England in 1908, but not until after it had logged 69,400 miles in Singapore, Malaya, Java, Scotland, and England.

In the first 10 years of the motor car in Singapore, it was a method of movement only the richest could afford. The cheapest was the Oldsmobile, which still set a buyer back by $1,250. Europeans were not the only ones snapping up motor cars; merchant Seah Liang Seah (1850–1925) and physician Dr Lim Boon Keng (1868–1957) also purchased Benzes imported by Katz Brothers. In all, there were just 214 licensed drivers in 1907. They chose from American (Rambler, Thomas, Oldsmobile), German (Benz), and British brands (Star, Wolseley). "Private transport" remained the realm of rickshaws and horse carriages for years to come.

In June 1907, the exclusive Singapore Automobile Club convened for the first time. The meeting of 30 or so motor car owners involved the most influential men in Singapore, lending credence to the motor car as the newest status symbol of the 20th century. The club's first president was Governor Anderson, and the committee included President of the Municipal Commission Edward George Broadrick (1864–1929) and Sir Walter Napier of law firm Drew & Napier. The gathering was held at Sultan Ibrahim's Tyersall Palace, who paraded his 70-horsepower Mercedes; meanwhile, Buckley turned up in his 1½-horsepower Benz!

Despite the ostentatiousness of the motor car, it malfunctioned often. When its fragile bicycle wheels were punctured, drivers had to trek to the nearest sawmill, fill up the tyre with sawdust, and wrap it with canvas or rope. If the whole car broke down, the driver had to suffer the indignity of arriving home in a bullock cart!

THREE DEVELOPMENTS popularised the motor car. One involved changes to the law, a second was the opening of an import and rental industry, and the third was an economic boom that created many overnight millionaires.

When the motor car arrived in Singapore, it was placed under the Light Locomotives Ordinance, even though it ran on petrol, not steam. That was problematic, for the ordinance allowed vehicles a maximum speed of just two miles an hour (three km/h) in the Town. Fortunately, in the same year, the Red Flag Act in Britain was repealed for the Locomotives on Highways Act, which raised the maximum speed of vehicles to 14 miles an hour (22.5 km/h). Consequently, the new maximum speed for vehicles was set at 10 miles an hour (16 km/h). Even then, motor car owners found this excessively restrictive.

Big changes to the ordinance came in 1905. The 10-mile-an-hour speed limit was repealed, and the governor now had power to introduce new regulations for motor cars. Six years later, in 1911, a new ordinance was passed for motor vehicles—the Traction Engines and Motor Cars Ordinance; similarly, the Hackney Carriage and Jinrikisha Department took on the jobs of registering and regulating motor cars, changing its name to the Registry of Vehicles (Hooper kept his job as the Registrar of Vehicles). No speed limit was imposed on motor cars. By now, motor cars in Singapore could exceed 30 miles an hour (48 km/h). Suddenly, it became clear who would become the future king of the road. Owning a motor car became a lot more appealing.

Singapore's first motor cars were imported on an ad-hoc basis. Then several people realised the need to create the demand for what was a very promising new form of private transport. The first was Kennedy, who opened Singapore's first motor car garage at Merbau Road, near the Singapore River, in 1902. He named it Howarth

Erskine Limited, importing Oldsmobile cars. Then came the famous Wearne brothers from Western Australia.

Charles and Theodore Wearne (born 1873 and 1878) migrated to Singapore at the ages of 13 and 14 respectively to work as apprentice engineers at the New Harbour Dock Company. They worked as sailors, bicycle shop owners, and engineers until 1906. That year, with just $700, the brothers started C. F. F. Wearne & Company, a motor car and truck import, rental, and repair company, in two shophouses at the junction of Orchard Road and Oxley Road. They saw the motor vehicle as the future of transport, and focused on importing cheaper vehicles to encourage the formation of a mass market. At first, cars moved slowly; the brothers could not sell more than three cars a month. But the rubber boom changed that.

Ironically, the boom was caused by rapid growth in the American motor industry, which created immense demand for rubber—a resource that could be tapped from trees grown en masse in Malaya. From 1906 to 1910, massive swathes of land in Malaya were converted to rubber plantations. In 1905, Malaya exported just 130 tons of rubber; by 1919, this increased 1,600 times to 204,000 tons, comprising half of all global exports! The boom created scores of millionaires in Malaya and Singapore—and they all wanted cars to flaunt their newfound wealth. The brothers struck gold; their business grew by leaps and bounds. Wearne Brothers was formed in 1912, a group that would eventually expand to nine companies, including Universal Cars Limited, which handled Ford cars, and Malayan Motors Limited. Branches opened in Malayan cities such as Kuala Lumpur, Penang, and Ipoh. Prominent Chinese merchants such as Tan Kheam Hock (1862–1922) and Tan Chay Yan (1871–1916) became shareholders; in fact, Tan Chay Yan, a grandson of Tan Tock Seng, had ordered the first Rolls Royce in Singapore through Wearne Brothers.[1]

Other car-importing firms soon followed: Borneo Company, Syme & Company, and Central Engine Works. But motor cars were not imported just for sale; they were also rented out. The benefits of hiring motor cars instead of owning them: it was cheaper than buying and maintaining a car, and paying for a syce and garage. In 1909, it was estimated that maintaining a 24-horsepower car cost 535 pounds ($4,586) every year!

Gradually, motor vehicles spread beyond the realm of private transport. The Public Works Department (PWD) imported Singapore's first Wolseley, a four-seater with a hefty price tag of $4,000. Orchard Road, a popular site for motor garages, also saw the debut of Singapore's first public motor bus service in 1906. A single-decker Straker-Squire was imported from Britain by "an anonymous gentleman of much enterprise". The route, number and location of stops, and fares were never recorded, but he apparently faced difficulties running the operation. York and Phillips wrote: "The mechanical facts of life soon became known to him in the form of numerous breakdowns, and the lesson of running a bus service went beyond simply sitting behind a steering wheel or collecting fares. The novelty soon went away, as did his few passengers." The following year, the Wearne brothers started their own motor bus service—Singapore's second—between Johnston's Pier and the Botanic Gardens. There were just four stops—Battery Road, Oxley Road, Orange Grove Road, then the Gardens. The fare was 10 cents a stop and 30 cents for the full journey. *The Straits Times* expected this service to take off, but it did not, and soon petered out.

The year 1906 was also a milestone for firefighting in Singapore. Previously, the Singapore Fire Brigade's fire engines were no more than water tanks mounted on horse carriages. The horses were stabled at Orchard Road (again!), far away from the carriage sheds at North Bridge Road. Often, fires burned out or were put out by the time the fire engines arrived. Now, the fire brigade received its first steam motor fire engine, named The Broadrick, after Municipal Commission President Broadrick. The fire engine carried a thousand feet of hose and could pump 400 gallons of water a minute. It was joined the following year by a second steam motor fire engine, the G. P. Owen, named after a former fire brigade superintendent. Soon, the motor fire engines took over all calls; by 1912, the fire brigade was entirely motorised.

In 1910, Wearne Brothers (again!) imported two 15-horsepower Rover cars and fitted them with taximeters. Yet another first was achieved: Singapore's first (metered) motor taxi cabs, only the second city in the Far East—after Calcutta, British India—to acquire this device, just years after they were introduced in European cities. The cabs charged 10 cents per quarter mile, or 40 cents a mile. At the time, rickshaws charged six cents a mile, and gharries 20 cents, but the cabs were faster, and their meters ensured lower fares than renting a car by the hour. A news article quipped: "One simply engages a cab, and the taxi does the rest—except pay." With motor buses and taxi cabs, Wearne Brothers became Singapore's first transport company to run two methods of movement as public services.

In 1914, the General Post Office took the fire brigade's cue and imported four modified motor cars to carry mail—again, to replace their tried and trusted horse carriages. Each car could carry one-and-a-half tons of mail and primarily served the Town and Keppel Harbour. And in 1917, the Wearne brothers presented a motor ambulance as a gift to the General Hospital.

As the "coffee grinder" became cheaper, and as horse carriage owners began to shed the romantic notion of slowly riding down shady boulevards with their equine companions in favour of getting to their destinations faster, the number of motor cars on the island grew. In 1913, there were just 535 cars, 92 motorcycles (they appeared before 1907) and 35 motor lorries in Singapore; by 1916, the number of cars had doubled to 1,000. The motor car was here to stay.

BLOOD ON THE STREETS

THE AGE of the engine did not mean the immediate demise of animal and human-powered transport, which persisted well into the second decade of the 20th century. In 1916, alongside the 1,000 motor cars, there were 8,270 rickshaws, 2,701 bullock carts, and about 1,500 horse-drawn vehicles. Numerous horse stables still stood in the heart of the Town: Messrs Lambert Brothers at Orchard Road; Clarke's Livery Stables (formerly Messrs Clarke & Company) at the junction of Stamford Road and Hill Street; Straits Horse Repository & Livery Stables at North Bridge Road, near Rochor Road; and Abrams' Horse Repository, first at Bras Basah Road, then Orchard Road. These stables rented out a couple of hundred horses every Sunday morning for recreational riding; close to a hundred people were employed to break and train these horses. The horses could be hired with carriages too; by 1907, they were classified as first-class hackney carriages and cost $10 a day or $5 a ride. A cheaper option were the gharries which could be flagged down off the streets, or hired at major landmarks in the

Town, such as Raffles Place and the Tan Kim Seng Fountain at Battery Road. They were classified as second-class hackney carriages and cost 10 cents every half mile (800 metres).

Meanwhile, the bullock cart was still the preferred method of movement when moving commodities, including moving house. And the bicycle was joined by the tricycle, which was first mentioned in Singapore newspapers in 1892. The tricycle was heavier, bulkier, and more expensive than the bicycle, but was popular among the elderly as it was more stable.

Such a mix of animal, human, and motor-powered vehicles made Singapore's roads doubly contested, congested, and dangerous. In the 1880s, rickshaws and steam trams dictated the pace of traffic and wrestled control of the roads away from pedestrians. Two decades later, rickshaws, electric trams, and most of all, motor vehicles, dictated the pace of traffic—and there were more of them than ever before.

Myriad traffic problems were identified by the authorities and in the newspapers between 1908 and 1917: congestion; noisy motor vehicles scaring horses and disturbing church services; rickshaw pullers and motor car drivers being unable to react to traffic conditions; ignorance of the rules of the road; reckless driving on the part of drivers and carelessness on the part of pedestrians; road hogging (the term "road hog" first appeared in a Singapore newspaper in 1911); the phenomenon of motor vehicles "rushing" pedestrians off the roads; and speeding. The pioneer generation of motor vehicle drivers had been handed command of a machine that could travel at high speed with almost no exertion needed. Passing requirements for driving tests were next to none, and many a speed demon with no road manners, judgement, or "road sense" were let loose. Many did not comprehend the power—and lethalness—of a motor vehicle until it was too late.

A 1909 letter to the *Singapore Free Press* newspaper reported:

> Some local chauffeurs are apparently under the impression that they have the principal claim to use the thoroughfares. They dash along at great speed with a good deal of "tooting" and compel everyone else to move for them. Now this is not right. Why should a pedestrian have to take a sudden flying leap into a ditch, and a man in a carriage throw his horse back on its haunches—often only to let an empty car driven by a Javanese or Boyan coolly pass. Orchard Road is by no means a safe place to go at 20 miles an hour!

And in 1917:

> The general position is that in the course of the last five or six years a type of fast street traffic has been introduced into a town essentially never planned to accommodate it… into a town still largely served by narrow streets without adequate footways, the commerce of which is very largely handled by bullock carts and handcarts and the passenger traffic by rikishas, has come the sudden incursion of fast, and to a degree heavy, motor traffic.

The nature of traffic accidents changed. Before 1905, most involved the passengers of horse carriages and rickshaws. From 1905 to 1917, a majority of casualties were pedestrians hit by vehicles. Over the year of 1912, 157 people were injured; 48 were caused by motor cars, while another 39 were caused by electric trams. Of six killed, two were by motor cars and two by electric trams. These figures worsened the following year. For the whole of 1913, traffic killed 24 people and injured 217—one casualty every one-and-a-half days.

It was only in 1914 that the police finally opened a Traffic Department, or Traffic Office, based in the Central Police Station—the humble ancestor of today's Traffic Police.[2] Its duties included controlling traffic, catching traffic offenders, and handing out summonses. However, the team remained too small to be effective. Three years after the department was formed, it only had an inspector-in-charge, a sub-inspector, five corporals, and 44 constables—51 souls in all. Their working hours were 7am to 8pm, which meant open season on the roads at night. The rural areas were also hardly patrolled. Nevertheless, the men did their best. In the year ending June 1917, there were 1,990 persecutions for traffic offences, 587 being motor car cases.

Even then, punishments were light and no deterrent—they were usually fines rarely exceeding $15. Taking a life through rash or negligent driving earned just a few months in prison. In 1917, motor car driver Sarja Sarban ran down Ramdawar at the junction of New Bridge Road and Cantonment Road, killing him. He received just six months.

THE GREAT War broke out in Europe in August 1914. Britain, allied with France and the Russian Empire, went to war with the German, Austro-Hungarian, and Ottoman empires. Singapore, on the other side of the world, was largely insulated from the terrible events that took the lives of millions. However, for seven days from 15 February 1915, terror gripped the Town. At the time, the only battalion responsible for the defence of the entire island was stationed in Alexandra Barracks off Alexandra Road. Out of 800 sepoys there, nearly half mutinied against their British masters. The predominantly Indian Muslim sepoys were unhappy with living conditions and rations, suffered from ill-discipline and insubordination, and were led astray by anti-British propaganda spread within mosques and their community. This was the Singapore Mutiny, an eruption of violence that nearly upended British rule in Singapore.

From the barracks, the armed mutineers headed east in groups over six kilometres of undulating country to the Sepoy Lines. Being travellers on foot, they naturally walked along the main roads—the same channels of movement that, in 1854 during the Hokkien-Teochew Riots, funnelled trouble from the Town into the country. This time, however, murder and mayhem travelled in the other direction, from the country to the Town. Different groups of mutineers moved through Pasir Panjang Road, Keppel Road, Outram Road, New Bridge Road, and South Bridge Road. They searched houses, stopped cars, and attacked police stations, and in all, killed 47 soldiers and civilians, mostly Britons.

For a few critical hours, the mutineers could have seized the Town if they had been organised and led by strong leaders. Fortunately, they were neither. The authorities also quickly appropriated a new and swift method of movement to assist them in suppressing the mutiny: the motor car. After martial law was declared on the first day, all civilian motor cars were requisitioned as staff cars or for the transport of troops; the cars' syces were temporarily conscripted for military service. Canvas hoods were slashed to allow for the swift embarking and disembarking of armed volunteers. The following day, motor cars were used for armed patrols and to transport volunteers to road junctions and key landmarks. The motor car allowed the authorities to quickly respond to trouble, allocate resources, and deny the enemy channels of movement. Imagine if mutineers had hijacked motor cars instead to head straight for the administrative buildings in the heart of the Town! But they never formulated such plans and they never took any cars. By the morning of the third day, the mutiny had petered out, with most of the mutineers killed, arrested or surrendered. In the end, 47 were executed for daring to shake the foundations of British rule in the Far East.

Like the 1854 Riots, the 1915 Singapore Mutiny spread through the main or trunk roads; but in 1915, unlike in 1854, the authorities used the motor car with great effectiveness against mutineers who mostly travelled on foot. This contributed to the authorities putting down the mutiny quickly. Not for another 27 years would military operations take place again on Singapore Island with mechanised vehicles.

SINGAPORE, IMAGINED
OVER FOUR decades from 1880 to 1918, myriad methods of movement changed the way Singapore moved. These also influenced the spatial and physical evolution of the Town of Singapore, drastically altered the shape of the Municipality, and transformed the European imagination of "Singapore".

Today, "Singapore" the sovereign city-state, and "Singapore" the island, are synonymous. However, in the past, the Town of Singapore and Singapore Island referred to different entities. After the British set up a port by the Singapore River, they referred to the town that grew up around it as "Singapore". This political and geographical delineation—and imagination—was cemented by the implementation of the Raffles Town Plan after 1822. The boundaries of "Singapore" were the boundaries of the Town. All else outside "Singapore" was "the country" or "Singapore Island".

The non-Europeans possessed their own sense of space. For example, the nexus of Chinese geographical identity was Da Po, or "Greater Town", which was Chinatown. But as the British, and by extension the Europeans, occupied the apex of a colonial hierarchy, controlling the island's political, administrative, and economic destiny, their sense of space—and their interpretations of it—carried the greatest consequences for Singapore's history of movement.

From the 1830s to the 1870s, the definition of "Singapore" slowly expanded as Europeans gradually set up home outside the Town. To the north, the Race Course was built off Serangoon Road; to the northwest, plantations; to the south, the docks and wharves of New Harbour. But this geographical expansion was limited by a largely unchanging transport scene. By the end of the 1870s, people still mostly got around by horse, donkey, buffalo, or on foot. Places such as Tanjong Katong to the east, Toa Payoh to the north, and Pasir Panjang to the west were considered "little excursions into the unknown 'wilds'".

In 1856, a Municipality of Singapore was formed, but the area within the municipal boundary remained largely synonymous with the Europeans' imagination and definition of "Singapore". However, from the 1880s, ribbon developments emerged along the main roads running out of the Town, such as Kallang Road, Serangoon Road, Thomson Road, Bukit Timah Road, Orchard Road, River Valley Road, and Tanjong Pagar Road. These developments were skewed to the east of the island, because to the east lay the flat, low-lying watersheds of the Kallang and

Geylang rivers; to the west, the land from Outram Road to Alexandra Road was replete with hills, and at least eight sprawling Chinese cemeteries, the combined area of which was the size of the Town north of the Singapore River. The cemeteries gave the area the unconventional name of Tiong Bahru; Tiong is Hokkien for "cemetery", while Bahru is Malay for "new"; its main road was Burial Ground Road. As for the ribbon developments, they were largely the result of affluent families fleeing the congestion and filth of an increasingly-crowded Town, birthing the concept of "suburbia" in Singapore. These developments, coupled with what the Europeans regarded as declining conditions inside the Town, meant that municipal reform was only a matter of time.

Under a new Municipal Ordinance implemented on 1 January 1888, the post of President of the Municipal Commission, previously unpaid, part-time, and elected by the commissioners, would now be paid, full-time, and appointed by the governor. The municipal boundary was extended for the first time, instantly growing the area of the Municipality by around 10 times to 28 square miles (72 square km)—around one-seventh of Singapore Island's land area. Out of 32 districts on the island in 1898, eight made up the Municipality—Singapore Town itself, Tanjong Pagar, Telok Blangah, Tanglin, Rochor, Geylang, Kallang, and Toa Payoh. More of Singapore Island's population now lived within the municipal boundary than ever before—from 68.5 per cent in 1881 to 83.2 per cent in 1891. The Municipality covered large swathes of agricultural land, marsh and swamp, hills, and Chinese cemeteries—places once considered "rural". For the first time in modern Singapore's history, the Municipality was far larger than the Europeans' imagination and definition of "Singapore". The municipal boundary would be revised marginally twice, in 1906 and 1918; the area around Tanjong Katong Road and Haig Road—named after Great War commander Douglas Haig (1861–1928)—would be added to the east of the Municipality.

However, what expanded the imagination and definition of "Singapore", and consequently, made "Singapore" seem smaller and more accessible, was not increasing the size of the Municipality overnight; it was the spread of rickshaws, motor cars, railway trains, and electric trams. These methods of movement made travel easier and faster. Larger distances could be covered within the same time by more people in greater comfort. The distances between residences and places of work and play grew. What mattered more than distance now was mobility.

When the Singapore Government Railway opened in 1903, the Municipality hoped the multitude of stations between Tank Road and Woodlands would bring "the country" closer to the Town, and encourage residents to move out of the congested Town. After all, it was the convention that "a railway built through undeveloped land (would) cause it to be settled and create its own traffic after construction". This came true to an extent. Several years after the opening of the railway, previously deserted buildings along Bukit Timah Road between Singapore and Bukit Timah stations became occupied again; new buildings, such as country houses and hotels, also came up. Property and rental prices rose. The area became a "popular resort".

The arrival of electric trams in 1905 pulled the rural areas of Paya Lebar and Geylang closer to the heart of the Municipality, encouraging ribbon developments along Serangoon Road and Geylang Road. A news columnist observed in 1908:

Since the invasion of the suburbs by the electric trams, there has been a marked change in those places traversed by the cars which hitherto were sparsely peopled. It is noticeable... that the route to Tanjong Katong, via Geylang, is now lined on both sides by houses of brick or wood, and what a short time ago were solitary spots are now either cultivated or built upon.

As more residents began living and working along Serangoon Road, a spike in addresses along the lengthy trunk road posed difficulties for the postal and utility services. Hence, sometime before 1907, Serangoon Road was separated into Serangoon Road and Upper Serangoon Road, at the junction with MacPherson Road. This was the first time a trunk road named x had been separated into x and upper x—and it would not be the last. Subsequently, the tiny village named 5¾ Mile Serangoon Road—the Paya Lebar terminus of the electric tram system—was renamed 5¾ Mile Upper Serangoon Road. Because of the tram terminus, by 1920, the village had expanded to a "small township of attap dwellings and shops".

With the arrival of the motor car, rich Europeans and Asians settled in suburbs further and further from the Town. Living in the "country" could now mean the sandy beaches of Pasir Panjang, former plantations along Upper Serangoon Road, or the shady coconut groves of Tanjong Katong. The last destination in particular became a favourite holiday location for Europeans eager to escape the crowded, polluted Town for some fresh air and sea breeze. There, the beach was considered the finest in Singapore.

Around the turn of the century, living in the "country" meant the shady coconut groves of Tanjong Katong Road. (Source: The New York Public Library Digital Collections)

With the spread of suburbs and the advance of the municipal boundary, new roads were laid down further into the interior of Singapore Island.

In the east, the municipal commissioners took over a private road in Tanjong Katong, extended it across the crocodile-infested mangroves and mudflats of the Geylang River to Geylang Road, and converted it to a public road named Grove Road. George Peet recalled: "The road… became a long causeway, with steaming mud and tangled black roots on either side at low tide." Grove Road got its name from Grove Estate, Thomas Dunman's coconut plantation. East of Tanjong Katong Road and the municipal boundary, Grove Road continued onto East Coast Road, named because it hugged the coastline. East Coast Road ran to Bedok Village by the Sungei Bedok, meeting Bedok Road.

In the northeast, a track running from Thomson Road to the *kangkar* of Yio Chu Kang was lengthened to connect the sprawling 2,500-acre Trafalgar Estate, a tapioca and coconut plantation in the upper reaches of the Sungei Punggol, to Serangoon Road. The completed, arcing road was named Yio Chu Kang Road.

In the south, Holland Road and Alexandra Road brought travellers to the municipal boundary. The western portion of Holland Road was subsequently realigned; it now curved north to meet Bukit Timah Road, the eventual site of Holland Road Railway Station. Nearby, Buona Vista Road was laid down to connect Holland Road to Pasir Panjang Road; curiously, it was the first road in Singapore Island with an Italian name, meaning "Good View", probably after impressive views of the sea from the hilly road. Also, Ayer Rajah Road was built to connect Alexandra Road to Reformatory Road. Ayer Rajah is Malay for "Water of the King".

In the west, a trunk road, Choa Chu Kang Road, was carved out from the 10th Milestone of Kranji Road at Bukit Panjang Village, past pepper and gambier plantations, to Choa Chu Kang Village. With its completion, only the extreme west of the island—filled with hilly terrain—remained free of trunk roads or main roads up to the 1910s; the remote districts of Lim Chu Kang, Tuas, Bajau, and Peng Kang were still reached by only cart tracks and footpaths.

Despite these developments, Singapore Island outside the municipal boundary remained sparsely populated, still mostly covered by farms, plantations, vegetable gardens, orchards, and secondary forest. People still travelled in convoys of horse and pony-drawn carriages, because tigers prowled the remote roads—Mandai Road, and Kranji Road north of Bukit Timah Village, were particularly notorious. After heavy rain, the soft, unmetalled, red laterite roads were flooded or washed out, with little difference from conditions a hundred years before. Numerous large estates appeared from the 1880s, growing new types of cash crops other than pepper and gambier. They included Confederate Estate (presently Joo Chiat) and Siglap Estate, growing coconuts; Perseverance Estate (4th Milestone Geylang Road), growing lemongrass; Tampines Estate; Teban Estate (presently the northern half of Paya Lebar Air Base); Chasseriau Estate (presently west of MacRitchie Reservoir), a tapioca and coffee estate owned by French landowner Leopold Es Chasseriau; Reliance Estate (Bukit Panjang Village), growing coconuts and coffee; and Tan Kim Seng's Estate (crisscrossed by Buona Vista Road and Ayer Rajah Road). Some were huge—Perseverance Estate was the size of Toa Payoh town today (around four square kilometres), while Chasseriau Estate was three-and-a-half times its size. However, most estate names above—save for "Siglap" and "Tampines"—have been lost to history. Generally, estate names did not survive the test of time.

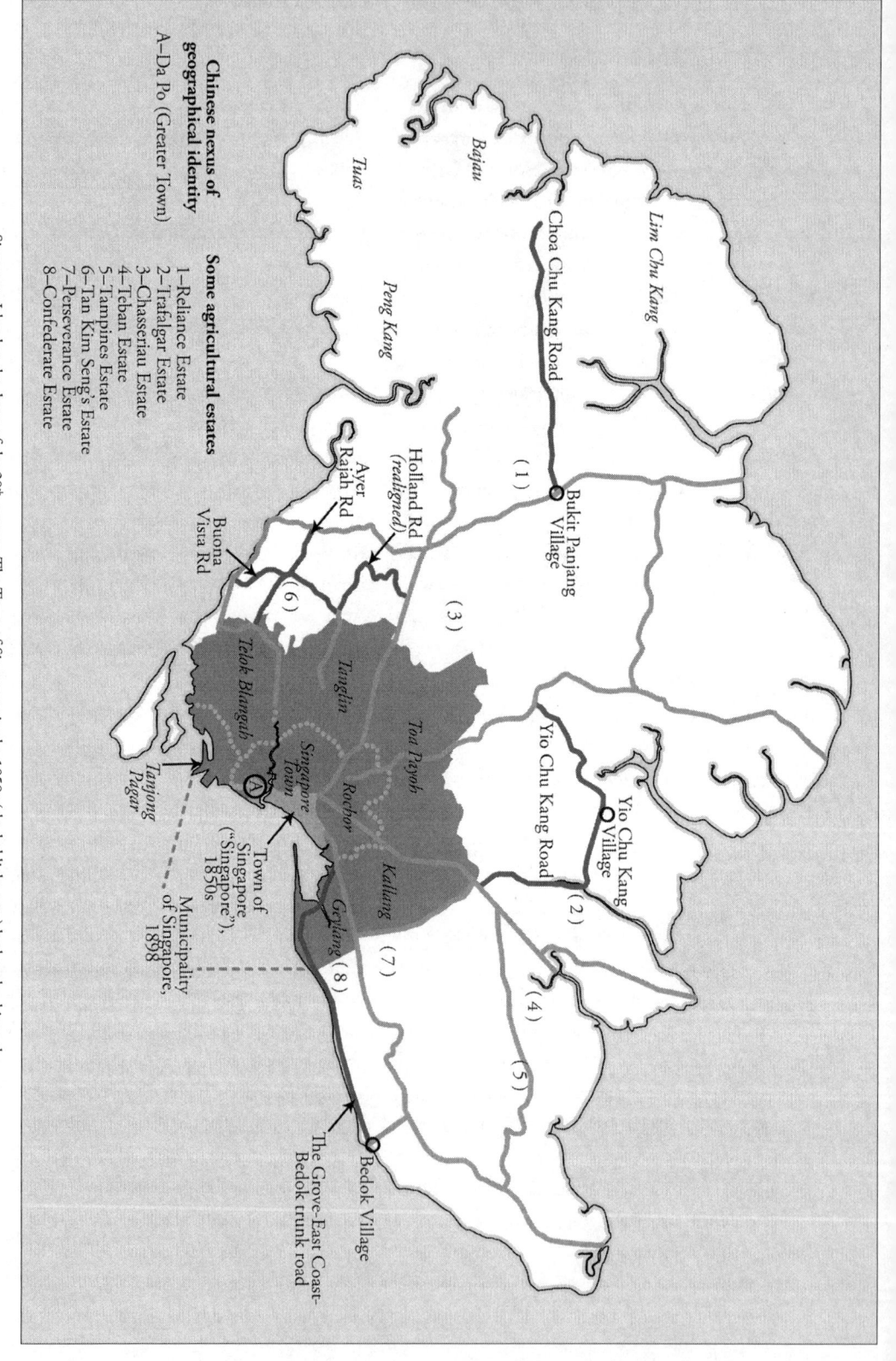

Chinese nexus of geographical identity
A—Da Po (Greater Town)

Some agricultural estates
1—Reliance Estate
2—Trafalgar Estate
3—Chasseriau Estate
4—Teban Estate
5—Tampines Estate
6—Tan Kim Seng's Estate
7—Perseverance Estate
8—Confederate Estate

Singapore Island at the dawn of the 20th century. The Town of Singapore in the 1850s (shaded light grey) had evolved into the Municipality of Singapore (shaded dark grey and divided into eight districts) half a century later, changing the European imagination of "Singapore". The Chinese nexus of geographical identity was different (labelled A). Meanwhile, trunk roads built between 1880 and 1918 are marked out in darker grey. Some agricultural estates mentioned in the text are labelled 1 to 8, while the regions of Lim Chu Kang, Bajau, Tuas, and Peng Kang remained unreached by the trunk road system. (Source: Eisen Teo)

After the turn of the century, the government encouraged the planting of rubber in Singapore. Thousands of acres of secondary forest, and pepper and gambier plantations, made way for swathes of "ugly, tired-looking" rubber trees. In 1910 and 1911, two rubber companies came into existence—Bukit Sembawang Rubber Company Limited, and Singapore United Rubber Plantation Limited. Bukit Sembawang's Teochew name was Buang Kok, or Wan Guo in Mandarin—meaning "10,000 countries", an auspicious name. Unlike other estate names, this place name would not disappear, but instead, grow in significance.

EVEN AROUND the turn of the century, Europeans still mistakenly believed that the Town of Singapore was divided spatially into three towns—Malay, English, and Chinese—with the Padang as the symbolic connection between the first two and the last. The reality was that Raffles' neat ethnic divisions were merely a figment of the imagination after almost a century's absence of urban planning. By the 1910s, the Europeans were still clustered in the old European Town (for example, along Queen Street, Waterloo Street, and Selegie Road) and the hills northwest of the Town. But the Chinese had spilled from Chinatown to the

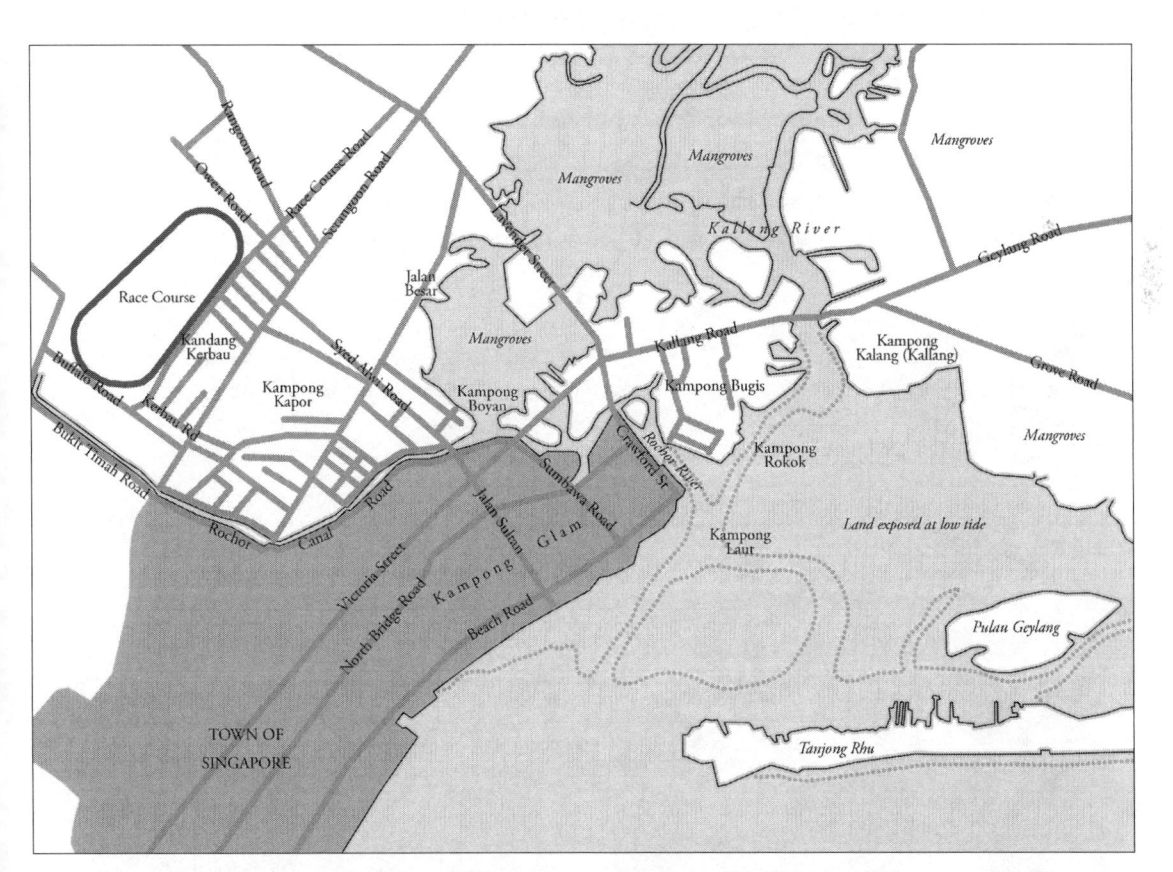

The mouths of the Rochor and Kallang rivers in 1913. Malay communities had arisen in the area, such as kampongs Kapor, Boyan, Bugis, Kalang, Rokok, and Laut. The houses of kampongs Rokok and Laut were built on stilts standing on land flooded at high tide. Meanwhile, Indian communities grew in and around Kandang Kerbau, next to the Race Course. (Source: Eisen Teo)

area north of the Singapore River. The Malays and other natives of the archipelago had spread from Kampong Glam to the mouths and mudflats of the Rochor and Kallang rivers, forming kampungs such as Kampong Kapor (Malay for "Chalk Village", because it was a depot for shell-lime); Kampong Boyan (named after the Boyanese); Kampong Bugis; Kampong Rokok ("Cigarette Village", because it produced cheap cheroots; it also had a reputation as an impenetrable hideout of smugglers); Kampong Laut; and Kampong Kalang (Kallang). The Indians settled in parts of Chinatown and around Raffles Place, and in Kandang Kerbau, giving rise to road names such as Buffalo Road, Lembu (Malay for "Cow") Road, and Hindoo Road (because many were Hindus).

Within Kampong Glam, the tradition of naming new roads after places in the Malay world or Muslim-majority West Asian countries persisted. In 1909, Muscat Street was named after the capital of Oman, and Kandahar Street after a city in Afghanistan. Sultan Road and Little Cross Street, both more than half a century old, were renamed Bussorah Street and Baghdad Street after cities in the Ottoman Empire.

Lasting signs of Chinese settling down in the old European Town and Government Ground included Tan Quee Lan Street, named after a merchant and landowner; Chin Nam Street, after dentist, merchant, and landowner Cheong Chin Nam; Hock Lam Street, after the name of a remittance company owned by businessman Low Kim Pong (1838–1909). "Hock Lam" is Hokkien for "Prosperity of the South".

In Chinatown, Scott's Hill was first renamed Gemmill's Hill after merchant and auctioneer John Gemmill; then it was renamed again to Ann Siang Hill after Chia Ann Siang (1832–1892), a Hokkien businessman. At the foot of the hill, Ann Siang Road was similarly named, although

South of the Singapore River, the greatest changes between 1880 and 1918 took place along Battery Road—all its buildings were rebuilt, and the road widened by up to three metres. This was Battery Road in 1905, crowded with rickshaws and horse carriages. (Source: Library of Congress)

Gemmill Lane survived on the other side. Nearby, Club Street was named after numerous rich men's clubs for Chinese along the road.

West of Ann Siang Hill, in the old Chinese Campong Extension, Smith Street gained a reputation as a red-light district; it had 25 brothels in 1901. Meanwhile, Sago Lane became known as Sei Yan Gai in Cantonese, meaning "Street of the Dead", after shophouses known as "death houses", where the old or terminally ill without kin in Singapore went to live out their final days. And Wayang Street, a small lane parallel to New Bridge Road, was named because of its numerous *wayang* theatres for street opera.

South of the Singapore River, the greatest changes between 1880 and 1918 took place along Battery Road—all its buildings were rebuilt, and the road widened by up to three metres. Three channels of movement opened between Raffles Place and Collyer Quay: Change Alley, literally an alley for merchants, brokers, and moneychangers; Prince Street, named in honour of John Prince, Singapore's first resident councillor; The Arcade, the first building to break the low skyline of Collyer Quay. Completed in 1909 by the Alkaff family, an influential Arab family of merchants and landowners, the four-storey structure had unique Moorish architecture, with onion domes and arches. It was also Singapore's first pedestrian mall, making it possible to walk from Collyer Quay to Raffles Place under shelter.

A tourist information book published in 1908 painted this portrait of the Town:

> High Street… is the home of native jewellers and silk-sellers, and should not be missed by the tourist in search of curios. Crossing High Street at right angles is North Bridge Road, which with its continuation, South Bridge Road, forms the longest thoroughfare in town and the main artery for traffic. Along its entire length, this street is lined with Chinese shops of all conceivable kinds—silversmiths', ivory workers', rice shops, pork chops, eating houses, hotels, and what not—whilst the side streets leading from it are simply thronged with stalls on which a medley of foodstuffs and peddlers' wares are exhibited…
>
> …The hub of the town in a commercial sense is Raffles Place… here at one time were situated all the big shipping and trading houses, banks, and stores… they have consequently spread to the neighbouring streets and to Collyer Quay, which is now almost wholly occupied by the shipping firms. The Square itself still remains the great shopping rendezvous for the European section of the community, and is a very busy place from (9am) till (5pm), after which hour, however, it is almost as deserted as the Sahara. In the daytime, the never-ceasing stream of traffic—carriages, gharries, rickshas, and foot passengers, with their wealth of colour, quaintness, and movement—makes a wonderfully interesting kaleidoscopic procession.

Raffles Place, the spot where "everybody knew everybody else by sight, if not by name", was dominated by two large, homegrown department stores frequented by Europeans—John Little and Robinsons. The latter was also known as Godown Merah ("Red Godown") and to the Chinese, Lo Ban Son. The centre of the square—bordered by

Connaught Drive was bordered by old, tall angsana trees. This photo probably dates to the 1920s, when motor cars had taken over the roads. (Source: The New York Public Library Digital Collections)

dusty, red laterite roads—was a garden with shady flame-of-the-forest trees. Carriage horses were tied to them to take shelter from the sun while their rich owners shopped. Under the same trees, there were also rickshaw pullers "sipping hot coffee with hot buns from a Bengali hawker, or gulping down ice-water, sweetened with doubtful syrup at half a cent a glass".

Similar soothing vistas greeted travellers through the Padang, flanked by Connaught Drive and St Andrew's Road. Old, tall, magnificent angsana trees bordered Connaught Drive. Rich Europeans still took their horse carriages—and soon, motor cars—there in the evenings. Brown recalled: "In the evening both sides of the drive were full of stationary carriages, the lady occupants of which would walk about or sit in each other's carriages and chat, while their husbands played their games on the Padang or discussed 'business' in the Singapore Club or the Cricket Club."

To the north, the scene along Beach Road had almost completely changed from when sailor George Windsor Earl visited in 1832. Nineteen of the 20 handsome villas he had observed—once homes to the cream of society such as Jose d'Almeida and William Renshaw George—had been torn down and replaced by two to three-storey shophouses. The only villa which survived was now the Raffles Hotel. On the seaward side of the road, the sea had retreated from the Beach Road Reclamation Ground.

Like in the 1830s, Orchard Road was still an arterial road running out of the Town into the "country", even though the "country" was now just a wealthy suburb well inside the Municipality. From the Dhoby Ghaut junction to the Emerald

Hill Road junction, horse stables and "native" shophouses lined the road, including Cold Storage, a frozen meat depot opened in 1903. Behind the shophouses were vegetable gardens and fruit trees cultivated in haphazard fashion. Further west, the road became "one of the most beautiful roads to be seen anywhere", as related by G. M. Reith; "one seeing it for the first time cannot fail to be delighted with the long vista of high trees with their variegated foliage and cool shade".

A RURAL BOARD, A "MINIATURE CITY"

A PERENNIAL problem the PWD had to grapple with was the poor state of roads, and that persisted between 1880 and 1918, with motor vehicles straining roads like never before. A letter writer to *The Straits Times* in 1897 gave this take:

> Carriages, cycles, gharries, rickshas, and even the less pretentious bullock carts are being shaken to pieces as they travel over the roads provided by our Municipal Engineer (Samuel Tomlinson). It is becoming a question with the public whether it would not be better to put up with the inconvenience of walking than to suffer the disagreeable, even painful, jolting experienced in riding. For years, the roads have not been so bad, while the system of patching them only makes them worse... A few years back, the roads of this town were considered unrivalled in the East: now, it is quite the other way.

Another persistent problem was dust. A motor car travelling over 20 miles an hour (32 km/h) left "a solid column of thick dust through which it was impossible to see". The spraying of roads with water loaded on bullock carts continued—more than 50 km of roads were treated every day. A more lasting solution was the tarring of macadam roads to create tarmacadam, or tarmac in short, patented in England in 1902. On tarmac, motor vehicles no longer caused ruts or raised dust. In all, there were 191 km of roads within the municipal boundary in 1919, compared to just 24 km of roads in 1821. A modest budget of $500,000 was spent every year to maintain them.

The PWD also tweaked the calibration of milestones, shifting the fixed point in the Town from which the locations of milestones were measured. Since the 1860s, the fixed point had been the Police Bahru Station along North Bridge Road. After 1896, the police moved out of the building. In 1910, the PWD's Survey Department moved the fixed point about half a mile south, to the 36-year-old General Post Office at the mouth of the Singapore River. Accordingly, all milestones across the island had to be shifted for the only time in Singapore's history, half a mile south. The junction of Kranji Road and Choa Chu Kang Road, where Bukit Panjang Village grew up, was known as the 10th Mile as it was Kranji Road's 10th Milestone, but even after the milestone shifted south, the junction's epithet persisted—to the present.

The PWD did receive a significant reprieve in its workload in 1908—when the Rural Board was formed. Before, roads outside the municipal boundary were maintained by the PWD, while rural police stations—mostly in villages—kept law and order. Little else was organised for rural residents. The Rural Board was convened to oversee matters such as road improvements and repairs, health improvement schemes, water supplies, markets, parks, and building inspections. In 1923, road maintenance took up 70 per cent of its $631,000 budget. After all, there were many trunk and rural roads needing constant upkeep.

Occasionally, merchants and landowners took on the role of the PWD and paid for urban development. In 1882, Cheang Hong Lim ordered the filling in of swamps along the upper reaches of the Singapore River skirting Kim Seng Road and River Valley Road. He built a market on the reclaimed land to serve residents in the vicinity, and around the market, erected "long rows of substantial and elegant-looking tenements until the place resembled a miniature city". The market, and the road serving it, were called Cheang Hong Lim Market; an adjacent creek was called Hong Lim Creek. His public works were so significant, many roads and places were named after him, his chop Wan Seng, and his sons, Jim Hean (1873–1901), Jim Kheng (1875–1939), and Jim Chuan (1878–1940). Around Cheang Hong Lim Market, there were Cheang Hong Lim Lane, Cheang Jim Kheng Street, and Cheang Jim Chuan Street. Between Havelock Road and Pearl's Hill, there were Cheang Wan Seng Road, Upper Cheang Wan Seng Road, Cheang Hong Lim Lane (again), Cheang Jim Hean Street, and Cheang Jim Chuan Lane. All these on top of Cheang Hong Lim Street and Cheang Wan Seng Place in the Telok Ayer Reclamation Ground, Hong Lim Quay by the Singapore River, and Hong Lim Green, a public park paid for by Cheang Hong Lim between North Canal Road and Upper Macao Street. With 14 landmarks, the Cheang clan was the family bequeathed the most place names in Singapore's modern history thus far—excluding the British royal family—bucking the trend of non-Europeans not having places named after them.

The Municipal Commission did not forget to engage in street renaming exercises to reduce what in their opinion was toponymic confusion caused by "the similarity of the names of several streets in different parts of the Town". As a result, the D'Almeida family came off poorer. In 1908, to prevent confusion over Almeida Road, Almeida Street, and D'Almeida Street, Almeida Road was renamed Balmoral Road (after Scotland's Balmoral Castle), while Almeida Street was renamed Temple Street (after the 81-year-old Sri Mariamman Temple).

Cheang Hong Lim's family was not spared either—they lost nine out of the 14 place names in their honour. First, in 1898, Upper Cheang Wan Seng Road was renamed Beng Hoon Road. Then, in 1915, Cheang Hong Lim Market was renamed Covent Garden, after a famous market in London's West End. Similarly, Cheang Hong Lim Lane, Cheang Jim Kheng Street, and Cheang Jim Chuan Street were renamed Covent Row, Covent Alley, and Covent Street respectively. By the Singapore River, Hong Lim Quay was merged with and renamed South Boat Quay. North of Pearl's Hill, Cheang Wan Seng Road became Taipeng Road, Cheang Hong Lim Lane became Hare Street, and Cheang Jim Hean Street became Calcutta Road. Only Cheang Jim Chuan Lane survived. For the rich and famous of Singapore, toponymics could be a fickle game—immortality granted in one instant, and taken away the next.

THE TOPONYMICS OF MALAYA

AFTER BRITISH intervention in Malaya began in the 1870s, British commercial and agricultural interests in the Malay sultanates grew. Singapore stood to gain from a vast Malayan hinterland. In 1886, the British declared Abu Bakar Sultan of Johor; the following year, the British compelled the Sultan of Pahang to accept a Resident for the running of its affairs. In the 1880s and 1890s, roads inside Kampong Glam were named after the sultanates and locations inside them. There were Pahang Street and Johore Road, and Jalan Kuantan and Jalan Pekan, named after towns in Pahang. Meanwhile, Mount Ophir, a mountain in Johor, gave its name to Ophir Road; the District of Muar, now part of Johor, gave its name to Muar Road.

The FMS was formed in 1896. In 1898, the municipal commissioners passed a resolution to "use the names of rivers and districts in the Malay Peninsula as being better adapted to the purpose (of naming streets) than the names of persons or families". These Malay names were preferred, because the commissioners felt they were "simpler and (could) be pronounced by all classes of the community". This was a significant departure from the usual practice of naming roads after people.

This resolution was honoured the same year when six new roads were laid down between Tanjong Pagar Road and Anson Road. They were Raub, Bernam, Enggor, Tapah, Gopeng, and Tras streets. Bernam was the name of a river between Perak and Selangor; Raub and Tras were towns in west Pahang; from north to south, Enggor, Gopeng (near Ipoh), and Tapah were towns in Perak.

A couple of years later, more new roads were built near the junction of Anson Road and Keppel Road, near the Tanjong Pagar wharves. They were named Siak Street, Patani Street, Selangor Street, and Deli Street. Selangor was one of the four sultanates in the FMS; Patani was a former Malay sultanate under the suzerainty of the Kingdom of Siam; Siak and Deli were sultanates in Sumatra under the Dutch East Indies.

Under the Bangkok Treaty of 1909, Siam transferred its rights over the Malay states of Perlis, Kedah, Kelantan, and Trengganu (the British spelling for Terengganu) to Britain; the four states were later known as the Unfederated Malay States. It was around this time that Kelantan Road and Kelantan Lane were named by the banks of the Rochor River, northwest of Kampong Glam; a small road named Trengganu Street was cut from Pagoda Street to Sago Street in the old Chinese Campong Extension. As the British were extending political and economic control over the Malay Peninsula, numerous roads in Singapore captured the zeitgeist of that period.

These street names possessed a Malayan significance only to those who understood the English language, who still formed the minority of residents in Singapore. The Chinese knew these roads by other names. For example, Raub Street, Bernam Street, and Enggor Street all shared the same name, Chin Seng Sua Khau, or Hokkien for "Mouth Of Chin Seng's Hill". Gopeng Street and Tras Street shared the same name too: Cho Su Kong Khau, or "Mouth Of The Cho Su Kong Temple". To the Chinese, the importance of Malaya to British Singapore did not matter to them as much as physical and community landmarks such as hills and temples.

CHAPTER NOTES

1 As of 2018, Wearne Brothers was known as Wearnes Automotive, based at Leng Kee Road. It represented luxury car brands such as Aston Martin, Bentley, and Jaguar in Singapore. At 112 years, Wearnes Automotive was Singapore's oldest transport company.

2 The Traffic Office moved from Central Police Station to a new headquarters at Maxwell Road in 1930. In 1999, as the Traffic Police, it moved to its current headquarters at Ubi Avenue 3. As of 2018, the conserved Maxwell Road complex was known as the Maxwell Chambers Suites, occupied by the Ministry of Law.

CHAPTER 4
1918 to 1941: Jams and Crashes

AT THE dawn of the 20th century, Singapore was a "city of rickshaws". Within 30 years, it was a "city of motor cars". The method of movement invaded the roads, conquered the free spaces, and most of all, appropriated the airwaves. British novelist and travel writer W. Robert Foran wrote in 1934:

> Singapore's streets are always seething with life. The noise is indescribable. London, New York, Paris and other great cities are bad enough; but they are a haven of peace in comparison with Singapore. The Malay drivers of motor vehicles have a failing which is highly objectionable. The horns or buttons of the mechanical hooters on cars and lorries prove quite irresistible to their childish minds. Their itching fingers are never off them for more than a few seconds at a time. They behave exactly like infants provided with a drum or cornet to amuse themselves, and make full use of this golden opportunity to render life hideous for others. It does not matter in the least to these native drivers that there is no real occasion to give warning of their approach. They argue that the hooter was provided for use, and are not niggardly in sounding it. They are an infernal nuisance in the city's streets, for they create bedlam by day and night…
>
> Sleep at night in the hotels, until you grow accustomed to this infliction (if you ever do), is practically an impossibility. Until 2 or 3 o'clock in the morning this hellish nightmare never ceases… three to four hours of sleep at night was about as much as I managed to get during the first few days in Singapore. In such a climate, this can lead only to the grave, murder or a lunatic asylum.

With narrow, dusty thoroughfares choked with motor vehicles, echoing with the cacophony of roaring engines and tooting horns, Singapore had truly entered the age of modernity. The era of roads belonging to pedestrians was long gone.

In the 23 years between the end of World War I in 1918 and 1941, movement on the island changed dramatically. Singapore had a population of 418,358 in 1921. Rickshaws were number one for both public and private transport, with 8,022 vehicles and 20,000 pullers working them in 1920. For public transport, electric trams covered much of the Town but were struggling as a business; the railway was taken by those who lived along the line. Motor cars were plying the streets for hire, but were few and far between. To move heavy goods, bullock carts were most frequented. For private transport, motor cars were an option for the very rich—or they could still rely on their trusty horse carriages.

The traffic scene of 1941 was very different. Singapore's population had increased by almost 75 per cent to more than 725,000. Diesel-powered motor buses and trolleybuses—an electric bus that drew electricity from overhead wires—had taken over as the main forms of public transport. The number of rickshaws had dropped by more than half to fewer than 4,000, while electric trams had disappeared altogether. Motor trucks had replaced bullock carts as a mover of goods.

This period was marked by several traffic phenomena. The "peak hour" or "rush hour" became pronounced, with traffic congestion on main roads, and overcrowding on public transport. Traffic management also took off with the introduction of traffic lights, pedestrian crossings, speed limits, road lines, and so on.

Channels of movement also saw significant changes. Part of the railway system was realigned for a growing Municipality. Two ring roads were completed to complement the trunk road system. A causeway linked the island with its hinterland.

Military bases were built all over the peripheries of Singapore as an outpost of empire. A world-class airport opened in 1937 at the mouth of the Kallang River.

For Singapore, entering modernity did not just mean a new phase in the history of movement. It also meant being plugged into an increasingly connected, ever-shrinking world, one which transformed Singapore's urban and rural landscapes—and invited war to its doorstep.

A LAND LINK AFTER 8,000 YEARS

FOR 300 years, Singapore Island was part of the Johor Sultanate. After sovereignty over the island was ceded to the British, an economic connection remained between Singapore and Johor. When the Bukit Timah–Kranji trunk road was built in

Robinson Road, sometime in the 1920s or 1930s. Note the absence of forms of traffic management we take for granted today—traffic lights, signallised pedestrian crossings, and lane markings. Rickshaws, horse carriages, and motor cars jostled for space. (Source: The New York Public Library Digital Collections)

the 1840s, it ran to the Straits of Johor, where a sampan service ferried people between Kranji and Johor. As British interests in Malaya grew from the 1870s, this Singapore–Johor transport connection also grew in importance. Hence, the Singapore Government Railway of 1903 also ran to the Straits of Johor. The site of the Woodlands terminus was chosen because the straits there was much narrower than at Kranji Road's end, reducing the time taken for ferry crossings. However, the Woodlands terminus was some distance away from Kranji Road, the nearest main road.

Hence, in 1907, a road was laid down between the Woodlands terminus and Kranji Road 13¾ Milestone. The new winding dirt road was called Woodlands Road, after the terminus. Over time, a village, Woodlands Village, grew up where the road and terminus met the sea, becoming one of Singapore Island's northernmost villages.

The railways on Singapore Island and Johor increased cross-strait traffic, but the ferries were a bottleneck. They struggled to keep up with rail traffic: in 1921, ferries transported 58,000 railway wagons across the straits—an average of 159 a day. Bridging the straits was a logical move. However, plans for a bridge were delayed by five years because of the economic strain caused by World War I. After 1918, engineers advised against building a bridge; the straits was too deep and the sea bed too unstable. Instead, a causeway—a solid bank of granite rubble—was suggested by W. Eyre-Kenny, Director of Public Works for the Federated Malay States (FMS). And so a causeway it was.

The following year, in 1919, engineers drew up plans for a causeway 1 km long and 18 metres wide, to be connected to the Woodlands terminus and Woodlands Road. Roughly 1.5 million cubic yards of granite had to be quarried from Bukit Timah and Pulau Ubin. The project took four years and cost $17 million, borne by the governments of the FMS, Johor, and the Straits Settlements. The Causeway, as it came to be known, opened to railway goods traffic on 17 September 1923; passenger trains were cleared to use it on 1 October; eight days later, a road over the Causeway was opened to pedestrian and vehicular traffic. Newspaper reports proclaimed that Bangkok was now just 60 hours from Singapore by train! For the first time in 8,000 years, since the end of the last glacial period, Singapore Island and the Malay Peninsula were connected by land.

The construction of such a significant channel of movement subsequently affected patterns of movement on Woodlands Road. Before, it was a sleepy, winding, single-lane carriageway, surfaced with red laterite, barely able to fit two motor cars passing by each other. It ran through hilly country covered by jungle, rubber estates, vegetable farms, and mangrove swamps. After it became a through passage to Johor, traffic volume suddenly shot up, with a regular stream of cars and trucks. A *Straits Times* article in July 1924 reported accidents occurring "practically every day":

> (The) road (is about) 15 feet wide, only permits of buses clearing each other by a few inches and the danger is greater in the case of large-sized cars meeting. The road winds practically the whole way, and the sides are precipitous. Yesterday two accidents occurred, and in one case a bus was piled up on the side of the road as the result of collision with a car...

It took three years for the authorities to carve out a separate, straighter, wider road next to Woodlands Road. In 1927, this new road was also named Woodlands Road; most traffic to and from the Causeway was diverted there; the old road, only 20 years old, went quiet again. It was renamed Marsiling Road, a name with its own history.

The turn of the century saw the rise of Lim Nee Soon (1879–1936), a Singapore-born Teochew merchant who made his fortune in rubber and pineapples. In the 1920s, Chan Chu Kang was renamed Nee Soon Village in his honour; the area became known as Nee Soon. To pay tribute to his ancestral hometown of Ma Xi Village in Guangdong, China, he named his properties "Ma Xi Lin", a portmanteau of the village's name and his surname in Mandarin. The British spelled the name as "Marsiling", and it stuck. There were Marsiling Building in Robinson Road, Marsiling Villa in Cairnhill, and Marsiling Estate in Woodlands—all owned by Lim. Hence, Marsiling Estate lent its name to Marsiling Road.

Further changes were to come. In 1929, the Rural Board decided to rename the stretch of Kranji Road from Bukit Timah Village to Bukit Panjang Village, to Bukit Timah Road; Kranji Road from Bukit Panjang Village to Woodlands Road became Woodlands Road. Now, Bukit Timah Road ran from the Town to Bukit Panjang Village; Woodlands Road ran from Bukit Panjang Village to the Causeway. Kranji Road was suddenly reduced in length from 11 km to 1.6 km.

Elsewhere, sometime between 1911 and 1924, Tanah Merah Road between Geylang Road and Changi Road was renamed Changi Road, lengthening the latter by three kilometres.[1] The length of a road could change not just because of physical extensions or expungements, but also bureaucratic decisions.

Even with the Causeway, the northern part of Singapore Island between Bukit Panjang Village and the straits remained largely rural and undeveloped. In the 1970s, George Peet reminisced about the experience of driving down Woodlands Road from the Causeway after dark, half a century before:

> … a marvellous memory of that drive through the hilly rubber estates beyond Woodlands is of the myriads of fireflies in the bushes on either side of the laterite road, switching on and off their jewelled lights in mysterious and perfect synchronisation. In later years fireflies became more and more rare on Singapore Island, and I suppose many people living there now have never seen a firefly at all.

Perhaps the history of movement in Singapore is a story of the gradual disappearance of fireflies along laterite roads?

THE NECESSARY "MOSQUITOES"

THE WEARNE brothers' first pair of motor taxis in 1910 marked not just the birth of Singapore's taxi system, but also the rise of Singapore's motor bus network. In the early days, there were few obvious physical or legal distinctions between a motor car plying for hire, or taxi cabs, and a motor omnibus, or bus—a larger, souped-up car could pose as a "bus". There was no separate ordinance for buses, and the government, with its usual hands-off approach to transport, was in no hurry to legally separate taxi cabs from buses, restrict the evolution of taxi cabs into buses, or control the number of buses. As a result, free market forces and unbridled competition took over.

From the 1910s to the early 1920s, there were three types of public motor vehicles: proper taxi cabs (usually older second-hand cars, which ferried one or two passengers at a time), proper motor buses (larger motor vehicles which ferried many passengers at a time), and taxi cabs which worked like buses.

In 1914, seven years after the Wearne brothers tried out a motor bus service, they launched Singapore's third motor bus service between Kampong Kapor and Seletar, possibly via Serangoon Road, Upper Serangoon Road and Yio Chu Kang Road. The service consisted of two Dennis buses and each ticket cost 15 cents. However, over the same route, motor cars were spotted taking passengers "eight to 10 at a go", charging 20 cents each; the cars were "run desperately hard". The same phenomenon was reported between Arab Street and Siglap, with as many as 12 passengers squeezed in five-seater cars, "with men clinging to the sides and hoods". These overcrowded cars drove at "mad speeds", possibly because of business rivalries among the owners and drivers. They were the genesis of what the authorities would later dub "mosquito buses". (The Kampong Kapor–Seletar bus run subsequently fizzled out.)

As for proper taxi cabs, most, if not all, were individually-owned. We know they existed because taxi cab stands were established alongside hackney carriage stands inside the Municipality, such as Beach Road in front of Raffles Hotel, and at the junction of Scotts Road and Stevens Road. As their numbers grew, the Registry of Vehicles began separating motor cars into three categories: private motor cars, cars hired out of garages as 1st-class motor cars, and taxi cabs as 2nd-class motor cars. In 1919, businessmen hatched plans to set up a Singapore Motor Taxi-Cab and Transport Company, but not enough capital was raised. Competition from rickshaws and gharries was still stiff, and the costs of running a taxi company were high.

Attempts to run motor bus services did not fare better—even though the Municipal Commission itself acknowledged their virtues. In a series of meetings in 1918, the commissioners agreed that a municipal motor bus system was the best way forward in encouraging people in the overcrowded Town to move out to outlying areas, and spurring the development of "backward" districts. "The question of transport is important", Commissioner W. Lowther Kemp stated, "because it is so inextricably intermingled with that question of health and housing".

Two years later, in 1920, the Municipal Commission took a small step towards fulfilling their wish, launching Singapore's first municipal bus services under the Singapore Municipal Omnibus Service—only the second time in Singapore's history the authorities paid for and managed a method of movement. Five Albion 17-seater buses plied a route between Telok Ayer Market and Pasir Panjang via Robinson Road; a second route, served by just one bus, covered Finlayson Green to Tanglin Barracks. The reception was not hot. The following year, the second route was withdrawn, and the bus placed on a new route, between Finlayson Green and Thomson Road. Later that year, a fourth service was started between Finlayson Green and Telok Kurau. However, these services suffered from little business, high costs, and competition from rickshaws and gharries, so the Municipality halted them all by June 1922.

Also in 1920, businessman Kam Teow Yang started two bus services under the banner of the Auto Buss Company. Each route had just one Ford bus (modified by the Wearne brothers!): one plied between Johnston's Pier and Serangoon; the other, between Johnston's Pier and Geylang. Both duplicated and competed with electric tram routes. Kam tried to keep fares low to attract the lower and middle classes, charging just five cents a mile—

rickshaws had recently raised their fares to 14 cents a mile. His services had order to them—the buses ran from 7am to 6pm daily on a regular timetable of 10 trips with fare stages. There were expansion plans involving 20 buses, but Auto Buss Company petered out shortly, possibly for the same reasons as the municipal bus services.

In 1922, a fateful municipal by-law was passed, allowing taxi cab drivers to take multiple passengers paying separately for their seats. This had the unexpected consequence of encouraging more taxi cab drivers to take on more separate passengers at a go—hence, the rise of more "mosquito buses".

THE MOSQUITO bus was usually an imported Model T or Model A Ford that received a new bus body made of wood in a Singapore workshop, capable of carrying up to seven passengers and a conductor. It swiftly became the new rickshaw of the early 20th century: cheap, convenient, fast—and was operated by mostly Chinese drivers with no proper training. In fact, many rickshaw pullers gave up pulling to become mosquito bus drivers to save their bodies from ruin. The mosquito bus industry differed from the rickshaw industry, though—the buses were mostly owned by individual drivers and conductors, not a handful of *towkays*.

While mosquito buses charged low fares to compete with rickshaws, the electric tram, and gharries, what made them succeed where proper motor bus services failed was their modus operandi: they had no fixed routes or timetables. To maximise income, a driver packed his bus to capacity, then travelled a route determined by the combined destinations of his passengers—Singapore's first form of dynamic vehicle pooling. And like rickshaw pullers, their drivers knew the importance of location. They hovered around the busiest thoroughfares in the Town, along the electric tram routes, and at terminuses and traffic junctions.

The buses were a boon to the lower classes because they were cheaper and faster than rickshaws, could potentially travel anywhere, and did not tire like pullers. The buses "moved around without much hurry, tickets were properly punched and handed out, all was in order". Then competition intensified. Eager to earn more, owners overworked their buses, and refused to send them for repairs or maintenance. Soon, many vehicles were "little better than masses of scrap iron"; one owner was running a bus with its steering gear "tied up with bits of wire". Brakes not working? No fear. Just engage the reverse gear to stop the bus!

The behaviour of drivers and conductors was no better. Conductors stopped issuing tickets; sometimes, they ejected passengers midway through rides without refunds, in order to take on new passengers going in another direction. Buses tore down streets trying to overtake each other and grab more passengers. A *Straits Times* editorial reported in 1927:

> Watch them come out of a side street at 20 miles an hour into a crowded main thoroughfare. With a cigarette between their lips, further obstructing their vision, they twist and turn their steering wheels into figures of eight with supreme nonchalance—and without a hoot from their horns… the streets are now replete with wild and financially-harassed drivers, irresponsible conductors, and vehicles rapidly shedding their worn-out constituent parts all over the roadsides.

Accidents happened; this time, the faster, hardier motor vehicles caused far more damage than rickshaws. The mosquito bus of the 1920s had become the rickshaw of the 1880s—mostly run by Chinese and a peril on the roads. But like the rickshaw, the mosquito bus was a necessary evil, meeting the demand for movement in Singapore.

The authorities were undoubtedly annoyed by these buses, but like the rickshaws, they barely raised a finger to control them, such as restricting vehicle numbers or setting and enforcing service standards. The exception was in 1924, when the Municipal Commission debated a resolution compelling bus owners to apply for motor insurance or pay a $250 deposit. In the end, only the latter was implemented, but it did little to improve the situation. By 1927, the mosquito bus contingent had grown to 445—Singapore's largest mechanised public transport fleet thus far.

Its biggest scalp was the electric tram system. The electric tram never made a lot of money from its inception in 1905, perpetually struggling to garner enough passengers. Stiff competition from rickshaws and now taxi cabs and mosquito buses meant death by a thousand cuts. The daily ridership of the tram was almost 37,000 in 1911, but declined to 34,800 by 1917—even though Singapore's population had grown 23 per cent over the same period.

Initially supportive of the private venture, the Municipal Commission gradually retreated. During their transport meetings of 1918, the commissioners were not in favour of an expansion of the electric tram system, citing reasons such as the high costs of maintaining the roads on which the tracks ran, difficulties of the trams in turning sharp corners, and excessive noise. According to Commissioner Roland Saint John Braddell (1880–1966), "the din of the trams… made a noise like machine guns in the trenches", which disrupted proceedings in the nearby courts. Even during performances at the Victoria Theatre in Empress Place, "just when the heroine was going to say something there came the rattle of the machine-gunning outside"!

Bleeding £50,000 ($428,600) a year, the company went into receivership in 1922, after which the receiver, Sir William Plender (1861–1946), contacted the Shanghai Electric Construction Company (SECC) for advice and expertise. The SECC recommended that Singapore's tram system be replaced by a trolleybus system.

Like the electric tram, the trolleybus—also called a "rail-less tram"—was powered by electricity, but it ran on the roads, not tracks. It was first tested in Berlin in 1882; trolleybus services opened in Leeds and Bradford in 1911. It had advantages over the electric tram. Firstly, its movement was not restricted to tracks that were costly to maintain, allowing a degree of manoeuvrability around road obstacles. Secondly, disabled vehicles could be easily detached and moved out of the way, reducing the impact of a breakdown on the entire route. However, the trolleybus had solid metal tyres, not pneumatic ones, so poorly-maintained roads meant sore bums for passengers!

Negotiations commenced amongst the receiver, the SECC, and the Municipal Commission. By 1925, a deal was struck. The Singapore Electric Tramways would be replaced by a new company set up by the SECC, called the Singapore Traction Company (STC). Trolleybuses would replace trams. The Municipal Commission would help the STC resurface roads to allow them to take the weight and impact of the hefty trolleybuses. Upon passing of the Singapore Traction Ordinance, the new company was granted a lucrative 30-year monopoly to run trolleybuses within the municipal boundary.

For the third time in Singapore's history, the authorities—dominated by Britons—assisted a company founded and run by Britons in importing a new, mechanised method of movement into Singapore. First, steam trams in 1886; then electric trams in 1905; now trolleybuses in 1925. It was clear that the Britons running Singapore supported commercial attempts to import new methods of movement from Britain, so long as the businesses were run by Britons and the methods of movement were "modern".

The trolleybus made its debut on 14 August 1926. Painted dark green and cream, each five-ton vehicle sat eight first-class and 30 second-class passengers, and was supplied by London-based vehicle manufacturer Associated Equipment Company. Thirty vehicles were put to work on the busy roads between Geylang and Tanjong Pagar, an old tram route. The second route to be converted was the one between Tank Road and Keppel Harbour, on March 1927. The final tram was pulled in 1928.

As the trolleybus was gradually introduced, the Municipal Commission took steps to ensure that the STC's monopoly would not be jeopardised. Hence, in November 1927, it decided to ban motorcycle taxis from Singapore's roads. President Roland John Farrer (1873–1956) explained it was because of "the further terror they would add to life… the introduction of a further, even more 'mosquito' type of vehicle than those at present would increase the danger and clog the streets".

One month later, the commissioners finally tried to slap some semblance of order on the mosquito buses, forcing them to apply for licences from the Registry of Vehicles; when applying for a licence, a bus owner had to choose one of three fixed routes for his vehicle. The routes: Pasir Panjang to Tanjong Pagar, Tanjong Pagar to Upper Serangoon Road, and Upper Serangoon Road to Finlayson Green. Accordingly, the bus would be painted red, blue, or yellow. Other rules: every bus had to carry a direction board, charge a fixed fare of three cents a mile, respect a speed limit of 20 miles an hour (32 km/h), and undergo an inspection four times a year; no dumping of passengers midway through rides was allowed. By restricting mosquito buses to just three routes, the STC was free to operate in the rest of the Municipality without as much competition.

The trolleybuses needed all the help they could get. At the start, they suffered teething issues such as buses frequently separating from their overhead wires—a problem that persisted because of unskilled or reckless drivers. But gradually, with the regulation of mosquito buses, the trolleybus system enjoyed robust patronage and growth. Its aforementioned advantages—no fixed tracks, ability to get around traffic obstacles—contributed to its success, as it was far cheaper to introduce, modify, or scrap routes, allowing the STC to quickly adapt and redeploy trolleybuses whenever patterns of movement changed. In September 1927, there were 66 trolleybuses plying six routes over 24 km; by 1930, the fleet had expanded to 108 trolleybuses plying 10 routes over 39 km. In 1917, the electric tram took on 34,800 passengers every day, or 9.3 per cent of Singapore's population; in 1930, the trolleybus managed 117,500 passengers daily, or 21.6 per cent of the population. Success had finally come to the STC where it had eluded the steam and electric trams, and in the 1930s, the STC boasted that they owned and operated "the largest trolleybus system in the world".

Trolleybuses debuted or cemented some innovations we take for granted in public transport today. One: unlike tramcars, service numbers were now displayed on trolleybuses, since routes overlapped one another. Two: like the electric tramway, stops were designated along trolleybus routes. Fare stages—three to 12 cents for first class, two to eight cents for second class—were calculated according to the stops. Most stops were simply marked by posts with a list of services tacked onto them. Bus stops were not sheltered, so passengers had to wait for their trolleybuses exposed to the elements.

As new suburbs opened, new routes and extensions rolled out, necessitating the building of Singapore's first bus terminals, transport nodes where trolleybuses were parked and organised, routes started and ended, and drivers and passengers gathered. One major terminal was at Finlayson Green, just south of Raffles Place. The earliest terminals were spartan: a single-storey hut for a timekeeper to ensure the departure of trolleybuses according to schedule; an awning for passengers to wait; a space reserved for hawkers; and sufficient road space to allow trolleybuses to turn around.

Some trolleybus routes within the municipal boundary covered undeveloped countryside, devoid of man-made landmarks, with just traction poles to power them. With the need to mark out fare stages, unique numbers were painted on some poles. Stages along Havelock Road, up to the junction with Alexandra Road, were marked in this manner. So was a prominent terminal near the 3rd Milestone of Geylang Road. It was marked "Post 310", identifying the traction pole along Geylang Road where it was convenient for trolleybuses to make a three-point turn and return where they came from. "Post 310" was near where Lorong 10 Geylang is today; the pole has long vanished without a trace.

The STC did not restrict itself to trolleybuses. In 1929, it opened a motor bus service of seven Dennis buses between Geylang and Finlayson Green. Like the trolleybuses, the buses were painted green and black, and each accommodated 20 people.

The STC had tasted success, but the mosquito buses remained strong competition. There were still hundreds of them and each could stop anywhere along its designated route, unlike trolleybuses, which had to stop at bus stops. It was only a matter of time before the Municipality targeted them again.

RISE OF THE CHINESE BUS COMPANIES

MUNICIPAL EFFORTS to clean up the mosquito bus industry in the 1930s were driven by a few motivations. One was a decaying mosquito bus fleet. In 1933, of the 455 licensed mosquito buses owned by 300 individuals, all but 38 were converted obsolete Ford Model T cars; most had been on the road for 10–15 years, and were literally falling apart from the strain of doing 100–170 miles (160–270 km) a day. Another was the mosquito buses' contribution to dangerous traffic conditions. Every morning, junctions such as North Bridge Road–Rochor Road and South Bridge Road–Cross Street were choked by buses waiting for passengers; many drivers disregarded the 20-mph (32-km/h) speed limit. A third motivation was support for the STC, of which race was probably a factor—the Briton-dominated Municipal Commission backing the Briton-dominated STC against the Chinese-dominated mosquito bus industry. In 1933, of the 455 mosquito buses, about half operated between

Geylang Road and Tanjong Pagar, 90 along Upper Serangoon Road, 59 along Bukit Timah Road, 46 on the Pasir Panjang route, and 34 on country runs to Seletar and Changi. This meant most buses covered the Municipality—the STC's turf.

Why didn't the Municipality ban all mosquito buses immediately? Because the mosquito buses were not all bad. Like the "annoying" rickshaws, they provided fast, affordable, convenient transport for the working classes, motivating many to relocate from the overcrowded Town to the suburbs of Geylang, Upper Serangoon, and Pasir Panjang.

The Singapore Motor Bus Transport Owners Association—formed in 1928 to give a voice to bus owners and drivers—also worked hard to hold back the inevitable. For four years from 1931, they lobbied against multiple decisions by the Municipal Commission to replace or scrap the mosquito bus fleet, with varying success. Eventually in 1935, despite a last-ditch petition to Governor Sir Shenton Thomas (1879–1962), mosquito buses were banned from all other routes, ending 21 years of operation. The Municipal Ordinance of 1935 decreed that henceforth, only companies could be granted omnibus licences; their buses had to follow fixed routes and pick up or set down passengers at specified bus stops; also, the routes could not compete with those of the STC. This meant that while their buses could still use the same roads as STC vehicles, they could not pick up or drop off passengers. In effect, many now had to ply outside the municipal boundary, where the STC did not operate.

Many owners and drivers headed north into Malaya, where they started afresh in towns such as Penang. The ones who stayed behind formed 12 Chinese bus companies—the start of a new era of motor buses. The dozen fanned out into the rural areas, each serving their own little corner of the island—what was remarkable was how the companies hardly trespassed on each other's turf. They imported new, larger motor buses. The companies are listed below.

Katong–Bedok Bus Service—12 buses, red livery; ran from Katong to Bedok via East Coast Road; route length 7.4 km.

Changi Motor Bus Service—15 buses, red and white livery; covered the length of Changi Road from Geylang Road to Changi Village; 15 km.

Paya Lebar Bus Service—14 buses, yellow and green livery; Route 1: from Geylang Road to Royal Air Force Seletar (finished 1928) via Paya Lebar Road and Yio Chu Kang Road; Route 2: the length of Tampines Road; 11.3 km.

Ponggol Bus Service—six buses, yellow livery; from 5¾ Mile Upper Serangoon Road (Village) to Punggol Village via Upper Serangoon Road and Punggol Road; 9.6 km.

Tay Koh Yat Bus Company—named after its founder Tay Koh Yat (1880–1957); two buses, yellow and white livery; covered MacPherson Road and part of Aljunied Road; 3 km.

Seletar Motor Bus Company—named after Seletar Road; 24 buses, red and black livery; ran from Beach Road to Toa Payoh, Ang Mo Kio, Nee Soon, and Sembawang; 22.5 km.

Green Bus Company—named after its green livery; 35 buses; Route 1: from Queen Street to Johor Bahru, via Bukit Timah Road and Woodlands Road; 24.5 km; Route 2: Queen Street to Lim Chu Kang, through Bukit Timah Road and Choa Chu Kang Road; 27 km.

Jurong Omnibus Service—four buses, green and white livery; covered the length of Jurong Road, which by the 1930s ran from Bukit Timah Village to Tuas Village by the sea; 17 km.

Ngo Hock Motor Bus Company—named after the Hokkien for "Five Blessings" ("Wu Fu" in Mandarin), an auspicious phrase; six buses, green and red livery; ran from Chinatown to Outram Road and Alexandra Road; 7.2 km.

Soon Lee Bus Company—named after the Hokkien for "smoothly" or "successfully" ("Shun Li" in Mandarin), an auspicious name; six buses, yellow and red livery; ran from Chinatown to Ulu Pandan via Tanglin Road and Holland Road; 12.4 km.

Kampong Bahru Bus Service—12 buses, blue and white livery; ran from the southern end of South Bridge Road over Neil Road and Kampong Bahru Road; 2.6 km.

Keppel Bus Company Limited—35 buses, blue livery; covered Keppel Road, Telok Blangah Road, and Pasir Panjang Road; 13 km.

The combined size of their bus fleets was 171.

The STC took advantage of the crackdown on mosquito buses to launch six new routes, serviced by 92 motor buses of its own. By 1937, the STC had 108 trolleybuses and 112 motor buses.

With so many different bus companies now, bus stop signs filled up with colourful labels, one for each company's livery. At the time, passengers identified services according to livery colours, not service numbers, since companies could use the same numbers. In the rural areas, some bus stops or terminals were identified by milestones. The northernmost terminal for the Seletar Motor Bus Company was called 15th Milestone, after the 15th Milestone of Sembawang Road, five miles north of Nee Soon Village.

Municipal efforts to kill the mosquito bus in the 1930s changed the face of public transport in Singapore. Before, driven by profits, trolleybuses and mosquito buses mostly trawled the busiest roads inside the municipal boundary. Only a handful of mosquito buses, rickshaws, and gharries willingly served the rural areas. After the transport reform, the Chinese bus companies were forced to ply the rural areas, covering most trunk roads. For the first time in modern Singapore's history, public transport spread to almost all parts of the island. Bus stops popped up in the most remote of areas. Never mind that waiting times could be up to an hour, or that bus transfers were still required for travel between the rural areas and the Municipality—the spread of bus coverage further hastened the decline of rickshaws and gharries as methods of movement.

WHILE the combined coverage of trolleybuses and buses expanded in reach, the depth of coverage in the busiest parts of the Municipality declined.

Problems emerged along the routes where the mosquitoes had been swatted away. The STC did replace the mosquitoes with their own motor buses, but their strength was significantly weaker. Along the busy Geylang–Tanjong Pagar route, 226 mosquito buses were replaced by just 50 STC motor buses. They were insufficient to handle traffic from the booming suburbs of Geylang, Katong, Serangoon, and Pasir Panjang.

Before the demise of the mosquito bus, trolleybus passengers took for granted that they never had to wait more than two or three minutes for an available trolleybus. They also took for granted that they could get on the first bus—and get seats. Now they were in for an unpleasant surprise. In the morning, between 8.30am and 9am, they could not board the first, second, or even third bus that pulled up at their stop; waiting times increased to 15 or 20 minutes; even if they could board, they could not get seats. They were forced to "strap-hang", the action of standing in a moving vehicle and hanging on to an overhead strap for dear life. The reality of a "rush hour", the unpleasant, stressful, grimy experience of overcrowded public transportation that was to become the hallmark of urban existence, was brought home to them. To add insult to injury, this experience of modernity was repeated in the evening, between 5pm and 5.30pm. It should be noted that these phenomena emerged only after the Municipality had actively intervened in public transport, and cut supply from areas of high demand without ensuring adequate replacements.

A commuter living along the Geylang–Tanjong Pagar route wrote in to *The Singapore Free Press* in July 1935, channelling the frustration and bewilderment of a population forced to adjust to a new experience of movement. In the morning, between 8am and 9am, he had to wait for a third or fourth bus before he could get on.

The earlier ones are packed like cattle trucks, with not even standing room available. In this way I waste from 10 to 15 minutes. When at last I am able to board a bus I usually have to stand for half the journey if I am lucky. If I am unlucky, I have to stand for the whole journey.

Returning in the evening between 4.45 and 5.15 the same thing occurs again, only I have to wait longer, because I will not board a bus unless I obtain a seat, as I do not fancy standing after a day's work.

(On the bus, there) were then 11 people standing and swaying about all over the place. At one moment someone would swing over towards my face and then swing away again. When the bus approached a crossing and the brakes were applied, the strap-hangers would all step back and bump against each other. When turning a corner all those standing would be thrown over towards those sitting on the right or left, as the case might be, and when the bus straightened up again they would surge over in the opposite direction. Of course, with all this motion, one's toes were constantly trodden on.

I would have liked to have smoked a cigarette or read my newspaper. It was impossible to open the paper or light the cigarette on account of the crowded condition of the bus... (When) I pay my fare I should be provided with a seat.

Until the services provide a seat for every passenger, they cannot be considered satisfactory. As things are now, the seats might as well be removed and the buses packed with humanity as close as possible like cattle in a truck.

Legitimate grievances, or self-entitled whingeing? I let the reader decide.

Another commuter even pined for the mosquito bus:

> Whatever might have been the failings of the mosquito bus, we should not forget that in those pre-slump days the bus was fast and cheap and transport needs were amply fulfilled without grousing comments appearing in press columns... The insufficient services in the Serangoon and the Katong districts cannot equal the smooth running provided by the defunct mosquito-buses.

He or she added: "As transport conditions are at present... there is no better alternative to an omnibus journey than a taxi-ride"—a comment that could pass off as being uttered in the present!

The STC also received brickbats for a perceived drop in the quality of service. Complaints included rude drivers and conductors, and buses stopping outside of bus stops, not stopping for passengers despite having space, and not waiting for passengers to board properly before driving off. These were attributed to the arrogance and complacency of a company enjoying a monopoly for too long. Again, inevitable comparisons were drawn with the mosquito buses, which, for all its faults, had served some commuters well:

> It is high time that the monopoly given to the STC was discontinued, because the monopoly enjoyed by the company is the cause of the high-handedness of the STC drivers and conductors... if mosquito buses are allowed to ply for hire I would rather travel by them, because drivers and conductors belonging to smaller bus companies are usually polite and obliging.

The only times the Chinese bus companies could pick up passengers on the STC's turf were when STC workers went on strike. In October 1936, 200 STC drivers and conductors—a quarter of its workforce—refused to work for three days, demanding improvements in working conditions, pay, and benefits. During the strike, the Municipal Commission had no choice but to allow the Chinese bus companies into the Municipality as relief buses. Commuters immediately commended the move:

> How nice it was driving to office this morning through streets unobstructed by green juggernauts (the STC trolleybuses)! And how splendid to see the humble, necessary mosquito craft back again... It took me five minutes less to get to the office. Long live the strike!

It was clear that the STC alone could not handle demand for public transport within the Municipality. Even the municipal commissioners began to change their minds. In May 1939, they discussed the possibility of limited competition on certain trolleybus and bus routes inside the Municipality—in other words, revoking the STC's 30-year monopoly 17 years early. But war clouds were gathering in Europe, so nothing came of this discussion.

FOR TAXI cabs, the main debate through the 1920s and early 1930s was over the installation of taximeters. Experiments of taximeter models were carried out in taxi cabs, but they were never made compulsory. Passengers frequently complained that drivers of cabs without taximeters tried squeezing excessive fares; drivers demanded a dollar for the shortest distances. What was the use of taxi cabs without taximeters, passengers asked? Many preferred cabs with taximeters, so there were taxi stands inside the Town set aside exclusively for such cabs. Locations included Johnston's Pier, Anderson Bridge, Raffles Hotel, and Jardine's Steps. In 1930, there were 527 taxi cabs plying in Singapore.

It was the gradual demise of the mosquito bus from 1933 that spurred further evolution in the taxi cab industry. With a sudden shortfall in public transport, and the STC seemingly unable to adequately cover this shortfall, enterprising taxi cabs stepped up to the plate. Again, it was the Wearne Brothers—the company who gave Singapore its first taxi cabs and its second motor bus service—who led the way forward. One of their companies, Universal Cars Limited, formed a "baby taxi" service in May 1933, comprising 60 Yellow Tops. These were pint-sized Ford Eights with yellow bonnets, each with a capacity of just two or three, and could have been inspired by the successful Yellow Taxis of Hong Kong and Shanghai.[2]

The Yellow Tops set a new standard in taxi service. Focusing on intra-town short-distance travel, they charged just 20 cents for the first mile—half the fare charged by other taxi cabs. Their drivers were Malays donning smart uniforms, and unlike other drivers, they were given a basic salary, with an additional 10 per cent of takings. Two more firsts: passengers were given insurance coverage of up to $5,000 each, and cabs could be booked by telephone—just dial 5484. The Yellow Tops soon gained a reputation for their clean interiors and courteous drivers. Wearne Brothers subsequently exported the Yellow Tops concept to Malayan towns such as Malacca, Kuala Lumpur, and Penang.

Taking the Wearne Brothers' cue, other taxi cab owners began introducing similar small cars onto the streets. They included Willys, Austin Tens, and other baby Fords. To differentiate themselves, fleets had their bonnets painted in various colours—there were red-tops, blue-tops, and brown-tops, adding a splash of colour to the Town's grimy streets.

These smaller, cheaper taxis were an immediate success. They craftily plied the routes where the mosquito buses had been swatted off, much to the relief of residents. However, some baby taxis began taking multiple passengers on the same ride—just as the passing of the by-law in 1922 had encouraged taxi cab drivers to take on multiple passengers, leading to the appearance of mosquito buses! More than 10 years on, it seemed as if history was repeating itself. The municipal commissioners were dismayed. They thought they had solved the mosquito bus "problem", and protected the STC's municipal monopoly; now, the same "problem" looked set to arise again, threatening the STC's monopoly once more.

Throughout 1934, the commissioners discussed what to do about the baby taxis. First, licences granted to light hackney carriages was capped at 550. Then, the commissioners discussed a by-law amendment to prohibit taxis from plying the streets for passengers, restricting them to waiting at taxi stands instead—which would have mortified cab drivers. Eventually, in January 1935, a by-law was added for "hackney carriages", which covered taxi cabs and baby taxis. It decreed that if the cab was not registered as a motor bus, it could not take up passengers "at any point on, or within 100 yards of any route upon which motor omnibuses or trolleybuses ply, except at a public stand". Taxi cabs and baby taxis could still ply the streets, and travel on STC routes, but now, it was almost impossible to steal the STC's passengers, or act like a mosquito bus. Once again, the STC's monopoly was safe, and once again, it was clear that the authorities would try their best to protect the STC from free market competition, at the expense of transport choices for commuters.

Nevertheless, baby taxis continued growing in number. In 1934, there were 164 baby taxis, then 206 in 1935, and 282 in 1936. Their growth in numbers was a consequence of the STC not fully exploiting its municipal monopoly.

THE NEW KING OF THE ROADS
IN 1918, the rickshaw was still Singapore's most popular form of private transport. By 1941, it had relinquished its position to the motor car. Sanctioned by the government, the motor car became the new king of the roads, and it has remained so ever since.

From Buckley's coffee grinder of 1896, motor cars rapidly progressed in technology and form, becoming more comfortable to drive and ride, improving in suspension, performance, and mileage, and having bonnets and windscreens attached to protect occupants from the elements. Windscreen wipers first appeared on cars in 1922. Cars also became cheaper—by almost 10 times over 30 years. In 1896, a car would have set someone back by £1,600 ($13,714). By 1921, a Morris Cowley—manufactured by British motor vehicle manufacturer Morris Motors—cost just £525; by 1926 its price had plunged further to £170 ($1,457).

In 1917, there were about 1,000 motor cars in Singapore, quadrupling to 4,000 in just four years. By 1930, there were 6,300 cars, and by 1941, there were 10,848. Meanwhile, the number of public rickshaws declined, from 9,047 in 1926, to 6,764 in 1930, and just 3,586 in 1938.

The rich and famous—from the governor and the municipal commissioners at the top, down to office managers and assistant managers—traded in their rickshaws for motor cars. And it wasn't just the Europeans acquiring this new status symbol—rich Asians did, too. The Chinese acquired the best cars, outdoing the Europeans in showing off. Many did not drive their own vehicles. They hired syces, who were usually Malay, Javanese or Boyanese; some were former gharry operators.

The reign of the motor car was buttressed by speed. The first cars of 1896 could go no faster than 18 miles an hour (29 km/h); by the 1930s, they could clock up to 50 miles an hour (80 km/h). With speed came impunity. One of the earliest mentions in a Singapore newspaper of a "hit-and-run" incident involving a motor car was in 1920:

> ...(There) comes to our knowledge now another instance where there was a collision, fortunately not dangerous, but where also the offender drove off without making any attempt to offer either assistance or apology. It is this aspect of motoring offences which is more reprehensible even than the actual offence of dangerous driving, and something should be done to stop it... It is the knowledge of practical freedom from detection which makes the motor car driver, who smashes and drives away, so ready to leave the victims to their fate...

Newspaper reports throughout the 1920s and 1930s identified a panoply of traffic problems, most brought on or exacerbated by motor vehicles: road-hogging; cutting across the flow of traffic; travelling on the wrong side of the road; overtaking hazardously; rounding corners and bends at high speeds; switching lanes without warning (motor vehicles had no indicator lights at the time); excessive horning; skidding after rain; indiscriminate parking and the loading and unloading of vehicles, causing congestion.

These problems persisted for years because traffic policing and punishments remained lax. Many offences were not caught or reported. The Traffic Office had a strength of just 161 in 1939—not sufficient to patrol the Municipality, let alone the rural areas. For offences that reached the courts, most earned the offender only a small fine. For example, in 1934, Noelle Frantle was learning to drive, so she drove a motor car without a licence at the junction of Oxley Road and Tank Road. For that, she was fined just $2—and was subsequently allowed to pass her driving test. In 1923, an unnamed driver took to the wheel of a motor bus without a licence, smashed a rickshaw and knocked down its puller along New Bridge Road, ran into a five-foot-way, and broke a parapet. The punishment? A $40 fine and no jail time!

Yet, despite the modest size of the Traffic Office, the number of recorded traffic offences was remarkably high for the number of vehicles in Singapore. In 1926, 855 licences were suspended and 89 revoked—one significant offence for every eight motor vehicles in Singapore. In 1927, there were 13,724 traffic cases, or three cases for every four motor vehicles and rickshaws on the island. In 1934, the number of traffic cases that went to court actually exceeded the number of motor vehicles and rickshaws on the island: 14,602 cases to 14,000 vehicles. Yet, just $47,958 in fines were collected, or $3.28 per case. Throughout the 1920s and 1930s, the Traffic Department had to deal with between 10,000 and 19,000 traffic cases a year. In 1933, a new Registry of Vehicles building opened in Middle Road, replacing the 34-year-old, "small and dingy" building that had debuted in 1899 as the Hackney Carriage and Jinrikisha Department. The new building was four times larger than its predecessor, and had "the most modern courtroom in Singapore", with a capacity of 150, to handle the huge volume of traffic cases—1,300 to 1,600 a month.

Motor vehicles brought death more than any other method of movement in Singapore's history. In 1922, 29 people were killed and 245 injured by motor vehicles; the toll for all other methods of movement was only three deaths and six injuries. In March 1937, a *Straits Times* article screamed "15 killed in 23 days"; more than 100 were hurt over the same period. The most accident-prone danger zones in Singapore lay in the heart of the Town, and along trunk roads leading out of the Town. One such "traffic disgrace" identified in 1937 was Bukit Timah Road, "a narrow road, a main traffic artery, cluttered up with bicycles, tricycles, pole coolies, huge lorries and fast-moving car traffic. It's a miracle there are so few fatal accidents on this road." More hazardous roads were named by the Traffic Department in 1938: New Bridge Road, which was "badly-lit and... crowded by poorly-educated pedestrians", Victoria Street, and Middle Road; Grove Road, a "wide, well-paved road", was "often an invitation to speeding".

Even the governor was not spared from motor accidents. In 1892, Governor Sir Cecil Clementi Smith's horse carriage was damaged in an accident with two rickshaws. Forty-five years later, in

November 1937, Governor Thomas' Daimler collided with a Ford V-8 as it was turning from Grange Road into Orchard Road on the way back to Government House. Both cars were driven by syces, and suffered slight damage. Just five weeks later, a Chevrolet allegedly stolen by three British soldiers crashed into the rear of another of the governor's cars at the junction of North Bridge Road and Stamford Road. This time, only his syce was in the car, and he was unhurt.

The proliferation in motor cars did not just impact patterns of movement, it also transformed the urban landscape. Parking—especially in the commercial quarters of Battery Road, Raffles Place, and Collyer Quay—became a headache. With almost no laws on parking, roadsides and vacant plots of land swiftly filled up in the mornings as office hours began, and emptied only after workers knocked off. A *Singapore Free Press* article in 1925 reported: "Raffles (Place) has fallen out of all proportion to the number of vehicles now able to use the centre as a parking ground, the fountain in Battery Road has been deprived of its border of trees, but the cars still come."

Parking became a concern for urban planners. Dedicated car parks appeared from the 1920s. In 1927, vacant land within the Telok Ayer Reclamation Ground was set aside for a covered car park, complete with telephone and refuelling facilities, a lot going for $10 a month. The following year, Collyer Quay got its own car park with a capacity for 150 cars, and in 1933, another car park opened along Orchard Road. By the 1930s, the garden with flame-of-the-forest trees in the centre of Raffles Place had disappeared, replaced by a car park filled with cars.

Raffles Place, sometime in the 1930s. The august square was now a glorified car park, although there was still space for rickshaws and horse carriages. (Source: The New York Public Library Digital Collections)

REINING IN A BEAST

THE AUTHORITIES took years to muster solutions to traffic problems wrought by the motor car. Solutions included the drawing of lines on roads, the installation of traffic lights, attempts to impose speed limits, and reducing the populations of slower vehicles.

In 1926, the Municipal Commission tried painting white lines on roads indicating where one lane began and ended, to guide vehicles travelling in opposite directions; and also at traffic junctions, to mark where vehicles should stop for passing traffic.

The experiment was conducted on three busy roads. Cross lines were painted on Stamford Road at all intersections to "indicate the limit to which vehicles might advance while traffic was proceeding along the relative cross street". At the junction of Orchard Road and Orange Grove Road, white lines were painted to indicate the centre of the two roads. However, motorists were not used to the lines; they were "not generally recognised, and the observance of them is not always insisted on by the police... white lines mean nothing to most drivers". The early experiment was a failure.

In the same year, N. L. Lindon, the Traffic Department's Assistant Superintendent of Police, came up with a novel idea to increase the effectiveness of policemen stationed at busy junctions: each man was given rattan "traffic wings" to wear. Now they had four arms instead of two, allowing them to better direct traffic. In subsequent years, other forms of traffic control at cross and T-junctions appeared in the Town: hand-operated Stop and Go signals, electrical hand-operated light signals, and automatic light signals. These were the first traffic lights in Singapore.

Into the 1930s, Empress Place had traffic lights controlled by a policeman stationed at the base of the pole; the junction of Stamford Road and North Bridge Road had an electrical control column; a Stop and Go signal was installed at the junction of Tanjong Pagar Road and Keppel Road. There was no coordinated system of traffic lights though, in which the changing of lights at one junction synchronised with the changing of lights at another junction for optimal traffic flow.

Imposing speed limits proved far more difficult. A debate over speed limits raged from 1908 into the 1930s. In 1908, a letter writer to *The Straits Times* called on people to trust the "honour and good sense of motorists to use the public roads with decency". During a 1914 Legislative Council meeting, a member maintained that "it should be a matter of judgement when occasion arose to decide what driving was dangerous instead of relying on a speed limit". In a similar meeting six years later, no less than the Inspector-General of Police opposed speed limits because of a lack of speed traps, and difficulties in accurately measuring speeds; to him, it was better to "attend to offences which, irrespective of speed, really cause danger to life and limb". To these detractors, the problem was not speed per se, but ignorance of the rules of the road.

However, the chorus of voices in favour of speed limits was louder. Dozens of letters and editorials appeared in local newspapers calling for curbs on speed—from members of the public, to legislative council members, car rental firm proprietor C. W. Abrams, and Rural Board Chairman W. S. Ebden. Hence, speed limits began appearing in Singapore by the mid-1920s.

The larger motor vehicles were targeted first. In 1923, a committee of municipal commissioners recommended that the speed of motor lorries should be fixed at 10–15 miles an hour (16–24 km/h) depending on tonnage. However, nothing more was heard of these recommendations; that said, a 12-mile-an-hour (19 km/h) speed limit on lorries was imposed outside the municipal boundary by 1927, apparently to prolong the quality of rural roads. By 1925, roads inside the Botanic Gardens had a speed limit of 15 miles an hour (24 km/h)—even though motorists reportedly exceeded it frequently. The same year, the Singapore Traction Ordinance also set the speed limit for trolleybuses at 25 miles an hour (40 km/h). Again, this did not stop trolleybuses from busting the limit, clocking 30 miles an hour (48 km/h) and rounding corners on three wheels! In 1927, the municipal commissioners approved a by-law decreeing the maximum speed of motor buses at 20 miles an hour (32 km/h). And in 1936, legislation was passed by Governor Thomas to impose a 30-mile-an-hour (48-km/h) speed limit on lorries island-wide.

Through it all, motor cars were free to speed. Even for vehicles restricted by speed limits, lax enforcement allowed many to get away. The rudimentary technology of the day—timing motorists with stop watches—made it hard for the Traffic Office to catch and charge offenders. In 1935, the police laid speed traps for motorists along rural roads such as Bukit Timah Road and Woodlands Road, where speeding was rife. Motorists who drove at "dangerous" speeds when passing through villages were booked. A private motor car was charged for clocking 36 miles per hour (58 km/h) zooming by Bukit Panjang Village. However, it was up to individual policemen to decide what speed was "dangerous". Punishments were also light—the aforementioned offender was fined only $4.

As it became more difficult for faster motor vehicles to share the roads with slower vehicles, the Municipal Commission sought to cut down on the latter—it was in their personal interests to do so. The first obvious target was the rickshaw, which they regarded as an outdated vehicle from a bygone era. In 1927, the commissioners decreed that for every two old rickshaws scrapped, only one new rickshaw could be licensed. As a result, the number of rickshaws dropped by almost two-thirds from 1927 to 1938, from 10,000 to 3,586. However, an outright ban was out of the question, as thousands of livelihoods were at stake, and for the lower classes, there was no alternative that was as cheap over short distances—it was half as expensive as the motor taxi in 1932. Tourists to Singapore also preferred the rickshaw as pullers remained a repository of local knowledge.

The decline of bullock carts and gharries was swifter. For the former, one and two-ton motor lorries took their place for transporting goods—and even serving as funeral hearses. Once numbering 2,701 in 1916, only 226 bullock carts were counted just 18 years later in 1934. Conversely, while in 1913 there were just 35 lorries, in 1934 there were 1,061—almost five times the number of carts. Meanwhile, there were 1,500 horse-drawn vehicles in 1917; by 1934, there were only 19 gharries left. Two gharry stands survived at Raffles Place and the Victoria Memorial Hall. The best gharries were well-painted, the coachwork good, with rubber tyres, but they did not venture far out of the Town; at most, a radius of three miles (five km) from the General Post Office, by now in the Fullerton Building, which officially opened in 1928 on the site of the old General Post Office. Once common in the Town, they were now a novelty.

Tricycles and bicycles were far more common. Between 1931 and 1940, the tricycle population grew a dozen times, from 546 to close to 7,000. The cheap vehicles were popular for transporting people and goods for small businesses, and they had taken the place of handcarts and even rickshaws in the rural areas. Not that the Municipal Commission did not try to hold back their growth. In the mid-1930s, tricycles were made to carry licence plates for easier tracking, the tax on commercial tricycles was raised from $2 to $6, and their numbers were capped at 7,000.

Bicycles were not spared either. While they had been introduced into Singapore in the 1860s, their popularity only surged in the 1930s. In 1936, the Municipal Commission decreed that bicycle owners had to register with the Traffic Office for $1 a year; in return, bicycles would be fitted with number plates, like motorcycles. By mid-1937, 50,000 bicycles were registered, leading some to suggest that Singapore was now the "bicycle capital" of the British Empire. Numbers were never restricted, probably because it was the only form of private transport the working class could easily afford; it was also one of the cheapest and easiest means of getting around in rural areas. By 1941, there were 120,000 registered bicycles; roughly one in seven persons owned a bicycle.

One vehicle introduced elsewhere in Malaya never had a chance in Singapore: the pedal rickshaw, or pedal ricksha, a cross between a rickshaw and a bicycle. By pedalling instead of pulling, it was easier for pullers to move their customers; pullers could now travel "three or four times" the distance with the same effort. It was patented in 1912 in the Straits Settlements and the FMS by an aspiring businessman named Christopher Pilkington. He tried raising up to $400,000 for a new company with 100 pedal rickshaws, but the venture never found its wheels. The chance for pedal rickshaws to break into the Singapore market, at a time when rickshaws were still popular and motor taxis were just getting off the ground, was lost. The pedal rickshaw appeared 20 years later, in 1936, in Penang.

Thereafter, the Municipal Commission discussed the possibility of introducing it in Singapore "as an improvement over the rickshaw". However, after the Traffic Office and the Registry of Vehicles tested one in the streets, the vehicle was deemed "not suitable" for public hire—the authorities were reluctant to have them fight motor vehicles for space on the roads. The pedal rickshaw appeared in Penang, Kuala Lumpur, Bangkok, and Shanghai, but never Singapore.

WE HAVE seen many official measures attempting to impose some form of order and control in Singapore's streets. Even the young were not spared. The "Safety First" education programme was rolled out for schoolchildren in 1937; in two years, 60,000 children in 452 schools were taught the dangers of jaywalking, and the need to be careful when riding bicycles. But the traffic chaos persisted. A more systematic approach was needed. In December 1937, Governor Thomas appointed a committee "to consider the present traffic conditions in the Town of Singapore including parking and the trial of traffic offences and to make recommendations for their improvement". The seven-strong committee was led by Sir George Trimmer, chairman of the Straits Settlements Harbour Boards.

The Trimmer Committee first carried out a comprehensive census of vehicles in Singapore for the year of 1937. For motor vehicles, they counted 9,382 motor cars and buses (excluding those owned by the STC), 2,753 motor lorries, and 620 motorcycles; for animal and human-powered vehicles, they counted 52,000 bicycles, 6,553 tricycles, 4,707 rickshaws, 1,332 hand and bullock carts, and nine horse-drawn vehicles. All these for a population of 603,200, according to the

1936 census. Never were there so many vehicles and vehicle types plying the roads. However, the committee noted that "most of the roads in Singapore were planned when less than half the volume of traffic now using them was in existence".

The Committee presented its recommendations to the Legislative Council in 1938. At least some were followed through, heralding a new era of traffic management in Singapore.

First, a dedicated Traffic Court was set up in July 1938 to try offenders in the grounds of the former Sepoy Lines Police Station along Cantonment Road. The following year, in 1939, the Singapore Traffic Advisory Committee was formed to advise the authorities on traffic issues. It introduced regulations giving the traffic police greater powers over errant road users. They included powers of arrest for offences that previously warranted only summons, such as illegal parking, failing to conform to a traffic signal, and jaywalking.

Also, in March 1939, a no-hooting ban was implemented in the Municipality between 11pm and 6am, and a "silence zone" around Raffles Place over nine hours of the working day. That November, a Road Traffic Bill was passed to align traffic laws across Malaya and Singapore. Aspiring drivers were issued with a provisional "learner" or "L" licence to differentiate them from certified drivers; a law was also passed to deal directly with motorists who drove under the influence of drugs or alcohol. In 1940, the government agreed on a speed limit of 30 miles an hour (48 km/h) for most of the Municipality, with plans for implementation in the near future.

Some road infrastructure made their debuts. The first coordinated system of traffic lights was introduced in Orchard Road in October 1938, operated from the Central Telephone Exchange. Unlike traffic lights elsewhere, the changing of lights at one intersection affected the changing of lights at another intersection. These enabled motorists to travel at a steady speed of 25 miles an hour (40 km/h) even during the rush hour. By early 1939, a similar system was introduced in Stamford Road.

Roundabouts—first introduced in Paris in 1901—were recommended for traffic intersections "where the volume of traffic was not large enough to require control by traffic lights or policemen". At least three opened by 1940. One was at the confluence of Tank Road and River Valley Road; another at the meeting point of Paterson Road, Paterson Hill, Grange Road, and Irwell Bank Road (named Grange Circus in 1950); a third at the convergence of Serangoon Road, Upper Serangoon Road, MacPherson Road, Kolam Ayer (Malay for "Pond Water") Lane, and Alkaff Avenue (rebuilt in 1953 and renamed Woodsville Circus after nearby Woodsville Road).

Other recommendations were not taken up, though. They included pavements and traffic crossings for pedestrians; dedicated lanes for bicycles; one-way road systems for congested, narrow two-way roads such as Battery Road and Dhoby Ghaut; and restrictions on street parking in the Town. At the time, motorists could park their cars for free in the middle or by the side of busy roads such as Raffles Place, Collyer Quay, and Robinson Road.

Despite some progress in traffic management, punishments remained lax up to the end of 1941. How much jail time did motor truck driver Tang Kong get for knocking down and killing rickshaw puller Tan Moi Kow, and injuring the rickshaw's two passengers, along Irwell Bank Road in 1937? None. He was fined $80.

BY THE end of 1941, the authorities were still far from reining in Singapore's transport chaos. They did implement lasting features and laws we take for granted today, such as synchronised traffic lights and traffic safety education. But these were not enough. The top priority of the authorities was not to protect the safety of pedestrians or road users, but to safeguard the position of the motor car as the number one method of movement in Singapore. This was clear from the absence of political will in implementing dedicated bicycle lanes and pavements for pedestrians—they would have taken away precious road space from motor cars. Furthermore, punishments for traffic violations were far from strict, emboldening many a motorist to act as if he or she owned the roads; instead, traffic safety education targeted pedestrians and cyclists first, exhorting them to watch out for traffic, subtly reinforcing the message that if they got into an accident, they were partly at fault. Finally, while there were restrictions on the number of slower vehicles such as bullock carts, rickshaws, and tricycles, no caps were ever imposed on motor cars, even though they killed more road users than any other vehicle. The lesson? The history of movement of a city at any point in its history will be heavily influenced by the method of movement favoured and used by the authorities at that point in time.

With the age of the engine entrenched, patterns and experiences of movement changed. More people could travel all over the island on cars, not just the rich, allowing them to know the land better. Slower methods of movement in the 19th century meant a slower pace of life, ensuring that almost everyone within the European ruling class knew each other; now, the pace of life was faster, increasing the emotional distances among people. Also, 19th-century social dinners were taken early because horse-drawn carriages and rickshaws took time to take people home before dark. Now, with cars and taxis guided by street lighting, dinners and social events ended later into the night. Customs and ways of life evolved with new methods of movement.

OF ENGLISH TOWNS AND MALAY NAMES

FUELLED BY the motor car, the expansion of suburbia and construction of roads continued between 1918 and 1941.

Ninety per cent of the *tuans besar* and municipal commissioners lived along Orchard Road. New suburbs for the wealthy arose along channels of movement, such as Nassim Road and Anderson Road in Tanglin District, Holland Road and Pasir Panjang Road on the western edge of the municipal boundary, and Grove Road and Tanjong Katong Road on the eastern edge. Grove Road was widened in the 1920s to accommodate heavier motor traffic between the Town and Tanjong Katong; meanwhile, the old Confederate Estate was developed into a housing estate, and the housing estate and its main road, Confederate Road, were renamed Joo Chiat after Hokkien business magnate Chew Joo Chiat (1857–1926).

The municipal boundary was further extended in 1928, mostly to the east. The extensions took in the land around 5¾ Milestone Upper Serangoon Village, Siglap District (including Joo Chiat and Frankel Estate, named after Lithuanian Jewish immigrant Abraham Frankel (1852–1928)), and parts of the districts of Paya Lebar, Bedok, and Ulu Bedok.

Inside the Municipality, there remained large areas of plantations, farms, bush, and marshes. At least six areas were developed in the 1920s and 1930s—Pek Kio, the Jalan Besar–Lavender

Street area, Tanjong Katong, Siglap, Tiong Bahru, and Kreta Ayer. Within these suburbs, new roads shared similar etymologies, commemorating significant world events, evoking images of another time and place, or honouring the contributions of community leaders—giving them unique identities.

Just north of the Race Course, the low-lying land surrounding a lake named Tasek Utara, Malay for "North Lake", was drained from 1921. New roads were named after English towns and counties such as Essex, Derbyshire, Suffolk, Norfolk, Shrewsbury, Carlisle, and Cambridge. Europeans and Eurasians moved to country houses there, turning it into another "Little England". But this "Little England" flooded very often. That contributed to the eventual decision in 1933 to uproot the 91-year-old Race Course and move it northwest, outside the municipal boundary, off the 6th Milestone of Bukit Timah Road. The Europeans did not mind the new, rural location as they had motor cars instead of horse carriages now. The old Race Course was converted into a sports field and renamed Farrer Park after former Municipal President Farrer.

The Chinese, however, knew "Little England" by other names. To the southwest of "Little England", Kampong Java Road ran by a canal, the Kampong Java Canal. There were two bridges over the canal, one white, one red. The former was known as Pek Kio, Hokkien for "White Bridge"; the latter, Ang Kio, or "Red Bridge" in English; Ang Kio was also known as Jambatan Merah in Malay. While the place names Ang Kio and Jambatan Merah have been lost in time, Pek Kio has persisted; also, today, there is still a red bridge under the Kampong Java Flyover, and two white bridges near the junction of Hertford Road and Kampong Java Road.

To the southeast of Pek Kio, the land bounded by Serangoon Road, Lavender Street, and the Rochor River was covered by mangrove swamps and the settlements of Kampong Kapor and Kampong Boyan. The main road that ran through the marsh, Jalan Besar—Malay for "Big Road"—was a favourite haunt of hunters searching for ducks, snipe, fish, mud lobsters, and snakes. Indian dhobies also used the water for laundry services.

By 1926, much of the swamps were reclaimed with rubbish, and ash from a municipal incinerator. The settlement of Kampong Boyan was resettled, and the hunting grounds and dhobies disappeared. The Municipal Commission then decided to commemorate the Great War by naming new roads built around Jalan Besar after prominent battle sites, or generals and admirals who had served in the war. Flanders, Marne, Mons, Somme, and Verdun roads were named after Western Front battlegrounds where hundreds of thousands of young men died. Falkland and Jutland roads were named after naval battle locations. Allenby, Beatty, Foch, Fisher (renamed Tyrwhitt after three years), French, Hamilton, Horne, Jellicoe, Kitchener, Maude, Petain, Plumer, Sturdee, and Townshend roads were named after British and French generals and admirals. They were tributes to a very traumatic period endured by Singapore's colonial master and her trusted ally. The only exception was King George's Avenue, which was named after Britain's King George V (who already had Prince of Wales Road off the 5th Milestone of Bukit Timah Road named after him in 1912). These roads were named over 1928 and 1929.

Some suburbs were built by an urban improvement department formed in 1927. This was the Singapore Improvement Trust (SIT), tasked with solving housing and sanitation problems caused by overpopulation in the Town. The SIT tore down houses unfit for habitation and resettled the occupants. The SIT had its origins in 1906, when the government appointed W. J. R. Simpson, a professor of hygiene at King's College, London, to study sanitary conditions in Singapore. The 1907 Simpson Report argued that poor housing conditions contributed to the spread of disease and death in the Town; Simpson suggested a town plan with building and land use regulations (none had existed since the time of Raffles), reordering the built environment through reconstruction work, and introducing back lanes and open spaces in the Town. None of these materialised. However, after acute housing shortages in 1917, a commission revisited these issues; the resultant Housing Commission Report of 1918 suggested an improvement trust to carry out Simpson's recommendations. Nine more years passed before legislation birthed the SIT.

Tiong Bahru Estate was the SIT's first housing project from 1926, located west of Pearl's Hill and Outram Road. A kampung, Kampong Tiong Bahru, made way for the estate, although the cemeteries around it were untouched. Burial Ground Road was lengthened to Alexandra Road and renamed Tiong Bahru Road. Bucking the trend, roads inside the estate commemorated Chinese pioneers. Hence, there were Lim Liak Street, Kim Cheng Street, Moh Guan Terrace, Yong Siak Street, Eng Watt Street, Eng Hoon Street, Seng Poh Road, Guan Chuan Street, Chay Yan Street (after Tan Chay Yan), Peng Nguan Street (after Lim Nee Soon's father Lim Peng Nguan), and Tiong Poh Road. These were the names of business magnates, the owners of rice mills, steamships, tin mines, and tapioca farms. Amongst these roads arose almost 30 blocks of Art Deco-style flats, numbered 55 to 82; they were two-to-five storeys high, hence the Chinese called the estate Gor Lau ("Five Storeys"). From this time, the word "estate" began to be associated with SIT housing projects—rather than plantations such as Confederate Estate.

The SIT's work was not restricted to outside the Town. Inside Kreta Ayer, in an area bounded by Smith Street, Trengganu Street, Sago Street, and New Bridge Road, the SIT erected four-storey Art Deco tenement blocks, each comprising shops on the first floor, and flats above with communal dining rooms, kitchens, and laundry facilities. These were completed by 1940. They were fresh architectural sights in an overcrowded, decaying urban landscape.

However, the SIT struggled to keep pace with a burgeoning population. From the mid-1930s, many lower-class Chinese moved from the Town to fringe areas surrounding the Town, following the arterial roads, similar to how the affluent classes moved out of the Town several decades before. Some fringe areas saw population increases of 50 per cent, a mushrooming of tightly-packed, wooden and palm-thatched huts. The authorities labelled such unauthorised, unregulated "urban kampungs" as "squatters" and "slums", presenting them as backward, dangerous, lawless, and unsanitary. This "problem" would only grow.

Outside the Municipality, one new settlement arose in the Paya Lebar and Ulu Bedok districts in 1929 due to the efforts of Mohamed Eunos Abdullah (1876–1933), a news editor, the first Malay member of both the Municipal Commission and the Legislative Council, and a progenitor of 20th-century Malay nationalism in Singapore. In 1926, he founded the Kesatuan Melayu Singapura (KMS), or Singapore Malay Union, Singapore's first Malay political association; KMS worked for the socioeconomic progress of the Malays. The following year, Eunos lobbied the government for land to be set aside for Singapore's Malays (numbering 65,014 in 1931) to preserve their traditional ways of life. Many Malays had been hit by rising property prices in the Town, and were forced to subsist in substandard rental housing. Thanks to the efforts of him and his KMS colleagues, the government raised $300,000 to purchase 620 acres of undeveloped land from the Frankel family east of Perseverance Estate. This became the Malay Settlement and Kampong Melayu, the second place officially set aside for Malays in Singapore's modern history—the first being Kampong Glam in 1822.

Subsequently, Eunos' contributions were commemorated by the naming of the approach road from Changi Road to Kampong Melayu, Jalan Eunos; Kampong Melayu was also renamed Kampong Eunos. As for roads inside the Malay Settlement, some were named after Eunos' colleagues in the KMS—Jalan Ambo Sooloh after businessman Haji Ambo Sooloh (1891–1963), and Jalan Engku Kadir after Tengku Kadir, a descendant of Sultan Ali Iskandar Shah. Others reflected a rural theme—Jalan Ladang ("Farm Road"), Jalan Singa ("Lion Road"), Jalan Punai ("Green Pigeon Road"), and Jalan Rimau ("Tiger Road"). In a British and Chinese-dominated toponymic landscape, the Malay Settlement was an island of Malay-ness, commemorating Malay attempts to organise themselves socially, economically, politically.

SHIFTING TRACKS, COMPLETING RINGS

AS SINGAPORE'S population grew, even existing channels of movement could be altered by urban development. In 1932, part of the Federated Malay States Railway (FMSR) was shifted to the west to accommodate urban growth—an unprecedented event in Singapore's history of movement.

When the railway was built in 1903, much of the stretch from Tank Road to Bukit Timah Village was sparsely developed. This changed over a quarter of a century. The railway line—and most of its 55 gate crossings and 23 public level crossings—became a "serious obstruction" to urban development and the laying down of roads for motor traffic. Furthermore, the government had expected residents between Tank Road and Bukit Timah to rely on railway trains as suburban transport. Instead, trolleybuses and motor buses did most of the work. By the 1920s, passengers travelling within Singapore formed only a small part of ticket receipts, as compared to cargo and passengers moving into and from Malaya. If the railway was removed, residents would not miss it.

In September 1928, the municipal commissioners and officials from the FMSR met to discuss "the railway deviation". They estimated the cost to be a million dollars, and another $430,000 to remove level crossings and bridges. It would be an expensive but necessary venture for the future of the Municipality. Unconventional, too—no other major urban centre in the world had shifted its main railway line just three decades into the line's existence!

The deviation would be 9¼ miles (15 km) long, hugging the relatively more undeveloped, western periphery of the Municipality. The existing stations of Pasir Panjang, Borneo Wharf, People's Park, Singapore, Newton, Cluny Road, Holland Road, and Bukit Timah would have to close. One commissioner suggested that the new railway terminus be located at Hill Street, but his colleagues eventually decided on a plot of land in Tanjong Pagar between Spottiswoode Park and Keppel Road, on what were mangrove swamps in

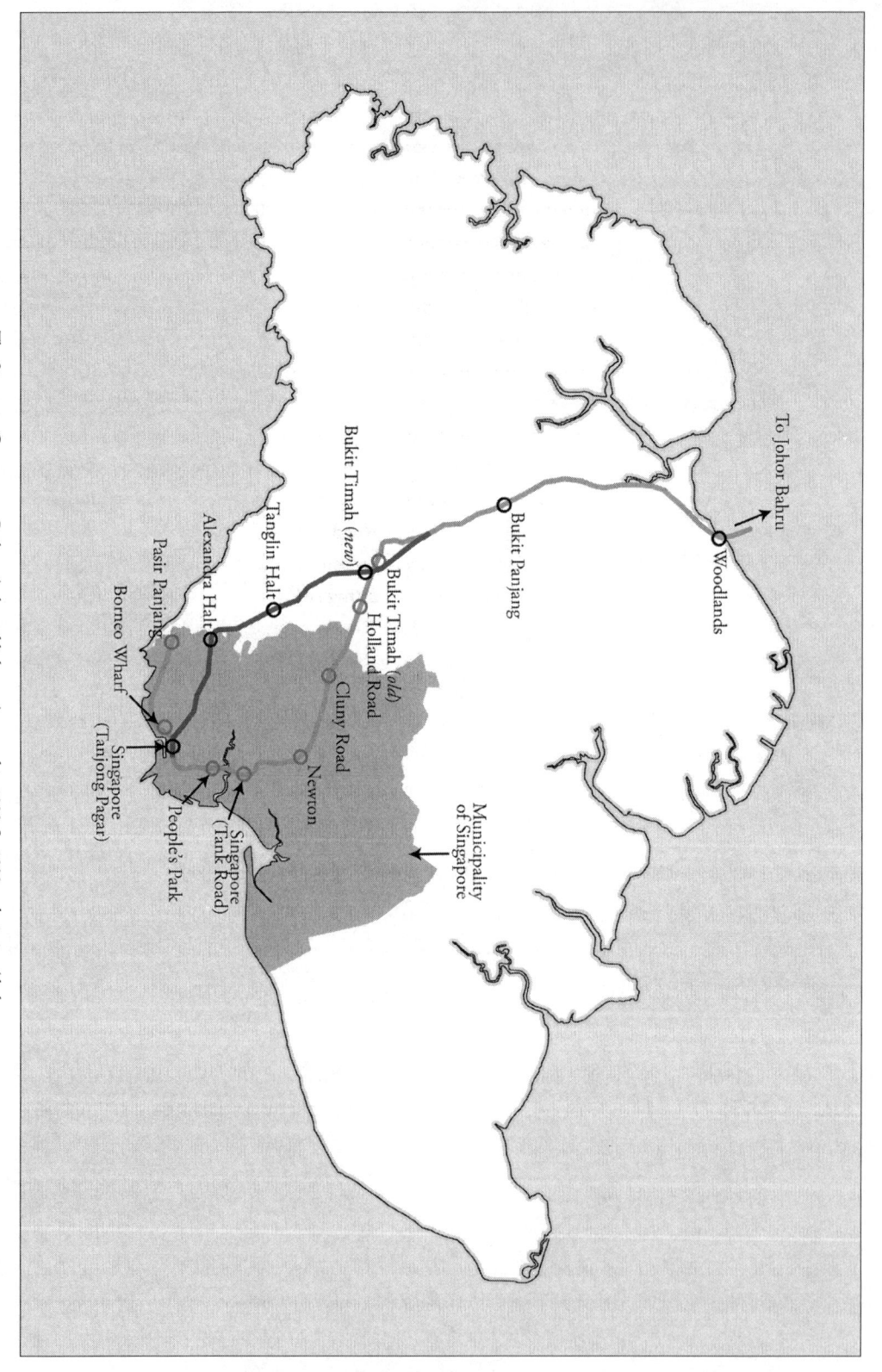

The Singapore Government Railway (coloured light grey) opened in 1903. In 1932, a deviation (dark grey) was built to allow urban and road development in the Municipality of Singapore to proceed without impediment. For this deviation, eight railway stations were replaced by four new ones. (Source: Eisen Teo)

the 1840s. From Singapore Station, trains would proceed past the cemeteries of Tiong Bahru to a new station next to Alexandra Road, on the edge of the municipal boundary, opposite the Alexandra Brickworks, Singapore's first modern brickyard owned by the Borneo Company; since trains halted at the station, it was called Alexandra Halt. From there, trains would proceed to Tanglin Halt Station, again named as such because trains halted there; however, the choice of the place name "Tanglin" is curious because Tanglin Halt lay outside Tanglin District and was nowhere near Tanglin Road. Finally, the railway would cross Buona Vista Road, and Holland Road twice, before pulling into a new Bukit Timah Station, a short distance away from its predecessor.

Work on the deviation started on 11 June 1929 and took nearly three years. The last train pulled out of Tank Road on 2 May 1932, the deviation opened the following day, and the old tracks were removed.

The Tanjong Pagar Railway Station was the jewel in the crown of the FMSR. It had four covered platforms, the longest at 365 metres, which could accommodate the longest trains at that time. The station building was designed by D. S. Petrovich, a Serbian architect with local architectural firm Swan and McLaren. Petrovich had been inspired by the Helsinki Railway Station in Finland, which was completed in 1914.

Alexandra Halt and Tanglin Halt stations did not last long. The former closed less than two years after it opened, on 20 March 1934; the latter, on 31 March 1939, as there were too few passengers using the stations to justify holding back cross-island trips. While the place name "Alexandra Halt" subsequently disappeared, "Tanglin Halt" survived—Tanglin Halt Road and Tanglin Halt Close would be built nearby in the early 1960s.

The railway deviation of 1932 had implications not just for the railway system in Singapore. An old tree that falls in a dense forest opens a space in the canopy for new trees. Similarly, the removal of railway tracks inside the Municipality freed up space for new roads and patterns of urban development. As soon as plans for the deviation were finalised in 1928, work began on new roads around the old line, and once the line closed, these roads opened.

Before 1932, there was a level crossing at Orchard Road, and another near Newton Railway Station, at the junction of Scotts Road, Newton Road, and Kampong Java Road. In 1932, these crossings were removed, and the junction was converted into a roundabout called Newton Circus—possibly Singapore's first roundabout. Instead of a crossing, which disrupted traffic, the Newton roundabout now promoted smoother traffic.

From the roundabout, a new arterial road was laid down past Emerald Hill and Fort Canning Hill to Orchard Road and River Valley Road, running over land once occupied by railway tracks. Since it ended at Clemenceau Bridge over the Singapore River, which had opened in 1922 and was named after a visiting French wartime premier Georges Benjamin Clemenceau (1841–1929), it was named Clemenceau Avenue. This channel of movement became a fresh route for travellers between Bukit Timah Road and the Town south of the Singapore River, allowing them to avoid the Town's congested roads.

The railway deviation also elevated the importance of Dunearn Road. It was completed in 1928 from Chancery Lane to the municipal boundary, parallel to Bukit Timah Road and the railway tracks. It was named after Dunearn House, an old mansion later converted to Oldham Hall, part of the present-day Anglo-Chinese School (Barker Road) campus; "Dunearn" could have originated from Scotland. Before the railway deviation, Dunearn Road only served an area north of the railway line; thereafter, 15 level crossings between Holland Road and Newton Road were removed. Now, it was possible to lengthen Dunearn Road to between Holland Road and Newton Circus. The land north of Bukit Timah Road could now be opened up, and Dunearn Road became a trunk road as important as Bukit Timah Road. Newton Circus became a key transport landmark. Seven roads in all directions—Bukit Timah Road, Dunearn Road, Newton Road, Keng Lee Road, Kampong Java Road, Clemenceau Avenue North, and Scotts Road—still meet at the roundabout; no other roundabout in Singapore's history connects so many roads.

After the tracks were removed, the government kept the strip of land between the Bukit Timah Canal and Dunearn Road as open space. Flower gardens were planted. Over time, both the canal and Dunearn Road were widened, swallowing up the gardens, and the old railway line faded into history.

Other than Newton Circus, two major road projects made possible by the railway deviation were the Inner Ring Road and Outer Ring Road. These ring roads were needed to relieve growing traffic congestion inside the Town. Also, by connecting the Municipality's trunk roads in concentric circles, the authorities hoped these ring roads would attract people inside the Town to move to previously undeveloped locations inside the Municipality.

The Inner Ring Road ($300,000) and Outer Ring Road ($700,000) were formed by connecting existing roads. Before 1929, there already existed Lavender Street and Balestier Road in the east; and in the west, Outram Road, Kim Seng Road, Irwell Bank Road, Paterson Road, Scotts Road, and Stevens Road. In 1929, a small reserve road was laid down between Stevens Road and Balestier Road, named Whitley Road after Michael Henry Whitley (1872–1959), an attorney-general. The road was subsequently lengthened and widened, and with the railway deviation, the 12-km Inner Ring Road was completed. Whitley Road was also one of the first roads in Singapore to come equipped with 4.5-metre-wide pavements for pedestrians.

The Outer Ring Road lay closer to the municipal boundary. There already existed Paya Lebar Road in the east, and in the west, Alexandra Road, Tanglin Road, Napier Road, and Holland Road. Braddell Road was laid down in the north, named after Thomas Braddell (1823–1891), the Straits Settlements' first attorney-general, and grandfather of Roland Saint John Braddell.[3] In the northwest, Adam Road, a short road "flanked with acacia trees", was named after Frank Adam (1856–1925), managing director of Pulau Brani Tin Smelting Works.

During the railway deviation, work started on a road to connect Holland Road and Adam Road. The "avenue of fragrant tembusu" was named Farrer Road after Municipal President Farrer (although it was nowhere near Farrer Park!). A second road was cut through jungle between MacRitchie Reservoir and Bukit Brown to link Adam Road to Braddell Road; the road was named Lornie Road after James Lornie (1876–1959), deputy president of the Municipal Commission. The final piece of the Outer Ring Road was completed in 1940, when Bartley Road was built to join Braddell Road to Paya Lebar Road; it was named after former Municipal President William Bartley (1885–1961). The Outer Ring Road's final length: 21.5 km.

The railway deviation ensured no level crossings cut across the ring roads; it took just 20 minutes to complete the Outer Ring Road by motor car. A 1937 *Straits Times* article proclaimed that the two arteries would "change out of all expectation the present suburban map of Singapore... within the next two decades". The Outer Ring Road cut through jungle, plantations, farms, and rural settlements. Braddell Road took "(a traveller) through flat country and over... fish ponds, market gardens, homes of squatters and a bit of jungle".

The completion of the ring roads and the railway deviation attested to the motor car as the method of movement favoured by the authorities in Singapore. Thirty years before, the railway was seen as the future of suburban transport; now, the motor car had taken over that mantle, and the railway had to give way to the car's demands on physical infrastructure.

OUTSIDE THE Municipal Boundary, the Rural Board built trunk roads into the last remote parts of Singapore Island. They were completed at the same time, around 1931.

For about 70 years, Jurong Road ended at the 11th Milestone by the Sungei Jurong; it was lengthened westwards by 11 km to the 18th Milestone, where another river, the Sungei Tuas, emptied into the sea. The coastal village there took on the name "18 Mile Jurong Road". In the northwest, eight kilometres of Lim Chu Kang Road were laid down from Choa Chu Kang Road to the Straits of Johor; it was named after the century-old *kangkar* of Lim Chu Kang. Finally, 100 years after work had started on the first trunk roads, every compass point of Singapore Island was now served by at least one trunk road. In particular, Lim Chu Kang Road would play a key role in Singapore's history in 10 years' time...

TENDING TO THE "NO-MAN'S LAND"

WITH THE age of the engine in full throttle, other than building new roads, the Public Works Department (PWD) and the Rural Board had to constantly maintain and upgrade existing roads suffering from wear and tear. For example, between 1931 and 1936, a princely sum of $700,000 was spent re-laying 22 km of Bukit Timah Road—one of the most heavily-used roads in Singapore—with concrete, asphalt, granite, and sand. A 1935 news article declared that when completed, the "new" Bukit Timah Road should become "one of the finest stretches of highway in the colonial empire and without equal in the Peninsula".

In 1932, after 65 years, the designation of Colonial Engineer of the Public Works Department was upgraded to Director of Public Works for the Straits Settlements and Advisor for Public Works for the Malay States. The eighth and last colonial engineer, George Sturrock, became the first Director of Public Works. By the end of the 1930s, the PWD of the Straits Settlements had grown to a staff of 45, 16 of which worked in Singapore. However, due to limited budgets and legal powers, and growing demands on movement, road users' experiences in the 1920s and 1930s were far from safe, smooth, or inclusive.

The name plates of roads were one example. We have seen how bazaar Malay was the lingua franca in Singapore, while English was spoken and read by only a fraction of the population. Yet into the 20th century, the name plates of roads bore English names only. In 1912, a Chinese municipal commissioner, Dr Suat Chuan Yin (1877–1958), proposed that Chinese and Malay script corresponding to these English road names be added to the name plates of roads in the Town. This way, the Chinese and Malays could understand the name plates too. A resolution was passed; however, nothing was done for 10 years. Then, the commissioners set aside $20,000 to fulfill Suat's vision. However, they ran into difficulties finding suitable Chinese and Malay names for each road. Some saw it as a waste of money, and impracticable, since there were so many Chinese topolect groups. In the end, the resolution was rescinded in 1925. Deputy President Lornie said that the budget for expenditure on roads was tight, so "any unnecessary expenditure which could be avoided should be avoided". The problem of linguistic heterogeneity in Singapore would persist into the 1960s.

Changing the names of individual streets was an easier endeavour. In 1922, Kling Street near Raffles Place was renamed Chulia Street. The term "Kling" had begun to be regarded as derogatory to Indians; Municipal Commissioner Dr H. S. Moonshi had suggested "King Street" as an alternative. However, there was already a King's Road off Bukit Timah Road, hence, "Chulia Street" was adopted to reflect the community of south Indians living there. Three years later, in 1925, Macao Street and Upper Macao Street were renamed Pickering Street and Upper Pickering Street respectively, to honour the first Protector of the Chinese, William Pickering (1840–1907). It was fitting that Pickering, an Englishman who could speak and write Chinese fluently, and did much to fight abuses in the Chinese coolie trade, was memorialised in the heart of Chinatown.

Road widening was tackled in earnest, with mixed results. Inside the Municipality, examples included Stamford Road, Kallang Road, Geylang Road, the Serangoon–Upper Serangoon trunk road, and Thomson Road. However, widening was very costly or impossible as land, with the buildings on them, had to be bought over. There were no laws for compulsory land acquisition, so if the land or building owners refused to sell, widening was out of the question. Hence, traffic gridlock remained a way of life inside the Town.

Street lighting, or the lack thereof, remained a problem. As the 1930s drew to a close, many roads near or beyond the municipal boundary remained unlit at night, endangering the lives of travellers. Examples included stretches of Paya Lebar Road, and Changi, Joo Chiat, Telok Kurau, and East Coast roads. Even inside the Town, where street lights were now commonplace, the gas supply was cut off half an hour before dawn, engulfing the Town in darkness. As a *Straits Times* journalist described in 1937:

> … on a pitch black morning, moonless and storm cloudy, Dhoby Ghaut—Princep Street—Selegie and Bras Basah Roads, with not a single lamp functioning—a common experience—become as fearsome as no-man's land between opposing trenches, to those who must negotiate them before daylight.

The Rural Board turned its attention to villages in 1938, when it embarked on an exercise to locate and name "unnamed" villages in rural areas. A committee, led by Lim Nee Soon's son and Rural Board member Lim Chong Pang (1904–1956), uncovered no fewer than 60 villages without official names. Most of them had arisen alongside trunk or main roads, and the villagers had taken on addresses "given as such-and-such milestones off certain roads". Eventually, all were given new names, usually taken from existing place names. For example, the village named 5¾ Mile Upper

Serangoon Road—once an electric tram terminus, now a trolleybus terminus—was renamed Paya Lebar Village; 5½ Mile Thomson Road was renamed Ang Mo Kio Village; 12 Mile Choa Chu Kang Road was renamed Keat Hong Village after nearby Keat Hong Estate (itself named after the Hokkien for "Luck and Abundance"); 18 Mile Jurong Road was named Tuas Village, and so on. This renaming exercise made life easier for postmen, the Rural Board, and the government. It also revealed the importance of roads as a birthplace of human settlements (60 villages!), and the role of road names and milestones in human consciousness (for example, their use as ad hoc addresses). Channels of movement were not just used for travelling between Point A and Point B, but were also an indissoluble part of social memory and identity.

ASSEMBLING A MILITARY JIGSAW

AFTER THE Great War, world events pushed the British Empire to turn Singapore Island into a military outpost serving imperial interests, leaving a lasting impact on Singapore's history of movement.

The British Empire emerged from the Great War as one of its victors, and gained more territory from the losers—the German and Ottoman empires—than any other participant. However, one of her wartime allies, Imperial Japan, also emerged from the war stronger. Britain and the United States grew wary of Japan—with colonies in Korea, Formosa, Shandong, and the Pacific—as a future rival power in East Asia. Malaya—exporting two-thirds of the world's rubber and 60 per cent of the world's tin—and Singapore had to be defended more resolutely.

At the time, the British naval base closest to the Far East was in Alexandria, Egypt, 8,000 km away. A new naval base was needed in the Far East. There were three choices—Hong Kong, Singapore, and Sydney. Hong Kong was deemed too close to Japan and unstable China; Sydney was too far from Southeast Asia. Hence, in 1923, the British government authorised the construction of a naval base in Singapore. The site chosen was in Sembawang facing the Straits of Johor. An air base was also to be built for the Royal Air Force (RAF) in Seletar—an acknowledgement of the new role air power played in warfare. To guard the eastern entrance to the Straits of Johor, coastal artillery defences would be built in the east of the island, in Changi. Blueprints were drawn up in 1926 and approved by London.

The chosen sites were remote and largely undeveloped, far from the Municipality, as the military bases needed space and security, and the land could be acquired cheaply. The site in Sembawang lay at the end of Seletar Road, covered by swamps of the Sungei Sembawang and rubber plantations of the Bukit Sembawang Rubber Company. The site in Seletar, north of Yio Chu Kang Village, was filled with rubber trees belonging to the Singapore United Rubber Plantation Limited. In Changi, there was just a Malay village, a police station, two government bungalows, and a Japanese hotel. Towering over them were grand, old, hundred-feet-tall trees.

RAF Seletar was finished in 1928. The Rural Board took over a private road connecting Yio Chu Kang Road to the air base and renamed it Air Base Road. However, in 1937, the RAF was granted permission to rename it Jalan Kayu (Malay for "Wood Road"), in honour of its late chief engineer, C. E. O. Wood. In and around the base, romantic visions of a cold, wintry London were evoked through street names that borrowed from landmarks in the capital of the British Empire.

These included Hyde Park Gate, Park Lane, Piccadilly, Hampstead Gardens, Baker Street, Oxford Street, and Maida Vale. Black-and-white bungalows for officers and their families lined many of these roads.

RAF Seletar also served civilian aircraft, but booming traffic quickly convinced Governor Sir Cecil Clementi (1875–1947, a nephew of former Governor Cecil Clementi Smith) that a purpose-built civilian aerodrome was needed. In August 1931, the mouths of the Kallang and Geylang rivers—right next to the Town—were chosen as the location for the aerodrome. This meant displacing the maritime Bugis and Orang Laut, who had called the area home for at least a century. The residents of Kampong Kalang, Kampong Rokok, Kampong Batin ("Chief"), and Kampong Laut had to be resettled. Tidal mudflats had to be reclaimed, joining Pulau Geylang to the mainland; the Geylang River was diverted. Construction of the aerodrome began the following year with an army of 800 labourers and several hundred trucks.

These large-scale construction projects required the movement of significant volumes of men, material, and equipment, necessitating the laying down of railway lines. In Changi, a 2.5-km Changi Express was built in 1928 to ferry troops and ammunition from the sea to gun sites. In Sembawang, a 5.75-km line connected Woodlands Station to the naval base site from around 1929. And from the early 1930s, a 6.5-km light railway moved tons of earth from quarries northeast of the Malay Settlement to the reclamation site for Kallang Aerodrome. Coincidentally, the Malays, Bugis, and Orang Laut displaced by the aerodrome were resettled in the other direction—the Malay Settlement.[4]

Japan's rise in the Pacific continued with the invasion of Manchuria in 1931, prompting the British to hasten the plodding construction of the naval base and build more air bases in Singapore. Work started on a second air base, Tengah, off Choa Chu Kang Road. Like the other bases, it was built on what was once bush, and rubber and pineapple plantations. RAF Tengah was swiftly completed and opened in 1935. Its roads were named after RAF plane models, such as Meteor, Stirling, Vampire, Hurricane, and Spitfire roads. Soon after, a third RAF base was finished south of the incomplete naval base; even though it was off Seletar Road, it was named RAF Sembawang, perhaps because it lay inside the District of Sembawang.

Kallang Aerodrome was officially opened on 12 June 1937 by Governor Thomas. It was served by Grove Road, upgraded and widened, no longer a humble cart track surrounded by swamps. Then some of the last pieces of the British military jigsaw came together in 1938 and 1941, with the completion of Sembawang Naval Base and Changi Artillery Base.

Although Changi was an artillery base, its roads were named after RAF bases in Britain. They included Netheravon, Turnhouse, Hendon, Northolt, Northweald, Aldergrove, Hawkinge, Martlesham, and Felixstowe roads.

Taking 15 years and £60 million ($514 million) to complete, Sembawang Naval Base was the crowning glory of the Admiralty in the Far East, able to accommodate the largest ships in the Royal Navy at the time—whenever they arrived from Europe. For Britain had a budget for only one fleet, not two, and this fleet, stationed in Europe, was supposed to sail over to Singapore whenever war broke out in the Far East.

Roads built to serve the barracks of the naval base—presently the site of Sembawang Camp—were fittingly named after British admirals. These roads included Hawke Road, Jervois Crescent, Drake Avenue, Exmouth Road, and Cochrane Road. The eight-kilometre road laid down to connect the barracks, the Naval Base, and the Causeway was named Naval Base Road. As for roads south of the Naval Base, they were named after territories, colonies or cities governed by the British Empire. Hence, there were Canberra Road, Delhi Road, Bermuda Road, Ottawa Road, Falkland Road, Fiji Road, Montreal Road, Tasmania Road, Hobart Road, Malta Crescent, Durban Road, and Kenya Crescent. These roads underscored the fact that the Naval Base was built not just to protect Singapore, but the Empire, and it was to be the lynchpin of British defence of the Far East.

Unfortunately, many of these roads with intriguing names are no longer in the public domain. Maps and street directories of Singapore in the 1980s still charted and listed roads inside military bases, but with the tightening of security, this has stopped.

It is in Sembawang where most of the former colonies and territories of the British Empire persist as a toponymic time capsule. Canberra has done exceptionally well. Canberra Road is a major road in Sembawang town, and has lent its name to a housing estate, electoral ward, schools, and future MRT station.

The Naval Base also altered the name of the trunk road leading to it. By the end of the 1930s, the municipal commissioners thought people might confuse Seletar Road with RAF Seletar off Jalan Kayu. Furthermore, a village had risen just south of the Naval Base at the 14th Milestone of Seletar Road, which the Rural Board named Sembawang Village. Hence, in 1939, Seletar Road was renamed Sembawang Road. For the second time in almost a hundred years, the place name "Seletar Road" disappeared. Meanwhile, the stretch of Thomson Road from Yio Chu Kang Road to Mandai Road was renamed Upper Thomson Road—again, to make life easier for the authorities and postal services.

1939. WAR looked to be on the horizon in Europe, but on the other side of the world in Singapore, people felt safe and secure. Life went on as usual in the ballrooms of the Raffles Hotel, the banks of Battery Road, the bazaars of South Bridge Road. With a proud naval base, multiple air bases, and fearsome coastal artillery defences, Singapore was regarded as the Gibraltar of the East, an impregnable fortress that protected not just its residents, but the British Empire stretching from Hong Kong to New Zealand.

The countryside remained covered with agriculture, with rubber making up two-thirds of cultivated land, followed by coconuts and pineapples. The convoys of horse and pony-drawn carriages of 30 years ago were gone; the rural roads belonged to motor cars now. George Peet wrote about how Changi Road was a journey through coconut plantations on hilly country; Thomson Road a winding ride on a narrow, hilly, laterite road through rubber estates; once tiger-infested Mandai Road especially popular for country drives. Tigers—once the scourge of many a cropper—were no more; the last wild tiger in Singapore was killed near Choa Chu Kang Village in 1930.

The Town of Singapore had grown into a bustling Municipality of more than half a million, with white-washed colonial buildings lining the seafront from Beach Road in the north to Robinson Road in the south. What was once the open fields of the Telok Ayer Reclamation Ground were rapidly filling up with godowns,

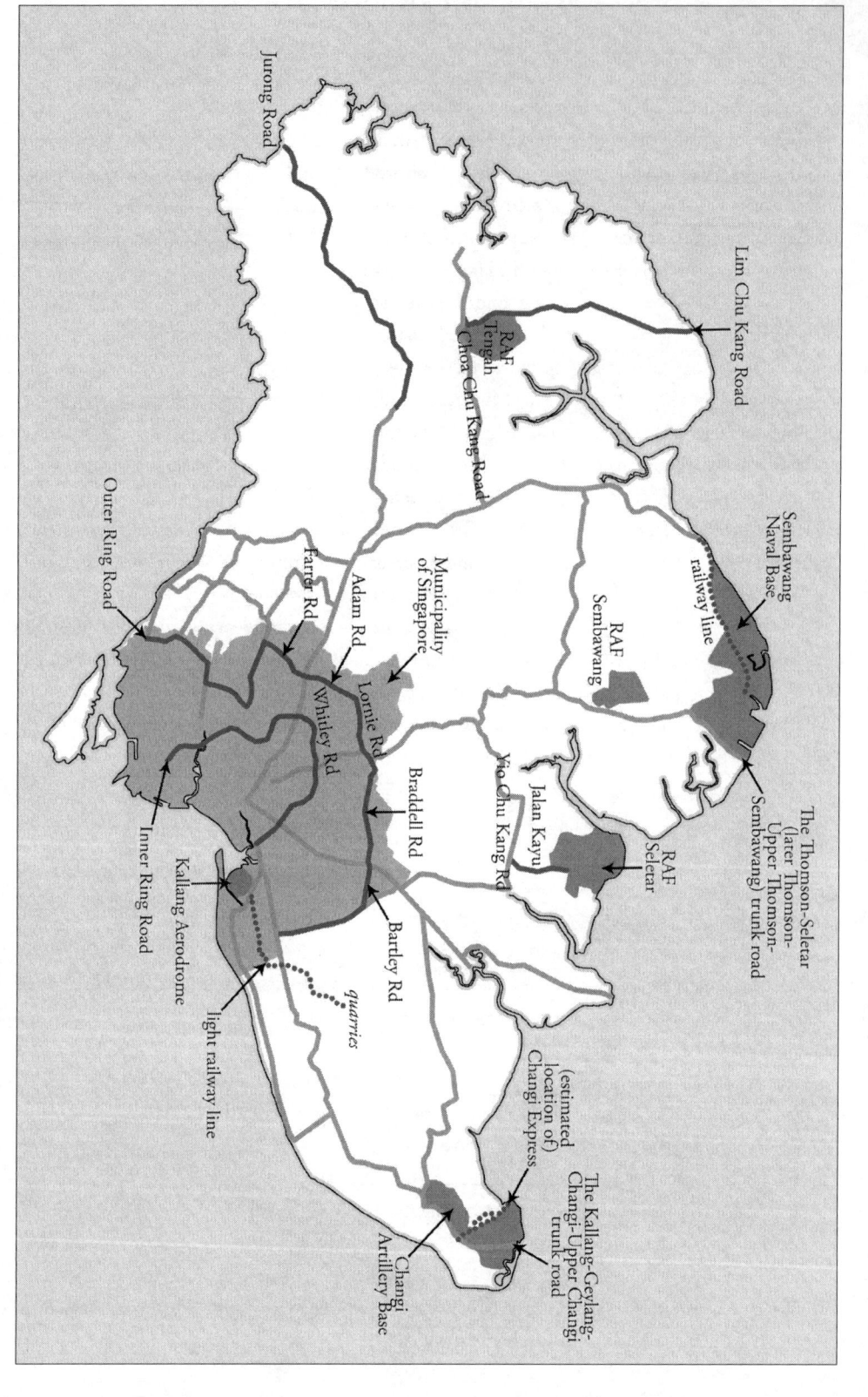

Singapore Island in 1941. The trunk road system was boosted by the completion of an Inner Ring Road and an Outer Ring Road connecting trunk roads concentrically. Lim Chu Kang Road and an extension of Jurong Road eased transport woes in the west of the island. Military bases were built on the peripheries of the island, while Kallang Aerodrome was sited near the heart of the Municipality. Three railway lines mentioned in the text—one serving Sembawang Naval Base, another serving the reclamation of land for Kallang Aerodrome, and the Changi Express—are indicated with dotted lines. (Source: Eisen Teo)

office buildings, and car parks crammed with hundreds of cars. New landmarks abounded. After 77 years, Johnston's Pier was replaced by Clifford Pier in 1933 as the site of choice for dignitaries coming in by sea; the new pier along Collyer Quay was named after Governor Sir Hugh Charles Clifford (1866–1941). A striking landmark at the mouth of the Singapore River was the Fullerton Building, completed in 1928. North of the river, opposite the Padang, a new Municipal Building opened in 1929, standing on what used to be the residences of William Montgomerie and Thomas Church in the 1850s. Next to it, a new Supreme Court opened in 1939 on the site of the former Hotel de L'Europe, once one of the finest hotels in Singapore. Change was a constant; writers lamented that the Singapore they knew decades before had all but disappeared. "New houses (are coming up) every day, and the past is soon buried", wrote Sir Robert Hamilton Bruce Lockhart in 1936. This state of flux seemed destined to go on indefinitely, for what could halt Singapore's prosperity?

CHAPTER NOTES

1. In 1911, "Tanah Merah Road" appeared in a Singapore newspaper with "5¼ Milestone" next to it. In a 1924 map, the trunk road east of Geylang Road was already named Changi Road. Hence, Tanah Merah Road was renamed Changi Road sometime between these two years. "Tanah Merah Road" still appeared in Singapore newspapers after 1911, and even after 1924, but without milestone numbers; it is possible these referred to Tanah Merah Besar Road or Tanah Merah Kechil Road instead.

2. As of 2019, Yellow Top taxis are still around in Singapore—but extinction looms on the horizon. Unlike most cabbies in Singapore who rent their vehicles from companies, Yellow Top cabbies privately own and operate their vehicles, but since the 1970s, the government has stopped issuing taxi licences to individuals. From a high of 3,800 Yellow Top taxis in the 1960s, their numbers dwindled to just 100 in 2018. The last Yellow Top taxi should disappear by 2035, as younger drivers reach the age of 75, the age ceiling for cabbies; the average age of Yellow Top taxi drivers is 67½ years.

3. There was a Braddell Road, off Martin Road near present-day Robertson Quay along the Singapore River. It was named sometime before 1906 after Thomas Braddell. However, when the Outer Ring Road was constructed and named Braddell Road, the original Braddell Road was renamed Pukat Road to avoid confusion. Pukat Road got its name after nearby Kampong Pukat (Pukat is Malay for "(Fishing) Net"). The road was expunged between 1991 and 1993.

4. Most of the Changi Express was torn up by the Japanese during the Japanese Occupation of 1942 to 1945; the rest was removed by the British soon after 1945. The railways for Sembawang and Kallang Aerodrome were removed by 1953, probably because they had outlived their original uses.

There were several more branch lines laid down from the Federated Malay States Railway (FSMR) line between 1909 and 1939. They included 1) tracks to ferry stone mined from quarries on Bukit Timah Hill. The first tracks appeared after 1909 and all were removed by 1978; 2) tracks to transport granite mined from Mandai Quarry to the main line at Yew Tee. They were completed by 1923 and were gone by 1953; 3) tracks from Tanglin Halt Station to Pasir Panjang Road, possibly to move troops to and from Pasir Panjang Ridge, which was strategic high ground in the southwest of the island. The tracks were built after 1937 and disappeared by 1953; 4) a military railway from the FMSR line near Holland Road to Buona Vista Battery, to supply ammunition to two 15-inch guns. The railway and battery were completed by 1939. The latter was removed by 1949; the railway followed by 1953.

CHAPTER 5
1941 to 1950: Gear Reversal

THE TRIP probably took only 15 minutes, but it was the saddest motor car ride in Singapore's history. After 4pm on 15 February 1942, two cars left Fort Canning Hill, one bearing a large white flag—the universal symbol of truce or surrender. They carried a delegation of four men, including Lieutenant-General Arthur Ernest Percival (1887–1966), General Officer Commanding Malaya Command, the head of the Allied army which defended Malaya and Singapore in World War II. Their destination was 13 km to the northwest, a motor car factory called the Ford Factory, at 8½ Milestone Bukit Timah Road. There, Percival was to meet his counterpart in war, Lieutenant-General Tomoyuki Yamashita (1885–1946), commander of the invading Japanese 25th Army, to discuss the impending surrender of Malaya Command.

In terms of Singapore's history of movement, the journey could not have been more symbolic. Earlier in the morning, surrounded by 11 men under his command, Percival had made the fateful decision to surrender inside an underground command centre called the "battle-box" inside Fort Canning Hill, once the seat and burial place of ancient Singapura's Malay kings, and the home of British governors. The route from the hill was never documented, but since Orchard Road had been heavily bombed, it was possible the cars went on Clemenceau Avenue, past Newton Circus, and onto Bukit Timah Road.

We can only guess as to what went through the minds of the delegation as their cars brought them up Bukit Timah Road—Brigadiers Kenneth Torrance and Thomas Newbigging, and interpreter Major Cyril Wild in the first car, Percival in the second. They could have been contemplating defeat, surrender, captivity, death. The scenery that greeted them would have been wanton destruction—the husks of bombed and shelled-out buildings, abandoned weaponry, dead bodies, black smoke against a clear blue sky.

The Adam Road junction was the frontline. Beyond the Outer Ring Road the British Empire ended. Everything to the north, for 800 km to the border with Thailand, now belonged to the Land of the Rising Sun. Percival's delegation had to leave their cars behind; the Japanese escorted them for an hour's walk over 6½ km to the Ford Factory, Yamashita's new headquarters in Singapore. The Ford Factory had opened just months before as Ford's first motor car assembly plant in Southeast Asia, a symbol of the popularity of the motor car in Singapore.

Yamashita met Percival after 5pm and negotiations began. Percival, already in a feeble state of mind, caved in to Yamashita's persistent demands for unconditional surrender. Fortress Singapore, and the British Empire in the Far East, had fallen. With an army three times smaller than that of Malaya Command, the Japanese had taken just 70 days to topple 123 years of British rule. Percival, his generals, the 120,000 men of Malaya Command, and Governor Sir Shenton Thomas, all became prisoners-of-war. Malaya and Singapore were renamed Marai and Syonan-to ("Light of the South"), and their five million people became subjects of Imperial Japan. Years later, British Prime Minister Winston Churchill would declare the fall of Singapore to be "the worst disaster and largest capitulation in British history". Arguably, the event also spelled the beginning of the end of the British Empire in the East.

WAR ON WHEELS

WORLD EVENTS caught up with Singapore in the 1930s. Fortress Singapore had a naval base designed to harbour a fleet that would protect British interests in both the Indian and western Pacific oceans. Naturally, it was a prime target for any enemy seeking to neutralise British dominion in Asia. Also, a majority of Singapore's population consisted of migrants from China, so events in China naturally had an impact on Singapore.

Imperial Japan invaded China in 1937, sparking off a merciless conflict known as the Second Sino-Japanese War. Millions were killed, injured, or displaced. The following year, Nazi Germany annexed its neighbours Austria and Czechoslovakia, a sure sign to Britain and its allies that the days of peace in Europe were numbered. These grave events cast a pall over Singapore. As more resources in Europe began to be directed towards the revving up of war machines, the availability of spare parts for motor vehicles declined, driving up their costs. Proposals to upgrade the once-proud trolleybus fleet were deemed too costly, and the buses were left to fend for themselves. Gradually, Singapore's public transport system wore down from a neglect in maintenance.

On 1 September 1939, Germany invaded Poland. Two days later, Britain declared war on Germany—for the second time in 25 years. From the start, the war went Germany's way. By June 1940, much of western Europe, including France, had fallen to the Nazis. Thereafter, Britain spent many months fighting for her survival against attacks from the air and at sea. Eventually, Britain prevailed, and the threat of a German invasion receded, but she still had her back against the wall. The export of spare motor parts from Britain to the Far East was out of the question. In March 1941, fuel rationing began in Singapore. As motorists cut back on using their private cars, they turned to public transport—but buses and taxis also had to scale back on services for the same reasons! Some trolleybus services reduced their off-peak frequency by up to half; as older buses were forced into service, breakdowns occurred almost daily. Buses became unbearably packed. To make things worse for the bus companies, there were cases of conductors overcharging fares and pocketing the differences. Despite these woes, some Chinese bus companies donated to the War Fund, an effort to raise money for the war effort in Europe. The Green Bus Company donated $500, the Ngo Hock Motor Bus Company gave $150, the Tay Koh Yat Bus Company gave $120, and the Kampong Bahru Bus Service, $100.

By late 1941, relations between Japan and the United States and Britain were deteriorating by the day. Japan occupied French Indochina, signifying her intentions in the rest of Southeast Asia. The U.S. responded with a crippling oil embargo to force Japan to stop the war in China and withdraw from French Indochina. Japan looked poised to strike at British and Dutch colonies in Southeast Asia, to attain the resources—oil, tin, rubber— she needed to continue the four-year-long war in China. The feeling of impending doom descended like a suffocating veil upon Singapore. People stocked up on canned food, sank wells for water, and grew their own vegetables. The desire for distractions grew—cinema and amusement park attendances soared. Wartime blackout regulations kicked in—for motor vehicles, all headlights, and interior lighting and destination displays on buses, had to be dimmed after dusk.

On 8 December 1941, in an impressive show of coordination, Japan launched near-simultaneous attacks on the U.S. Pacific Fleet at Pearl Harbor in Hawaii, and Guam, Wake Island, the Philippines, and southern Thailand. In the wee hours of the morning, Japanese troops landed in northern Malaya, while Singapore was bombed from the air for the first time. Seletar and Tengah airfields were hit, as were locations inside the Town, mostly around Raffles Place, the Singapore River, and Chinatown. At daybreak, Dr John Cuylenburg drove into the Town to survey the damage:

> ... in nearby Boat Quay I witnessed a harrowing sight: bodies were laid out for identification alongside the carriageway. Some were unrecognisable from terrible injuries, others seemed just asleep, probably having been killed by the blast from the explosions. Men and women were weeping—in fact, pandemonium reigned in this locality. Those killed were mostly well-to-do people of this business centre, including some of my patients...
>
> I then parked my car in Chulia Street and walked into Raffles Place. I was stunned! Most of the damage seemed to have been done here. I noticed at once a tremendous amount of broken glass, which literally paved Raffles Place, forming a layer over six inches thick... Every glass show-window in Raffles Place had been destroyed and every building in this square had pockmark holes on its exterior, and some inside as well...

In one fell swoop, the death and destruction of war was brought home to the residents of Singapore. This air raid was only the beginning.

Over the next eight weeks, the Japanese 25th Army raged a "lightning war" in Malaya, racing armoured columns down rural roads. Even the infantry was mobile, travelling on motor trucks and bicycles in "bicycle brigades". Malaya Command—comprising British, Australian, Indian, and local forces—were outfought, outgunned, and outmanoeuvred, forced on a fighting retreat. One by one, the states of Malaya fell to the Japanese. As the Royal Air Force (RAF) disintegrated, nightly air raids over Singapore started from 16 December, and daytime raids started from 12 January 1942. And the Royal Navy? Fully stretched in the Atlantic and the Mediterranean, most warships could not be spared for Singapore. Sembawang Naval Base remained a naval base without a navy.

Singapore's public transport system, already ailing, unravelled with the rest of the population. Discipline among drivers and conductors broke down. The incidence of dangerous driving rose. Bus and taxi drivers, and even rickshaw pullers, overcharged commuters by as much as 300 per cent. Absenteeism skyrocketed; it was "every man for himself". Vehicles, rolling stock, depots, and workshops—including the Singapore Traction Company (STC) headquarters at MacKenzie Road—were destroyed by wave after wave of bombings. By 24 January, the operating hours of bus services were cut to between 6am and 7pm.

Malaya Command also ordered the STC to dispatch a convoy of between 20 and 30 motor buses to Malaya to help in the war effort. The orders were swiftly carried out, and the buses crossed the Causeway with fitters and a service van loaded with spare parts and fuel. The buses—and personnel—were never seen or heard of again.

Private transport was not spared either. Motor cars and bicycles were requisitioned. The police took up strategic positions at main thoroughfares, stopped cyclists, and confiscated their bicycles.

Malaya Command, with thousands of refugees in tow, retreated across the Causeway on 31 January 1942—and in a desperate attempt to stop the Japanese advance, blew a 21-metre gap in it. The Causeway had lasted just 18 years. British Malaya ceased to be. Singapore Island was now under siege.

THE 25th Army, led by Yamashita—one of Japan's most brilliant generals—had done their homework before the outbreak of war. In 1940, Japanese officers had visited Singapore to assess its defences; they took the popular seafront route from Tanjong Katong to Pasir Panjang via East Coast Road and Pasir Panjang Road. They also travelled up Bukit Timah Road and Woodlands Road, from the Municipality to Johor Bahru. Like the spokes of a wheel, roads ran from all corners of Singapore Island to the heart of the Town. The Japanese could not afford protracted siege warfare or house-to-house fighting in Singapore; the key to taking Singapore swiftly was to exploit its well-developed trunk and arterial road system. One major thoroughfare that was singled out in battle plans was the century-old Bukit Timah–Woodlands trunk road, with the adjoining hills of Bukit Mandai, Bukit Panjang, and Bukit Timah. Terrain was a crucial element of warfare and Yamashita and his staff mastered it.

The Japanese gave Malaya Command little time to catch their breath. After a week's pause, on the night of 8 February, four waves of 4,000 men from the 15th and 18th Divisions braved heavy fire to storm the coast of Singapore's northwest, a stretch from Lim Chu Kang to present-day Poyan Reservoir. For a few critical hours, it looked as if the Australians defending that sector were going to hold the Japanese, but Yamashita kept his nerve and his men gained beachheads. Once they did so, they went for the nearest road, Lim Chu Kang Road, built just 10 years before. A new trunk road intended by the Rural Board to advance agriculture in Singapore's northwest now contributed to the defenders' undoing. One of the first villages to fall under Japanese occupation was Ama Keng Village along Lim Chu Kang Road. By the afternoon of 9 February, the Australians had been pushed back to a defensive line straddling Choa Chu Kang Road, around Bulim Village. By the dawn of 10 February, the defenders—plagued by confusion, chaos, and a paralysed leadership—retreated further east, to the historic 10th Mile of Bukit Timah Road.

Japanese reconnaissance maps of Singapore trunk roads came in handy. The interim target was Bukit Timah Hill, the highest point on the island. Shortly after dusk on 10 February, the 5th and 18th Divisions attacked Choa Chu Kang Road and Jurong Road simultaneously. With the northwest secure in Japanese hands, the 18th Division floated at least 50 tanks across the Straits of Johor on barges and set them loose. Making use of the trunk road system, the tanks rumbled down Lim Chu Kang Road, Choa Chu Kang Road, and then Bukit Timah Road, smashing into the heart of Bukit Timah Village. Choa Chu Kang Road, Jurong Road, Bukit Timah Village, and Bukit Timah Hill were all lost after heavy fighting by the evening of 11 February.

Meanwhile, chaos reigned inside the Town. It had been hit by air raids every day for a month now, and as Japanese artillery came within range, it also suffered from daily bombardment. Orchard Road, the quays around the Singapore River, and the godowns and docks of Keppel Harbour were hit especially hard. Untold thousands died. Major thoroughfares became impassable to traffic, choked by debris, burning vehicles, and dead bodies. Dense columns of smoke from fires burning out of the control hung low over the Town. Fire brigade member B. C. J. Buckeridge recalled:

> The face of Singapore changed, the sky darkened by day by billowing smoke, and lightened by flames reflected at night; poles and lamp posts lying drunkenly and in pieces… litter and wreckage of war all over the roads, amidst burning buildings, bombs and shells, and flying shrapnel…. there were thousands of fires, and in the 70 days which the actual hostilities lasted, I estimate some 3,000 calls must have been made upon the Fire services. It was as if Japan had declared war on the Fire Brigade, as indeed it had.

By 13 February, Japanese troops had moved four kilometres southeast of Bukit Timah Village, to Pasir Panjang Ridge in the south, and the Outer Ring Roads of Lornie Road, Adam Road, and Farrer Road in the north. These roads, built just 10 to 20 years before, now saw heavy fighting and shelling. Within two days, both lines were breached. In the north, the 5th Division pushed the British back to Bukit Brown and Mount Pleasant, while in the south, the 18th Division overran the Malay Regiment after a valiant last stand, a battle that has since become legend. On the morning of 15 February, the Japanese were just six kilometres and a single breakthrough from the Municipal Building opposite the Padang. Malaya Command was running out of food and ammunition, and the Municipality had just 24 hours' worth of water left. Hence, the fateful decision to surrender. A ceasefire took effect that night.

Churchill had previously wanted Percival and his men to fight to the death. However, Percival's controversial decision to surrender rather than risk a Japanese breakthrough and house-to-house fighting inside the Town saved the lives of untold thousands of civilians, and the Town itself from certain destruction. Even though continuous bombing and shelling had destroyed many parts of the Town, the destruction was not total, and whatever rebuilding that took place did so on the original town blocks. Despite the physical trauma of the Battle of Singapore, the urban composition and road system of the Town remained largely unchanged.

The lesson from the Battle of Singapore—and previous conflicts in Singapore's history—must not be forgotten. In 1854, when rival Chinese factions took up arms against each other, the British made use of the trunk road system to restore order. In 1915, when hundreds of sepoys threatened to overturn British rule, the British made use of motor cars on arterial roads to swiftly crush the revolt. Now in 1942, an invader used the trunk road system with outstanding effect, forcing the British to capitulate in eight days. If a ground conflict broke out in Singapore again, the island's well-connected expressway network could be the key to victory or defeat.

The morning after capitulation, on 16 February, the 25th Army rode into the Town of Singapore on motor trucks. For the next three-and-a-half years Syonan came under Japanese occupation. There was a lot to do. The devastation of war had to be cleared and repaired. Dead bodies lying in the

In January and February 1942, Singapore came under heavy Japanese bombing. Roads became impassable to traffic, choked by debris, destroyed vehicles, and dead bodies. (Source: State Library of Victoria)

streets and buildings had to be disposed. Gas, water, and electricity were in short supply.

One of the priorities of the Japanese military police, or Kempeitai, was security. They occupied all major road junctions and bridges in the Town and set up roadblocks to search passers-by and commuters. Syonan's major thoroughfares, once bustling with continuous flows of pedestrians and vehicular traffic, suddenly cleared overnight. People stayed home; they were afraid of getting into trouble at the roadblocks. Everyone had to bow low before the sentries; not doing so could get one slapped or detained for hours!

On 17 February, a series of marches took place from the Town eastward along the historic Geylang–Changi trunk road to the far east of the island. The Japanese forced tens of thousands of Allied soldiers and civilians to walk the roughly 21 km from the Town to Changi Gaol, to begin three-and-a-half years of incarceration. To botanist E. J. H. Corner, the trudge "must have been the saddest sight to the inhabitants of Singapore, the saddest in its history"—because it showed the Asians how far the British had fallen. The sorry spectacle would be forever seared in their minds.

The Chinese were next. The Japanese saw them as loyal to Britain or China, which made them sworn enemies. From 18 February, all Chinese males in Syonan between the ages of 18 and 50 were ordered to gather at "screening centres" all over the Municipality. Over the next few days, military police and auxiliary officers "screened" them for "anti-Japanese elements"—in reality, they mostly selected men indiscriminately. These unlucky ones were loaded onto trucks, driven to remote locations mostly in the east of the island—and were never seen again. This was the infamous Sook Ching (Cantonese for "Cleansing Through Elimination") massacre; estimates of the eventual death toll range between 5,000 and 50,000—which meant most Chinese in Syonan knew someone who had disappeared because of Sook Ching. The trunk roads of Changi Road and Serangoon Road carried these ill-fated men to what were most certainly violent deaths in places such as Punggol Beach, the 8th milestones of Upper Serangoon Road and Changi Road, Changi Beach, Tanah Merah Besar Beach, Katong, and Siglap. Of course, at the time, their families did not know they had been murdered, and instead hoped for their eventual return. This tragic faith kept the Chinese community in Syonan cowed and subservient.

After the Europeans were locked away and the Chinese terrorised into silence, daily routine took over again. People knew they had to get used to a new, usually unpleasant reality. The same applied to movement. Syonan's history of movement under Japanese rule reflected a vastly changed world order. The colonial hierarchical structure remained largely the same. But Europeans and laissez-faire commerce no longer sat at the apex. They had been brutally replaced by the Japanese and harsh, austere autarky.

TURNING BACK THE CLOCK

UNDER THE Japanese, the clock for Syonan's transport system was rewound by at least 60 years, to when rickshaws first arrived. Before the war, the trolleybus was the number one form of public transport, closely followed by the motor bus, then the rickshaw. By 1945, a new method of movement, the trishaw, was doing a roaring business, followed by the rickshaw, then a struggling trolleybus and motor bus system. For private transport, the motor car was once king of the roads, followed by the rickshaw, then the bicycle. After three-and-a-half years, only the Japanese and those who worked for them had uninhibited access to cars; for the rest of Syonan, the bicycle was the main form of private transport. Like the pre-war established order, Syonan's methods of movement were turned on their heads. In fact, by 1945, a large proportion of Syonan's population had reverted to walking—the result of a harsh wartime occupation replete with shortages, an administration preoccupied with self-preservation, and an almost complete absence of free trade, free enterprise, and rule of law.

Syonan was ruled by the Gunseikanbu, or Central Military Administration, which followed a chain of command going back to the General Inspection Bureau of the Imperial Japanese Army in Tokyo. Reporting to the Gunseikanbu was the Tokubetsu-Shi, or Municipal Administration. Transport matters were considered municipal issues under the purview of the Tokubetsu-Shi. The Registry of Vehicles resumed operations at Middle Road, but the registrar was Japanese of course.

Before the war, there were some 120 trolleybuses and 260 motor buses owned by the STC and Chinese bus companies. The former was run by Britons, while the latter was run by local Chinese; hence, they were not allowed to resume their businesses. The Tokubetsu-Shi appropriated all buses under the authority of the Syonan Shiden, or Singapore City Electric.[1] However, because of the fighting, only 53 trolleybuses and 69 motor buses—which were not in great condition—were salvaged. The Tokubetsu-Shi also took over the former STC headquarters at MacKenzie Road to repair and refit scores of buses. There was a wartime shortage of paint, so pre-war liveries were never painted over; instead, buses carried coloured boards as a new form of route identification. Old buses, once repaired, were made to ply new routes—with destination displays written in Japanese.

Syonan Shiden's first trolleybus service resumed on 16 March 1942, running from Moulmein Road through the Town to the railway terminus at Tanjong Pagar. The following day, the Tokubetsu-Shi issued an edict declaring themselves the only authority permitted to run bus services. No company or individual could start a bus service. For the first time in Syonan's history, all buses were unified under one operator—the government of Syonan.

The Syonan Shiden took its time to resume public transport services. Its first motor bus service began only on 15 April, running from Katong to Post 310 in Geylang. By October, there were six trolleybus and 23 motor bus routes serving both the Municipality and rural areas—only a small fraction of pre-war services, yet the most that would ever be achieved during the occupation. This, despite Syonan's population having grown to exceed a million! There were also four free bus services for the Japanese military departing from a central terminal along Orchard Road to military installations across the island.

In February 1943, the Syonan Shiden abolished the class system in buses, a staple in public transportation since the steam tram arrived from Europe 60 years before. All fares were now fixed at former second-class rates—two cents for every fare section. Separate compartments for different classes were also removed. These changes would never be reversed.

One benefit the Japanese brought to public transport and traffic in Syonan was discipline. In July 1942, the Tokubetsu-Shi launched "Safety First Week", later known as "Traffic Safety Week"—similar to the pre-war "Safety First" campaign. They ordered the people of Syonan to respect traffic signals and stop lines, and "train morality in trolleybuses". No longer should commuters smoke or spit in buses; neither should they rush to board or exit buses in a disorderly manner. Motorists were also ordered to respect speed limits, which the Japanese introduced in April 1942—the British had struggled for years to implement them. By 1944, motor cars and motorcycles could not exceed 25 miles an hour (40 km/h) inside the municipal boundary, and 45 miles an hour (72 km/h) outside it; for motor trucks, it was 25 miles an hour inside and 35 miles an hour (56 km/h) outside; at night, all were restricted to 20 miles an hour (32 km/h). Under the British, many might have disregarded these rules, but under harsher Japanese rule, they were taken more seriously.

By late 1942, an uneasy peace had returned to Syonan, which lay in the centre of a Japanese Southeast Asia—much of British Burma, the Dutch East Indies, and the American Philippines had been conquered by June. But war with the Allies raged on in faraway places such as New Guinea and the southwest Pacific. Tokyo wanted a swift conclusion to the conflict, but instead, they found themselves in a quagmire—just like in China. As the war of attrition dragged on, public transport in Syonan gradually disintegrated. Spare parts for motor vehicles could not be acquired from Britain or the United States, while wartime austerity in the Japanese Home Islands and American submarine warfare meant maritime imports of new vehicles and spare parts dwindled over time. Whatever did make it through served the military first. Self-sufficiency became the mantra of Syonan. Existing buses had to go without maintenance for months on end. Over time, the number and frequency of bus services declined.

Syonan also suffered from a severe shortage of petrol, which had to be rationed. Local workshops stepped in with an ingenious alternative—charcoal-burning, gas-powered engines. It was claimed that converted buses could each carry up to 35 passengers at 30 miles an hour (48 km/h) for just one cent a mile. But the reality was a litany of breakdowns and even minor engine explosions!

The Tokubetsu-Shi tried to manage the expectations of commuters through their official mouthpiece, the *Syonan Shimbun*, formerly *The Straits Times*. Newspaper articles encouraged commuters to walk short distances instead of "burdening the buses with additional weight", be "more methodical and public-spirited", and "make adjustments to their departure times". "Talk of putting more buses on the road in circumstances at present prevailing savours of thoughtlessness."

By July 1945, only a handful of bus services remained. Some routes were served by just a single vehicle. Vehicle lubricants were so short in supply, coconut oil was used as a substitute. The only thing that grew was the size of the scrap heap at MacKenzie Road.

PRIVATE TRANSPORT in Syonan was also turned on its head by autocratic Japanese policies. Before the occupation, the ownership of motor cars was an expression of a social and economic hierarchy—only the Europeans and rich Asians rode in cars. Now, only the Japanese could own them. All motor cars on the island were confiscated. According to writer Low Ngiong Ing, "car owners surrendered ignition keys with as good a grace as they could muster". Of course, they were given no compensation! The requisitioned cars were first mothballed in open areas such as the Padang, the Raffles Reclamation Ground, Balestier Road, and Farrer Park. Cuylenburg recalled: "It made our hearts ache, when we trudged past these dumping areas, to see beautiful Packards left in the open alongside shabby Fords." Soon, the more expensive models were taken by Japanese officers and officials. The rest were eventually shipped to other occupied territories around Southeast Asia, or to Japan itself, either for use or to be sold as scrap iron.

The only time a non-Japanese civilian could commandeer a car was when he was employed by the Japanese administration for important work. Cuylenburg, for example, was employed as a doctor at the Labour Department, hence he obtained permission to use a requisitioned car—"a godsend"; but even then, he was granted only 15 gallons of petrol a month, "hardly enough to take me to the office and back", forcing him to brave the black market for more petrol.

The Ford Factory, a proud landmark for the Japanese because it was the site of the British surrender, was eventually reopened in the middle of 1943, producing motor trucks for the military administration. Nissan Motors, a major Japanese automobile manufacturer, took over the assembling plant. The first truck was completed in July 1943. Up to half a dozen Japanese and 300 local Asian workers were stationed there, producing 150–200 trucks a month. An unknown number of cars were also assembled, ensuring Japanese officials and high-ranking officers enjoyed new cars throughout the occupation.

Nevertheless, just like Syonan's motorised public transport system, its car and truck productions were hit hard by submarine warfare and a shortage of spare parts and petrol as the war dragged on. From almost 11,000 cars in 1941, Syonan was home to no more than 4,000 cars by 1945. The car was king no more.

A CITY OF WALKERS

BEFORE THE war, human and animal-powered methods of movement were either restricted by the authorities or seemed destined for the dustbin of history. The unforeseen overturning of the established order in Syonan changed their fates. With the decline in motor vehicles, civilians were forced to revert to human or animal-powered transport.

Previously prohibited before the war, the trishaw now found its way into Syonan to "solve the transport problem". Known as the rickshacycle (a combination of "rickshaw" and "bicycle") and the sanricksha (the Japanese name for the trishaw), 10 of these public hire vehicles made their debut on 7 August 1942, charging 15 cents a mile. They were manufactured and rented out by the Syonan Tricycle Company, which in the tradition of other transport companies, had its headquarters at Orchard Road. The trishaw was an instant hit with people eager to find work, as it was not as taxing as pulling a rickshaw. Other syndicates subsequently produced and rented out trishaws, too. Individuals also flexed their creativity in times of need, coming up with improved versions of the three-wheeled vehicle. The *Syonan Shimbun* reported two designs invented separately by young local-born Chinese in October and November 1942—Sunny Tan and Lim Hong Bee's creations could be purchased for $300 and $275 respectively. By November 1942, there were 500 public and 20 private trishaws on Syonan's roads. The trishaw and rickshaw replaced the trolleybus and motor bus as key forms of public transport. By 1945, there were about 4,000 trishaws and 3,500 rickshaws plying for hire.

However, trishaw riding was not without its dangers. One rider, Chia Kee Huat, who was 18 years old in 1942, knew the peril of running into Japanese soldiers:

> A trishaw rider's life was not too bad then. Our only worry was meeting soldiers on the road... Some of them paid and some refused. It was worse near midnight, when

I had to take them from the downtown shopping area to their barracks in Bukit Timah, Holland Road or Pasir Panjang where you could not expect to pick up passengers on the return trip… It was sheer bad luck if I should meet other soldiers on the return trip. They would order me to take them back to the barracks. There were nights when I had to make many trips until dawn—and all for nothing.

Rickshaw passengers also had to be careful. It was not uncommon for Japanese sentries to force rickshaws to stop and make the passenger pull the rickshaw—just for a cruel laugh. Low remembers one such incident outside the Municipal Building:

A Chinaman, spruce and dapper, was passing in a rickshaw. A Japanese soldier stopped the rickshaw, pulled the Chinaman down and, firmly grasping him by his tie, gave him a good shaking. Next he motioned the puller to climb onto the seat and made the dandy pull the rickshaw in his turn.

Even cyclists had to be on their guard. The number of bicycles in Singapore hit an all-time high in 1941 at 120,000, but during the Malayan Campaign, thousands were confiscated by the British. After the fall of Singapore, tens of thousands more were seized by the 25th Army and sent overseas to equip other "bicycle brigades" conquering Southeast Asia. Whatever remained became valuable private transport. Even then, Japanese soldiers and sentries frequently divested cyclists of their wheels on a whim. For the Chinese, of course, he was lucky to get away without an extra slap or kick to add insult to injury; for the other races, they usually received at least a dollar in compensation. This was one manifestation of a divide-and-rule policy along racial lines. Low remarked that "in 1942, there were many who were pro-Japanese and anti-British; it took the Japanese three years to make us all anti-Japanese".

With motor trucks destroyed, confiscated, or mothballed, tricycles took over their pre-war role of moving heavy goods. Tricycle owners started a new business—renting out their vehicles. Hundreds of tricycles could be hired at three locations in the Town—opposite the Beach Road Market at the junction of Beach Road and Rochor Road, Coleman Bridge, and Tew Chew Street in Chinatown. A tricycle could be had for $4 a day, although it was more lucrative to transport freight by the mile—for example, 20 cents a mile for one bag of rice (a tricycle could hold five bags).

As for bullock carts and horse-drawn carriages, their stay in Syonan was prolonged by the occupation. However, their numbers did not grow, perhaps because it was tough to feed and upkeep large animals in times of food shortages (and it would be tempting to slaughter them for food!), and harder still to import animals from overseas (what with the submarine blockade). In 1934, there were 226 bullock carts and 19 gharries in Singapore; in July 1942, 206 bullock carts and just nine gharries—five public, four private—remained registered. In May 1944, the Tokubetsu-Shi formed the Gyu Basya Unyu Kumiai, or the Bullock Cart and Horse Drawn Carriage Association, to oversee the "smooth distribution of transport"—probably a euphemism for appropriating them for municipal duties. At the first general meeting of bullock cart and carriage owners in June, 51 turned up, surely lured by the promise of animal feed rations.

With so many difficulties and dangers in using methods and channels of movement, the last option for the civilians of Syonan was, as Edwin Brown had put it, to "hoof it". Bowing low to sentries multiple times during a journey became second nature. Cuylenburg remembers how "thousands walked the streets all day, trying to sell something at black market prices… those who had bicycles were the privileged few." Another Syonan resident recalled: "Either you used your bicycle mostly, or else you walked. It was common for people to walk many miles those days." If we wish to imagine a dystopian Singapore, the Syonan of 1945 is one good place to start.

YET, WHAT if Japan had brokered a peace with the United States six months after Pearl Harbor, as she had hoped? Japan had grand plans of economic self-sufficiency for her empire in the Far East—what she dubbed the Greater East Asia Co-Prosperity Sphere, an imperialist propaganda concept justifying her occupation and exploitation of territories throughout East and Southeast Asia.

Like other colonial powers before her, Japan had been making use of the railway to consolidate her overseas empire, starting with Manchukuo in the early 1930s. As her empire grew, a high-speed, standard-gauge railway was needed to unify different gauges and cover great distances swiftly—by 1945, the Co-Prosperity Sphere had 380 million people spread over an area 18 times the size of the Japanese Home Islands. This new trunk line was literally called the "New Trunk Line", or Shinkansen in Japanese. First, it had to connect the capital Tokyo to mainland East Asia. Hence, the first part of the plan was to link Tokyo to Shimonoseki at the western end of Honshu Island with a railway of unprecedented speed—up to 200 km per hour, covering the distance of 1,000 km in just nine hours. Then in 1939, railway official Yumoto Noboru proposed an underwater tunnel between Japan's Kyushu Island and the Korean Peninsula; two years later, engineering studies began on the tunnel.

This was where Syonan came in. In August 1942, Japan's South Manchurian Railway Company formulated plans for an 8,000-km rail network—the Trans-Greater East Asian Railway—stretching from Manchukuo in the north, through China, Indochina, and Marai, to Syonan in the south. Noboru further suggested extending the railway from Syonan south across the Java Sea to Jakarta, freshly seized from the Dutch. The total distance between Tokyo and Jakarta was 11,618 km, and with high-speed trains, he estimated it could be covered in only four-and-a-half days. Syonan would be plugged into a railway line grander than any the British had ever dreamed.

Alas, with the war going badly for Japan from 1943, these grand plans were shelved and never revived. The Shinkansen in its current form was eventually opened between Tokyo and Osaka in 1964; in 2016, Malaysia and Singapore signed off on plans for a high-speed railway between Kuala Lumpur and Singapore, which should begin operations by 2031. If Noboru's Tokyo–Jakarta railway line had come true, Singapore—or Syonan—might have acquired a high-speed railway even before the 1950s came around. This would have changed Singapore's history of movement beyond all recognition—an attractive notion for fans of alternate history! It was a sign of how far the Co-Prosperity Sphere's fortunes had fallen that, by 1945, people walked in Syonan instead of boarding a high-speed rail to Tokyo.

VISIONS OF A "NEW CITY"

WE HAVE seen how the dominant road-naming system in modern Singapore became a British one with British naming conventions. Most place and road names in Singapore were in English, Chinese, or Malay. After Singapore became Syonan in 1942, the Japanese renamed some major landmarks in the Town. For example, Clifford Pier became Yamato (an ancient province in Japan, and the name of a powerful Imperial Japanese Navy battleship) Sanbashi ("Pier"), Raffles Hotel became Syonan Ryokan ("Inn"), and Capitol Theatre, Kyo-ei Eigakan ("Co-Prosperity Cinema"). But these were outside the norm. For road names, the Japanese transliterated virtually all of them into Japanese. Thus, the names were in Japanese script, but phonetically, they sounded like the original English, Chinese, or Malay words.

There could have been one exception. Before Yamashita was reassigned from Syonan to Manchukuo in July 1942, his officers suggested to him that Stamford Road be renamed Yamashita Road in his honour. It would have been fitting as Stamford Road was one of Syonan's oldest roads, had been named after Stamford Raffles, and was a key road connecting Orchard Road to the Padang. But Yamashita, a humble, principled man, declined the honour, and passed on his opportunity at toponymic immortality.

The reasons why almost no roads in Syonan were given fresh Japanese names were twofold. One: the Tokubetsu-Shi had more important municipal priorities to grapple with; two: the Japanese did not stay around long enough to conduct renaming exercises or build new roads and housing estates. If they had won the war and Syonan had remained Japanese for the next 100 years, it was possible that eventually all roads in Syonan would have been Nipponised. If not a Yamashita Dori (Japanese for "Street"), then perhaps a Tojo Dori after Prime Minister Hideki Tojo, or Tokyo Odori ("Boulevard"). It could have been a matter of time, because the Japanese community in Syonan was growing rapidly. After the Pacific War broke out in December 1941, about 1,000 Japanese civilians in Singapore were interned in British India, but after an exchange of internees with the British, about 700 returned. More Japanese then flocked to Syonan from other parts of the Empire. Japanese companies were invited to set up shop in Syonan, and Japanese officials, engineers, and technicians were needed to replace the Europeans who were incarcerated. Possibly thousands of Japanese civilians were living in Syonan by 1945, on top of 70,000 Japanese soldiers posted there. They formed the new apex of the social, political, and economic hierarchy in Syonan.

Also, given enough time, Japanese architects and urban planners could have come around to the massive task of overhauling the overcrowded, congested Town of Syonan. A hint of how this remodelling could have been carried out lay in the north of the Empire.

Shinkyo (Japanese for "New Capital"), or Xinjing in Mandarin, formerly Changchun, was the capital of Manchukuo, but it had been under Japanese influence for almost 40 years. After the Russo-Japanese War of 1905, the Japanese supplanted the Russians in what was then Manchuria of Qing China. In 1907, they set up a railway town northwest of the old walled city of Changchun. This new town had a rectangular plan with straight streets, regular blocks, and diagonal boulevards running to large plazas—a town plan Raffles would have approved! Major landmarks such as the post office, railway station, and regional office building were all European in architecture—representations of progress, civilisation, cosmopolitanism, and modernity. After Manchukuo was established in the 1930s and

Changchun was renamed Shinkyo and declared its capital, urban planners worked on it as a model city for the rest of the Japanese protectorate. New buildings were spaced far apart with wide facades; housing estates were separated from industries to reduce the effects of pollution. Thousands of trees were planted, lining major thoroughfares. Traffic strips separated vehicular and horse-drawn traffic.

Shinkyo was a world of difference from the Town of Syonan—tightly-packed shophouses and tenement houses bent over narrow roads choked with seething traffic, a morass of pollution and noise. Urban land use was haphazard, and greenery rare. It is not a leap of imagination to picture Japanese urban planners ordering the tearing down of the Town and building another Shinkyo from the ground up—with fresh Japanese place and road names. In reality, large-scale urban renewal in Singapore began from the 1960s. It could have started far earlier if the Japanese had won the war.

One lasting place name in Syonan borne out of the Japanese occupation was not Japanese, but Malay. Wartime food shortages led to the administration encouraging civilians to plant food crops such as tapioca. So much tapioca was planted in Perseverance Estate west of the Malay Settlement, that part of it took on the name Kampong Ubi, after *ubi kayu*, Malay for "tapioca". Today, the place name Ubi is a reminder of hard times during the occupation.

Syonan never remained Japanese long enough to become another Shinkyo. From 1943, the war was as good as lost for Japan. The Japanese were gradually pushed back in the Pacific. The Allies invaded the Philippines in October 1944, Iwo Jima in February 1945, and Okinawa—just 145 km from the Home Islands—in April. In Europe, Nazi Germany surrendered to the Allies in May, leaving Japan to fend for itself.

The fighting seemed destined to reach Syonan again. The Allies drew up plans to land forces in Malaya and strike south to Syonan. Operation Zipper foresaw landings in Malaya for September 1945, while the invasion of Syonan was part of Operation Mailfist, to take place between December 1945 and March 1946. The Allies had 100,000 men, while 70,000 Japanese soldiers awaited them in Syonan. A bloodbath was imminent; Syonan looked set to suffer the fate of Manila in the Philippines, destroyed by house-to-house fighting in February 1945, killing an estimated 125,000 civilians and soldiers.

Other events intervened. On 6 and 9 August 1945, the Allies dropped two nuclear bombs on Japan, wiping out the cities of Hiroshima and Nagasaki; on 8 August, the Soviet Union declared war on Japan and invaded Manchukuo. These events culminated in Japan's unconditional surrender on 15 August—sparing Syonan further destruction. The darkest chapter in modern Singapore's history mercifully came to a close. Syonan became Singapore again. Joy and relief swept through the population.

Mamoru Shinozaki (1908–1991), a Japanese diplomat and occupation-era administrator who has been nicknamed "Singapore's Oskar Schindler" for saving the lives of thousands through the liberal issue of safety passes, believed that the occupation was a "historical necessity for Singapore". In terms of a history of movement, the occupation was necessary—to show us how a regression in movement under autocratic rule could unfold. The occupation took Singapore on a different historical trajectory. It was a Singapore in which motor vehicles were monopolised by the ruling power, while most of the population had to revert to human and animal-powered transport; the government exercised an iron grip over methods of movement; spare parts and fuel for motor vehicles were in very short supply; and unpredictable, arbitrary rule triumphed over rule of law. For the first time in Singapore's modern history, movement was seriously curtailed, crippling economic growth and the quality of life.

After the surrender, the Allies took two weeks to return to Singapore. The British Military Administration (BMA) took control of Malaya and Singapore pending a return to civilian rule. Singapore was purged of all things Japanese. All Japanese soldiers were rounded up, interned, and eventually repatriated. The entire Japanese community—almost as old as modern Singapore itself—was also expelled.

Even Japan Street in Telok Ayer—a road more than a century old—had to go. A letter writer to *The Straits Times* in November 1945 called the road name a "disgusting eyesore", and urged its renaming, claiming that "servicemen would certainly be pleased to know that 'Japan' is wiped off the map here". Suggested alternatives included Chungking Street (after Nationalist China's wartime capital, known as Chongqing today), Chiang Kai Shek Street (after Nationalist China's wartime leader), and Mountbatten Street (after Allied commander Lord Louis Mountbatten (1900–1979)). The Municipal Commission—which took over from the BMA in April 1946—came to a decision in June: Boon Tat Street, after Ong Boon Tat (1888–1941), a businessman and former municipal commissioner.

Other new place names emerged to commemorate the Allies' triumphant return to Singapore. By November 1945, there were Chungking Theatre (along Kim Seng Road), Atlantic Cinema (the Atlantic was a major theatre of war), a Leyte Café (after another great battle in the Pacific), and an Atomic Restaurant! None has survived to the present. But one road did—Mountbatten Road. Grove Road was renamed in May 1946 to honour the commander.

An unusual experience of movement emerged after the occupation—the first airport crossings in Singapore. During the occupation, the Japanese used prisoner-of-war labour to construct an airfield in Changi, east of Changi Road. They also decided to extend the landing radius of Kallang Aerodrome to accommodate larger bombers, starting work on a 1.6-km runway cutting across Grove Road onto the open land beyond, and closing the road to traffic.

After the British returned, the Changi airfield, named RAF Changi, was upgraded; an airport crossing was necessary near 13½ Milestone Changi Road. Kallang Aerodrome's runway was also completed; the Municipality negotiated the reopening of Grove Road (now Mountbatten Road) by December 1946, necessitating another airport crossing. Motorists using the busy road did not appreciate this—if planes landed or took off, they had to wait up to 15 minutes for the gates to open!

RETURN OF THE OLD ORDER

After the Japanese occupation, the authorities had their work cut out rebuilding Singapore's transport system. Senior BMA officer Brigadier P. A. B. MacKerron said in December 1945: "Singapore's transport problem is one of the greatest obstacles in the return of the country to normalcy."

Since Singapore was fortunate not to have become a battleground in the Allied endeavour to retake Southeast Asia, it did not suffer heavy or complete destruction of its urban and transport infrastructure, unlike other cities. For example, the total annihilation of Manila led to the post-war decision not to revive its electric tramway system; instead, jeepneys—public jeeps similar to mosquito buses—took over. Singapore experienced no such sea change in its public transport system. Instead, the BMA allowed the STC and Chinese bus companies to restart their bus networks. However, out of the 53 trolleybuses and 69 motor buses surrendered to the Japanese in 1942, only 20 trolleybuses and 22 motor buses remained roadworthy by the end of the occupation—just one in nine buses survived the war.

The 20 trolleybuses, still in their original green-and-white colours, were given a fresh coat of paint and dispatched on two routes on 16 September 1945: Tanjong Pagar to Geylang, and Finlayson Green to Paya Lebar. Fares remained at pre-war rates, between four and 10 cents. Thirteen days later, railway trains between Singapore and Malaya resumed service.

In the years after the occupation, the public bus system suffered from a host of problems, most of all a case of too few buses and too many commuters. The bus companies took years to restore their numbers to pre-war standards. Orders for new buses were only delivered from war-ravaged Britain from 1947. Nevertheless, orderly queues formed at bus stops, and no one rushed when a bus finally arrived—the effect of years of harsh Japanese discipline! The BMA also helped by supplying military lorries converted at short notice into "lorry-buses": a canvas sheet propped up at the back to provide the coachwork; holes cut into the sheets as windows; makeshift steps tacked onto the tailboard. These hardy, 30-seater lorries worked the roads for the next decade or so.

Meanwhile, every bus packed in the crowds. Despite an official cap of 45 passengers per bus instead of the usual 55, drivers and conductors frequently flouted it—with tragic results. Buses did not come with doors then, and it was not uncommon for passengers to stand on the steps while buses moved. Occasionally, passengers tumbled out onto the road to their deaths. Alarmed, the traffic police suggested automated sliding doors, but they were too costly to install.

Other problems plaguing buses included lawlessness and corruption, symptomatic of a society pulling itself together after a brutal occupation. Fights and pickpocketing on buses abounded, and conductors were frequently assaulted and robbed. Conductors also cheated their companies, issuing tickets with lower values than actual fares paid, collecting used tickets to be sold again, or collecting fares without issuing tickets. This way, the STC lost more than a thousand dollars in revenue every day. Stealing became so lucrative it was said that anyone who wanted to be employed as a bus conductor had to pay $50 upfront in "coffee money" to get the job!

Bus strikes were rife. Because of the war and occupation, people in Singapore became more politicised and combative to protect their rights, so post-war trade unions grew in membership and influence, and strikes became a frequent instrument to get demands met or addressed. The first post-war transport strike started on 26 October 1945, as returning STC workers demanded a 40 per cent increase in wages plus bonuses. The strike collapsed within a week as the BMA stepped in with military servicemen to drive the buses. But a precedent had been set. Strikes would become a mainstay for the next 15 years.

These problems notwithstanding, the Municipal Commission saw the trolleybus-motor bus system as the future of public transport in Singapore. In its view, the trishaw and rickshaw were relics from another era. Hence, the Commission put in place legislation against them. 30 April 1947 was set as the final day of operation for rickshaws in Singapore. Rickshaw pullers accepted their fate—reluctantly. Many returned to China, while others stayed on and turned to trishaw riding. It was the end of a 67-year era.

As rickshaws checked out, trishaw numbers rose from 6,908 in 1946 to a peak of 8,948 the following year. The Municipal Commission tried to rein them in by registering all trishaws by 1 June 1947, and setting uniform fares of 20 cents for a half mile (800 metres), or $1.50 for one hour and 40 cents for every additional 15 minutes. Private trishaws had to be painted pill-box red while public trishaws went in olive green. But the Commission refrained from getting rid of the trishaw altogether—just as it did not abolish the rickshaw in the 1930s—as Singapore's beleaguered public transport system needed all the vehicles that could be had. By the end of 1950, trishaw numbers had dipped to 7,065, with 7,500 riders.

As shipping recovered after the occupation, vehicle imports into Singapore resumed. Motor taxis thrived. The number of taxis—still dubbed "hackney carriages" by the authorities—reached a post-war high of 1,947 in November 1948. The following year, the Municipal Commission decided to cap taxis at 1,500; by the end of 1950, there were 1,443 taxis. Fares were fixed in 1946 at 30 cents for the first mile (1.6 km) and 15 cents for each half mile thereafter, or $2 for an hour or less, and 50 cents for every 15 minutes thereafter. These rates roughly matched the trishaw's. Of course, taxi drivers could charge their own exorbitant fees. Taximeters were still not compulsory, although some taxis had them—each device was as large as a kitchen toaster!

By 1950, Singapore's public bus system had again become the island's number one form of public transport, followed by trishaws, then taxis. There were now 11 Chinese bus companies, one fewer than before the war: the Green Bus Company took over the Jurong Omnibus Service, monopolising rural bus services in the west of Singapore Island; the Tay Koh Yat Bus Company took over the Seletar Motor Bus Company; the Easy Bus Company (with a livery of black and yellow) was formed. The Chinese bus companies now had 274 motor buses, while the STC had 50 trolleybuses and 233 motor buses. With a population of 1,022,000 in 1950, that meant one bus for 1,835 people in Singapore, compared to one for 2,024 people in 1941. And buses were better in quality—the STC's new Ransomes, Sims & Jefferies trolleybuses came with pneumatic tyres instead of solid metal wheels—no more sore butts!

MEANWHILE, IN the realm of private transport, the motor car swiftly regained its pre-war position of number one. On 30 September 1946, the Registry of Vehicles logged 4,156 cars, about as many as there were 25 years before. Just four years later, in December 1950, the number had quadrupled to 16,000, or one car for every 64 people. With the car population slashed to a third during the occupation, the chance was there to move Singapore away from a car-first culture and encourage alternate methods of movement to relieve urban congestion. But the post-war European and Chinese political and economic elite remained beholden to cars, and the chance was lost. Allowing car numbers to grow without restrictions, while abolishing or cutting back on slower vehicles, was the path of least resistance.

Singapore's roads quickly returned to pre-war levels of chaos and danger. With strict Japanese rule a thing of the past, reckless driving, bad road manners, even excessive use of the horn, all returned with a vengeance. During the Japanese occupation, over six months from June to December 1942, there were just 22 fatal and 143 non-fatal traffic accidents—fewer than one accident a day. Over the 31 days of December 1946, there were 522 accidents—almost 17 a day!—with 23 deaths and 127 injuries, setting a record for the highest monthly casualty rate since record-keeping began in 1928. For the year of 1946, 140 died in accidents—two deaths every five days. "Traffic control as we used to know it," an October 1946 *Straits Times* report proclaimed, "is almost completely absent."

The Municipal Commission tried to tackle the newfound chaos. One solution was an idea conceived by the Trimmer Committee in 1938—one-way roads. The first area to test this scheme was Raffles Place and the old Telok Ayer Reclamation Ground. In February 1946, Market Street, D'Almeida Street, De Souza Street, Malacca Street, Robinson Road, Cecil Street, Telegraph Street, Finlayson Green, and Raffles Quay became one-way. In a month, with no serious accidents and a reduction in congestion, traffic police chief C. J. R. Pembroke declared the scheme a "success". With the exception of De Souza Street, which was expunged in the 1980s for Raffles Place MRT Interchange, these roads have remained one-way to this day.

As more one-way schemes spread throughout the Town, the inflexibility of the trolleybus system became clear. When two-way carriageways were converted to one-way, traffic could be easily diverted, but not trolleybuses, because they relied on traction poles and overhead cables. Relocating them cost money that the STC could ill afford. Hence, on Kallang Road, the Municipal Commission granted permission to town-bound trolleybuses to move against the flow of traffic—the only time in Singapore's history that any vehicle was officially allowed to travel against the flow of traffic. This practice spread to other converted one-way roads that carried trolleybus routes.

Another solution to traffic chaos was speed limits. Back in 1940, the Traffic Advisory Committee had suggested a speed limit of 30 miles an hour (48 km/h) within the municipal boundary. Finally, on 1 January 1949, this was implemented for all motor vehicles. Three months later, the same speed limit was also laid down inside large villages. In January 1950, this ruling spread to trunk and arterial roads with built-up areas outside the municipal boundary, such as Upper Serangoon Road, Changi Road, and Yio Chu Kang Road.

Despite these measures, accident and fatality records continued to be broken. In 1947, 158 died in 7,036 accidents, or one accident every 75 minutes—a new record. A new high was also reached for monthly accident figures in July 1949, with 622 accidents; December 1949 saw 684 accidents, close to one accident an hour—resulting in seven killed, 221 injured. The most treacherous roads were Bukit Timah Road, Geylang Road, Orchard Road, and the Serangoon–Upper Serangoon trunk road.

It became clear to the government that traffic reform was sorely needed. But traffic reform had to go together with urban reform, as channels of movement are inseparable from the urban milieu in which they exist. Hence, the government set in motion plans to study and overhaul the urban landscape, a monumental endeavour never attempted since the day Raffles set sail from Singapore in 1823.

While officials were contemplating the future of movement in Singapore, the old was going quietly into the night. In 1950, *The Straits Times* tracked down Singapore's last three surviving gharries. They were all owned by a Muslim man named Hupsah, Singapore's only gharry licensee.

The 76-year-old, who had run carriages for hire for 65 years, housed four ponies for his carriages in a stable in Towner Road, off Serangoon Road:

> The gharries are used mainly for cinema advertising, but Hupsah often gets calls to children's parties where his ponies are great fun for the youngsters… Hupsah is allowed to drive his gharries anywhere in town except in the streets around Raffles Place.
>
> He has memories of better days. He remembers hitching his horses to the shady trees in Raffles Place when it was a laterite road… He used to take sightseers around the island but could only go as far as Woodlands because there was no Causeway. And his gharries have drawn up at Government House carrying people attending official functions as he says— "only the wealthy could ride in my gharries in those days".
>
> …During the Japanese occupation he did a roaring business because of the transport difficulties. His gharries were used for funerals, to take children to school, to deliver laundry and to carry people about their business.

Hupsah represented the end of an era—the end of animal-powered transport, the end of slow movement, the end of a time before modernity in Singapore. The time had arrived for an urban and transport revolution to take Singapore's history of movement into a new era.

CHAPTER NOTES

1. *Syonan Shimbun* articles printed the name "Syonansi Siden". However, photos of trolleybuses during the Japanese Occupation show the vehicles stamped with the kanji "昭南市電" ("Zhao Nan Shi Dian" in Mandarin), which is "Syonan Shiden".

CHAPTER 6
1950 to 2011: Urban Revolution

MADAM GOH Poh Thuan was born in 1883 during the term of Governor Sir Frederick Weld, just three years after the rickshaw began operations in Singapore. During the Japanese Occupation, her family moved into Perseverance Estate west of Jalan Eunos, where they eked out a living on a vegetable farm rearing chickens, ducks, and pigs. There they lived for the next three decades… until 1979, when a government order came for the kampung dwellers of Perseverance Estate to be resettled for urban redevelopment. For 96-year-old Goh, it was the shattering of a dream. She told *The Straits Times*:

> I had dreamt of a large, happy family of children, grandchildren and great-grandchildren living together under the same roof… I thought this was possible and I have a few years more to live at most. Now the family will be split up as our new flat in Ang Mo Kio cannot possibly accommodate all of us.

Goh's story was similar to that of hundreds of thousands of Singaporeans, swept up in an urban and transport revolution from the 1960s to the 1990s, one that forever changed the history of movement in Singapore.

Over just 30 years, a large proportion of Singapore's population was resettled from what was the Municipality to rural areas of the island—into new towns, a concept born in England and in reaction to the devastating effects of urbanisation and industrialisation on nature and the human body. This large-scale resettlement entailed the destruction of rural communities that had thrived for generations, and the effacement of trunk and rural roads that had served travellers for decades. After resettlement, centuries-old city blocks and roads inside the Town of Singapore were also razed for a new city to be built atop the ashes of the old. A new generation of Singaporeans—now citizens of a nation-state independent after 1965—grew up in entirely different surroundings from that of their parents.

Such a feat was possible only through urban and transport planning on an unprecedented scale. As the dust of World War II settled, Singapore's colonial masters started a process of drafting master plans to chart the island's urban and transport development; after the island gained self-rule in 1959, its successor government inherited these plans. To execute them, however, a bureaucratic apparatus on a scale and complexity hitherto unseen in colonial Singapore was constructed—meticulous, efficient, coldly pragmatic, leaving no (mile)stone unturned and no corner of the island untouched. Departments grew into ministries, which hired thousands to accomplish more in years what the British had wished to do in decades. This facilitated the transformation of a city and the way people in the city moved.

But let us not forget that such feats of planning and execution from the top down were impossible without general acquiescence on the ground—accepting what they saw as the inevitable march of history, seeing their sacrifices as necessary for the progress of a nation, and keeping faith that even the entire dislocation of communities and shared memories was fair exchange for a better future for their children and grandchildren. Goh's neighbour, coffee shop owner Sim Kim Bei, then 51, was born in Perseverance Estate; his parents had lived there for 65 years—like Goh, they had to move. "Of course, I shall miss this old place," he said. "But it is no use getting fed up. One must adapt to the future." It is to people like him that this chapter is dedicated.

NEW TOWN, OLD CONCEPT

THE RAFFLES Town Plan of 1822 was modern Singapore's first and last town plan for 130 years, during which the island's population grew 110 times from 10,000 to 1,100,000.

After Raffles left Singapore in 1823, the authorities adopted a laissez-faire approach towards urban and transport planning in favour of free trade and mass immigration. There was little coordination among officials who studied or oversaw the island's population, housing, and traffic patterns.

There was also little control over land use and allotment. Outside the Town, however, the authorities freely parcelled out irregular plots of land for developers and speculators. Many parcels came with freehold leases, giving landowners the right to rebuff later efforts by the authorities to acquire their land for redevelopment.

While the Public Works Department (PWD) oversaw the building and maintenance of roads, drains, and bridges, the closest pre-war Singapore came to an organisation charting and implementing urban change was the Singapore Improvement Trust (SIT). From 1927, the SIT surveyed land use, acquired land for building and widening roads, checked dwellings to ensure they were fit for habitation, and rehoused people in dwellings deemed unfit for habitation.

However, Singapore persistently suffered from an acute housing shortage. The private sector, which constructed bungalows and other upscale housing, was reluctant to build houses for the poor because doing so did not turn a profit, and the government was reluctant to pick up the slack because great expenditure was required. From 1920 to 1941, the SIT built only 2,112 housing units.

But it is erroneous to assume that the SIT had completely shirked its alleged "duty" of providing high-density housing for thousands of "Singaporeans". This assumption was borne from the popular post-independence nation-building narrative describing how the SIT's successor, the Housing and Development Board (HDB), had succeeded where the SIT had failed by swiftly constructing thousands of high-rise flats. In fact, the HDB's eventual achievement was never one of the SIT's missions. The SIT was not a public housing authority with clearly defined statutory housing powers. When the SIT built new estates such as Tiong Bahru, it was often going beyond the call of duty.

The end of WWII set in motion the wheels of political change. The British set Malaya and Singapore on a peaceful path to self-government. In April 1946, the Straits Settlements, Federated Malay States, and Unfederated Malay States were dissolved to form a Malayan Union under a centralised government in Kuala Lumpur. However, Singapore was kept out as a separate Crown Colony—a fateful decision. The governor of the Straits Settlements became the governor of Singapore, the first being Sir Franklin Charles

Gimson (1890–1975); the PWD of the Straits Settlements became the PWD of Singapore.

A post-war baby boom intensified the pre-war housing shortage in the Town. Town blocks bordered by major thoroughfares were crisscrossed by small lanes. These blocks were densely packed with two to four-storey, century-old shophouses; each had a frontage of only 16 feet (4.8 m), but a depth of up to 200 feet (60 m). Many were formerly the family houses of wealthy merchants. Now, the ground floors—each originally intended to house one or two families—were occupied by businesses, while the upper floors were divided and subdivided into cubicles of about nine square metres each. Each cubicle—without windows, swathed in permanent semi-darkness, claustrophobic, insanitary—could house a family of half a dozen. Daily living and working spilled out onto the narrow streets, side lanes, back alleys, and five-foot-ways. In 1947, the most densely populated area in Singapore was the 12 hectares bounded by South Bridge Road, Upper Nankin Street, New Bridge Road, and Smith Street; the eight town blocks accommodated 22,000 people!

Saturation in the Town accelerated the movement of low-income families to urban kampungs at the fringes of the Town, especially along arterial roads such as Geylang Road, Upper Serangoon Road, Tiong Bahru Road, and Kampong Bahru Road. These urban kampungs were packed with wooden houses with attap or corrugated zinc roofs built without planning approval, and had no paved roads, only narrow tracks which turned to mud after heavy rain. Their combined population topped 127,000 in 1947.

In the same year, an eight-man housing committee appointed by the government to study housing conditions in Singapore and make recommendations for improvement, published its report. The report framed housing as a crisis of congested, dangerous, insanitary "slums" and "squatters" that necessitated a radical solution: urban renewal. (Never mind that many "squatters" were in fact rent-paying tenants; the label gave the impression that they illegally occupied land.) Urban kampungs were singled out as the "worst type of slum", with "living conditions which (were) not fit for animals to live in". This was because urban kampungs were semi-autonomous communities that defied official planning and control—which the authorities were anxious to subdue.

To accomplish urban renewal, the committee proposed a "Master Development Plan" for Singapore—"a plan for the whole island, showing not only roads as at present but what land is to be developed, and how it is to be developed, and what land is not to be developed". Never since 1823 had such a master plan been drawn up. The committee also proposed resettling thousands of people from the Town and surrounding urban kampungs to the rural outskirts, to new, self-contained satellite towns, or new towns. The "new town" was an unprecedented idea for Singapore, but its origins went back half a century, to Britain.

London, 1898. Ebenezer Howard (1850–1928), a parliamentary record keeper, published *To-Morrow: A Peaceful Path to Real Reform*, after witnessing a decade of bitter parliamentary debates over land issues, housing, and the poor. With rampant urbanisation and industrialisation, the capital's population had almost doubled since 1871, from 3.9 million to 6.6 million; the government was divided over what to do about the city's sprawling, overcrowded slums. Howard's "Garden City Concept" advocated resettling part of the population to the countryside around London. The new settlements were radical in form. Each "garden city" would be circular in shape, with a park in the centre. Houses, gardens, roads, and railway lines would form concentric rings radiating outwards from the central park, with factories and a green belt forming the outer rings. More roads and railway lines would make up the spokes of a wheel. This way, 32,000 people could comfortably inhabit 1,000 acres. The virtues were many. Everything would be within walking distance—people could get around on foot or by rail. Land use would be economised. Residential areas would be surrounded by green spaces. Once a garden city was full, another one could be built a short distance away, then another—the result would be a polycentric cluster housing up to 250,000 people, all connected by rail to London itself. Howard's emphases were on the quality of life, green spaces, careful planning and design, and the urban space as organic, not hostile—everything London (or Singapore) was not in 1898.

Howard's revolutionary ideas caught on among some architects and planners. They formed the Garden City Association, which advocated the development of garden cities, or new towns, instead of uncontrolled urban sprawl. The Association did not catch on among mainstream urban planning; nevertheless, two new towns inspired by Howard's ideas were built in 1902 and 1919—Letchworth and Welwyn Garden City, both north of London.

During WWII, an Association member and town planner, Patrick Abercrombie (1879–1957), was tasked with coming up with a plan for the redevelopment of London. The metropolis had been ravaged by years of German bombing and here was a chance for the government to rebuild the city and improve land use and transport. Abercrombie came up with the County of London Plan in 1943, followed by the Greater London Plan in 1944; the latter involved relocating 500,000 people to 10 new towns 30–45 km from the city.

Abercrombie's plans, and post-war construction of new towns in Britain, subsequently inspired Singapore's Housing Committee in 1947—hence the latter's references to a "Master Plan", "New Towns", and a recommended satellite town size of 50,000. In fact, in its report, the committee mentioned the County of London Plan, and recommended that Abercrombie be summoned to assist in framing a master plan. Unfortunately, Abercrombie's plans only drew inspiration from Howard's ideas, and did not replicate his original concentric garden city plan—hence, down the line, the Housing Committee's new towns idea made no mention of concentric settlements either. Otherwise, that would have made for an interesting sight on a map of Singapore Island! Nevertheless, the 1947 Housing Committee Report laid a basic framework for urban and transport development in Singapore for the next 60 years—and by extension, its history of movement.

FROM A Town to a City. In 1951, Singapore was conferred city status—the Town and Municipality of Singapore were now officially the City of Singapore. The 22-year-old Municipal Building was renamed City Hall; the Municipal Commission, a century-old institution, was replaced by the City Council, comprising a President and 18 elected and nine nominated councillors. The City Council retained control of the PWD and the Registry of Vehicles, and its first president was T. P. F. McNeice.

The last governor of the Straits Settlements, Shenton Thomas, was also honoured in the same year despite inept and uninspiring leadership during the Malayan Campaign. His decision to stay after the fall of Singapore and endure captivity for the next three-and-a-half years redeemed him in the eyes of the British. When Raffles Quay was lengthened south to Palmer Road, the stretch south of Boon Tat Street was renamed Shenton Way.

The Housing Committee Report of 1947, and its recommendations of decentralisation and new towns, had an impact on the SIT's direction in the early 1950s. Before, its housing projects were mostly inside the old Town; now, most were located outside the Town. However, since there was no master plan to follow, these estates were built close to the Town or along major channels of movement, so residents could still travel around easily.

Within the old Town, several SIT estates were constructed, including Upper Pickering Street (1952) and Outram Hill (1953). Upper Pickering Street Estate, next to Hong Lim Green in the heart of Chinatown, had five nine-storey blocks, the first high-rise public housing in Singapore—at the time, nine storeys were considered high-rise! The blocks soon became infamous as a favourite spot for committing suicide.

Just north of the old Town, in the Pek Kio area, the SIT built Durham, Owen, and Norfolk estates, named after the respective roads. Tasek Utara Estate was also built next to the lake of the same name. All were completed by 1950. Temple Estate at Kim Keat Road off Balestier Road was added in 1954. The cluster of 38 three-storey blocks was named after a religious landmark, the Siong Lim Temple, completed in 1907 as Singapore's first Buddhist monastery.

In the south of the island, the SIT concentrated six housing projects—Kampong Silat, Delta, Alexandra Road (North) and Alexandra Road (South) (built over Chinese cemeteries), Redhill/Bukit Merah (built over a village named Kampong Selomoi), and Henderson estates, named after nearby roads or landmarks. All were completed between 1952 and 1955. As for Delta Estate, named after Delta Road, its roads were named after famous rivers around the world, such as Brahmaputra Road, Ganges Avenue, Indus Road, Mekong Walk, Nile Road, and Tigris Walk. Alexandra Road (South) Estate used the names of Nordic gods and goddesses: Bragi Road, Iduna Road, Thor Terrace, Vulcan Terrace, and Odin Square. Those were the days when creativity and flair were employed in the naming of roads.

To the west of these estates, on land occupied by rubber plantations and attap huts, the SIT commenced building of Singapore's first "satellite town" in 1952, as envisioned by the Housing Committee Report. Even though the new town was on what was once Tan Kim Seng's Estate, it was named Queenstown to honour Queen Elizabeth II's coronation. The town was to be built in stages. The first two estates were Princess Margaret and Duchess estates, respectively named after the Queen's younger sister and their mother's title, Duchess of York. Roads inside Queenstown were given names associated with the Queen: Margaret Drive; Strathmore Avenue, after the Queen's maternal grandfather, Claude Bowes-Lyon, 14th Earl of Strathmore and Kinghorne; Dawson Road, after Bertrand Dawson, physician to the Royal Family; and Clarence Lane, after Clarence House, the Queen's royal home from 1953 to 2002. In all, four SIT estates built in the 1950s were named in association with the Queen. This underlined Singapore's close links with Britain despite embarking on a journey towards independence, and the peaceful nature of that journey.

However, the SIT could not build estates and homes fast enough to solve the housing "crisis". By 1955, there were over 50 urban kampungs surrounding the old Town, housing 41,000 families and 246,000 people. The SIT painted them as a "black belt... infested with, and providing shelter to, dangerous secret societies". But like the mosquito bus, urban kampungs were a necessity the authorities had to tolerate, at a time when SIT housing was in short supply and too expensive for the lower classes.

THE FIRST URBAN PLAN IN 130 YEARS

IN 1953, taking to heart the Housing Committee Report, the SIT assembled a "diagnostic survey team" under its manager Sir George Pepler. In 1822, six men took just weeks to come up with a town plan. Now, Pepler's team took more than two years to complete the first ever Master Plan of Singapore, encompassing detailed land surveys, volumetric traffic censuses, and a population census—to plan for the future, they first had to study the existing situation in detail. Such unprecedented bureaucratic dedication set the tone for future plans.

The Master Plan of 1955 divided Singapore Island into three zones. The Central Area—with 12 planning districts—measured roughly four miles by one mile (6.4 km by 1.6 km), covering the old Town and its fringes. Even though it made up just two per cent of Singapore Island, 30 per cent of the island's population lived inside it in 1953—about 340,900 out of 1,120,800 people. Its average residential density was 400 persons per square acre, but in some neighbourhoods, this went up to 1,000 persons.

The Urban Planning Area—with 16 planning districts—covered about 30 per cent of the island, which was the City of Singapore (formerly the Municipality) excluding the Central Area. The Urban Planning Area was considerably less crowded than the Central Area, with 60 persons living in a square acre; in all, half of Singapore's population, or 552,700 people. Its three most populous planning districts were Geylang (125,300, or one in nine persons in Singapore), Tiong Bahru (98,400, or one in 11), and Toa Payoh (64,000, including Temple Estate)—all replete with urban kampungs.

Finally, the Rural Planning Area—with 11 planning districts—covered the island beyond the city limits. It had 18 per cent of Singapore's population, or 203,200 people, mostly in villages along trunk roads, road junctions, or outside British military bases, a major source of employment. Significant ribbon developments lined Bukit Timah Road between Bukit Timah Village and Bukit Panjang Village, and Upper Thomson Road around Nee Soon Village.

The Master Plan echoed the 1947 Housing Committee Report in highlighting two problems. One was "considerable overcrowding in buildings which are structurally sound", mainly in and around the Central Area. Another was that "a large number of existing residential buildings (were) so dilapidated that they must be replaced"—the surveyors estimated almost four in 10 people in Singapore lived in such dwellings, more than half of them in urban kampungs.

Hence, the Master Plan suggested what the Housing Committee Report had previously put forward, echoing Abercrombie's plans and Britain's new towns programme: resettling at least half the population in the Central Area—170,000 people—to the Urban and Rural Planning Areas, while embarking on an ambitious building programme. With resettlement and Singapore's rapid population growth (now through natural increase and not immigration), it was estimated that 1,050,000 people would need permanent homes between 1953 and 1972; that meant building 11,000 homes every year from 1953 to

1972. In 12 years from 1947 to 1959, the SIT built just 20,907 units of housing—1,742 homes a year.

The Master Plan also recommended that new estates in the Urban and Rural Planning Areas be organised as "New Towns"—keeping alive a strain of Howard's "Garden City Concept" conceived half a century earlier. The Master Plan defined a new town as a self-sufficient satellite town physically separate from the rest of the City, "with places of work and community services adequate for the majority of its population". Three possible locations in the Rural Planning Area were identified. One was in Woodlands; the second was around Bulim Village along Choa Chu Kang Road; the third was at the junction of Upper Thomson Road and Yio Chu Kang Road. However, they would have to wait. The Master Plan, privy to the future plans of the SIT, expected that Queenstown and Toa Payoh (both just inside the city limits) would be developed first. Queenstown was a "satellite suburb", while Toa Payoh, replete with farming communities, would "be developed as a suburb along the lines of Queenstown".

Furthermore, the Master Plan surveyed patterns of movement. Pepler's team carried out censuses of vehicle numbers in 1953, revealing an exponential growth in traffic since the end of WWII. By January 1954, there were more than 250,000 vehicles of all varieties for 475 km of roads, including 31,451 motor cars—a doubling of the car population in just four years.

Some of the heaviest morning and evening peak hour traffic in the City occurred along the Kallang Road–Mountbatten Road stretch, Serangoon Road, and Bukit Timah Road, arteries that connected the Central Area with the rest of the island. There was also congestion at the intersection of trunk roads and the Outer and Inner Ring Roads. During these peak hours, 10,000 motor vehicles—one in five motor vehicles in Singapore—approached the inner ring roads every hour; 5,500 vehicles moved through Kallang Road alone. Within the Central Area, most major thoroughfares suffered from moderate to heavy congestion, with Collyer Quay and Raffles Quay getting the worst of it. One-way traffic schemes had not worked, while laying down new roads within the overcrowded Central Area was virtually impossible.

The Master Plan also critiqued different methods of movement. They condemned the trishaw as a "slow-moving" vehicle that "takes almost as much room as a car, and is a source of delay to speedier traffic". However, they suggested the bicycle as a substitute for the motor car—in essence, they hoped for a "car-lite" Singapore, even though the term would only appear 60 years later. In January 1954, there were 192,376 bicycles in Singapore—one for every six persons. The Master Plan said: "The bicycle must be recognised as a principal form of road transport... and, where practicable, measures to aid cyclists must be taken, such as separate cycle tracks on main roads." On the cusp of change in the 1950s, this was a golden opportunity for Singapore to wean itself off a car culture and work cycling lanes into developmental plans. Unfortunately, the political will was never there, and the chance was lost.

Finally, the Master Plan also mooted the ideas of expanding the existing railway line in Singapore, building branch lines or a suburban railway, and a subway system to relieve traffic congestion. A suburban railway was a concept briefly floated in the 1920s; for the subway idea, the team probably had in mind the New York Subway, the London Underground, or the Tokyo

Metro.¹ But they concluded it would be too costly for Singapore. The technology and building materials at the time did not allow for affordable tunnels or raised platforms through Singapore's complex geological and urban landscape. Instead, extending and improving the existing railway line was more feasible.

Through the Master Plan of 1955, Pepler's team highlighted the urban and transport chaos stemming from 130 years of laissez-faire governance. Now the onus was on the government and the City Council to use the information to improve housing and transport in the colony. It was evident that the solution to housing problems in Singapore was inseparable from the solution to transport problems.

THE GOVERNMENT that would take over the Master Plan of 1955 also took on a new form that year. Limited self-government came to Singapore. The 1955 General Election was called to elect 25 out of 32 members of a new Legislative Assembly, including a chief minister who would report to the governor; for this, the colony was carved into 25 wards. For the first time, a majority of lawmakers would be elected by the people and not chosen by the British—residents in Singapore were on the road to becoming "Singaporeans".

On 2 April, 158,075 people, 52.7 per cent of the electorate, voted; the Labour Front won the most seats, 10, and its chairman, lawyer David Marshall (1908–1995) and Assembly Member for the ward of Cairnhill, became Singapore's first Chief Minister. Marshall led a Council of nine ministers, five of whom he picked from the Legislative Assembly; acting like a cabinet, they took charge of ministries which oversaw all matters except external affairs, internal security,

and defence. Marshall and four of his five picks were born in Singapore or Malaya, not Britain— part of a process called Malayanisation. Among them was Abdul Hamid Haji Jumat (1916–1978), Minister of Communications and Works; his ministry took over the PWD. England-born Francis Thomas (1912–1977) became Minister for Local Government, Lands and Housing; his ministry took over the SIT.²

As political change chugged along, efforts were underway to relieve perennial traffic congestion between the Central Area and the suburbs of Geylang and Katong. In 1956, the $12-million Nicoll Highway—named after Sir John Fearns Nicoll (1899–1981), governor from 1952 to 1955—was laid down across the Raffles Reclamation Ground and the mouth of the Kallang River. Its working name was Esplanade Road, almost 50 years after another Esplanade Road was renamed St Andrew's Road! As for the $8-million bridge across the Kallang River over which Nicoll Highway ran, it opened as the Merdeka (Malay for "Independence") Bridge to reflect the "confidence and aspirations" of the people of Singapore for self-government.

Nicoll Highway was unique as there were no traffic junctions or lights along its entire span from Bras Basah Road to Guillemard Road. With its completion, for the first time in 130 years, Beach Road no longer offered direct access to the sea. Its name now signified what was, not what is.

Sweeping toponymic changes came to the north of the island in 1956. The catalyst was the death of Lim Chong Pang. He had owned land at the entrance of the Naval Base in Sembawang; a village for local employees of the Naval Base arose, called West Hill Village after a hill in the area. After his death, West Hill Village was renamed Chong Pang Village in his honour; 16

roads inside were also gradually renamed over the next seven years.[3] Thirteen of these new names honoured the Lim clan: Chong Pang, Chong Nee, Chong How, Chong Sin, and Huang Long after Lim and his other names; Hock Chwee after his father-in-law Chia Hock Chwee; Bah Tan, Kee Ann, and Soon Keat after his uncles; Wei Hua and Kee Hua after his father Lim Nee Soon's other names; Eng Hock after Lim Nee Soon's maternal uncle Teo Eng Hock; Teo Lee after his maternal grandfather. As one headed south from the village along Sembawang Road, one would also meet Bah Soon (another name of Lim Nee Soon) Pah Road and roads in Nee Soon Village with names related to Lim Nee Soon: Nee Soon (officially named in 1950), Chong Kuo (another of his sons), Thong Aik (his rubber factory), and Thong Bee (his chop).[4] Throw in Peck Hay (his wife) Road off Clemenceau Avenue, Peng Nguan (his father) Street in Tiong Bahru Estate, Marsiling Road in Woodlands, and Huat Choe (another of his names) Village at the 14th Milestone of Jurong Road, and it was clear that by the early 1960s, the Lim clan had defeated Cheang Hong Lim's family to become, other than the British Royal Family, the family honoured with the most place names in Singapore—an impressive 24!

Reform also came to the City Council. In July 1957, the Legislative Assembly passed the Local Government Bill to expand the City Council to 32 seats, all elected. The president would be replaced by a mayor, chosen by the councillors. On 21 December, elections were held; 161,703 people cast their votes. The People's Action Party (PAP) won the most seats, 13, and Malacca-born Ong Eng Guan (1925–2008), councillor for Hong Lim, became Singapore's first mayor.

The opening of Nicoll Highway was timely, as it served the residents of a new SIT estate completed in 1958. Three years before, Kallang Airport, merely 18 years old, closed. Aviation traffic had grown exponentially after WWII, and a larger airport was needed further away from the Central Area. Hence, a $37-million Singapore International Airport was built in the rural countryside east of Paya Lebar Road and the city limits; it was also later known as Paya Lebar Airport. Three hundred families had to be resettled. Airport Road was laid down to connect the airport to Paya Lebar and MacPherson roads. Tampines Road also had to be diverted around the airport's main runway. The 90-year-old trunk road received a new bend, and the rump roads on either side of the runway were renamed Tampines Drive and Tampines Avenue.

With Kallang Airport closed, much of it was turned into Kallang Park; the airport crossing at Mountbatten Road also closed, to the delight of motorists! The grounds east of Mountbatten Road were developed into Old Kallang Airport Estate, with 70 low-rise blocks. Part of the former runway was converted into Old Airport Road.

As the 1950s drew to a close, Singapore's relations with Britain remained cordial, but some local politicians wanted more than just Malayanisation in government—Singapore's 140-year-old British road-naming system had to go, too. In May 1958, the City Council saw an intense debate over the naming of a new road off Balestier Road. Some opted for Jalan Kebun Limau, as the area was known to locals as Kebun Limau, Malay for "Lemon Garden". Others preferred Balestier Way, as "Balestier Road was familiar to everyone, while 'Jalan Kebun Limau' was difficult to remember and spell". After an hour, Jalan Kebun Limau won. Mayor Ong then declared that "when Singapore achieves

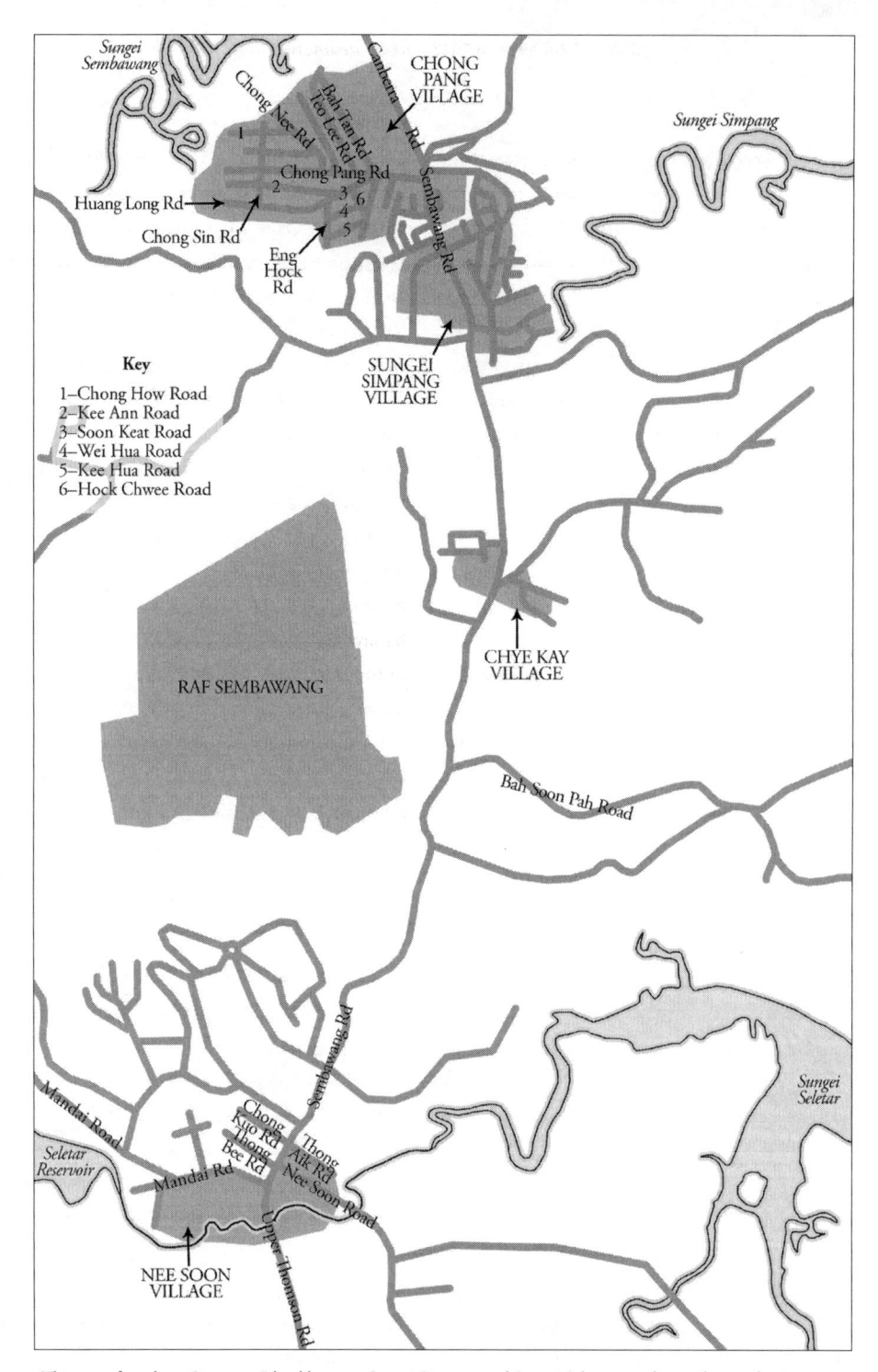

This area of northern Singapore Island between Sungei Simpang and Sungei Seletar once bore tribute to businessman Lim Nee Soon's clan—there were 20 unique place names honouring members of his clan, including Chong Pang Road and Nee Soon Road. All of them appear here. Other key place names such as that of water bodies, Sungei Simpang Village, Chye Kay Village, Canberra Road, Sembawang Road, RAF Sembawang, Mandai Road, and Upper Thomson Road, are also highlighted. Today, just five place names related to Lim's clan remain—Chong Pang, Bah Soon Pah Road, Chong Kuo Road, Thong Bee Road, and Nee Soon Road. That said, the land east of Sembawang Road in this map is now occupied by Yishun town—itself named after Lim Nee Soon. (Source: Eisen Teo)

independence, most of its roads would be given new Malayan names". He continued:

> No self-respecting nation will allow its streets to be used to perpetuate the memory of ex-governors and other colonial officials. We are determined to give expression to our national sentiments. We shall no longer allow our streets to be named after ex-governors who, in addition to drawing big emoluments from the coffers of our people, expect to retire in the countryside of England with the certain knowledge that a street in Singapore will be named after them.

> The name of a street is not an unimportant thing. It is as important as the throwing away of the mace. It is as important as an independent country changing its flag.

The time had not yet come to rename the streets, Ong said, but when it came, "national sentiment would be manifested in the new street names". He promised Guillemard Circus would be renamed Merdeka Circus, Nicoll Highway to Merdeka Highway, Shenton Way to Merdeka Way, and Collyer Quay to Merdeka Quay. To him, the government of an independent Singapore had to forge a new identity divorced from that of her colonial master.

BIG GOVERNMENT, BIG BUREAUCRACY

SINGAPORE'S FIRST master plan called for an urban and transport revolution. Executing it was a monumental task that took time, money, imagination, political will, and deft hands—the uprooting of entire communities was a political minefield that if handled roughly, could explode in the government's face. An organised army of bureaucrats and technical experts working across multiple departments and agencies was required for an unprecedented level of top-down intervention into the lives of people. In the 1950s, the PWD and SIT, by themselves, could not accomplish the impossible. Big government and big bureaucracy—built on the bedrock of a stable political system—were needed. These were fulfilled through the creation of ministries and statutory boards from the late 1950s.

Full internal self-government came to Singapore in 1959, after a general election on 30 May to elect an expanded Legislative Assembly of 51 lawmakers. In all, 527,919 people, 92.9 per cent of the electorate, voted; the PAP won a landslide of 43 seats, forming the new government. The PAP's Central Executive Committee convened and chose lawyer and Assembly Member for Tanjong Pagar Lee Kuan Yew (1923–2015) as Singapore's first prime minister—he defeated Ong Eng Guan (who had resigned as mayor to contest in Hong Lim—and won) by just one vote. Sir William Goode (1907–1986), the fourth and last governor, made way for a Yang Di-Pertuan Negara, or head of state, Perak-born Yusof Ishak (1910–1970).

The ministerial portfolios were reshuffled. Curiously, the Ministry of Communications and Works was dissolved, and Singapore would have no Communications Ministry until 1968. Transport issues, and the PWD and SIT, now came under the Ministry of National Development (MND), with Ong as its first minister.

The PAP also moved to consolidate political power. The City Council and Rural Board had operated as centres of power separate from the Legislative Assembly. For "greater efficiency and economy", the PAP transferred most of their departments to various ministries. For example, the Registry of Vehicles was taken over by the Traffic Police, under the Ministry of Home Affairs, led by Kuala Lumpur-born Ong Pang Boon (born 1929). Future Council polls were suspended, its councillors retired. The 51-year-old Rural Board was abolished in 1959; the City Council remained to oversee the supply of water, electricity, and gas until 1963, when a new statutory board, the Public Utilities Board, took over these functions; the City Council, with a lineage of 114 years, disappeared into history.

The PAP knew its limitations though. In a Legislative Assembly seating in February 1960, Perak-born Deputy Prime Minister Toh Chin Chye (1921–2012) stated it was the government's policy "to nationalise public road transport"; however, "the complicated machinery of public transport was not within the capabilities of any government department at the moment". Instead, staff could be trained to form a future Road Transport Authority, as a prerequisite to nationalisation.

Dissension soon arose within the PAP's ranks—coming from none other than Ong Eng Guan. He had grown unhappy with the policies and direction of his party. Embroiled in several public disputes with colleagues, he filed 16 resolutions against his party in June 1960—a move seen as a challenge to collective leadership. In August, he was sacked as minister and expelled from the PAP (but retained his Assembly seat). Assembly Member for Paya Lebar Tan Kia Gan was appointed the second Minister for National Development.

Before urban renewal of the Central Area could take place, the housing problem had to be solved first—if people were chased out of their homes with no alternative housing, mass unrest could break out. Hence, the PAP's five-year budget for 1960–65 put public housing and public works as top priorities. $194 million was set aside for public housing and economic planning, and another $150 million for public works. They rolled up their sleeves and set to work. First, the 33-year-old SIT was dissolved, to be replaced by the Planning Department and the Housing and Development Board (HDB). The HDB, chaired by Lim Kim San (1916–2006), was a proper housing authority under the MND, backed by legislation. It took over all SIT estates and projects and started a Five Year Plan to build 51,000 housing units—just as the 1955 Master Plan had recommended. High-density, high-rise blocks were the way forward to attain as many flats as possible within the shortest time. From 1960 to 1965, most new blocks were built within a radius of eight kilometres from the city centre, in estates such as Bukit Ho Swee, Tiong Bahru, MacPherson, and Kallang—spelling the start of the demise of urban kampungs.

The HDB also expanded Queenstown New Town and started work on Toa Payoh New Town. For Queenstown, the estates of Commonwealth, Tanglin Halt, and Queen's Close were built. Commonwealth was named after the Commonwealth of Nations, a voluntary association of former British colonies; Queen's Close was named after Queen Elizabeth II (again); Tanglin Halt was named after the former railway station. Two arterial roads were built—Commonwealth Avenue and Queensway. Such pro-British names might not have been possible if Ong Eng Guan had remained as minister for national development!

As for Toa Payoh, for more than a century after John Turnbull Thomson mapped it in the 1840s, it remained on the periphery of the City, a hilly landscape dominated by vegetable and pig farms, orchards, and rural settlements housing 3,000 families, with no paved road between Balestier

Road and Braddell Road. But from 1961, its hills were flattened and carted away—just like what Raffles did in the 1820s. Every day for five months, 60 lorries moved 4,000 tons of earth to the marshes of the Kallang River north of Kallang Road. The reclaimed marshes became the new neighbourhoods of Kallang Bahru and Geylang Bahru (Malay for "New"). Meanwhile, flat land was readied for thousands of flats for Toa Payoh New Town. The first homes were put up for sale in 1966 and by the end of the decade, Toa Payoh had become Singapore's most populous new town and the darling of the HDB. Whenever overseas dignitaries visited Singapore, the HDB would take them to tour Toa Payoh; when Queen Elizabeth II dropped by in 1972, she visited Toa Payoh instead of Queenstown. In 1973, Toa Payoh was chosen to be the Games Village for the 7th Southeast Asian Peninsular Games.

In the HDB's first five years, it constructed twice as many flats as the SIT had built in all its existence—a feat that has become the stuff of legends. What contributed to this achievement was the PAP holding on to power and weathering all challenges without violence. In 1961, Prime Minister Lee survived a vote of no-confidence in the Legislative Assembly by a razor-thin 26 to 25. In the 1963 General Election, the PAP fended off a stiff challenge from a splinter party, the Barisan Socialis. The election came just five days after the Crown Colony merged with Malaya (which had won independence in 1957), British North Borneo (now Sabah) and Sarawak to form Malaysia. After another two tumultuous years, Singapore separated from Malaysia in August 1965 to become an independent city-state. Racial and political tensions were high, but they never led to civil war, foreign invasion, or the overthrow of Singapore's leaders. In the 1968 General Election, Singaporean citizens rallied around the incumbent PAP and gave it another landslide victory. The PAP would monopolise all seats in Parliament (formerly the Legislative Assembly) for the next 13 years, and command a super-majority after that—a political dominance that has persisted until the present. Lee himself would remain Prime Minister until 1990. Hence, the PAP was free to employ its ministries and enact legislation to enable whatever radical urban and transport changes were needed.

BY THE end of the HDB's first Five Year Plan in 1965, Singapore's housing crisis had been somewhat alleviated. Now, it could properly turn to urban resettlement and renewal in the Central Area for its second Five Year Plan from 1965 to 1970. The means of achieving this? Another level of bureaucracy. The HDB formed the Urban Renewal Unit in 1964, renamed the Urban Renewal Department (URD) two years later. It started out with just three people—an architect-planner Alan Choe (born 1931), who would later become its general manager, and two assistant architects—but grew to 76 by 1965. The department's aims were to "rejuvenate the old core of the City centre" and "rebuild the (Central Area) completely", not only to improve residents' lives, but also allow economic development and investment through freeing up prime land for private developers.

The department divided 1,700 acres of the old Town—stretching from Outram Road to Kallang—into 19 "Urban Renewal Precincts", and set to work. They needed the law to be on their side. With the PAP's super-majority in Parliament, they got the backup. A Resettlement Department was set up in 1964 to clear the Central Area and rehouse communities in new flats, while the

Compulsory Land Acquisition Act was passed two years later, allowing the government to acquire land without having to obtain permission.

The Act was prompted by families who had refused to move, delaying entire housing projects; the construction of Toa Payoh New Town itself was held back for months. Some could demand up to $150,000 in compensation, and when bulldozers pulled up outside their shacks, they brandished blunt weapons and threatened violence. Critics slammed it as draconian and heavy-handed, but for the government, the ends justified the means. All the MND had to do now was issue orders to move two years in advance, assign new flats to the affected, and pay them compensation calculated beforehand. In the 1960s, each affected tenant family was compensated $400, while a house owner received $600. Each family was also paid $20–40 for fruit trees, and $741 per hectare for vegetable beds. Even then, some Singaporeans used creative tricks to try to squeeze as much compensation as possible—as recounted by Choe:

> On (compensation for) resettlement, Singaporeans were good at improvising. On Friday, they stocked up the building material. On Monday, you saw a brand-new house, but they stained it as though it had been there a long time: "That's a house. Pay compensation." Fruit trees, the same. Suddenly you found, so many papaya, pineapple, banana trees.

Fifteen per cent of Singapore Island's land area was acquired by the government under the Act by 1973; more than half was used for housing. Most leases issued were no longer freehold—now, 99-year leases were the norm. This ensured land could be easily taken back for further urban renewal.

Even street naming was bureaucratised. In February 1967, a Street-Naming Advisory Committee (now the Street and Building Names Board) was formed. It recommended to the government new street names and changes to existing street names, and in turn, took instructions from the government on what street names to suggest. After the domination of a British road-naming system for more than 140 years, what would a Singapore road-naming system be like?

At the time, in Malaya—especially cities such as Kuala Lumpur and Penang—there were official toponymic exercises to replace colonial names with local, Malay names. Pragmatic Singapore did no such thing—which was uncommon among decolonised states in Asia and Africa. For example, HDB rejected calls to change colonial names in Queenstown to Malay ones, because they wanted to "avoid confusion and inconvenience", and because "Queenstown was well-known throughout the world and should be preserved". But for new roads, the committee experimented moving away from the old British road-naming system. In March 1967, the government instructed the committee to steer clear of "old colonial nuances, British snob names, towns, and royalty", and give priority to Malay names, to "signal Singapore's allegiance to the Malay world". English-language names could still be used, but they had to "reflect the historical background of the area, current affairs of public interest in Singapore, local flora and fauna, and the physical nature of the area". And as much as possible, no person should have a street named after him while he was still alive.

However, the sudden proliferation of Malay street names was not universally embraced. Some Chinese topolect-speaking residents found the

Malay names to be "tongue-twisters", while developers and residents of private housing estates saw English names as superior to Malay ones. In the interests of multiracialism, the government decided to move away from favouring Malay over other languages. By January 1968, the committee was given new guidelines: street names should now "reflect the multi-lingual, multi-racial and multi-cultural context of the society", and "be easily translated or pronounced" across Singapore's four official languages—English, Mandarin, Malay, and Tamil. In May, the committee was even told to "stop naming streets after flowers, fruits, animals etc. in Malay, avoid the use of 'Jalan', and carefully review any objection to existing street names in Malay". "Mathematical naming"—naming roads sequentially, such as Avenue 1, 2, 3, etc., which had no racial overtones—was also tried out. These toponymic twists and turns, part of the growing pains of a newly-independent nation-state finding its place in a newly-configured Malay world, had long-lasting repercussions on Singapore's history of movement.

Chinese place names were not spared either. In 1968, a Committee on the Standardisation of Street Names in Chinese was convened to standardise Chinese translations for more than 500 street names, to avoid confusion. In this bureaucratic exercise, existing Hokkien, Teochew, and Cantonese place names were largely overlooked for literal translations or transliterations in Mandarin. For example, North Bridge Road's Toa Beh Lo became Qiao Bei Lu (Mandarin for "Bridge North Road"); Fort Canning's Ong Keh Sua (Hokkien for "Hill of Royalty", a reference to Singapura's Malay kings) became Fu Kang Ning (which sounds like Fort Canning). This supported a post-independence national bilingual education policy, which promoted Mandarin over other Chinese topolects, relegating their statuses to "dialects".

The Ministry of Communications was formed again in 1968, with Negri Sembilan-born Yong Nyuk Lin (1918–2012) as minister, to oversee, among other things, transport-related issues. During the two years Singapore was part of Malaysia, the Registry of Vehicles was part of the Federation's Transport Ministry; after separation, it was placed under Singapore's Prime Minister's Office. Now, with the Communications Ministry revived, the Registry was moved there.

By the mid-1960s, the Master Plan of 1955 was deemed obsolete. A new long-term plan guiding development for the next 20 years was needed; it was completed in 1971 as Singapore's first Comprehensive Long-Range Concept Plan, providing for a population of four million (Singapore's population in 1970 was 2,074,507). This was a four-year, $17-million endeavour by the URD, the State and City Planning Department, the PWD, and consultants from the United Nations Development Programme; extensive land, building, population, and transport surveys were conducted.

The Concept Plan, hailed as a "bold and ambitious" approach in long-term planning, integrated the planning of land use and transportation, coordinated ministry efforts, and painted the future of urban space in Singapore in broad strokes. In essence, it was a "ring plan": corridors of commercial, industrial, and residential development in a ring around the Central Catchment Area and across the island from Jurong to Changi, continuing the narrative of decentralisation. Some radical ideas eventually became reality: a network of expressways connecting the new towns and new centres of development to replace the age-old trunk and ring road systems; a mass rapid transit system to serve the heart of the Central Area, by now known as the Central Business District (CBD); and relocating the international airport (again) from Paya Lebar to the east of the island, at Changi.

The broad ideas and concepts sketched by the Concept Plan were subsequently expanded upon in successive Master Plans, revised every five years. Today, the Concept Plan guides development over 40–50 years, while Master Plans do so over 10–15 years; through the latter, the government tightly controls land use, sets aside land parcels for transport infrastructure, and ensures new development projects submit traffic impact assessments. The result? Orderly development along predetermined land use and transport planning principles—an achievement not many cities or city-states can claim.

By 1974, the URD's work had grown so much in size and scope, it was upgraded to a full statutory board, the Urban Redevelopment Authority (URA), and moved from the HDB to directly under the MND.

Whenever the government saw a major problem, a popular solution was to form a committee drawing on manpower from different ministries. In this manner, numerous committees were formed in the 1970s. The Bus Services Reorganisation Committee was formed by Minister Yong in 1973 to reform the ailing public bus industry. The Road Transport Action Committee was formed in 1974 to tackle traffic congestion and improve public bus service standards. Singapore's bus stops too few, small, poor in quality? Enter the Bus Stops Committee in 1975, headed by the Registrar of Vehicles to oversee the siting and construction of 120 bus shelters. These committees, while short-lived, ensured specific goals were met within fixed timelines.

Throughout Singapore's modern history, public transport was usually controlled by multiple private companies or individuals looking after their own interests. Fares and service standards could be fixed by municipal laws, but took years to pass, and were difficult to uphold. Integration across different methods of movement, in terms of infrastructure and services, was also non-existent. In 1987, as envisioned by the Concept Plan, Singapore's Mass Rapid Transit (MRT) system opened, and there was a need to integrate it with the existing public transport system. Hence, the Communications Ministry set up the Public Transport Council (PTC), to work with public bus companies, taxi companies, and the company formed to handle the operations of the MRT system, the Singapore Mass Rapid Transit (SMRT). The PTC regulated fares and service standards across all forms of public transport, and balanced public interest with the need for public transport operators to make money.

The pace of urban change accelerated. In the late 1980s, urban redevelopment began inside older new towns. This process would no longer be confined to dilapidated or hundred-year-old buildings; any piece of land—and the buildings on it—was fair game if it was valuable enough. Hence, in 1989, the URA absorbed the Planning Department, by now the Planning Authority; the expanded URA became the national planning authority in charge of land use.

The Concept Plan of 1971 received an upgrade in 1991. In 1990, Singapore's population was 3,047,132, so the 1991 Concept Plan addressed land use and transportation planning for three future stages: up to 2000, 2010, and Year X, when the population of Singapore reached 4 million (this was achieved in the year 2000). Among other things, the plan envisioned a new "Downtown Core" built on land reclaimed just east of the old Town, named Marina Bay; four regional centres in Tampines, Seletar, Woodlands, and Jurong East; and expanding the transportation system, including the MRT system. The Concept Plan has been revised twice, in 2001 and 2011, to account for land use changes and population growth.

To improve day-to-day coordination of transport policies across public and private transport, four public sector entities were merged into one statutory board in 1995. They were the Registry of Vehicles, possessing a lineage of 128 years; the PWD's Roads and Transportation Division, in charge of the building and maintenance of roads and expressways, and traffic management; and the Communications Ministry's Land Transportation Division and MRT Corporation (a department tasked with constructing MRT lines). The resultant statutory board, the Land Transport Authority (LTA), was placed under the Communications Ministry. The LTA immediately put together a White Paper, a road map which aimed to create nothing less than a "world-class" transport system in 15 years, by 2011.

The rest of the PWD was subsequently corporatised in 1999. After 142 years of existence, the PWD was renamed CPG Corporation; today, it remains a major architectural, engineering, and construction business. In 2001, the Communications Ministry, by now the Ministry of Communications and Information Technology, was absorbed into the Ministry of Transport; the first Transport Minister was Yeo Cheow Tong (born 1947).

From 1959, the PAP ran the city-state of Singapore as a tight ship. They inherited the PWD, SIT, and Registry of Vehicles, and built a new state machinery around them. Ministries, statutory boards, departments, and committees were birthed, reshuffled, or reformed to do the hard, sometimes seemingly impossible, work. These bureaucracies hire thousands of people—including some of the brightest minds in the country. At the top are the Ministries of Transport and National Development. The HDB, URA, LTA, and PTC handle everything and anything to do with housing, land use and planning, and private and public transport planning and management, controlling and influencing all aspects of movement.

There may be dissenting views on the desirability of big government and big bureaucracy, but Singapore is one of the few countries in the world with a government and state machinery with the mandate, will, and capability to invest in public infrastructure, coordinate land use and transport, and balance the profit motive of transport companies and the public interest. Far from being an "invisible hand", the "big visible hand" will continue to influence the history of movement in Singapore for many decades to come.

THE DEATH OF A CITY

AFTER THE necessary bureaucratic and legal machinery needed to transform the Central Area was set in place in the mid-1960s, the 150-year-old settlement was changed beyond all recognition in the name of progress. The authorities and the press sang the same tune, presenting the Central Area as "slum-ridden", where urgent work was necessary to relieve the "suffering" of its residents. A 1966 *Straits Times* article summed it up: "Singapore has become the first city in Asia to comprehensively tackle slum clearance and urban renewal… The skyscrapers have begun to march on the old city, replacing crumbling tenements where people are packed into nightmarish cubicles."

First, thousands were resettled. Some were moved to new housing inside the Central Area, but most were moved out of the Central Area to new towns. The last HDB flats inside the Central Area—Albert Centre (next to Albert Street), Rowell Court (off Jalan Besar), and Kreta Ayer Complex (Smith Street)—were completed by 1984; thereafter, land inside the Central Area was reserved for commercial use. The government made sure new accommodation was ready when residents had to move, and as much as possible, entire communities were moved together to the same location. This somewhat soothed the sense of being uprooted, and prevented urban renewal from becoming a political hot potato or destabilising PAP hegemony in Singapore.

After resettlement, the bulldozers moved in. Untold numbers of two to four-storey shophouses and godowns, each bearing an unspoken history going back to more than a hundred years, were pulled down. A new city had to rise above the ashes of the old—and heritage and conservation be damned. As URA General Manager Alan Choe wrote in 1969: "Unlike England or Europe, Singapore does not possess architectural monuments of international importance. There are therefore few buildings worthy of preservation."

To maximise land use, no longer would new buildings be constructed like shophouses. Urban renewal heralded a new form of land use—the mixed-use, high-rise complex, going up, up, up. There was a podium block of three to eight storeys, comprising a concrete sandwich of shops on the lower floors, then offices, then a multi-storey car park. The top of the podium block was a "void deck", an open space for residents to mingle and organise community activities such as weddings and funerals. Atop the void deck rose one or more tower blocks of residential flats that could top 20 to 30 storeys. After 150 years, the low, ground-hugging skyline of the Central Area was broken.

Urban change was not just vertical. The footprint of a complex was far larger than an old shophouse's. At the time, there were many small city blocks bordered by small roads and back lanes nestled between major thoroughfares. To accommodate new complexes, city blocks had to be enlarged or combined, expunging the small lanes. Entire branches from Singapore's toponymic tree were shaved off and thrown into the fire. But the main thoroughfares survived the cull: arteries such as Beach Road, North Bridge Road–South Bridge Road, Stamford Road, and Upper Cross Street–Cross Street; also, what the Chinese knew as Da Ma Lu to Qi Ma Lu. The grid system of the Raffles Town Plan stood the tests of time and development—many of its roads remained the grid system of a reborn Central Area.

URBAN RENEWAL first came to Kampong Glam in the mid-1960s on its reclaimed land, the old Raffles Reclamation Ground. The government proclaimed a one-mile strip of seafront between Beach Road and Nicoll Highway the "Golden Mile", to encourage developers to build offices there to relieve congestion in the Central Area. One form of encouragement—the land cost just $1 per square foot! Two of the first mixed-use, high-rise complexes in Singapore—the 15-storey Golden Mile Complex and the 18-storey Golden Mile Tower—were completed by 1973 and 1974 respectively.

Meanwhile, 2,500 families living inside the area bounded by North Bridge Road, Jalan Sultan, Beach Road, and Crawford Street were resettled for it to be razed; the only surviving building was the Masjid Hajjah Fatimah, completed 1846. The project was assisted by United Nations experts and lauded as "visionary" and "ambitious". It also led to the disappearance of Minto Road, Java Road, Palembang Road, and part of Sumbawa Road.[5] In their place, a "concrete mosaic" of 17 residential blocks eight to 15 storeys in height arose, housing 5,000 families; the blocks of flats are now known as Beach Road Garden and Golden Beach Vista. To serve the residents, the 25-storey Textile Centre was finished in 1974, complete with a bowling alley and cinema, also taking in 150 textile shops displaced by urban renewal. Jalan Sultan Centre followed by 1977, and Golden Sultan Plaza—with 250 shops spread over nine storeys—in 1981.

Some distance away, Clyde Terrace, Beach Street, and Lim Chiak Street were expunged; in their place, the Hotel Merlin Singapore was finished in 1971. A 32-storey residential and commercial tower block was added by 1978, becoming the tallest structure in Kampong Glam. Today, the buildings are known as PARKROYAL on Beach Road, and The Plaza.

In the 1970s, three small lanes between Ophir Road and Rochor Road—Tiwary Road, Anguillia Road, Muar Road—were expunged. The six city blocks within were merged for Rochor Centre, completed by 1977. The complex had a three-storey podium block and atop it, four residential blocks—1 to 4 Rochor Road—reaching the 17th floor.

Meanwhile, the historic roads of Jalan Pekan, Jalan Kuantan, and the remains of Sumbawa Road were cleared for Crawford Centre, a cluster of 11 buildings, and a new campus for Hong Wen School, a primary school.[6] Crawford Centre, completed by 1978, was named after Crawford Street.

Further down North Bridge Road, Blanco Court, a $19.6-million, 15-storey complex, was completed in 1980. It was built at the junction of North Bridge Road and the lane Blanco Court which gave it its name; two theatres and two lanes—Diamond Theatre, Theatre Royal, Lorong Kassim, and Swatow (the original English spelling of Shantou, a city in Guangdong, China) Street—were destroyed. North Bridge Road was losing its decades-old reputation as a "road of theatres".

The lane Blanco Court—laid down before 1871—did not last long; neither did its old neighbour, Shaik Madersah Lane. By 1981, both were swallowed by the extension and realignment of Ophir Road. Once a small road, the lengthened and widened Ophir Road became a significant part of the grid system, linking Bukit Timah Road to Beach Road and Nicoll Highway.

The 1980s saw the disappearance of more historic landmarks in Kampong Glam. By 1984, 111-year-old Clyde Terrace Market was razed; the URA dismissed it as "out of place" and "incompatible" in "an area of towering hotels, shopping complexes and cinemas". In its place rose The Gateway, two (literally) cutting-edge 37-storey office towers. Off Arab Street, a 150-year-old *keramat* known as the Keramat Arab Street or Keramat Fakeh Haji Abdul-Jalil after an imam to Sultan Hussein Shah, was replaced by Golden Landmark Shopping Complex by 1983. As for Kampong Bugis, it was cleared of houses and shipyards. As late as 1978, housewives living there still took sampans over the Rochor River to travel to and from markets in Crawford Centre.

More skyscrapers came up in the 1990s. The Concourse was completed in 1994 as the final piece in the "Golden Mile" jigsaw. At 43 storeys and 175 metres, it became Kampong Glam's tallest building… for only 23 years.

Between the new Ophir Road and Rochor Road, six roads—Clyde Street, Jeddah Street, Ark

Lane, Fraser Street, Sin Koy Lane, and Garden Street—and five city blocks were expunged for Parkview Square, a 24-storey Art Deco office building completed in 2002. A 130-year-old mosque off Jeddah Street, the Masjid Maarof, was demolished.

Nearby, Johore Road was expunged by 2000 to make way for the Victoria Street Wholesale Centre, which itself moved to Kallang Avenue after 2009. And the building Blanco Court, barely 20 years old, was given a makeover and reopened as Raffles Hospital in 2002, erasing the place name "Blanco Court" from history.

Over 40 years from the 1960s, Kampong Glam changed beyond recognition. Many old roads with unique names vanished, including some reflecting themes of the Malay world and Middle East. A handful of historic landmarks have survived—the Masjid Sultan, Masjid Hajjah Fatimah, and the Istana Kampong Glam. Today, the Istana is the nucleus of an enclave of preserved and restored shophouses between Jalan Sultan and Ophir Road—the dwellings of "brick and lime… roofed with red tile" John Crawfurd described in the 1820s. Kampong Glam's basic grid network has also been retained: Victoria Street, Beach Road, Jalan Sultan, Arab Street, North Bridge Road—including the kink past the former Sultan's compound, the legacy of a feud between two empires. Still around, too, are the "Tombs of the Malayan Princes" and Jalan Kramat off Victoria Street, presently named Jalan Kubor Cemetery and Jalan Kubor (Malay for "Grave Road"). But like many historical sites in Singapore, the future of the oldest Muslim cemetery in Singapore is uncertain—it has been earmarked for residential development since 1998.

FOR THE old European Town, once allocated to the tiny European community, change came at a slower pace at first. Singapore's first residential complex in the Central Area was completed in 1963 at the junction of Selegie Road and Short Street. Selegie House cost $3.8 million and comprised a 20-storey block and two 10-storey blocks linked by two-storey blocks—505 housing units in all. At the time, it was one of the tallest buildings in Singapore, and attracted crowds at its opening. Neighbouring Selegie Integrated School, at 10 storeys, was the tallest school in Southeast Asia.[7] The buildings came at the price of Veerappa Chitty Lane, Annamalai Chetty Lane, and Swee Hee Lane.

The next skyscraper over the old European Town was also another Beach Road landmark—Shaw Tower at 35 storeys, completed in 1976 at the intersection with Middle Road. Shaw Tower was named after local film theatre chain Shaw Organisation. Further up Middle Road, the landmarks of Waterloo Girls' School and Queen Street Post Office were replaced by $40-million, nine-storey Midlink Plaza, and Waterloo Centre, with three residential blocks—262, 263, and 264 Waterloo Street.[8]

At the corner of Victoria Street and Bain Street, another residential complex was completed in 1980, erasing Carver Street and Theng Hai Place. The $15.2-million, 700-unit Bras Basah Complex has two 21-storey towers rising over a four-storey podium. The area was previously known for its bookstores and stationery shops, so when they were resettled, many were commendably allocated shops in the complex, retaining the character of the area. Curiously, Bras Basah Complex is some distance from Bras Basah Road; its address is 231 Bain Street.

North of Bras Basah Complex, three city blocks and the two lanes within—Holloway Lane

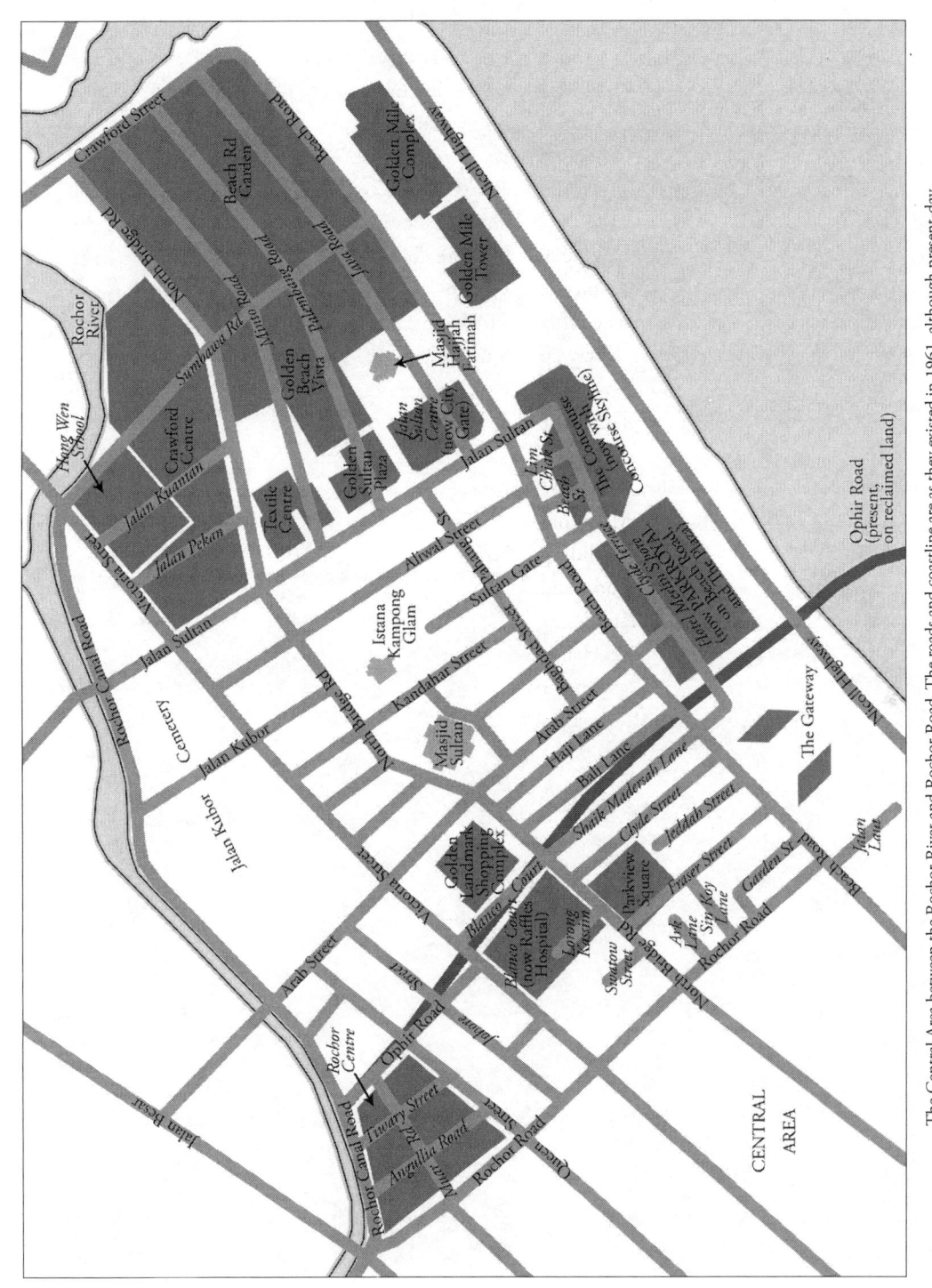

The Central Area between the Rochor River and Rochor Road. The roads and coastline are as they existed in 1961, although present-day Ophir Road is also marked out in the darkest shade of grey. Place names in italics no longer exist; roads have been expunged, and buildings have been torn down, revamped, or renamed. Buildings or sites in darker grey, such as Crawford Centre and PARKROYAL on Beach Road, were constructed between 1961 and 2019 at the cost of expunged roads such as Jalan Kuantan and Clyde Terrace. (Source: Eisen Teo)

An oasis of heritage inside the Central Area: Kampong Glam, surrounded by skyscrapers. This photo was taken from the 24th floor of the Textile Centre off Jalan Sultan. The white band marks the rough boundaries of the Sultan's compound of the Raffles Town Plan, drawn up by 1822. Soon after, North Bridge Road and Victoria Street were cut through the residence. Presently, (1) is the former Sultan's Palace, now the Istana Kampong Glam; (2) is the Masjid Sultan, and (3) is Jalan Kubor Cemetery. Beach Road used to face the sea, but presently features skyscrapers such as (from extreme left) Concourse Skyline, The Plaza, The Gateway, and DUO. (Source: Eisen Teo)

Tucked away off busy Victoria Street are the "Tombs of the Malayan Princes", presently known as Jalan Kubor Cemetery, named after Jalan Kubor, a small lane which bisects it. The cemetery is at least 200 years old, but a question mark lies over its future. (Source: Eisen Teo)

and Lorong Sidin—were razed in the 1980s. It remained a grass patch for two decades (!) until the National Library moved from Stamford Road into a new 16-storey building in 2005. South of the complex, 32-year-old Odeon Theatre was demolished in 1985; the commercial building erected on the site 20 years later was named Odeon Towers in its memory.

The 1980s saw big changes to the area once known as Kampong Bencoolen. Lorong Krishna off Waterloo Street was expunged for 20-storey Fortune Centre, another mixed-use complex completed in 1983. The face of Albert Street was transformed by Sim Lim Square, Fu Lu Shou Complex, Albert Centre, and Albert Complex in the space of several years. Albert Centre spelled the demise of Lorong Kranji, a curious name because it was nowhere near Kranji!

Even the historic campus of Raffles Institution—the school envisioned by Raffles to educate the sons of East India Company employees—was not immune to urban renewal. The 150-year-old compound was demolished for a complex of hotels, offices, a shopping mall, and a convention centre. The complex was named Raffles City in memory of the school, which had moved to Grange Road. Raffles City opened in 1986, boasting the world's tallest hotel, the Westin Stamford, at 73 storeys and 226 metres. It is now Swissôtel The Stamford.[9]

From the 1950s to the 1980s, the area around Bugis Street was world-famous for its food, *pasar malams*, and transgender sex workers. Bugis Street and nearby Malabar Street, Malay Street, and Hylam Street were expunged in the late 1980s; they were reborn as walkways—complete with faux street signs—inside an air-conditioned shopping mall, Bugis Junction, which opened in 1995. Across the road from Victoria Street, a cluster of 34 shophouses was preserved as a shopping enclave, named Bugis Village. The section of Albert Street running through it was renamed New Bugis Street in an ultimately unsuccessful bid to recreate the bustling roadside shopping experience Bugis Street once boasted. Today, the place name "Bugis" is associated with Bugis Junction and Bugis MRT Interchange, and not Kampong Bugis to the northeast.

At the junction of Bras Basah Road and Waterloo Street, Beng Swee Place was expunged by 1993 for 11-storey Plaza By The Park, presently the Manulife Centre. As for Farquhar Street and Bernard Street, tributes to Singapore's first Resident and his son-in-law, they were expunged between 1995 and 1998. Back in the former Kampong Bencoolen, Lorong Mandai—near Middle Road and another oddity since it was nowhere near Mandai—made way for a new campus for the Nanyang Academy of the Fine Arts.

The Government Ground was once allocated to "purposes of government", but from the 1970s, urban renewal saw parcels of land converted to commercial use. Peninsula Shopping Centre was completed first in 1971, for which George Coleman's 136-year-old residence, 3 Coleman Street, was demolished. The following year, Colombo Court, a 10-storey shopping centre and office block, opened; it was named after the neighbouring lane Colombo Court. Then Ford Street, a lane off High Street, was expunged for 32-storey High Street Centre and 11-storey High Street Plaza. The construction of the former also entailed the clearing of shophouses and godowns along North Boat Quay, including Singapore's oldest godown, completed in 1843 by Yeo Kim Swee, a merchant who had hired Seah Eu Chin as a bookkeeper. Capitol Shopping Centre opened in 1976 next to the historic Capitol Theatre, leading to the demise of Flag Road.[10] Peninsula

Malay Street in the early 20th century, at the junction with Hylam Street. This small lane between Victoria Street and North Bridge Road had appeared by the 1850s, and by the end of the 19th century, was famous as a red-light area.

Today, Malay Street is a pedestrian walkway inside Bugis Junction, a shopping mall. The shophouses that used to line the street have been conserved, and now house shops and eateries. Faux street signs remind shoppers of what used to exist before the mall was built in the 1990s. (Sources: The New York Public Library Digital Collections, Eisen Teo)

Plaza—opposite Peninsula Shopping Centre—was finished in 1980. And Hoo Ah Kay's former ice house, known as Whampoa's Ice House, was torn down in 1981 to widen River Valley Road at the junction with Hill Street, ending its existence at 127 years.

The Old Lines of Singapore—named and described by Crawfurd in the 1820s—disappeared as the British developed the Town, but the "Freshwater Stream" in front of it survived into the 1980s as the Stamford Canal, running along Stamford Road. By 1984, it was completely covered; one of the last visual reminders of ancient Singapura as it had existed 700 years before was removed from sight.

Just south of Peninsula Shopping Centre, Hock Lam Street, Chin Nam Street, and Hong Hin Court were all expunged for Funan Centre, which opened in 1985. Funan Centre was unique as it adopted the name of a small lane over which it was constructed—"Fu Nan" is Mandarin for "Hock Lam".[11]

In the 1990s, the area around High Street was transformed. High Street was separated into High Street and Parliament Place; nearby, the building named Colombo Court, not even 30 years old, was demolished for a new Supreme Court, which opened in 2005. The road Colombo Court was then renamed Supreme Court Lane, erasing the 90-year-old place name "Colombo Court" from history.

Over 40 years from the 1960s, the old European Town and Government Ground lost much of their original character. The mix of colonial and Asian that had attracted tourists the world over disappeared along with iconic streets and landmarks, such as the colourful and sleazy Bugis Street, the tastes of Hock Lam Street, and the regal campus of Raffles Institution. Colonial bungalows, shophouses, and small lanes reflecting Singapore's ethnic potpourri were replaced by modern towers such as Bras Basah Complex, High Street Centre, and Raffles City. Individual historic buildings have been conserved, such as St Andrew's Cathedral, the Central Fire Station, and Raffles Hotel, but they are islands of heritage in a sea of relatively new developments.

SOUTH OF the Singapore River, in the densely-populated area once known as the Chinese Campong, urban renewal first unfolded at the foot of Pearl's Hill. People's Park was a welcome evening retreat for Chinatown residents, who flocked there after sunset for its hawker stalls, storytellers, and street performers. People's Park Market opened in 1922, but a fire destroyed it in 1966. Then the government acquired the site for a new complex named People's Park Complex. The $10-million complex, with a six-storey podium and 25-storey residential tower, was finished in 1973, becoming Chinatown's tallest building.

Fire was also a catalyst for change near the Singapore River. It destroyed 123-year-old Ellenborough Market in 1968. Soon after, it was torn down, and Fish Street was also expunged for a new complex of three blocks and a resurrected Ellenborough Market. 1, 2, and 3 Tew Chew Street were completed around 1972.

In 1976, the People's Park legacy grew with the opening of another mixed-use complex, People's Park Centre. It comprised a six-storey podium block below a 22-storey residential tower and seven-storey office tower. Six city blocks were combined for its footprint, and Lim Eng Bee Lane and part of New Market Road had to go. People's Park Centre was closely followed by Pearl's Centre, completed in 1977 by Pearl's Hill Terrace. It had a

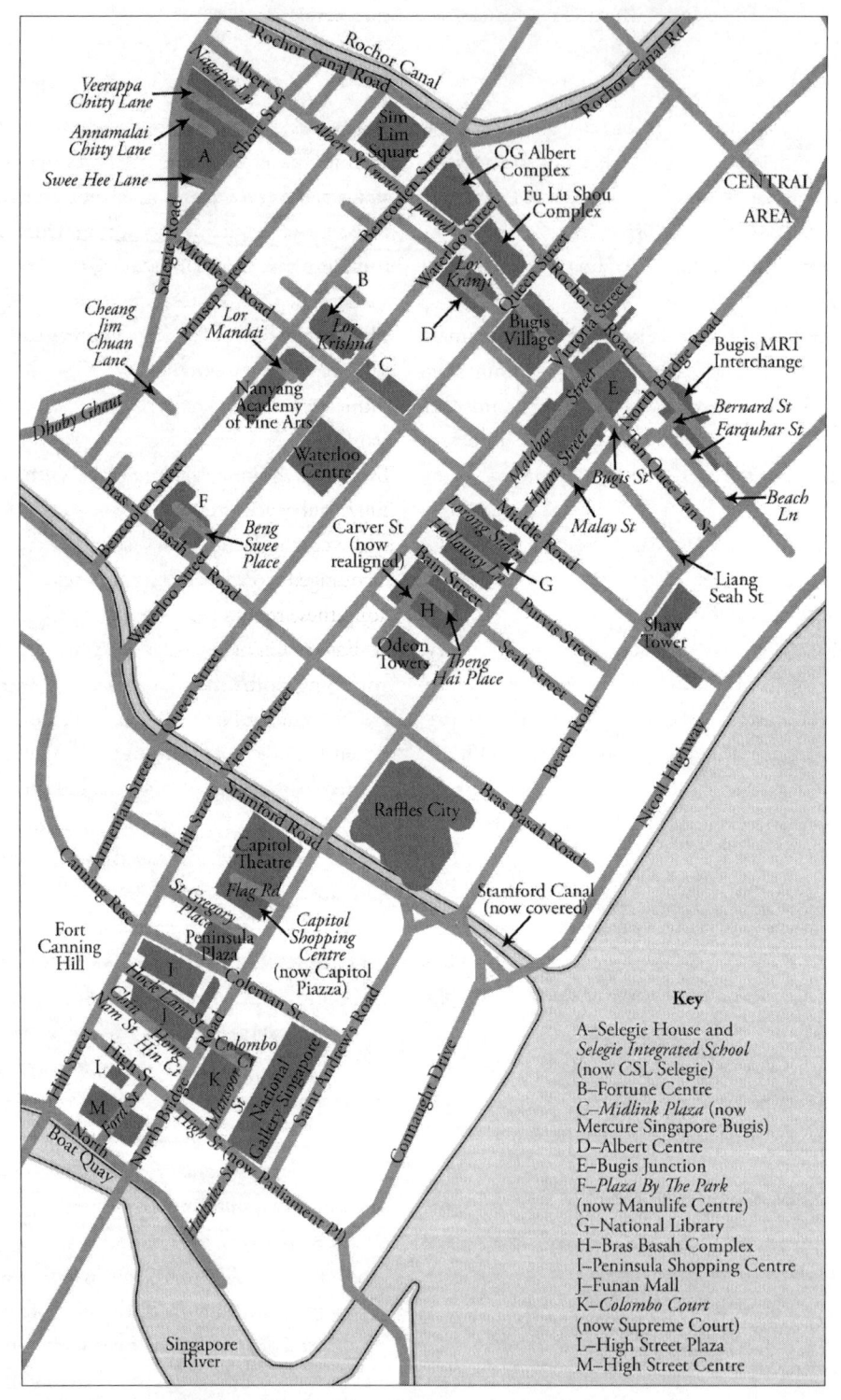

The Central Area between Rochor Road and the Singapore River. The roads and coastline are as they existed in 1961. Place names in italics no longer exist; roads have been expunged, and buildings have been torn down, revamped, or renamed. Buildings or sites in darker grey, such as Bras Basah Complex and Funan Mall, were constructed between 1961 and 2019 at the cost of expunged roads such as Theng Hai Place and Hock Lam Street. (Source: Eisen Teo)

10-storey podium block with 12 storeys of luxury apartments above; its cinema, Yangtze Cinema, developed a seedy reputation in the 1990s for screening Asian and European softcore films.

Across New Bridge Road, 140-year-old Upper Nankin Street and Upper Chin Chew Street made way for Hong Lim Complex, curiously named since Hong Lim Green—presently Hong Lim Park—was two city blocks away. The complex, with 1,000 flats in four residential towers topping at 18 storeys, opened in 1980.

The "death houses" of Sago Street and Sago Lane, much of the two roads, and the SIT's four-storey Art Deco tenement blocks, were all cleared by the early 1980s for Kreta Ayer Complex, an $18-million development with a three-storey podium block and two 21 and 25-storey towers atop it. The complex was named after Kreta Ayer Road. But its 400 stallholders suggested to the HDB that it be renamed Chinatown Complex, in their opinion a more tourist-friendly name. And so in 1984, Kreta Ayer Complex became Chinatown Complex.

Opposite Hong Lim Park, the Central Police Station, a Neo-Palladian structure opened in 1933, was demolished for South Bridge Centre, a 13-storey, $77-million commercial building, completed in 1984. Like Bras Basah Complex, South Bridge Centre took in displaced jewellers and goldsmiths in the area, hence retaining a link with a past community.

The PWD decided to widen New Bridge Road to relieve congestion south of the Singapore River, turning the two-lane dual carriageway into four lanes. However, instead of just widening the existing road, New Bridge Road was converted into a one-way four-lane street; traffic could only proceed southbound. Eu Tong Sen Street, once a small lane between Park Road and Havelock Road, named after businessman Eu Tong Sen (1877–1941), was widened to four lanes and lengthened until it became New Bridge Road's twin—a one-way street with traffic proceeding northbound. The four-year operation was completed in 1988 at the expense of Wayang Street.

Into the 21st century, some historic roads in Chinatown were converted to pedestrian malls in an attempt to resurrect a street vibe and outdoor ambience lost to redevelopment. Hokien Street, Nankin Street, Chin Chew Street, Sago Street, and Trengganu Street were closed to vehicular traffic by 2007, and paved over for pedestrians. Pagoda Street followed the following year. Pedestrianisation encouraged more foot traffic for shops and eateries along these roads.

East of Chinatown, Raffles Place was birthed from Singapore's first urban renewal exercise of the 19th century. Now, 20th-century urban renewal hurled the old Raffles Place into a glass-and-steel encased 21st century. Its colonial architecture was gradually lost to skyscrapers, underscoring the Republic's bid to "progress" from old-world colony to "First-World" city-state.

One of Raffles Place's first urban renewal projects in the 1960s was seven-storey Market Street Car Park, Singapore's first standalone multi-storey car park, completed 1964. One of the first iconic colonial buildings to go was the Ocean Building, a five-storey landmark along Collyer Quay, headquarters of the Straits Steamship Company. When it was completed in 1923, it was the tallest building in Singapore, at 49 metres. It was demolished in 1970 to make way for a new 28-storey tower named Ocean Tower.

The same year, rent control was lifted for Raffles Place, Collyer Quay, and much of the old Telok Ayer Reclamation Ground, allowing landlords to repossess their properties from tenants and sell their land to private developers. This accelerated urban renewal. *The Straits Times* coined a nickname for the 32 hectares of prime land resembling an upturned shoe—the Golden Shoe, to match the Golden Mile north of the Singapore River. This spelled the end of Raffles Place as a popular shopping venue. In November 1972, Robinsons Department Store, a mainstay of Raffles Place for 80 years, was entirely gutted by a fire; nine people died. Amazingly, the store reopened by Christmas—but in Orchard Road. The original site was given over to a new skyscraper, the Overseas Union Bank (OUB) Centre, which became Singapore's tallest building at 280 metres and 63 storeys when it opened in 1986.

For 150 years, Malacca Street, Market Street, and Chulia Street were known for their Indian traders and Chettiar moneylenders; they were ordered to vacate in 1975. All along Market Street, Cecil Street, Chulia Street, Phillip Street, and Robinson Road, pre-war stationery and provision shops, restaurants, wholesale and retail dealers, commodity handlers, and finance houses had to uproot a way of life they had known for decades.

In 1978, The Arcade's time ran out. For five generations, it was one of Singapore's best-known seafront landmarks, with small shops running the length of its pedestrian mall, selling a plethora of goods ranging from watches to cameras and sports gear. It was demolished to make way for a 20-storey complex of the same name which opened two years later.

Several roads in Raffles Place were expunged in the 1980s. Union Lane, off Collyer Quay, disappeared by 1984, making way for 24-storey Tung Centre.[12] Then, to create a through road from Chinatown to Collyer Quay, Church Street was lengthened to join Cecil Street and Market Street at the expense of Guthrie Lane. The resultant triangular-shaped city block was used to build the Golden Shoe Car Park. And to make way for the construction of Raffles Place MRT Interchange, De Souza Street and the road named Raffles Place were removed.

More of Market Street's heritage disappeared by 1988 when the Masjid Moulana Mohammed Aly, which served Indian Muslims in the area, was expunged. In its place rose the United Overseas Bank Plaza complex, with Tower 1 rising to 280 metres, tying with the OUB Centre as the tallest building in Singapore. The mosque subsequently reopened in the basement of the complex.

The last of the old Raffles Place and Collyer Quay died out in 1989, with the closure of Change Alley, once a shopping belt to rival The Arcade. Two old buildings—Winchester House, built in 1905, and Singapore Rubber House, built in 1960—were demolished, too. After they were replaced by 33-storey Caltex House and 37-storey Hitachi Tower, an indoor pedestrian mall was opened between them, also named Change Alley, but not quite the historic tourist attraction.[13]

South of the Singapore River, historic Chinatown and Raffles Place experienced different fates over 40 years of urban renewal. Even though the former lost numerous roads and old landmarks to complexes such as People's Park Centre and Hong Lim Complex, five neighbourhoods of shophouses have been conserved—areas around the Singapore River, China Street, Pagoda Street, Club Street, and Keong Saik Road—more than anywhere else in the Central Area. As for Raffles Place, excluding places of worship, only two buildings presently remain as they were in the early 20th century—the octagonal Lau Pa Sat, and the Fullerton Building, now the Fullerton Hotel, the lone survivor of what was once a seafront replete with colonial architecture. Similarly, almost nothing of the early 20th century has remained of the old Telok Ayer Reclamation Ground, save for the resilient grid road network—Cecil Street, Robinson Road, and Shenton Way are now skyscraper canyons. Presently, nine of Singapore's 20 tallest buildings are here, including three—OUB Centre (now One Raffles Place), UOB Plaza One, and Republic Plaza (completed 1995), all at 280 metres—towering over what was once Commercial Square of the dusty laterite roads, flame-of-the-forest trees, carriage horses, and rickshaw pullers.[14]

Urban renewal was not confined to the Central Area. It spread to Tanjong Pagar to the south, Orchard Road and River Valley to the west, and Jalan Besar to the north. From the 1980s, Orchard Road took over High Street and North Bridge Road as the shopping mecca of Singapore. What was once "a well-shaded avenue to English mansions", lined with shophouses, plantations, and cemeteries, became a boulevard of gleaming malls such as The Centrepoint, Ngee Ann City, and Ion Orchard.

Types of land use which contributed to traffic congestion, such as markets, motor repair shops, and schools, were relocated from the Central Area. From the 1970s to the 1990s, seven schools within the old European Town and Government Ground moved. Other than Raffles Institution, they included the Convent of the Holy Infant Jesus, which moved from Bras Basah Road to Toa Payoh New Town in 1983; St Joseph's Institution, which moved from Bras Basah Road to Whitley Road in 1988; and St Anthony's Convent, which moved from Middle Road to Bedok New Town in 1995.

Businesses and trades unique to specific areas for generations were forever displaced. The street hawkers of Albert Street and Queen Street were resettled in Albert Centre. Tradesmen dealing in car spare parts and accessories along Rochor Road and Sungei Road moved to Waterloo Centre. Hardware and canvas goods tradesmen in Syed Alwi, Kitchener, French, and Kelantan roads were consolidated in Jalan Besar Plaza. And with the lifting of rent control, businesses which once paid around $100 a month in shophouse rent now faced rents of $2,000–3,000 in HDB shops.

In 1953, 340,900 people, or 30 per cent of the colony's population, lived inside the Central Area. This dropped to 100,000 by 1990, or 3.7 per cent of Singapore's resident population. This further declined to only 18,230 people—0.5 per cent—by 2016.

All over what was once old Singapore, the experience of movement—what a traveller saw if he looked out a moving vehicle—changed irrevocably. Crumbling shophouses and five-foot-ways were replaced by modern facades and concrete pavements. Old traffic lights and signs, street name plates, and lamp poles were replaced and standardised. Roadside hawkers were spirited away to hawker centres. Trees and bushes sprouted everywhere, the product of Prime Minister Lee's 1967 "Garden City" vision. The volume of street litter diminished with the launch of the "Keep Singapore Clean" campaign the following year. The result: order, uniformity, cleanliness. But street culture, traditional lifestyles, and open-air nightlife were irretrievably lost.

When urban renewal began, heritage conservation was largely left out of the picture. It was not until 1971 that conservation was recognised as an "indispensable" element in urban renewal, and not until 1989 that conservation was statutorily institutionalised through a Conservation Master Plan. Even then, it had to take place within the framework of

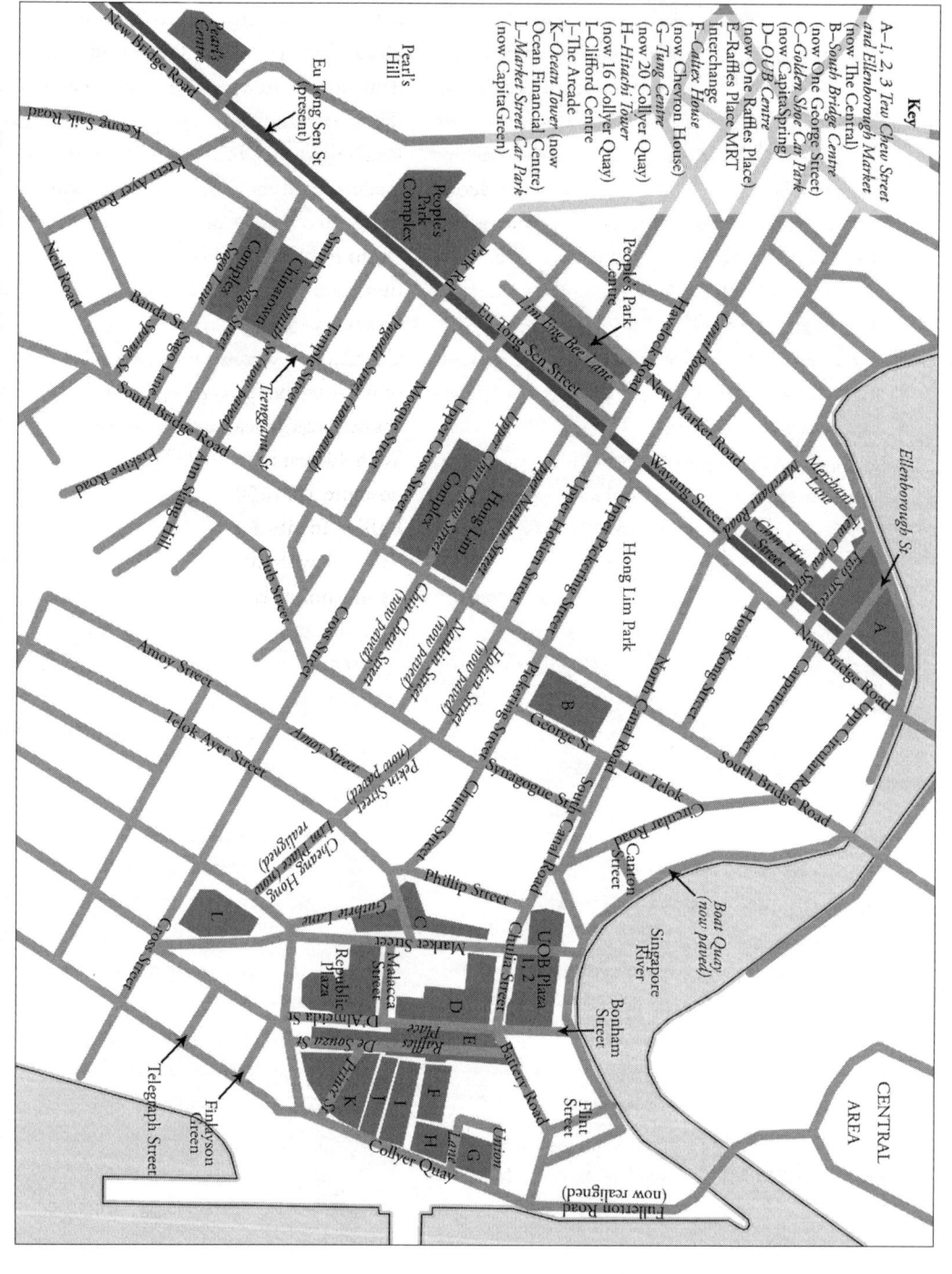

214 **Jalan Singapura**: 700 Years of Movement in Singapore

Key

A–1, 2, 3 *Teu Chew Street and Ellenborough Market* (now The Central)
B–*South Bridge Centre* (now One George Street)
C–*Golden Shoe Car Park* (now CapitaSpring)
D–*OUB Centre* (now One Raffles Place)
E–*Raffles Place MRT Interchange*
F–*Caltex House* (now Chevron House)
G–*Tung Centre* (now 20 Collyer Quay)
H–*Hitachi Tower* (now 16 Collyer Quay)
I–*Clifford Centre*
J–*The Arcade*
K–*Ocean Tower* (now Ocean Financial Centre)
L–*Market Street Car Park* (now CapitaGreen)

The Central Area south of the Singapore River. The roads and coastline are as they existed in 1961, although present-day Eu Tong Sen Street is also marked out in the darkest shade of grey. Place names in italics no longer exist; roads have been expunged, and buildings have been torn down, revamped, or renamed. Buildings or sites in darker grey, such as People's Park Centre and Hong Lim Complex, were constructed between 1961 and 2019 at the cost of expunged roads such as Lim Eng Bee Lane and Upper Chin Chew Street. (Source: Eisen Teo) economic pragmatism. Usually, if an old building was to be saved, it had to make money, either in becoming a tourist attraction, or being converted to commercial use. In 1989, just four per cent of the Central Area was earmarked for conservation as "historic districts". They included the "ethnic enclaves" of Chinatown, Little India, and Kampong Glam, and Emerald Hill and the Singapore River. Much of the rest of the Central Area was fair game for urban renewal.

Some lamented irreplaceable losses. Two years after Raffles City and the Westin Stamford opened over the site of the former Raffles Institution, *Straits Times* journalist Russell Heng wrote:

> We swopped the oldest English school in Singapore for the tallest hotel in the world. But with the oldest school building, the record is for keeps. The tallest hotel in the world is just good for until somebody else builds a taller one.

The Westin Stamford held the title of the world's tallest hotel for just 11 years. As of 2018, it was joint 17th.

LIKE HISTORY, urban renewal in Singapore goes in cycles. Some pioneer buildings erected in the 1960s and 1970s have themselves become victims of urban renewal. North of the Singapore River, Jalan Sultan Centre has been torn down for a new mixed development, City Gate. Rochor Centre was levelled for a future transport corridor; most of its residents were relocated to Kallang Trivista near the mouth of the Kallang River. South of the Singapore River, the resurrected Ellenborough Market and three blocks of Tew Chew Street—not even 30 years old—were demolished for the construction of Clarke Quay MRT Station in 2000. Further south, South Bridge Centre was demolished for One George Street, a $191-million, 23-storey office building, which opened in 2004. Pearl's Centre, with its iconic Yangtze Cinema, has made way for the upcoming Thomson-East Coast MRT Line.

In Raffles Place, the Ocean legacy entered its third generation in 2010, when 28-storey Ocean Tower was replaced by 43-storey Ocean Financial Centre. The Golden Shoe Car Park and its hawker centre—to the dismay of the lunchtime crowd—has been razed for a new, 280-metre office building. With 99-year leases the norm now, there would be no more 120–150-year-old buildings such as the Raffles Institution campus gracing the Central Area. Now, buildings approaching 40–50 years in age are in danger of being sold for hundreds of millions of dollars to private developers. The very structures that once heralded the destruction of the old Town are now themselves icons of heritage, nostalgia, and a growing grassroots effort to combat the relentless tide of redevelopment—Rochor Centre was one example.

Was it a must that a new CBD had to be constructed over the ashes of the old Central Area? In most accounts of Singapore history, yes. But recall that the hills of Toa Payoh were used to fill the swamps of the Kallang River in the 1960s. Could the banks of the Kallang River north of Kallang Road, and neighbouring Jalan Besar, have been the site of the new CBD, hence saving much of the old Central Area from destruction? Much of historic Paris has been preserved while the modern business district of La Défense was constructed 10 km away in the 1950s and 1960s. Similarly, Pudong, Shanghai's modern business district, was built on the other side of the Huangpu River from Puxi, its historic quarter. Imagine if most of the old

Rochor Centre was completed in 1977 as part of an immense wave of urban renewal which swept over the Central Area. Ironically, it became a victim of urban renewal in the 2010s, when it was torn down to make way for the North-South Corridor. This photo was taken in 2016, just before its residents moved out. Demolition commenced in 2018. (Source: Eisen Teo)

Town from Kampong Glam to Outram Road had been preserved, while the Kallang River became the new commercial and financial heart of a post-independence Singapore. Unfortunately, we will never know how this version of Singapore would have turned out.

A BRIEF ode to Cheang Hong Lim's family. Urban renewal was harsh to their toponymic legacy. Between 1898 and 1924, nine of these names were renamed; of them, only Chin Swee Road survives today at the foot of Pearl's Hill.[15] Of the five names which survived after 1924, Hong Lim Creek and Cheang Jim Chuan Lane have vanished; only three—Hong Lim Green (now Park) in Chinatown, and Cheang Hong Lim Street (now Place) and Cheang Wan Seng Place near Raffles Place—still exist today. Yet urban renewal has gifted the Cheang clan another place name: Hong Lim Complex.

NEW TOWNS AROUND THE ISLAND

WHILE URBAN renewal transformed the Central Area, the rest of Singapore Island experienced its own sea changes through the building of 21 new towns over 50 years. Powerful land acquisition laws enabled the government to acquire vast tracts from villagers and landowning companies such as the Bukit Sembawang Rubber Company. Myriad rural communities and landscapes were homogenised into carefully-planned, manicured satellite towns. Hundreds of rural kampungs were resettled to concrete, vertical kampungs—high-rise flats, with each block housing roughly the number of people living in an average-sized kampung. Winding dirt tracks made way for paved roads through towering flats. Hills and valleys were levelled, the green of forests and plantations replaced by the grey and white of concrete walls and pavements. The distinctions between "town" and "country", "urban" and "rural", disappeared. City limits became redundant. Most of Singapore Island became an urban city-state.

Each new town that arose was intended to be almost self-sufficient—a town centre, neighbourhoods each with its own centre, retail and entertainment facilities, car parks, industrial estates, and transport nodes such as bus interchanges. Arterial roads were built to link each new town with other towns and the Central Area.

In the 1960s, ground broke on two new towns. Efforts focused on Toa Payoh, which by 1970 had become Singapore's most populous new town with 150,000 residents. Toa Payoh New Town absorbed Temple Estate, including part of Kim Keat Road and Kim Keat Avenue. Fourteen roads were built inside the town. As they were laid down after the 1967 Street-Naming Advisory Committee guidelines of Malay names and mathematical naming, 10 were named Lorongs 1, 1A, 8A, and 2–8 Toa Payoh; the rest were named Toa Payoh North, East, West, and Central. The town's road layout was unique at the time—a series of concentric arcs and circles; for the outer perimeter, Jalan Toa Payoh was laid down to connect Thomson Road to Serangoon Road at Woodsville Circus. Unlike the Town of Singapore, these roads did not follow a regular pattern, because the north of Toa Payoh New Town was built first, and not what would become Toa Payoh Central. Hence, Lorong 1 was eventually joined to Lorong 6, Lorong 6 turned into Lorong 4, Lorong 5 turned into Lorong 7, and so on—confusing for newcomers. Unfortunately, that was a harbinger of future new town road systems. The regular grid system used for the Town of Singapore was never replicated for most new towns.

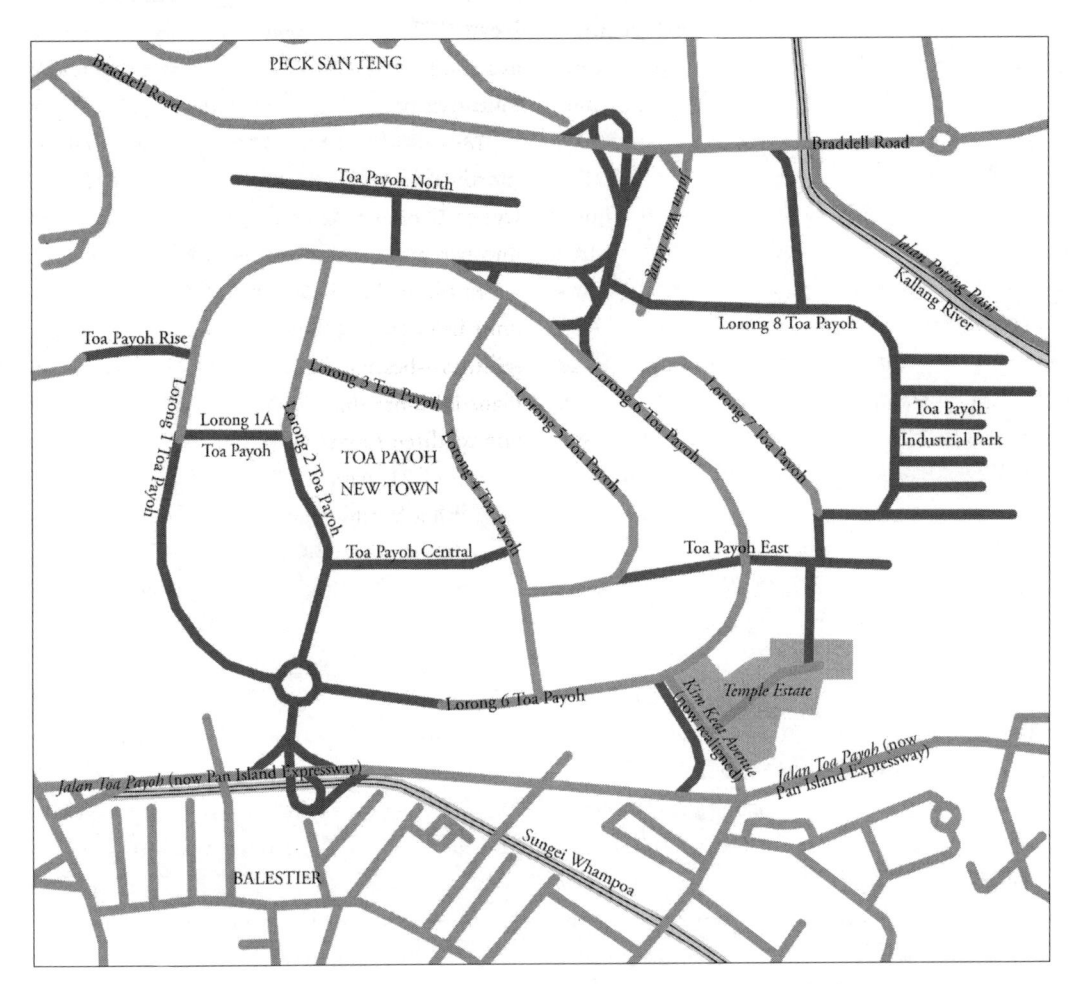

Toa Payoh New Town. The regular grid system used for the Town of Singapore was not replicated. The town was constructed in stages; the north was built first, then the south and east. Roads in light grey existed in 1969; roads in dark grey, such as Toa Payoh Central and Lorong 8 Toa Payoh, were laid down between 1969 and 1978. (Source: Eisen Teo)

In the west of the island, Jurong New Town came up to house workers and their families for Singapore's largest industrial project to date, the Jurong Industrial Estate. Both were named after Jurong Road. Around 1961, the trunk road was separated into Jurong Road and Upper Jurong Road at the junction with Boon Lay Road (named after landowner Chew Boon Lay (1851–1933)), later renamed Jalan Boon Lay. From 1963, a cluster of roads was laid down west of the Sungei Jurong. Connecting the new town and industrial estate to the Central Area were Jurong Road and a new arterial road, New West Coast Road; New West Coast Road was soon renamed Jalan Ahmad Ibrahim to honour Ahmad Ibrahim (1927–1962), who was Labour Minister and a PAP assemblyman for Sembawang.

As for the cluster of roads, many took on Malay names with references to industry—indicative of Singapore's post-independence drive towards industrialisation. Names included Jalan Utasan ("Utilities"), Jalan Gerabak ("Carriage"), Jalan Pabrik ("Factory"), Jalan Rehat ("Rest"), Jalan Gudang ("Warehouse"), Jalan Jentera ("Machinery"), and Jalan Tukang ("Artisan"). There were also Jalan Peng Kang (named after the historic District of Peng Kang, although it was not near Peng Kang at all) and Taman Jurong ("Jurong Park"), where the first flats came up. However, after new street-naming guidelines in 1968 shifted the focus from Malay to Singapore's four official languages, the first five aforementioned roads were renamed International Road, Tractor Road, Jurong Pier Road, Quality Road, and Jurong Port Road. Jalan Peng Kang and Taman Jurong were also renamed Corporation Road and Corporation Drive to maintain the spirit of industriousness, although residents still refer to the estate around Corporation Drive as Taman Jurong. West of Jalan Boon Lay, Enterprise Road and Pioneer Road were named; other roads were given more auspicious Chinese names such as Fan Yoong ("Prosperity") Road and Soon Lee ("Smooth-Sailing") Road; Neythal (Tamil for "Weaving") Road was named as a tribute to both the Tamil language and textile industries there.

Meanwhile, plans to develop Bulim Village (north of Jurong New Town) and the junction of Upper Thomson Road and Yio Chu Kang Road into two more satellite towns never materialised.

In all, the HDB constructed 117,225 housing units from 1960 to 1970, about one flat every 49 minutes—beating the targets of the two Five Year Plans by more than 6,000 units. Most flats had one to three rooms. A Singapore citizen above the age of 21, with an income of $500 a month and with a family of up to five, could be housed in days. From a country of kampung dwellers, Singapore was on its way to becoming a country of high-rise flat dwellers. In 1960, just nine per cent of the population, or 148,176 people, lived in flats, mostly low-rise blocks not exceeding half a dozen storeys. By 1970, 726,075 Singaporeans, or 35 per cent of the population, lived in mostly high-rise flats reaching 10–15 storeys. Even then, there were still 60,000 families on the waiting list for a flat in 1972.

THE CONSTRUCTION of four new towns began between 1970 and 1980, more than doubling the number of new towns to seven. In the far north, Woodlands New Town emerged just south of the Causeway as a frontier town complementing Johor Bahru, with the Woodlands–Bukit Timah trunk road linking it to the Central Area. (In 1959, Bukit Timah Road was separated into Bukit Timah Road and

Upper Bukit Timah Road at the junction with Clementi Road; at the same time, the stretch of Thomson Road from Braddell Road to Yio Chu Kang Road was renamed Upper Thomson Road, more than doubling its length to 9.6 km.) The first roads laid down in the town included Admiralty Road (after nearby Admiralty Road West, formerly Naval Base Road), Marsiling Drive, Marsiling Rise, and an extension of existing Marsiling Road. Woodlands Town Centre was completed in 1981, next to the Causeway.

In the central part of the island, Ang Mo Kio New Town emerged next to Upper Thomson Road on land Thomson once surveyed in the 1840s, not far from the planned Yio Chu Kang New Town. An arterial road was built to channel traffic to Thomson Road and the Central Area; it was named Marymount Road after Marymount Convent School.

In the east, work began on Bedok New Town east of Frankel Estate, and either side of Upper Changi Road, which connected it to the Central Area. (Sometime before 1953, Changi Road was separated into Changi Road and Upper Changi Road around the 6th Milestone.)

In the south, Telok Blangah (later Bukit Merah) New Town was formed. Neighbourhoods built over what was once the sprawling Chinese cemeteries which gave Tiong Bahru its name, were amalgamated with existing SIT estates such as Tiong Bahru, Redhill/Bukit Merah, and Kampong Silat. The wilderness on either side of the Federated Malay States Railway—renamed the Keretapi Tanah Melayu (KTM, Malay for "Malayan Railways") in 1962—disappeared; now, the tracks cut through the town.

In all, 251,489 flats were built between 1971 and 1980, one every 21 minutes. By 1980, 1.62 million Singaporeans, 67 per cent of the population, lived in flats. The average size of a flat also grew with affluence—from 37 square metres and one or two rooms in the 1960s, to 65 square metres and three or four rooms in the 1970s.

Into the 1980s, the pace of building accelerated to clear the long waiting list of 107,000 applicants in 1983. Work on 11 new towns began, more than doubling the number to 18. This was when language policies set Singapore's road-naming nomenclature on another course.

In 1979, Prime Minister Lee launched the Speak Mandarin Campaign to bolster the national bilingual education policy. This extended to toponymics—existing Chinese "dialect" place names were changed to Mandarin, spelled in pinyin; henceforth, new Chinese place names were to be only in Mandarin. For example, when Tekka Market in Kandang Kerbau was torn down and replaced by a new multi-use complex in 1982, it was renamed Zhujiao ("Foot of the Bamboo") Centre. Officials in charge of renaming were so zealous, they even dreamed up Mandarin transliterations for non-Chinese names! When plans for a new town in Seletar were unveiled in 1984, the suggested name, "Shilida", raised eyebrows. A public outcry over changing a place name with a history predating the founding of modern Singapore (think Orang Seletar) swiftly forced the HDB to ditch "Shilida" (the new town never materialised either), and before the decade was out, the toponymic exercise was discontinued in the face of public unhappiness. Some Mandarin names reverted to their old "dialect" names—for example, Zhujiao Centre was renamed Tekka Centre in 2000—but others were retained, leaving a colourful toponymic landscape.

In the southwest of the island, work on Clementi New Town started between Clementi

Road (renamed from Reformatory Road after Sir Cecil Clementi in 1947) and Upper Ayer Rajah Road—the first new town named after a place name taken from a person. To complement Upper Ayer Rajah Road and West Coast Road in connecting the town to the Central Area, Commonwealth Avenue West was laid down as an extension of Commonwealth Avenue.

In the west, Jurong New Town was enlarged and separated into Jurong East and Jurong West new towns on either side of the Sungei Jurong. Taman Jurong was now part of Jurong West. Boon Lay Way was built to connect the two towns to the Central Area via Commonwealth Avenue West, hence creating a continuous channel of movement from Jalan Boon Lay to New Bridge Road in Chinatown—a distance of about 18 km.

Among the hills that gave Bukit Panjang its name, three new towns emerged—Bukit Batok west of Bukit Timah Hill, and Choa Chu Kang and Bukit Panjang on either side of 10th Mile Upper Bukit Timah Road. Initially, Choa Chu Kang was pinyin-ised to Caicuogang, and Bukit Panjang to Zhenghua, the pinyin spelling of Cheng Hwa (Hokkien for "Honesty and Brilliance"), taken from Jalan Cheng Hwa, a main road inside Bukit Panjang Village. However, by 1987, the government decided to revert to their old names, as work on the towns was still in its early stages.[16] Bukit Batok New Town was constructed over part of Jurong Road, hastening its demise as a trunk road; similarly, Choa Chu Kang New Town was built over part of historic Choa Chu Kang Road, absorbing Teck Whye Estate.

In the north, a new town came up at the 11th Milestone of Sembawang Road. As it was near Nee Soon Village, it was named Nee Soon—the first new town named after a place name taken from an Asian person. However, Nee Soon was pinyin-ised to Yishun. Lentor Avenue (named after nearby Lorong Lentor, a track off the 10½th Milestone of Yio Chu Kang Road) and Seletar Avenue 1 were built to link Yishun with Ang Mo Kio New Town and the Central Area. By 1988, Seletar Avenue 1 was renamed Lentor Avenue too.

Between Ang Mo Kio and Toa Payoh new towns, a new town was planned over one of the largest cemeteries in Singapore, a Cantonese and Hakka graveyard for more than 100,000 souls called Peck San Theng, meaning "Jade Mountain Pavilion". The new town took on the name Peck San, later pinyin-ised to Bishan. Bishan Road was laid down to connect Ang Mo Kio, Bishan, and Toa Payoh new towns.

In the northeast, along Upper Serangoon Road, plans were made for Au Kang New Town. Au Kang was a Teochew name for the area between the 5th and 7th Milestones of Upper Serangoon Road, meaning "Back of the River", a reference to the Sungei Serangoon. However, it was pinyin-ised to Hougang. Unlike Caicuogang and Zhenghua, the new town names of Hougang, Yishun, and Bishan were not reverted, because when HDB made the decision, the trio were "developments already well populated and their names widely accepted... it would inconvenience the public to have their names changed".

To the southwest of Hougang New Town, Serangoon New Town came about, incorporating two new HDB neighbourhoods called Serangoon Central and Serangoon North with the existing private estates of Serangoon Gardens and Braddell Heights. In the east of the island, Pasir Ris and Tampines new towns came up. The former was named after Pasir Ris Village, while the latter was named after the road and district that used to cover the area.

In all, from 1981 to 1990, the HDB completed one flat every 16 minutes, or 321,777 flats. By 1990, 2.41 million people, or 88 per cent of the resident population, lived in one. Flats continued growing in size and height. Twenty-five storey blocks appeared in Ang Mo Kio and Bishan; five- and six-room apartments in Bishan and Yishun.

The last rural settlements disappeared by the 1990s. Urban renewal even began within the oldest of new towns—Queenstown, Toa Payoh, Jurong (now part of Jurong West). By 1988, Temple Estate's 38 low-rise blocks, just 34 years old, were demolished; in their place, 19 high-rise blocks came up, forcing the realignment of Kim Keat Avenue. From 1988, another 60 blocks of 13,000 one- and two-room flats made way for four and five-room flats.

In the 1990s, work began on three new towns. Between Woodlands and Yishun new towns, Sembawang New Town appeared; Sembawang Way and Gambas Avenue were built to connect the towns. The rural northeast receded as Sengkang (Teochew for "Prosperous Harbour") and Punggol new towns arose. Unlike previous towns, they adopted grid road systems. And as Woodlands New Town spread to the east, its town centre shifted east from Woodlands Town Centre to Woodlands Square; Woodlands Town Centre became Old Woodlands Town Centre.

Between 1991 and 2015, another 434,579 flats were built, or one flat every 30 minutes. In 2016, there were 3.25 million people—almost 83 per cent of Singapore's resident population—living in 1,011,000 HDB flats, a ratio of 3.2 people to one flat, compared to 1968's ratio of 6.5 people to one flat. With the maturing of new towns, the HDB has replaced the term "new town" with "town". In 2016, the three most populous towns in Singapore were Bedok, with a population of 287,170, Jurong West with 270,350, and Woodlands with 249,780. The two oldest towns of Queenstown and Toa Payoh had just 99,350 and 122,780 residents respectively.

We can see the differences between Ebenezer Howard's Garden City vision and the reality of new towns in Singapore. The latter has far larger populations—even the smallest new town, Sembawang, had 77,350 residents in 2016, as compared to Howard's estimate of 50,000 per garden city. New towns also never took on the garden city's circular shape or concentric land use plan; the concrete and asphalt of arterial roads and expressways separate towns today, not green belts; the geographical sizes of towns do not allow most residents to go around on foot. Howard may have provided the vision for satellite towns in Singapore, but the reality was an urban concept unique to the city-state.

THE RURAL was no more. In 1953, 18 per cent of Singapore's population, or 203,200 people, lived inside the Rural Planning Area. By 2016, its population had increased almost 16 times to 3,180,370, or 81 per cent of Singapore's resident population. Around 1950, out of a land area of 541.9 square km, 35 per cent of Singapore was cultivated for agriculture, while another 30 per cent was secondary forest. In 2016, just one per cent of Singapore's 719.7 square km was agriculture, while nature reserves took up 4.4 per cent. The result: lost landscapes, lost communities, lost traditions, lost experiences of movement.

Before Toa Payoh New Town came about, areas in historic Toa Payoh were known to locals by different names in different topolects. What became part of Lorong 8 Toa Payoh was once known as Hup Choon Hng, Teochew for "United

Spring Garden"; another part was known as Puay Tian Keng, or "Flying Sky Temple". Near where Lorong 6 Toa Payoh is today, there was also an Ang Siang Suah—"Ang Siang Hill" in Hokkien, not to be confused with Chinatown's Ann Siang Hill. With the building of the new town and relocation of the original inhabitants, these place names have been forgotten.

In the east, Bedok was once known for its jungles, hiking tracks, and red cliffs mapped by the Portuguese in the 1600s. Tampines possessed vast sand quarries and rolling hills stretching for miles. No longer. The tracks have been removed, sand quarries cleared, rolling hills flattened, the earth carted to the beaches off East Coast Road for the creation of what was to become Marine Parade, East Coast Park, and Marina Bay.

Just half a century after its creation, in the mid-1980s, much of the Malay Settlement and Kampong Eunos made way for the flats of Eunos and the industrial estate of Kaki Bukit (Malay for "Foothill") in Bedok New Town. The descendants of the Malays, Bugis, and Orang Laut resettled from the mouth of the Kallang River for Kallang Airport had to be resettled themselves. Dozens of historic roads were expunged, although two names were retained for new roads built for the HDB neighbourhoods—Jalan Tenaga (Malay for "Energy") and Jalan Damai (meaning "Peaceful"). The place name Eunos has also survived as a reminder of the rise of Malay nationalism in early 20th-century Singapore.

Sengkang's "prosperous harbour" was a fishing port named Kangkar, in existence from as early as the 1850s at the mouth of the Sungei Serangoon. Into the 1980s, it was home to 100 fishing vessels, and its market traded 40 tons of fish every day. It was said that anyone born and bred in Kangkar could tell the freshness of fish with just one look,

and the predominantly Teochew village was also known for its operas during the annual 7th Lunar Month Festival. But in the era of new towns, there was no place for Kangkar and its expert fishermen. In 1984, the government resettled a few hundred villagers and demolished the port to create Hougang and Sengkang new towns; the Sungei Serangoon was first canalised, then converted into a reservoir in 2011. The place name "Kangkar" only lives on today in the name of an LRT station near the Serangoon Reservoir, and a mall near Hougang MRT Station.

Punggol Village, one of the oldest villages in Singapore predating Raffles' arrival in 1819, did not survive urban renewal either. A *Straits Times* reader wrote an appeal in 1985 to preserve the 500-strong village as a "model Malay fishing village", but his plea fell on deaf ears. Punggol's villagers and farms were resettled by the dawn of the 21st century, and Punggol Road, once a forested, remote trunk road, gradually saw the flats of Sengkang and Punggol new towns rise around it.[17]

In the north, Chong Pang Village, a cluster of zinc-roofed houses with shops and bars serving British servicemen from the naval base, was razed in 1989 for Sembawang New Town. Like Cheang Hong Lim's family, the Lim clan has seen many unique place names in their honour extinguished by urban renewal. All 14 place names linked to their family in Chong Pang Village disappeared; nearby Nee Soon Village was also resettled. Today, only seven of the original 24 place names connected to the Lim clan have survived: Bah Soon Pah, Chong Kuo, Thong Bee, Nee Soon, Peck Hay, and Marsiling roads, and Peng Nguan Street.

Ulu Sembawang—bounded by Woodlands, Sembawang Road, and Mandai—was one of the widest expanses of rural countryside in Singapore, covered with farms and rubber plantations. For generations, it was home to mostly Hokkien families with surnames Ang or Toh, subsisting on animal, vegetable, and fish farms. By 1948, Jalan Ulu Sembawang—a dirt road barely wide enough for two trucks to pass each other—was cut through the area from Sembawang Road to Mandai Road, becoming one of the longest dirt roads in Singapore; in 1972, it served 8,500 people. In the 1970s, illicit *samsu* (moonshine) distillers played cat-and-mouse games with the police in the jungle; in the 1980s, the fledgling Singapore Armed Forces staged war games with thunderflashes and blanks. Between exercises, people trawled the jungle for the fruits of hundreds of durian trees.

But Ulu Sembawang gradually made way for Woodlands New Town. *The Straits Times* reported the impending end of an era in 1985:

> House number 285 (Jalan Ulu Sembawang) stands on a slope. A climb to the top reveals a vista of the HDB flats in Woodlands and Marsiling. Away to the right, the twin spires of Senoko Power Station break the skyline.
>
> Master of the house, 40-year-old Mr Toh Bon Poh, strode up to welcome the visitor. He has lived here since he was born. He is an orchid grower who used to rear pigs.
>
> Mr Toh's family consists of his brothers, their families, his four sisters and his parents and their grandchildren, all in about 40 people. "When we cook rice, we use two big pots. You look around, where in Singapore can you find a family like ours?" he asked proudly.

He isn't looking forward to resettlement. "They can give me five HDB flats, and they will never be able to replace this place."

Alas, Toh had to move.

The once-common experience of travelling on dusty, muddy tracks through forest, plantations, and farms, occasionally past crumbling shophouses and squat huts made of wood and zinc, was replaced by the experience of travelling on concrete pavements and asphalt roads past towering flats painted in different colours and hues, and manicured flora amidst car parks and covered walkways.

New spaces emerged for HDB dwellers. The void deck became a community space for myriad activities. The common corridor replaced dirt tracks and private gardens in kampungs, used by residents for potted plants, furniture, and airing laundry. For playtime, children moved from trees, drains, and makeshift swings in the great outdoors into the void decks and corridors. Unfortunately, they also took to pressing lift buttons for amusement, and before urine-detection devices and close-circuit cameras were installed in lifts, public urination was a common problem.

Many first-time HDB dwellers suffered anxieties. Many multi-generational families could not be relocated to the same block of flats. The oldest family members usually took it hardest. They found themselves living alongside strangers and confronted by an atmosphere of aloofness. The open, ground-hugging spaces of the kampung were replaced by the claustrophobia of high-rise pigeonholes with doors locked for fear of criminals. The lift was a harrowing experience for many first-time users.

The staples of a kampung, such as the provision store and market, and familiar professions such as the neighbourhood tailor and cobbler, were lost

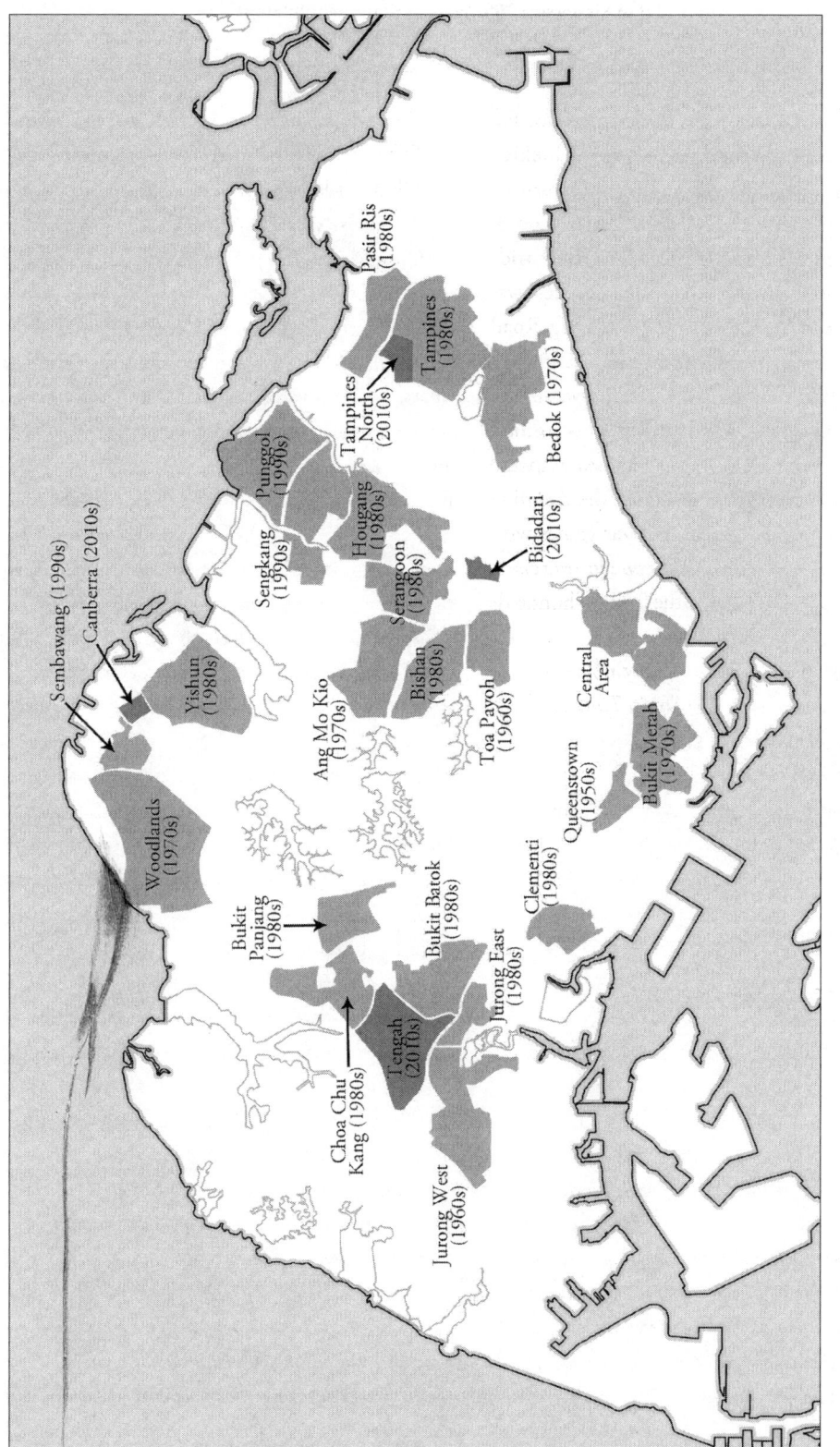

New Towns built in Singapore from the 1960s, shaded light grey. With each place name is the decade in which construction of flats started. Four major housing estates / towns started in the 2010s—Tengah, Canberra, Bidadari, and Tampines North—are shaded a darker grey. (Source: Eisen Teo)

in the move. So were traditional coffeeshops, where proprietors dressed in singlets and shorts grilled bread over charcoal and served customers at marble-topped tables. Artisan trades were hit hardest because the new ground-floor shop spaces in HDB blocks only allowed tenants to display and sell goods, not craft them.

Providing better physical living conditions through urban renewal did not automatically translate to a happier life. A 1977 study of over 400 low-income families living in one-room flats in Telok Blangah New Town revealed that many were stressed with their electricity and water bills—their water supply used to be free from a well or communal pipe, and they were used to blackouts anyway. They found their new environment oppressive, with a feeling of little control and escape. They accepted that urban renewal was a reality, and that living conditions had "improved", but derived little solace from them.

Like other revolutions in history, the urban revolution was a double-edged sword. It radically improved many lives, at the same time consigning others to an irreversibly bleak existence.

THERE ARE still small pockets of land in Singapore Island that retain a semblance of the rural, mostly in the west, northwest, north, and northeast—for example, Pasir Laba, Lim Chu Kang, Kranji, Mandai, and Seletar. Even so, these pockets are decreasing in size. After 2010, construction started on four new estates in areas once covered by secondary forest or open fields: Canberra in the north between Sembawang and Yishun towns, named after Canberra Road; Tampines North in the east, once a bike park; Bidadari along Upper Serangoon Road, formerly a cemetery serving Christians, Muslims, Hindus, and Sinhalese Theravada Buddhists; and Tengah in the west, billed by the HDB as a "forest town", set to take the place of an actual forest untouched since the last villages north of Jurong West town were resettled in the 1980s. Meanwhile, the cranes and excavators are still working overtime in Jurong West, Sengkang West, and Punggol North; soon, the farms of Seletar Farmway and the wilderness of Punggol North will exist only in history books.

Cranes and excavators have not gone silent in older towns either—like in the Central Area, urban renewal in the suburbs continues relentlessly. Most SIT estates—the likes of Durham, Owen, Delta, and Alexandra Road (North and South)—have disappeared; only former Tiong Bahru Estate has a significant concentration of conserved buildings today—20 blocks. In 1995, the HDB started an urban redevelopment scheme called the Selective En bloc Redevelopment Scheme (Sers), which identifies blocks of flats for demolishment to "renew older housing estates". Usually, shorter blocks spaced further apart would be replaced by taller, closely-packed blocks, to house more people in the same area. As of 2016, 80 Sers projects have been announced for old neighbourhoods such as Margaret Drive, Ang Mo Kio Avenue 1, and Commonwealth Drive, with 76 completed. An entire former town centre can fall to the wrecking ball—Old Woodlands Town Centre was demolished in 2018 for an extension of the Woodlands Checkpoint.

Today, the only place on Singapore Island one can relive authentic kampung life and get a sense of the experience of movement common in the 1960s, is Kampong Lorong Buangkok, near Yio Chu Kang Road. Founded by traditional Chinese medicine seller Sng Tow Koon in 1956, the kampung housed 40 families at its peak in the 1960s, but as of 2017, there were just 26

Singapore Island's last authentic kampung is Kampong Lorong Buangkok, off Gerald Drive. When I visited in 2010, the kampung was crisscrossed by dirt tracks which turned muddy after rain—giving a good idea of how rural roads in Singapore were like up to the 1980s. (Source: Eisen Teo)

households left, occupying 1.22 hectares. The dirt tracks and wooden huts give one the feeling of being frozen in time. The community has escaped at least two cycles of urban renewal. But for how long? New flats of Hougang town tower above the kampung, and while there were plans to build schools and a major road on the land as of 2017, there was "no intention" to carry them out "in the near future". Meanwhile, the 26 families continue their quiet lives outside the urban sprawl.

A TOPONYMIC REVOLUTION

THE CONSTRUCTION of new towns from the 1960s influenced road building and naming, and the geographical imagination associated with place names, more than any other event in modern Singapore's history. Hundreds of new roads were built; hundreds of old roads, villages, agricultural estates, and other physical landmarks were cleared. The geographical imagination of place names outside the Central Area grew, shifted, or shrunk. This was a toponymic revolution to match the urban revolution.

As new towns rose, their assigned names imprinted themselves onto the collective psyche of hundreds of thousands of residents, irrevocably latching onto daily experience and popular memory. As these residents travelled to, within, and from the new towns, these assigned names became part of their experiences of movement. Today, we may not think much upon the mention of household names such as Jurong, Choa Chu Kang, Ang Mo Kio, or Tampines. But we are used to these names because they have been seared into our collective consciousness. We come across these names every day when travelling from one place to another. What strengthened this etching onto popular consciousness was an exercise in uniformity and homogenisation.

SIT estates built in the 1950s had roads with unique themes, such as Delta Estate's rivers and Alexandra Road (South) Estate's Nordic gods. When the old British road-naming system was replaced by an evolving Singaporean road-naming system in the 1960s, one guideline handed to the Street-Naming Advisory Committee was to give priority to Malay names. It coincided with bureaucratic efforts to bequeath names to unnamed rural tracks. As a result, the number of roads starting with "Jalan" and "Lorong" surged: In 1966, out of 2,646 roads in Singapore, there were 617 roads starting with "Jalan" and 188 roads starting with "Lorong", making up 30 per cent of all roads; by 1975, these numbers had increased to 692 and 419 respectively out of 3,296 roads, making up 33.7 per cent of roads. Such toponymic creativity was discontinued when the Committee was handed the guideline on mathematical naming in July 1967. Most new towns thereafter followed this sterile pattern of road-naming: first, the new town's name; followed by "Street", "Avenue", or "Drive"; then a number at the end. For example: Yishun Street 11, Serangoon North Avenue 1, Pasir Ris Drive 3.

In 1966, the names that were eventually assigned to 18 new towns appeared in just 21 roads, or 0.8 per cent of all roads in Singapore. In 2016, these names appeared in 528 roads, or 12 per cent of all roads.

What complicated this toponymic revolution was that not all the assigned names were definite shoo-ins. When decisions were made to name a new town, other place names could have been adopted, and the decisions to choose certain names over others was the difference between toponymic immortality and total effacement from history. The following shows the origins of the names of 13 new towns, alternative names for these towns, and how place and road names—and the geographical imagination associated with them—changed as a result.

JURONG EAST and WEST New Towns
- Named after: Jurong Road.
- Could have been named: PENG KANG, the historic district on which Jurong New Town was built in the 1960s, now part of Jurong West town.[18]
- Could also have been named: BOON LAY, after Jalan Boon Lay.
- In 1966: Two roads starting with the name "Jurong"; one road each with the names "Peng Kang" and "Boon Lay". 2016: 55 roads and an MRT interchange starting with "Jurong"; five roads with the name "Boon Lay". Jalan Peng Kang has been renamed Corporation Road.[19]
- The geographical imagination of "Jurong": Shifted west, subsuming historic Peng Kang. What used to be known as "Jurong" is now part of Bukit Batok town. This is why Old Jurong Road is next to Bukit Batok town.

BUKIT BATOK New Town
- Named after: The hill called Bukit Batok, part of the Bukit Timah Granite Formation, 235–250 million years old.
- Could have been named: PERANG, after Jalan Perang, a track that connected Jurong Road to Choa Chu Kang Road. "Perang" is Malay for "Battle" or "Auburn".
- Could also have been named: GOMBAK, after Bukit Gombak II, a hill next to the town, presently Little Guilin.
- In 1966: No roads starting with "Bukit Batok" or "Gombak"; one road with the name "Perang". 2016: 31 roads and an MRT station starting with "Bukit Batok"; two roads and an MRT station with the name "Gombak"; Jalan Perang has been expunged.
- The geographical imagination of "Bukit Batok": Shifted west and expanded, covering what was once part of "Jurong".

CHOA CHU KANG New Town
- Named after: Choa Chu Kang Road.
- Could have been named: TECK WHYE (Cantonese for De Hui, or "Virtue and Kindness"), after the name of the estate it absorbed.
- Could also have been named: KEAT HONG or KRANJI. Keat Hong Village lay inside the present-day town; the town was also built within the historic district of Kranji.
- In 1966: One road starting with the names "Choa Chu Kang" and "Teck Whye"; two roads with the name "Kranji". 2016: 28 roads and an MRT interchange starting with "Choa Chu Kang"; five roads and an LRT station with the name "Teck Whye"; five roads and an MRT station with the name "Kranji"; two roads and an LRT station with the name "Keat Hong".
- The geographical imagination of "Choa Chu Kang": Shifted east, away from Choa Chu Kang Village towards the historic 10th Mile Upper Bukit Timah Road.

WOODLANDS New Town
- Named after: Woodlands Road.
- Could have been named: MARSILING or ADMIRALTY, after Marsiling Road

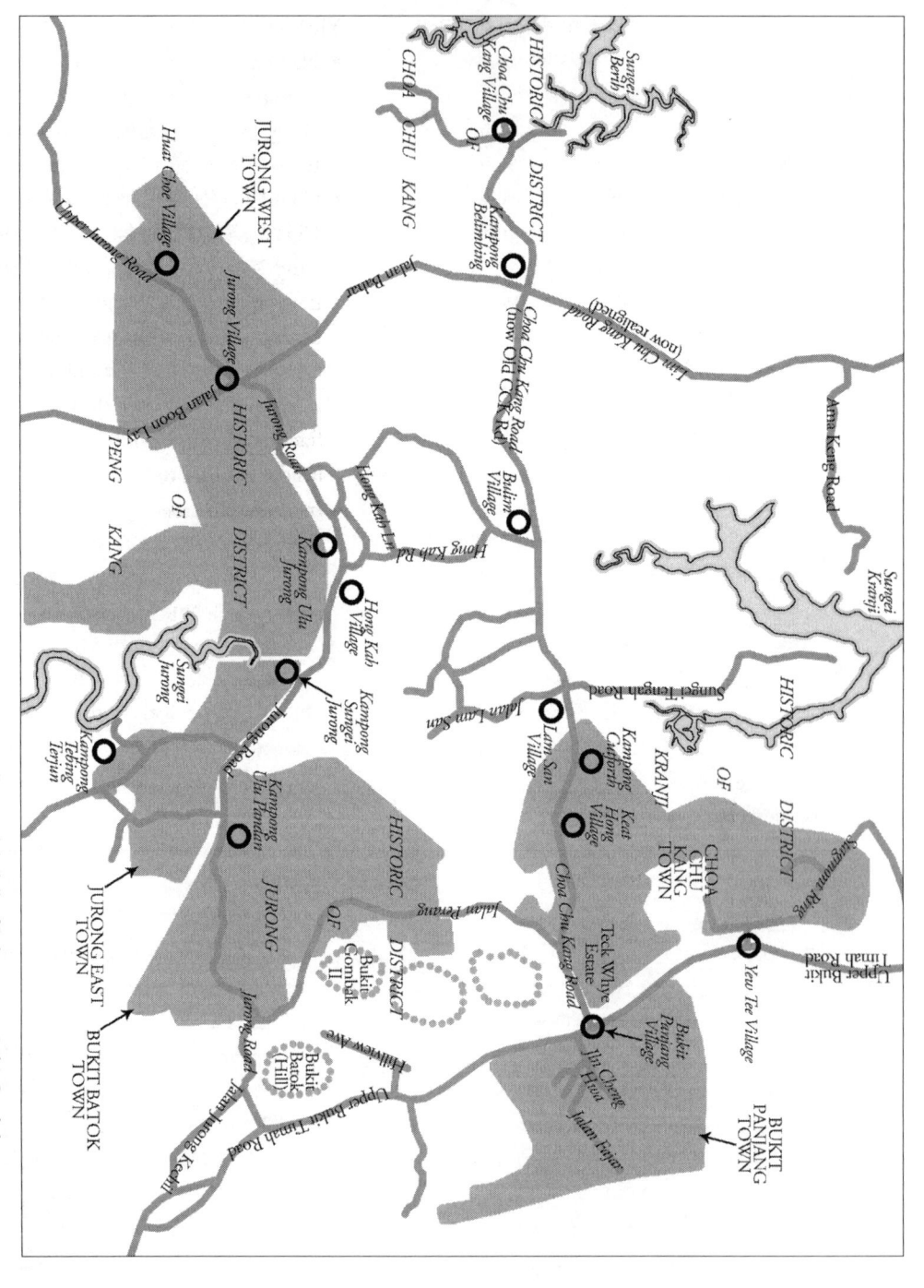

The west of Singapore Island. The roads and rivers are as they existed in 1966, with major villages and the hills of Bukit Panjang, Bukit Gombak, and Bukit Batok marked out with black rings and light grey dots respectively. The historic districts of Choa Chu Kang, Peng Kang, Kranji, and Jurong are highlighted in capital letters. Place names in italics highlight expunged villages and roads, or partially expunged, realigned, or renamed roads. The present-day towns of Jurong East, Jurong West, Bukit Batok, Choa Chu Kang, and Bukit Panjang are shaded in light grey; the towns followed the demise of roads such as Choa Chu Kang Road and Jurong Road, and villages such as Keat Hong and Huat Choe. (Source: Eisen Teo)

and Admiralty Road, roads that lie inside the town today.
- Could also have been named: SEMBAWANG, as the town lay within the historic district of Sembawang.
- In 1966: One road each starting with "Woodlands", "Marsiling", and "Admiralty". 2016: 72 roads, an MRT station and two future MRT stations starting with "Woodlands"; 15 roads and an MRT station starting with "Marsiling"; seven roads and an MRT station starting with "Admiralty".
- The geographical imagination of "Woodlands": Expanded southeast from Woodlands Road and the Causeway, subsuming the historic region of Ulu Sembawang.

SEMBAWANG New Town
- Named after: Sembawang Road. However, the road and Sembawang Village lay outside the new town.
- Could have been named: CHONG PANG, after the village and road off Sembawang Road.
- In 1966: Two roads starting with "Sembawang"; one road starting with "Chong Pang". 2016: 23 roads and an MRT station starting with "Sembawang". Chong Pang Road and Chong Pang Village have been expunged. "Chong Pang" lives on as the name of a neighbourhood and a ward, but in Yishun town to the southeast.
- The geographical imagination of "Sembawang": Shrunk from Sembawang Village, the Naval Base, and the region of Ulu Sembawang.

YISHUN New Town
- Named after: Nee Soon Village, itself named after Lim Nee Soon. However, the village lay to the south of the town, closer to Mandai than Yishun town today.
- Could have been named: NEE SOON, CHYE KAY, or BAH SOON PAH. Chye Kay, or Cai Qi in Mandarin, was the name of a village and road around the present-day town; it was taken from Tan Chye Kay, a rubber and pineapple plantation owner from the late 1800s. A fraction of Bah Soon Pah Road still lies inside the town today.
- In 1966: One road each with the names "Nee Soon", "Chye Kay", and "Bah Soon Pah". 2016: 34 roads and an MRT station starting with "Yishun"; one road each with the names "Nee Soon" and "Bah Soon Pah". Chye Kay Road has been expunged.
- The geographical imagination of "Nee Soon" or "Yishun": Shifted northeast, away from Nee Soon Village and Nee Soon Road.

ANG MO KIO New Town
- Named after: The historic district of Ang Mo Kio, and Ang Mo Kio Village. However, Ang Mo Kio Village lay outside the town.
- Could have been named: CHENG SAN (Hokkien for Qing Shan, or "Green Hill"), after Cheng San Road, which spanned the width of the present-day town.
- In 1966: No roads starting with "Ang Mo Kio"; one road starting with "Cheng San". 2016: 41 roads and an MRT station starting with "Ang Mo Kio". Cheng San

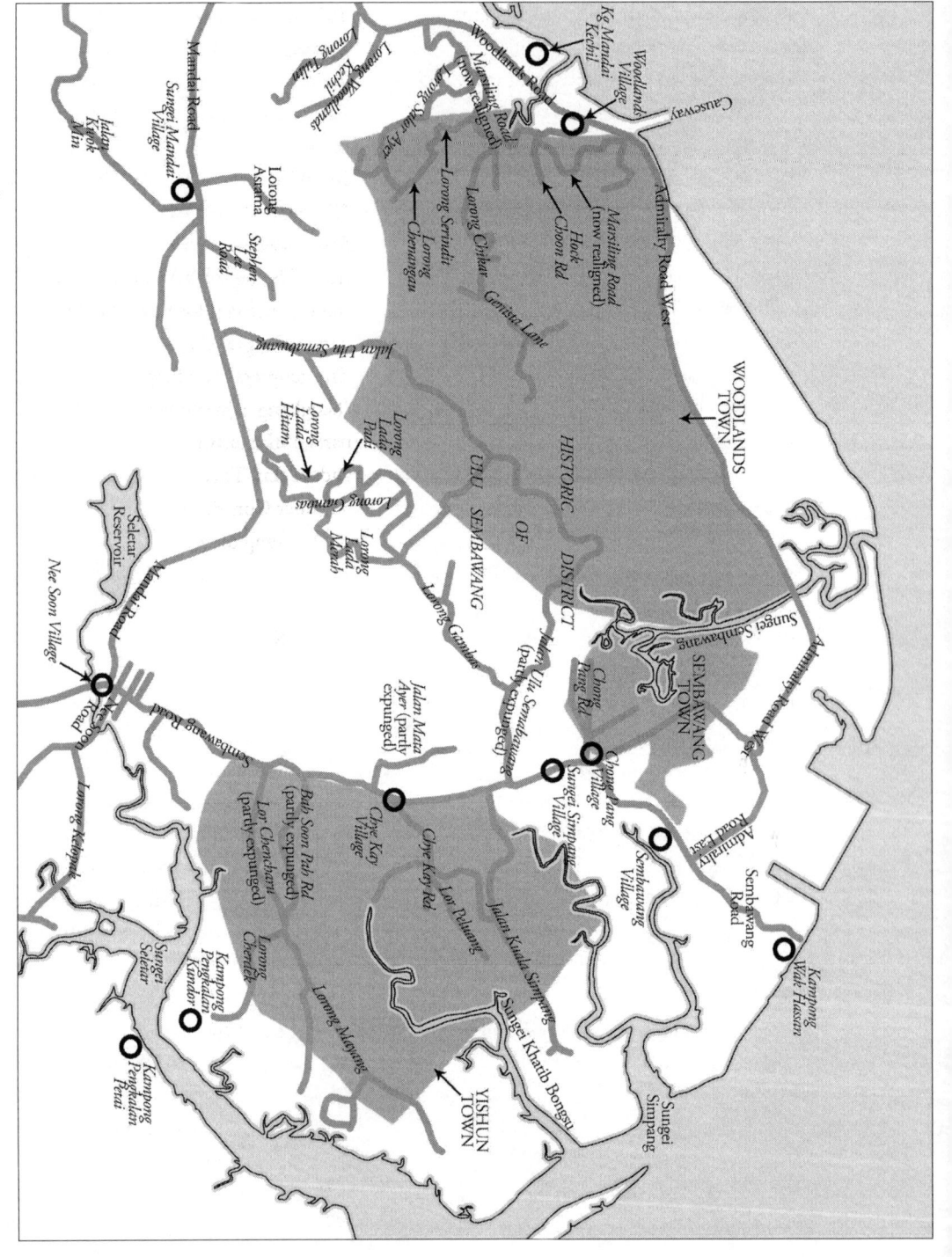

The north of Singapore Island. The roads and rivers are as they existed in 1969, with major villages marked out with black rings. The historic district of Ulu Sembawang is highlighted in capital letters. Place names in italics highlight expunged villages and roads, or partially expunged, realigned, or renamed roads. The present-day towns of Woodlands, Sembawang, and Yishun are shaded in light grey; the towns followed the demise of roads such as Jalan Ulu Sembawang and Jalan Kuala Simpang, and villages such as Chong Pang and Chye Kay. (Source: Eisen Teo)

Road has been expunged; the place name lives on in a community club, a library, and the ward of Cheng San-Seletar (part of Ang Mo Kio Group Representation Constituency).
- The geographical imagination of "Ang Mo Kio": Shifted northeast, away from Ang Mo Kio Village, subsuming the region of Cheng San. The area around Ang Mo Kio Village is now part of Bishan town.

HOUGANG New Town
- Named after: Au Kang.
- In 1966: No roads starting with "Au Kang". 2016: 22 roads and an MRT station starting with "Hougang".
- Renamed road: The southern end of Punggol Road was renamed Hougang Avenue 8 and Hougang Avenue 10.
- The geographical imagination of "Hougang": Expanded north and east, subsuming the southern part of what was once "Punggol". This is why Punggol Park is in Hougang town. "Hougang" now refers to a town, not a river or road.

SENGKANG New Town
- Named after: Lorong Sengkang, and the historic fishing port along the banks of the Sungei Serangoon, now Serangoon Reservoir.
- Could have been named: BUANGKOK. Lorong Buangkok ran across much of the town, connecting Yio Chu Kang Road via Jalan Woodbridge to Punggol Road. "Buangkok" was the Teochew name for Bukit Sembawang Rubber Company, which owned land in the area. In the late 1970s, nine tracks were carved out from Lorong Buangkok—Buangkok North Farmways 1–4, and Buangkok South Farmways 1–5. All were expunged for the town.
- In 1966: One road each with the names "Buangkok" and "Sengkang". 2016: Seven roads and an MRT station with the name "Buangkok"; 11 roads, an MRT station, and two LRT systems with the name "Sengkang".
- The geographical imagination of "Sengkang": Spread west, subsuming parts of the historic districts of Punggol and Seletar. This is why the Single Member Constituency of Punggol East is in Sengkang town, and there is a mall in Sengkang West called The Seletar Mall.

PASIR RIS New Town
- Named after: Pasir Ris Road, Pasir Ris Village, and Kampong Pasir Ris.
- Could have been named: TAMPINES, as the town was sited along the historic trunk road of Tampines Road, and inside the historic district of Tampines.
- Could also have been named: LOYANG, after Jalan Loyang Besar and Kampong Loyang.
- In 1966: No roads with the name "Pasir Ris"; two roads with the name "Loyang". 2016: 41 roads and an MRT station with the name "Pasir Ris"; 19 roads with the name "Loyang".
- The geographical imagination of "Pasir Ris": Expanded east, subsuming part of the historic regions of Tampines and Loyang. This is why much of Sungei Tampines flows through Pasir Ris town.

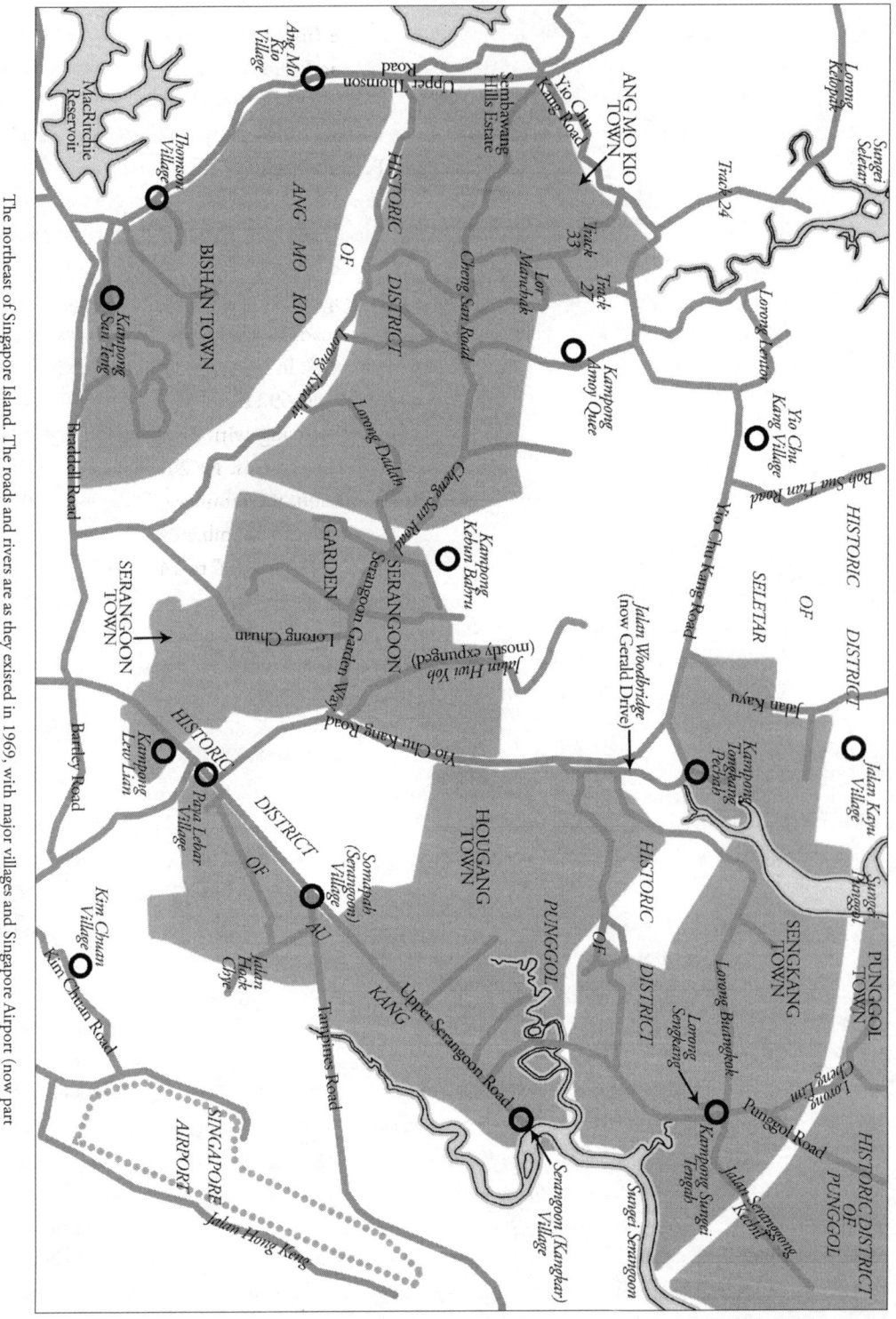

The northeast of Singapore Island. The roads and rivers are as they existed in 1969, with major villages and Singapore Airport (now part of Paya Lebar Air Base) marked out with black rings and light grey dots respectively. The historic districts of Ang Mo Kio, Seletar and Punggol are highlighted in capital letters. Place names in italics highlight expunged villages and roads, or partially expunged, realigned, or renamed roads. The present-day towns of Ang Mo Kio, Bishan, Serangoon, Hougang, Sengkang, and Punggol are shaded in light grey; the towns followed the demise of roads such as Cheng San Road and most of Lorong Buangkok, and villages such as Kampong San Teng and Kampong Sungei Tengah. (Source: Eisen Teo)

TAMPINES New Town
- Named after: Tampines Road and the district of Tampines.
- Could have been named: ULU BEDOK. Part of the town lies within the historic district.
- In 1966: Seven roads with the name "Tampines". 2016: 68 roads, an expressway, and three MRT stations with the name "Tampines".
- The geographical imagination of "Tampines": Shifted south, subsuming part of Ulu Bedok.

BEDOK New Town
- Named after: Bedok Village, Bedok Road, and the historic district of Bedok. However, the village and road lay outside the town.
- Could have been named: CHANGI. Upper Changi Road lay within the town.
- In 1966: Two roads starting with "Bedok". In 2016: 38 roads, three MRT stations, and two planned MRT stations with the name "Bedok".
- The geographical imagination of "Bedok": Spread northwest, subsuming the historic region of Chai Chee and part of Ulu Bedok.

Certain place names like Woodlands, Bedok, and Hougang have survived. On the other hand, many roads, villages, and agricultural estates that could have lent their names to new towns and their neighbourhoods were effaced, not just from physical existence, but from human experience and popular memory too. Some examples of agricultural estates named after their owners or the companies that managed them—Mok Peng Hiang Estate (near Admiralty MRT Station today), Aik Chiang Estate (Bukit Panjang town), and Ho Tong Jen Estate (Tampines town). Rural roads that used to span whole regions of Singapore, such as Jalan Perang, Jalan Ulu Sembawang, and Cheng San Road, were wiped off the map. Immortality in the national consciousness once lay within their grasp.

To get an idea of the extent of the homogenisation of place names, look no further than roads beginning with the words "Jalan" and "Lorong". In 1975, out of 3,296 roads in Singapore, there were 692 roads starting with "Jalan" and 419 roads starting with "Lorong", making up 33.7 per cent of roads. By 2016, because of the urban revolution, the number of roads had increased to 4,396, but the number of "Jalans" had dropped to 443, and "Lorongs" to 144, forming just 13.3 per cent of roads. In 41 years, the combined number of "Jalans" and "Lorongs" declined by almost half. Over the same period, all 132 villages listed in the 1966 street directory had vanished; 51 of them had unique names such as O'Carroll Scott, Padang Terbakar, and Tua Kong Lye. Gone too were the unique names of urban kampungs, such as Si Kah Teng and Kuchai. The new towns that replaced them employed little creativity in road-naming. For example, in Yishun town, roads such as Jalan Kuala Simpang, Lorong Mayang, and Chye Kay Road were replaced by the likes of Yishun Avenue 7, Yishun Street 71, and Yishun Ring Road.

Occasionally, there were attempts to depart from this mathematical naming system, with varied results. When Bedok New Town was birthed in the mid-1970s, planned roads included Bedok Highway (at the expense of Jalan Puay Poon), View, Walk, Plain, Place, and Drive. However, by 1978, they were renamed Bedok South Avenues 1–3, Bedok South Road, Bedok North Road, and Bedok North Avenue 3. As for Tampines

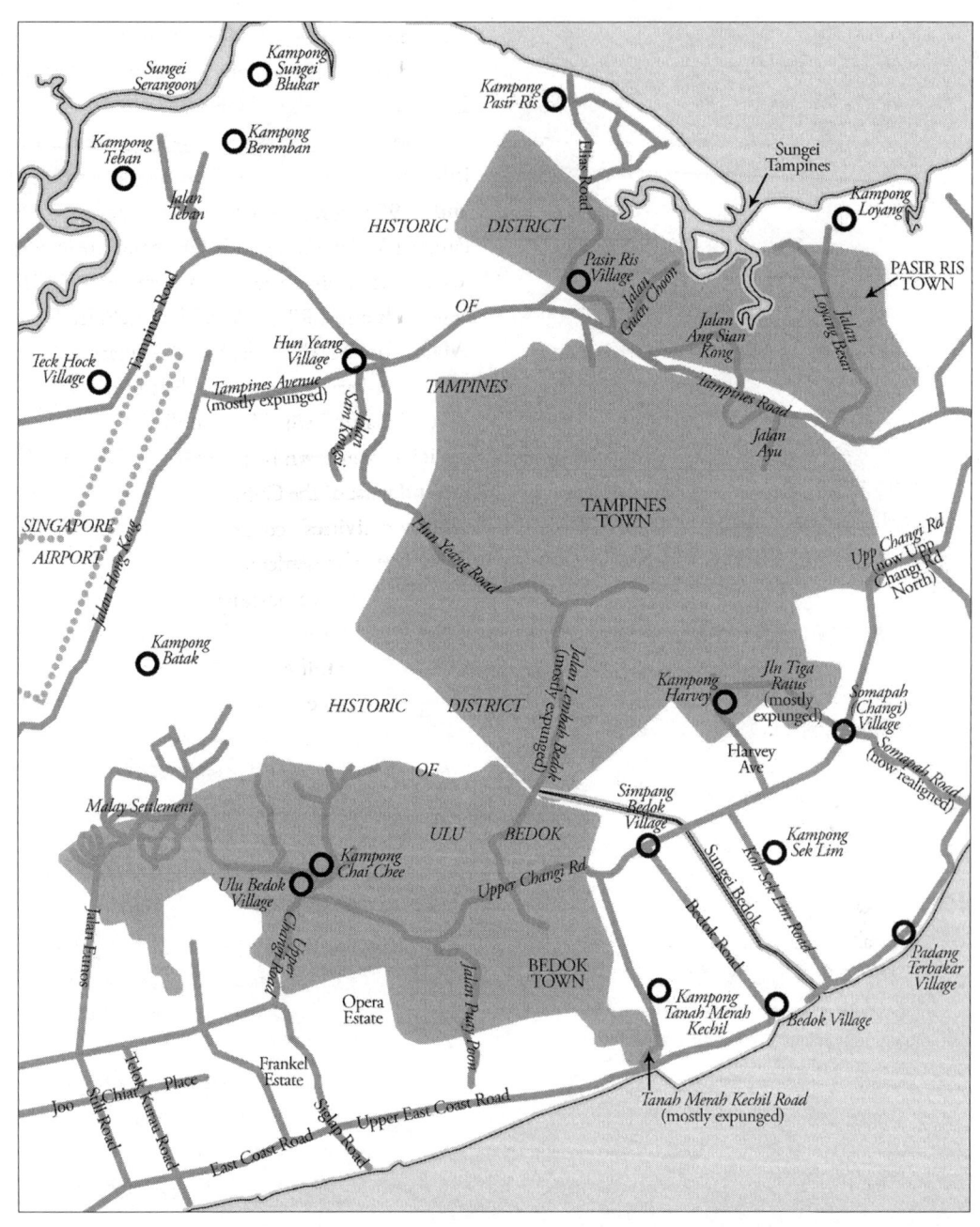

The east of Singapore Island. The roads and rivers are as they existed in 1966, with major villages and Singapore Airport (now part of Paya Lebar Air Base) marked out with black rings and light grey dots respectively. The historic districts of Tampines and Ulu Bedok are highlighted in capital letters. Place names in italics highlight expunged villages and roads, or partially expunged, realigned, or renamed roads. The present-day towns of Pasir Ris, Tampines, and Bedok are shaded in light grey; the towns followed the demise of roads such as Hun Yeang Road and most of Tampines Road, and villages such as Pasir Ris and Ulu Bedok. (Source: Eisen Teo)

New Town, not all neighbourhoods began with "Tampines". One estate launched in 1986 at the expense of Jalan Tiga Ratus was named Simei, Mandarin for "Four Beauties"; its four main roads were named Xishi, Diaochan, Guifei, and Zhaojun roads, after the Four Great Beauties of ancient China—this was when Singapore was still gripped by the Speak Mandarin Campaign! However, after just one year, the HDB gave in to pressure that the Mandarin names were too hard to pronounce, and went for the tried and tested, renaming the roads Simei Streets 1–4.

Two relatively younger towns, Sengkang and Punggol, also moved away from the mathematical naming system. The former adopted the names of Rivervale, Compassvale, Anchorvale, and Fernvale for its streets. The first three are a nod to the region's legacy as a riverine fishing port; the last pays tribute to its densely-wooded past. Meanwhile, Punggol took on the fancy prefixes of Edgefield, Edgedale, Waterway, and Northshore for some of its roads. But these names were conjured up during the construction of the towns, with no roots in the locality.

The LRT systems for Sengkang and Punggol fare better in preserving the physical, social, and zoological history of the region. Out of 27 LRT stations in Sengkang and Punggol, seven took on old road or place names. For example, Cheng Lim LRT Station took its name from Lorong Cheng Lim, an expunged road off Punggol Road, while Soo Teck took its name from Soo Teck Chinese School. Meanwhile, five stations were named after local plants and animals, such as Rumbia, a type of sago palm; Bakau, Malay for "Mangrove"; and Ranggung, the water bird that gave Serangoon its name. Finally, four stations were named after notable people or human activities of yesteryear. For example, Layar is Malay for "Sail (of a Ship)", a reference to the area's shipping past; Sumang was derived from Wak Sumang, a Malay warrior who had founded Punggol Village.

The town that best carried over its history into the present is Bukit Panjang. In the 1980s and 1990s, rural roads and tracks east of Bukit Panjang Village were gradually expunged for the town, but their place names were retained for new roads and LRT stations. They included Segar (Malay for "Fresh"), Jelapang ("Granary"), Fajar ("Dawn"), Pending (a type of belt buckle), Senja ("Dusk"), and Petir ("Thunder"). Unfortunately, Bukit Panjang town is the exception, not the rule.

And what of the Chinese and Indian "signposts of daily activities" covered in Chapter 2? With urban renewal, resettlement of entire communities, and an aggressive national bilingual education policy, such toponymic heterogeneity in and around the Central Area has largely vanished. Only a handful of place names have survived: Pek Kio, Tekka Centre, Lau Pa Sat, and the most popular name, Niu Che Shui ("Bullock Cart Water") as the Mandarin name for Chinatown.

CLAIMING LAND FROM THE SEA—AGAIN

"SINGAPORE IS land-scarce"—a common refrain, but the reality is more complex. Modern Singapore's urban development over the first 130 years of its existence was concentrated in the southeast of the island, closely hugging the sea. Other than urban renewal, land reclamation was another option for the Central Area to (literally) expand. As other parts of the island became new nodes of urban development, reclamation was also employed to create more space for their respective needs. Reclamation was favoured because the seas off the south, southwest, and southeast coasts of the island were shallow. In

1960, Singapore's total land area—of the main and offshore islands—was 581.5 square km; by 2017 this had grown to 721.5 square km—an expansion of 24 per cent over 57 years! No account of urban development in Singapore is complete without covering reclamation and its various impacts, such as the loss of roads, villages, and natural landscapes.

Since the Central Area had historically grown up in the southeast of Singapore Island, naturally, the first big reclamation project in the 1960s took place in the southeast. This was the East Coast Reclamation Project, dwarfing all reclamation projects that had come before. Launched by the HDB in 1965, the year of Singapore's independence from Malaysia, it lasted 20 years over seven phases, and saw the reclamation of more than 1,500 hectares of land from the Telok Ayer Basin to Tanah Merah Besar. Previously, the largest reclamation project—the Kallang Aerodrome—covered no more than 137 hectares.

Phases 1 and 2 of the project advanced the coastline from Tanjong Rhu to Bedok at a cost of $44 million. The hills of Bedok and Tanah Merah were flattened for the fill; the flattened land later became part of Bedok New Town. Phase 3 covered the sea off Nicoll Highway, from the Esplanade to the mouth of the Kallang River. Phase 4, starting in 1970, the largest at 529 hectares, filled the sea off Bedok to Tanah Merah Besar. The cut site for Phases 3 and 4 created what is now Bedok Reservoir. Phase 5 completed the triangle of reclaimed land off Nicoll Highway, later known as Marina Centre, and created a strip of land east of the Telok Ayer Basin. Phase 6 created Marina East, while Phase 7 completed Marina South, filling up what was once the Inner Roads and surrounding the South Pier of the Telok Ayer Basin with land; finished by 1985, the 360 hectares of Phases 6 and 7 were the priciest of the project at $385 million. Their cut site were the hills and quarries of Tampines; the flattened land became part of Tampines New Town.

This was the creation of new land on an industrial scale, a symbol of the bold ambitions and dreams of the newly-independent republic. Modern, industrial machinery was used for all cut sites, a far cry from the cangkuls and shovels employed for Commercial Square in 1822. For Phases 6 and 7, two 420-ton excavators moved 79,000 tons of earth every day onto conveyor belts stretching 7 km from Tampines to the sea. The earth was then loaded onto barges which sailed 12 km to the fill sites at Marina East and South.

The intangible costs of the project were hefty. The natural beaches along the island's southeast coast vanished, including the coastline that had attracted Manuel Godinho de Eredia to map it in 1604. A thousand families living at the cut sites and along the coast were resettled. Most small roads and lanes south of the East Coast–Upper East Coast trunk road survived, but the trunk road was no longer a coastal road. Marine Parade Road, first named in 1931, no longer fronted the sea either; the famous Sea View Hotel lost its sea view. The shoreline receded from historic Bedok Village, which was eventually expunged.

With loss comes creation. 16 km of artificial beaches were created in East Coast Park, a new recreational zone; the reclaimed land was also used for a new expressway, the East Coast Parkway. A housing estate was completed in 1976 with 8,015 housing units for 40,000 residents; it was named Marine Parade after the road, which was extended to three times its original length to connect the estate to Bedok New Town. Now, East Coast Parkway and a service road parallel to the expressway, East Coast Park Service Road, hugged the new coastline.

Even as the East Coast Reclamation Project was in full swing, in 1975, Prime Minister Lee confirmed that Changi would become the site of Singapore's main civilian airport, replacing Paya Lebar, just 20 years old. There were cogent reasons for its relocation—Changi was less populated than Paya Lebar, so expanding the airport would displace fewer people; new flight paths could cross over the sea, reducing noise pollution. The new Changi Airport with two runways would cost $1.3 billion; eight times the size of Paya Lebar Airport, most of it would be built on reclaimed land.

Over just 37 months from 1976, 745 hectares of land were reclaimed off Changi and Tanah Merah Besar, costing $239.1 million. Most of Changi Air Base (formerly RAF Changi), and Singapore's last airport crossing at 13½th Milestone Upper Changi Road, made way for the new airport.

The airport opened in 1981, transforming the east coast of Singapore Island. Most of Changi's natural beaches, known to the locals as Pantai Chantek (Malay for "Beautiful Beach"), were sacrificed with its popular government bungalows. Kampong Ayer Gemuroh ("Roaring Water"), and part of historic Tanah Merah Besar Road and its coastal cliffs, also had to go. The coastal roads of Siak Kuan Road and Windsor Drive (both expunged later) no longer ran by the sea; now, it was a new Changi Coast Road. The historic Changi trunk road no longer ran to Changi Village—part of the northern end of Upper Changi Road was sliced off at the 12½th Milestone; the sliced-off end was eventually renamed Changi Village Road. Changi, once known for its prison, trunk road, village, and beaches, was now known for its international airport.

In the southwest of the island, reclamation started in 1974 for new port facilities called the Pasir Panjang Wharves. With urban renewal, most shipping in the Singapore River and Kallang Basin were resettled to Pasir Panjang in the 1980s. As a result, Pasir Panjang Road and West Coast Road no longer faced the sea; the famed coastal drive, with the sea on one side and rolling hills on the other, was no more. Sharing the reclaimed land with the wharves, West Coast Park became the lesser cousin of East Coast Park, while an arterial road was built to connect Jurong Industrial Estate to the wharves—West Coast Highway. In 2006, the highway was extended to twice its length over part of Pasir Panjang Road by means of a 5-km elevated viaduct, Singapore's longest viaduct, to allow faster travel from Jurong to the Central Area. It has become the equivalent of East Coast Parkway in the east, connecting the west end of the island to the Central Area.

Meanwhile, in the far west of the island, reclamation off the historic Tuas Village and Sungei Tuas commenced from 1975, headed by the Jurong Town Corporation. It aimed to develop Tuas for industries and shipping, due to its proximity to Jurong Industrial Estate and its wide coastline. The hills south of Upper Jurong Road were levelled for their earth; the flattened land later became part of Jurong West New Town. By the end of the decade, the mouth of Sungei Tuas had made way for the Northern Tuas Basin, part of the waters of the new Tuas Shipyard; Tuas Village's 10,000 residents were gradually resettled.

Tuas Village was formerly the fishing centre of the west of Singapore Island, famous for its fishermen, rich fishing grounds, seafood restaurants—and *wayang*. It had one main street—Upper Jurong Road—running to a jetty; the road was surrounded by wooden shophouses occupied by tailors, clockmakers, and merchants. Every morning, up to 200 boats came in loaded with fresh fish. This unique community all but disappeared by the early 1980s; Tuas became synonymous with chemical and engineering industries, and brick and cement works. Much of Upper Jurong Road, once one of Singapore's most remote roads, had to be widened and levelled due to a sharp rise in traffic.

Unlike the smooth coastline of Changi, Tuas had a rugged shoreline marked by numerous capes and river mouths; these were all wiped off the map as the coastline was straightened. Lost place names included Tanjong Karang (Malay for "Coral") and Teritip ("Barnacle"), and Sungei Blukang, Blukang Kechil, Laboh Gandom, Merawang, Buntu, and Piatu. Only Tuas and Gul have survived as the names of roads.

The second stage of reclamation off Tuas began in 1983 and was completed by 1988. The $2-billion project reclaimed 600 hectares over three phases and created a piece of land shaped like a hockey stick—hence it was nicknamed the Tuas Hockey Stick.

The government reserved the boldest of dreams for the reclaimed land nearest to the Central Area—Marina Centre, South, and East, a "clean canvas" 690 hectares in area for planners to craft "a new downtown". Marina Centre was developed first. Between 1983 and 1985, its road system was laid down to connect it to the grid road system of the Central Area. As the young republic approached 20 years of independence from Malaysia, the roads were given "Singaporean" names—Raffles Avenue and Boulevard, Temasek Avenue and Boulevard, and Merlion (later Republic) Avenue and Boulevard. Three sprawling commercial complexes mushroomed—Marina Square in the 1980s, and Suntec City and Millenia Walk in the 1990s. Once facing the sea, Beach Road and Nicoll Highway now faced the skyscrapers of a new shopping and tourism quarter.

Development in Marina South and Marina East proceeded slower. The URA first set aside most of Marina South as a temporary "playground"; buildings and land use there were guaranteed a lifespan of just 20 years. Marina South City Park, a 30-hectare "green jewel", opened in 1989; it joined two bowling alleys, steamboat joints, and Marina Bay Golf and Country Club in providing recreation not far from the Central Area. As land use was not intense, the only roads built in Marina South were to connect these recreational spots and Marina Bay MRT Station to the Central Area.

The final reclamation of the rest of the Telok Ayer Basin and its North Pier—38 hectares—began in 1990 as a natural extension of Raffles Place and Shenton Way. After 180 years, the Inner Roads—the destination of ships the world over, mentioned by travel writers—were no more.

Between 1960 and 1992, 59.5 square km of land was reclaimed at a cost of $3.15 billion. Other than the aforementioned projects, new land was also created in the northeast, off Seletar, Punggol, and Pasir Ris. Pulau Punggol Barat and Pulau Punggol Timor emerged from the sea, while Coney Island (Pulau Serangoon) was greatly enlarged. From 1992 to 2016, another 78.7 square km of land was reclaimed, mostly in Tuas South, Jurong Island, and Changi East.

The Tuas Hockey Stick has lost its shape, ballooning to twice its size—and it is still growing today. Its southern end will host Tuas Terminal, a mega port to be developed in four phases over 30 years from 2016. The grand plan is to move all of Singapore's port activities to Tuas South by 2027, freeing up land in Tanjong Pagar and Pasir Panjang for redevelopment. From the Singapore River in 1819, New Harbour in the 1850s, to Pasir Panjang in the 1980s, Tuas South will be the final stage of evolution of the modern port of Singapore.

Today, 5.5-km Tuas South Boulevard has the twin honour of being Singapore Island's westernmost and southernmost channel of movement.

East of Changi Airport and Changi Coast Road, Changi East has materialised, a parcel of land twice as large as the land reclaimed for the airport in the 1970s. The airport's Terminal 5 is currently being built there for 2030; in 2017, Changi Coast Road, just 36 years old, was closed to be expunged for the project. Tanah Merah Coast Road, 11 km long, now runs along much of the coastline of Changi East and is Singapore Island's easternmost road—even though it is far from de Eredia's red cliffs.

The growth of Tuas South and Changi East has turned Tuas and Changi into two of Singapore Island's largest regions. In 1966, just one road had the place name "Tuas"; in 2016, 87 roads started with "Tuas". Only its remoteness and industrial identity have hindered its prominence in the social consciousness of Singaporeans. Instead, it is Changi which is known the world over, because of its world-class airport.

As for Marina South, urban renewal has already

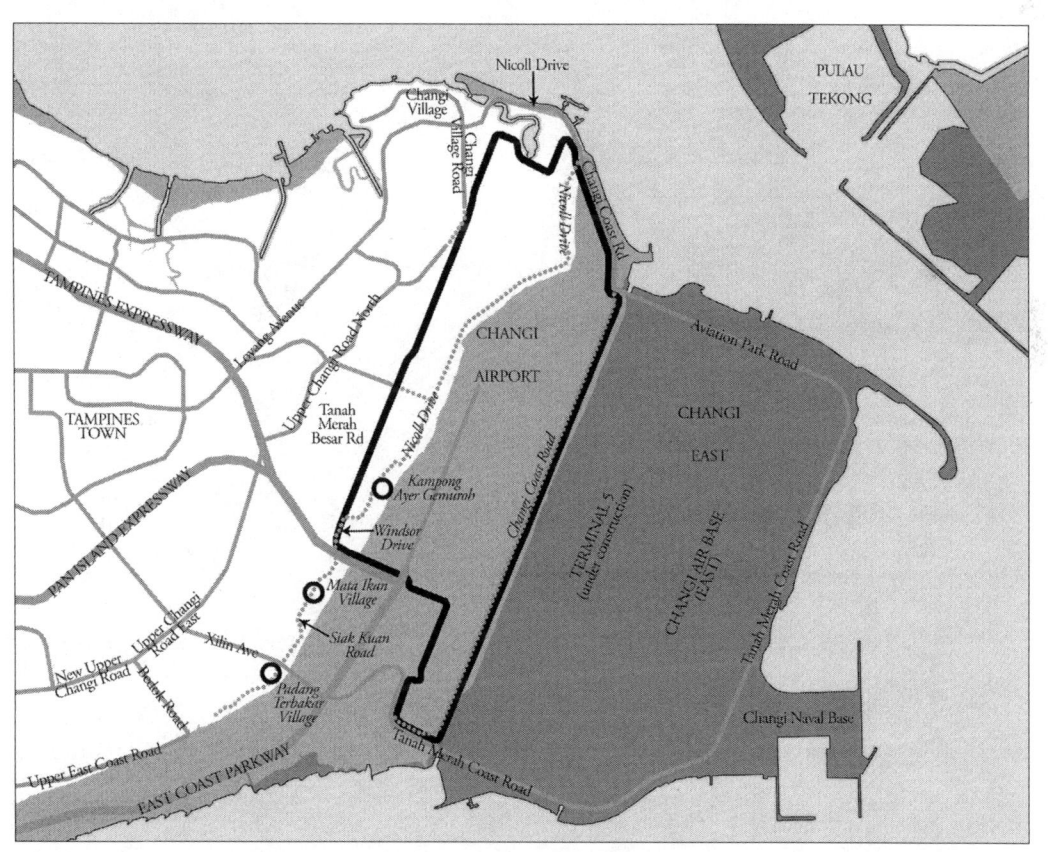

The east of Singapore Island. Most of Changi's natural beaches, and historic landmarks such as Kampong Ayer Gemuroh and Siak Kuan Road, have disappeared; place names in italics and roads in dotted lines no longer exist. The land in white is what existed in 1923; light grey land was reclaimed between 1923 and 1993, enabling the construction of Changi Airport and East Coast Parkway; dark grey land was reclaimed between 1993 and 2019, leading to the expungement of Changi Coast Road, while enabling the construction of Changi Naval Base, Changi Airport Terminal 5, and Changi Air Base. Light grey solid lines are the present-day road and expressway system, with Tanah Merah Coast Road as Singapore Island's easternmost road. (Source: Eisen Teo)

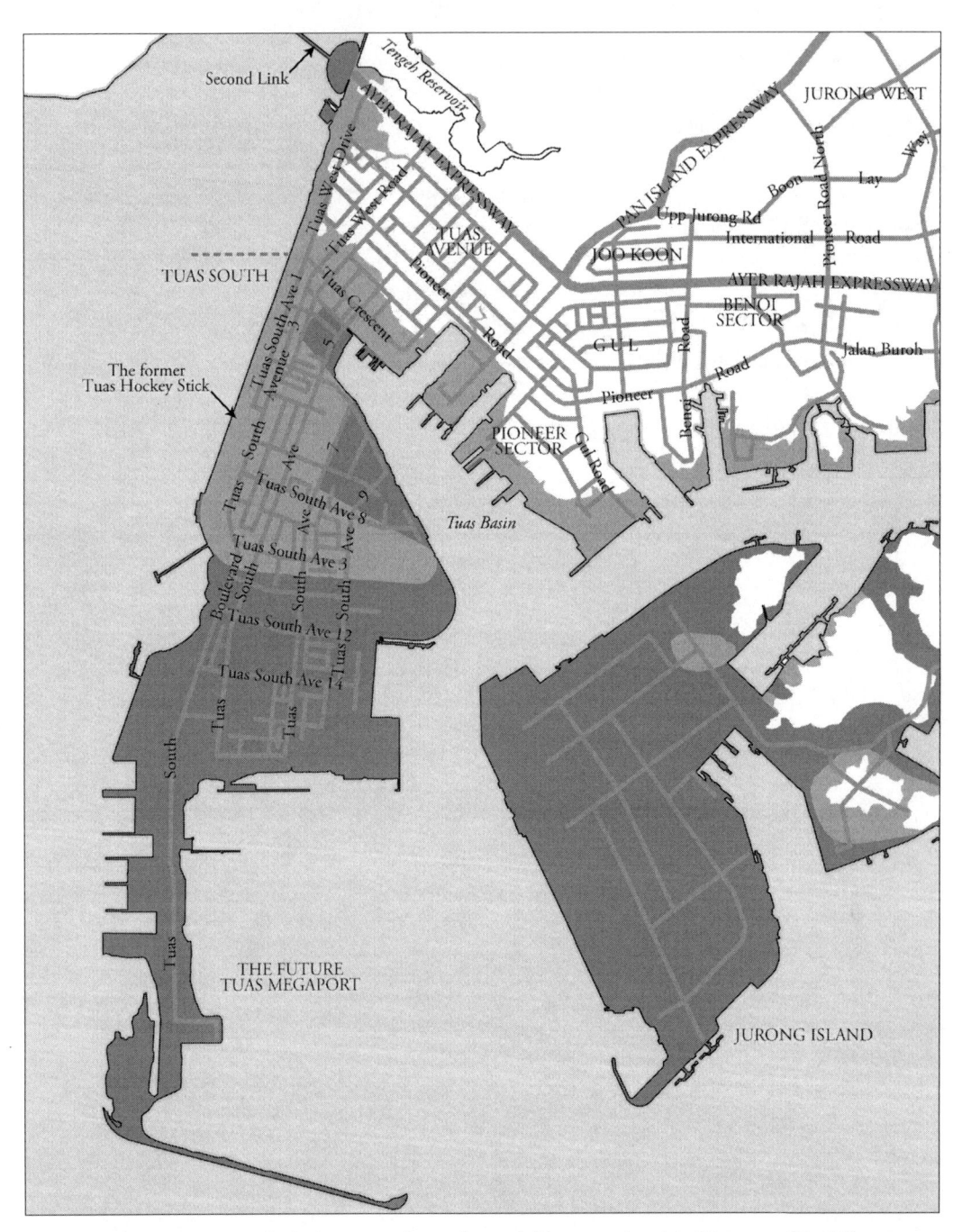

The southwest of Singapore Island. The area, once known for its rich fishing grounds and the fishing port of Tuas Village, is now replete with industries and shipping facilities. The land in white is what existed in 1923; light grey land was reclaimed between 1923 and 1988, creating Tuas Basin and the Tuas Hockey Stick; dark grey land was reclaimed between 1988 and 2019, creating Jurong Island, Tuas South, and the foundations of the future Tuas Megaport. Light grey lines are the present-day road and expressway system, with Tuas South Boulevard as Singapore Island's westernmost and southernmost road. Neighbourhoods include Tuas South, Tuas Avenue, Pioneer Sector, Gul, Joo Koon, and Benoi Sector. (Source: Eisen Teo)

kicked in just 30 years into its existence. The time has run out for its "temporary playground"; the new "downtown" envisioned in the 1980s is finally materialising, with complexes such as the Marina Bay Financial Centre and Marina One coming up as an extension of Raffles Place and Shenton Way. As a result, the grid road system of the former Telok Ayer Reclamation Ground has spread east into Marina South, wiping out landmarks from the 1990s. Marina City Park, and the once-popular steamboat joints and bowling alleys of Marina Mall, made way for a billion-dollar artificial garden, Gardens By The Bay, served by Marina Gardens Drive. Roads such as Marina Street, Place, and Way were expunged; part of Marina Station Road was renamed Straits Boulevard. Parts of Marina Mall and Grove have survived as deserted, dusty roads mostly used by trucks building the new downtown, but their days are numbered.

Just as some of modern Singapore's earliest roads were given generic English names such as High Street, Hill Street, and Middle Road, the Marina Downtown's new roads have been given similar names such as Marina View, Straits View, Central Boulevard, and Park Street. Almost 200 years after Commercial Square was created at the mouth of the Singapore River, Commerce Street was laid down to the south. Only one road bears the name of a prominent Singaporean—Sheares Avenue, after Benjamin Henry Sheares (1907–1981), Singapore's second Yang Di-Pertuan Negara. Time will tell if the government decides to name more roads in the Marina Downtown after personalities—like the British did for Raffles, Farquhar, and Crawfurd.

In the 1990s, Marina South was popular for its bowling alleys and cheap steamboat joints along the road named Marina Mall. When I took this photo in 2008, the road was devoid of traffic, and the tenants had already moved out. These buildings and stretch of road no longer exist—Gardens by the Bay now stands in their place. (Source: Eisen Teo)

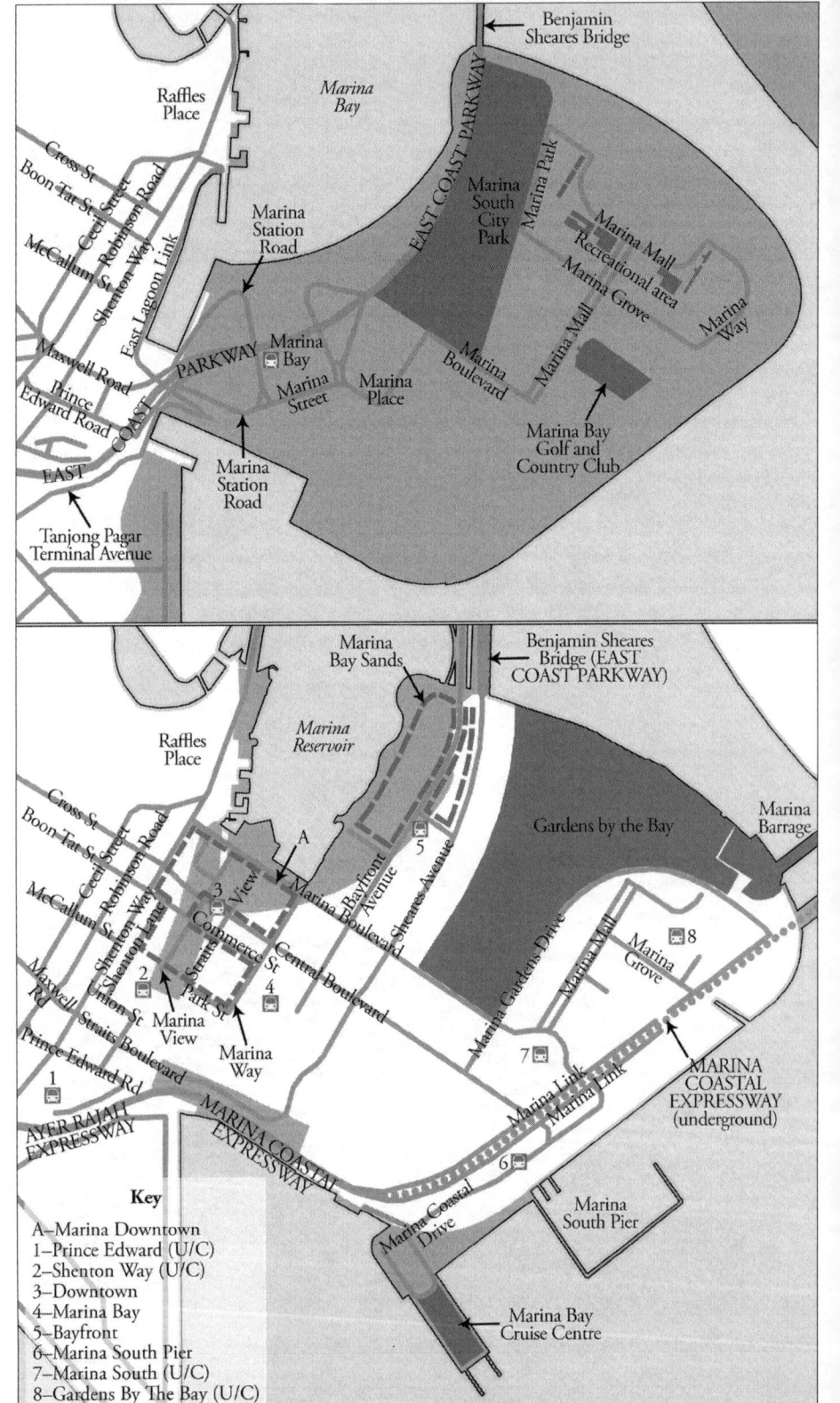

Marina South in 1993. The land in white is what existed in 1975; light grey land was reclaimed between 1975 and 1993, enabling the construction of Marina South City Park and the recreational area along Marina Mall. Light grey solid lines are the road and expressway system in 1993. There was just one MRT station in Marina South at the time—Marina Bay.

Marina South in 2019. The land in white is what existed in 1993; light grey land was reclaimed between 1993 and 2019, enabling the construction of the Marina Downtown and Marina Bay Sands (both in dashed lines). Light grey solid lines are the road and expressway system in 2019; dots indicate the underground section of Marina Coastal Expressway. The urban landscape of Marina South has changed beyond recognition since 1993. (Source: Eisen Teo)

Key
A–Marina Downtown
1–Prince Edward (U/C)
2–Shenton Way (U/C)
3–Downtown
4–Marina Bay
5–Bayfront
6–Marina South Pier
7–Marina South (U/C)
8–Gardens By The Bay (U/C)

CHAPTER NOTES

1. In 1928, *The Straits Times* reported a proposal to construct a railway branch line "in the dim and distant future". The line would start at the junction of Bukit Timah Road and Whitley Road, run parallel to Balestier Road, cover Lavender Street, and cross the Kallang River to Geylang and Katong. However, the idea never saw the light of day.

2. Marshall resigned in 1956; his Minister for Labour and Welfare Lim Yew Hock became Singapore's second Chief Minister. When he picked his ministers, Abdul Hamid and Thomas switched ministerial portfolios.

3. While Chong Pang Village was at 13½ Milestone Sembawang Road, there was another Chong Pang Village near the 12th Milestone, opposite RAF Sembawang. This village was named by the Rural Board in 1938 also in honour of Lim Chong Pang. After 1958, much of the original Chong Pang Village made way for a veterinary station. Today, the area is still an agricultural enclave around Bah Soon Pah Road.

4. The "Pah" in Bah Soon Pah Road referred to a type of banana.

5. The place name "Minto Road" was resurrected between 1981 and 1984, as a lane off Jalan Sultan; "Java Road" was resurrected between 1993 and 1995 as a lane between Beach Road and Nicoll Highway.

6. Hong Wen School was relocated to Towner Road in 2009. As of 2018, its former premises along Victoria Street were used by the Elections Department as a training centre.

7. Selegie Integrated School (later Selegie Primary School) was merged with Stamford Primary School in 1987 and shifted out of its campus. As of 2018, the campus was used as a student hostel.

8. Midlink Plaza, just over 30 years old, was torn down in 2014 for a 15-storey hotel, the Mercure Singapore Bugis, which opened in 2016.

9. As of 2018, Raffles Institution was in Bishan.

10. Capitol Shopping Centre (later the Design Centre, then Capitol Centre) was torn down in 2013 for part of an integrated complex which includes Capitol Piazza and Eden Residences Capitol.

11. Funan Centre (later Funan The IT Mall, then Funan DigitaLife Mall) was torn down in 2016 for a new Funan mall, to be opened in 2019.

12. Tung Centre was renamed 20 Collyer Quay in 2013.

13. As of 2018, Caltex House was known as Chevron House, and Hitachi Tower was known as 16 Collyer Quay.

14. As of 2018, the tallest building in Singapore was Tanjong Pagar Centre at 290 metres.

15. Beng Hoon Road and Calcutta Road have been expunged. Hare Street made way for Chin Swee Estate. In the early 1970s, Covent Garden, Row, Alley, and Street made way for 88–92 Covent Garden Estate—themselves demolished in 2014.

16. The place name "Zhenghua" has survived elsewhere, though. It is the name of primary and secondary schools, a park, a community club, a flyover, and a ward in Holland-Bukit Timah Group Representation Constituency.

17. A stretch of the northern part of Punggol Road was closed in 2018 for the Punggol Digital District Plan. The closed portion will be converted into a pedestrian walkway and a 1.3-km heritage trail.

18. In September 1962, a *Straits Times* letter writer by the name of "L.E.L." called for Jurong Industrial Estate to be named Peng Kang instead. The Economic Development Board wrote back to give its justifications for using the place name Jurong, promising that the "name of Peng Kang will not be forgotten". Of course, it was forgotten.

19. Peng Kang lives on in the name of a hill in Pasir Laba Camp famous to many National Servicemen. It will lend its name to Peng Kang Hill MRT Station of the Jurong Region Line, which will be completed by 2028.

CHAPTER 7
1950 to 2011: Mergers and Laws

7 NOVEMBER 1987—the dawn of a new era in Singapore's history of movement. That morning, the Republic's $5-billion Mass Rapid Transit (MRT) electric railway system, the most expensive and ambitious infrastructure project in its history, was launched by the man who pushed for it more than anyone else—Second Deputy Prime Minister Ong Teng Cheong (1936–2002). Five MRT stations over 5.9 km—Yio Chu Kang, Ang Mo Kio, Bishan, Braddell, and Toa Payoh—opened, the start of a three-year roll-out that would involve 42 stations over 67 km of track. For Ong, it was the culmination of 20 years' of conceptualising, debating, planning, and finally, building. He said: "The baby is born—we have a bouncing one. This is only the beginning. To say that I am happy would be an understatement. This is fantastic. I am very thrilled."

Singaporeans took to the MRT from the word go. On the first day, 120,000 people from all over the island turned up for their maiden rides in air-conditioned comfort. Some appeared at the stations as early as 7am, three hours before the first train, forming queues that snaked out of Toa Payoh MRT Station. There was a party mood on the trains—excited chatter, photos snapped, children pressing their noses to window panes. Many took multiple trips from one end of the line to the other. Salesman K. Sarvaswaram, 29, was with his wife and son: "This is the sixth time we're going up to Yio Chu Kang. We're going to do this until we're satisfied!"

As more stations opened, uptake soared. Within two months, 1.1 million trips were made a week; this grew to 1.6 million trips after a year, and 2.1 million trips by 1989—up to one in 10 Singaporeans took the MRT fewer than two years into its existence. The MRT had become the new pride of Singapore.

The MRT scored with commuters because it ran on its own channels of movement. Like the railway train, it had dedicated tracks, freeing a traveller from congested roads and chaotic traffic. But unlike the railway train, the MRT was far more accessible—the locations of the first 42 stations were determined such that half the population and offices were within 1 km of a station.

Meanwhile, from the 1960s, motor vehicles also received new channels of movement designed for swifter, higher-volume traffic flow—an expressway system which replaced the hundred-year-old trunk road system. Like the MRT, the intention was for expressways to free travellers from congested roads, transforming the urban landscape in the process.

But what set apart this age of movement from previous epochs were mergers and laws, ushering in an unprecedented level of government involvement in movement. Successive mergers created transport companies of unprecedented size. ComfortDelGro and SMRT Corporation are multi-modal transport giants, simultaneously managing bus, taxi, and MRT services; their staff strengths run into the thousands, their annual

In December 1987, when I was three years old, my parents took me on my maiden MRT ride. My mother held me up for a photo on the platform of Yio Chu Kang MRT Station—the tennis courts in the background were still around in 2019—while my father posed with me inside a train carriage, vintage advertisements on the tunnel walls behind us. (Sources: Eisen Teo)

revenues worth hundreds of millions of dollars, and they move millions of people every day.

As for laws, they formed a framework upon which traffic management was attempted at a level hitherto unseen. Entities such as the Traffic Police and the Land Transport Authority (LTA) combined forces to separate pedestrians from motor traffic, free up road space for motor traffic, manipulate patterns of movement, and punish travellers for breaking laws. Complex schemes such as the Certificate of Entitlement (COE) and Electronic Road Pricing (ERP) did not just restrict the growth of the motor vehicle population, they also taxed motorists for using channels of movement.

All these have made private transport in Singapore smoother, but more expensive than ever before; public transport has become world-class, but power lies in the hands of only a few entities. Together, they move a population approaching six million people. Overall, movement has become a well-oiled, highly-complex machine; but when the machine stutters or breaks down, the potential for chaos is greater than ever before.

FROM TRUNK ROADS TO EXPRESSWAYS

SINCE THE 1920s, the number one method of movement in Singapore has been the motor car, except for a brief dethronement during the Japanese occupation. After WWII, the car population in Singapore grew exponentially, aided by several factors. One was population growth, from 1.1 million in 1953 to more than 5.6 million as of 2017. Another was the rapid spread of affluence as Singapore's economy boomed, and the persistence of the car as a status symbol for many Singaporeans. A third factor was the government's longstanding policy in accommodating the car as a premier method of movement. They may have come up with creative forms of traffic management to reduce car population growth rates, but it was growth nonetheless. Only in recent years has there been official talk of a "car-lite" Singapore, but achieving this remains a mammoth task. The phenomenal growth in the car population over 60 years has had tremendous impact on the island's channels, patterns, and experiences of movement.

The 1955 Master Plan logged about 50,000 motor vehicles in 1953, of which 31,451 were cars. In just 20 years, in 1975, there were 280,378 motor vehicles, including 143,155 cars. These figures hit an all-time high in 2013—974,170 motor vehicles—a growth of almost 20 times in just 60 years—and 607,292 cars. This meant that in 1955, one in 30 persons owned a car; in 1975, one in 16 owned a car; by 2013, one in nine had a car. Only after 2013 did car numbers dip, to 575,353 cars in 2015.

It is obvious that if Singapore Island's road system had remained as they were in the 1950s, with its urban area concentrated in the southern third of the island, the traffic situation would have become more abysmal than Jakarta's or Bangkok's. The fact that this has not happened was due to a slew of radical government measures over 60 years. One, as we have seen, was urban renewal and resettlement, thereby spreading out the concentration of people and cars. Another was simply building more roads and expressways to accommodate more motor vehicles. A third was curbing the growth of the car population by progressively making it costlier to own a car. A fourth was traffic management on a scale never practised before. A fifth was far stricter control over methods of movement—on one hand fostering and overseeing improvements in public transport and striving to make it world-class, hence persuading car owners to give up their cars;

on the other hand, consigning slower methods of movement to history. These measures were borne out of necessity, and they have shaped movement in Singapore into what we are familiar with today.

With urban renewal and resettlement, new housing estates and towns outside the Central Area meant that networks of roads had to be built to transport people and goods. In 1965, with three new towns established, there were 2,646 roads in Singapore; in 2015, this had increased by two-thirds to 4,396 roads. In 1968, there were 1,607 km of roads, which more than doubled to 3,496 km in 2014. These roads are also wider—two and three-lane dual carriageways are now the norm.

The historic trunk road system, established from the 1830s and subsequently supplemented by rural roads branching off trunk roads, was no longer suitable for movement around the island. Gradually, from the 1960s, it was dismantled by urban renewal. Much of Tampines Road was expunged for Pasir Ris New Town, part of Choa Chu Kang Road for Choa Chu Kang New Town, and much of the Jurong–Upper Jurong trunk road for new towns, industries, and an expressway. What is left includes Old Tampines Road, Old Choa Chu Kang Road, and Old Jurong Road. And 2.5-km Jurong Road is much like what it was in the 1960s: a narrow, two-lane road without pavements for long stretches.

Other branches of the trunk road system have been realigned. For the Thomson–Sembawang trunk road, dangerous curves north and south of the Yio Chu Kang Road junction were straightened in the 1950s; the original curves remain, and the 4.3-km time capsule is now Old Upper Thomson Road. As for Yio Chu Kang Road, three parts were straightened between 1963 and 1981. The original road around the 8th Milestone is known as Gerald Drive today; a stretch near the 10th Milestone was renamed Ang Mo Kio Street 66; part of the original road around the 12th Milestone was renamed Old Yio Chu Kang Road.[1]

Most major rural roads supplementing the trunk road system have been largely lost to development. Admiralty Road West–Admiralty Road East and Jalan Bahar are significant exceptions, only because they exist on the peripheries of the island.

Mostly lost to history too are numbered dirt tracks branching off trunk roads. The practice of naming tracks after numbers—for example, Yio Chu Kang Road Track 14—began around the 1950s; curiously, some trunk roads, such as Bukit Timah–Woodlands, escaped this practice. By 1969, there were more than 240 numbered tracks; Jurong Road had 51 of them, the Changi–Upper Changi trunk road had 39, and Yio Chu Kang had 35. By 2016, this had dwindled down to 12, mostly in undeveloped, forested areas; of these, just four were accessible to the public: Choa Chu Kang Road Tracks 14 and 33, Mandai Road Track 7, and Upper Changi Road North Track 39.

The 140-year-old practice of using milestones as geographical points of reference—recording tiger attacks, registering addresses, calculating rickshaw fares—died out in the 1970s, as Singapore transitioned from the imperial system to the metric system. The transition started in 1972 and was completed by 1974. A solitary milestone survived the cull—the 3rd Milestone of Geylang Road between Lorongs 6 and 8, hidden among the roots of a tree—but sadly, was removed by the LTA in 2014 for road works. Today, the milestone has been largely forgotten as a symbol of movement, except in several isolated place names: Junction 10 (shopping mall) and Ten Mile Junction (LRT station) after 10th Mile Upper Bukit Timah Road; Golden Mile Tower and Golden Mile Complex after the Golden Mile of Beach Road.[2]

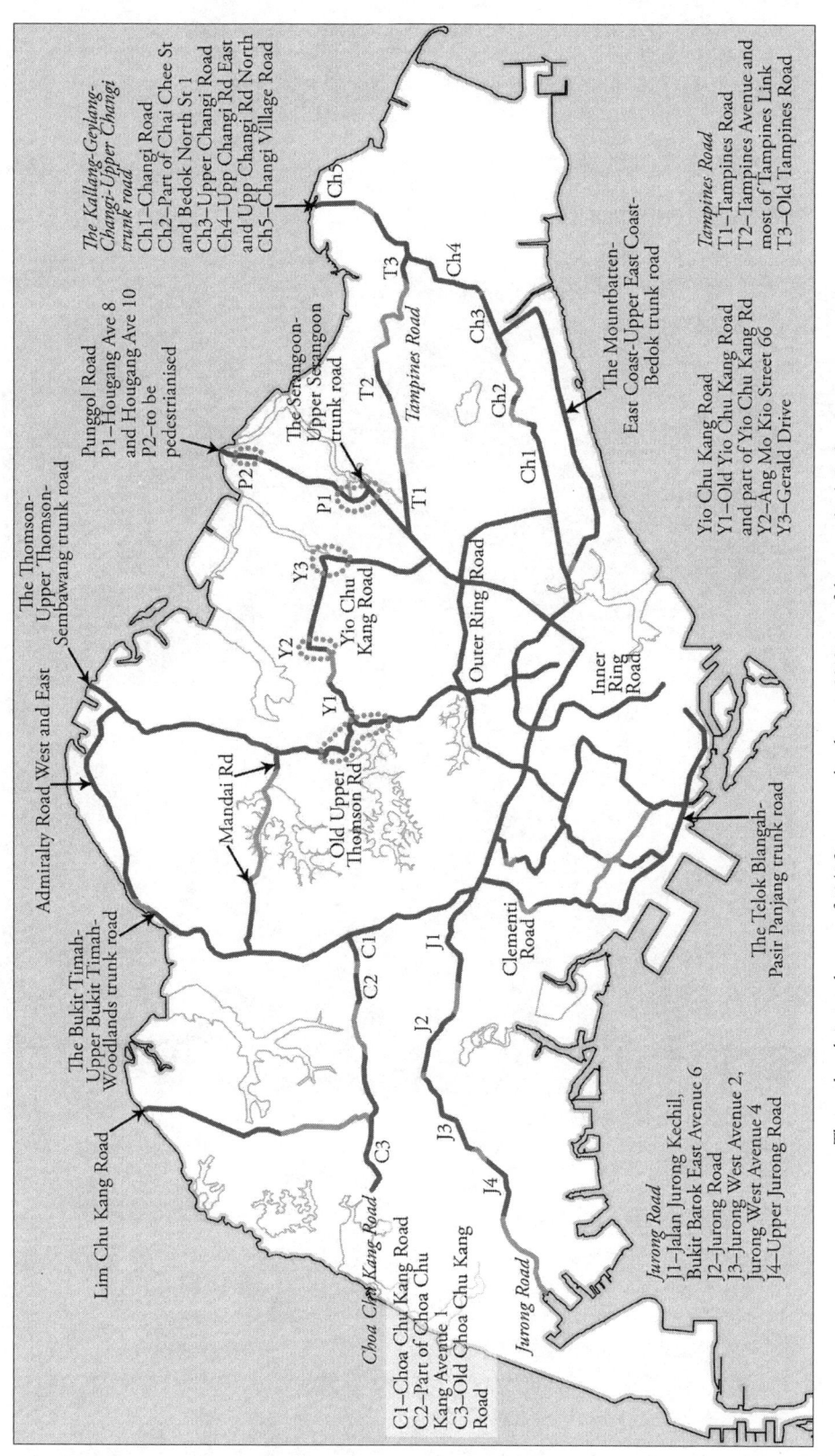

The trunk and ring road system of 1941 Singapore, placed onto a 2019 map of the same island. Dark grey portions still exist today, even though many have been renamed—examples include Old Choa Chu Kang Road, Ang Mo Kio Street 66, and Upper Changi Road North; they are either labelled ("Y2", "P1", etc.) or circled with dots. Light grey portions have been expunged. Names in italics highlight trunk roads which have been broken up for towns and expressways. (Source: Eisen Teo)

The Kallang-Geylang-Changi-Upper Changi trunk road
Ch1–Changi Road
Ch2–Part of Chai Chee St and Bedok North St 1
Ch3–Upper Changi Road
Ch4–Upp Changi Rd East and Upp Changi Rd North
Ch5–Changi Village Road

Punggol Road
P1–Hougang Ave 8 and Hougang Ave 10
P2–to be pedestrianised

Tampines Road
T1–Tampines Road
T2–Tampines Avenue and most of Tampines Link
T3–Old Tampines Road

Yio Chu Kang Road
Y1–Old Yio Chu Kang Road and part of Yio Chu Kang Rd
Y2–Ang Mo Kio Street 66
Y3–Gerald Drive

Choa Chu Kang Road
C1–Choa Chu Kang Road
C2–Part of Choa Chu Kang Avenue 1
C3–Old Choa Chu Kang Road

Jurong Road
J1–Jalan Jurong Kechil, Bukit Batok East Avenue 6
J2–Jurong Road
J3–Jurong West Avenue 2, Jurong West Avenue 4
J4–Upper Jurong Road

The Thomson-Upper Thomson-Sembawang trunk road

The Bukit Timah-Upper Bukit Timah-Woodlands trunk road

Admiralty Road West and East

Lim Chu Kang Road

Mandai Rd

Old Upper Thomson Rd

The Serangoon-Upper Serangoon trunk road

The Mountbatten-East Coast-Upper East Coast-Bedok trunk road

Outer Ring Road

Inner Ring Road

Clementi Road

The Telok Blangah-Pasir Panjang trunk road

252 **Jalan Singapura**: 700 Years of Movement in Singapore

Hundreds of numbered dirt tracks used to branch off trunk roads, but almost all of them have disappeared. Punggol Road Track 24 off Punggol Road was expunged in 2016, not long after this photo was taken. (Source: Eisen Teo)

NEW, LARGER channels of movement were needed for the swift movement of high-volume motor traffic around the island. The 1971 Concept Plan suggested expressways, which gradually supplanted the trunk road system. For better or for worse, the expressway network has had a significant impact on Singapore's geographical and toponymic landscape.

The Pan Island Expressway (PIE) is Singapore's oldest and longest expressway, but was constructed in phases to serve different needs at different times. The first phase was built in the 1960s to serve Toa Payoh New Town as an alternative to the congested Outer Ring Road. From 1966, Kolam Ayer Lane off Woodsville Circus was upgraded to become Jalan Kolam Ayer; Paya Lebar Way was constructed between Jalan Kolam Ayer and Paya Lebar Road. By 1972, Jalan Toa Payoh, Jalan Kolam Ayer, Paya Lebar Way, and part of Whitley Road were incorporated into the PIE. The PIE had no traffic lights—this would become a feature of expressways—and to avoid a traffic intersection at Thomson Road, Singapore's first expressway flyover, the Thomson Flyover, was built for $3.2 million. The expressway permanently impacted the landscape, cutting the Kallang River watershed in half, separating historic Toa Payoh from Balestier. Kim Keat Avenue and Temple Estate were separated from Kim Keat Road at the Kim Keat Flyover; thereafter, they were absorbed into Toa Payoh New Town.

Work on the PIE's second phase started in 1969 and was completed in 1975. It ran west from Whitley Road over Adam Road, meeting Jalan Anak Bukit (Malay for "Child of Hill") near Upper Bukit Timah Road. It was now possible to travel between Paya Lebar and Jurong bypassing busy Bukit Timah Road and the Central Area altogether.

Singapore's second expressway was the East Coast Parkway (ECP), built in four phases between 1971 and 1981 almost entirely on freshly reclaimed land. It ran from Keppel Road through Marina South, crossed over the sea to Marina Centre via the Benjamin Sheares Bridge, crossed over the sea again to Tanjong Rhu, ran past Marine Parade and on to Changi Airport, which also opened in 1981. The 19-km expressway bypassed the congested Kallang–New Upper Changi trunk road to connect the Central Area and Changi Airport. Three years after opening, traffic volume in Nicoll Highway dropped by 20 per cent, while that of Robinson Road and Cecil Street dropped by 40 per cent.

The third phase of the PIE, opened in 1981, ran past Jalan Eunos and Ulu Bedok and joined the ECP at the Changi Flyover. This gave travellers from Changi Airport another fast route to Jurong, and connected young Bedok New Town to the Central Area. However, Jalan Eunos was sliced in half at the Eunos Flyover, spelling the start of the end of the Malay Settlement. The last phase of the PIE also opened in the same year, running from Jalan Anak Bukit west across Jurong to Jalan Bahar. This connected the future Jurong East and Jurong West New Towns, and Jurong Industrial Estate, to the east of the island. In return, historic Jurong Road was separated from Upper Jurong Road at the junction with Jalan Bahar. The final length of the PIE: 35 km.

Part of Phase 1 of Singapore's third expressway opened in 1983. It was originally planned as Sembawang Expressway, even though the proposed route lay nowhere near Sembawang; eventually it opened as the Central Expressway (CTE), named because it ran through the off-centre part of the island. Part 1 of Phase 1 ran from Ang Mo Kio Avenue 1 to the PIE at the

Whampoa Flyover. It permanently separated Toa Payoh New Town from Potong Pasir. Part 2 of Phase 1 was completed in 1985, running from the Whampoa Flyover southwest to Thomson Road. This connected Ang Mo Kio, Bishan, and Toa Payoh New Towns to the Central Area, allowing the Thomson–Upper Thomson trunk road to be bypassed. As the expressway crossed historic Balestier Road, Jalan Kebun Limau was absorbed into the channel of movement. Nearby, the expressway separated Norfolk Estate from the rest of Pek Kio; part of Norfolk Road was expunged for the Moulmein Flyover. Eventually, Norfolk Estate's 17 low-rise Singapore Improvement Trust blocks were levelled, its 2,000 residents resettled; today, the area remains an open field in the shadow of the mighty CTE.

Thereafter, the pace of construction of expressways quickened; four expressways opened in the next six years. In 1986, 11-km Bukit Timah Expressway (BKE) opened, named because it ran past Bukit Timah Hill. It starts at the Woodlands Checkpoint and ends at the PIE at the Chantek Flyover, named as such because Kampong Chantek Bahru (Malay for "New Beautiful Village") was expunged for it. The expressway cut through the secondary forest of the Central Catchment Area, severing the Bukit Timah Nature Reserve, sparking criticism from environmentalists. Nevertheless, the BKE connected Johor Bahru, and Woodlands, Choa Chu Kang, and Bukit Panjang New Towns to the Central Area, bypassing the busy Woodlands–Upper Bukit Timah trunk road.

The following year, in 1987, Phase 1 of the Tampines Expressway (TPE) opened between the up-and-coming flats of Tampines and Pasir Ris new towns, running from the Upper Changi Flyover to Elias Road. It connected the towns to the Central Area through the PIE, relieving traffic pressure on the Serangoon–Upper Serangoon trunk road. However, the TPE caused the demise of Pasir Ris Village and a large part of historic Tampines Road. Phase 2 followed two years later, extending the TPE northwest to Tampines Road.

The expressway system spread to the southwest of the island in 1988, with the completion of Phases 1 and 2 of the Ayer Rajah Expressway (AYE), from the ECP and Keppel Road, past Bukit Merah and Clementi new towns, to Jurong Town Hall Road. The AYE was named as such because much of it was upgraded from the existing Ayer Rajah–Upper Ayer Rajah arterial road. As a result, Clementi New Town was sliced in half. The AYE provided a new route between Jurong and the Central Area. Instead of converting Keppel Road from an arterial road to an expressway, a 2-km $67-million Keppel Viaduct was built over it, creating Singapore's first two-tier channel of movement.

By 1989, the rest of Phase 1 of the CTE—from Yio Chu Kang Road to Ang Mo Kio Avenue 1, and from Thomson Road to Bukit Timah Road—opened. Now at 11.8 km, the expressway physically separated Ang Mo Kio New Town from Serangoon New Town.

1990 saw the opening of Phase 1 of Singapore's seventh expressway, the Seletar Expressway (SLE), from the CTE at the Boh Sua Tian Flyover to Upper Thomson Road, giving residents of Yishun and Woodlands New Towns access to the CTE and a faster journey to the Central Area. The SLE got its name from Lower Seletar Reservoir to the north, formerly the Sungei Seletar. Boh Sua Tian Flyover was named as such because the CTE extension from Yio Chu Kang Road to the SLE was constructed over Boh Sua Tian Road, a track off Yio Chu Kang Road; both the road and Boh Sua Tian Village, a farming community largely populated by Hokkiens with the surname Toh, were named after a nearby wireless station; "wireless" is "boh sua tian" in Hokkien. After the road and village were expunged for the expressway, the flyover was renamed Seletar Flyover, consigning the place name "Boh Sua Tian" to history.

Now the time came for different expressways to be connected to one another. In 1991, Phase 2 of the CTE extended it by 3.7 km to the AYE at the Radin Mas Flyover. To minimise urban destruction near the Central Area, two tunnels were bored—a first for an expressway in Singapore; the 1.7-km south tunnel travelled under Orchard Road, Fort Canning Hill, and the Singapore River, splitting Chin Swee Road down the middle. The tunnels were a challenging engineering endeavour, quadrupling the cost of Phase 2 to a hefty $313 million. Part of 70-year-old Clemenceau Avenue had to be expunged, splitting the road into Clemenceau Avenue and Clemenceau Avenue North. By the Singapore River, Pulau Saigon was joined to the mainland through land reclamation; Pulau Saigon Road was expunged, while century-old Pulau Saigon Bridge was demolished. After the Public Works Department (PWD) dismissed the steel bridge as not having "special architectural value to merit preservation", it was dismantled and sold as scrap for $22,000. The CTE's final length: 15.5 km.

In 1994, the 8.4-km Kranji Expressway (KJE) was completed, joining the BKE to the PIE. The western end of the PIE was also realigned and extended by almost 8 km to meet the KJE and then Jalan Ahmad Ibrahim at the Tuas Flyover, not far from the former Tuas Village. The KJE cut through forest, disused rubber plantations, farms, and dirt roads. It also sliced in half Choa Chu Kang New Town and historic Choa Chu Kang Road. But the latter had outlived its significance. The new KJE–PIE connection linked Bukit Panjang and Choa Chu Kang New Towns with Jurong West New Town, and industries in Jurong and Tuas with the Causeway. A former 2-km section of the PIE from Jurong Road to Jalan Bahar was downgraded to a main road and renamed Jurong West Avenue 2. Now, the western end of the PIE demarcates the northern boundaries of Jurong East and Jurong West New Towns. The PIE remains Singapore's longest expressway, at 42.8 km.

From 1996 to 1998, the final phases of the TPE, AYE, and SLE were completed; all were extended west. The TPE was lengthened from Tampines Road to meet the SLE and CTE at the Seletar Flyover—a final length of 14.4 km. The farms and plantations of Seletar West Farmway 10, Cheng Lim Farmway 1, and Punggol Farmway 1 had to make way for this extension, but this plugged up-and-coming Sengkang New Town and the future Punggol New Town into the expressway system. Meanwhile, the AYE was lengthened from Jurong Town Hall Road over the old Jalan Ahmad Ibrahim; now, a new version of the arterial road runs on either side of the AYE. The AYE ends at the Tuas Second Link, Singapore's second land link with Malaysia, opened in 1998 to relieve congestion at the Causeway. With the extension, the AYE now connects the Second Link and Tuas' industries to the Central Area and Changi Airport, and is Singapore's second-longest expressway at 26.5 km. Finally, the SLE was extended from Upper Thomson Road to the BKE at the Woodlands South Flyover. Part of its 12 km now forms the southern boundary of Woodlands town.

Historically, the eastern half of Singapore Island has experienced more urban development than the western half. The continuation of this pattern was evident in persistent congestion on both the CTE and the Serangoon–Upper Serangoon trunk road as the 21st century dawned. To ease pressure on them, the Kallang–Paya Lebar Expressway (KPE) was opened by 2008. It connects the TPE, PIE, and ECP—a parallel of the Serangoon–Upper Serangoon trunk road, giving residents of Punggol, Sengkang, and Hougang towns another route to the Central Area. However, a historic route between Tanjong Katong and the Central Area was severed. With Nicoll Highway and the ECP as alternatives, Mountbatten Road—almost a hundred years old—was cut in two for Sims Way, an entrance-exit road for the KPE. The rump off Geylang Road was renamed Geylang Drive, and subsequently expunged for Kallang Airport Drive and Way.

Unlike expressways before it, most of the KPE—nine out of 12 km—runs underground through built-up areas: under sewage pipes of the Kim Chuan Treatment Plant, a Paya Lebar Air Base taxiway, MRT lines and tunnels, the Pelton Canal (a tributary of the Kallang River), the Geylang River, Nicoll Highway, and the ECP. To accommodate construction of the KPE, subterranean power cables, water and gas pipes, communication lines, and parts of the Pelton Canal and the PIE had to be diverted. One of Singapore's biggest infrastructural projects in terms of technical complexity, its price tag was $1.74 billion, Singapore's most expensive expressway yet.

Yet the KPE held this title for just five years. In 2013, Singapore's 10th and newest expressway, the Marina Coastal Expressway (MCE), opened at a cost of $4.1 billion. At just 5 km—Singapore's shortest expressway—it cost more than $800 million per km. In comparison, all other expressways excluding the KPE—eight in all—cost "only" $1 billion. Sixty per cent of the MCE is underground; at its deepest, 20 metres under the seabed. It runs from where the KPE meets the ECP at Tanjong Rhu to under Marina East and South, meeting the AYE at the Keppel Viaduct. Since 1981, the ECP had split Marina South in two; now, the MCE allowed part of the ECP in Marina South to be downgraded to a main road called Sheares Avenue, freeing up Marina South to be developed as a whole.

AS SOLID rivers of concrete and asphalt, expressways have been both a boon and a bane to movement. Three to four lanes wide in both directions and unimpeded by traffic intersections, they allow for the movement of a large volume of traffic at higher speeds. The default speed limit on expressways in the 1970s was 70 km an hour, then 80 km in 1981, and is presently 90 km. But while the trunk roads of yesteryear allowed people to live along them and traverse them, hence fostering the growth of villages and communities, the expressways of the present are walls dividing neighbourhoods, towns, and regions. Save for overhead bridges and underpasses, expressways are impassable to pedestrians, and in 1981 it became illegal to cross them. As vehicles cannot stop in expressways, communities cannot thrive along them. Most flats near expressways have ended up in such close proximity because the channels of movement were laid down after the flats were built, engulfing their residents in a sea of noise and dust. Traffic on the CTE roars past the flats of Potong Pasir Avenue 1 and Whampoa Estate every day, while the PIE is a permanent fixture for residents of Kim Keat Avenue and MacPherson Estate.

For residents living along roads that were upgraded to expressways, such as Jalan Toa Payoh and the Ayer Rajah–Upper Ayer Rajah arterial

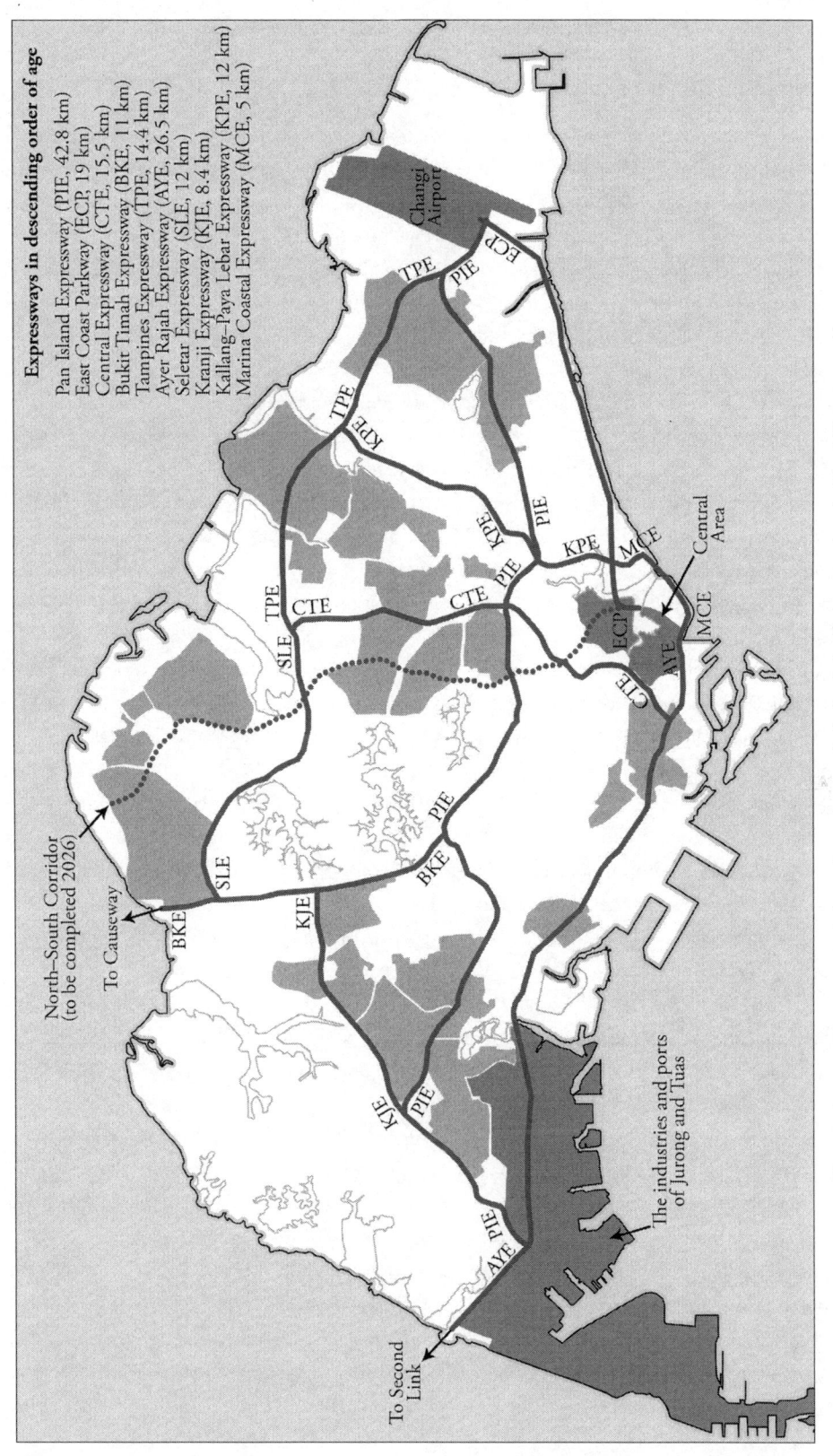

Expressways in descending order of age

Pan Island Expressway (PIE, 42.8 km)
East Coast Parkway (ECP, 19 km)
Central Expressway (CTE, 15.5 km)
Bukit Timah Expressway (BKE, 11 km)
Tampines Expressway (TPE, 14.4 km)
Ayer Rajah Expressway (AYE, 26.5 km)
Seletar Expressway (SLE, 12 km)
Kranji Expressway (KJE, 8.4 km)
Kallang–Paya Lebar Expressway (KPE, 12 km)
Marina Coastal Expressway (MCE, 5 km)

Singapore's expressway system—in dark grey lines—is presently the lynchpin of motor travel on the island. They connect the island's new towns—shaded light grey, including the four new housing estates / towns of Tengah, Canberra, Bidadari, and Tampines North—to the Central Area, Changi Airport, and the industries and ports of Jurong and Tuas. (Source: Eisen Teo) road, the changes in movement could not have been greater, immediately blocking access to the other side. People had to make lengthy detours to get to places a stone's throw away. One region that suffered was Pek Kio; according to residents, the CTE "divided the community": "Old neighbours no longer visit each other as often, hawkers and shopkeepers have lost many of their favourite customers, and a visit to the outpatient clinic a short walk away now means having to catch a bus or taxi." Fortunately, the present trend is for expressways to be built underground, minimising impact on the urban environment.

Singapore's expressway system—10 expressways with a combined length of 166.6 km—is presently the lynchpin of motor travel on the island. Supplementing this concrete web are old trunk roads that survived urban renewal with modifications, the Inner and Outer Ring Roads, and a new breed of inter-town arterial super-roads that arose from connecting multiple roads across towns.

What began as Thomson Road in the 1840s now runs 18.9 km from Kampong Java Road to Canberra Road, connecting the Central Area and five towns. The old Kallang–Changi trunk road still starts at Kallang Road, but ends at the sea off Loyang Way, 17.1 km in all. The old Serangoon Road now ends at Punggol East in Punggol town after 13.7 km. The old Bukit Timah–Kranji trunk road now ends at Woodlands MRT Station after 23.2 km—the longest of the former trunk roads.

The 12-km Inner Ring Road is mostly unchanged since 1932, save for a small stretch of Whitley Road which has been upgraded into the PIE. The Outer Ring Road is now a 32.4-km closed ring incorporating the original stretch from Paya Lebar Road to Farrer Road, and relatively newer roads such as West Coast Highway, Esplanade Drive, and Nicoll Highway.

Some of the longest inter-town super-roads include one running 18.2 km through five towns from Woodlands Avenue 7 in Woodlands to Marymount Road in Bishan; another running 22 km through five towns from Upper Jurong Road in Jurong West to Jalan Bukit Merah; and a third running 27.9 km from Pioneer Road to Keppel Road, connecting the industries of Tuas and Keppel Harbour.

Presently, Singapore's combined expressway and road network is the most comprehensive in its history, connecting most of the Republic's residents to each other. What literally hinders such connectivity and movement on a daily basis is the sheer volume of motor vehicles. It was in the areas of managing vehicle populations and traffic that Singapore has taken the path less travelled.

THE ROADS ARE FOR MOTORISTS— TO PAY

EVEN THOUGH the Trimmer Committee of 1938 had achieved a breakthrough in terms of analysing Singapore's traffic situation, and identifying problems and solutions, a lot remained on paper. At the beginning of the 1950s, Singapore's roads were chaotic, with unprecedented numbers of accidents, deaths, and injuries. Again, big government intervened. From the 1950s, the Traffic Police and the PWD, and the LTA from the 1990s, cooperated in six areas: the separation of pedestrians and motor traffic, permanently ceding control of the roads to the latter; freeing up and growing road space; tighter control and management of patterns of movement; making motorists pay for the use of roads; quotas on motor vehicle ownership; the imposition of laws and a complex system of punishments as deterrence. As a result, Singapore's roads are nowhere as gridlocked as that of other Southeast Asian cities,

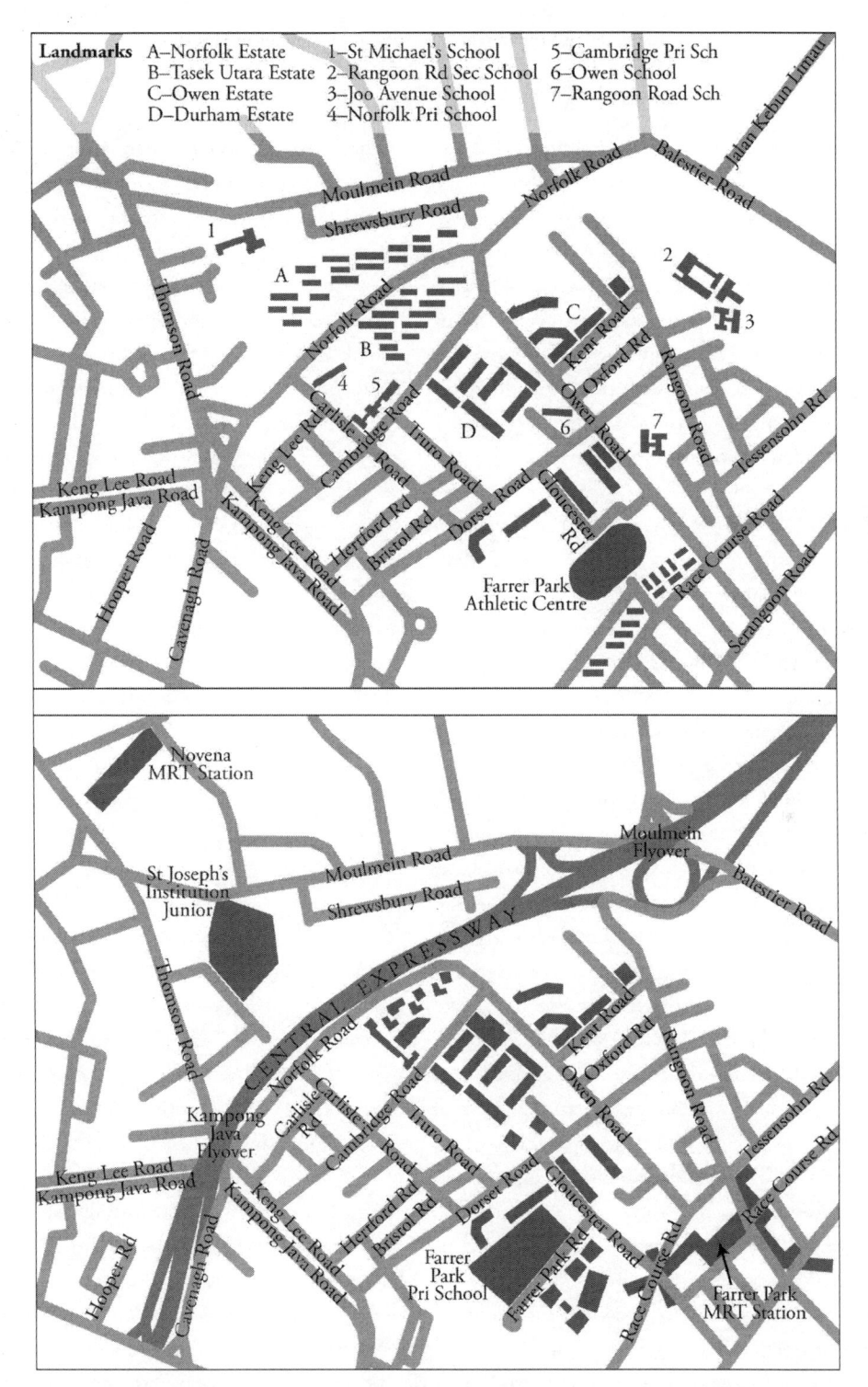

Top: Pek Kio in 1984, just before construction of the Central Expressway started in the area. It had Singapore Improvement Trust (SIT) estates such as Norfolk and Tasek Utara, and at least seven schools such as St Michael's School and Norfolk Primary School.
Bottom: Pek Kio in 2019. The Central Expressway now cuts across the historic area, separating Shrewsbury Road from what is left of Norfolk Road. The SIT estates and schools of 1984 are gone. (Source: Eisen Teo)

and Singapore's rates of accidents, deaths, and injuries have declined even as its population and volume of motor traffic have grown.

Separating pedestrians and motor traffic was imperative, for while the motor car was king of the roads, jaywalking was still second nature to pedestrians. The Trimmer Committee had suggested pedestrian crossings at traffic junctions, and pavements to keep pedestrians off the roads, but concrete action to implement them was not taken until the 1950s.

In 1949, the zebra crossing—an invention designed to allow pedestrians to traverse roads lawfully and safely—debuted in England. In 1952, three zebra crossings were introduced at Collyer Quay, one of the busiest roads on the island. Traffic police had to be stationed there to ensure pedestrians had right of way. By 1954, pedestrian crossings at traffic junctions were installed at six locations across City Hall, Orchard Road, Collyer Quay, and New Bridge Road; they were pedestrian-operated, push-button crossings. By 1966, there were 40 zebra crossings. However, pedestrians and motorists frequently battled over their usage. The former claimed motorists ignored them at crossings, nearly running them over; the latter claimed pedestrians took their time to cross. It seemed that motorists prevailed again, for in the 1960s, overhead bridges—structures raised 32 steps above roads, which removed the need for motorists to halt for pedestrians—began replacing zebra crossings.

Singapore's first overhead bridge opened in April 1964—again, over Collyer Quay, after calls for one for 15 years. It opened to great fanfare—banners, flags, VIPs, a TV crew, the works. The choice of location was apt because by 1974, 10,000 pedestrians used the steel bridge every day to avoid 112,000 motor vehicles on the road. (As for Singapore's first pedestrian underpass, it opened under Connaught Drive in February 1964 at a cost of $85,000.) The island's second overhead bridge, costing $20,000, was over Upper Serangoon Road next to the Lim Tua Tow Market at the 5½ Milestone. Overhead bridges then were so rare, a Member of Parliament (Sia Kah Hui, for Upper Serangoon) graced its opening ceremony! By 1970, the number of overhead bridges had grown to 25, and by 1973, there were 52. Yet only five per cent of pedestrians used them. A *New Nation* columnist wrote in 1974: "Every evening just after office hours, you find huge crowds streaming onto the roads against the traffic lights. Their reasoning is that there's safety in numbers, and you won't dare run into all of them." At the time, nearly half the people who died in road accidents every year were pedestrians. More had to be done to separate them from motorists.

The authorities began installing more pedestrian crossings at traffic junctions, which pedestrians accepted more readily than overhead bridges; it was in the early 1970s that the familiar green man-red man signals debuted. Several concessions were handed to pedestrians: in 1976, they were given right of way over motorists turning left and right at signalised traffic junctions, first introduced at the busy junction of North Bridge Road and High Street. In 1977, zebra crossings were introduced across slip roads; the first was at the junction of Marine Parade Road and Joo Chiat Road. And in 1980, zigzag markings were introduced 50 metres before zebra crossings; no overtaking was allowed for motor vehicles within these markings.

It was also in the 1970s that pavement construction picked up considerably, almost four decades after the Trimmer Committee. As urban renewal transformed the Central Area, the PWD took the chance to replace five-foot-ways choked with vendors and merchandise with open pavements. It set up a Walkway Unit in 1977 dedicated to constructing walkways in the Central Area; in four years, the Unit built 76 stretches of pavement along 50 roads, including Stamford Road, North Bridge Road, South Bridge Road, and Beach Road. New roads in new towns around the island also came with pavements.

Jaywalking was finally outlawed on 1 July 1977 under the Pedestrian Crossing Rules of the Road Traffic Act. Pedestrians caught crossing a road within 50 metres of a designated crossing could be fined up to $50. Even then, pedestrians took their time relinquishing their claim over the roads. During a two-month grace period over July and August, 96,801 pedestrians were issued warning tickets instead of fines—an average of more than 1,600 a day. Today, pedestrian crossings are ubiquitous at traffic junctions, and as of 2018, there were 552 overhead bridges and underpasses across the island—10 times the number in 1973. The Republic's first two overhead bridges are no longer around, but the oldest still dates back to 1967, near the junction of Serangoon Road and St Michael's Road.

WHILE NEW expressways and roads were being constructed all over Singapore, existing roads were widened—a municipal practice dating back to the 1850s. However, from the 1950s, road widening significantly grew in scope, costs, and its adverse impact on the immediate environment and its residents. Single carriageways were converted into dual carriageways with centre dividers or islands; budgets ballooned into millions of dollars; entire communities had to be relocated.

Road widening happened everywhere. Stretches of Yio Chu Kang Road were widened in 1957, 1965, 1976, and 1984, gradually converting the road into a dual carriageway with a centre divider and towering trees. Upper East Coast Road was widened in 1964 from 6.7 metres to 12 metres. Upper Paya Lebar Road's width was more than doubled in 1969. 1976 saw Clementi Road transform from a two-lane single carriageway to a three-lane dual carriageway with pavements for $6.6 million, while $9 million was spent on the creation of a two-lane dual carriageway for Sembawang Road.

A boon for motorists, a bane for local communities. When Sungei Road was widened in 1980, 65-year-old Tekka Market was demolished. The community of 544 stalls, many ran by families for up to 50 years, was uprooted. When it was Still Road's turn in 1985 to be widened from two lanes to six lanes, pre-war houses, shops, terrace houses, and 59-year-old Telok Kurau School were demolished. Across the island, countless house owners had to relinquish driveways and gardens for noise, dust, even occasional flooding caused by raised roads. To add insult to injury, they were given tough options: give up their land without compensation, or claim compensation but at rates frozen at 1973 market levels—and pay road-building charges. Many quietly opted for the former because choosing the latter might have required them to pay the government for losing their land! Such land acquisition laws allowed the authorities to carry out road widening swiftly and efficiently, but left a bitter taste in the mouths of those affected.

But it was not enough to just widen roads. Removing obstacles to the flow of traffic was crucial too. One such obstacle was motor vehicles themselves—parked at the sides of roads. Before WWII, motorists enjoyed unrestricted free roadside parking even in the Central Area, a problem identified by the Trimmer Committee. This paradise for motorists disappeared after the war; by 1964, roadside parking in the Central Area cost 40 cents an hour. But the long-term solution was to move roadside parking to multi-storey car parks. In 1964, Singapore's first multi-storey car park, Market Street Car Park, was completed over an existing ground-level car park at the junction of Market Street and Cross Street, with a price tag of $2.5 million and a capacity of 900 cars and 130 motorcycles. No less than National Development Minister Lim Kim San turned up at the opening ceremony. The car park charged 50 cents an hour; monthly season tickets cost $30. Parking charges would only climb thereon.

From 1977, roadside parking began to be phased out. Roadside lots were gradually removed, while more and more roads were painted with double yellow lines, indicating that parking was disallowed. To replace them, the Urban Redevelopment Authority (URA) began building multi-storey car parks in and around the Central Area. One of the largest was Golden Shoe Car Park, a 10-storey, 1,000-lot car park a short distance away from Market Street Car Park; it was completed in 1984. The URA also required all private developers to provide car parks—usually multi-storey ones—in new buildings.

It was also in 1977 that multi-storey car parks became a must for HDB estates in the Central Area, and from 1985, new towns. At the time, the cost of building multi-storey car parks was far more expensive than surface lots—$25,000 to $30,000 versus $2,000. But for the sake of conserving land, the costlier path had to be taken.

Today, roadside parking in the Central Area and along arterial roads is unheard of, and almost all major commercial buildings in the Central Area come with their own car parks. Parking there during office hours hits the wallet hard: One Raffles Place and Republic Plaza, for example, charge $3 every 30 minutes from 7am to 5pm! Accordingly, the need for standalone multi-storey car parks has diminished. We have seen what has happened to Golden Shoe Car Park; 47-year-old Market Street Car Park was torn down in 2011 for a 40-storey skyscraper called CapitaGreen.

SMOOTHENING THE flow of motor traffic on channels of movement is a science that the authorities have studied, analysed, and experimented with for decades. Converting two-way roads into one-way streets—another Trimmer Committee suggestion—had succeeded in the Central Area in the late 1940s, so the authorities continued this from the 1950s. In 1953, Singapore's largest one-way scheme thus far came into operation—a loop covering Sumbawa Road, North Bridge Road, South Bridge Road, Upper Cross Street, New Bridge Road, Hill Street, and Victoria Street, spanning Kampong Glam to Chinatown. Up to 150 policemen had to be dispatched to tackle what the press called "Operation Headache". But even that ailment was eventually cured. In 1963, Bukit Timah Road and Dunearn Road were both made one-way, the former carrying traffic away from the Central Area, the latter Central Area-bound. In 1969, part of Serangoon Road, Selegie Road, Bencoolen Street, and Jalan Besar become one-way; south of the Singapore River, Telok Ayer Street, Robinson Road, Shenton Way, and parts of Cecil Street and Anson Road followed suit.

Occasionally, when a road became one-way, a new road had to be laid down to take traffic in the other direction. In this manner, Orchard Road became one-way and Central Area-bound in 1974;

a small lane off Grange Road, Woodstock Drive, was expunged for five-lane Orchard Boulevard, carrying traffic away from the Central Area. Today, most major roads in the Central Area are one-way. Notable exceptions are most of Beach Road, Victoria Street and Hill Street (reverted between 1991 and 1995), and part of Collyer Quay.

While one-way streets became the norm in the Central Area, roundabouts disappeared from the City. The Trimmer Committee had suggested building roundabouts; the authorities took up this suggestion just before the war, and for another 20 years after the war ended. By the 1960s, there were 40-odd registered traffic circuses around the island, mostly at major traffic junctions. They included Orchard Circus at the junction of Orchard Road, Clemenceau Avenue, and Edinburgh Road; and Tanglin Circus at the junction of Tanglin Road, Grange Road, Napier Road, and Middlesex Road. In 1957, Bukit Panjang Circus opened by Bukit Panjang Village at the historic 10th Mile Bukit Timah Road.

The decline of roundabouts began just after Singapore's independence from Malaysia in 1965. On approaching a roundabout, drivers automatically slow down to watch out for traffic; hence, roundabouts handle traffic well only up to a critical mass, and the PWD calculated that to be 3,000 vehicles an hour. Beyond that, traffic jams could arise. As Singapore's vehicle population climbed, more and more roundabouts were converted into traffic light junctions with left-slip roads and right-turn storage lanes, in a bid to raise the flow of traffic by 10–30 per cent.

Orchard Circus was converted in 1967; Tanglin Circus disappeared by 1977; Farrer Circus—at the junction of Farrer Road, Holland Road, and Queensway—by 1978. Tanglin Circus and Farrer Circus were beautiful landmarks, green circuses with fountains, adorned with colourful lights giving a carnival air at night, but they made way for asphalt. Bukit Panjang Circus was converted by 1980, and in 1987, even Newton Circus—Singapore's oldest and largest roundabout—received two sets of traffic lights, to be switched on during peak periods. From 40-odd registered circuses in the 1960s, there were 23 in 1976, eight in 2008, and just six as of 2018. They are Pioneer Circus (built 1972), at the junction of Pioneer Road and Jalan Ahmad Ibrahim; Nepal Circus (built by 1966), off Portsdown Road, named after Nepal Park; Central Circus (built between 1945 and 1953), inside the Singapore General Hospital compound; Newton Circus; Serangoon Gardens Circus (built 1952), inside Serangoon Gardens Estate; Piccadilly Circus (built 1930s), at the junction of Piccadilly, Edgware Road, and Jalan Kayu.[3] At current volumes of traffic, it is highly unlikely the circus will make a comeback.

Two more road features introduced before WWII to regulate the flow of traffic were traffic lights and guiding lines. In 1949, double white lines appeared on roads, usually narrow ones or with dangerous bends, to prohibit overtaking. Throughout the 1950s, automatic traffic lights—many ordered from Britain—began appearing at junctions, sometimes replacing policemen.

In 1969, the single yellow line was introduced by the sides of roads to prohibit parking, at first on Bendemeer Road. Two years later, in 1971, yellow boxes were introduced at four traffic junctions in the Central Area to reduce congestion: motorists were not allowed to enter a yellow box junction if they could not leave it before it was the turn of cross traffic to enter it. The junctions were at the intersections of Stamford Road with North Bridge Road and Hill Street, and where Bras Basah Road met North Bridge Road and Victoria Street. In three years, there were 21 yellow box junctions in the Central Area, including one at the junction of High Street and North Bridge Road. Also, in 1972, the symbolism of single yellow lines along sides of roads changed; now, a single yellow line meant parking was allowed at certain times of the day, while double yellow lines were introduced to prohibit parking altogether. In 1974, lane markings were introduced en-masse. Today, they are ubiquitous in Singapore, double yellow lines are a must for arterial and Central Area roads, and yellow boxes are present at all major intersections.

No man is an island; the same applies to traffic lights. Singapore's first coordinated system of traffic lights was introduced along Orchard Road in 1938, but the timings of the changing of lights were pre-set. As decades passed, advances in technology boosted the sophistication of traffic lights. In 1981, a computerised traffic light system was introduced for the Central Area. Two central computers in the Ministry of National Development (MND) headquarters at Maxwell Road controlled 151 traffic lights through telephone cables. Instead of one plan of pre-set timings, each junction now had six plans for different times of the day, based on historical traffic count data; each plan was updated every two years. The aim was to maximise the number of "green waves"—an uninterrupted series of green lights—across the Central Area.

A traffic light system that responded to real-time movements was finally implemented in 1988. Under the Green Link Determining System, or GLIDE, wire sensors were installed beneath road surfaces to detect traffic volume; for junctions with higher volume, the computerised system kept the lights green for longer, and vice versa. This system covered pedestrian crossings too. Previously, the green man appeared even if there were no pedestrians; now, traffic light poles were installed with push buttons, and the green man appeared only if the button was pushed.

DESPITE MEASURES to smooth the flow of motor traffic, congestion of arterial roads in and out of the Central Area persisted due to the sheer number of vehicles. The problem intensified from the 1960s as car ownership skyrocketed, with traffic jams a daily occurrence on key roads such Nicoll Highway, Serangoon Road, Bukit Timah Road, and Orchard Road. In March 1975, one out of every four vehicles in Singapore entered or passed through the Central Area during the peak period of 7.30am to 9.30am!

The newly-appointed Road Transport Action Committee came up with radical ideas to solve this problem, even suggesting closing the Central Area to cars. They eventually decided to make motorists pay for the use of congested roads. For the first time in Singapore's history, the authorities intervened not in controlling the numbers of vehicles, but in the decisions of vehicle users as to when and where to use their vehicles. This was the principle of the Area Licensing Scheme (ALS), the world's first intra-city cordon road-pricing system, which sought to discourage motorists from using cars to commute to and from work.

An imaginary cordon called the Restricted Zone (RZ) was set up in the Central Area, covering 610 hectares. Overhead gantries came up on 28 roads leading into the RZ. During the hours of restriction—7.30am to 9.30am every day except Sundays and public holidays—certain categories of vehicles such as private cars had to purchase and display an area licence on their windscreens to enter the RZ (emergency vehicles such as police cars, fire engines, and ambulances were exempted).

The licences were available as dailies (for $3, granting a motorist the right to enter the RZ as many times as he wanted for one day only) or monthlies ($60) at post offices and roadside booths. The authorities strongly encouraged alternatives: Park and Ride, which was the parking of cars at the Central Area fringe and taking a City Shuttle Service into the RZ;[4] forming a carpool of four to enter the RZ for free; or taking the bus. A small army of auxiliary policemen was deployed at gantries to spot with the naked eye errant motorists driving in without an area licence and a carpool of four. These motorists were not stopped, but their licence plate numbers were taken down; they were served fines within two weeks.

On the morning of 1 June 1975, motorists woke up to a new reality. The ubiquitous peak hour jams vanished. Traffic on usually congested roads inside the RZ, such as North Bridge Road, New Bridge Road, and Shenton Way, was light; at times, buses had the roads to themselves. From 23 June, taxis were ordered to pay for area licences too, angering them into a boycott of the RZ during the restricted hours. On 1 August, the restricted hours were extended to 10.15am. From 1976 to 1980, the ALS charge for private cars rose to $4, then $5; the fee for taxis was reduced to $2. In 1986, as Marina Centre was developed, the RZ absorbed it, growing to 33 gantries over 720 hectares.

The ALS was declared a success. Almost immediately, motorists got used to the gantries. There were cases of forgetful motorists slamming the brakes just before a gantry, or attempting to make illegal U-turns to avoid one, but these were rare. The number of motorists fined $50 each for lacking valid area licences eventually stabilised at 1,600–1,700 a month, and by 1980, 1,050 motorists a month, or around 35 a day—a tiny fraction of the total who entered the RZ.

The ALS drastically altered patterns of movement in and around the RZ. The number of motor vehicles entering the RZ during the restricted hours plunged by 44 per cent; by 1988, the volume of traffic entering the RZ during the restricted hours was still 31 per cent lower than before the ALS was implemented, despite employment in the Central Area growing by a third, and the motor vehicle population growing by 77 per cent. Instead, many motorists left for work earlier or later. Traffic thickened on roads leading into the RZ before and after the restricted hours, drawing out the morning peak period to four hours. Some motorists even waited for the restricted hours to end before driving into the RZ. Others gave up driving altogether, braving packed buses.

Motorists who used to go through the RZ when travelling between the east and west of the island searched for alternate routes. Consequently, the Inner Ring Road experienced daily jams, necessitating the widening of Newton Road and Scotts Road.

An unprecedented phenomenon came about— hitchhiking into the Central Area. Some Central Area-bound bus passengers hitched rides in cars that were short of carpoolers; these formed the majority of carpoolers, not car owners as the authorities had hoped. Cars waited by bus stops or the roadside before gantries, offering lifts. This led to the official designation of carpool pick-up spots.

The government raised significant revenue from the ALS, which it poured back into road development. It was revealed in 1977 that every month, the sale of area licences brought in $560,000, while policing and maintaining RZ gantries cost just $23,000—an annual profit of $6.4 million.

With the management of morning peak period congestion, the authorities turned to the evening. On 1 June 1989, the ALS was extended to the evening peak period of 4.30pm to 7pm on weekdays; private cars had their area licence fee reduced to $3. A month later, motorcycles were charged $1 each to enter the RZ. By December, the evening restricted hours were shortened to 6.30pm. But on 3 January 1994, the ALS was extended to the full working day—7.30am to 6.30pm on weekdays, and 7.30am to 3pm on Saturdays, reflecting the five-and-a-half-day work week at the time.

A similar Road Pricing System (RPS) was implemented for Singapore's expressways, starting with the ECP in 1995 to cover 7.30am to 9.30am on weekdays. The system was extended to the CTE and PIE two years later.

By then, there were compelling reasons for a complete overhaul of the ALS and RPS. One was their complexity. When the ALS began in 1975, it only taxed cars and taxis; by 1997, there were 14 different licences to choose from depending on type of vehicle, the hour of the day, and the day of the week, causing confusion and leading to fines. Another was the licence itself—it granted a motorist unlimited entries into the RZ on a given day, defeating the purpose of congestion pricing. Thirdly, the ALS and RPS were labour-intensive, requiring 70 people to sell licences and 78 gantry enforcers. Again, technology stepped in. On 1 April 1998, the LTA replaced the ALS and RPS with Electronic Road Pricing (ERP), a system using computers, cameras, radio waves, and smart cards, instead of people and paper licences; the first of its kind in the world for congestion pricing.

The overhead gantry was given a makeover: optical sensors to detect vehicles passing below, radio antennae to communicate with vehicles via radio waves, and cameras to take electronic photographs of the rear licence plates of vehicles not equipped to pass the gantry. As for motor vehicles, each was installed with an in-vehicle unit (IU) about the size of a small pocket diary, fixed permanently to the windscreen. The IU was needed to hold an integrated chip contact card, or CashCard, containing a stored value; when a vehicle passed under the gantry, the ERP charge would be deducted automatically by the IU communicating with the gantry's radio antennae.

The ERP debuted with 28 gantries surrounding the RZ, switched on from 7.30am to 7pm on weekdays; five gantries were placed in expressways, switched on from 7.30am to 9.30am on weekdays. This number, and its geographical reach, has grown. As of 2018, there were 77 ERP gantries in Singapore, 25 of which lay in or on the edge of the Central Business District (CBD). Twelve formed the Orchard Cordon around Orchard Road and Penang Road, nine covered the PIE, while seven graced the CTE. Charges varied according to location and the time of the day. For example, for the gantry on the CTE southbound after Braddell Road, the charge for a motor car could climb from $1 at 7am to a hefty $6 by 8.35am, then drop to $1 by 9.25am. These charges are reviewed every three months based on vehicle speeds achieved during half-hour blocks. The result is a dynamic system that regularly responds to changes in patterns of movement, instead of a more rigid ALS. The choices offered to motorists under the ALS have also carried over to the ERP: they can modify their routes to avoid the ERP, change the timings of their journeys to pay lower charges—or choose to pay full charges. In 2018, a peak-hour drive down the CTE from Yishun into the CBD took one through three ERP gantries—and a maximum combined charge of $9.50. This has translated to more revenue for the government: an estimated $144 million a year in 2009.

THE COST of buying a motor car gradually climbed through the 1970s and 1980s as road taxes and registration fees were progressively raised. By 1990, a car was subject to a customs duty of 45 per cent, and a registration fee of 175 per cent. This meant that the cost of a car could jump from $11,000 to $42,000!

Yet few people were deterred from buying a car. The car population in Singapore grew from 143,155 in 1975 to 244,722 in 1990, an increase of almost 71 per cent in just 15 years. Hence, in April 1990, the government introduced a Vehicle Quota System, a world-first like the ALS and ERP. In order to purchase a motor vehicle, motorists must obtain a Certificate of Entitlement (COE). A quota of COEs would be issued each quarter, later amended to every month. Motorists who wanted to purchase a class of vehicle had to enter bids for a COE; the price for a COE would be set at the lowest accepted bid. A COE lasts only 10 years before it must be renewed. The results: the government has absolute control over the motor vehicle population in Singapore, and the cost of owning a motor vehicle was raised by tens of thousands of dollars, further raising the bar for motor vehicle ownership.

The Vehicle Quota System has persisted to this day, but it is not without its criticisms. The auction-style system for COEs favours the wealthy, who can afford multiple cars; lower-income households are forced to pay COE prices driven up by demand. Those who can afford the high COE prices then feel compelled to use their cars as much as possible, contributing to long-term traffic congestion. Since COEs expire in 10 years, car owners are discouraged from keeping road-worthy cars, and cars in Singapore are overwhelmingly younger than 10 years. Finally, businesses which rely on transport—including taxi companies—are hit by high overhead costs. Meanwhile, the government has raked in handsome revenues. For the financial year of 2016 alone, motor vehicle taxes netted $2.308 billion, while COEs brought in $6.863 billion—more than enough to pay for the KPE and MCE.

THE FINAL factor in traffic management is the behaviour of motorists themselves. Careless driving ups the accident rate, which causes traffic jams. The roads of Singapore in the 1920s and 1930s were like the Wild West partly because traffic laws and enforcement were so lax. Attempts were made to change this after WWII.

From 1949, 30 miles an hour (48 km/h) gradually became the default speed limit for most of the island. Long stretches of arterial or trunk roads with high traffic volume, such as Nicoll Highway, Lornie Road, and Dunearn Road, enjoyed 40 miles an hour (64 km/h). When Singapore switched to the metric system, the law was amended in 1975 to make the speed limit for all roads 50 km an hour. Over time, some roads had their speed limits raised to allow for smoother traffic; others, lowered for safety. In 1980, for example, Bukit Timah Road, Commonwealth Avenue 1, and Ang Mo Kio Avenue 1—major arterial or trunk roads—had their speed limits adjusted to 70 km an hour.

The current Road Traffic Act, which covers Singapore's traffic laws, was passed in 1961. On 1 March 1975, the authorities introduced the Points Demerit System, to better keep track of a motorist's track record over time, and punish him or her for accumulated offences. Under this system, a motorist could earn demerit points for 11 types of traffic offences such as speeding, reckless driving, and failing to give way to pedestrians at a pedestrian crossing. If he earned 12 or more points within a year, his licence would be suspended. Thirteen months into the system, more than 10,000 motorists had received demerit points, while 14 had received six-month suspensions. The authorities decided to up the ante. From August 1977, the system covered 21 offences instead of 11, and the number of demerit points awarded per offence rose from four to six, to three to nine. In 1981 alone, 7,707 motorists were suspended!

The authorities then decided brandishing the stick was not enough; carrots should also be dangled. In March 1983, the Driver Improvement Points System (DIPS) replaced the Points Demerit System; now, a motorist was suspended only if he accumulated 24 points within two years. Furthermore, his existing points could be wiped out if he committed no offence for a year, and all previous suspensions could be expunged if he stayed clean for two years. These rewarded motorists for being law abiding rather than just punishing them. DIPS has persisted to the present.

The law had to continually keep abreast of new motoring trends. From the 1970s, the roads were plagued by motorcycle gangs called "hell riders", who used channels of movement as racing circuits, endangering lives; the Road Traffic Act was amended in 1984 to throw the book at them, such as mandatory jail time for first-time offenders, and a DIPS penalty of nine demerit points instead of three for exceeding the speed limit by more than 40 km an hour. The following year, the Act was amended again to make it illegal for motorists to refuse a breathalyser test when stopped by the police, aiding a clampdown on drunken driving. The Act also had to be amended to deal with motorists wearing headphones to listen to music while driving, then the use of car telephones while driving, then the use of mobile phones—as technology advanced, the law had to keep pace.

Seat belts in motor cars were made compulsory in 1983, increasing the chances of survival in accidents. All new cars and station wagons registered on or after 1 January 1978 had to install front seat belts; at the time, just 20 per cent of cars and vans were fitted with them. In 1992, it became mandatory for rear passengers to don seat belts too.

These measures have collectively made Singapore's roads safer for both motorists and pedestrians. In 1950, there were 114 deaths and 2,537 injuries for 29,926 motor vehicles, a casualty rate of roughly one for every 11 vehicles. In 1972, there was an absolute high of 390 deaths, with 10,819 injuries; but with 337,364 motor vehicles, the casualty rate had still dropped to one for every 30 vehicles. As traffic laws and disciplinary measures kicked in, the casualty rate plunged to one for every 50 vehicles in 1985, with 265 deaths and 9,506 injuries for 486,760 vehicles; in 2015, there were 151 deaths and 10,412 injuries for 957,246 vehicles, or one casualty for 91 vehicles.

However, the penalties for causing death by reckless or dangerous driving, or rash or negligent driving, are still light compared to the harm caused. There is a historical basis to this—since motor vehicles started taking over the roads in the 1920s, penalties have been light; we have seen examples in chapters 3 and 4. Even in 1979, a driver convicted on a charge of causing death by rash and negligent driving was just fined $2,500 and disqualified from driving for five years. As of 2018, the maximum sentence for the aforementioned offences was five years; in reality, sentences meted out usually do not exceed a few months. Driving a motor vehicle remains the only way you can (accidentally) kill someone and get away with a few months in jail!

Motorists would never be persuaded to give up their cars altogether if there were no good alternate methods of movement. Fortunately, giant strides have been made in public transport in Singapore from the 1950s, slowing down the growth of Singapore's motor vehicle population.

FROM 12 TO ONE... THEN TWO

SINGAPORE'S PUBLIC transport system experienced a revolution from the 1950s to the 1980s. The bus industry went through three phases. From 1950 to 1962, there was a mighty struggle within the industry, with trade unions battling companies and the authorities; the trolleybuses of the Singapore Traction Company (STC) made a quiet exit. The second phase from 1962 to 1973 saw the amalgamation of 10 bus companies, the government midwifing the creation of a united Singapore Bus Service (SBS). Meanwhile, the STC was allowed to die a natural death. The third phase from 1973 to 1987 saw the SBS grow from strength to strength, cementing its position as Singapore's premier transport company. Even then, a new bus company, Trans-Island Bus Services (TIBS), was formed to keep SBS on its toes. All this while, pirate taxis—the post-war version of mosquito buses—flourished, served the masses where bus companies and licensed taxis fell short, and were finally eliminated by the government. In return, the authorities shored up the taxi industry and grew it to a size and quality capable of serving Singaporeans who did not want to drive, yet desired a more private form of public transport.

In 1951, two bus companies merged—the Ngo Hock Motor Bus Company and the Soon Lee Bus Company, to form the Hock Lee Amalgamated Bus Company. The green and red of the former combined with the yellow and red of the latter to form a new livery of green, yellow, and red—the most colourful of bus companies. Their turf covered Havelock Road, Tiong Bahru, and Alexandra Road.

The strike years of the 1950s convinced the authorities to permit Chinese bus companies to service City routes, eroding the STC monopoly. These were times of student and worker activism, and trade unions with great power. Many bus drivers and conductors belonged to three unions. STC workers joined the STC Employees' Union; Chinese bus company workers belonged to the Singapore Bus Workers' Union (SBWU) and the Singapore Transport Workers' Union.

Bus strike activity reached unprecedented levels in the 1950s. Trade unions called them for a variety of reasons. The more common ones were for higher pay and bonuses, and better working conditions. Workers could also strike to protest against their companies denying them the right to join trade unions. They could be forcing their companies to reinstate colleagues who had been sacked for infractions such as giving union members free lifts or pocketing ticket receipts. They could be showing solidarity when workers in other industries, such as ports or factories, went on strike. They could be protesting against government crackdowns on student activism in Chinese-medium schools.

When bus workers went on strike, they could give up to 14 days' notice—opening the door to negotiations—or none at all. There was strength in numbers—a strike could involve thousands. In October 1956, 7,000 workers from nine out of the 10 Chinese bus companies stopped work. And there was no telling how long a strike could last. The shortest lasted just 10 minutes; some ran into months. In 1957, 87 Tay Koh Yat Bus Company employees stopped work for 87 days, while 230 Hock Lee employees did so for 112 days. But the record hit the STC from 27 September 1955 to 16 February 1956—450 buses and 50 trolleybuses grounded for 142 days.

Each time the wheels stopped turning, the public suffered, a testament to how crucial buses were as public transport. Before the war, rickshaws were still an able substitute; after the war, trishaws and taxis were only distant seconds to the bus. So when buses were out, people were forced to "hoof it", just like in the 19th century. The authorities and affected companies also commissioned lorries. Throughout the 142-day STC strike, lorries ferried 12,000 schoolchildren to and from school.

These dire times brought out the best and worst of humankind. Lorries plied busy roads, such as Serangoon Road, offering rides at double the bus fares. Taxi drivers also upped their fares by up to six times—fixed meter rates be damned. Some of these (unlicensed) taxis were actually driven by striking bus drivers themselves; each made $10–20 a day from a situation that was of his causing; often, they set aside money for fellow strikers.

Yet others lent a hand to the stranded. During the 142-day STC strike, motor car owners offered free lifts; they pasted stickers on windscreens showing off specific destinations. People in Joo Chiat did not have to wait more than 20 minutes for a lift to the Central Area in the morning. Even Chief Minister David Marshall set a good example, picking up three people a day from his home in Changi en-route to his office in Assembly House in High Street.

But motorists could only do so much. Hence, the authorities decided to allow other bus companies to cover the routes of a strike-hit company. During the 142-day STC strike, the Katong–Bedok Bus Company and the Easy Bus Company extended their suburban services from Guillemard Road and Alexandra Road respectively to Finlayson Green in the Central Area. Ironically, even as STC workers went on strike to fight for a better life, their actions jeopardised their company's City monopoly.

Occasionally, bus strikes took a more sinister turn. Violence during a Hock Lee strike on 12 May 1955, involving a mob of 2,000 workers and students attacking policemen, police posts, road blocks, and vehicles, has been remembered as the "Hock Lee Bus Riot"—a textbook example of the harm antagonistic trade unions wrought on Singapore. The toll of four dead and 31 injured overshadowed the Hock Lee workers' cause against poor working conditions and low pay. During other strikes, when some workers chose to strike and others did not, the former would intimidate the latter, such as stoning their buses, slashing tyres, or even forcing their buses off the roads. However, these criminal acts were the exception rather than the norm. Most strikes proceeded peacefully. In the long run, trade unions did secure better contracts for their workers. By 1960, the SBWU had signed agreements with all Chinese bus companies in Singapore—no easy feat. Thanks to the efforts of Fong Swee Suan (1931–2017), the union's advisor and political secretary to the Ministry of Labour and Law (also the man blamed in some quarters for instigating the Hock Lee Bus Riot), the bus companies' employees received bonuses that year.

After the People's Action Party (PAP) took over the reins of government in 1959, the general stance of trade unions in Singapore gradually shifted from combative to cooperative. The PAP amended the Trade Unions Ordinance to empower its Registrar to deregister or reject the registration of unions; as a result, many splinter trade unions disappeared; other trade unions amalgamated.

In 1961, after the left-wing Barisan Socialis split from the PAP, the Singapore Trades Union Congress—the island's largest congress of trade unions—also split into the pro-PAP National Trades Union Congress (NTUC) and the pro-Barisan Singapore Association of Trade Unions (SATU). Two years later, the PAP executed Operation Coldstore, a covert security operation which detained over 100 people without trial, officially to cripple communism in Singapore; this also led to the arrest of many leaders of SATU, which subsequently went into decline. Conversely, the NTUC went from strength to strength, taking in more trade unions. By the end of 1964, 55 registered unions representing 102,000 workers—65 per cent of organised workers in Singapore—were affiliated to the NTUC. The days of strikes and violence were over.

Meanwhile, on 15 December 1962, the STC pulled the last of its 50 trolleybuses off the streets, ending 36 years of the trolleybus in Singapore. One-way roads had exposed the inflexibility of the trolleybus system. Trolleybuses kept "coming off the wire" whenever drivers were too zealous in turning a corner or overtaking. Also, the STC had to grapple with lengthy strikes, competition from Chinese bus companies, and erosion of its City monopoly; expensive trolleybus infrastructure burdened it further. It was easier and cheaper to replace trolleybuses with motor buses, and the STC did just that.

From 233 STC and 274 Chinese bus company motor buses—a total of 507—in 1950, numbers doubled to 405 STC and 631 Chinese bus company buses—a total of 1,036—by 1962. After a very trying decade, the motor bus had cemented its position as the number one form of public transport in Singapore.

AFTER SINGAPORE'S separation from Malaysia in 1965, the government promised to devote attention to reforming the country's ageing public bus system. Australian transport consultant R. P. Wilson filed the Wilson Report in November 1970; the government implemented many of its recommendations in Parliament two months later. These included merging Singapore's bus companies. Merger would solve the problem of service duplication. Some roads were served by multiple services, while other roads had none. The existence of so many companies made it difficult to adjust supply to meet demand. Also, without economies of scale, it was hard to implement new technologies and service standards.

The bus companies accepted the recommendations of the Wilson Report. In April 1971, Singapore's 10 Chinese bus companies reorganised themselves into three companies serving the west, north, and east of the island.

Hock Lee, Keppel, and the Kampong Bahru Bus Service merged to form the Amalgamated Bus Company covering the west of the island. The companies' respective fleets were combined to form a new fleet of 296 buses with a livery of royal blue, similar to Keppel's livery, serving 22 routes.

The Tay Koh Yat, Green, and Easy bus companies formed the United Bus Company covering the north with a fleet of 448 buses, sporting a livery of yellow, covering 39 routes.

Paya Lebar, Changi, Katong-Bedok, and the Ponggol Bus Service merged into the Associated Bus Services covering the east. Their respective fleets were combined to form the largest fleet of 479, taking on Katong-Bedok's red livery, serving 30 routes. Meanwhile, the STC remained the largest bus company—510 buses serving 37 routes. In all, the four bus companies had 1,733 buses; with a population of 2.113 million in 1971, there was one bus for 1,219 people, as compared to one bus or trolleybus for 1,835 people in 1950.

With reorganisation came the merging, revising, and removal of bus routes. Transfers were avoided as much as possible. The three merged bus companies could now stop inside the City, ending the STC's 55-year monopoly. The authorities also imposed a unified fare structure. Previously, fares ranged from five to 80 cents; the new fare structure started from 10 cents and progressed every 10 cents to a maximum of 50 cents. Schoolchildren under the age of 18 paid a flat fee of 10 cents upon flashing a bus pass.

Singapore's revised bus routes came into operation on 12 April 1971—a day of confusion, frustration, and anger. Everything had changed: bus numbers, liveries, routes, fares. It was a time before the internet, social media, and smartphones, when bus guides were in short supply and bus stops lacked information—many passengers did not know which buses to board and where to get off. Bus stops were abuzz with chatter as commuters consulted each other for help. Some turned up late for work; others were horrified when they realised that they now had to pay more than twice the fare for the same routes. Bus conductors were swamped with inquiries, and they had to give running commentaries on routes. Other buses even lost their way! Some commuters gave up and chose to walk instead, some up to five kilometres. It took a full month for them to get used to the new routes and fares.

The government soon lost patience with the STC. For years, Singapore's oldest and largest public transport company had failed to raise its performance and service standards to meet passenger growth. From 1964 to 1971, it accumulated $5 million in losses. In February 1971, Minister for Communications Yong Nyuk Lin said in Parliament: "The large crowds waiting helplessly at bus stops during peak periods in the (Central Area)… is a clear indication that STC has failed in its task to provide an adequate public bus service." It was a damning indictment; the pre-war days of the authorities favouring the STC were long gone.

By the end of the year, the STC had folded. The dissolution of its City monopoly had all but broken the ageing camel's back. In a deal brokered by Yong and the STC Employees' Union, its three competitors bought most of its buses, took over its routes, and hired 2,000 of its 2,824 workers. One laid-off worker was 51-year-old ticket inspector Lim Lye Huat, who received just $168 after serving 30 years and 14 days with the firm. He had started out as a trolley boy, then was promoted to ticket collector and timekeeper, and finally ticket inspector for the last 20 years. (He was grateful for the severance pay, though, calling it a "timely *ang pow* [red packet]" and a "welcome birthday gift".)

The STC, with a proud heritage going back to 1925, could not adapt with the times and stay competitive. Its demise is a lesson for even the biggest transport companies today.

But the government was not satisfied with three bus companies. Finally, Yong arm-twisted them into merger on 1 November 1973, forming the Singapore Bus Service. For only the third time in Singapore's history—the first in 1906, the second in WWII—there was only one public bus operator covering the island. After 50 years, what began as a poorly-organised, chaotic, ill-disciplined substitute to rickshaws and electric trams, had evolved into the largest public transport company in Singapore, with 1,800 buses and 10,000 workers. To commemorate the event, the SBS launched 40 new "jumbo" buses, each with a capacity of 73, a new SBS logo, and a new livery of red and white.

TURNING AROUND THE BUS INDUSTRY

THE NEW SBS, with the government as midwife, came at the right time. New towns were coming up in rural Singapore. Urban renewal was transforming the old Central Area. The success of a transport company partly depends on its ability to adapt to changes in patterns of movement. The SBS was poised to do so more effectively than a dozen smaller bus companies. But there was still a long way to go.

After merger, the SBS was burdened with up to 14 bus models of different ages, which complicated maintenance. Buses persistently broke down. But vehicles were only part of its worries—the performance levels of bus drivers and conductors were poor. Conductors were rude and argued with passengers over tickets and change. Drivers did not keep to schedules, and when they fell behind, skipped bus stops and refused to stop for passengers. A usual 10-minute wait for a bus could exceed 30 minutes. In 1975, *The Straits Times* reported that a clerk lost her job after turning up late for work three times in a week—buses had sped past her without stopping. On the roads, drivers drove dangerously without regard for standing passengers. They braked hard at bus stops or traffic lights, and moved off from bus stops even while passengers were still on the steps.

Bus infrastructure was wholly inadequate. Bus stops near schools, entertainment areas, shopping centres, and in the Central Area each overflowed with queues of more than 150 people during peak hours. In new towns such as Ang Mo Kio, morning peak period bus stop queues could be up to 50-strong, running into the void decks. Many bus stops still had no shelter from the sun or rain. People living in the rural areas had it worst. In 1974, Sembawang residents complained that buses came three in a row after an hour's wait. In Changi, the wait could go up to two hours!

In 1974, *Straits Times* journalist Wong Lai Wah took the bus 30 times in two days, and filed this damning report:

> They jostled, they elbowed one another, they pushed and squeezed—no, they were not fleeing from a scene of disaster, but were merely taking a bus. This mad stampede—almost an obscene spectacle of men, women and children not giving any quarter to anyone, regardless of sex or age— is a daily occurrence in Singapore…
>
> One weary commuter—a receptionist who waited 15 minutes for service 13A in Orchard Road—said: "I can't recall the number of times buses have let me down and I had to take a taxi to reach the office on time. It's maddening when you know the office is only 20 minutes away and you have to wait nearly an hour to get a bus."
>
> Waiting aside, commuters have to put up with nerve-racking journeys with heavy bone-shaking bumps along the way. Curves and bends are often negotiated too fast, causing commuters to sway and slide in their seats… Like all other commuters, I had to bear with pneumatic drill-like vibrations, loose-window rattlings, wheel wobbles, damaged seats, jammed or paneless windows, even squeaky windscreen wipers.

I saw two conductors quarrelling with passengers. One issued a middle-aged woman a 30-cent ticket when she wanted a 20-cent ride. When she asked for change, he refused, raised his voice—loud enough for passengers seven rows behind to hear— and then walked away, without changing her ticket.

… I saw in bus commuters pent-up frustrations, witnessed frayed tempers and heard loud and often vehement criticism of the inefficient system.

That year, Parliament discussed nationalising the SBS. That would have been unprecedented, for the British had rarely taken over any form of public transport, save for a short-lived municipal bus service in 1920. Many Singaporeans were in favour of nationalisation. But after three months of deliberation, the government decided that it did not have the expertise to run a bus company. Communications Minister Yong declared in Parliament: "Nationalisation involving heavy subsidies does not necessarily result in a more efficient service." However, the government did assign its officials to senior posts in the SBS to oversee operations and personnel.

Gradually, with government prodding and assistance, the SBS pulled up its socks. First, it overhauled its fleet of buses, scrapping up to 100 old vehicles every year. Hundreds more were refitted with two automated doors instead of one manual door. From 1,800 buses in 1974, or one bus for 1,219 people in Singapore, the SBS fleet grew to 3,000 buses in 1983, or one for every 894 people. The SBS also introduced a regular maintenance programme for its buses, which drastically reduced the number of breakdowns.

In 1974, 800 buses broke down; this alarming number was slashed to just 19 in 1981.

New buses would not please commuters if their drivers and conductors were not professional. The SBS drew up a new disciplinary code, issued new uniforms and identification tags, gave out quarterly incentive payments to high performers, and sent staff for seminars on safe driving, service, and courtesy. For those who stepped out of line, the SBS was prepared to sack them. Over eight months in 1974, it dismissed 499 drivers and conductors (out of a workforce of 10,000) for ill discipline. These measures were somewhat effective, halving the number of commuter complaints from 1979 to 1983.

The SBS cut back on surging labour costs by converting its buses from a two-man operation to a one-man operated service, or OMO. From 1979, it spent more than $16 million to convert its entire fleet; by 1984, the post of the bus conductor, introduced with the steam tram in 1886, was rendered obsolete by a driver-side coin box and ticket-dispensing machine. From a high of 4,100 conductors, the SBS retrenched 1,400 in five years, assigning the rest to other jobs. This bore financial fruit: The company saved $30 million a year.

Commuters took time to get used to the OMO. After paying their fares, many walked to their seats leaving tickets dangling from dispensers! They also had to pay exact fares instead of getting change from a conductor, forcing some to buy tissue paper or sweets at interchanges to get small change. Bus interchanges were installed with coin-changing machines, but the next phase of fare payment arrived soon after. In 1985, SBS tested the use of fare cards—magnetic stored-value cards—on Service 282 in Clementi New Town. Passengers slid the credit card-sized fare card through the top of a box-like machine mounted next to the driver; the machine automatically deducted the fare. At the time, Singapore was only the third city in the world to test this technology on buses, behind San Diego and Hong Kong. The SBS implemented this on all buses the following year.

A smaller wage bill and greater economies of scale convinced the SBS to introduce air-conditioning in buses. In April 1984, Service 168 between Ang Mo Kio and Orchard Road took on eight 41-seater air-conditioned buses. Fares were 50 per cent more expensive, going up to $1.20. The SBS was afraid that passengers would be cool to this, but they gradually warmed up to the service—they no longer had to endure sweltering heat or wet seats when it rained.

The SBS also had the deep pockets to pay for double-decker buses. In 1977, it debuted seven Atlantean double-deckers imported from British Leyland. Service 86 from Tampines Way Bus Terminal to Shenton Way was launched by Senior Minister of State for Communications Ong Teng Cheong.[5] Each bus could accommodate 87 sitting passengers instead of 55 for a single-deck bus, and at 4.4 metres, was the tallest method of movement to grace Singapore's roads. The service became popular with schoolchildren from rural Punggol, who made use of the flat fare of 10 cents to take joyrides to the Central Area and back. By 1983, the SBS double-decker fleet had grown to 300—one in 10 SBS buses.

All the new buses in the world were useless if they were not deployed where commuters needed them most. The SBS laboured to figure out the best routes for a rapidly-changing urban landscape while watching its profit margins. "Rationalisation" was commonplace—the amending or withdrawing of services with low demand, a practice disliked by commuters. The spread of new towns made it unprofitable for the SBS to offer direct services between every new town and the Central Area. Hence the rise of feeder services: short-distance services moving people from HDB flats to trunk or arterial roads, where they transferred to other Central Area-bound buses. The first feeder services in Singapore served Jurong, Sembawang Hills Drive, Bedok New Town, and Changi Village. In terms of planning, the SBS had advantages over the old Chinese bus companies: it could plan for an entire island, not just one region; and from 1983, it started employing computer technology to track bus routes and travel patterns. In 1971, four bus companies ran a total of 128 routes; in 1978, the SBS alone ran 217 routes.

Improvements for a method of movement should not be limited to just vehicles and their handlers, but also supporting infrastructure. In the 1970s and 1980s, more resources were poured into boosting supporting infrastructure for buses than any other mode of public transport in Singapore's history. The SBS was fortunate in that it had the government's backing—millions of dollars of taxpayers' money were spent to bolster a private transport company.

A reserved bus lane was trialled for two months along New Bridge Road in 1972—the first time part of a channel of movement was reserved for just one method of movement, in a bid to improve bus scheduling and reliability. It was deemed a success. Two years later, permanent bus lanes stamped "Bus Only" were rolled out in and around the Central Area. Starting with Robinson Road, 23 roads from Jalan Besar to Anson Road, a combined length of 14.2 km, received bus lanes. These roads were picked as they carried at least 100 buses an hour; Robinson Road carried 300 buses an hour during peak hours. Taxi stands and roadside parking lots had to make way for these bus lanes, and motorists had to keep out, or be fined at least

$400. These measures paid off. Bus lanes helped increase bus speeds by at least 15 per cent, and accommodate more travellers on one lane—in 1974, 7,000–21,000 bus passengers an hour, as compared to 1,300 travellers in motor cars. Full-day bus lanes were introduced by the LTA in 2005, and as of 2018, there were 58 roads with normal bus lanes and 28 roads with full-day bus lanes all over Singapore.

Bus stops were upgraded from mere poles with service numbers tacked on. In 1977, the PWD started building shelters for 120 stops at a cost of $600,000. In 1985, service information signs were put up at 150 major CBD and other popular stops, displaying route details, bus arrival timings, peak and off-peak frequencies, and fares—bus stops still carry such travel aids today.

From the genesis of Chinese bus companies in the 1930s, bus terminals sufficed as transport nodes for the start and end of bus services. These terminals were usually by roadsides, with parking space for up to a dozen buses. In 1978, the SBS operated 64 terminals with a capacity of 640 buses. However, the growth of new towns and feeder services necessitated the creation of something bigger: the modern bus interchange. The SBS footed the bill at first, building interchanges in five new towns by the end of 1979: Jurong, Bedok, Ang Mo Kio, Telok Blangah, and Clementi. Ang Mo Kio Interchange was soon torn down and rebuilt again by 1983; Version 2 had 63 bus bays for almost 30 services. That year, the government took over the building and maintenance of interchanges and terminals, in order to better coordinate urban renewal projects. By the end of 1983, new interchanges had opened in Woodlands, Hougang, and Toa Payoh New Towns; Jurong East New Town got its interchange in 1985; Serangoon and Tampines interchanges came along in 1987. The latter cost $5 million, was as large as three football fields, and hosted 85 bus bays.

In 1980, a *Straits Times* forum contributor, J. Foo, painted this scene:

> Ever since I moved into Ang Mo Kio New Town two months ago, I cannot help but sense this perpetual movement of people everywhere—people with anxious looks on their faces. This is especially evident during the mornings at the SBS (terminal) next to Block 324 where staggered lines of commuters have to wait for their respective services.
>
> Each time the sardine-packed feeder service buses arrive to drop off their passengers, you see everyone caught in this moving stream of people trying to get an early place in the queues for the external buses.
>
> Heading for your queue is not a smooth and easy journey. You have to manoeuvre through narrow gaps in the lines of commuters, be alert so as not to step on people's feet, watch out for oncoming commuters and look out for your bus. It becomes chaotic when these queues start moving up for their buses.

Bus interchanges became nexuses of a wave of modernity, a new experience of movement that transformed the rural areas of Singapore: a torrent of humanity, the intersection of a thousand paths, where time was measured by bus schedules.

In the space of just a dozen years, the SBS transformed itself from an entity beset with myriad problems ranging from rickety buses and abusive drivers to inadequate bus infrastructure,

CHAPTER 7 1950 to 2011: Mergers and Laws 277

Bus interchanges are hives of constant activity, a new experience of movement that came about in the late 1970s. This was Woodlands Temporary Bus Interchange in 2019. (Source: Eisen Teo)

into the pride of Singapore's public transport system, with air-conditioned double-decker buses, fare cards for easy payment, and exclusive bus lanes to keep passengers moving during peak periods. Government assistance—both talent and cash—greatly helped. But given the importance of buses to movement in Singapore, the assistance was justified. The SBS became a publicly-listed company in 1978; in 1985, passengers made a record 818.6 million trips on 2,633 SBS buses, or 2.24 million trips every day (for a population of 2.736 million), boosting the company's after-tax profits to a healthy $9.5 million. More than one in two working adults and one in three students took the bus every day—a ridership figure unseen since the heyday of the rickshaw. But unlike the rickshaw of old, bus coverage extended to almost all corners of the island, serving bustling new towns that, 10 years before, were plantations and farmland.

But as the number of new towns grew, as Singapore's population surged past 2.5 million in 1981, one public bus company was not enough. The government desired limited competition to keep it on its toes. Hence, in 1982, it granted an operating licence for a public bus company to the Singapore Shuttle Bus (SSB), a company formed by seven school bus operators. The SSB set up a subsidiary called Trans-Island Bus Services, or TIBS, with Ng Ser Miang (born 1949) as managing director. For the first time in nine years, the SBS had competition. As a sign of its intent, TIBS purchased 90 45-seater buses for $8 million, painting them in a livery of yellow and orange.

Just as the government had poured in resources and talent to the SBS, it also orchestrated the rise of TIBS to ensure the fledgling company was not crushed by the SBS. It set aside the northern regions of Woodlands, Sembawang, and Yishun for TIBS, and existing SBS services were handed over to TIBS. The government took care to give TIBS a fair share of the transport pie without hurting the SBS' bottom line. In April 1983, TIBS commenced its first two services: Service 167 between Sembawang Shipyard and Anson Road, and 160 between Admiralty Road West and Crawford Street. For the rest of the year, TIBS took over another 10 SBS services, and also management of Woodlands Bus Interchange.

TIBS became a commercial success, proving that a second bus company in Singapore was viable. By 1987, it had 361 buses, 1,300 staff, a new bus depot at Ang Mo Kio Street 62, and the first bus interchange exclusive to TIBS buses and services at Yishun Avenue 2, to serve Yishun New Town.

A quiet exit came in 1984—the former STC's MacKenzie Road depot was demolished. Built in 1905 to house, repair, and generate electricity for electric trams, the depot later took in trolleybuses and motor buses. The government bought the property in 1971 and leased it to the SBS for its headquarters and bodyworks division. In 1983, the SBS moved to a new headquarters in Braddell Road, which it still occupies. The depot, with leaking zinc-roofed sheds and old tram tracks embedded onto the concrete floor, disappeared into the abyss of history. Today, in its place lie a car park and an open field near Little India MRT Interchange.

COMFORT FOR THE TAXI INDUSTRY

IN THE early 1950s, the City Council tried to raise the service standards of Singapore's 1,500 motor taxis by ordering them to be fitted with two devices. One was taximeters, laying to rest decades of debate. Another was radiophones, to better connect commuters to available taxis. While the former came to pass by 1 January 1954, the latter did not, as many fleet owners protested against the high costs of installation—$800 per radiophone. They had won, but a bigger battle lay ahead: the pirate taxi.

Lax laws, the lure of money, and an ailing public transport system, gave birth to pirate taxis. After WWII, the prices of motor cars plunged. A second-hand car could be had for just $1,500. Many began seeing the benefits of illegally using one's car as a pirate taxi. A licensed taxi driver had to pay three times the car insurance and 10 times the road tax; he also had to submit his vehicle for safety inspections twice a year. A pirate did not have to do all of this, saving up to $3,000 a year. No wonder he could charge rock-bottom fares. In 1966, a pirate charged 10–20 cents a mile, far below the licensed taxis' charge of 40 cents a mile. With the bus industry far from world-class, there was significant demand for movement at a speed and level of convenience exceeding that of buses and trolleybuses. In a year, a pirate could pocket a couple of thousand dollars in profit—a fortune for the working class. People took up driving lessons just so they could become pirate taxi drivers. In 1955, out of Singapore's 6,600 taxis, some 5,000 were pirate taxis; many were licensed taxi drivers who could not purchase or rent taxis.

The illegal business became one of the "most open of open secrets in the Colony". Locals knew where to look for them—Rochor Canal Road, the tiny lanes off North Bridge Road and Beach Road, certain hotels and nightspots. Purvis Street and Beach Road were headquarters for organised services of pirate taxis; Havelock Road and Chinatown were "pirate taxi paradises". The vehicles and their occupants mostly blended in—but if one took a careful look, "sometimes a car can be identified as moving along prescribed routes with a very odd assortment of passengers for a private car. Its passengers may consist of a humble labourer, an anxious-looking farmer's wife from the outlying districts of Singapore, a clerk who lives in Katong, maybe a salesman who lives in Bedok and a shop assistant returning to Seah Street."

The authorities and print media demonised pirates as robbing from the government, the bus companies, and legitimate taxi drivers. The facts seemed to support their argument. In 1955, it was estimated that licensed taxi drivers lost almost $17,000 a month in earnings to pirates, while the Registry of Vehicles ended every year short of $1.38 million in fees.

However, this was not the full picture. Like the rickshaw and mosquito bus, the pirate taxi was a service of the people and for the people. The vehicles were hired for family trips, weddings, and funerals. They ferried workers and schoolchildren on a daily basis—in 1957, arranging a pirate taxi to take a child to and from school cost as little as $20 a month, compared to $48 for a legitimate taxi. People appreciated pirate taxis at a time when the public transport system was not up to scratch—bus strikes were common, and buses came infrequently and were overcrowded. The licensed taxi industry was no better: rude drivers, drivers refusing to stop for customers, drivers choosing their fares. The pirates were praised for being willing to drive any distance for any fare.

Many pirates were poor and lived hand-to-mouth, just like the passengers they ferried. One gave this account in 1970:

All of us have families and if we stop running these taxis, who will feed us and our families? My children are in school. By running a pirate taxi, I earn a few dollars a day, sometimes more. I know it is illegal but I don't have any other way out. I only live for tomorrow. I cannot look ahead. We are not a public nuisance. We provide cheap and fast transport for people in areas not serviced by buses or taxis.

Not all pirates were "of the people", though. Where there was money, organised gangs stepped in. Pirates pooled money to hire thugs to protect their "territory". Some even held entire estates hostage. In 1959, *The Straits Times* reported a syndicate of 10 pirate taxis operating in Opera Estate off Siglap Road. A gang barred licensed taxis from entering the estate of 7,000, allowing the pirates to charge exorbitant rates; the residents' only alternative was walking 800 metres to the nearest bus stop.

The City Council first declared war on the pirates in 1951, starting a pattern that would repeat for the next 20 years: parties who stood to lose from the pirates—taxi drivers, bus companies, public transport workers' unions—complained to the authorities; the authorities launched blitzes on the pirates, making arrests and convictions; scores of pirates were fined, disqualified from driving for months and had their cars confiscated; they laid low; they bounced back. Laws punishing pirates stiffened through the years, but with little impact. Organised gangs intimidated vehicle inspectors and struck fear into the hearts of passengers, making them reluctant to testify against pirates, forcing the courts to drop cases.

The end only came in July 1970, when a government White Paper announced plans to eliminate them within a year. With sufficient political will, this drive succeeded where others have failed.

What made the difference was that the authorities came up with systemic solutions, not just carrying out raids and strengthening laws. First, the reorganisation of Singapore's public bus system from 1971 to 1973 encouraged more people to take the bus instead of pirate taxis. Next, confiscated cabs were no longer put on the market, allowing pirates to buy them back; instead, they were sold $100 apiece as scrap—a draconian move. Third, the Communications Ministry encouraged pirates to come forward and register for a job conversion scheme, which included applying for legitimate taxi-driving jobs with a new taxi association.

This association was Comfort, affiliated with the 10-year-old NTUC. NTUC Comfort entered the taxi market at the right time—when pirates were being forced off the streets. Before, taxi drivers had to rent Yellow Top taxis on a daily basis from fleet owners, which did not grant them long-term job security. Some drivers even had to grease the palms of clerks renting out the vehicles. Now, Comfort taxi drivers could "own" taxis for up to seven years after paying off loans in monthly instalments. They also enjoyed unprecedented benefits such as diesel rebates, discounts on spare parts, and assistance in traffic incidents and insurance claims. Such radical changes in the form of taxi ownership encouraged almost 1,000 pirates to turn legitimate. The first 1,000 Comfort taxis hit the roads by mid-1971.

Four years later in 1975, when NTUC Comfort provided 28 buses to run part of the City Shuttle Service, it was the first time in about five decades that a public transport company had put out vehicles for more than one mode of public transport—previously, the STC had added motor buses to its fleet of trolleybuses.

Providing credible alternatives for both pirates and their customers made the government's anti-pirate drive a success. One year after the

White Paper, no arrests of pirates were made. Singapore's 5,500 pirates were finally gone—or so the authorities thought. The public bus system strained to keep pace with the spread of new towns. Where the buses were inadequate, pirates returned. Between 1974 and 1977, pirate taxis reappeared sporadically in the still rural areas of Sembawang, Marsiling, Woodlands, Tampines, and Jurong. They popped up during peak periods, ferrying office workers frustrated by overcrowded or tardy buses; they gave lifts to kampung residents between their homes and the main roads; after 9pm, when the frequency of buses dipped, they turned up to take people home. They only petered out again with the improvement of bus and taxi systems in the 1980s.

Like the bus industry, the government ensured NTUC Comfort had measured competition—they granted taxi licences to three more companies. The Singapore Airport Bus Services (SABS)—of which the SBS was a shareholder and managing agent—launched a fleet of 50 air-conditioned green and cream Datsun taxis in 1979. Four years later, the Singapore Commuter—a subsidiary of Singapore Automotive Engineering, owned by the Ministry of Defence—rolled out 105 red-topped, white-bodied cabs; as opposed to Yellow Tops, they were dubbed "Red Tops". Also in 1983, the first 20 SBS taxis hit the roads. Gradually, the composition of the taxi industry shifted from groups of fleet owners to taxi companies. By 1987, NTUC Comfort was the biggest player in the industry with 6,300 cabs; the Singapore Commuter had 500; SABS had 300; SBS Taxi, 200; and there were 3,000 Yellow Tops. In all, there were 10,300 taxis, or one taxi for 248 people; in 1971, there were just 4,800 taxis, or one taxi for 444 people.

The taxi industry progressed in other ways. The taxi radiophone finally materialised—in 1976, the first 60 radiophone taxis began plying the Jurong area between Upper Ayer Rajah Road and Boon Lay Gardens. The taxis belonged to the Taman Jurong Taxi Service, and their "headquarters" was a two-man operation at a Taman Jurong taxi stand.[6]

Another improvement was more taxi stands and kiosks. Travellers and taxis could wait for each other at the stands, while kiosks had telephones for travellers to dial for cabs. Roadside kiosks started appearing in the early 1970s, small wooden sheds no larger than half the size of an HDB bedroom, for drivers to relax in between shift changes and long drives. By 1976, there were 114 stands and 25 kiosks in Singapore.

The authorities also set minimum mileage quotas for taxis, forcing them to spend more time on the road instead of going for long coffee breaks. In 1983, NTUC Comfort introduced a 260-km minimum daily mileage, or 40,000 km every six months. Similarly, SBS Taxi imposed a 180-km minimum daily shift mileage.

A fourth measure was incentivising taxi drivers to travel to areas of higher passenger demand. The incentives were to come from passengers' pockets—enter the taxi surcharge. In 1980, an airport surcharge of $1.50 was implemented for Paya Lebar Airport. The following year, a $1 peak-period surcharge was imposed on taxi rides from the CBD. By 1985, cabbies enjoyed a midnight surcharge of 50 per cent of the metered fare between midnight and 6am. Taxi surcharges have survived to the present day.

MOVING MOUNTAINS FOR THE MASS RAPID TRANSIT

CONSIDERING HOW critical the MRT is to public transport in Singapore today, it seems incredible that it took years to decide whether or not to build it. As early as 1953, a *Straits Times* transport columnist, Manning Blackwood, wrote that "rail transportation is the main solution to Singapore's traffic problem (congested roads)". In 1966, one year after independence, the MND and the Planning Department toyed with plans for an MRT system from Kallang Park to the Central Area. Comparing the subway, the aboveground electric train, and the monorail, they identified the first option as "aesthetically the most acceptable and also the most efficient, since all its track and machinery are hidden from view". However, they decided that costs were prohibitive, and the system not suitable in Singapore because of poor soil conditions and a high water table.

Then came the four-year project that culminated in the 1971 Concept Plan. The team included a certain Ong Teng Cheong, then a 31-year-old architect in the Planning Department; they concluded that by 1992, no matter how much the bus system was improved, there would be chaos in city streets; hundreds of buses would jam the roads during peak periods. Singapore needed the MRT. The Concept Plan incorporated an MRT system in the City, from Toa Payoh to Kallang and the Central Area, then swinging to the west through Tiong Bahru to Queenstown.

Presented with a nightmarish scenario, the government took action to turn the MRT vision to reality. In 1972, it initiated the Mass Transit Study, to assess the need for an MRT and the shape the project would take. Phase I took two years; a two-line MRT system was proposed, one running east to west from Jurong through the Central Area to Siglap, the other running north to south from Ang Mo Kio to the Central Area. Phase II took three years from 1975 to 1978, concluding that the MRT was technically and economically feasible—unlike in the 1960s. Still, a hefty price tag of $1.75 billion was set. Phase III took a year from 1979 to 1980; it focused on design and engineering, and the price tag was revised to $4 billion. In 1980, the government formed a Provisional MRT Authority to implement the MRT project.

The end was near, but the project threatened to derail before construction even started. Ong, now Communications Minister and the project's strongest advocate, faced strong opposition from other cabinet ministers and MPs, including First Deputy Prime Minister Goh Keng Swee and Trade and Industry Minister Tony Tan. They took issue with the MRT's stiff price tag; wouldn't an all-bus system be cheaper and work just as well? A review team from Harvard agreed with them. Finally, after 10 studies and $10 million spent over 15 years, the government made the decision in May 1982—the MRT project would go ahead.

The government moved fast. There would be 42 stations—15 underground, 27 aboveground—over three lines, similar to the 1971 Concept Plan. In October 1983, the Mass Rapid Transit Corporation (MRTC) was formed to build the infrastructure needed for the MRT. More infrastructure would be needed than any other method of movement in Singapore's history. Hence, the MRTC was handed wide-ranging powers: acquiring land, digging tunnels, building viaducts—even across private property. Work began that month at Shan Road off Balestier Road.

Originally, the 42 stations were scheduled to be completed in eight years, but they were finished in just six—a titanic feat of planning and engineering. More than 5,000 people worked around the clock on the stations, tracks, tunnels, and viaducts simultaneously. Digging was done with 110-ton drilling machines; 10,000–14,000 lorry loads of earth and clay were excavated for each underground MRT site. To create a tunnel between Newton Circus and Orchard Road, workers had to deal with very soft and waterlogged soil under Scotts Road, peppered with massive boulders that had to be sliced and blasted away. The Singapore River had to be dammed in stages for a 95-metre tunnel to be built under it. Tunnelling had to be carried out amidst built-up areas. Cracks appeared in HDB blocks and factories near the Toa Payoh and Braddell MRT station worksites; cracks also damaged the stained glass windows of the 80-year-old Convent of the Holy Infant Jesus (CHIJ), next to the City Hall MRT Interchange worksite. But by and large, there were no major damages to buildings.

Many significant landmarks had to make way for MRT stations and tunnels. A Jewish cemetery made way for Novena MRT Station. The century-old Sri Sivan Temple, and the Amber Mansions—one of Singapore's earliest shopping centres built in the 1920s—were torn down for Dhoby Ghaut MRT Station. Almost half of the CHIJ complex had to go for City Hall's worksite (SMRT's headquarters was later built there). Raffles Place MRT Interchange spelled the demise of the road called Raffles Place, De Souza Street, and parts of Change Alley and The Arcade; the iconic, six-storey Chartered Bank Building, which opened in 1952, had to be torn down too. Outside of the Central Area, Commonwealth Avenue and Commonwealth Avenue West were split into two carriageways to accommodate in the middle the MRT viaduct connecting Queenstown, Commonwealth, and Clementi MRT stations.

Japanese company Kawasaki Heavy Industries won the contract to deliver 396 train cars to MRTC at a bargain price of $581 million. Each train consisted of six cars, and was 138 metres long and 3.2 metres wide—at 12 times the length of a standard bus, and with a capacity of 1,800 passengers, the MRT train became the largest method of movement in Singapore's history. A train travelled at an average of 40–45 km/h, but crucially, was not subject to road congestion or traffic lights. A train arrived every two minutes during peak periods, and five to seven minutes during off-peak hours.

On the big day of 7 November 1987, the Singapore Mass Rapid Transit (SMRT) took over the daily operations of the MRT system from the MRTC. SMRT was a company wholly owned by Temasek Holdings, the government's sovereign wealth fund, which meant indirect governmental control over the running of the MRT. Like the SBS, the MRT was too precious to leave at the mercy of free market forces.

From that day until 6 July 1990, the 42 stations opened over nine phases. The 15-station North South Line ran from Yishun in the north to Marina Bay in the south, connecting four new towns to the Central Area. The 26-station East West Line started at Boon Lay in the west and ended at Pasir Ris in the east, linking eight new towns to the Central Area. The four-station Branch Line ran from Jurong East north to Choa Chu Kang, serving two new towns. Three stations were interchanges—Raffles Place, City Hall, and Jurong East. Raffles Place and City Hall each has two platform levels for commuters to transfer between the North South and East West lines; Raffles Place was the deepest MRT station in Singapore, with four levels below ground.

When work began on the stations, working names were assigned to them, but some were eventually changed to "better reflect the locality of the stations" and "for a more local flavour". Of the 42 stations, just 16 ended up with English-language names. Fifteen have names of Malay origin, eight have Chinese names, one is a

Raffles Place MRT Interchange, as seen from Exit A, facing north. The European-style buildings that once graced the square have been replaced by glass-and-steel skyscrapers; John Little Department Store lives on in the façade of Exit B (centre), which was modelled after it. The road called Raffles Place disappeared when the interchange was built. Once filled with cars, the square is now open to pedestrians only. (Source: Eisen Teo)

Chinese-Malay hybrid (Tiong Bahru), one is of Indian origin (Dhoby Ghaut, even though the road has been expunged), and one is Italian (Buona Vista). Twelve names are those of new towns, evidence of the MRT's connectivity. Nine names are those of places named after people—Yishun, Braddell, Newton, Raffles Place, Outram Park, Boon Lay, Clementi, Aljunied, and Eunos.[7] In 1985, the Singapore Tourist Promotion Board (now the Singapore Tourism Board) had requested MRTC to rename Outram Park MRT Station to Chinatown, to "make it easier for tourists to find their way to their favourite destination", but it was not taken up; the station was on the edge of Chinatown, not inside it.

Just as the place names chosen for new towns entered toponymic immortality at the expense of other names, the place names chosen for MRT stations also impressed themselves upon the population, becoming household names. Good for little-known place names like Khatib; since the 1840s, a river north of the Sungei Seletar was known as Khatib (Arabic for a person who delivers the sermon during Friday prayers in Islam) Bongsu (Malay for "Last" or "Youngest"). Conversely, the place names of Maxwell (after Maxwell Road, named after the family of the chief justice of the Straits Settlements Sir Peter Benson Maxwell [1816–1893]) and Victoria (after Victoria Street) lost out to Tanjong Pagar and Bugis respectively.[8]

Singaporeans swiftly got used to taking the train, including buying tickets and using fare gates. There were teething problems in the early days—coin-changing machines breaking down, ticket-vending machines overwhelmed by crowds, trains not stopping precisely where they should—but they were eventually ironed out. A plethora of rules were imposed, prohibiting smoking, carrying large luggage, pets, placing feet on seats, eating, drinking, and playing the radio, among other things. Durians were banned from trains six months after the MRT opened, and chewing gum, 18 months after.

The SBS and TIBS had good reason to be fearful of the MRT's arrival. MRT fares were competitive, just 50 cents to a maximum of $1.10. The SBS feared that a third of its fares would be lost to the MRT, but the reality was only a slight dip in ridership—3.3 per cent from 1989 to 1990. Its after-tax profits actually rose from $36.9 million in 1987 to $49.9 million in 1990. TIBS did not fare too badly either—its after-tax profits were $8.73 million in 1991, and its bus fleet grew from 361 in 1987 to 478 that year.

In the past, concurrent forms of public transport—such as rickshaws and electric trams—competed with each other. Now, bus and rail companies complemented each other. Both bus operators lost some long-distance passengers, but also gained trunk and feeder service commuters between housing estates and MRT stations. Again, rationalisation kicked in. Just two months after the MRT opened, five services from Ang Mo Kio and Toa Payoh to the Central Area were cut—they had lost a third of their passengers to the MRT—much to the chagrin of commuters.

On 10 February 1996, the North South Line grew from 15 stations to 25, and from 21.5 km to 44 km of track (overtaking the East West Line in length of track), with the addition of the Woodlands Extension—six aboveground stations and 16 km of track at a cost of $1.3 billion. To the north of Yishun, there were Sembawang (previously the working name of Khatib MRT Station), Admiralty, Woodlands, Marsiling, Kranji, and Yew Tee MRT stations. Since the line connected to the 6.5-km Branch Line, the latter was absorbed into the former, and the North South Line's western terminus was now Jurong East. Nineteen six-car trains were purchased from German conglomerate company Siemens AG for the extension.

The extension served Woodlands and Sembawang towns. Woodlands MRT Station opened with Woodlands Bus Interchange, Singapore's first below-ground bus interchange; the station became the new town centre of Woodlands, replacing (Old) Woodlands Town Centre.

Three years later, on 6 November 1999, Singapore saw the debut of its first light electric railway system, the Light Rapid Transit (LRT). This was the culmination of an eight-year journey starting with proposed LRT systems in Yishun, Punggol, and Tampines in the 1991 Concept Plan. Studies were subsequently done to assess the suitability of the LRT in the Beach Road–Nicoll Highway area, the area that is now Sengkang town, Ang Mo Kio, Toa Payoh, and Buona Vista, but the authorities eventually decided on Bukit Panjang town. The result: the Bukit Panjang LRT Line, an elevated, 7.8-km, 14-station, fully-automated and driverless system run by the SMRT. LTA, which in 1995 had absorbed the MRTC, built the system for $285 million to connect Bukit Panjang town with Choa Chu Kang town and the MRT network at Choa Chu Kang MRT Station, which became Singapore's fourth MRT interchange. Train cars were purchased from German company ADtranz; each car accommodates 105 passengers and completes a loop in 28 minutes. After the LRT opened, the SBS withdrew or re-routed 19 bus services in Bukit Panjang town.

By the beginning of the new millennium, SMRT had grown into a transport giant to match the likes of SBS and TIBS. From 300,000 trips in 1989, daily MRT ridership had almost quadrupled to 1.1 million trips in 2001, netting SMRT an after-tax profit of $115.4 million for the year 2000. In 1998, SBS's 2,747 buses over 196 services garnered an after-tax profit of $39 million. With 670 buses, TIBS's after-tax profit for 1999 was $3.72 million. That year, SBS's share of the public transport market was 60 per cent, SMRT controlled 25 per cent, while TIBS had 15 per cent.

The conditions were ripe for mergers of a scale not seen in Singapore's history of movement since the formation of the SBS in 1973.

TRANSPORT GIANTS, MASS MOVEMENT

THE FIRST significant merger occurred in the taxi industry in 1995. Singapore Commuter, SBS Taxi, and SABS merged to form CityCab, which became the Republic's second largest taxi operator. NTUC Comfort, which had reorganised into Comfort Group, still led the pack with 9,000 taxis; CityCab was now second with 3,200 taxis, while there were about 2,000 Yellow Tops, and 500 taxis belonging to TIBS Taxis—TIBS had rolled out a cream-coloured taxi fleet in 1990. Eventually, the government decided to deregulate the industry and open it to market forces, ending a period of control dating back to the 1970s, when they dealt the death blow to pirate taxis. Taxi fares were deregulated in 1998, allowing taxi firms to set fares instead of the LTA; in 2003, deregulation was completed, allowing more taxi firms to enter the industry. These new firms included Premier Taxis, SMART Cab, and Trans-Cab in 2003, and Prime Taxi in 2007.[9]

The second merger happened in December 2001, when SMRT bought over 19-year-old TIBS and its fleet of 730 buses and 2,000 taxis for $194 million. TIBS' boldness in introducing new services and vehicles cannot be understated. In 1996, it rolled out articulated buses called Bendy Buses in Yishun and Woodlands; at 17.5 metres, 50 per cent longer than a standard bus, the air-conditioned, three-door bus became the longest public transport vehicle on the roads, capable of packing in 150 passengers. In the year 2000, TIBS launched an after-midnight bus service called the NightRider from Marina Centre to Yishun, offering a transport service between midnight and 3am far cheaper than a taxi. In the end, TIBS was absorbed into SMRT, which became Singapore's first multi-modal public transport company to run MRT lines, an LRT line, buses, and taxis. TIBS' bus operations became SMRT Buses, and its taxi fleet became SMRT Taxis; by 2005, their liveries were replaced by SMRT's colours of red, black, and grey.

The SBS was not resting on its laurels. In 1997, SBS Private Limited changed its name to DelGro Corporation, although the name "SBS" was kept for the bus industry. DelGro competed with TIBS for the tender to run a new MRT line, the North East Line—and won, becoming Singapore's second MRT operator. It also won the contracts to run two new LRT lines in Sengkang and Punggol towns. As SBS was no longer running just buses, in 2001, it was renamed SBS Transit. Then in 2003, Comfort Group merged with DelGro Corporation to become ComfortDelGro; Comfort Group also acquired CityCab. By 2005, ComfortDelGro had become Singapore's largest taxi operator with almost 70 per cent of all taxis; its fleet of 2,708 buses commanded 75 per cent of the bus industry and a daily ridership of 2.05 million; it ran an MRT line and two LRT lines—a transport titan to match SMRT. Their dominance persists today. No other company has the resources to simultaneously run rail, bus, and taxi operations.

A new device for paying for MRT and bus fares debuted in the year 2000. The LTA phased out the magnetic stored-value fare card, and replaced it with a tap-and-go, contactless smart card. The EZ-Link card allowed passengers to cross MRT fare gantries and board buses more quickly, since there was no longer a need to slot cards into gantries or ticketing machines.

The MRT system continued growing in size. In 2001 and 2002, three stations were added to the 26-station East West Line. Tanah Merah MRT Station became Singapore's fifth MRT interchange with the opening of the 6.4-km, $700-million Changi Airport Branch Line, making the East West Line (at 45.4 km) the longer of the two MRT lines in Singapore again. The branch line's first station had the working name of Somapah, after nearby Somapah Road, in turn named after Indian landowner Hunmah Somapah (died 1906); it eventually opened as Expo, after the neighbouring Singapore Expo, on 10 January 2001. On 18 October that year, Dover MRT Station opened; it was the first MRT station built over existing track. On 8 February the following year, the Changi Airport Branch Line's second station, Changi Airport MRT Station, opened inside Singapore's main international airport, allowing tourists to take the MRT directly to and from the airport.

The North East Line, Singapore's third and shortest MRT line at 20 km, opened on 20 June 2003, the culmination of 17 years of studies, planning, and construction—even as the North South and East West lines were being built. Early proposals conceptualised a line ending in two forks, one at Jalan Kayu, another at Punggol, but the former was eventually dropped.

The North East Line cost $4.6 billion, almost as much as the MRT's first 42 stations. It was Singapore's first fully underground MRT line with fully automated, driverless trains, and the first to be run by SBS Transit. The six-car trains were supplied by French multinational company Alstom.

The 16 stations started at HarbourFront—near the former Telok Blangah Village and Jardine's Steps—and ended at Punggol, connecting the Central Area with Serangoon, Hougang, Sengkang, and Punggol towns. Dhoby Ghaut overtook Raffles Place to become Singapore's deepest MRT station, with five underground levels. In all, Singapore's MRT network now had 65 stations, of which seven were interchanges, with 109.4 km of track.

While the rest of the North East Line opened in 2003, Woodleigh and Buangkok stations were mothballed. The Ministry of Transport explained that there were fewer than 2,000 housing units within 400 metres of each station, which did not justify opening them. Local residents, who were told of the mothballing just three days before the line opened, saw yet another example of profits being put before passengers' interests. In August 2005, just before a ministerial visit to the area, eight cardboard elephants were put up in protest around Buangkok MRT Station, a reference to the term "white elephant"—a daring move in a city-state where protests without permits are outlawed. After intense grassroots lobbying, Buangkok finally opened on 15 January 2006, two years before schedule—a decision that reportedly cost SBS Transit $1 million a year because of low passenger turnout. Interest in Woodleigh was not as keen, so it opened only on 20 June 2011—eight years after the rest of the line. In 2009, the Transport Ministry declared that it would no longer mothball completed MRT stations, perhaps to avoid stirring more popular discontent.

The rationalisation controversy continued, with SBS Transit withdrawing or re-routing 12 bus services a month after the opening of the North East Line. Between 1987 and 2006, more than 80 bus services across Singapore were removed because of the MRT. For many commuters, this meant longer travelling times or costlier trips.

Meanwhile, Singapore's aboveground LRT system also grew, with the completion of the 10.7-km, 14-station Sengkang LRT Line in 2003, and the 10.3-km, 15-station Punggol LRT Line in 2005, for a combined $656 million. Each line had an east loop and a west loop meeting at Sengkang and Punggol MRT stations respectively, which became interchanges. Forty-one train cars from Japanese engineering company Mitsubishi Heavy Industries were purchased for the lines.

While the Bukit Panjang LRT Line was built after much of the town and its road system, Sengkang and Punggol's lines came up before much of the towns. This absence of coordination in town planning meant the lines were opened in phases, with stations mothballed until enough housing units appeared. Sengkang's Kupang LRT Station opened on 27 June 2015, 10 years after the opening of the West Loop. The aboveground tracks and stations of the Punggol West Loop stood mothballed amidst secondary forest for nine years. They made a curious, post-apocalyptic sight in highly-urbanised Singapore. As of 2018, one station—Teck Lee—remained unopened.

AS SINGAPORE'S population climbed, so did pressure on its public transport infrastructure. When the MRT began operations in 1987, the city-state had a population of 2.775 million; by the time the North East Line opened in 2003, the population had swelled almost 50 per cent to

CHAPTER 7 1950 to 2011: Mergers and Laws 289

Construction of the Punggol LRT Line's West Loop was completed by 2005, but because much of Punggol town in the area was not built yet, the stations were mothballed for at least nine years. I took this photo of Samudera station in 2011—a curious sight of an LRT system lying in the midst of forest and bush. Samudera eventually opened in 2017. As of 2019, a road called Punggol Way ran below the station, but many blocks of flats around it were still under construction. (Source: Eisen Teo)

4.115 million. The government had to make the MRT network the backbone of Singapore's public transport system.

In 2009, another extension was added to the 29-station East West Line. The 3.8-km, $436-million Boon Lay Extension ran west from Boon Lay to Pioneer and Joo Koon MRT stations, connecting more of Jurong West town and Jurong Industrial Estate to the MRT network. Both opened on 28 February. After 19 years, Joo Koon replaced Boon Lay as the western terminus of the East West Line.

From the 1920s, the Municipality recognised the need for ring roads to connect major trunk roads concentrically; 70 years later, the government recognised the need for an orbital MRT line to connect existing MRT lines concentrically, allowing commuters to avoid the Central Area when transferring lines. The result was a circular MRT line that mirrored the Outer Ring Road.

As work on the North East Line was nearing completion in 2002, work started on the Circle Line, Singapore's fourth MRT line and its second fully-underground, automated, and driverless line. It had 28 stations over 33.3 km, with a price tag of $10 billion—Singapore's costliest line yet. However, unlike previous lines, stations accommodated three-car trains supplied by Alstom. The line opened in phases between 2009 and 2011, with Dhoby Ghaut Interchange as the eastern terminus and HarbourFront Interchange as the western terminus. Bras Basah overtook Dhoby Ghaut as the deepest station in the network at 35 metres below ground, but Dhoby Ghaut became the only interchange thus far to be the meeting point of three lines. A 2.4-km Marina Bay extension—from Promenade to Bayfront and Marina Bay—opened on 14 January 2012.

For the first time, the LTA engaged the public in naming the new stations. They put forward possible names for each station, then allowed the public to give feedback on these names through the internet. Alternative names were also welcomed. After considering the hundreds of responses, LTA then finalised the names and sent them to the Street and Building Names Board for final approval. Travellers could now draw upon their experiences of movement to suggest and vote for the names of portals for a new channel of movement—unprecedented in Singapore's history of movement, and a far cry from the days of municipal commissioners mulling over the names of roads.[10]

Further plans for MRT lines included the Bukit Timah Line, which would hug the historic Bukit Timah–Upper Bukit Timah trunk road and connect Bukit Panjang town to the Central Area; and the Eastern Region Line, a loop that would mirror the Pan Island Expressway and the East Coast–Upper East Coast arterial road. By 2005, the former was combined with part of the latter, meeting in the Central Area. The consolidated line was called the Downtown Line, Singapore's fifth MRT line, its third fully-underground, automated, and driverless line, and the world's longest line with automated and driverless trains. At 41.9 km and 34 stations, the Downtown Line is Singapore's most expensive ever, costing $20.7 billion. Like the Circle Line, its rolling stock comprised three-car trains, supplied by Changchun Bombardier Railway Vehicles, a Canadian-Chinese joint venture.

The Downtown Line opened in three phases from 2013 to 2017, with Bukit Panjang MRT Station as the western terminus and Expo Interchange as the eastern terminus. When Promenade's Downtown Line section opened in

2013, it overtook Bras Basah as the deepest MRT station in the network, at 42 metres below ground; however, Bencoolen trumped it by one metre when it opened in 2017. It takes five escalator rides to get from ground level to the train!

Twenty-five years after Marina Bay MRT Station opened, it ceased being the eastern terminus of the North South Line; on 23 November 2014, Marina South Pier MRT Station opened to serve its namesake. And on 18 June 2017, the four-station, 7.5-km Tuas West Extension extended the East West Line westward from Joo Koon to Tuas Link, connecting more of Tuas' industries to the MRT network.

As of 2018, Singapore's MRT network had 119 stations, of which 26 were interchanges, spread over 199.3 km of track. These stations are portals into a relatively fast, air-conditioned, generally comfortable form of travel, which can move a commuter from one end of the island to the other for at most $2.02. Because of the MRT's reach, speed, and general reliability, ridership has climbed as the network expanded. In 2002, a year before the North East Line opened, 1.081 million trips were made on the MRT every day; this climbed to 1.698 million in 2008 (before the Circle Line opened), 2.525 million in 2012 (just before the Downtown Line opened), and 3.302 million in 2018. Between 2002 and 2016, the number of MRT stations more than doubled, and Singapore's population grew by 34 per cent, resulting in MRT ridership almost tripling. Like bus interchanges, MRT stations have become spaces of continuous movement, intersections of a thousand paths.

MRT ridership may be booming, but the bus remains Singapore's most popular mode of public transport—from 3.197 million trips a day in 2002 to 4.037 million trips a day in 2018. Increased connectivity between MRT lines and buses has fostered the simultaneous growth of MRT and bus use.

From the turn of the century, air-conditioned bus interchanges were built seamlessly linked to adjoining MRT stations and shopping malls, allowing commuters to shop, eat, and travel easily. The bus-MRT infrastructural combo is called an Integrated Transport Hub (ITH). The first ITH was Toa Payoh, which opened in 2002, replacing the 16-year-old Toa Payoh Bus Interchange. The new bus interchange is integrated with Toa Payoh MRT Station and office complex HDB Hub. Singapore's second ITH was Sengkang in 2003, serving Sengkang town. As of 2018, there were nine ITHs—Ang Mo Kio, Bedok, Boon Lay, Bukit Panjang, Clementi, Joo Koon, and Serangoon make up the other seven. These infrastructural combos, which cut down on MRT-bus transfer times, were only possible because one authority—LTA—oversees the development of all transport infrastructure.

Considering the scale of construction works and daily operations for five MRT lines, major accidents have been few in the MRT's first 30 years of existence. The MRT's first train collision took place six years after its inception, on the morning of 5 August 1993. A maintenance train had accidentally spilled hydraulic oil onto the westbound tracks between Buona Vista and Clementi stations on the East West Line, causing passenger trains to overshoot Clementi station upon arrival. One train applied the emergency brakes, and had to stop at Clementi for longer than usual for the brakes to recharge; the train behind could not stop in time because of the oil. The resultant collision at 7.46am injured 156 commuters.

Eleven years later, at around 3.30pm on 20 April 2004, an MRT tunnel being constructed near Nicoll Highway MRT Station of the Circle

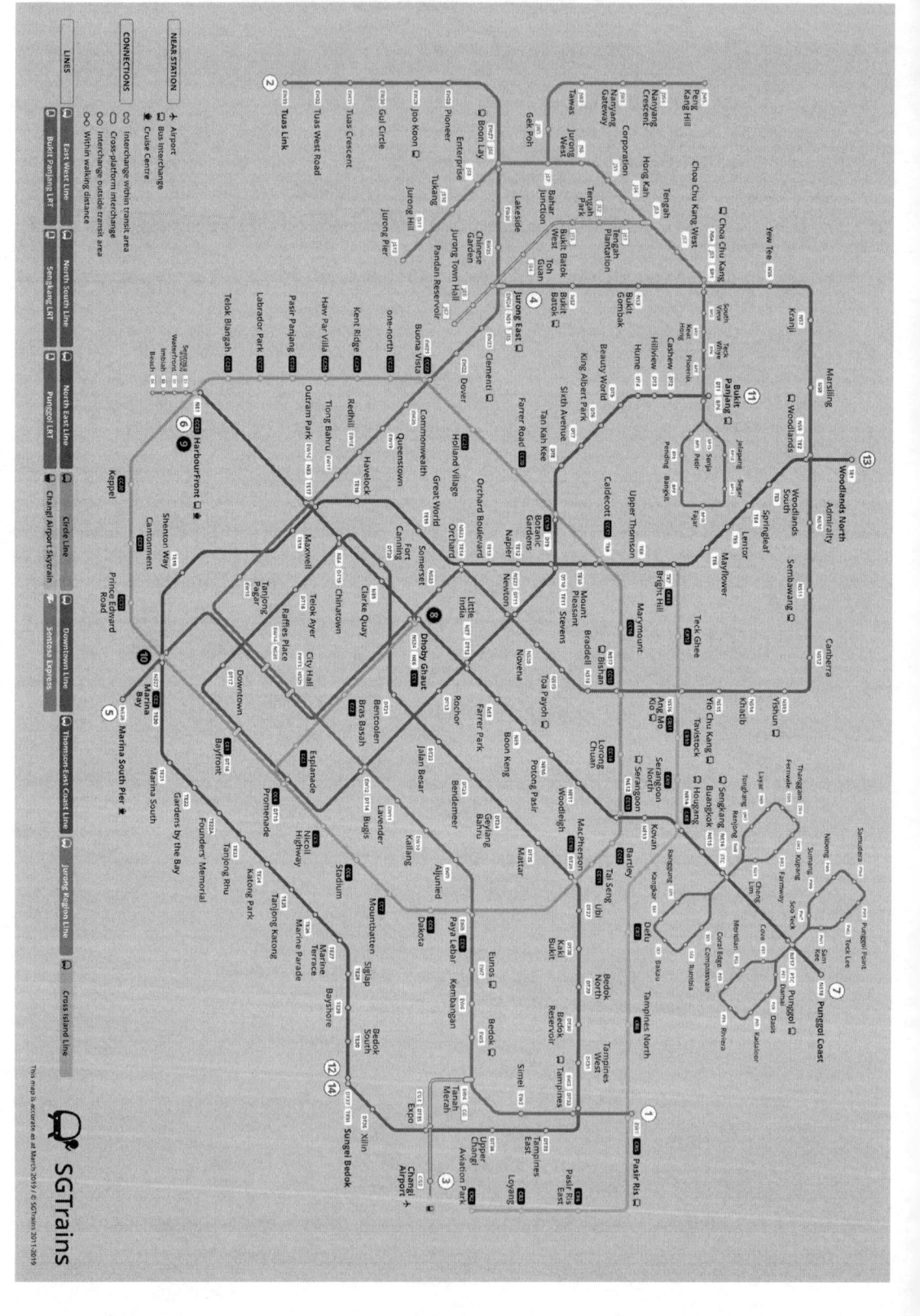

Singapore's MRT and LRT network as of March 2019, including the future Thomson–East Coast, Jurong Region, and Cross Island lines. (Source: SGTrains)

Singapore's Light Rapid Transit (LRT) system debuted in 1999, serving Bukit Panjang and Choa Chu Kang towns. This is a first-generation, rubber-tyred Bombardier Innovia train in double-car formation, pulling into Keat Hong LRT Station. (Source: Eisen Teo)

Singapore's Mass Rapid Transit (MRT) system moves millions every day. Spotted pulling into Admiralty MRT Station on the North South Line is a first-generation, six-car Kawasaki Heavy Industries C151 train that was introduced with the system in 1987. (Source: Eisen Teo)

The construction of MRT lines and stations is a monumental task, at least in scale and complexity. This is a view of the construction of the Downtown Line section of Little India MRT Interchange in 2013. Part of Bukit Timah Road (left) and Rochor Canal in front of the Land Transport Authority corporate headquarters (right) had to be diverted for tunnelling. The station opened in 2015. (Source: Eisen Teo)

Line collapsed after its retaining wall gave way. The cave-in was 30 metres deep, destroyed six lanes of Nicoll Highway, killed four workers, and injured three—Singapore's most serious MRT construction accident. Tremors hit nearby Golden Mile Complex and its residents had to be temporarily evacuated. The historic highway was not reopened until December that year and the station had to be shifted 100 metres away from the original site, delaying completion of the line for a year. It is easy to forget how monumental MRT construction projects can be—until something goes terribly wrong.

FORSAKEN BY THE "BOOK OF FATE"

THE GOVERNMENT saw the MRT and the bus as the future of movement in Singapore. Other methods of movement, not so.

The bullock cart was one of them. There were still 79 vehicles in 1952, but they were not allowed within the city limits. In 1954, there were still occasional newspaper articles about bullock cart drivers who were fined $1 to $25 by the court for riding their carts inside the City. By 1956, there were just four bullock carts left; we do not know what happened to them.

Bicycle numbers were not restricted, and the authorities eventually relinquished control over them. After WWII, bicycle registration persisted, each vehicle issued a metal registration plate attached to the back. From 110,733 in 1950, its numbers grew to 266,496 in 1960, 372,276 in 1970, and 570,000 by October 1981—when the Registry of Vehicles decided to cease registration to reduce paperwork.

As for the trishaw, in 1950, it was still the number two mode of public transport in Singapore, after buses. But it was downhill from there. Its numbers were capped at 7,000, and the authorities frowned upon it, thinking it antiquated. That year, the Trishaw Industry Proprietors and Manufacturers' Association applied to the Municipality for motor trishaws—the third such application since 1933. Again, the answer was a firm no.

Left on its own, the trishaw faltered. The urban revolution changed the face of the Central Area, resettling much of the trishaw's customer base; riders lost much of their frequent customers and old routes. Simultaneously, rival methods of movement such as the bus and the taxi progressed rapidly, convincing many travellers to switch from the trishaw. In 1956, the trishaw's numbers were cut to 5,000; by 1972, 3,300; and by 1983, there were just 1,000 left.

The trishaw experienced a mild comeback in the late 1970s, when younger men began plying their vehicles around tourist spots such as the Raffles Hotel and Orchard Road. They usually held other jobs and took tourists on rides only as a side line. Meanwhile, the old breed of riders, most of them over 55 years of age, avoided tourists, partly because of their lack of proficiency in the English language. Instead, their customer base comprised the local working class—housewives, small traders, schoolchildren, prostitutes—covering Chinatown, the Buffalo Road area around what is now Tekka Centre, Geylang, Katong, and Joo Chiat. Housewives heading to and from markets preferred trishaws to taxis because the former was cheaper, and used small lanes to accomplish swifter journeys. Trishaws offered the convenience of a taxi at the cost of a bus. These riders charged 60 cents to $1.50 for about 1 km, earning $10 a day. They had to retire at the age of 70, because from 1977, no one above that age was eligible for a trishaw licence.

Into the 1980s, rotten apples amongst the new breed of riders generated bad press for the

A relic of a bygone era. Trishaws once numbered in the thousands in the 1950s; today, there are only a handful left, existing because of the tourist trade. This photo was taken in 2015 outside Bugis Junction, near the junction of Victoria Street and Rochor Road. (Source: Eisen Teo)

trishaw—they charged tourists exorbitant fares. For example, they would agree on a fare of $3, but then take their passengers to a dark alley and demand $300. Other tricks included insisting later that an agreed price was in US dollars and not Singapore dollars, or that the quote price of "three-four" meant $34 and not $3.40. The Traffic Police and the Registry of Vehicles were forced to take these errant riders to task, and impose measures such as designating pick-up and drop-off points, colour-coding trishaws, and making riders don ID tags.

From 2001, the LTA stopped issuing new licences to individual trishaw riders. Instead, the only way to become a new rider was to do so under a trishaw operator licensed by the LTA and the Singapore Tourism Board. As of 2018, there was only one such licensed operator in Singapore—Trishaw Uncle, with a stable of 100 riders. They offered novelty tourist rides to popular locations such as Bugis, Little India, and the Singapore River. A 30-minute ride cost $39, and a rider could earn $1,200 a month. Other than them, there were perhaps a dozen or so freelance riders scouring the tourist areas in the Central Area—individuals who had acquired trishaw licences before 2001.

Once a chief method of movement during and after WWII, the trishaw has been reduced to nostalgia on wheels, a curious oddity in an era of motor vehicles and mass rapid transit. The tourist dollar has saved it from total extinction.

THE RAILWAY came to Singapore at a time when its colonial masters desired to connect its port to the resource-rich hinterland of Malaya. As the geopolitics and economics of the Malay Peninsula changed, the railway struggled to stay relevant, right to its very end.

Passenger demand for the railway within Singapore was never significant; far larger numbers took the trolleybus, motor bus, or rickshaw. After WWII, the Federated Malay States Railway (FMSR) still ran five suburban stations for passengers: Tanglin Halt (which had been shut in 1939, but reopened sometime between 1942 and 1945), Bukit Timah, Bukit Panjang, Kranji, and Woodlands. In April 1946, the FMSR closed Tanglin Halt, Bukit Panjang, and Kranji, allowing faster travel between Woodlands and Tanjong Pagar stations.

With the formation of the Federation of Malaya in 1948, the FMSR changed its name to the Malayan Railway Administration (MRA); five years after Malaya gained independence from Britain, in 1962, its name was changed again to Keretapi Tanah Melayu (KTM), or Malayan Railways. Even as Singapore was outside Malaya, the railway tracks and land in Singapore remained leased to the KTM; it had been leased to them in a 1918 ordinance for 999 years.

A vision of an alternate future flickered for a brief moment in November 1955, when suburban passenger train services were revived—but only because of the 142-day STC strike. The Ministry for Communications and Works worked with the MRA to run three passenger trains a day from Singapore to Johor Bahru, and two in the opposite direction. Other than Bukit Timah, four stations—Telok Blangah (formerly Alexandra Halt), Tanglin Halt, Bukit Panjang, and Kranji—were dusted off for passengers again. Passengers paid five cents a mile up to 65 cents, which relieved them of paying up to $3 for a pirate taxi. Free lorry services also connected the stations and selected locations, such as Collyer Quay, Waterloo Street, and Holland Village. Up to 2,000 people benefited from this arrangement, which resembled a present-day MRT station and feeder bus model. There was talk of this temporary service becoming a permanent fixture, but after the strike ended, it was discontinued, and all suburban stations were closed to passengers once again.

Official interest in the railway spiked when industrialisation came to Jurong from 1960. The Singapore government was keen on using the railway to transport raw materials from Malaya to Jurong, and send completed products the other way. This tied in with dreams of an eventual merger with Malaya. A freight-only Jurong Line was first announced in July 1960, together with plans for Jurong Industrial Estate. Work started in 1963, and the first trains ran from 12 November 1965. Singapore's Economic Development Board worked with the KTM on the infrastructure—the former built 22 culverts, eight steel bridges, and three tunnels, and reclaimed swamps and levelled hills, readying the landscape for 19 km of tracks. A main line ran west from Bukit Timah Railway Station under Clementi Road, through the wilderness of Ulu Pandan, under a roundabout at Upper Ayer Rajah Road and Jalan Ahmad Ibrahim, and separated into three branch lines snaking into Jurong Industrial Estate.

The authorities had high hopes for the Jurong Line, expecting 2–3 million tons of goods to be moved every year, but the line never reached its full potential. In the short five years between the announcement of the Jurong Line and its completion between 1960 and 1965, Singapore had merged with Malaya, then acrimoniously separated from it. Trade still continued between the two countries, but no longer was Malaysia the vast, rich hinterland as envisioned. The Singapore government largely left the Malaysia-owned KTM to its own devices, never engaging the operator in any grand transport plan.

In 1969 and 1970, the Automobile Association of Singapore suggested that the KTM line could take on new services to ferry passengers between the Central Area and Jurong via Queenstown, to relieve pressure on the roads and the beleaguered bus system. Again in 1979 and 1980, as studies for an MRT system in Singapore were nearing an end, there were public calls in Singapore for the KTM line to be upgraded to take on rapid transit cars, as it could be cheaper and swifter to implement than an MRT system. Nothing came of these suggestions as the KTM line did not belong to Singapore, and any modifications to the line required a revision of the 1918 ordinance, which specified that KTM's land in Singapore be used only for railway operations. This required years of complicated diplomatic negotiations between Singapore and Kuala Lumpur, whose relations were far from rosy.

It was not just Singaporeans who were thinking about greater involvement of the KTM line in Singapore transport. When the KTM launched a new two-car railbus service between Tanjong Pagar and Johor Bahru in 1984, it also pitched the idea of reviving passenger stops between the two stations. Even though the railbus was a hit with passengers, the idea never took off.

1987 saw the debut of the MRT system. Because the railway remained Malaysian, seamless integration with Singapore transport was almost impossible now. With the exception of crossings, KTM trains in Singapore travelled in a world of their own.

The Jurong Line lasted just three decades; in the mid-1990s, it quietly closed. Subsequently, the authorities removed most of its tracks. Scattered remnants remain—tunnels, a truss bridge, some rusting tracks—tucked away in the footnotes of Singapore's urban history.

Ultimately, Singapore coveted the 217 hectares of KTM land. On 27 November 1990, Singapore's Prime Minister Lee Kuan Yew and Malaysia's Finance Minister Daim Zainuddin signed a landmark Points of Agreement (POA), for the KTM to withdraw north to Woodlands and give up its railway land, in exchange for three parcels of Singapore land to be developed by a company owned 60 per cent by Malaysia and 40 per cent by Singapore. However, the two countries subsequently disagreed on the terms of the POA, and years passed without any progress.

In 1998, as per the terms of the POA, Singapore moved its Customs, Immigration and Quarantine (CIQ) facilities at Tanjong Pagar to Woodlands, expecting Malaysia to follow suit. This did not materialise. Hence, Malaysia-bound passengers at Tanjong Pagar experienced the curious phenomenon of being cleared by Malaysian customs for entry into Malaysia before being cleared by Singapore customs for exit from Singapore. Malaysian customs got around this by not stamping passports.

This unique cross-border experience lasted for another 13 years. Finally, on 20 September 2010, Singapore's Prime Minister Lee Hsien Loong and his Malaysian counterpart Najib Razak agreed on a deal to close the loop on the 1990 POA. KTM would retreat to Woodlands with its CIQ facilities by 1 July 2011, in exchange for two parcels of land in the Ophir-Rochor area, and four parcels in Marina South. A rapid transit system between Johor Bahru and Singapore would also be jointly developed.

It was the death knell for the small but tightly-knit community that had grown up in Tanjong Pagar Railway Station, where old-school Malaya melded with 21st-century Singapore. It included Habib Railway Bookstore, which had called the station its home since 1938. Ajimul Naseerullakhan, 35, a worker at the shop for more than 10 years, said: "I was very sad when I saw the news of the station's move. We have been here since my great-grandfather's time." There were also two 24-hour coffee shops named M. Hasan Railway Food Station and M. Hasan Railway Station Canteen, run by Indian migrants Mahmoodol Hasan, 66, and his younger brother, Masudul Hasan, 63. Said a taxi driver: "I know most of the vendors here and they are very friendly. This reminds me of kampung days back in the 1970s. The homely feeling is something I can feel here but not outside."

In 1913, *The Straits Times* wrote: "It is written in the book of fate that in the year 2000 Singapore will be one of the greatest railway termini in the world." Alas, on the night of 30 June 2011, hundreds thronged Tanjong Pagar Railway Station to take photos and videos of the last train pulling out of it. At the helm was Sultan Ibrahim Ismail of Johor, who had received training from the KTM. He had expressed a wish to commandeer the last train, since his great-grandfather Sultan Ibrahim had been present at the official opening of the Causeway in 1924. Earlier in the day, many also thronged Bukit Timah Railway Station to witness the final manual exchanges of key tokens between passing train drivers and station crew, an antiquated procedure granting permission to trains to proceed.

It was the end of an era of rail, one that lasted 108 years, a relic of a colonial system of political control and economic development. The tracks themselves were soon dismantled and returned to Malaysia. The sliver of land where the tracks once lay, surrounded by wilderness, was renamed the Rail Corridor.

The railway in Singapore had left its mark on urban development, which carefully circumvented

On the historic night of 30 June 2011, the last train pulled out of Tanjong Pagar Railway Station before it closed for good, ending a 108-year era of rail. (Source: Eisen Teo)

the railway tracks. An eastern stretch of the AYE runs parallel to the Rail Corridor. The corridor also makes up Queenstown town's western boundary, and separates Choa Chu Kang and Bukit Panjang towns.

Now that the Rail Corridor is no longer exclusively railway land, what will become of it? Fortunately, Singapore has entered a period in its history in which heritage is more valued by the authorities and the populace alike than any other time in its post-1965 history. As of 2018, there were no official plans to erase the Rail Corridor with urban development. Meanwhile, Bukit Timah and Tanjong Pagar railway stations have been given conservation status. The URA will convert the former into a heritage gallery by 2021, while the latter will be incorporated into the future Cantonment MRT Station, part of a three-station extension to complete the Circle Line by 2025—finally, an integration of old rail and new rail. Only time will tell if the Rail Corridor can survive the encroachment of urbanisation, but for now, some of Singapore's railway heritage is here to stay.

CHAPTER NOTES

1   The original road around the 8th Milestone was first renamed Jalan Woodbridge between 1963 and 1966 after nearby Woodbridge Hospital, a facility for the mentally ill. After the facility was relocated to the present Institute of Mental Health at Buangkok View, Jalan Woodbridge was renamed Gerald Drive in 1998, after neighbouring Gerald Crescent. In turn, Gerald Crescent was named in 1953 after Gerald Mugliston, chairman of the Bukit Sembawang Rubber Company.

2   Ten Mile Junction LRT Station of the Bukit Panjang LRT Line, which opened in 1999, closed for good on 13 January 2019 due to low ridership. It was converted into a holding and testing area for rolling stock of the LRT system.

3   Nepal Circus is an oddity—it curves out from and back to Portsdown Road. It originally connected Portsdown Road and North Buona Vista Road, but between 1981 and 1984, the latter was straightened, bypassing the circus altogether, removing the circus' raison d'être. Somehow, the circus was never expunged.

4   Park and Ride did not take off. Most either drove or took public transport the whole way. The last City Shuttle Service was withdrawn in 2007, and the LTA ceased Park and Ride in 2016.

5   By 1984, Tampines Way was renamed Hougang Avenue 3, part of Hougang New Town. The bus terminal has been demolished, replaced by a bus stop next to Hougang Community Club. As of 2018, there was no direct bus service between that bus stop and Shenton Way.

6   As of 2018, the Taman Jurong Radiophone Taxi Service was still going strong. It had 140 drivers, and its taxi kiosk at Yung Kuang Road received about 300 calls a day.

7   As of 2018, of 119 station names, 56 were in English or of English origin, 41 were of Malay origin, 18 were of Chinese origin, two were Chinese-Malay hybrids, one was of Indian origin, and one was Italian. Twenty-five names (one in five) were of places named after people, but only one—Tan Kah Kee—was directly named after a person for whom there was no existing toponym.

8   The place name Maxwell made a comeback eventually—it became the name of Station TE18 of the Thomson–East Coast Line, located next to the Jinrikisha Station at the junction of South Bridge Road, Maxwell Road, Tanjong Pagar Road, and Neil Road.

9   In 2013, SMART Cab's operator licence was not renewed by LTA. In 2018, HDT Singapore Taxi became Singapore's seventh taxi operator, managing a fleet of electric taxis.

10 Public consultation exercises for the Downtown and Thomson-East Coast lines have given commuters more say. There was a two-step process: LTA called for suggestions, then worked with the Street and Building Names Board (SBNB) to shortlist up to three names per station. The names were put to an internet vote; the results were sent to the SBNB for final approval.

CONCLUSION:
Speed and Slowness

IN *THE History Manifesto*, historians Jo Guldi and David Armitage write: "History explained communities to themselves. It helped rulers to orient their exercise of power... it provided citizens with the coordinates by which they could understand the present and direct their actions towards the future." The same applies to a history of movement from ancient times to the present. By focusing on the *longue durée* and constructing a narrative over hundreds of years, weaving stories of channels, methods, patterns, and experiences of movement, I have shown connections spanning the geological past to the dawn of the 21st century.

Before 1880, the predominant form of movement in Singapore was by foot. In 1880, the reign of mass public transport began with the arrival of the rickshaw from China, fuelled by cheap labour also from China. The early 1920s saw the start of the reign of motor vehicles and motor cars; public transport began to transition from predominantly animal and human-powered vehicles to motor vehicles, largely in the form of trolleybuses, motor buses, and mosquito buses. The Japanese Occupation of 1942–1945 was an interregnum, when the tide of motor vehicles temporarily receded for human-powered vehicles. After 1945, a second reign of motor vehicles and cars began. In 1987, a new phase of mass public transport began with the arrival of the MRT.

From 1819 to the 1950s, the colonial authorities mostly left movement to market forces—with the exception of the Japanese Occupation, when movement was nationalised. From the 1960s, the post-independence government became deeply involved with movement.

Does this mean Singapore's history of movement is a history of progress in the endeavour to move between Point A and Point B? Yes and no. In his book *What Is History?*, E. H. Carr argued that progress does not have a beginning or an end, and it does not mean equal and simultaneous advancement for all. Likewise, Singapore's history of movement is not a straightforward narrative of uniform progress. For channels of movement, we have seen how hundred-year-old trunk roads, once vital for travel into the interior, were expunged for new towns. Different methods of movement entered Singapore at different points in time; some prospered, then receded in reach; others disappeared altogether. For patterns of movement, peak-period congestion has existed in and around the Central Area since the 1920s, but exact locations and timings have shifted over time, depending on the building of arterial roads and expressways, and the introduction and evolution of the ALS and ERP. As for experiences of movement, travelling times have not necessarily become shorter as methods of movement increased in speed; instead, many commuters travel longer distances for work within the same times. The rush hour, be it on trolleybuses along Upper Serangoon Road in the 1930s, or on the North South Line or the CTE in 2019, remains very much a stressful, unpleasant experience. And as the second decade of the 21st century has shown, Singapore's history of movement is as colourful, chequered, and full of twists and turns as ever.

THE CAR-LITE DRIVE

SINGAPORE IS car-heavy, no doubt about it. In 1913, there were just 535 private cars in Singapore; in 2014, this number had grown by more than a thousand-fold to 600,176. But that year, the government made an unprecedented declaration: it wanted the Republic to become "car-lite". Launching the Sustainable Singapore Blueprint on 8 November 2014, Prime Minister Lee Hsien Loong declared: "We have to rely less on cars on the road, because we can't keep building… more roads for more cars." He was right. At the time, roads already made up 12 per cent of land use in Singapore—just behind housing, which took up 14 per cent.

There are many roads to a car-lite Singapore. Some entail greater governmental involvement, such as expanding the MRT network and growing the public bus fleet. Conversely, the government has tried to steer clear of hindering the spread of private-hire cars, bicycles, and personal mobility devices (or PMDs, comprising electric scooters or e-scooters, kick-scooters, hoverboards, and unicycles). In 2013, 63 per cent of peak period trips were by public transport; the government aims to bump this up to 75 per cent by 2030, and at least 85 per cent into the 2050s.

Meanwhile, car-friendly infrastructural projects such as the Singapore Underground Road System (SURS) were scrapped. SURS was conceptualised in the late 1980s as a 30-km, underground ring-road system around the fringe of the Central Area, to complement the Inner Ring Road. However, in August 2017, the LTA and the URA binned SURS. Singapore was shifting to a car-lite society, they declared, and the city centre was already well-served by a comprehensive public transport network.

A few months later in February 2018, the LTA implemented zero growth on the Vehicle Quota System. This meant no increase in the number of COEs in Singapore for the first time in the system's 28 years. The rate of growth had been declining for years, from three per cent in the system's early years, to 0.25 per cent in recent years. This has caused the number of private cars to decline by more than nine per cent from a peak of 607,292 in 2013, to 551,575 in 2018. If zero growth continues, 100,000 families—around 400,000 people—who had access to a private car in 2013 could lose it by 2023. They could contribute an additional one million trips on trains and buses every day.

But can public transport cope?

The MRT was supposed to be the engine powering the car-lite drive. When "car-lite" became a thing in 2014, 2.762 million trips were made every day on the MRT, and in terms of the combined factors of capacity, speed, connectivity, and the price of a trip, the MRT as public transport was unbeatable. However, not all was well. After its debut in 1987, it became Singapore's pride, a bright symbol of the young Republic's technological advancement. But as the system aged, it shed its lustre with alarming speed. After the turn of the century, trains became more and more packed; during peak periods on the North South and East West lines—the system's oldest lines—it became normal to have to wait for two or three trains to be able to board. Breakdowns and delays increased in frequency and severity, disrupting thousands. The proliferation of social media brought greater attention to each incident. In the eyes of many Singaporeans, the MRT was reduced to an embarrassment. Frustration on a national level was exacerbated because many relied on it for daily travel with no alternatives.

In December 2011, the MRT experienced its worst service disruptions in its 24-year history—three breakdowns over five days, on 13, 15, and 17 December. The most serious incident on the 15th stranded 127,000 commuters during the evening peak period, after services in both directions between Bishan MRT Interchange and Marina Bay MRT Station on the North South Line were disrupted for five hours due to a power failure. The third breakdown on the 17th over a similar stretch of line affected 94,000 commuters over five hours. The disruptions prompted the government to appoint a Committee of Inquiry, which uncovered significant shortcomings in SMRT Corporation's maintenance regime. Chief executive Saw Phaik Hwa was criticised for focusing on growing SMRT's retail business instead of engineering during her nine years in charge; she resigned not long after, to be replaced by former Chief of Defence Force Desmond Kuek.

The problems did not stop with her exit; almost a decade of neglect, and years of overloaded trains, took their toll on ageing infrastructure. On 7 July 2015, a power trip during the evening peak period shut down much of the North South and East West lines in both directions for 3½ hours, stranding 250,000 commuters.

Another unprecedented "achievement" was to follow on 7 October 2017, exactly a month shy of the MRT's 30th anniversary. Following torrential rain, the North South Line tunnels between Bishan and Braddell stations flooded for the first time, causing a 21-hour, overnight shutdown of train services between Ang Mo Kio and Newton stations, affecting 231,000 commuters. Investigations by the LTA and SMRT revealed a lack of proper maintenance, audits, and supervision; tunnels had flooded because the team responsible for maintaining the storm water sump pit and pump system at Bishan had neglected its duties, and worse, falsified maintenance records for almost a year.

More ignominious history was to be made. Just weeks after the flooding, on 15 November 2017, a train at Joo Koon station on the East West Line suffered a signalling fault. A second train, carrying 517 passengers, pulled up behind it. A minute later, the second train unexpectedly accelerated and rear-ended the first train, injuring 38—only the second MRT collision in Singapore's history. A software failure in the signalling system was the cause. Both LTA and SMRT were criticised for being slow in reporting the full severity of the incident, even describing the collision as one train "coming into contact" with another in their initial media releases.

The MRT's decline in standards, despite immense public reliance on it for daily long-distance travel, has made it, and by extension the transport ministerial portfolio, a political hot potato. Raymond Lim became Transport Minister in 2006; he lasted only one term of five years before relinquishing the portfolio. (Former Prime Minister Lee Kuan Yew once told him helming the portfolio was a "thankless job".) Lim was replaced by Rear-Admiral Lui Tuck Yew, who lasted just four years, during which major train disruptions grew in frequency. As for the chief executive position of SMRT, Kuek lasted just five-and-a-half years before resigning in April 2018. Months before, he admitted to not being able to resolve "deep-seated cultural issues" within the organisation, which led to a lack of accountability and ownership of problems.

The weekday peak period MRT is not for the faint-hearted. This photo of the Circle Line platform in Bishan MRT Interchange—a major interchange with the North South Line—was taken on a Thursday, 7 March 2019, at 7.50am. I cross this platform every workday—and this crowd size is the norm. (Source: Eisen Teo)

But even as the MRT system struggles with infrastructural wear and tear and organisational rot, it is set to grow. The 32-station, 43-km Thomson–East Coast Line will open in six stages from 2019 to 2025, connecting Woodlands, Ang Mo Kio, Bishan, and Toa Payoh towns, and the regions of Katong, Marine Parade, Siglap, and Changi, to the Central Area and Marina South. The 24-station, 24-km Jurong Region Line will open from 2026 to 2028, a regional line connecting parts of Jurong West, Choa Chu Kang, Tengah, and Bukit Batok to the rest of the MRT system. Construction for Stage 1 of Singapore's eighth MRT line, the Cross Island Line, will begin in 2020; the whole line should open by 2030. Like the East West Line, it will cross the island from Changi to Jurong. In all, the MRT network is set to grow in length from close to 200 km in 2018 to 360 km by 2030. However, new MRT lines are not being built fast enough to meet surging demand, especially during peak periods. Even if an MRT line is conceived in planners' minds tomorrow, it could take an average of close to 13½ years before it becomes reality. The car-lite push is commendable, and a pivotal moment in Singapore's history of movement, but it will not work if public transport is not ready to meet the growth in commuter numbers.

Fortunately, the public bus system has fared significantly better than the MRT in recent years, thanks again to timely government intervention. In September 2012, as SBS Transit and SMRT struggled to cope with rising demand for bus services, the LTA launched the Bus Service Enhancement Programme (BSEP), adding 1,000 government-funded buses to the companies' combined fleet of 4,500 over five years at a cost of $1.1 billion. The additional buses were put to work on 80 new routes, and 218—or 70 per cent—of existing routes, raising trip frequencies and cutting back on waiting times and overcrowding.

At first, some criticised the government for using taxpayers' money to purchase vehicles that should have been paid for by SMRT and SBS Transit. However, in 2014, the LTA introduced a new Bus Contracting Model (BCM), once again transforming the bus industry. Under this model, the government takes over ownership of all buses and bus infrastructure, and contracts out packages of routes for operators to run. For each package, operators—both local and overseas—can bid for a five-year contract; the winning operator will be paid a fixed fee to manage the routes, maintain the buses and infrastructure, and ensure service standards are met. All revenue goes back to the government; this way, it takes over revenue risks. This is not full nationalisation—the government does not operate the routes. But the BCM allows the LTA to respond more quickly to changes in ridership patterns; also, operators can focus on service and maintenance, and not worry about meeting revenue targets, a key source of criticism in the past. No longer will commuters have their favourite bus route removed because an operator was not making enough money off them.

The LTA separated Singapore's bus routes into 14 regions, each served by 300–500 buses. Since 2016, four packages have been put up for tender: two (Seletar and Bukit Merah, 44 routes in all) went to SBS Transit; one (Bulim in Jurong West, 26 routes) was won by Tower Transit Singapore, part of British-based Tower Transit Group; another (Loyang, 25 routes) was bagged by Go-Ahead Singapore, a subsidiary of the Go-Ahead Group, also from Britain. Tower Transit and Go-Ahead are Singapore's third and fourth bus operators respectively, and their debuts in 2016 marked the entries of the first overseas-based public transport companies in Singapore since the Singapore

Traction Company in 1925. But their presence in Singapore is still small compared to incumbents SBS Transit and SMRT—the former ran 208 routes in 2017, the latter, 106 in 2016.

To ease the bus industry into the BCM, the incumbents SBS Transit and SMRT were allowed to keep 10 of the 14 packages for up to 2021 to 2026, whereupon they would be up for tender too. After 2026, most public buses in Singapore would be owned by the authorities—a scenario not seen since the Japanese Occupation.

The BCM is commendable because bus companies can now focus on serving commuters. As long as the LTA is competent, the bus industry has the ability to handle future commuter demand. A similar model, the New Rail Financing Framework, has been applied to the MRT system—the government has taken over all rail assets, such as trains and signalling systems, from SMRT and SBS Transit, freeing them to focus on service and maintenance. In 2016, LTA paid SMRT $1.06 billion for its assets on the North South, East West, Circle, and Bukit Panjang lines; two years later, it paid SBS Transit $30.8 million for its assets on the North East, Sengkang, and Punggol lines. However, unlike the BCM, SMRT and SBS Transit pay licensing fees in return for a share of fare revenue. Also, their contracts to operate the rail lines last 15 years—although this is already a significant reduction from the previous licence period of 30 to 40 years. It remains to be seen if this will improve rail performance in the same manner the BCM has boosted the bus industry.

Meanwhile, Singapore's taxi industry has been upended by a new, yet almost identical method of movement—the private-hire car. The global spread of touchscreen smartphones and apps from 2007 paved the way for the formation of ride-hailing companies. These companies create apps that make use of a smartphone's Global Positioning System and mobile broadband access to connect a network of drivers to a network of commuters. In 2009, UberCab, later renamed Uber, was founded in San Francisco. In 2012, Malaysians Anthony Tan and Tan Hooi Ling founded GrabTaxi, later Grab, to connect taxi drivers to commuters; the service GrabCar for private-hire drivers was launched in 2014. Both Uber and Grab entered Singapore in 2013; their impact was immediate. In 2014, Singapore's combined taxi fleet hit an all-time high of 28,736; by the end of 2017, it had shrunk to 23,140. Over the same period, Uber and Grab's private-hire car fleets had outgrown the taxi fleet by more than two times—46,903. A Public Transport Council survey conducted in 2017 revealed that 70 per cent of commuters took a private-hire car ride in the last seven days, compared to just 30 per cent of commuters for a taxi ride.

The force behind Uber and Grab's devastating success was billions of dollars in venture capital, which allowed them to throw incentives at both drivers and commuters; in 2017 alone, Uber lost nearly $1.5 billion every quarter. Financially, taxi companies could not compete. The government has also helped by largely staying out of the picture, avoiding stifling regulations—perhaps because of the car-lite push; after all, a robust private-hire car industry may persuade more people to give up their cars. Commuters have mostly benefited. They have more travel choices; they can order rides to their doorstep; fares can be fixed beforehand; and drivers' service standards have generally improved since apps allow commuters to grade them. While some taxi drivers have complained about Uber and Grab stealing their lunch, most of the taxi companies

In the 1930s, public buses came in a flood of colours. Today, all "SG Buses" under the Bus Contracting Model get a standard livery of "Lush Green". These vehicles spotted in Woodlands Temporary Bus Interchange are a MAN A95 double-decker bus, capacity 139 (82 seating, 57 standing), introduced in 2017; and a Mercedes-Benz O530 Citaro single-decker bus, capacity 88 (37 seating, 51 standing), introduced between 2015 and 2017. Large, spacious, sleek, and well-maintained, they are a far cry from the "mosquito buses" of a century ago. (Source: Eisen Teo)

First introduced in 1996, Bendy Buses remain the longest public transport vehicles on the roads. This is a MAN A24 at 18 metres in length, capacity 131 (51 seating, 80 standing), introduced between 2013 and 2015. (Source: Eisen Teo)

have collaborated with them; for example, in March 2017, Grab partnered five taxi companies in pooling their vehicles under one booking platform called JustGrab.

It remains to be seen if the good times will last. In March 2018, after five bloody years of battle, Uber shocked its fans in Southeast Asia by withdrawing from the region of 620 million people, selling its business there to Grab. Almost immediately, Grab drivers and commuters in Singapore complained about cutbacks in driving and riding incentives—to be expected, as Grab now controlled the lion's share of the private-hire car industry. Meanwhile, rival apps like Ryde, Tada, and Go-Jek have tried to fill the vacuum left behind by Uber. Will the government now lay its "big visible hand" on the ride-hailing industry? We will have to wait and see.

Part of the car-lite push also involves improving first- and last-mile connectivity, usually the journey between one's doorstep and the nearest MRT station or bus stop. To this end, the government has encouraged "active mobility"—cycling and using PMDs. In 2017, the LTA set a target of five to 10 years to grow the number of people using bicycles or PMDs by four times—a target they look set to achieve.

Bicycle-sharing has helped. It entered Singapore in January 2017 on the back of smartphone apps, which use GPS to display the locations of bicycles for short-term hire; again, like with ride-hailing, the government avoided heavy-handed regulations. Singapore-based oBike started with 1,000 bicycles; 15 months later, their fleet had grown to around 50,000 bicycles, with a million reported users. oBike was closely followed by Mobike and ofo, companies headquartered in Beijing, and Singapore-based GBikes and SG Bike. By April 2018, there were around 100,000 bicycles available for sharing at rates of 25–50 cents per 15 minutes—so successful that a government-backed bicycle-sharing scheme was scuttled.

A successful cycling network also needs proper infrastructure—bicycle paths and crossings, racks for parking, ramps to go up overhead bridges. Under the National Cycling Plan released in 2010, a 700-km, island-wide cycling network will be completed by 2030, with every HDB town getting their own intra-town network. Almost 80 years after the 1938 Trimmer Committee's suggestion of bicycle lanes, historic Bencoolen Street was revamped with a dedicated cycling lane in 2017, the first road in the Central Area to have one.[1] And original plans for an $8-billion, 21.5-km North–South Expressway to run from Woodlands in the north to the East Coast Parkway in the south, were redrawn to incorporate dedicated bus and cycling lanes; when completed in 2026, the North–South Corridor will be Singapore's first expressway with such car-lite features.

However, much of this infrastructure will appear in the future. In 2018, the sight of shared bicycles littering pavements, bus stops, and other public spaces around the island indicated a dearth of docking spaces, poor bicycle-sharing etiquette, and a saturated bicycle-sharing market. In March, the LTA belatedly imposed licensing requirements on the industry, setting standards such as capping the number of bicycles offered by a firm and ensuring users do not park indiscriminately. Then, an astonishing collapse.

First, oBike abruptly exited the industry, leaving 220,000 users with $9 million in unrefunded deposits. GBikes and ofo subsequently ceased operations in Singapore; Mobike then applied to withdraw from the market in March 2019, leaving only SG Bike and Anywheel as viable operators with just 4,000 bicycles. Meanwhile, most roads in Singapore have no dedicated cycling lanes, and parts of intra-town cycling networks consists of existing pavements, which means cyclists and pedestrians have to jostle for space. And they have been joined by another method of movement that only appeared around 2013 or 2014: PMDs.

At first, there were not many users, as PMDs were not allowed on roads, pavements, or park connectors. In 2014, the Traffic Police said: "Singapore's footways are not wide enough for shared purposes. Given (PMDs') construction and their ability to move at higher speeds, the risk of collision resulting in serious injuries to the users as well as pedestrians is significant." However, enforcement was lax. PMDs, which could be had for a few hundred dollars, started appearing everywhere; the car-lite push started, and the government began considering PMDs to enhance first and last-mile connectivity.

The point of no return came in January 2017, when Parliament passed the Active Mobility Act for PMDs and bicycles, which effectively legalised PMDs on footpaths and shared paths, and electric bicycles on shared paths and roads. The Act also introduced limits on the speeds, sizes, and weights of PMDs, penalties for reckless behaviour and injuring others, and a code of conduct, such as giving way to pedestrians, slowing down when approaching bus stops, and walking devices in crowded areas. However, it took 16 months for the authorities to commence active enforcement of the Act in May 2018, during which the incidence of accidents involving PMDs on public paths escalated. From 19 accidents in 2015, there were 42 in 2016, 132 in 2017, and 251 in 2018—an increase of 13 times over just three years.

In its eagerness to go car-lite, the authorities have allowed at least 40,000 PMDs to take over the pavements—pedestrians' final domain—and render them unsafe for pedestrians, without first setting up a proper regulatory framework, or ensuring existing infrastructure can handle demand. As of mid-2018, PMD users were not required to go for safety riding courses or pass riding tests; riding a PMD required no licence or registration; speed limits for PMDs were 25 km/h for shared paths and 15 km/h for footpaths—far faster than a sprinting pedestrian. Being hit by an e-scooter at 15 km/h packs a force nine times that of an average person's punch. It remains to be seen whether stricter regulations and enforcement will be able to unravel the chaos plaguing the pavements.

THE ROAD AHEAD

A SURVEY of Singapore's history of movement over hundreds of years reveals numerous parallels in history, which further reinforces my argument that it is not a straightforward narrative of uniform progress.

Parallel 1: For hundreds of years, most travellers in Singapore went around on foot. As motor vehicles started to proliferate from the 1910s, pedestrians began to be chased off the roads. The separation of motor vehicles from pedestrians was completed in the 1970s with the island-wide construction of pavements. In the 2010s, as PMDs, electric bicycles, and shared bicycles started to proliferate, pedestrians began to be crowded out of pavements.

Parallel 2: Public transport in Singapore has continuously seen new methods of movement, or modifications of existing methods of movement, upend established norms. In the 1880s, rickshaws became an instant success, leaving the gharry and steam tram trailing in its wake. From the 1910s to the 1930s, mosquito buses contributed to the demise of the electric tram, and frustrated trolleybus operators. From the 1940s to the early 1970s, pirate taxis nearly overwhelmed the legitimate taxi industry; their next threat came in the 2010s with the rise of private-hire cars. Each time, the success of a transport "disruptor" indicated significant traveller demand that was not being met—until the arrival of said method of movement.

Parallel 3: Steam trams were novel in the 1880s because they ran on dedicated tracks. However, the tracks were laid on existing roads, which allowed other vehicles to cross, affecting the tram's efficiency. The railway train also had dedicated tracks, but as the tracks avoided built-up areas, ridership was not high. Since 1987, the MRT has dedicated tracks running through urban areas, so it has more than attained its potential of moving millions of commuters every day.

Parallel 4: Mosquito buses were on-demand vehicles that (generally) allowed passengers to get on and disembark anywhere within a driver's operating area for an affordable price. About 80 years after they were forced off the roads, in 2017, the LTA called a tender to develop on-demand public bus services. The services would allow commuters to use a smartphone app to request pick-ups and drop-offs at any bus stop within an operating area, instead of relying on fixed timetables or routes, allowing for shorter waiting and travelling times—the same factors that had made mosquito buses so attractive.

Parallel 5: The Chinese bus companies carved rural Singapore into different regions. LTA's Bus Contracting Model of 2014 also divided Singapore into 14 regions, for which public bus companies can bid to run services.

Parallel 6: The 19th-century trunk road system connected travellers in the Municipality to the furthest corners of Singapore Island. Its mantle was passed to the expressway system, which presently connects motorists between the Central Area and towns spread around the island.

Parallel 7: The Outer Ring Road was completed in 1940 as an orbital road connecting different trunk roads running like the spokes of a wheel. The Circle Line opened about 70 years later as an orbital MRT line connecting different MRT lines running like the spokes of a wheel.

What lessons can we glean from Singapore's history of movement, then?

Lesson 1: The flourishing or decline of a method of movement during a period in history depends on these factors: (a) its speed; (b) geographical reach; (c) the percentage of the distance of a trip it can cover; (d) affordability to the general population; (e) the presence of competing methods of movement; (f) the level of governmental involvement. For public transport, there are three more factors: (g) the level of service it provides; (h) ease of access (for example, if I need a taxi, how easy is it for me to get hold of one); (i) the ability of the entity running it to ensure revenue meets costs. These explain why certain methods of movement looked good on paper, but failed in reality. For instance, the steam tram was generally affordable, but faced stiff competition from the rickshaw, which was fatal to its bottom line, and its geographical reach was limited. The Kranji Electric Line of 1891 did not get off the ground because it had only one backer, who might have run out of interest or funds or both. The first two public motor bus services of 1906 and 1907 petered out because there were too few buses plying routes of low demand. These methods of movement either arrived at the wrong time, or before their time.

Lesson 2: Before a new method of movement enters Singapore, both the infrastructure to handle it, and the appropriate regulatory framework to oversee its use, must be in place first. Otherwise, there will be chaos, even injuries and deaths. Examples from history abound—rickshaws, mosquito buses, and of course, the motor car. Its numbers climbed exponentially from the 1910s to 1941, and again from 1945, but for decades, roads were devoid of traffic lights, white lines, and pedestrian crossings, and laws and enforcement were lax. The result? The killing and maiming of thousands every year. Now history has repeated itself with the authorities belatedly coming in with regulations for the bicycle-sharing industry and PMDs, after they have taken over the pavements and other public spaces. The only consolation is that the casualty rate is much lower.

Lesson 3: Singapore's channels of movement have almost always grown in number and total length to meet the demands of the dominant mode of private transport at the time. In the 1800s, roads in the Town had to be continuously maintained to sustain the rigours of horse carriage traffic. But it was the motor car that spurred the building of roads (and expressways) for over a hundred years to the present—roads now take up 12 per cent of Singapore's land area. It was only in 2014 that the government acknowledged this could not go on indefinitely. If all 2.62 million of Singapore's resident population aged 20 to 64 owned a car, we would need 30.2 square km of parking space—almost as large as the Central Catchment Area.

Lesson 4: Peak period congestion in and around the Central Area has come about ever since (a) significant populations have moved out of the Central Area; (b) animal and human-powered methods of movement began to be replaced en-masse by motorised methods of movement; (c) the ratio of mass public transport vehicles (such as rickshaws) to private transport vehicles (such as motor cars) has dropped, and reversed. And this peak period congestion has never gone away.

Lesson 5: For mass public transport that requires expensive infrastructure and vehicles, the government should pay for it as a public good; companies with a profit motive should only run the services and maintain the infrastructure and vehicles. We have seen how the steam and electric tram systems gave way under high overhead costs such as replacing tracks; the current bus and rail financing models have freed up bus and rail companies such as SMRT and SBS Transit to focus on serving commuters.

Lesson 6: The first method of movement in Singapore that drastically slashed the time it took to travel anywhere was the motor car. The next method of movement which drastically slashed the time it took to travel anywhere was the MRT.

So where do we go from here?

According to *The History Manifesto*, "thinking with history… may help us to choose which institutions to bury as dead and which we might want to keep alive". Singapore's history of movement can offer solutions to problems plaguing the city-state in the present. And there are quite a few. For methods of movement: too many cars, and the cars are too expensive; the trains and buses are packed during peak periods, and even outside the peak periods. For channels of movement: the road and expressway networks are not sufficient to handle peak period congestion, and there are physical limits to expanding these networks further. For patterns of movement: peak period congestion in and around the Central Area, and on arterial roads and expressways, shows no signs of abating, and these peak periods are growing in length.

My solutions, based on a study of Singapore's history of movement:

Solution 1: Depart from history and get rid of Singapore's century-old car culture once and for all. The car-lite push and zero growth for COEs are small steps in the right direction. For long-lasting effect, the number of private cars in Singapore should be progressively cut by two-thirds, from 551,575 in 2018 to around 200,000, a figure surpassed back in 1984. This would also reduce the total number of motor vehicles in Singapore by a third—instantly reducing peak hour congestion, and removing pressure to further expand the island's road and expressway networks. However, keep the COE and its high prices for at least another 10–15 years to defray the costs of building more public transport infrastructure. COE prices would no longer be determined by bidding, but artificially set by the government as a tax. To determine who gets a COE, use a needs-based points system. Points could be awarded for household size, the number of young and elderly dependents, distance of household address from the Central Area, and so on. This way, people with the greatest needs, not the deepest pockets, get access to a limited pool of private cars.

Solution 2: Since fewer travellers have access to cars, significantly expand the MRT, bus, and taxi networks. The greatest efforts should be expended on the MRT, because it has its own dedicated channel of movement, and it greatly increases the mobility of residents living near stations. On top of lines currently being planned or built, at least another four MRT lines should be built over the next 10–15 years: (a) a Nanyang Line connecting Nanyang Technological University, the towns of Jurong West, Clementi, and Queenstown, and Orchard MRT Interchange; (b) a Seletar–Jurong Line connecting Seletar Airport, the towns of Sengkang, Serangoon, and Toa Payoh, Pek Kio, Dhoby Ghaut MRT Interchange, Tanglin, Bukit Batok town, Jurong, and Tuas; (c) a North Shore Line connecting Kranji, the towns of Woodlands, Yishun, Punggol, and Pasir Ris, Changi Village, and Changi Airport; (d) an Arch Line connecting Telok Blangah and Queenstown towns, Stevens, Balestier, Boon Keng, Geylang, and Tanjong Katong. Also, the Downtown Line should be extended from Bukit Panjang to Marsiling. A medium rail system—smaller than the MRT but larger in capacity than an LRT system—should be built just for the Central Area. At least two lines could be built: (a) a Kampong Glam–Chinatown Loop, covering the old Raffles Town Plan; and (b) an Orchard–Marina Loop linking Orchard Road to Marina Bay.

Meanwhile, the public bus system should have its fleet doubled in strength, from 5,665 in 2017 to at least 11,000. If all additional buses were double-decker, each with a capacity of 139 passengers, it means being able to move an additional 740,000 commuters. Some of the new buses should be deployed as on-demand services—each service plies an operational area, and the route and stops depend on real-time demand through a smartphone app; one operational area should cover the Central Area only. Other buses should be deployed as express services connecting towns, or towns and the Central Area, making use of arterial roads and expressways as much as possible. With fewer private cars on the roads, more roads and expressways should be installed with full-day bus lanes to allow buses complete right-of-way.

For the MRT and bus networks, as per Lesson 5, the government should continue paying for all infrastructure and vehicles—MRT tracks, bus interchanges, trains, and so on—and taking on as much revenue risk as possible, while tendering out service and maintenance to bus and rail companies. With more MRT lines and bus routes to run, the tenders should be opened up to more overseas companies such as Tower Transit and Go-Ahead Singapore. This would keep long-time home-grown companies SMRT and SBS Transit on their toes.

To keep Singapore car-lite, the government should not grow the taxi and private-hire car industries as much as the MRT and bus networks. Cap private-hire car numbers at 50,000, and as much as possible keep market forces in control of these industries. However, to cater to people who are forced to give up their cars but are reluctant to switch full-time to the MRT and bus, the government should set up a new premium private-hire car company, offering on-demand taxi services through a smartphone app at higher prices than regular taxis and private-hire cars. This premium service could have a fleet of no more than 5,000 cars.

Solution 3: Allow bicycles and PMDs to flourish—on roads. With the number of private cars reduced, road lanes could be converted into lanes exclusively for bicycles and PMDs, something that should have been implemented decades ago. The pavements would be handed back to pedestrians to go about on foot safely.

Solution 4: Areas in the Central Area to be declared car-free zones. Major thoroughfares in these No-Car Zones could be handed over to public buses, goods and emergency vehicles, bicycles, PMDs, and pedestrians; smaller roads could be made off-limits to buses, and designated primarily for bicycles, PMDs, and pedestrians. This means keeping 19th-century arterial roads such as Victoria Street, New Bridge Road, and Beach Road for cars, but not other age-old roads like North Bridge Road and South Bridge Road. There could be four No-Car Zones: (a) Kampong Glam, from Jalan Sultan to Ophir Road; (b) Civic District, from Stamford Road to the Singapore River; (c) Boat Quay, from the Singapore River to Upper Pickering Street; (d) Kreta Ayer, from Cross Street to Maxwell Road. With a denser bus network and a medium rail system serving the Central Area, this should encourage more people to switch from cars to an alternate method of movement to travel to, from, and within the Central Area.

Solution 5: WWII-era Japan had grand plans to bring the *shinkansen* to Singapore. Now, something similar should be done—build underground mini-*shinkansen* lines for peak period long-distance travel between highly-populated regions and the Central Area, serving motorists who have given up their cars and do not mind paying more for swift, cross-island travel. The island's size is too small to accommodate high-speed rail services, but medium-speed rail might be viable. Stations could be built next to existing MRT stations in high-density suburbs such as Woodlands, Boon Lay, Bishan, Sengkang, and Tampines, all connecting to Raffles Place.

Japan has two medium-speed rail lines or mini-*shinkansen*, the Yamagata and Akita Shinkansen, both of which operate at a maximum speed of 130 km/h, slower than the regular *shinkansen*'s maximum speeds of 240–320 km/h. The shortest distance between two stations on the Yamagata Shinkansen is just 5.4 km, covered in four minutes. Following the timetables for the Yamagata and Akita Shinkansen, Singapore's mini-*shinkansen* could cover Woodlands to Bishan to Raffles Place (19.4 km) in 14 minutes, Boon Lay to Raffles Place (17.3 km) in 12 minutes, Tampines to Raffles Place (12.9 km) in nine minutes, and so on. These durations are shorter than existing peak period MRT travel times by between 66 and 76 per cent, and peak period car travel times by between 76 and 86 per cent. Even if mini-*shinkansen* tickets were priced significantly higher than MRT rides, regular

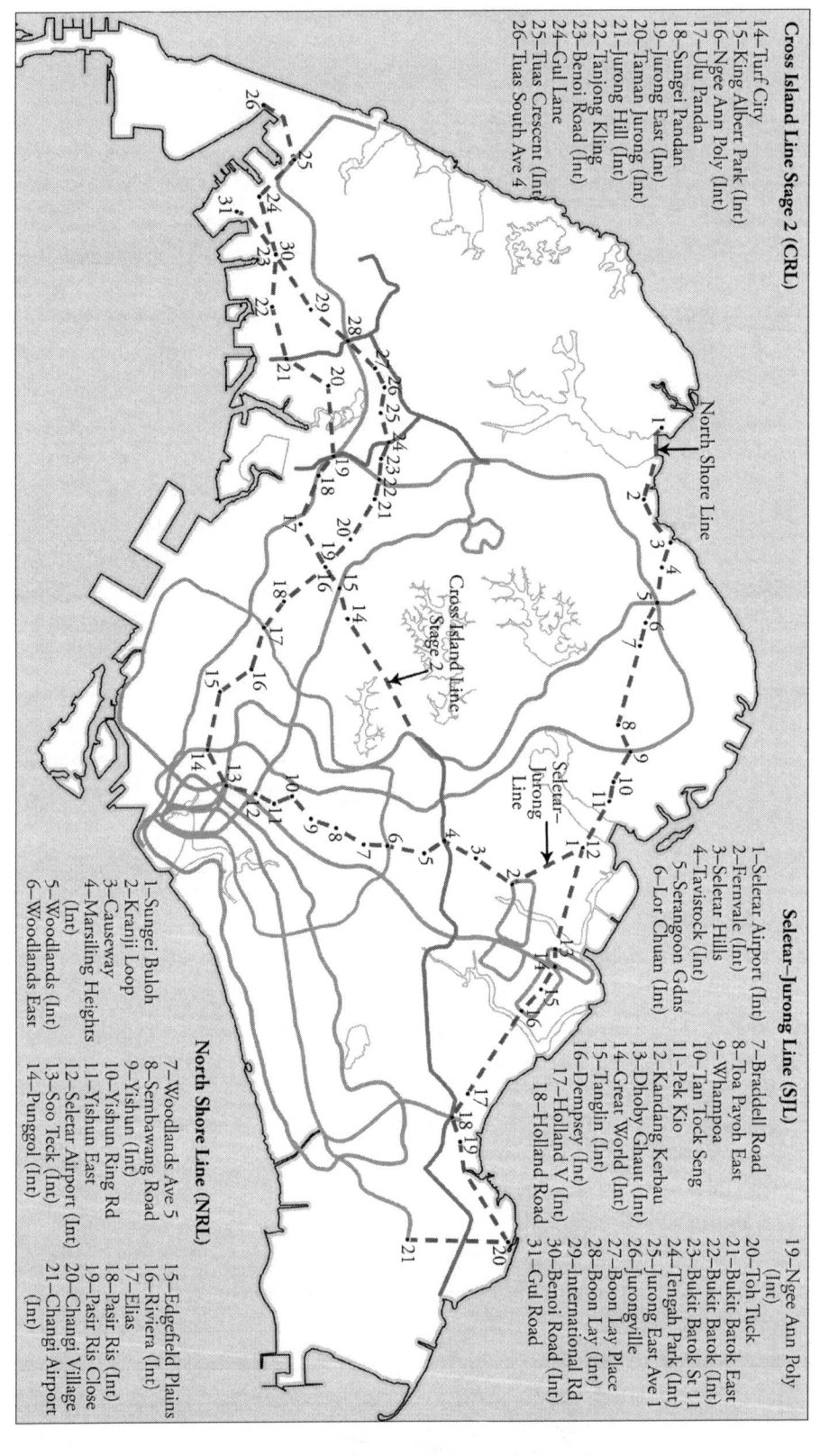

Cross Island Line Stage 2 (CRL)

14—Turf City
15—King Albert Park (Int)
16—Ngee Ann Poly (Int)
17—Ulu Pandan
18—Sungei Pandan
19—Jurong East (Int)
20—Taman Jurong (Int)
21—Jurong Hill (Int)
22—Tanjong Kling
23—Benoi Road (Int)
24—Gul Lane
25—Tuas Crescent (Int)
26—Tuas South Ave 4

Seletar-Jurong Line (SJL)

1—Seletar Airport (Int)
2—Fernvale (Int)
3—Seletar Hills
4—Tavistock (Int)
5—Serangoon Gdns
6—Lor Chuan (Int)
7—Braddell Road
8—Toa Payoh East
9—Whampoa
10—Tan Tock Seng
11—Pek Kio
12—Kandang Kerbau
13—Dhoby Ghaut (Int)
14—Great World
15—Tanglin (Int)
16—Dempsey
17—Holland V (Int)
18—Holland Road
19—Ngee Ann Poly (Int)
20—Toh Tuck
21—Bukit Batok East
22—Bukit Batok (Int)
23—Bukit Batok St 11
24—Tengah Park (Int)
25—Jurong East Ave 1
26—Jurongville
27—Boon Lay Place
28—Boon Lay (Int)
29—International Rd
30—Benoi Road (Int)
31—Gul Road

North Shore Line (NRL)

1—Sungei Buloh
2—Kranji Loop
3—Causeway
4—Marsiling Heights (Int)
5—Woodlands (Int)
6—Woodlands East
7—Woodlands Ave 5
8—Sembawang Road
9—Yishun (Int)
10—Yishun Ring Rd
11—Yishun East
12—Seletar Airport (Int)
13—Soo Teck
14—Punggol (Int)
15—Edgefield Plains
16—Riviera (Int)
17—Elias
18—Pasir Ris (Int)
19—Pasir Ris Close
20—Changi Village
21—Changi Airport

Singapore has an extensive MRT network, but to truly turn the city-state car-lite, it must be significantly expanded. This map shows some of my suggested MRT lines and extensions; the rest are in the map on the next page. Existing lines at the time of writing are in light grey; the Cross Island Line Stage 1 and Jurong Region Line are in medium grey; my proposed lines and extensions—the Cross Island Line Stage 2, North Shore Line, and Seletar-Jurong Line—are in dark grey. "Int" stands for an MRT interchange. (Source: Eisen Teo)

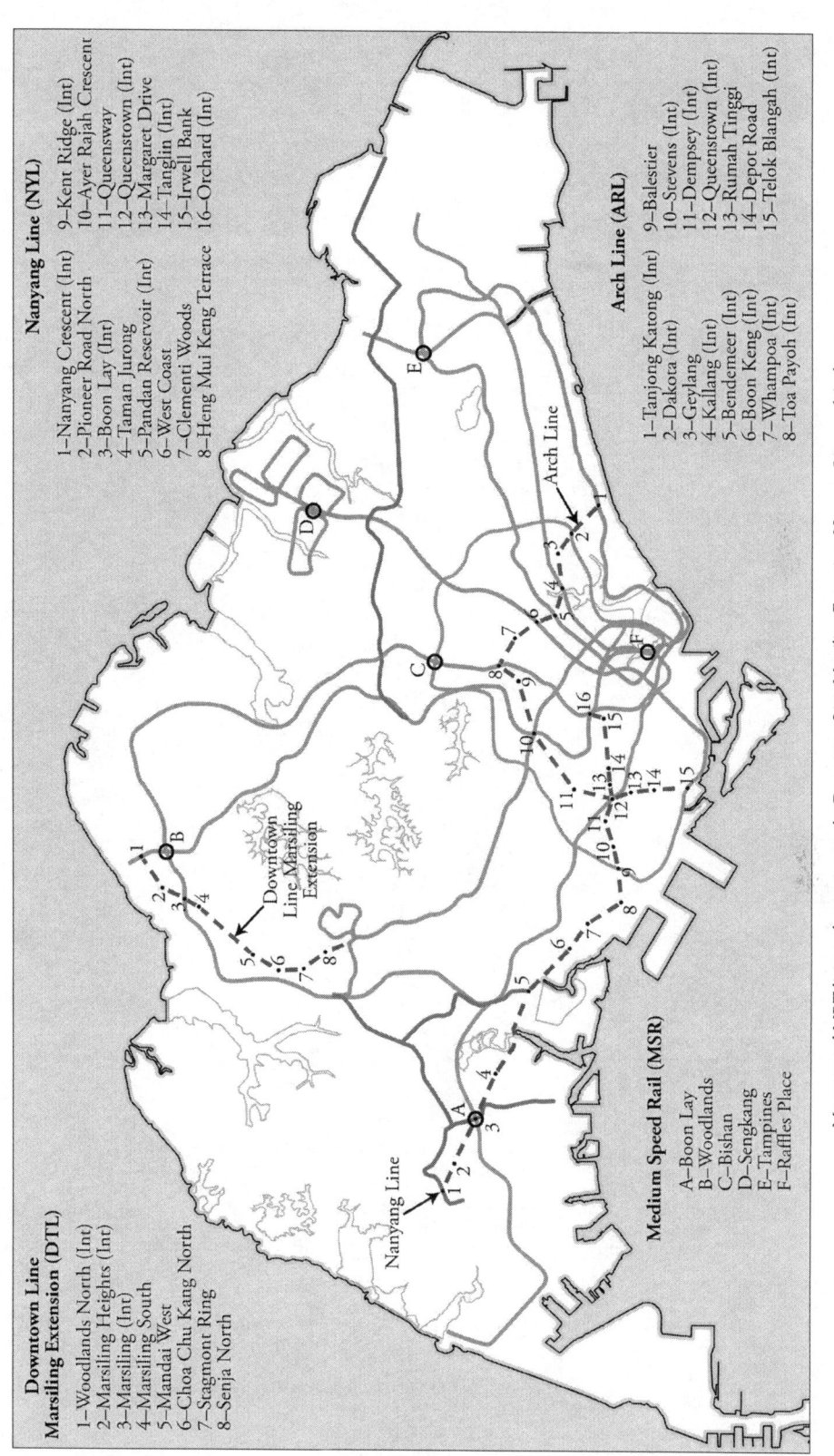

Downtown Line Marsiling Extension (DTL)

1—Woodlands North (Int)
2—Marsiling Heights (Int)
3—Marsiling (Int)
4—Marsiling South
5—Mandai West
6—Choa Chu Kang North
7—Stagmont Ring
8—Senja North

Nanyang Line (NYL)

1—Nanyang Crescent (Int)
2—Pioneer Road North
3—Boon Lay (Int)
4—Taman Jurong
5—Pandan Reservoir (Int)
6—West Coast
7—Clementi Woods
8—Heng Mui Keng Terrace
9—Kent Ridge (Int)
10—Ayer Rajah Crescent
11—Queensway
12—Queenstown (Int)
13—Margaret Drive
14—Tanglin (Int)
15—Irwell Bank
16—Orchard (Int)

Arch Line (ARL)

1—Tanjong Katong (Int)
2—Dakota (Int)
3—Geylang
4—Kallang (Int)
5—Bendemeer (Int)
6—Boon Keng (Int)
7—Whampoa (Int)
8—Toa Payoh (Int)
9—Balestier
10—Stevens (Int)
11—Dempsey (Int)
12—Queenstown (Int)
13—Rumah Tinggi
14—Depot Road
15—Telok Blangah (Int)

Medium Speed Rail (MSR)

A—Boon Lay
B—Woodlands
C—Bishan
D—Sengkang
E—Tampines
F—Raffles Place

My proposed MRT lines and extensions—the Downtown Line Marsiling Extension, Nanyang Line, and Arch Line—are in dark grey. My proposed Medium Speed Rail (Mini-*shinkansen*) stations are marked out with black rings. Collectively, my suggestions would vastly improve public transport, especially for the north, west, and northeast of the island, and ensure most towns are served by two to four MRT lines. (Source: Eisen Teo)

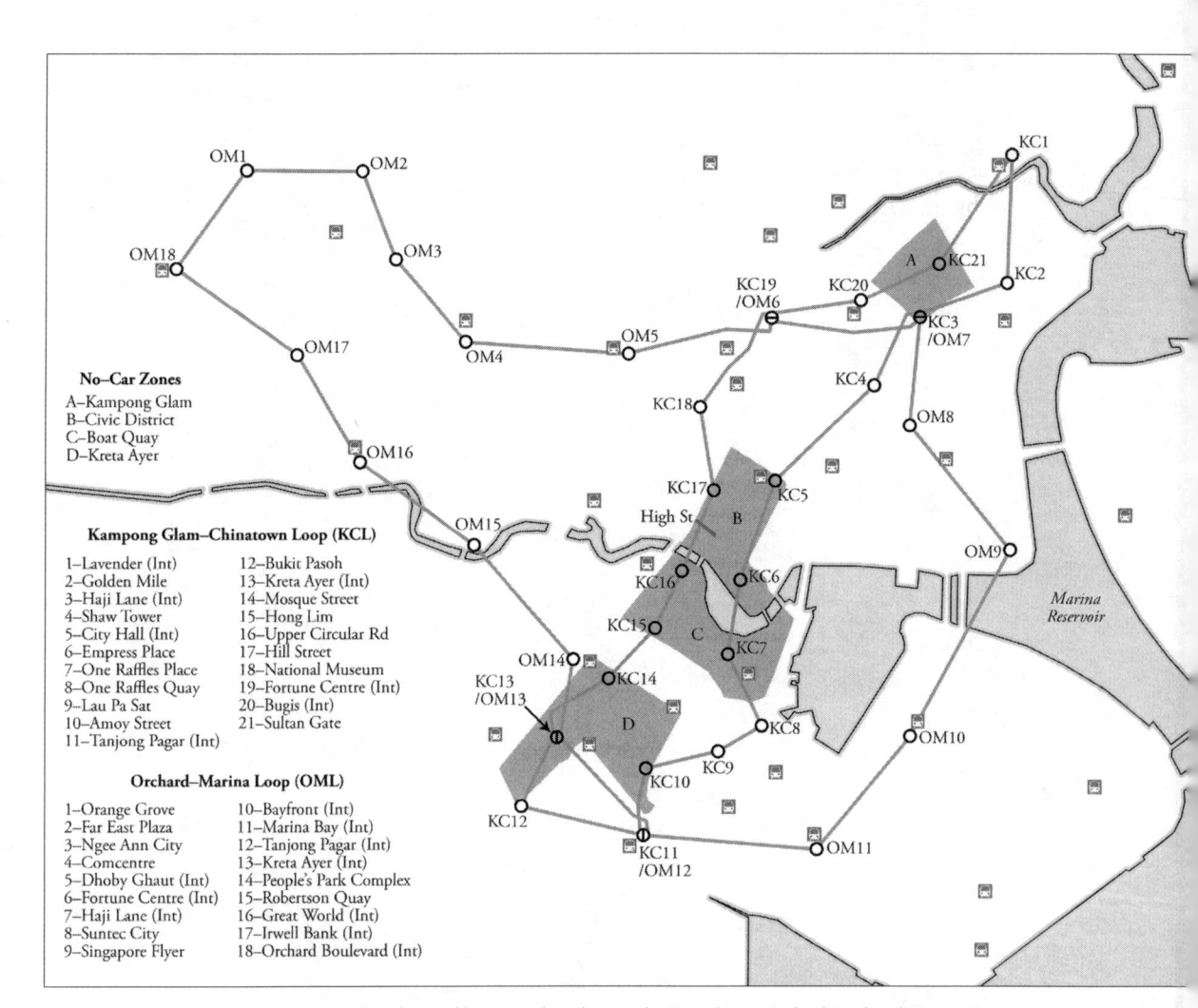

No–Car Zones
A–Kampong Glam
B–Civic District
C–Boat Quay
D–Kreta Ayer

Kampong Glam–Chinatown Loop (KCL)

1–Lavender (Int)
2–Golden Mile
3–Haji Lane (Int)
4–Shaw Tower
5–City Hall (Int)
6–Empress Place
7–One Raffles Place
8–One Raffles Quay
9–Lau Pa Sat
10–Amoy Street
11–Tanjong Pagar (Int)
12–Bukit Pasoh
13–Kreta Ayer (Int)
14–Mosque Street
15–Hong Lim
16–Upper Circular Rd
17–Hill Street
18–National Museum
19–Fortune Centre (Int)
20–Bugis (Int)
21–Sultan Gate

Orchard–Marina Loop (OML)

1–Orange Grove
2–Far East Plaza
3–Ngee Ann City
4–Comcentre
5–Dhoby Ghaut (Int)
6–Fortune Centre (Int)
7–Haji Lane (Int)
8–Suntec City
9–Singapore Flyer
10–Bayfront (Int)
11–Marina Bay (Int)
12–Tanjong Pagar (Int)
13–Kreta Ayer (Int)
14–People's Park Complex
15–Robertson Quay
16–Great World (Int)
17–Irwell Bank (Int)
18–Orchard Boulevard (Int)

My proposed medium rail lines to exclusively serve the Central Area, Orchard Road, and Marina Bay—the Kampong Glam–Chinatown Loop and the Orchard–Marina Loop. Existing and planned MRT stations are marked out with square train icons; proposed medium rail stations are marked out with black rings. The four areas shaded light grey are my proposed No-Car Zones. Each zone will be served by multiple MRT and/or medium rail stations to ensure the absence of cars will not be felt. High Street falls inside the Civic District No-Car Zone. (Source: Eisen Teo) travel should still be far cheaper than buying and maintaining a car, or ordering taxis or private-hire cars; the stress of movement would disappear too. This could persuade many motorists to give up their cars altogether.

With my solutions, I imagine a Singapore where major patterns of movement during peak periods are served by numerous public and individual transport alternatives—the mini-*shinkansen*, multiple MRT lines, on-demand and express buses, taxis and private-hire cars, bicycles, and PMDs—giving travellers ample choices based on budget, time, and destination. The government's aim of having 85 per cent of peak period trips on public transport would be easily achieved. There would be little or no travel stress, and congestion on MRT trains, buses, expressways, and arterial roads would be a thing of the past.

And what would become of High Street, the genesis of my story? As it is inside the Civic District No-Car Zone and not a major thoroughfare, it would be turned over to bicycles, PMDs, and pedestrians. More than a century after motor vehicles took over Singapore's channels of movement, pedestrians would be free to walk on High Street again without the fear of getting run over by a motor car. The glass-and-steel facades of the Treasury and High Street Plaza might never revert to the crumbling shophouses of the 1960s, but pedestrians would find themselves back in the 1880s, before the arrival of the motor car. High Street going car-free would be both a departure from current trends, as well as a continuation of history.

SIX HUNDRED years ago, a flourishing kingdom in Singapore was destroyed by foreign invaders, and the island "went back to jungle", observed Sir Robert Hamilton Bruce Lockhart in 1936. He continued: "In the light of the thousand new problems which confront the East today it is just (as) conceivable that in another 600 years (Singapore) may go back to jungle again." He may have written these words more than 80 years ago, but they are no less true today. No empire lasts forever, no matter how powerful or prosperous, much less a tiny city-state. History is cyclical; cities and institutions rise from the dust, attain their golden ages, and then return to dust.

Until the day this metropolis returns to jungle again, I hope this book has made the reader realise that we all play a role in a history of movement. Our decisions on travelling between Point A and Point B all day, every day—where we travel, when we travel, what means we choose to get to our destination, our experiences and interactions while travelling—add up to a historical narrative that is constantly being written and rewritten. This narrative has its origin going back millions of years to when the very terrain was forged, multiple chapters saw human settlements coming and going from ancient times to the present, and the writing will continue into the future, the work of our children and grandchildren. Transient monuments to history exist all around us in the forms of channels and methods of movement, and through them, we are but transient beings leaving our own little marks on history.

Bon voyage, and stay safe.

CHAPTER NOTES

1   The first road in Singapore Island to be fitted with a dedicated cycling lane was Tanah Merah Coast Road in April 2017, a month before the launch of Bencoolen Street's cycling lane. The former's cycling lane is 10 km long and two metres wide.

BIBLIOGRAPHY

BOOKS

Abdullah Abdul Kadir. *Hikayat Abdullah*. Kuala Lumpur: Oxford University Press, 1970.

Abercrombie, Patrick. *Greater London Plan, 1944: A Report Prepared on Behalf of the Standing Conference on London Regional Planning by Professor Abercrombie at the Request of the Minister of Town and Country Planning*. London: H.M. Stationery Off., 1945.

Bastin, John. *The Founding of Singapore 1819: Based on the Private Letters of Sir Stamford Raffles to the Governor-General and Commander-in-Chief in India, the Marguess of Hastings, Preserved in the Bute Collection at Mount Stuart, Isle of Bute, Scotland*. Singapore: National Library Board, c2012.

Bellwood, Peter. *Prehistory of the Indo-Malaysian Archipelago*. Honolulu: University of Hawaii Press, 1997.

Bogaars, George. *The Tanjong Pagar Dock Company, 1864–1905*. Singapore: G.P.O., 1956.

Brown, Edwin A. *Indiscreet memories: 1901 Singapore Through the Eyes of a Colonial Englishman*. Singapore: Monsoon Books, 2007.

Bruce Lockhart, Robert. *Return to Malaya*. London: Putnam, 1936.

Buckley, Charles Burton. *Anecdotal History of Old Times in Singapore: From the Foundation of the Settlement Under the Honourable the East India Company on February 6th, 1819 to the Transfer to the Colonial Office as Part of the Colonial Possessions of the Crown on April 1st, 1867*. Singapore: Oxford University Press, 1984.

Carr, E. H. *What Is History?* London: Penguin Books, 1987.

Castells, Manuel. *The Urban Question: A Marxist Approach*. Cambridge, Mass.: MIT Press, 1977.

Cheong, Colin. *Building Singapore's Longest Road Tunnel: The KPE Story*. Singapore: Published for the Land Transport Authority by SNP International Publishing, c2008.

Cheong, Colin. *Framework and Foundation: A History of the Public Works Department*. Singapore: Times Editions for PWD, 1992.

Chronology of Trade Union Development in Singapore 1940–1984. Compiled by Lim-Ng Bee Eng. Singapore: Singapore National Trades Union Congress, 1985.

Chua, Beng Huat. *The Golden Shoe: Building Singapore's Financial District*. Singapore: Urban Redevelopment Authority, 1989.

Colonialism and the Modern World: Selected Studies. Edited by Gregory Blue, Martin Bunton, and Ralph Croizier. Armonk, N.Y.: M.E. Sharpe, c2002.

Concept Plan: The Future Direction for Planning. Singapore: Singapore Institute of Planners, 1993.

Cook, John Angus Bethune. *Sunny Singapore: An Account of the Place and its People, with a Sketch of the Results of Missionary Work, by the Rev. J. A. Bethune Cook*. London: E. Stock, 1907.

Corden, Carol. *Planned Cities: New Towns in Britain and America*. Beverly Hills, Calif.: Sage Publications, c1977.

Corner, E. J. H. *The Marquis: A Tale of Syonan-to*. Singapore: Heinemann Asia, 1981.

Crawfurd, John. *Journal of an Embassy from the Governor-General of India to the Courts of Siam and Cochin China*. Kuala Lumpur, London, New York, OUP, 1967.

Cree, Edward. *The Cree Journals: The Voyages of Edward H. Cree, Surgeon R.N., as Related in His Private Journals, 1837–1856*. Exeter, Devon: Webb & Bower, 1981.

Dale, Ole Johan. *Urban Planning in Singapore: The Transformation of a City*. Shah Alam, Selangor: Oxford University Press, 1999.

Daniels, P. W., and A. M. Warnes. *Movement in Cities: Spatial Perspectives on Urban Transport and Travel*. London; New York: Methuen, 1980.

De Albuquerque, Afonso. *The Commentaries of the Great Afonso Dalboquerque, Second Viceroy of India*. New York: B. Franklin, 1970.

De la Garza, Andrew. *Mughals at War: Babur, Akbar and the Indian Military Revolution, 1500–1605*. London; New York, NY: Routledge, 2016.

Dick, Howard W., and Peter J. Rimmer. *Cities, Transport and Communications: The Integration of Southeast Asia Since 1850.* New York: Palgrave Macmillan, 2003.

Drabble, J. H. *Rubber in Malaya, 1876–1922: The Genesis of the Industry.* Kuala Lumpur, New York: Oxford University Press, 1973.

Early Singapore 1300s–1819: Evidence in Maps, Text and Artefacts. Edited by John Miksic and Cheryl-Ann Low. Singapore: Singapore History Museum, c2004.

Faretable. Singapore Bus Service Ltd., 1978.

Farrell, Brian P. *The Defence and Fall of Singapore 1940–1942.* Singapore: Monsoon Books Pte Ltd, 2015.

Gaur, R. C. *Excavations at Fatehpur Sikri: A National Project.* New Delhi: Aryan Books International, c2000.

Geology of the Malay Peninsula (West Malaysia and Singapore). Edited by D. J. Gobbett and C. S. Hutchison. New York: Wiley-Interscience, 1973.

Gill, Simryn. *Guide to the Murals at Tanjong Pagar Railway Station.* Singapore: Simryn Gill & Singapore Biennale, 2006.

Guldi, Jo, and David Armitage. *The History Manifesto.* Cambridge: Cambridge University Press, 2014.

Hall-Jones, John, and Christopher Hooi. *An Early Surveyor in Singapore: John Turnbull Thomson in Singapore, 1841–1853.* Singapore: National Museum, 1979.

Hamilton, Alexander. *A Scottish Sea Captain in Southeast Asia, 1689–1723.* Chiang Mai, Thailand: Silkworm Books, 1997.

Hancock, T. H. H. *Coleman's Singapore.* Kuala Lumpur: The Malaysian Branch of The Royal Asiatic Society in association with Pelanduk Publications, 1986.

Hiroshi, Shimizu, and Hirakawa Hitoshi. *Japan and Singapore in the World Economy: Japan's Economic Advance into Singapore, 1870–1965.* New York: Routledge, 1999.

Hon, Joan. *100 Years of the Singapore Fire Service.* Singapore: Produced & published for Singapore Fire Service by Times Books International, 1988.

Hood, Christopher P. *Shinkansen: From Bullet Train to Symbol of Modern Japan.* London; New York: Routledge, 2006.

Hornaday, William. *The Experiences of a Hunter and Naturalist in the Malay Peninsula and Borneo.* Kuala Lumpur: Oxford University Press, 1993.

Howard, Ebenezer. *To-morrow: A Peaceful Path to Real Reform.* London; New York: Routledge, 2003.

Kampong Days: Village Life and Times in Singapore Revisited. Edited by K. F. Tang. Singapore: National Archives, 1993.

Karni, Athsani, and Bernard Chen. *Singapore Road Development Programme: A Comparison with Selected Countries.* Singapore: Economics Section, Economic Development Division, Ministry of Finance, 1969.

Kaur, Amarjit. *Bridge and Barrier: Transport and Communications in Colonial Malaya, 1870–1957.* Singapore: Oxford University Press, 1985.

Kennedy, Paul M. *The Rise of the Anglo-German Antagonism, 1860–1914.* London; Boston: Allen & Unwin, 1980.

Korea at the Center: Dynamics of Regionalism in Northeast Asia. Edited by Charles K. Armstrong, Samuel S. Kim, Gilbert Rozman, and Stephen Kotkin. Armonk, N.Y.: M.E. Sharpe, Inc., c2006.

Lee, Imm Yew, et. al. *80 Years of Bus & Coach: The Soon Chow Story.* Singapore: busfansunlimited, 2007.

Lee, Kim Woon, and Zhou Yingxin. *Geology of Singapore* (2nd edition, 2009). Singapore: Defence Science and Technology Agency in collaboration with Nanyang Technological University, Building and Construction Authority, 2009.

Leibbrand, Kurt. *Transportation and Town Planning.* London: L. Hill, 1970.

Leinbach, Thomas R. and Chia Lin Sien. *South-east Asia Transport: Issues in Development.* Singapore: Oxford University Press, 1989.

Lim, William S. W., and Philip Motha. *Land Policy in Singapore*. Singapore: DP Architects, 1979.

Loh, Kah Seng. *Squatters into Citizens: The 1961 Bukit Ho Swee Fire and the Making of Modern Singapore*. Singapore: Asian Studies Association of Australia in association with NUS Press and NIAS Press, c2013.

Low, N. I. *When Singapore was Syonan-to*. Petaling Jaya: Eastern Universities Press Sdn. Bhd., 1983.

Marryat, Frank. *Borneo and the Indian Archipelago: With Drawings of Costume and Scenery.* Singapore: ASCANIO Books, 2007.

Marriott, John Arthur Ransome. *Anglo-Russian Relations: 1689–1943*. London: Methuen & Co., 1944.

McNair, John Frederick Adolphus. *Prisoners Their Own Warders*. Westminster: A. Constable, 1899.

Menon, Gopinath. *Transport*. Singapore: Institute of Policy Studies: Straits Times Press Pte Ltd, 2016.

Menon, Gopinath, and Lam Soi Hoi. *Singapore's Road Pricing System: 1975–1989*. Singapore: Centre for Transportation Studies, Nanyang Technological University, 1992.

Mills, L. A. *British Malaya, 1824–67*. Singapore: Malayan Branch: Royal Asiatic Society, 1961.

Miksic, John. *Archaeological Research on the "Forbidden Hill" of Singapore: Excavations at Fort Canning, 1984*. Singapore: National Museum, c1985.

Miksic, John. *Singapore and the Silk Road of the Sea, 1300–1800*. Singapore: NUS Press, 2013.

Modern Singapore. Edited by Ooi Jin-Bee and Chiang Hai Ding. Singapore: University of Singapore, 1969.

Murray, J. F. N. *A Report on Control of Land Prices, Valuation and Compulsory Acquisition of Land*. Singapore: Printed at the Govt. Print. Off., 1956.

One Hundred Years of Singapore. Edited by Walter Makepeace, Gilbert E. Brooke, and Roland St J. Braddell. Singapore: Oxford University Press, 1991.

Ooi, Giok Ling. *Future of Space: Planning, Space and the City.* Singapore: Eastern University Press, 2004.

Oppenheimer, Stephen. *Eden of the East: The Drowned Continent of Southeast Asia*. London: Weidenfeld and Nicolson, 1998.

Pearson, H. F. *A History of Singapore*. London: University of London Press, 1956.

Pearson, H. F. *People of Early Singapore*. London: University of London Press, 1955.

Pearson, H. F. *Singapore: A Popular History, 1819–1960*. Singapore: Published by D. Moore for Eastern Universities Press, 1961.

Peet, George L. *Rickshaw Reporter*. Singapore: Eastern Universities Press, 1985.

Pelras, Christian. *The Bugis*. Cambridge, Mass.: Blackwell Publishers, 1996.

Pfeiffer, Ida. *A Woman's Journey Round the World: From Vienna to Brazil, Chili, Tahiti, China, Hindostan, Persia, and Asia Minor*. Kila, Mont.: Kessinger Pub., 19--.

Pires, Tome. *The Suma Oriental of Tome Pires, an Account of the East, from the Red Sea to Japan, written in Malacca and India in 1512–1515*. London, Hakluyt Society, 1944.

Probert, Henry. *The History of Changi*. Singapore: Changi University Press, c2006.

Reith, G. M. *Handbook to Singapore*. Singapore; New York: Oxford University Press, 1985.

Rimmer, Peter J. *Rikisha to Rapid Transit: Urban Public Transport Systems and Policy in Southeast Asia*. Sydney: Pergamon Press, 1986.

Roff, William R. *The Origins of Malay Nationalism*. Kuala Lumpur: Oxford University Press, 1994.

Savage, Victor R., and Brenda S. A. Yeoh. *Singapore Street Names: A Study of Toponymics*. Singapore: Marshall Cavendish Editions, 2013.

Saw, Swee-Hock. *The Population of Singapore* (Third Edition). Singapore: ISEAS Pub., 2012.

Sejarah Melayu (Malay Annals). Translated by C. C. Brown. Kuala Lumpur: O. U. P., 1970.

Sejarah Melayu (Malay Annals). Translated by John Leyden. Kuala Lumpur: Silverfish Books, c2012.

Sharp, Ilsa. *The Journey: Singapore's Land Transport Story*. Singapore: Published for the Land Transport Authority by SNP Editions, 2005.

Shinozaki, Mamoru. *Syonan, My Story: The Japanese Occupation of Singapore*. Singapore: Asia Pacific Press, 1975.

Singapore: 150 years. Edited by Tan Sri Dato Mubin Sheppard. Singapore: Published for the Malaysian Branch of the Royal Asiatic Society by Times Books International, 1982.

Song, Ong Siang. *One Hundred Years' History of the Chinese in Singapore*. Singapore: Oxford University Press, 1984.

Sopher, David Edward. *The Sea Nomads: A Study of the Maritime Boat People of Southeast Asia*. Singapore: National Museum, 1977.

The Development of Nee Soon Community. Singapore: The grassroots organisations of Nee Soon Constituency: National Archives: Oral History Department, 1987.

The Land Transport of Singapore: From Early Times to the Present. Singapore: Published for Archives and Oral History Dept. by Educational Publications Bureau, 1984.

The MND Network: Shaping the Future. Singapore: Ministry of National Development, 1994.

The Underside of Malaysian History: Pullers, Prostitutes, Plantation Workers. Edited by Peter J. Rimmer and Lisa M. Allen. Singapore: Singapore University Press for Malaysia Society of the Asian Studies Association of Australia, c1990.

Thomson, John Turnbull. *Glimpses into Life in Malayan Lands*. Singapore: Oxford University Press, 1984.

Travellers' Singapore: An Anthology. Compiled by John Bastin. Kuala Lumpur; New York: Oxford University Press, 1994.

Travellers' Tales of Old Singapore. Compiled by Michael Wise. Singapore: Times Books International, c1985.

Trocki, Carl. *Prince of Pirates: The Temenggongs and the Development of Johor and Singapore, 1784–1885*. Singapore: Singapore University Press, 1979.

Turnbull, C. M. *The Straits Settlements, 1826–67: Indian Presidency to Crown Colony*. London: Athlone Press, 1972.

Tyers, Ray. *Singapore: Then & Now*. Singapore: University Education Press, 1976.

Urban Redevelopment Authority: Towards a Tropical City of Excellence. Singapore: URA, 1993.

Van Cuylenburg, John Bertram. *Singapore: Through Sunshine and Shadow*. Singapore: Heinemann Asia, 1982.

Wallace, Alfred Russel. *The Malay Archipelago: The Land of the Orang-utan, and the Bird of Paradise*. Singapore: Oxford University Press, 1986.

Warren, James Francis. *Rickshaw Coolie: A People's History of Singapore 1880–1940*. Singapore: Singapore University Press, c2003.

Wheatley, Paul. *The Golden Khersonese: Studies in the Historical Geography of the Malay Peninsula before A. D. 1500*. Kuala Lumpur: University of Malaya Press, 1961.

Wong, Tai-Chee, and Yap Lian-Ho Adriel. *Four Decades of Transformation: Land Use in Singapore, 1960–2000*. Singapore: Eastern University Press, 2004.

Yeoh, Brenda S. A. *Contesting Space in Colonial Singapore: Power Relations and the Urban Built Environment*. Singapore: Singapore University Press, c2003.

Yang, Daqing. *Technology of Empire: Telecommunications and Japanese Expansion in Asia, 1883–1945*. Cambridge, Mass.: Harvard University Asia Center: Distributed by Harvard University Press, 2010.

York, F. W., and A. R. Phillips. *Singapore: A History of Trams, Trolleybuses and Buses, Vol. I, 1880s to 1960s*. Surrey: DTS Publishing Ltd., 1996.

JOURNAL ARTICLES

Corlett, Richard T. "The Ecological Transformation of Singapore, 1819–1990", *Journal of Biogeography*, Vol. 19, No. 4 (July 1992), pp. 411–420.

Dobby, E. H. B. "Singapore: Town and Country", *Geographical Review*, Vol. 30, No. 1 (January 1940), pp. 84–109.

Fraser, James M. "Town Planning and Housing in Singapore", *The Town Planning Review*, Vol. 23, No. 1 (April 1952), pp. 5–25.

Gibson-Hill, C. A. "Singapore: Notes on the History of the Old Strait, 1580–1850", *Journal of the Malayan Branch of the Royal Asiatic Society*, Vol. 27, No. 1 (165) (May 1954), pp. 163–214.

Heng, Derek. "Reconstructing Banzu, a Fourteenth-Century Port Settlement in Singapore", *Journal of the Malaysian Branch of the Royal Asiatic Society*, Vol. 75, No. 1 (282) (2002), pp. 69–90.

Jensen, Rolf. "Planning, Urban Renewal, and Housing in Singapore", *The Town Planning Review*, Vol. 38, No. 2 (July 1967), pp. 115–131.

Lee, David K. C., and Winston T. H. Koh. "Auctions for Transferable Objects: Theory and Evidence from the Vehicle Quota System in Singapore", *Asia Pacific Journal of Management*, Vol. 10, Issue 2 (October 1993).

Menon, Gopinath, and Sarath Guttikunda. "Electronic Road Pricing: Experience & Lessons from Singapore", *SIM-air Working Paper Series: 33–2010*, January 2010.

Miller, H. Eric. "Extracts from the Letters of Col. Nahuijs", *Journal of the Malayan Branch of the Royal Asiatic Society*, Vol. 19, No. 2 (139) (October 1941), pp. 169–209.

Smith, Peter. "Controlling Traffic Congestion by Regulating Car Ownership: Singapore's Recent Experience", *Journal of Transport Economics and Policy*, Vol. 26, No. 1 (January 1992).

Teo, Siew Eng. "Planning Principles in Pre- and Post-Independence Singapore", *The Town Planning Review*, Vol. 63, No. 2 (April 1992), pp. 163–185.

Yeoh, Brenda S. A. "Street-Naming and Nation-Building: Toponymic Inscriptions of Nationhood in Singapore", *Area*, Vol. 28, No. 3 (September 1996), pp. 298–307.

Yeoh, Brenda S. A. "Street Names in Colonial Singapore", *Geographical Review*, Vol. 82, No. 3 (July 1992), pp. 313–322.

UNPUBLISHED ACADEMIC EXERCISES

Chia, Hock Chuan. *Gambier and Pepper Industry in Singapore and Johore (1819–1917): A Study of Chinese Agricultural Economy*. Dept. of History, Faculty of Arts, Nanyang University, 1977.

Ng, Peck Hear. *A Study on the HDB Annual Reports*. Dept. of Economics & Statistics, Faculty of Arts & Social Sciences, National University of Singapore, 1995.

Tan, Choon Kiat. *A History of Tanjong Pagar: 1823–1911*. Dept. of History, Faculty of Arts & Social Sciences, National University of Singapore, 1989.

Tan, Kim-chia. *Public Housing in Singapore 1947–70 (The Work of the SIT and the HDB)*. Dept. of History, University of Singapore, 1974.

Yeo, Hsuyin. *Queenstown: A History of Singapore's First New Town*. Dept. of History, Faculty of Arts & Social Sciences, National University of Singapore, 1995.

NEWSPAPERS AND MAGAZINES

Channel Newsasia

New Nation

Singapore Chronicle and Commercial Register

Singapore Free Press and Mercantile Advertiser

Singapore Standard

Straits Observer

Straits Times Overland Journal

Straits Times Weekly Issue

The New Paper

The Star Online

The Straits Times

Today

Torque

MUNICIPAL, CITY, AND GOVERNMENT RECORDS AND REPORTS

"2016/2017 Annual Report", *Housing & Development Board. Administrative Reports of the Singapore Municipality.*

Annual Report of the Registry of Vehicles 1965.

Annual Report of the Registry of Vehicles 1976.

"Annual Vehicle Statistics 2017", downloaded from *Land Transport Authority.*

"Estimated Singapore Resident Population in HDB Flats", *Data.gov.sg,* 15 December 2017. URL: https://data.gov.sg/dataset/estimated-resident-population-living-in-hdb-flats

"Investigation findings on flooding of MRT tunnels between Bishan and Braddell stations from 7-8 October 2017", *Land Transport Authority,* 5 December 2017. URL: https://www.lta.gov.sg/apps/news/page.aspx?c=2&id=2181b69a-db90-419a-9693-f5872ff00ff6

Master Plan: Report of Survey. Singapore: Govt. Print. Off., 1955-1958.

Master Plan (1980). Singapore: Planning Department, Ministry of National Development, 1980.

"Population and Population Structure", *Department of Statistics Singapore,* 9 May 2018. URL: https://www.singstat.gov.sg/find-data/search-by-theme/population/population-and-population-structure/latest-data

Profile of Residents Living in HDB Flats. Edited by Moey-Khoo Hsiao Pi, et al. Singapore: Research & Planning Dept., Housing & Development Board, 2000.

"Public Transport Utilisation – Average Daily Public Transport Ridership", *Data.gov.sg,* 2017. URL: https://data.gov.sg/dataset/public-transport-utilisation-average-public-transport-ridership

Report of the Committee Appointed by His Excellency the Governor of the Straits Settlements to Enquire into and Report on the Present Traffic Conditions in the Town of Singapore. Singapore: Straits Settlements: Committee Appointed to Enquire into and Report on the Present Traffic Conditions in the Town of Singapore, 1938.

"Report of the Committee of Inquiry into the disruption of MRT train services on 15 and 17 December 2011, *Ministry of Transport,* 3 July 2012. URL: https://www.mot.gov.sg/news/COI%20report%20-%20Executive%20Summary.pdf

"Road Accident Casualties and Casualty Rates (2004–2016)", downloaded from *Singapore Police Force.*

"Road Length In Kilometer (end-of-year)", downloaded from *Land Transport Authority.*

"Singapore Residents By Age Group, Ethnic Group And Gender, End June, Annual", *Data.gov.sg,* 27 August 2018. URL: https://data.gov.sg/dataset/resident-population-by-ethnicity-gender-and-age-group

"Singapore Residents by Planning Area/Subzone, Age Group and Sex, June 2000–2017", downloaded from "Geographic Distribution", *Department of Statistics Singapore,* 9 May 2018. URL: https://www.singstat.gov.sg/find-data/search-by-theme/population/geographic-distribution/latest-data

The Work of the Singapore Improvement Trust (1949). Singapore: Singapore Improvement Trust, 1949.

The Work of the Singapore Improvement Trust (1958). Singapore: Singapore Improvement Trust, 1958.

"Total land area of Singapore", *Data.gov.sg,* 9 August 2018. URL: https://data.gov.sg/dataset/total-land-area-of-singapore

"Transcript of Prime Minister Lee Hsien Loong's Speech at Clean & Green Singapore 2015 Launch on 8 November", *Prime Minister's Office Singapore,* 8 November 2014. URL: http://www.pmo.gov.sg/newsroom/transcript-prime-minister-lee-hsien-loongs-speech-clean-green-singapore-2015-launch-8

ANNUAL REPORTS OF TRANSPORT COMPANIEs

SBS Transit Annual Report 2017

SBS Transit Ltd Annual Report 2005

Singapore Bus Service (1978) Ltd Annual Report 1990

Singapore Bus Services Limited Annual Report 1998

SMRT Corporation Ltd Annual Report 2016

TIBS Holdings Limited Annual Report 1991

ONLINE ARTICLES, BLOGS, AND WEBSITES

"1980s", *Land Transport Authority*, 27 April 2017. URL: https://www.lta.gov.sg/content/ltaweb/en/about-lta/our-history/1980s.html

"Akita Shinkansen", *East Japan Railway Company*. URL: http://www.eki-net.com/pc/jreast-shinkansen-reservation/english/wb/common/timetable/e_akita_d/index.html

"Akita Shinkansen", *Wikipedia*, 14 July 2018. URL: https://en.wikipedia.org/wiki/Akita_Shinkansen

"Bencoolen Street gets a car-lite makeover", *Land Transport Authority*, 10 November 2016. URL: https://www.lta.gov.sg/apps/news/page.aspx?c=2&id=53a6b1b8-0ade-4323-8a52-2867a493e725

"Bus Contracting Model", *Land Transport Guru*, 2018. URL: http://landtransportguru.net/bus/bus-contracting-model/

"Bus lane schemes", *OneMotoring*, 13 October 2017. URL: https://www.onemotoring.com.sg/content/onemotoring/en/on_the_roads/traffic_management/full_day_bus_lanes.html

Chen, Johnny. "Selegie House and Selegie Integrated School", *Stories of Our Singapore*, 25 August 2013. URL: http://www.ghettosingapore.com/selegie-house-and-selegie-integrated-school/

"Completed SERS Projects", *Housing & Development Board*, 29 August 2017. URL: https://www.hdb.gov.sg/cs/infoweb/residential/living-in-an-hdb-flat/sers-and-upgrading-programmes/completed-sers-projects

"Completion of the Bus Service Enhancement Programme (BSEP)", *Land Transport Authority*, 9 December 2017. URL: https://www.lta.gov.sg/apps/news/page.aspx?c=2&id=fa0bb307-b327-4132-b4c9-65dee82ea989

"Cycling for All", *Urban Redevelopment Authority*, 17 August 2018. URL: https://www.ura.gov.sg/Corporate/Planning/Master-Plan/Key-Focuses/Transport/Cycling-for-All

"Driver's Guides", *SGCarMart.com*, 2018. URL: http://www.sgcarmart.com/news/carpark_index.php

"Electronic Road Pricing (ERP)", *Land Transport Authority*, 6 October 2017. URL: https://www.lta.gov.sg/content/ltaweb/en/roads-and-motoring/managing-traffic-and-congestion/electronic-road-pricing-erp.html

"ERP Guide", *SGCarMart.com*, 2018. URL: http://www.sgcarmart.com/news/carpark_index.php?TYP=erp&LOC=all

"Factsheet: Active Mobility Bill", *Land Transport Authority*, 10 January 2017. URL: https://www.lta.gov.sg/apps/news/page.aspx?c=2&id=2e0d9c1a-55ab-4647-9b08-4cd4ff6d44cb

"FAQ", *Mobike*, 2018. URL: https://mobike.com/sg/faq#faq4

"FAQs", *oBike*. URL: https://www.o.bike/sg/faqs/

"First multi-storey carpark of Singapore walks into history", *Remember Singapore*, 22 April 2011. URL: https://remembersingapore.org/2011/04/22/first-multi-storey-carpark/

Ginsburg, Lisa. "A Jewish family story", *Asian Jewish Life*, 2015. URL: http://asianjewishlife.org/pages/articles/AJL_Issue_15_Oct2014/AJL_Issue15_CoverStory_Worlds_Apart_in_Singapore.html

Goh, Lee Kim. "First Light Rail Transit system", *Singapore Infopedia*, 2016. URL: http://eresources.nlb.gov.sg/infopedia/articles/SIP_538_2005-01-05.html

"Heritage", *Ministry of Transport*, 11 December 2017. URL: https://www.mot.gov.sg/about-mot/corporate-profile/heritage

"In-Progress SERS Projects", *Housing & Development Board,* 29 August 2017. URL: https://www.hdb.gov.sg/cs/infoweb/residential/living-in-an-hdb-flat/sers-and-upgrading-programmes/in-progress-sers-projects

"Kampung Gelam – from the Istana to Masjid Bahru (Masjid Maarof)", *Our Stories, Singapura Stories.* URL: http://singapurastories.com/kampung-gelam-rochor-kallang/kampung-gelam-from-the-istana-to-masjid-bahru-masjid-maarof-ian-lloyd-1985-singapore-from-the-air-pp36-37/

Lee, Abraham. "The Great Rail Meltdown: 2011 vs 2015", *The Middle Ground,* 8 July 2015. URL: http://themiddleground.sg/2015/07/08/great-rail-meltdown-2011-vs-2015/

Lee, Michael. "People's Park Complex", *Singapore Infopedia,* 2016. URL: http://eresources.nlb.gov.sg/infopedia/articles/SIP_1597_2009-10-31.html

Lee, Timothy B. "Uber, losing $1 billion a quarter, sells its Southeast Asian business", *Ars Technica,* 26 March 2018. URL: https://arstechnica.com/cars/2018/03/uber-sells-southeast-asian-business-to-regional-rival-grab/

Lim, Tin Seng. "1955 Legislative Assembly general election", *Singapore Infopedia,* 24 January 2018. URL: http://eresources.nlb.gov.sg/infopedia/articles/SIP_2014-07-07_134339.html

Lim, Tin Seng. "Area Licensing Scheme", *Singapore Infopedia,* 15 August 2014. URL: http://eresources.nlb.gov.sg/infopedia/articles/SIP_777_2004-12-13.html

"LTA awards Bukit Merah bus package to SBS Transit Ltd", *Land Transport Authority,* 23 February 2018. URL: https://www.lta.gov.sg/apps/news/page.aspx?c=2&id=a0d4d08f-32f9-4a7a-804b-a0e97e9c19e6

"LTA awards first tendered bus package to Tower Transit Group Limited", 8 May 2015. URL: https://www.lta.gov.sg/apps/news/page.aspx?c=2&id=6bc7cedf-2390-4c4f-904c-de12115b1354

"LTA awards second bus package to Go-Ahead Group PLC", 23 November 2015. URL: https://www.lta.gov.sg/apps/news/page.aspx?c=2&id=b788c5ef-a7cc-4de3-b5d8-9fc1cd1d1b2e

"LTA awards third bus package to SBS Transit Ltd", *Land Transport Authority,* 19 April 2017. URL: https://www.lta.gov.sg/apps/news/page.aspx?c=2&id=d4fd0825-966d-4796-817f-ae2907b2494f

"Maintaining our roads and facilities", *Land Transport Authority,* 17 July 2018. URL: https://www.lta.gov.sg/content/ltaweb/en/roads-and-motoring/road-safety-and-regulations/maintaining-our-roads-and-facilities.html

"MAN A95 (Euro 6) – First Production Batch", *Land Transport Guru,* 2018. URL: https://landtransportguru.net/man-a95-euro-6-first-production-batch/

"Network", *SGTrains,* 2018. URL: https://www.sgtrains.com/network.html

"North-South Corridor", *Land Transport Authority,* 6 June 2017. URL: https://www.lta.gov.sg/content/ltaweb/en/roads-and-motoring/projects/north-south-corridor.html

"Our History", *Land Transport Authority,* 11 October 2012. URL: https://www.lta.gov.sg/content/ltaweb/en/about-lta/our-history.html

"Our nature reserves are small", *Chope For Nature,* 2016. URL: http://www.chopefornature.org/our-nature-reserves/it-is-small/

"Overview of Vehicle Quota System", *Land Transport Authority,* 8 May 2017. URL: https://www.lta.gov.sg/content/ltaweb/en/roads-and-motoring/owning-a-vehicle/vehicle-quota-system/overview-of-vehicle-quota-system.html

"Population, total (Singapore)", *The World Bank,* 2018. URL: https://data.worldbank.org/indicator/SP.POP.TOTL?locations=SG

"Riders", *ofo,* 2018. URL: https://www.ofo.com/sg/en

"Rules and Code of Conduct", *Land Transport Authority,* 1 August 2018. URL: https://www.lta.gov.sg/content/ltaweb/en/walk-cycle-ride/rules-and-code-of-conduct.html

"SERS", *Housing & Development Board,* 2 October 2017. URL: https://www.hdb.gov.sg/cs/infoweb/residential/

living-in-an-hdb-flat/sers-and-upgrading-programmes/overview-of-sers

"Shanghai's classic trolley buses and trams are on a resurgence", *Global Times,* 23 February 2016. URL: http://www.globaltimes.cn/content/970005.shtml

Singapore Elections. URL: http://www.singapore-elections.com/

"SMRT Trains and SMRT Light Rail to transit to new rail financing framework", *Land Transport Authority,* 15 July 2016, https://www.lta.gov.sg/apps/news/page.aspx?c=2&id=aa0d44f9-e909-46f2-92af-792f2efe4992

"The Genealogy of the Lim Family of Marsi Village: Its Discovery and Historical Values", *Kua Bak Lim's Blog,* 9 July 2013. URL: http://kuabaklim.blogspot.sg/2013/07/blog-post_1154.html

"The Merlin Hotel at Beach Road", *Roots,* 4 July 2018. URL: https://roots.sg/learn/collections/listing/1146555

Thulaja Naidu Ratnala. "Bugis Junction (indoor streets of Bugis)", *Singapore Infopedia,* 2004. URL: http://eresources.nlb.gov.sg/infopedia/articles/SIP_297_2004-12-20.html

"Types of vocational licence", *Land Transport Authority,* 13 April 2018. URL: https://www.lta.gov.sg/content/ltaweb/en/industry-matters/vocational-licences/types-of-vocational-licence.html

"World's population increasingly urban with more than half living in urban areas", *United Nations,* 10 July 2014. URL: http://www.un.org/en/development/desa/news/population/world-urbanization-prospects-2014.html

"Yamagata Shinkansen", *East Japan Railway Company.* URL: http://www.eki-net.com/pc/jreast-shinkansen-reservation/english/wb/common/timetable/e_yamagata_d/index.html

"Yamagata Shinkansen", *Wikipedia,* 18 August 2018. URL: https://en.wikipedia.org/wiki/Yamagata_Shinkansen

"Zion Road Estate", Singapore: *Lost & Found,* 21 June 2013. URL: https://lostnfiledsg.wordpress.com/2013/06/21/zion-road-estate/

MAPS
Maps of Singapore Island and/or the Town of Singapore, 1839 to the present

Mighty Minds Singapore Street Directory 2016

Singapore Guide and Street Directory 1966

Singapore Guide and Street Directory 1969

Singapore Guide and Street Directory 1975

INTERVIEWS
Cheng, Tun Wah. Interview conducted on 10 March 2013.

Caldwell, George. Interview conducted on 1 June 2012.

INDEX

Numbers

10th Mile Bukit Timah Road 119, 125, 168, 221, 229, 250, 263

A

Abdul Rahman (Temenggong) 26, 33, 42, 44–5, 54

Abrams, Harry 81, 113

Abu Bakar (Sultan) 54, 90, 102, 126

Airport crossing 179, 193, 239

Alexandra 58–9, 104, 115, 117, 119, 137, 139, 152, 155–6, 189, 226, 228, 269–70, 297

Ang Mo Kio 53, 59, 138, 159, 220–2, 226, 231, 233–4, 247, 250, 253–4, 267, 275–6, 278, 282, 285–6, 291, 305, 307

Anson Road 86, 88, 127, 262, 275

Area Licensing Scheme 264–6

Au Kang—*see Hougang*

Ayer Rajah 119–20, 221, 254–6, 281, 298

B

Balestier 55, 57, 78, 156, 173, 189, 193, 245, 253–4, 282, 314

Battery Road 41, 66, 82, 97–8, 112, 114, 122–3, 145, 149, 161

Beach Road 35, 40, 46, 61, 75, 78, 87–8, 124, 133, 138, 161, 175, 192, 202–6, 240, 245, 250, 261, 263, 279, 286, 315

Bedok 21–2, 25–7, 51, 58, 60, 69, 119–20, 138, 150, 152, 213, 220, 222–3, 235–8, 253, 270–1, 275–6, 291

Bencoolen Street 41, 75, 77, 262, 310

Bicycle 62–3, 101, 105, 147–9, 150, 167–8, 171–2, 175–6, 191, 295, 304, 310–1, 313, 315

Bicycle-sharing 310–1, 313

Bishan 221–2, 233–4, 245, 247, 254, 258, 305–7, 315

Bonham 37, 67, 71, 75

Boon Tat Street 88–9, 179

Bras Basah 41, 75–6, 99–100, 106, 109, 113, 158, 192, 204, 207, 213, 263, 290–1

Broadrick 111, 113

Buangkok 121, 226–7, 233–4, 288

Buckley, Charles 35, 68–9, 79, 102–4, 110–1

Bugis 25–6, 35–6, 39, 41, 122, 160, 203, 207, 209, 223, 285, 297

Bukit Batok 221, 229–30, 307, 314

Bukit Larangan—*see Fort Canning Hill*

Bukit Panjang 21, 50, 58, 60, 93, 104, 119, 125, 132, 147, 168, 190, 221, 230, 235, 237, 254–5, 263, 286, 288, 290–1, 297, 301, 308, 314

Bukit Timah 21, 49, 50–1, 53, 56–60, 67–9, 100, 102–5, 109–10, 116–7, 119, 130–2, 138–9, 144, 147, 151, 153, 155–8, 163, 165, 168–9, 175, 182, 190–1, 203, 219–21, 229, 245, 250, 253–4, 258, 262–4, 267, 290, 297–9, 301

Bullock cart 62–3, 67, 73, 78, 82, 90–1, 104, 108, 111, 113–4, 125, 129–30, 147–8, 175, 237, 295

Buona Vista 119–20, 155, 163, 285–6, 291, 301

Bus 106, 112–3, 131–3, 137–9, 166–8, 172, 179–80, 269–78, 287, 301, 307–9, 312, 314–5

Bute Map 34–6, 38

C

Car 109–16, 125, 129–30, 143–50, 157–8, 165, 173–4, 181–2, 249, 267, 304, 311–4

Car-lite 191, 249, 304, 307–8, 310–1, 314–5, 319

Car park 145, 163, 202, 211–2, 215, 217, 262

Causeway 131–2, 161, 168, 183, 220, 255, 299

Central Business District 10, 200, 215, 266, 281

Certificate of Entitlement—*see Vehicle Quota System*

Chan Chu Kang—*see Nee Soon*

Changi 21, 27, 51, 53, 55, 58–9, 68–9, 132, 138, 153, 158–61, 163, 171, 179, 182, 199–200, 220, 235, 239–41, 250–1, 253–5, 258, 270–1, 273, 275, 287, 307, 314

Cheang, Hong Lim 85, 126, 217

Chinatown 39–40, 42, 46–7, 57, 67, 77, 91, 97, 101–2, 116, 121–3, 127, 139, 158, 167, 175, 189, 209, 211–2, 214–5, 221, 237, 262, 279, 285, 295, 314

Chinese Campong—*see Chinatown*

Choa Chu Kang 53, 119–20, 125, 139, 157, 159–61, 168, 191, 221, 229–30, 250–1, 254–5, 283, 286, 301, 307

Chong Pang 158, 192–4, 223, 231–2, 245

Chulia Street 41, 158, 167, 212

Circus—*see Roundabout*

City Council 188, 193, 195–6, 278, 280

City Hall 163, 169, 175, 188, 260, 283

Clementi 21, 58–9, 85, 99, 119, 160, 220–1, 251, 254, 261, 274, 276, 283, 285, 291, 298, 314

Clifford Pier 163, 177

Coleman, George Drumgoole 37, 40, 47, 50, 67–8, 76, 209

Coleman Street 35, 40, 99, 104, 207, 209

Collyer Quay 82–3, 86, 92, 123, 145, 149, 163, 191, 195, 211–2, 245, 260, 263, 297

ComfortDelGro 280–1, 287

Commercial Square—*see Raffles Place*

Compulsory Land Acquisition Act, 198

Concept plan 199–201, 253, 282, 286

INDEX

Conductor (Bus, Tram) 95–6, 106, 108, 134, 141, 166–7, 180, 269, 272–4

Crawford Street 71, 76, 95–6, 202–3, 278

Crawfurd, John 29, 44–6, 48–9, 71–2, 76, 79, 204, 209

D

D'Almeida 54–6, 69, 76, 124, 126, 182

Daeng Ibrahim (Temenggong) 54, 69, 73

Dare, Mrs G. M.—*see Earnshaw, Annie Dorothea Caroline*

De Eredia, Manuel Godinho 25, 27, 51, 238, 241

Dhoby Ghaut 75, 103, 124, 149, 158, 283, 285, 288, 290, 314

Driver Improvement Points System 267–8

Dunearn Road 155–6, 262, 266

E

Earnshaw, Annie Dorothea Caroline 79, 110

East Coast Road 76, 119, 138, 158, 168, 223, 261

Electronic Road Pricing 266–7

Ellenborough 47, 209, 215

Esplanade—*see Padang*

Estate (agricultural) 55–7, 75, 119–21, 131–2, 150, 153, 159, 161, 178, 185–6

Eu Tong Sen Street 211

Eunos 152–3, 185, 223, 253, 285

Expressway 169, 199, 201, 238, 250–1, 253–9, 266, 290, 310, 312–4

F

Farquhar, William 33–5, 37–8, 41–2, 44, 72, 76, 207

Ford Factory 165, 174

Fort Canning Hill 10–1, 13, 23–4, 29, 34–7, 40, 43–4, 48, 55–6, 65, 69–70, 103, 105, 155, 165, 199, 255

G

Garden City (Ebenezer Howard)— *see New town*

Geylang 21–2, 26, 51, 53, 55, 59, 106–7, 109, 116–9, 132–3, 136–8, 140, 158, 160, 163, 171–2, 180, 182, 187, 190, 192, 197, 245, 250, 256, 295, 314

Gharry—*see Horse carriage*

Golden Mile 202–3, 212, 250, 295

Golden Shoe 212, 215, 262

Government Hill—*see Fort Canning Hill*

Grove Road—*see Mountbatten Road*

H

Hackney carriage—*see Horse carriage*

Hackney Carriage (and Jinrikisha) Department 62, 91, 100, 111, 144

High speed rail 176, 315, 317

High Street 10–3, 29, 34–5, 38, 40, 70, 75, 87, 99, 106–8, 123, 207, 209, 213, 243, 260, 264, 270, 318–9

Hill Street 13, 35, 40, 47, 69, 113, 153, 209, 243, 262–3

Hokkien-Teochew Riots 69–70, 115

Holland (in Singapore) 58–9, 103, 119–20, 139, 150, 153–6, 163, 175, 263, 297

Hooper, William Edward 100, 111

Horse carriage 12, 32, 35, 47, 60–2, 64, 66, 68, 78, 81–2, 90–2, 95–9, 101, 104, 113–4, 122–5, 130, 133, 139, 143, 145, 147–8, 150, 175–6, 182–3, 311

Horse-drawn omnibus 63–4, 104

Hougang 221, 223, 228, 233–4, 256, 276, 288, 301

Housing and Development Board 186, 196–8, 200–2, 211, 213, 217–26, 237–8, 262, 275, 291, 310

Hussein Shah (Sultan) 33, 35, 41, 44–5, 54, 203

I

Inner Ring Road 156, 162, 191, 258, 265, 304

J

Jackson, Philip 37, 66

Jalan Besar 150–1, 202, 213, 215, 262, 275

Japan Street—*see Boon Tat Street*

Johor Sultanate 10, 24–6, 29, 31, 33, 41, 44, 54, 130

Jurong 21–2, 49–50, 57, 59–60, 139, 157, 159, 162, 168, 181, 193, 199, 201, 219, 221–2, 226, 229–230, 239–40, 242, 245, 250–1, 253–5, 257–8, 275–6, 281–3, 286, 290, 292, 298, 301, 307, 314, 316–7

K

Kallang 21–2, 26, 39, 48–9, 51, 53, 55, 59, 67, 71, 106, 108, 116–7, 121–2, 130, 158, 160, 162–3, 179, 182, 191–3, 196–7, 204, 215, 217, 223, 238–9, 245, 253, 256, 258, 282

Kampong Glam 26, 39, 41, 45–6, 49–50, 64, 67, 70–1, 78, 122, 126–7, 153, 202–6, 215, 262, 314–5, 318

Kampong Malacca 40, 47, 67, 76–7

Kandang Kerbau 50, 78, 103, 106, 121–2, 220

Kangkar 48–9, 53–4, 58–9, 119, 157, 223

Kennedy, William 110–1

Keppel Road 86, 96, 104, 115, 127, 139, 146, 153, 253–4, 258

Keretapi Tanah Melayu 220, 297–301

Kim Seng 70, 76, 114, 119, 126, 156, 176, 189

Kranji 21–2, 49–50, 53, 57–9, 63–4, 68–9, 93, 102–4, 119, 125, 130–2, 207, 226, 229–30, 255, 258, 285, 297, 312, 314, 316

L

Land Transport Authority 201, 249

Lane markings—*see Road lines*

Lee, Kuan Yew 195, 197, 213, 220, 239, 299, 305

Light Rapid Transit 223, 229, 233, 237, 250, 286–9, 292–3, 301

Lim Chu Kang 21, 53, 119–20, 139, 157, 162, 168, 226

Lorong Tambangan 35–6, 38–9

M

Malay Settlement 153, 160, 178, 223, 253

Malay Street 41, 94, 207–8

Mandai 58–60, 119, 161, 163, 168, 194, 207, 223–4, 226, 231–2, 250–1

Marina Bay / Centre / East / South 201, 223, 238, 240–1, 243–4, 253, 256–7, 265, 283, 287, 290–1, 299, 305, 307, 314, 318

Market Street 41, 66, 71, 84–6, 182, 211–2, 262

Marshall, David 192, 245, 270

Marsiling 132, 193, 220, 223–4, 229, 231–2, 281, 285, 314, 317

Mass Rapid Transit 12, 200, 247–8, 281–8, 290–5, 298, 304–8, 312, 314, 316–8

Master plan 37, 187–92, 196, 199–200, 249

Middle Road 40, 87, 95–6, 98, 100, 144, 172, 204, 207, 213

Milestone 51, 53, 125, 139, 158–9, 250

Montgomerie, William 37, 54–5, 57, 76, 163

Mosquito bus 132–43, 311–2

Motorcycle 113, 148, 173, 262, 266, 268

Motorcycle taxi 136

Mountbatten Road 119–20, 144, 150, 160, 179, 191, 193, 256

Municipal Building—*see City Hall*

Municipal Committee / Commission 40, 68–71, 73, 76, 83–4, 111, 117, 126–7, 133, 135–8, 141–3, 146–8, 150–3, 156–8, 161, 179–82

N

Nee Soon 53, 58, 60, 132, 138–9, 152, 158, 190, 193–4, 221, 231–2

Neil Road 71, 73–4, 77, 84, 86, 102, 139

New Bridge Road 47, 66, 71, 84, 108, 115, 123, 144, 152, 187, 211, 221, 260, 262, 265, 275, 315

New town 60, 187–91, 200, 202, 217–26, 229–35, 250, 275–6, 283, 285

Newton Circus 155–6, 165, 263, 282

Nicoll Highway 192–3, 195, 202–3, 238, 240, 245, 253, 256, 258, 264, 267, 286, 291, 295

North Bridge Road 13, 41–2, 45, 51, 64, 68, 71, 76–7, 96, 98, 106, 108–9, 113, 123, 125, 137, 146, 199, 202–6, 208, 213, 260–5, 279, 315

O

One-way road 149, 182, 191, 211, 262–3, 271

Ong, Eng Guan 193, 195–6

Ong, Teng Cheong 247, 275, 282

Orang Laut 21, 24–6, 32, 35, 51, 54, 72, 160, 223

Orchard Road 21, 56–7, 71, 75, 103, 105, 112–4, 116, 124, 145–6, 149–50, 155, 165, 169, 172, 174, 182, 212–3, 255, 260, 262–4, 266, 273, 275, 282–3, 295, 314, 318

Outer Ring Road 156–7, 162–3, 165, 169, 253, 258, 290, 312

Outram 71, 115, 117, 139, 152, 156, 189, 197, 285

Overhead bridge 260–1, 310

Owen, Mrs G. P.—*see Earnshaw, Annie Dorothea Caroline*

P

Padang 12–3, 19, 31, 35, 38, 62–3, 67, 71, 87, 121, 124, 163, 169, 173, 177, 192

Pasir Panjang 58–9, 68, 104, 115–6, 118–9, 133, 136, 138–40, 150, 153, 163, 168–9, 175, 239–40

Pasir Ris 221, 233, 236, 240, 250, 254, 283, 314, 316

Pavement 97, 149–150, 156, 260–1, 310–1, 313, 315

Paya Lebar 53, 59, 69, 106–7, 109, 117–9, 138, 150, 152, 156, 158–9, 180, 193, 200, 234, 236, 239, 253, 256, 258, 261, 271, 281

Peck San—*see Bishan*

Pedal rickshaw 148

Pedestrian crossing 260–1

Pek Kio 150–1, 189, 237, 254, 258–9, 314, 316

Personal mobility device 304, 310–1, 313, 315

Pirate taxi 279–81, 286, 297, 312

Private-hire car 308, 310

Public Works Department 12, 70–2, 112, 125, 157, 186–8, 192, 195, 199, 201, 255, 258, 260, 263, 276

Punggol / Ponggol 21–2, 26, 28, 58–9, 119, 138, 171, 222–3, 226, 233–4, 237, 240, 245, 251–2, 255–8, 275, 286–9, 308, 314

Q

Queenstown 21, 189, 191, 196–8, 222, 282–3, 298, 301, 317

R

Raffles, Stamford 10, 23, 26, 33–5, 37–44, 48, 55–7

Raffles Place 31, 39, 41, 43, 46, 66, 71, 76, 78, 81, 83–7, 92, 109, 114, 122–3, 137, 145, 147, 149, 167, 182–3, 211–5, 243, 262, 283–5, 288, 315, 317

Raffles Town Plan 37–44, 73, 82, 116, 186, 202, 206, 314, 318

Railway 90, 102–5, 117, 131, 153–7, 160, 162–3, 180, 191–2, 196, 220, 245, 297–301, 312

Ralfe, Henry 10, 35, 37–8, 66

Rationalisation 275, 285, 288

Reclamation 12, 38–9, 67, 82–9, 160, 237–44, 255

Reformatory Road—*see Clementi*

Registry of Vehicles 111, 133, 136, 144, 148, 172, 181, 188, 196, 199, 201, 279, 295, 297

Rickshaw 81, 90–4, 97–102, 104, 108–9, 113–4, 117, 122, 124, 129–30, 133–4, 143–5, 147–8, 167, 174–5, 180–1, 279, 285, 311–3

River Valley Road 43, 47, 71, 116, 126, 149, 155, 209

Road lines 146, 263–4

Robinson Road 85–6, 88–9, 130, 132–3, 149, 161, 182, 212–3, 253, 262, 275

Rochor Centre 203, 205, 215–6

Roundabout 149, 155–6, 165, 195, 217, 253, 263, 282–3, 298, 301

Royal Air Force air bases 138, 159–61, 167, 179, 194, 239

Rural Board 125–6, 132, 146, 157–9, 161, 195–6, 245

Rush hour 61, 140–1, 149, 191, 265–6, 273, 275, 283, 306

S

Salat Road 39, 42–3, 47, 71–5

Sang Nila Utama 19, 21–3, 25

SBS Transit 272–8, 287–8, 307–9

Scandal Point 38, 41, 61–2, 87

Selective En bloc Redevelopment Scheme 226

Seletar 21, 26, 49, 51, 53, 133, 138–9, 159–62, 194, 201, 220–1, 226, 233–4, 240, 254–5, 307, 314, 316

Seletar Road—*see Thomson Road*

Sembawang 21–2, 51, 53, 60, 138–9, 159–63, 167, 192–4, 219, 221–6, 231–2, 235, 245, 250–1, 253, 261, 273, 278, 281, 285–6

Sembawang Naval Base 159–62, 166–7, 192, 220, 231

Sengkang 21, 222–3, 226, 233–4, 237, 255–7, 286–8, 291, 308, 314–7

Serangoon 21–2, 49–50, 53, 55, 58–60, 62, 67–9, 75, 95, 106–9, 116–9, 133, 136, 138, 140–1, 149–51, 158–9, 171, 182–3, 187, 191, 217, 221, 223, 226, 233–4, 240, 254, 256–8, 260–4, 270, 276, 288, 291, 314, 316

Shenton 138, 165, 188–9, 195, 213, 240, 243, 262, 265, 275, 301

Singapore Improvement Trust 151–2, 186, 188–190, 196, 254, 259

Singapore River, 10, 12–3, 19, 22–3, 25–6, 29, 33–47, 61, 64–6, 72, 75, 82, 92, 106–7, 116, 121–2, 125–6, 155, 163, 167, 169, 209–11, 214–5, 239–40, 255, 283, 297, 315, 318

Singapore Traction Company 135–43, 148, 167, 172, 180–2, 269–72, 278, 280, 297

SMRT Corporation 200, 283, 286–7, 304–5, 307–8, 313, 315

South Bridge Road 42–3, 46–7, 67, 84, 95–6, 98, 102, 106–8, 110, 115, 123, 137, 139, 161, 187, 202, 261–2, 301, 315, 318

Speed limit 97, 111, 136–7, 146–7, 149, 173, 182, 256, 267–8, 311

Stamford Road 40, 43, 56–7, 87, 96, 99–100, 113, 145–6, 149, 158, 177, 202, 207, 209, 261, 263, 315, 318

Street and Building Names Board 198, 290, 301

Street lighting 66, 68, 109, 150, 158

Strike 91, 100–2, 141, 180, 269–71, 279, 297–8

Sundaland 20

Sungei Singapura—*see Singapore River*

Superintendent of Public Works and Convicts 50, 67–70

Syce 61–2, 86, 110, 112, 115, 143, 145

T

Tampines 21, 58–60, 75, 119, 138, 193, 201, 221, 223, 225–6, 233, 235–8, 250–1, 254–5, 257, 275–6, 281, 286, 301, 315–7

Tanah Merah 25–7, 51, 59, 69–70, 132, 163, 171, 238–9, 241, 287, 319

Tanglin 53, 55–6, 59, 117, 133, 139, 150, 155–6, 163, 196, 263, 297, 314, 316–7

Tanjong Katong 55, 79, 116–9, 150–1, 168, 256, 314, 317

Tanjong Pagar 39–40, 42–3, 53, 55, 57, 59, 62, 72–4, 82, 84, 86, 88, 95–6, 102, 106–7, 109, 116–7, 127, 136, 138, 140, 146, 153, 180, 195, 213, 240, 245, 285, 301

Tanjong Pagar Railway Station 154–5, 297–301

Tanjong Rhu 25, 27, 238, 253, 256

Taxi 113, 132–5, 141–3, 147, 163, 166–7, 181, 200, 265–7, 270, 278–81, 286–7, 295, 297, 301, 308, 310–2, 314–5

Telok Ayer 36–8, 41–3, 84–90, 95, 126, 133, 145, 161, 163, 179, 182, 211–3, 238, 240, 243, 262

Telok Blangah 21, 42, 44, 53–4, 58–9, 69, 72–4, 86, 106–7, 117, 139, 220, 226, 276, 288, 297, 314, 317

Thomson, John Turnbull 50–1, 53–4, 56, 196

Thomson Road 51–4, 58–9, 67–9, 71, 116, 119, 133, 158–61, 190–1, 194, 217, 219–20, 250–1, 253–5, 258–9

Tiong Bahru 117, 150–2, 155, 187, 190, 193, 196, 220, 226, 269, 282, 285

Toa Payoh 53, 59, 116–7, 138, 190–1, 196–8, 213, 215, 217–8, 221–3, 247, 253–4, 256–8, 276, 282–3, 285–6, 291, 307, 314, 316

Track (numbered) 233, 250, 252

Traffic Department / Office 115, 127, 144, 146–8

Traffic light 97, 106, 130, 146, 149, 192, 213, 253, 260, 263–4, 313

Tram (Electric) 105–9, 114–5, 117–8, 133–7, 158–9, 278, 311, 313

Tram (Steam) 86, 94–100, 102, 107, 172, 274, 311–3

Trans-Island Bus Services 278, 285–7

Tricycle 62, 114, 144, 147–8, 150, 174–5

Trimmer Committee 148–9, 182, 258, 260, 262–3, 310

Trishaw 148, 174–5, 180–1, 191, 295–7

Trolleybus—*see Singapore Traction Company*

Tuas 119–20, 139, 157, 159, 239–42, 255, 257–8, 291, 314, 316

U

Note: For road names in the form of "Upper x", please look up "x".

Ubi 127, 178

Ulu 59–60

Ulu Sembawang 59–60, 223–4, 231–2, 235

Urban kampung 152, 187, 189–90, 196, 235

Urban Redevelopment Authority 197–8, 200, 262

V

Vehicle Quota System 267, 304

Victoria Street 41, 51, 77, 144, 204–8, 245, 262–3, 285, 296, 315

W

Wallich 37, 57, 79, 86, 105

Wearne, Charles / Brothers / Theodore 112–3, 127, 132–3, 142

Whampoa (Hoo Ah Kay) 55, 209, 253–4, 256

Widening (of roads) 73, 109, 122–3, 150, 156, 158, 160, 186, 203, 209, 211, 240, 261, 265

Woodlands 21, 60, 104–5, 117, 131–2, 139, 147, 160, 168, 183, 191, 193, 201, 219–20, 222–6, 229, 231–2, 250, 254–5, 258, 276–8, 281, 285–7, 297, 299, 307, 309–10, 314–7

Y

Yamashita, Tomoyuki 165–71, 177

Yellow Top (taxi) 142, 163, 280–1, 286

Yio Chu Kang 53, 119–20, 133, 138, 159, 161, 182, 191, 219–21, 226, 233, 247–8, 250–1, 254–5, 261

Yishun 194, 221–2, 226, 231–2, 235, 254, 266, 278, 283, 285–7, 314, 316

Z

Zebra crossing 260

ACKNOWLEDGEMENTS

The endeavour of historical research and writing is like a solitary drive down a deserted expressway. However, between the genesis of this book in 2011 and its completion in 2019, there have been a few who have contributed in their own ways to its evolution.

I will like to thank, in no particular order of importance:

- Professor Brian Farrell and Professor Bruce Lockhart of the National University of Singapore's History Department. They gave critical academic assessments of my completed manuscript, and strong feedback where it was needed.

- Mr Jeya Ayadurai of the Singapore History Consultants, for supporting this project. He gave me the green light to present an outline of my book to the firm, allowing me to flesh out ideas and concepts. Thereafter, he passed me valuable feedback.

- Tiak, my beloved wife, for being by my side through my ups and downs. She accompanied me on many explorations around Singapore, walking the ground for the book.

- George Caldwell, for our long conversations on transport and urban studies. His wisdom, ideas, and humour were an inspiration. Rest in peace.

- Melvin Neo, from my publisher Marshall Cavendish, for giving me a chance.

- Michael Spilling, my editor, for paring my manuscript down to length, making it more concise and to-the-point.

- The Buddies, my companions during the long hours of researching and writing.

- And finally, all of you who gave me encouragement when I mentioned that I was working on a book.

ABOUT THE AUTHOR

Born and bred in Singapore, Eisen Teo is Assistant Director of Special Projects at Singapore History Consultants, a Singapore-based heritage consultancy. He graduated valedictorian with a first class honours in History from the National University of Singapore. He spends his free time researching on Singapore history, transport, and urban issues, and exploring historic or disappearing places in Singapore—such as Punggol Road Track 24 (above), which was expunged in 2016. This is his first book; he is working on his second. To reach out to him, visit his website at www.historybyeisen.com.

Made in the USA
Monee, IL
02 December 2024